OUTSIDE CRIMINOLOGY:
SELECTED ESSAYS BY STANLEY COHEN

PIONEERS IN CONTEMPORARY CRIMINOLOGY

Series Editor: David Nelken

The titles in this series bring together the best published and unpublished work by the leading authorities in contemporary criminological theory. By drawing together articles from a wide range of journals, conference proceedings and books, each title makes readily available the authors' most important writings on specific themes. Each volume in this series includes a lengthy introduction, written by the editor and a significant piece of scholarship in its own right, which outlines the context of the work and comments on its significance and potential. The collected essays complement each other to give a retrospective view of the authors' achievements and a picture of the development of criminology as a whole.

Titles in the series

A Criminological Imagination
Pat Carlen

Working Out of Crime
David Downes

Crime, Law and Society
Malcolm Feeley

Building Modern Criminology: Forays and Skirmishes
David F Greenberg

Breaking Criminological Convention: Selected Essays of Richard Ericson
Kevin D. Haggerty, Aaron Doyle and Janet Chan

Policing, Popular Culture and Political Economy
Robert Reiner

Victims, Policy-making and Criminological Theory
Paul Rock

Essays on Transnational Crime and Policing
James Sheptycki

Thinking about Punishment
Michael Tonry

Outside Criminology
Selected Essays by Stanley Cohen

Edited by
TOM DAEMS
KU Leuven

PIONEERS IN CONTEMPORARY CRIMINOLOGY SERIES

LONDON AND NEW YORK

First published 2016
by Routledge
2 Park Square, Milton Park, Abingdon, Oxon OX14 4RN

and by Routledge
711 Third Avenue, New York, NY 10017

Routledge is an imprint of the Taylor & Francis Group, an informa business

Editorial material and selection © 2016 Tom Daems; individual owners retain copyright in their own material.

The right of Tom Daems to be identified as the author of the editorial material, and of the authors for their individual chapters, has been asserted in accordance with sections 77 and 78 of the Copyright, Designs and Patents Act 1988.

All rights reserved. No part of this book may be reprinted or reproduced or utilised in any form or by any electronic, mechanical, or other means, now known or hereafter invented, including photocopying and recording, or in any information storage or retrieval system, without permission in writing from the publishers.

Trademark notice: Product or corporate names may be trademarks or registered trademarks, and are used only for identification and explanation without intent to infringe.

British Library Cataloguing in Publication Data
A catalogue record for this book is available from the British Library

Library of Congress Cataloging in Publication Data
A catalog record for this book has been requested

ISBN: 978-1-4724-6743-0 (hbk)

Typeset in Times New Roman
by Servis Filmsetting Ltd, Stockport, Cheshire

Contents

Acknowledgements vii
Publisher's Acknowledgements ix
Introduction: From the Banal to the Grand xi
Bibliography of Stanley Cohen (1966–2014) xxviii

Rock, P. (2014), 'Stanley Cohen, 1942–2013', in British Academy, *Biographical Memoirs of Fellows of the British Academy, XIII*, pp. 65–88. xxxviii

1. Cohen, S. (1967), 'Mods, Rockers and the Rest: Community Reactions to Juvenile Delinquency', *Howard Journal of Criminal Justice*, **12**, 2, pp. 121–130. 1

2. Cohen, S. (1968), 'The Politics of Vandalism', *New Society*, 12 December, pp. 872–874. 11

3. Cohen, S. (1968), 'The Nature of Vandalism', *New Society*, 12 December, pp. 875–876. 17

4. Cohen, S. (1968), 'Can it be Controlled?', *New Society*, 12 December, pp. 877–878. 21

5. Cohen, S. (1974), 'Criminology and the Sociology of Deviance in Britain: A Recent History and a Current Report', in P. Rock and M. McIntosh (eds), *Deviance and Social Control*. London: Tavistock, pp. 1–40. 25

6. Cohen, S. (1979), 'How Can We Balance Justice, Guilt and Tolerance?', *New Society*, 1 March, pp. 475–477. 65

7. Cohen, S. (1979), 'Community Control – a New Utopia', *New Society*, 15 March, pp. 609–611. 71

8. Cohen, S. (1979), 'Some Modest and Unrealistic Proposals', *New Society*, 29 March, pp. 731–734. 79

9. Cohen, S. (1979), 'The Punitive City: Notes on the Dispersal of Social Control', *Contemporary Crises*, **3**, 4, pp. 339–363. 89

10. Cohen, S. (1983), 'Social-Control Talk: Telling Stories about Correctional Change', in D. Garland and P. Young (eds), *The Power to Punish*. London: Heinemann, pp. 101–129. 115

11	Cohen, S. (1989), 'The Critical Discourse on "Social Control": Notes on the Concept as a Hammer', *International Journal of the Sociology of Law*, **17**, pp. 347–357.	147
12	Cohen, S. (1991), 'Alternatives to Punishment – The Abolitionist Case', *Israel Law Review*, **25**, 3, pp. 729–739.	159
13	Cohen, S. (1991), 'Talking about Torture in Israel', *Tikkun*, **6**, 6, pp. 23–30, pp. 89–90.	171
14	Cohen, S. (1993), 'Intellectual Skepticism and Political Commitment: The Case of Radical Criminology', *Studies in Law, Politics, and Society*, **13**, pp. 187–209.	181
15	Cohen, S. (1995), 'State Crimes of Previous Regimes: Knowledge, Accountability, and the Policing of the Past', *Law and Social Inquiry*, **20**, pp. 7–50.	205
16	Cohen, S. (1996), 'Government Responses to Human Rights Reports: Claims, Denials, and Counterclaims', *Human Rights Quarterly*, **18**, 3, pp. 517–543.	249
17	Cohen, S. (1996), 'Crime and Politics: Spot the Difference', *British Journal of Sociology*, **47**, 1, pp. 1–21.	277
18	Cohen, S. (1997), 'Conference Life: The Rough Guide', *The American Sociologist*, pp. 69–84.	299
19	Cohen, S. (2002), 'Moral Panics as Cultural Politics', in S. Cohen, *Folk Devils and Moral Panics. The Creation of the Mods and Rockers*. Third Edition. London: Routledge, pp. vii–xxxvii.	315
20	Cohen, S. (2005), 'Post-Moral Torture: From Guantanamo to Abu Ghraib', *Index on Censorship*, **34**, 1, pp. 24–30.	347
21	Cohen, S. (2009), 'Carry on Panicking'. Address on receiving the Award for 'Outstanding Achievement' from the British Society of Criminology at its Annual Conference, Cardiff, 29 June 2009, *British Society of Criminology Newsletter*, **64**, pp. 5–10.	355
Index		361

Acknowledgements

A major part of the research for this book was completed while I was a visiting scholar at the Mannheim Centre for Criminology of the London School of Economics and Political Science (LSE) (November–December 2014). I am most grateful to Jennifer Brown for making this visit possible and for being such a great host. During my visit I had numerous talks with some of Stan Cohen's old colleagues and friends at LSE – or visiting LSE – about this project, including David Downes, Janet Foster, David Garland, Nicola Lacey, Tim Newburn and Paul Rock. The staff at LSE's Centre for the Study of Human Rights – Zoe Gillard and Sara Ulfsparre – kindly facilitated access to the Stan Cohen collection.

I am very grateful to Judith Suissa who has been helpful and supportive throughout the project. David Downes, Malcolm Feeley, Daphna Golan, Elena Larrauri, Mike Nellis, Ken Plummer, Paul Rock, Sharon Shalev and Laurie Taylor have at various points offered feedback on different versions of Stan Cohen's bibliography or they have been so kind as to send me difficult to access papers. I am in particular grateful to Mike Nellis for offering me his collection of RAP publications and newsletters which included some hard-to-find published material by Stan Cohen.

I would like to acknowledge the financial support of the Research Foundation Flanders (FWO) for a travel grant to finance my stay at LSE. I am grateful to my current academic home, the Faculty of Law of the University of Leuven, for flexibility in arranging my teaching schedule. Cedric De Koker offered some much appreciated assistance when I was still at Ghent University and Jonas Visschers did the same when I moved to Leuven.

I also would like to express my gratitude to Series Editor David Nelken for welcoming this volume to the Series and Dymphna Evans and Hayley Kennard for their help and support in getting this book published.

Most of my thanks go out to my family – in particular to my wife Eva for running and managing the family while I was on research leave in London.

All royalties for this book will be donated to 'Freedom from Torture', http://www.freedomfromtorture.org/.

Tom Daems
Leuven, 17 August 2015

Publisher's Acknowledgements

The chapters in this volume are taken from the sources listed below. The editor and publishers wish to thank the authors, original publishers or other copyright holders for permission to use their material as follows:

Paul Rock, 'Stanley Cohen 1942–2013', *Biographical Memoirs of Fellows of the British Academy*, XIII, 2014, pp. 65–88. Permission by the British Academy.

Chapter 1: 'Mods, Rockers and the Rest: Community Reactions to Juvenile Delinquency', *Howard Journal of Criminal Justice*, 12, 1967, pp. 121–130. Permission by John Wiley & Sons.

Chapter 2: 'The Politics of Vandalism', *New Society*, 12 December, 1968, pp. 872–874. Permission by PMI Publishing.

Chapter 3: 'The Nature of Vandalism', *New Society*, 12 December, 1968, pp. 875–876. Permission by PMI Publishing.

Chapter 4: 'Can It Be Controlled?', *New Society*, 12 December, 1968, pp. 877–878. Permission by PMI Publishing.

Chapter 5: 'Criminology and the Sociology of Deviance in Britain: A Recent History and a Current Report', in P. Rock and M. McIntosh (eds), *Deviance and Social Control*, 1974, (London: Tavistock), pp. 1–40.

Chapter 6: 'How Can We Balance Justice, Guilt and Tolerance?', *New Society*, 1 March, 1979, pp. 475–477. Permission by PMI Publishing.

Chapter 7: 'Community Control – A New Utopia', *New Society*, 15 March, 1979, pp. 609–611. Permission by PMI Publishing.

Chapter 8: 'Some Modest and Unrealistic Proposals', *New Society*, 29 March, 1979, pp. 731–734. Permission by PMI Publishing.

Chapter 9: 'The Punitive City: Notes on the Dispersal of Social Control', *Contemporary Crises*, 3, 4, 1979, pp. 339–363. Permission by Springer Science+Business Media.

Chapter 10: 'Social-Control Talk: Telling Stories about Correctional Change', in D. Garland and P. Young (eds), *The Power to Punish*, 1983, pp. 101–129. Permission by Heinemann.

Chapter 11: 'The Critical Discourse on Social Control: Notes on the Concept as a Hammer', *International Journal of the Sociology of Law*, 17, 1989, pp. 347–357. Permission by Elsevier.

Chapter 12: 'Alternatives to Punishment – The Abolitionist Case', *Israel Law Review*, **25**, 1991, pp. 729–739. Permission by the Faculty of Law, The Hebrew University, Israel.

Chapter 13: 'Talking About Torture in Israel', *Tikkun*, **6**, 6, 1991, pp. 23–30, pp. 89–90. Permission by Duke University Press.

Chapter 14: 'Intellectual Skepticism and Political Commitment: The Case of Radical Criminology', *Studies in Law, Politics, and Society*, **13**, 1993, pp. 187–209. Permission by Elsevier.

Chapter 15: 'State Crimes of Previous Regimes: Knowledge, Accountability, and the Policing of the Past', *Law and Social Inquiry*, **20**, 1995, pp. 7–50. Permission by John Wiley & Sons.

Chapter 16: 'Government Responses to Human Rights Reports: Claims, Denials, and Counterclaims', *Human Rights Quarterly*, **18**, 3, 1996, pp. 517–543. Permission by the Johns Hopkins University Press.

Chapter 17: 'Crime and Politics: Spot the Difference', *British Journal of Sociology*, **47**, 1, 1996, pp. 1–21. Permission by John Wiley & Sons.

Chapter 18: 'Conference Life: The Rough Guide', *The American Sociologist*, **28**, 1997, pp. 69–84. Permission by Springer Science+Business Media.

Chapter 19: 'Moral Panics as Cultural Politics', in *Folk Devils and Moral Panics. The Creation of the Mods and Rockers*, 2002, pp. vii–xxxvii. Permission by Taylor & Francis Ltd.

Chapter 20: 'Post-Moral Torture: From Guantanamo to Abu Ghraib', *Index on Censorship*, **34**, 1, 2005, pp. 24–30. Permission by *Index on Censorship*.

Chapter 21: 'Carry on Panicking', Address on receiving the Award for 'Outstanding Achievement', from the British Society of Criminology at its Annual Conference, Cardiff, 29 June 2009, *British Society of Criminology Newsletter*, **64**, pp. 5–10. Permission by the British Society of Criminology.

Every effort has been made to trace all the copyright holders, but if any have been inadvertently overlooked the publishers will be pleased to make the necessary arrangement at the first opportunity.

Publisher's Note
The material in this volume has been reproduced using the facsimile method. This means we can retain the original pagination to facilitate easy and correct citation of the original essays.
   It also explains the variety of typefaces, page layouts and numbering.

Introduction
From the Banal to the Grand

TOM DAEMS
KU Leuven

Following the principle
that monkeys don't make the best zoologists,
the outsider's view
is sometimes to be preferred
(Cohen 1991a: 2)

In May 1990 Stanley Cohen was interviewed by Herman Franke for the Dutch newspaper *NRC Handelsblad*. This happened at the occasion of the inaugural Willem Bonger Memorial Lecture at the University of Amsterdam. 'I've always been more interested in the question how people think about crime then in crime itself', he told Franke (1990) when he was asked about his views on left realism. Franke was at that time a rising star in Dutch criminology. His 900-page dissertation had just been published and he would soon earn international fame for its shortened and translated edition, *The Emancipation of Prisoners* (Franke 1995). However, soon thereafter Franke left criminology and became a successful and prizewinning novel writer until his untimely death in August 2010.

Also Stan Cohen has in the meantime sadly passed away (on 7 January 2013) but unlike Franke he never really broke with criminology. It could have happened though. His early work was deeply critical about (British) mainstream criminology and aimed to introduce the new sociology of deviance that had flourished in the United States (that is, the work of Becker, Erikson, Lemert, Matza, Scheff and the like) to a new cohort of students of crime and its control. In his PhD dissertation, *Hooligans, Vandals and the Community: A Study of Social Reaction to Juvenile Delinquency*, Cohen wrote about a sceptical revolution in criminology and the sociology of deviance. The new tradition, so he explained there, '... is sceptical in the sense that when it sees terms like "deviant", it asks, "deviant to whom?", or "deviant from what?"; when it deals with social problems, it asks "problematic to whom?"; when it is told that certain actions are not functional, it asks "functional to whom?"' (Cohen 1969: 16). And, indeed, in his early work – as well as via the institutional fora he helped create (in particular the National Deviancy Conference in 1968 and some years later the European Group for the Study of Deviance and Social Control) – Cohen was very much directed at questioning conventional criminology and creating a space to think differently about crime and its control. Cohen also contributed empirically to the new tradition, in particular through his PhD dissertation on vandalism and reactions to youth delinquency which included a case study on the

1960s phenomenon of the Mods and Rockers. This study of the Mods and Rockers – which was covered in the fourth part of his thesis (Cohen 1969: Chapters 12–17) – was reworked and published a couple of years later as *Folk Devils and Moral Panics* (1972) which is still his most influential book.

Cohen's unease and dissatisfaction with criminology culminated in a book with the telling title *Against Criminology*. On the first page of this book is a quote from Theodor Adorno: 'One must belong to a tradition to hate it properly.' In the second chapter Cohen described his relation towards criminology as 'repressive tolerance', a term he borrowed from Herbert Marcuse: 'Every attempt I have ever made to distance myself from the subject, to criticize it, even to question its very right to exist, has only got me more involved in its inner life' (Cohen 1988: 8). These words were probably at the back of his mind two decades later when he was awarded the inaugural Outstanding Achievement Award from the British Society of Criminology. Indeed, receiving this honour implied that he was now considered to be part of the newly created gallery of most prominent British criminologists – as its first recipient he now *was* fully absorbed in criminology's inner life. As was to be expected, however, Cohen (2009) had his response ready at the award ceremony: criminology, in his view, was not to be considered as an end-point but rather as a starting-point to arrive at the much wider questions which had really interested him throughout his career. Indeed, as he had suggested already three decades earlier: 'Criminology is successful not to the extent that it solves the state's problems but to the extent that it becomes a vehicle for understanding society. This is itself a moral goal in so far as crime and punishment are ultimately only markers to what sort of society we live in, and want to live in' (Cohen 1979a: 734). Or as he explained at yet another occasion, it is all about '… to move "down" from the grand questions of social and political theory to the banal questions of crime and punishment – and then "up" again from the banal to the grand' (Cohen 1990a: xiv).

This volume

This book brings together a selection of Stan Cohen's published work which testifies to his lasting contribution to criminology. However, it has not been easy to make this selection. Stan Cohen was a prolific writer whose work has been published in an unusually wide range of formats: from newspapers (such as *The Guardian* or the *Jerusalem Post*), through magazines (such as *Anarchy*, *New Society*, *Index on Censorship* or *New Humanist*) and reports (for *Radical Alternatives to Prison*, *B'Tselem* and *Ford Foundation*) to academic sociology and criminology journals as well as books. The result is an utterly diverse and rich body of work which addresses multiple audiences. In order to make our selection we have applied the following criteria.

First, we did not want to include any material that was republished in *Against Criminology*. For that book (which was first published in 1988) Stan Cohen made a selection from his own work from the 1970s and early 1980s. *Against Criminology* is a wonderful collection of essays and it has a great (new) chapter where Cohen reflects upon the title of the book (see above), but since it is still available on the market we thought it would make more sense to select publications from his oeuvre which were not included in that book. Seen from that perspective *Outside Criminology* can be considered as a complement to *Against Criminology*. This also explains why we devote relatively more space in this volume to his published work from the 1990s and early 2000s. Indeed, in the last phase of his career Cohen moved – as he put it – from 'doing' criminology to 'doing' human rights (Cohen 1993a: 97). Reactions to torture and other human rights violations – or the lack thereof – were themes that he started to explore and write about from the late 1980s onwards and these were therefore, evidently, not covered in *Against Criminology*.

Second, in *Outside Criminology* readers will only find single-authored publications by Stan Cohen. Given the pool of work we could choose from and in view of the spirit of the book series, which focuses on the work of pioneers in contemporary criminology, we think our choice is justified. We do realize, however, that this second criterion is debatable. Like most academics Stan Cohen also has, at various points throughout his long career, joined forces with colleagues – for example with Paul Rock ('The Teddy Boy', 1970), Jock Young (*The Manufacture of News*, 1973), Andrew Scull (*Social Control and the State*, 1983), Daphna Golan (*The Interrogation of Palestinians During the Intifada: Ill-Treatment, 'Moderate Physical Pressure' or Torture?*, 1991 and its 1992 follow-up report) and Bruna Seu ('Knowing Enough Not to Feel Too Much: Emotional Thinking about Human Rights Appeals', 2002).

His friendship and collaboration with Laurie Taylor in particular proved to be immensely productive. Together they wrote a number of papers as well as three books which were all published in the 1970s, that is, *Psychological Survival* (1972), *Escape Attempts* (1976; re-issued in 1992) and *Prison Secrets* (1978). *Psychological Survival* (1972) grew somewhat haphazardly out of a series of sociology classes which Cohen and Taylor offered to a group of inmates in Durham prison. Their students were long-term prisoners who were locked up in a high security wing. In the book they attempt '... to understand E-Wing as a particular extreme situation and to interpret the men's behaviour as attempts to survive in this situation' (Cohen and Taylor 1972: 9). Cohen and Taylor refer to their book as the outcome of a 'collaborative research project'. It was explicitly influenced by David Matza's views on appreciative inquiry (Matza 1969). As they observe in Chapter 8 of the book (with the title 'Taking Sides'): 'This involves abandoning ideas of correction, and any attempts to get rid of the deviant phenomenon, and instead favours attempts to empathize with and thus comprehend the subject of inquiry' (Cohen and Taylor 1972: 182).[1] Their second joint prison book – that is, *Prison Secrets* (1978) – is a short pamphlet which was in part informed by their experience with doing research at Durham's E-Wing. *Prison Secrets* is a damning critique of the secrecy of the British prison administration – as they put it elsewhere, a 'policy of secrecy at all costs in the name of security' (Cohen and Taylor 1977: 85). This 'policy of secrecy' not only proved to be an insurmountable obstacle for their own research,[2] but also, and in particular, it affected significantly the ways in which inmates could relate to the outside world. *Prison Secrets* includes some early observations on the 1975 case Golder *vs.* UK (under the beautiful heading 'All that Glitters is not Golder') which is generally considered to be a landmark case of the European Court of Human Rights in the development of prisoners' rights throughout Europe. Here they note how the Home Office actually neutralized the reforms that were requested by the Court: 'By virtue of the arrangements explained ... it does not appear that staff should in practice feel at substantially greater risk of involvement in litigation than now' (Home Office, cited in Cohen and Taylor 1978: 43). The Home Office's 'obsession with secrecy as a form of general social control', so Cohen and Taylor argued, had led to '... the creation of a system which seems almost totally designed to block the prisoners' intentions at every turn – a system in which double-talk and hypocrisy have almost become elevated into principles' (Cohen and Taylor 1978: 48). Their third book, *Escape Attempts* (1976), addresses the various ways in which we deal with routine and repetition in everyday life.[3] At first sight the book's subject seems somewhat unrelated to their other joint ventures – indeed, the whole project had been like '... a hobby, a property which we have kept to ourselves over all these years ... It is ... our own "escape attempt"' (Cohen and Taylor 1976: xiv). The links with the themes they had explored for *Psychological Survival* are, however, evident and these are also made explicit at the start of the book: whereas *Psychological Survival* touches upon the experience and coping strategies of inmates facing the extreme predicament of long-term imprisonment in a security wing, *Escape Attempts* charts the multiple ways in which people in free society invent somewhat related ways to survive the ordinary predicament of the routines, habits and boredom of everyday life. The book reminds us that we *all* are – in some way – permanently busy trying to escape reality, irrespective of whether we find ourselves in a prison, factory, kitchen, pub, class room, office or the matrimonial bed.[4]

The three books Cohen wrote with Taylor are important – and this explains why we briefly introduced their content here so that readers who wish to explore these joint enterprises further can more easily find their way to them. But, as explained above, we have decided not to select any co-authored material for this book. Also in this respect *Outside Criminology* follows the lead of *Against Criminology* where Cohen only included work of which he was the sole author.

Third, the selection for this volume aims to do justice to the wide variety of themes that are addressed in his published work. These are – roughly speaking – the following: reactions to deviance – including moral panics (from the late 1960s till the mid-1970s); punishment and social control (from the early 1970s till the late 1980s); and reactions to human rights violations – including denial (from the late 1980s onwards). His three major books – that is, *Folk Devils and Moral Panics* (1972), *Visions of Social Control* (1985) and *States of Denial* (2001) – are to some extent representative of these three phases in his career. Moreover, because the concept of moral panic refers to over-reaction (to deviance) and the concept of denial to under-reaction (to human rights violations) it becomes possible to establish a link between his early and later work. Indeed, as Cohen suggested in his address when he received the Outstanding Achievement Award of the British Society of Criminology: 'The critique behind the concept of moral panics, is that too much attention (human resources, moral indignation, social construction) is given to the particular problem at issue. The critique behind the concept of denial is too little attention of the same type is given to a particular problem' (Cohen 2009: 9). Or as he concluded towards the end of the new introduction to the third edition of *Folk Devils and Moral Panics*: 'Studying them [moral panics] ... allows us to identify and conceptualize the lines of power in any society, the ways we are manipulated into taking some things too seriously and other things not seriously enough' (Cohen 2002: xxxv).

In addition, Cohen's various research projects have been accompanied by an ongoing 'sociology of knowledge'-type of reflection[5] on developments in and outside of criminology: from his early observations on British criminology and the sociology of deviance in the late 1960s and early 1970s to his various commentaries on the critical, new, abolitionist and realist criminologies throughout the 1970s and 1980s. Indeed, Cohen was not only a sharp critic of mainstream criminology but he also pointed at the weak spots of the newer streams in criminology which had emerged in the wake of the sceptical revolution in criminology. *Outside Criminology* includes published work which reflects his own substantive contributions to criminological research as well as essays where he reflects on the criminological enterprise as such.

Fourth, our last criterion has to do with style and audience. The style of Cohen's writing and the content of his work have been informed by a deep familiarity with literature and poetry.[6] It is probably not a coincidence that his first publications were a handful of poems that appeared in the mid-1960s in a magazine called *International Breakthru*. When Cohen was interviewed in 2001 by Paul Thompson for his oral history project on pioneers in qualitative research he recalled that, during his thesis years, he came to realize that he loved writing and '... that it came very easily' (Thompson 2014: 43). And, indeed, his writing style is characterized by a clarity and a care for words that is quite unusual in the world of academia. The Norwegian criminologist Nils Christie once suggested that you should always keep your favourite aunt in mind when writing. The chances that Cohen often thought about his favourite aunt when he wrote are probably small but nonetheless he clearly was as sensitive as his old friend to the multiple ways in which words can illuminate as well as obscure. Cohen's worries about how the uses and abuses of language can hamper understanding – a theme which was also at the centre of his later work on human rights violations and denial – at times even led to an openly expressed aversion towards some forms of scientific communication.[7]

Cohen's love for writing and the accessibility of his style also explain why he could serve so many audiences: from academics to social workers, from newspaper readers to human rights activists. As he wrote in his editorial introduction to *Images of Deviance*, the first volume of papers that emanated from the National Deviancy Conference, under the heading 'Connecting with the Public': '...we can be credible only to the extent that we are intelligible. Without our talking down or being patronizing, the accounts and theories we give of deviance should be interesting and meaningful to the layman' (Cohen 1971a: 16). Cohen was not a passive armchair academic: he was clearly – and explicitly[8] – preoccupied with the question 'What is to be done?' This sense of commitment is also revealed by his biography: from his work for Radical Alternatives to Prison (RAP) in Britain in the 1970s to his active involvement in the human rights movement in Israel in the 1980s and 1990s.[9] On several occasions in his academic work Cohen aimed to clarify the policy implications of the various theoretical options and analyses available on the criminological market of ideas. In the mid-1970s he wrote for example a paper which addressed the critique 'it's all right for you to talk', that is, the observation that the sociology of deviance and the various new and critical criminologies were unable to offer any practical guidance to those who are doing the 'dirty work'. As he wrote: 'The implication is that, however interesting, amusing, correct and even morally uplifting our message might be, it is ultimately a self-indulgent intellectual exercise, a luxury which cannot be afforded by anyone tied down by the day-to-day demands of a social-work job' (Cohen 1975a: 76). In the paper Cohen painstakingly demonstrated why some strands in criminology, indeed, failed to formulate a positive strategy but he also pointed a way out of the impasse, which was – at that time – a cautious endorsement of Thomas Mathiesen's (1974) idea of 'the unfinished' (see also Cohen 1980). This refusal to separate academic work from practical involvement also explains why later in his career, when he started to focus on torture and other human rights violations, Cohen was so vehemently opposed to postmodernism: 'I do believe that the idea (and ideal) of core and universal human rights is the last meta-narrative still alive – and that it deserves defending against the excesses of post modernist rhetoric' (Cohen 2000: 2). The tensions between doubt and action were most directly addressed in his Willem Bonger Memorial Lecture where he referred to the 'double loyalty' of intellectual scepticism and political commitment (Cohen 1990c, 1993b). Towards the end of his Bonger lecture Cohen made the predicament a bit more complex. Here he wrote about a *triple* loyalty: '... first, an overriding obligation to honest intellectual enquiry itself (however skeptical, provisional, irrelevant and unrealistic), second, a political commitment to social justice, but also (and potentially conflicting with both) the pressing and immediate demands for short term humanitarian help. We have to appease these three voracious gods' (Cohen 1993b: 204–205).

The four criteria that we have clarified in this section have guided us in making our selection. We will introduce the selected essays briefly in the next section. In addition to Stan Cohen's work we have also included two other pieces in *Outside Criminology*. First, shortly after Stan Cohen's death Paul Rock wrote a biographical memoir for the British Academy. This memoir not only offers readers essential information on Cohen's personal and professional background but it also makes some of his thematic choices and research strategies more intelligible. Our private and public lives are often closely intertwined – and this also holds for Stan Cohen, as he himself acknowledged on several occasions (see e.g. McMahon and Kellough 1987; Thompson 2014). Second, for this volume we have compiled a bibliography of Stan Cohen's published work. This bibliography covers the period 1966–2014, from his first academic articles (published in 1966 in *Anarchy*) to a memorial speech (for Harold Wolpe) that was reprinted in a book in 2014 to celebrate 50 years of sociology at the University of Essex.[10]

Selected essays

The first essay (**'Mods, Rockers and the Rest: Community Reactions to Juvenile Delinquency', 1967**) is a lecture Cohen gave for the Howard League in December 1966. It was published two years before he earned his PhD at the LSE.[11] This paper is one of his first publications and it offers a good introduction to what later became his highly influential *Folk Devils and Moral Panics* (1972). Cohen's PhD dissertation consisted of three studies: (1) a study on vandalism (Part II: Chapters 3–6); (2) a survey of views about delinquency held by control agents in a London Borough which he termed 'Northview' (Part III: Chapters 7–11); and (3) a study of the phenomenon of the Mods and Rockers (Part IV: Chapters 12–17). These three studies were preceded by a lengthy discussion of developments in the sociology of deviance and an introduction to the so-called 'transactional perspective' (Part I: Chapters 1–2) and followed by a conclusion (Part V: Chapter

18). The next essays are a series of three short articles which were published in 1968 in *New Society* (**'Vandalism – 1. The Politics of Vandalism', 'Vandalism – 2. The Nature of Vandalism', 'Vandalism – 3. Can it be Controlled?', 1968**). Here Cohen draws on the research he had undertaken for the second part of his PhD, that is, his study of vandalism, a phenomenon that had attracted a great deal of attention in Britain in 1963–1964, when he started his study. These essays are somewhat difficult to access these days as *New Society* no longer exists. *New Society* was published between 1962 and 1987 and was then incorporated into the *New Statesman*. The magazine had a unique format, making social science research and debate on issues of social concern available to a large audience in short articles and reviews (Frith 1995; Savage 2013). A quick glance at Stan Cohen's bibliography, which can be consulted elsewhere in this book, reveals that he published a large number of articles and reviews in *New Society*. It is indicative of how Cohen aimed to engage with a readership that goes beyond the immediate circle of fellow academics. The fifth selected essay is one of his first 'sociology of knowledge'-type of papers (**'Criminology and the Sociology of Deviance in Britain', 1974**). Here Cohen criticizes mainstream British criminology and he introduces the new sociology of deviance. The paper also discusses at length the birth of the National Deviancy Conference in July 1968 in Cambridge during the Third National Conference of Teaching and Research on Criminology (see also Cohen and Taylor 1975b). Three decades later Leon Radzinowicz – whose work was directly attacked by Stan Cohen in the selected essay – disclosed in his autobiography that the events of 1968 made him think of a group of '… naughty schoolboys playing a nasty game on their stern headmaster' (Radzinowicz 1999: 229). Cohen's analysis was later updated for his 1981 essay 'Footprints in the Sand' (Cohen 1981).

The next essays introduce the reader to some of his work on punishment and social control. As we discussed earlier, throughout the 1970s Cohen wrote prolifically on the experience of imprisonment and prison policy (see above). But alongside his collaborative work with Laurie Taylor he also started to reflect on the historical origins and recent trends in punishment and social control. In this period Cohen became deeply interested in the new wave of revisionist history writing which questioned explanations of penal change in terms of reform, progress, humanitiarianism or benevolence.[12] The revisionists, as he and Andrew Scull pointed out in their introduction to *Social Control and the State*, started from a different position: '… scepticism about the professed aims, beliefs and intentions of the reformers; concern with the analysis of power and its effects; curiosity about the relationship between intentions and consequences; determination to locate the reform enterprise in the social, economic and political contexts of the period. The problem of maintaining the social order … becomes dominant' (Cohen and Scull 1983: 2). At this stage in his career Cohen also began to reflect on recent trends in social control and punishment, in particular on the origins and effects of the so-called 'destructuring impulse', that is, the longing for forms of community control, as it was expressed in various calls for decarceration, decentralization, deprofessionalization, demedicalization, antipsychiatry, abolitionism, and the like.

We have, again, selected a series of three short articles from *New Society* (**'Crime and Punishment: 1. How Can We Balance Justice, Guilt and Tolerance?', 'Crime and Punishment: 2. Community Control – A New Utopia', 'Crime and Punishment: 3. Some Modest and Unrealistic Proposals', 1979**). In these essays Cohen outlines in an accessible way some of the ideas which he elaborated over the coming years. The second of these short articles – on community control as new utopia – for example, formed the backbone of his famous article on 'The Punitive City', which we have also selected for this volume (**'The Punitive City: Notes on the Dispersal of Social Control', 1979**). In this often cited essay Cohen elaborates his well-known 'fishing net' metaphor (widening the net, thinning the mesh, etc).[13] This essay is followed by his chapter for the book *The Power to Punish* (1983) (**'Social Control Talk: Telling Stories about Correctional Change', 1983**). *The Power to Punish* has been tremendously important for setting an agenda for research in the sociology of punishment.[14] This chapter offered – together with 'The Punitive City' – inspiration for his second major book, *Visions of Social Control* (1985). The next essay is his 1989 commentary on the literature on 'social control' (**'The Critical Discourse on Social Control: Notes on the Concept as a Hammer', 1989**). Here he warns his readers that the term 'social control' risks becoming a 'hammering concept'. Like little children who sometimes use their toy hammers to bang on the floor, attack a baby sibling or enjoy the sound of breaking glass, so the concept of 'social control' has often been used to render different bits and pieces of reality manageable and comprehensible but, unfortunately, without much attention for the consequences. The final essay of this period is one of his contributions to the debate on abolitionism (**'Alternatives to Punishment – The Abolitionist Case', 1991**). In this paper Cohen expresses his own views – and doubts – about abolitionism: 'My own position towards abolitionism is that of a sympathetic, but critical fellow traveller: I agree with much, want to believe more but am skeptical about some' (Cohen 1991c: 729). In the paper Cohen also presents a useful summary of some of the ideas that he had elaborated at length in *Visions of Social Control*.

Throughout the 1990s and the early 2000s Cohen's work touches in particular upon two themes: first, he continues his 'sociology of knowledge'-type of reflection on developments in criminology; and, second, he starts focusing his research on reactions to torture and other human rights violations. In 1979 Cohen moved from Britain to Israel where he became a professor at Hebrew University. From a professional point of view this did not turn out to be his best decision: 'Conditioned, of course, by my immersion in these debates elsewhere, my personal reactions to Israeli criminology in the eight years I've worked here have sometimes been like travelling back in a time machine. The mainstream of the discipline is frozen at the place it was, say, in Britain and Western Europe 20 years ago – and there are no visible sidestreams' (Cohen 1990b: 7). When Cohen was asked in June 2001 about the worst thing in his life, he replied that moving to Israel had been a 'mistake' and that he had spent 'a lot of unhappy time there' (Thompson 2014: 116).

But living and working in Israel also implied that he now – after growing up in Apartheid South Africa – came to be exposed – as he put it – to yet another rather extraordinary society (Cohen 1991a: 2). Life in Israel would impact upon his academic work, in particular from December 1987 onwards, when the *Intifada* started. Indeed, Cohen became actively involved in the human rights movement and was *inter alia* co-author (with Daphna Golan) of the 1991 B'Tselem report *The Interrogation of Palestinians During the Intifada: Ill-Treatment, 'Moderate Physical Pressure' or Torture?* This report documented the torture and ill-treatment of Palestinian prisoners during the *Intifada*. The focus was on interrogation techniques that were used by the security forces on the

West Bank and in Gaza. The report included drawings of the interrogation techniques in order to make readers aware that what had been named 'moderate physical pressure' (in the wake of the 1987 report of the Landau Commission) amounted, in fact, to torture and serious ill-treatment. As Cohen explained: 'We wanted to undermine the function of political language ("moderate physical pressure") that Orwell pointed to: "Such phraseology is needed if one wants to name things without calling up mental pictures of them"' (Cohen 1991b: 27). In a follow-up report that was released in March 1992 Cohen and Golan reflected upon the reception of their original report. Here they were disappointed about the lack of debate and decisive action (Cohen and Golan 1992). Ten years later, in the preface to *States of Denial,* Cohen looked back upon the reactions to the B'Tselem report as follows: '... we were immediately thrown into the politics of denial. The official and mainstream response was venomous: *outright denial* (it doesn't happen); *discrediting* (the organization was biased, manipulated or gullible); *renaming* (yes, something does happen, but it is not torture); and *justification* (anyway "it" was morally justified)' (Cohen 2001: xi, italics in original). These experiences with the B'Tselem report sparked his interest in mechanisms of denial. Between 1992 and 1994 Cohen conducted a study, with financial support from the Ford Foundation, about how human rights organizations (in particular Amnesty International) aim to get their message out there and to move people to donate or otherwise support the good cause. As he described the project in the opening pages of his report *Denial and Acknowledgement: The Impact of Information about Human Rights Violations*: 'My project might be called "After The Report." Its aim is to place on the agenda of the human rights community some serious consideration about what happens to all the knowledge that we generate. There is a paradox in the heart of the human rights movement: we believe that if people "only knew" what was happening they would do something, but we have learnt that just letting know is not enough' (Cohen 1995: iv). The B'Tselem and Ford Foundation reports contain the seeds for what later became his third major book, that is, *States of Denial* (2001). Indeed, the central question of that book is: 'what do we do with our knowledge about the suffering of others, and what does this knowledge do to us?' (Cohen 2001: x).

From this last major phase in his career we have selected the following publications. The first article is an early essay published in *Tikkun* (**'Talking about Torture in Israel', 1991**). In this essay Cohen reflects directly on the torture debate in Israel as well as on the reception of the B'Tselem report. The paper discusses the debate on torture as a 'struggle to define reality' and an 'epistemological politics' and, in doing so, it offers a wonderful introduction to some of the themes that return later on in his work. The next essay is his famous Willem Bonger Memorial Lecture which he delivered in Amsterdam on 14 May 1990.[15] The lecture was part of a high-profile but unfortunately short-lived series that ran between 1990 and 1995.[16] In this lecture Cohen reflects upon the recent history of various critical strands in criminology from the 1960s up to the late 1980s (**'Intellectual Skepticism and Political Commitment: The Case of Radical Criminology', 1993**). This 'sociology of knowledge'-type of paper is followed by two of his mid-1990s publications on human rights and denial: the first paper is a contribution to the debate on 'transitional justice', that is, the question of how societies confront serious human rights abuses committed by previous regimes (**'State Crimes of Previous Regimes: Knowledge, Accountability, and the Policing of the Past', 1995**); the second paper usefully summarizes and reflects on some of the findings of the Ford Foundation report, *Denial and Acknowledgement* ('**Government Responses to Human Rights Reports: Claims, Denials, and Counterclaims**', **1996**). In the next essay – which is the published version of his 1995 Centenary Lecture in Law and Society – Cohen revisits the relationship between crime and politics – a topic that had interested him since the early beginning of his career ('**Crime and Politics: Spot the Difference', 1996**). We have also included his essay on 'Conference Life' ('**Conference Life: The Rough Guide', 1997**). This is probably one of the funniest pieces that has ever been published in an academic journal: in this paper Cohen introduces the neophyte to the customs and habits of attending academic criminology conferences. Our selection continues with Cohen's introduction to the third edition of *Folk Devils and Moral Panics* ('**Moral Panics as Cultural Politics', 2002**). Here he reviews thirty years of research and debate on moral panics and he establishes a link with his later work on denial. The penultimate essay is an article that was published in a special issue on torture that Cohen edited for *Index on Censorship* ('**Post-Moral Torture: From Guantanamo to Abu Ghraib', 2005**). Here Cohen reflects on the debate on torture following the controversy related to the prison camps of Guantanamo and Abu Ghraib. The book concludes with the speech he delivered when he accepted the inaugural Outstanding Achievement Award from the British Society of Criminology ('**Carry on Panicking', 2009**).

Beyond *Outside Criminology*

In this volume we can only include a small selection of Stan Cohen's published work. For readers who wish to explore his oeuvre further we give here a few guidelines and suggestions. The most obvious starting-point is his three major books, *Folk Devils and Moral Panics* (1972), *Visions of Social Control* (1985) and *States of Denial* (2001), as well as the essays that Cohen selected for *Against Criminology* (1988). The 2002 edition of *Folk Devils and Moral Panics* also includes the introduction ('Symbols of Trouble') that he wrote for the second edition of the book which appeared in 1980. Cohen's PhD dissertation has recently been made available through 'LSE Theses Online', the online archive of PhD theses for the London School of Economics and Political Science.[17] The 1991 and 1992 reports on torture which he wrote together with Daphna Golan have been utterly important for his work on denial and can be consulted at the webpage of B'Tselem, The Israeli Information Center for Human Rights in the Occupied Territories.[18] The 1995 report *Denial and Acknowledgement: The Impact of Information about Human Rights Violations* has, again, been very significant for what later became *States of Denial* but, unfortunately, no e-version has ever been made publicly available.[19] For his other published work we invite readers to consult Stan Cohen's bibliography which has been included in the present volume. This bibliography covers most of his published work from 1966 till 2014.

For those who are interested in learning more about his biography and intellectual development there are a number of instructive interviews in the public domain. In 1987 *Canadian Criminology Forum* published a lengthy interview where Cohen reflects *inter alia* upon the place of values in his work, his early influences, the National Deviancy Conference, the work of David Matza and Michel Foucault, abolitionism and, in particular, his second major book, *Visions of Social Control*, which had only just been published (McMahon and Kellough 1987).[20] In 2004 Laurie Taylor interviewed Stan Cohen for *New Humanist*. This interview was later reprinted in *Social Justice* (in 2005) as well as in the 2007 LSE *Festschrift*. Here Cohen is asked about his experience in Israel and how his work on the torture of Palestinian detainees in the Occupied Territories led to his third major book, *States of Denial*. The German journal *Neue Kriminalpolitik* published a so-called 'portrait' of Stan Cohen in 1994 (Herz 1994). The Dutch-language interview Herman Franke conducted on the occasion of the Willem Bonger Memorial Lecture which we referred to at the start of this chapter is also still worth reading. The most comprehensive guide to his life and work (up till mid-2001) is the transcripts of the interviews which Paul Thompson conducted in London on 2 and 30 May 2001 and 14 June 2001 for his oral history project on 'Pioneers of Qualitative Research, 1996–2012'. Here Cohen reflects at length on his personal and professional life, from growing up in South Africa and moving to Britain, through his experiences and disappointments during his time in Israel, up to the writing of *States of Denial*. In 2007 his colleagues at LSE published a *Festschrift* on the occasion of his retirement from the position of Martin White Professor of Sociology at the LSE. Many of the contributions to this *Festschrift* – in particular the editors' introduction – contain a great deal of information on his biography as well as insightful reflections on his work (Downes *et al.* 2007).

Immediately after Cohen's death a number of obituaries and tributes to his life and work were published (Taylor 2013; Downes 2013; Hudson 2013; Super 2013). Shorter messages from his former colleagues, friends, students and others were posted – and can still be read – at LSE's condolences page.[21] The journal *Crime, Media & Culture* invited a number of Cohen's old friends and colleagues to reflect on his life and work (Ben-Yehuda 2013; McLaughlin 2013; Moon 2013; Young 2013). The 2013 Spring edition of *Critical Criminologist* has a section entitled 'Reflections on Stan Cohen and his Legacy' (Novelozo 2013; McDermott 2013). The 2013 Autumn edition of the newsletter of the *European Group for the Study of Deviance & Social Control* also paid special tribute to Stan Cohen (Scott 2013, Feyling 2013; Munro 2013; Potter 2013). There are also a number of reflections on his life and work in Spanish and Dutch (Anitua 2013; Bernal Sarmiento 2013; Daems 2014). On 18 February 2013 the BBC's Radio 4 show *Thinking Allowed*, hosted by his old friend Laurie Taylor, devoted a special programme to Stan Cohen.[22] On 10 December 2013 a memorial event 'From Moral Panics to States of Denial: A Celebration of the Life and Work of Stan Cohen' took place in London with interventions from Robin Cohen, David Downes, Daphna Golan, Thomas Hammarberg and Harvey Molotch. Video and audio recordings of this event have been made publicly available through the website of LSE.[23]

There is in the meantime also a burgeoning secondary literature on Stan Cohen's work. The concept of moral panics, in particular, has become massively influential in academic literature and popular culture, as he recalled himself in his 2002 introduction for the third edition of *Folk Devils and Moral Panics*, which has been reprinted in this volume. In 2009 the *British Journal of Criminology* devoted a special issue (issue 1, volume 49) to the concept (see Ben-Yehuda 2009). In 2013 Ashgate published *The Ashgate Research Companion to Moral Panics* (Krinsky 2013; see also Thompson 1998). The British Academy hosted a special event 'Moral Panics: Then and Now' on 9 March

2007 with Stan Cohen, David Garland and Stuart Hall (see also Garland 2007, 2008). An audio recording of this event has been made available through the Academy's website.[24] In the late 1990s Stan Cohen was interviewed by Steve Taylor for 'The Classic Collection' about *Folk Devils and Moral Panics*. The interview with accompanying video footage and press cuttings about the Mods and Rockers events was released in 1999 as a 25-minute DVD intended for use in education. Stan Cohen was also included in *Fifty Key Thinkers in Criminology* (Findlay 2010).

Stan Cohen's personal library was entrusted by his family to the LSE. The 'Stan Cohen Collection' is hosted by the Centre for the Study of Human Rights in a room named after him.[25]

References:

Anitua, G.I. (2013). Stanley Cohen (1942–2013): la mirada crítica. *Revista de derecho penal y criminología*, 1 February, 131–138.

Ben-Yehuda, N. (2009). Moral Panics – 36 Years On. *British Journal of Criminology*, 49(1), 1–3.

Ben-Yehuda, N. (2013). Stan. *Crime, Media, Culture*, 9(2), 188–189.

Bernal Sarmiento, C.E. (2013). Stanley Cohen: Escepticismo intelectual, compromiso político y justicia social. In memoriam. *Revista Crítica Penal y Poder*, 4, 216–224.

Cohen, S. (1969). Hooligans, Vandals and the Community: A Study of Social Reaction to Juvenile Delinquency. Thesis submitted for the degree of PhD, University of London.

Cohen, S. (1971a). Introduction. In: S. Cohen (ed.), *Images of Deviance*. Harmondsworth: Penguin Books, 9–25.

Cohen, S. (1971b). Directions for Research on Adolescent Group Violence and Vandalism. *British Journal of Criminology*, 11(4), 319–340.

Cohen, S. (1972). *Folk Devils and Moral Panics. The Creation of the Mods and Rockers*. London: MacGibbon and Kee.

Cohen, S. (1974). Asylum in Chains. Review: D.J. Rothman, *The Discovery of the Asylum: Social Order and Disorder in the New Republic*; Y. Bakal (ed.), *Closing Correctional Institutions*. *New Society*, 7 February, 332–333.

Cohen, S. (1975a). It's All Right for You to Talk: Political and Sociological Manifestos for Social Work Action. In: R. Bailey and M. Brake (eds), *Radical Social Work*. New York: Pantheon Books, 76–95.

Cohen, S. (1975b). Good Dreams. Review: C. Bukowski, *Life and Death in the Charity Ward*. *New Society*, 10 April, 89–90.

Cohen, S. (1978). The Archaeology of Power. Review Essay: M. Foucault, *Discipline and Punish: The Birth of the Prison. Contemporary Sociology*, 7(5), 566–568.

Cohen, S. (1979a). Crime and Punishment: 3. Some Modest and Unrealistic Proposals. *New Society*, 29 March, 731–734.

Cohen, S. (1979b). Guilt, Justice and Tolerance: Some Old Concepts for a New Criminology. In: D. Downes and P. Rock (eds), *Deviant Interpretations*. Oxford: Martin Robertson, 17–51.

Cohen, S. (1979c). Review: A.T. Scull, *Decarceration: Community Treatment and the Deviant – A Radical View*. *British Journal of Sociology*, 30(2), 250–251.

Cohen, S. (1980). Introduction. In: L. Dronfield, *Outside Chance: The Story of the Newham Alternatives Project*. London: Radical Alternatives to Prison, 2–6.

Cohen, S. (1981). Footprints in the Sand: A Further Report on Criminology and the Sociology of

Deviance in Britain. In: M. Fitzgerald, G. McLennan and J. Pawson (eds), *Crime and Society: Readings in History and Theory*. London and Henley: Routledge and Kegan Paul, 220–247.

Cohen, S. (1985a). *Visions of Social Control: Crime, Punishment and Classification.* Cambridge: Polity Press.

Cohen, S. (1985b). Review: E.H. Mizruchi, *Regulating Society: Marginality and Social Control in Historical Perspective*. *Sociological Review*, 33(1), 159–161.

Cohen, S. (1986). Review: D. Garland, *Punishment and Welfare: A History of Penal Strategies*. *British Journal of Criminology*, 26(4), 409–411.

Cohen, S. (1988). Against Criminology. In: S. Cohen, *Against Criminology*. New Brunswick: Transaction, 8–32

Cohen, S. (1990a). Preface. In: W. de Haan, *The Politics of Redress: Crime, Punishment and Penal Abolition*. London: Unwin Hyman, xiii–xiv.

Cohen, S. (1990b). Politics and Crime in Israel: Reactions from the Home Front. *Social Justice*, 17(1), 5–24.

Cohen, S. (1990c). *Intellectual Scepticism and Political Commitment: The Case of Radical Criminology*. Amsterdam: Stichting W.A. Bonger-Lezingen.

Cohen, S. (1991a). *The Human Rights Movement in Israel and South Africa: Some Paradoxical Comparisons. Lecture in Memory of Professor Michael Wade*. The Truman Institute. Occasional Papers No. 1. The Hebrew University of Jerusalem, 12 November.

Cohen, S. (1991b). Talking about Torture in Israel. *Tikkun*, 6(6), 23–30, 89–90.

Cohen, S. (1991c). Alternatives to Punishment – The Abolitionist Case. *Israel Law Review*, 25(3), 729–739.

Cohen, S. (1993a). Human Rights and Crimes of the State: The Culture of Denial. *Australian & New Zealand Journal of Criminology*, 26, 97–115.

Cohen, S. (1993b). Intellectual Skepticism and Political Commitment: The Case of Radical Criminology. *Studies in Law, Politics, and Society*, 13, 187–209.

Cohen, S. (1995). *Denial and Acknowledgement: The Impact of Information about Human Rights Violations*. The Hebrew University of Jerusalem: Center for Human Rights.

Cohen, S. (1996). Review, J.I. Ross, *Controlling State Crime: An Introduction*. *British Journal of Sociology*, 47(4), 733–734.

Cohen, S. (2000). Preface. In: C. Banks (ed.), *Developing Cultural Criminology: Theory and Practice in Papua New Guinea*. Sydney: Sydney Institute of Criminology Monograph Series No 13, 1–4.

Cohen, S. (2001). *States of Denial. Knowing about Atrocities and Suffering*. Cambridge: Polity Press.

Cohen, S. (2002). Moral Panics as Cultural Politics. Introduction to the Third Edition. In: S. Cohen, *Folk Devils and Moral Panics: The Creation of the Mods and Rockers*. Third Edition. London: Routledge, vii–xxxvii.

Cohen, S. (2009). Carry on Panicking. Address on receiving the Award for 'Outstanding Achievement' from the British Society of Criminology at its Annual Conference, Cardiff, 29 June 2009. *British Society of Criminology Newsletter*, 64, 5–10.

Cohen, S. and Golan, D. (1991). *The Interrogation of Palestinians during the Intifada: Ill-Treatment, 'Moderate Physical Pressure' or Torture?* Jerusalem: B'Tselem, The Israeli Information Center for Human Rights in the Occupied Territories.

Cohen, S. and Golan, D. (1992). *The Interrogation of Palestinians during the Intifada: Follow-up to March 1991 B'Tselem Report*. Jerusalem: B'Tselem, The Israeli Information Center for Human Rights in the Occupied Territories.

Cohen, S. and Scull, A. (1983). Introduction: Social Control in History and Sociology. In: S. Cohen and A. Scull (eds), *Social Control and the State: Historical and Comparative Essays*. Oxford: Martin Robertson, 1–14.

Cohen, S. and Taylor, L. (1972). *Psychological Survival: The Experience of Long-Term Imprisonment.* Harmondsworth: Penguin.
Cohen, S. and Taylor, L. (1975a). Prison Research: A Cautionary Tale. *New Society,* 30 January, 253–255.
Cohen, S. and Taylor, L. (1975b). From Psychopaths to Outsiders: British Criminology and the National Deviancy Conference. In: H. Bianchi, M. Simondi and I. Taylor (eds), *Deviance and Control in Europe. Papers from the European Group for the Study of Deviance and Social Control.* London: John Wiley & Sons, 3–33.
Cohen, S. and Taylor, L. (1976). *Escape Attempts: The Theory and Practice of Resistance to Everyday Life.* London: Allen Lane.
Cohen, S. and Taylor, L. (1977). Talking about Prison Blues. In: C. Bell and H. Newby (eds), *Doing Sociological Research.* London: George Allen and Unwin, 67–86.
Cohen, S. and Taylor, L. (1978). *Prison Secrets.* London: National Council for Civil Liberties & Radical Alternatives to Prison.
Cohen, S. and Taylor, L. (1992a). *Escape Attempts: The Theory and Practice of Resistance to Everyday Life. Second Edition.* London: Routledge.
Cohen, S. and Taylor, L. (1992b). Have We Got to Get Out of This Place? *The Guardian,* 25 August.
Cohen, S. and Taylor, L. (1992c). The Supermarket of the Self. *The Guardian,* 26 August.
Daems, T. (2014). Stanley Cohen (1942–2013): een beknopte bio- en bibliografie. *Panopticon,* 35(5), 468–473.
Downes, D. (2013). Stanley Cohen: Distinguished Criminologist. *The Independent.* 24 February.
Downes, D., Rock, P., Chinkin, C. and Gearty, C. (eds) (2007). *Crime, Social Control and Human Rights. From Moral Panics to States of Denial, Essays in Honour of Stanley Cohen.* Cullompton: Willan Publishing.
Feyling, R. (2013). 'Folk Devils' and Release from Prison: How the Work of Stan Cohen Helps us to Understand Post-prison Reintegration. *Newsletter of the European Group for the Study of Deviance and Social Control.* Autumn I (Special 40th Anniversary Edition), 23–25.
Findlay, M. (2010). Stanley Cohen. In: K. Hayward, S. Maruna and J. Mooney (eds), *Fifty Key Thinkers in Criminology.* London: Routledge, 242–249.
Franke, H. (1990). Stanley Cohen over misdaad en straf. 'Twee dingen tegelijk kan niet: moeilijke vragen stellen en criminaliteit bestrijden'. *NRC Handelsblad,* 8 May.
Franke, H. (1995). *The Emancipation of Prisoners.* Edinburgh: Edinburgh University Press.
Frith, S. (1995). Speaking Volumes: *New Society* (1962–87). *Times Higher Education.* 30 January. http://www.timeshighereducation.co.uk/162372.article.
Garland, D. (2007). Moral Panics: Then and Now. *British Academy Review,* 10, 4–5.
Garland, D. (2008). On the Concept of Moral Panic. *Crime, Media, Culture,* 4(1), 9–30.
Garland, D. and Young, P. (1983). Preface. In: D. Garland and P. Young (eds), *The Power to Punish.* London: Heinemann, ix–x.
Herz, R. (1994). Stanley Cohen – Der Engagierte. *Neue Kriminalpolitik,* 6(2), 50–52.
Hudson, B. (2013). Professor Stanley Cohen: An Appreciation. *Criminal Justice Matters,* 92(1), 40.
Krinsky, C. (ed.) (2013). *The Ashgate Research Companion to Moral Panics.* Farnham: Ashgate.
McDermott, V. (2013). Adding Legitimacy to the Moral Panic Toolkit. *The Critical Criminologist,* 21(3), 8–16.
McLaughlin, E. (2013). Start Worrying: Details to Follow. *Crime, Media, Culture,* 9(2), 190–192.
McMahon, M. and Kellough, G. (1987). An Interview with Stanley Cohen. *Canadian Criminology Forum,* 8, 132–149.
Mathiesen, T. (1974). *The Politics of Abolition.* London: Robertson.
Matza, D. (1969). *Becoming Deviant.* Englewood Cliffs, NJ: Prentice-Hall.

Moon, C. (2013). 'Looking without Seeing, Listening without Hearing': Cohen, Denial and Human Rights. *Crime, Media, Culture*, 9(2), 193–196.

Munro, B. (2013). On Words and the Logic of Things: Some Notes on Stan Cohen's Visions of Social Control. *Newsletter of the European Group for the Study of Deviance and Social Control*. Autumn I (Special 40th Anniversary Edition), 21–22.

Novelozo, A. (2013). The Last Seminar: 'Their' Story. *The Critical Criminologist*, 21(3), 2–8.

Potter, G. (2013). Stan Cohen: Critical Criminology's Theoretical Curmudgeon. *Newsletter of the European Group for the Study of Deviance and Social Control*. Autumn I (Special 40th Anniversary Edition), 18–20.

Probyn, W. (1977). *Angel Face. The Making of a Criminal*. London: George Allen and Unwin.

Radzinowicz, L. (1999). *Adventures in Criminology*. London: Routledge.

Savage, M. (2013). Revisiting New Society. http://www.discoversociety.org/2013/10/01/revisiting-new-society/.

Scott, D. (2013). A Disobedient Visionary with an Enquiring Mind – An Essay on the Contribution of Stan Cohen. *Newsletter of the European Group for the Study of Deviance and Social Control*. Autumn I (Special 40th Anniversary Edition), 8–14.

Super, G. (2013). Stan Cohen – In Memory. Centre of Criminology, Law Faculty, University of Cape Town, 7 March.

Taylor, L. (2004). The Other Side of the Street. *New Humanist*, July–August.

Taylor, L. (2013). Stanley Cohen Obituary. *The Guardian*, 23 January.

Thompson, K. (1998). *Moral Panics*. London: Routledge.

Thompson, P. (2014). *Pioneers of Qualitative Research, 1996–2012 [computer file]. 2nd Edition*. Colchester, Essex: UK Data Archive [distributor], January 2014. SN: 6226.

Young, J. (2013). Early Days. *Crime, Media, Culture*, 9(2), 197–201.

Notes

1 Five years later Cohen adopted a similar appreciative approach when he offered his assistance to Walter Probyn for his autobiography *Angel Face* (1977). Probyn was one of his former students at Durham prison's E-Wing. Cohen wrote an introduction, a reflection and a postscript to Probyn's book.

2 Cohen and Taylor's enduring struggle with the Home Office drove them to the highly unusual decision to return a research grant which had been awarded to them by the Social Science Research Council (see Cohen and Taylor 1975a, 1977).

3 *Escape Attempts* was first published in 1976. In their original preface Cohen and Taylor highlighted the influence of Erving Goffman and Georg Simmel (Cohen and Taylor 1992a: xv). In the preface to the second edition they acknowledged that the book would have been different if they had been able to take Michel Foucault's work into account: '… a continual source of delight and an intellectual inspiration which would make this a different book if we started writing it now' (Cohen and Taylor 1992a: ix). Cohen had a somewhat mixed relationship towards the legacy of Michel Foucault. In his 1978 review of *Discipline and Punish* he expressed some reservations about Foucault's approach but these were overshadowed by his overall praise for the book. He found Foucault's study 'dazzlingly creative' and '… the most stimulating and revealing history of prisons and punishment ever written … Foucault has become our supreme archaeologist of power' (Cohen 1978: 566, 568). In *Visions of Social Control* Cohen wrote the following: '… to write today about punishment and classification without Foucault, is like talking about the unconscious without Freud' (Cohen 1985a: 10). In a 1987 interview

Cohen disclosed how he had read Foucault: 'When I moved to Israel in 1979, I'd already read *Discipline and Punish* and *Madness and Civilization*, but after that I was reading Foucault on my own, totally insulated and isolated from everybody's discovery of Foucault in the West, and the criticism, and the massive industry about it. Nobody knew anything about it in Israel' (McMahon and Kellough 1987: 140). In this interview (as well as in *Visions of Social Control*) Cohen discussed how he disagreed with Foucault's structuralist denial of human agency but also why his views on power appealed to him so much (see Cohen 1985a: 9–10; McMahon and Kellough 1987: 140–142).

4 The book was re-issued in 1992 with a new introduction, 'Life after postmodernism' (Cohen and Taylor 1992a: 1–29). On 25 and 26 August 1992 *The Guardian* devoted two full pages to excerpts of this new edition, see Cohen and Taylor 1992b,c.

5 'I think many of the things I've written about criminology ... are really exercises in the sociology of knowledge. I'm interested in ideas, and how ideas change: this fascinates more than any other intellectual problem' (McMahon and Kellough 1987: 136).

6 Throughout his career Cohen pointed repeatedly at the added value of fiction, e.g. '... it seems as if (not for the first time) the sociologist's task is being carried out with more credibility and imagination by novelists. One "appreciates" (in Matza's sense) the violence in, say, *Last Exit to Brooklyn* in a way that one does not in most sociological accounts' (Cohen 1971b: 334); on Charles Bukowski: 'Somehow he had survived 14 years working in the Los Angeles post office, an experience which was the basis of his 1971 novel, *Post Office*. This is my favourite of his writings and – to take for a moment the entirely philistine attitude of the sociologist who plunders literature for "material" – it is a superb description of work and the pleasures that make it at all tolerable' (Cohen 1975b: 89). Or in a reflection on the sociology of deviance: 'Any comparisons of sociological naturalism with naturalism in the novel (or "social realism" in another tradition) were quite deliberate and indeed most sociologists working in this vein began to see themselves as novelists manqué. Sociology of deviance booklists were (and still are) full of those works of fiction that we told our students would give a more realistic view of the world than our own research: *Last Exit to Brooklyn, Junkie, Our Lady of the Flowers, One Flew over the Cuckoo's Nest* – these would tell it like it is' (Cohen 1979b: 18).

7 Cohen seemed to dislike in particular the American way of communicating. See e.g. '... the truly awful prose style of American sociology' (Cohen 1985b: 161); or '...a mixture of social scientese and that mangled way in which Americans inflate English' (Cohen 1996: 734).

8 Most notably in the final chapter of *Visions of Social Control* which carried the title 'What is to be done?' (Cohen 1985a: 236–272).

9 For more details, see Paul Rock's biographical memoir, reprinted in this volume. Also see McMahon and Kellough, 1987; Thompson 2014.

10 Since we are not aware of any existing complete list of his published work we have compiled this bibliography ourselves. Different versions of this bibliography have been seen by several of Stan Cohen's former colleagues and friends. Their names are listed in the acknowledgements of this book.

11 Terence Morris was his supervisor at the LSE. In the preface to his PhD Cohen also explicitly extends his thanks to David Downes (Cohen 1969: 3). In 2001 he told Paul Thompson that if it were not for the encouragement of Downes he would probably have dropped out (Thompson 2014: 38–39).

12 See also his reviews of David Rothman's *The Discovery of the Asylum* (Cohen 1974), Michel Foucault's *Discipline and Punish* (Cohen 1978), Andrew Scull's *Decarceration* (Cohen 1979c) and David Garland's *Punishment and Welfare* (Cohen 1986).

13 Interestingly, the notion of 'net widening' had already appeared on several occasions throughout his PhD, see e.g.: '... the "widening of the net" effect ... the result is that a number of

non-hooligan deviants are drawn into the same net of sensitization. In the phase after the inventory, other targets became more visible, and, hence, candidates for social control' (Cohen 1969: 482). See also Cohen 1969: 483, 494, 520, 566 (note 24).

14. The book's title '... intended to signify a shift away from traditional moral and technical penology towards a political and social analysis of the institutions, practices and techniques through which that power is exercised. However, it should not be thought that penality is exclusively "political" or that there exists, behind the penal complex, a newly discovered subject of history – "power" itself' (Garland and Young 1983: x).
15. Stan Cohen's Bonger lecture was originally published as a small booklet with an introduction by Elisabeth Lissenberg (Cohen 1990c). It was later reprinted with small changes in *Studies in Law, Politics, and Society*. It is this 1993 edition which we have included in this volume.
16. Stan Cohen's 1990 inaugural lecture was followed by lectures from Ernest Zahn (1991), Jaap Goudsblom (1992), Pat Carlen (1993), Jac. van Weringh (1994) and Zygmunt Bauman (1995).
17. LSE Theses Online can be accessed via http://etheses.lse.ac.uk/; Stan Cohen's PhD dissertation is available at http://etheses.lse.ac.uk/48/.
18. Both reports are available at http://www.btselem.org/publications.
19. Unfortunately it is also not easy to get access to hard copies of the report. I had to order a copy from the library of Utrecht University as I was unable to find a copy in a Belgian university library. The Stan Cohen Collection at LSE's Center for the Study of Human Rights also has a copy.
20. This interview has recently also been published online, on the website of the European Group for the Study of Deviance and Social Control: http://www.europeangroup.org/?q=node/25.
21. See http://blogs.lse.ac.uk/condolences/2013/01/08/stancohen/.
22. An audio-link is available at http://www.bbc.co.uk/programmes/b01qjc37.
23. See http://www.lse.ac.uk/humanRights/events/2013/stanCohen.aspx#ad-image-0.
24. See http://www.britac.ac.uk/events/2007/moral-panic/.
25. The catalogue can be consulted online at http://www.lse.ac.uk/humanRights/research/Library.aspx.

Bibliography of Stanley Cohen (1966–2014)

Cohen, S. (1966). Observations on Anarchy 57: Anarchism and Crime. *Anarchy*, 59, 29–30.

(1966). Vandalism and the Social Structure. *Anarchy*, 64, 181–187.

(1967). Mods, Rockers and the Rest: Community Reactions to Juvenile Delinquency. *Howard Journal of Criminal Justice*, 12(2), 121–130.

(1967). Review: K.T. Erikson, *Wayward Puritans: A Study in the Sociology of Deviance*. *British Journal of Criminology*, 7(3), 346–348.

(1967). Review: A.K. Cohen, *Deviance and Control*; E.M. Lemert, *Human Deviance, Social Problems and Social Control*. *British Journal of Criminology*, 7(4), 459–461.

(1967). Violence: Why Vandalism? *The Guardian*, 15 November.

(1968). Politics of Vandalism. *The Nation*, 11 November, 497–500.

(1968). Criminal Behaviour. Review: F.H. McClintock and N. Howard Avison, *Crime in England and Wales*. *New Society*, 5 December, 852–853.

(1968). Vandalism – 1. The Politics of Vandalism. *New Society*, 12 December, 872–874.

(1968). Vandalism – 2. The Nature of Vandalism. *New Society*, 12 December, 875–876.

(1968). Vandalism – 3. Can it be Controlled? *New Society*, 12 December, 877–878.

(1969). Hooligans, Vandals and the Community: A Study of Social Reaction to Juvenile Delinquency. Thesis submitted for the degree of PhD, University of London.

(1969). Review: N. Christie, *Aspects of Social Control in Welfare States*. *British Journal of Sociology*, 20(3), 352–353.

(1969). Chicago Segments. Review: G.D. Suttles, *The Social Order of the Slum*. *New Society*, 15 May, 762.

(1969). Notes on Detention Centres. *Anarchy*, 101, 210–222.

(1969). The Politics of Violence. *Phalanx*, 2.

(1970). Review: J. Landesco, *Organised Crime in Chicago*. *British Journal of Criminology*, 10(1), 92.

(1970). Seized Bootlaces. *The Times*, 3 April.

(with P. Rock) (1970). The Teddy Boy. In: V. Bogdanor and R.K. Skidelsky (eds), *The Age of Affluence: 1951–1964*. London: Macmillan, 288–320.

(with L. Taylor) (1970). The Experience of Time in Long-term Imprisonment. *New Society*, 31 December, 1156–1159.

(ed.) (1971). *Images of Deviance*. Harmondsworth: Penguin Books.

(1971). Introduction. In: S. Cohen (ed.), *Images of Deviance*. Harmondsworth: Penguin Books, 9–25.

(1971). Postscript. In: S. Cohen (ed.), *Images of Deviance*. Harmondsworth: Penguin Books, 246–252.

(1971). Directions for Research on Adolescent Group Violence and Vandalism. *British Journal of Criminology*, 11(4), 319–340.

(1971). Review: J.D. Douglas, *Deviance and Respectability: The Social Construction of Moral Meanings*. *British Journal of Sociology*, 22(1), 105–106.

(1971). Inside Out. Review: R.F. Sparks, *Local Prisons: The Crisis in the English Penal System*. *New Society*, 23 September, 578–579.

(1971). Review: J.R. Lambert, *Crime, Police and Race Relations: A Study in Birmingham*. *British Journal of Criminology*, 11(3), 296–297.

(1972). *Folk Devils and Moral Panics: The Creation of the Mods and Rockers.* London: MacGibbon and Kee.
(1972). Writing from Inside. *New Society*, 31 August, 447–449.
(1972). Review: J. Irwin, *The Felon. Sociology*, 6(1), 141–142.
(with L. Taylor) (1972). *Psychological Survival: The Experience of Long-Term Imprisonment.* Harmondsworth: Penguin Books.
(1973). Protest, Unrest and Delinquency: Convergences in Labels and Behaviour. *International Journal of Criminology and Penology*, 1, 117–128.
(1973). Review: R. Hood and R. Sparks, *Key Issues in Criminology*; J.F. Short, *Modern Criminals. Sociology*, 7(1), 154–155.
(1973). Cry Murder. Review: R. Heppenstall, *The Sex War and Others: A Survey of Recent Murders, Principally in France*; R.D. Altick, *Victorian Studies in Scarlet. New Society*, 3 May, 256–257.
(1973). Living with Crime. *New Society*, 8 November, 330–333.
(1973). Property Destruction: Motives and Meanings. In: C. Ward (ed.), *Vandalism.* London: The Architectural Press, 23–53.
(1973). Campaigning against Vandalism. In: C. Ward (ed.), *Vandalism.* London: The Architectural Press, 215–258.
(1973). Some Sociological Problems in the Study of Adolescent Violence. *Proceedings of the Royal Society of Medicine*, 66, 1131–1132.
(1973). Review: L. Radzinowicz and M.E. Wolfgang, *Crime and Justice. Sociology*, 7(3), 475–476.
(1973). Bars that Split Families. *The Guardian*, 7 July.
(1973). The Failures of Criminology. *The Listener.* 8 November, 622–625.
(with J. Young) (eds) (1973). *The Manufacture of News. Deviance, Social Problems and the Mass Media.* London: Constable.
(1974). Criminology and the Sociology of Deviance in Britain: A Recent History and a Current Report. In: P. Rock and M. McIntosh (eds), *Deviance and Social Control.* London: Tavistock, 1–40.
(1974). Breaking Out, Smashing Up and the Social Context of Aspiration. *Working Papers in Cultural Studies*, 5, 37–63.
(1974). Act of Faith. Review: T. Parker, *The Man Inside. New Society*, 10 January, 78.
(1974). Asylum in Chains. Review: D.J. Rothman, *The Discovery of the Asylum: Social Order and Disorder in the New Republic*; Y. Bakal (ed.), *Closing Correctional Institutions. New Society*, 7 February, 332–333.
(1974). Make and Mend. Review: K. Soothill, *The Prisoner's Release. New Society*, 28 March, 784–785.
(1974). Arts of Deception. Review: K. Meyer, *The Plundered Past. New Society*, 18 July, 170–171.
(1974). Law Addicts. Review: J.B. Williams, *Narcotics and Drug Dependence*; L.R. Simmons and M.B. Gold (eds), *Discrimination and the Addict*; J.A. Inciardi and C.D. Chambers (eds), *Drugs and the Criminal Justice System. New Society*, 5 September, 624.
(1974). Human Warehouses: The Future of our Prisons? *New Society*, 14 November, 407–411.
(1974). Simply Doing Nothing. Review: E.M. Schur, *Radical Non-Intervention: Rethinking the Delinquency Problem. New Society*, 21 November, 494–495.
(1974). Review in Brief. I. Waller, *Man Released from Prison. New Society*, 30 May, 526
(1974). Carry On Bombing? Review: A. Burns, *The Angry Brigade. The Guardian*, 24 January.
(1974). Mummy is the Root of all Evil. Review: T. Wiseman, *The Money Motive: A Study of an Obsession. The Guardian*, 6 June.
(1974). Who Says Jack's a Dull Boy? Review: A. Clayre, *Work and Play: Ideas and Experience of Work and Leisure. The Guardian*, 5 September.

(1974). Dionysus Revisited. Review: F. Musgrove, *Ecstasy and Holiness*; A. Rigby, *Alternative Realities*; A. Rigby, *Communes in Britain*. The Guardian, 17 October.

(1975). It's All Right for You to Talk: Political and Sociological Manifestos for Social Work Action. In: R. Bailey and M. Brake (eds), *Radical Social Work*. New York: Pantheon Books, 76–95.

(1975). Teaching Method. Review: C. Fletcher, *Beneath the Surface: An Account of Three Styles of Sociological Research*. New Society, 6 February, 336.

(1975). Outside In. Review: J. Mitford, *The American Prison Business*. New Society, 27 March, 801.

(1975). Good Dreams. Review: C. Bukowski, *Life and Death in the Charity Ward*. New Society, 10 April, 89–90.

(1975). Prison on Report. Review: L. Blom-Cooper (ed.), *Progress in Penal Reform*. New Society, 22 May.

(1975). Horror Tale. Review: A. Holden, *The St Albans Poisoner: The Life and Crimes of Graham Young*. New Society, 14 August, 385–386.

(1975). The Home Office Honeymoon that Wasn't. *The Guardian*, 29 July.

(1975). Fitting in the Misfit. Review: G. Pearson, *The Deviant Imagination: Psychiatry, Social Work, and Social Change*. The Guardian, 23 October.

(with L. Taylor) (1975). Prison Research: A Cautionary Tale. *New Society*, 30 January, 253–255.

(with L. Taylor) (1975). From Psychopaths to Outsiders: British Criminology and the National Deviancy Conference. In: H. Bianchi, M. Simondi and I. Taylor (eds), *Deviance and Control in Europe. Papers from the European Group for the Study of Deviance and Social Control*. London: John Wiley & Sons, 3–33.

(1976). Dark Thoughts. Review: J.Q. Wilson, *Thinking about Crime*. New Society, 22 January, 174–175.

(1976). Crime in a City. Review: J. Baldwin and A.E. Bottoms, *The Urban Criminal: A Study in Sheffield*. New Society, 13 May, 368.

(1976). A Hidden Consensus? Review: Glasgow University Media Group, *Bad News:* vol. 1. New Society, 9 September, 559–560.

(with L. Taylor) (1976). *Escape Attempts: The Theory and Practice of Resistance to Everyday Life*. London: Allen Lane.

(with D. Downes and L. Taylor) (1976). Shouldn't the Public be Allowed to See the Unveiled Face of Authority? *The Guardian*, 24 March.

(1977). Prisons and the Future of Control Systems: From Concentration to Dispersal. In: M. Fitzgerald, P. Halmos, J. Muncie and D. Zeldin (eds), *Welfare in Action*. London and Henley: Routledge and Kegan Paul, 217–228.

(1977). Introduction. In: W. Probyn, *Angel Face. The Making of a Criminal*. London: George Allen and Unwin, 11–17.

(1977). Commentary: Notes on the Reformation of a Criminal. In: W. Probyn, *Angel Face. The Making of a Criminal*. London: George Allen and Unwin, 232–251.

(1977) Postscript. In: W. Probyn, *Angel Face. The Making of a Criminal*. London: George Allen and Unwin, 253–254.

(1977). None Too Scared. Review: S.C. Heilman, *Synagogue Life*. New Society, 13 January, 77–78.

(1977). Letters. Race Indictment. *New Society*, 27 January, 195.

(1977). Moral Contours. Review: E. Lustgarten, *The Illustrated Story of Crime*; C. Steinbrunner and O. Penzler (eds), *Encyclopedia of Mystery and Detection*; H.S. Nelli, *The Business of Crime: Italians and Syndicate Crime in the United States*. The Guardian, 13 January.

(1977). Return of the Champ. Review: L. Radzinowicz and J. King, *The Growth of Crime: The International Experience*. The Guardian, 16 June.

(1977). The Official Secrets Act & Prisons. *Christian Action Journal*, Summer, 13.

(1977). Human Warehouses: The Future of our Prisons. *Christian Action Journal*, Summer, 18–20.

(with L. Taylor) (1977). Talking about Prison Blues. In: C. Bell and H. Newby (eds), *Doing Sociological Research*. London: George Allen and Unwin, 67–86.

(with L. Taylor) (1977). Letter. Prison Secrecy. *New Society*, 28 April, 188.

(1978). Back to Justice. Review: A. von Hirsch, *Doing Justice: The Choice of Punishments*. *New Society*, 16 February, 380–381.

(1978). Reviews in Brief: P. Bean, *Rehabilitation and Deviance*. *New Society*, 8 April, 94.

(1978). The Archaeology of Power. Review Essay: M. Foucault, *Discipline and Punish: The Birth of the Prison*. *Contemporary Sociology*, 7(5), 566–568.

(with L. Taylor) (1978). *Prison Secrets*. London: National Council for Civil Liberties and Radical Alternatives to Prison.

(1979). The Punitive City: Notes on the Dispersal of Social Control. *Contemporary Crises*, 3(4), 339–363.

(1979). Guilt, Justice and Tolerance: Some Old Concepts for a New Criminology. In: D. Downes and P. Rock (eds), *Deviant Interpretations*. Oxford: Martin Robertson, 17–51.

(1979). Review: A.T. Scull, *Decarceration: Community Treatment and the Deviant – A Radical View*. *British Journal of Sociology*, 30(2), 250–251.

(1979). Crime and Punishment: 1. How Can We Balance Justice, Guilt and Tolerance? *New Society*, 1 March, 475–477.

(1979). Crime and Punishment: 2. Community Control – A New Utopia. *New Society*, 15 March, 609–611.

(1979). Crime and Punishment: 3. Some Modest and Unrealistic Proposals. *New Society*, 29 March, 731–734.

(1979). The Last Seminar. *Sociological Review*, 27(1), 5–20.

(1979). Review: R.A. Marsh, *Alabama Bound: Forty-Five Years Inside a Prison System*. *British Journal of Criminology*, 19(3), 297–299.

(1979). Review: D. Hamparian *et al.*, *The Violent Few: A Study of Dangerous Juvenile Offenders*. *The Abolitionist*, 4, 24.

(1979). Only a Public Inquiry Will Do. *The Guardian*, 18 December.

(1979). *Crime and Punishment: Some Thoughts on Theories and Policies*. London: Radical Alternatives to Prison.

(with L. Taylor) (1979). *Prison Secrets (With Postscript October 1979)*. London: National Council for Civil Liberties and Radical Alternatives to Prison.

(1980). Symbols of Trouble. Introduction to the New Edition. In S. Cohen, *Folk Devils and Moral Panics: The Creation of the Mods and Rockers*. Oxford: Martin Robertson, i–xxxiv.

(1980). Crimes of State. Review: L. Tifft and D. Sullivan, *The Struggle to Be Human: Crime, Criminology and Anarchism*. *New Society*, 23 October, 192.

(1980). The Crisis for Sociologists. *New Society*, 24 January, 196–197.

(1980). Review: J.W. Moore, *Homeboys: Gangs, Drugs, and Prisons in the Barrios of Los Angeles*. *Urban Studies*, 17(1), 86–87.

(1980). Introduction. In: L. Dronfield, *Outside Chance: The Story of the Newham Alternatives Project*. London: Radical Alternatives to Prison, 2–6.

(with J. Young) (eds) (1980). *The Manufacture of News. Social Problems, Deviance and the Mass Media. Revised Edition*. London: Constable.

(1981). Footprints in the Sand: A Further Report on Criminology and The Sociology of Deviance in Britain. In: M. Fitzgerald, G. McLennan and J. Pawson (eds), *Crime and Society: Readings in History and Theory*. London and Henley: Routledge and Kegan Paul, 220–247.

(1982). Western Crime Control Models in the Third World: Benign or Malignant? In: S. Spitzer and R.J. Simon (eds), *Research in Law, Deviance and Social Control*, Volume 4, Greenwich: JAI Press, 85–119.

(1982). When Speaking Out Exposes the Ugly Face of Zionism. *The Guardian*, 26 July.

(1983). Social-Control Talk: Telling Stories about Correctional Change. In: D. Garland and P. Young (eds), *The Power to Punish*. London: Heinemann, 101–129.

(with A. Scull) (eds) (1983). *Social Control and the State: Historical and Comparative Essays*. Oxford: Martin Robertson.

(with A. Scull) (1983). Introduction: Social Control in History and Sociology. In: S. Cohen and A. Scull (eds), *Social Control and the State: Historical and Comparative Essays*. Oxford: Martin Robertson, 1–14.

(1984). Sociological Approaches to Vandalism. In: C. Lévy-Leboyer (ed.), *Vandalism: Behaviour and Motivations*. Amsterdam: Elsevier Science, 51–61.

(1984). The Deeper Structures of the Law or 'Beware the Rulers Bearing Justice': A Review Essay. *Contemporary Crises*, 8, 83–93.

(1985). *Visions of Social Control: Crime, Punishment and Classification*. Cambridge: Polity Press.

(1985). Review: D. Black, *Towards a General Theory of Social Control*. *American Journal of Sociology*, 91(3), 714–717.

(1985). Review: E.H. Mizruchi, *Regulating Society: Marginality and Social Control in Historical Perspective*. *Sociological Review*, 33(1), 159–161.

(1985). Review: R. Evans, *The Fabrication of Virtue: English Prison Architecture, 1750–1840*. *British Journal of Criminology*, 25(3), 288–290.

(1985). Review: G. Avanesov, *The Principles of Criminology*; N. Struchkov, *Correction of the Convicted: Law, Theory, Practice*. *Contemporary Sociology*, 14(2), 184–185.

(1986). Bandits, Rebels or Criminals. African History and Western Criminology. *Africa*, 56(4), 468–483.

(1986). Community Control: To Demystify or Re-affirm? In: H. Bianchi and R. van Swaaningen (eds), *Abolitionism: Towards a Non-repressive Approach to Crime*. Amsterdam: Free University Press, 127–132.

(1986). Review: D. Garland, *Punishment and Welfare: A History of Penal Strategies*. *British Journal of Criminology*, 26(4), 409–411.

(1986). Editorial Introduction. *Contemporary Crises*, 10, 3–4.

(1987). Review: M. Akerstrom, *Crooks and Squares: Lifestyles of Thieves and Addicts in Comparison to Conventional People*. *Contemporary Sociology*, 16(4), 535–536.

(1987). Editorial Introduction. *Contemporary Crises*, 11, 335.

(1987). Taking Decentralization Seriously: Values, Visions and Policies. In: J. Lowman, R.J. Menzies and T.S. Palys (eds), *Transcarceration: Essays in the Sociology of Social Control*. Aldershot: Gower, 358–379.

(ed.) (1988). *Against Criminology*. New Brunswick: Transaction.

(1988). Against Criminology. In: S. Cohen (ed.), *Against Criminology*. New Brunswick: Transaction, 8–32.

(1988). The Object of Criminology: Reflections on the New Criminalization. In: S. Cohen (ed.), *Against Criminology*. New Brunswick: Transaction, 235–276.

(1988). Criminology and the Uprising. *Tikkun*, 3(5), 60–62, 95–96.

(1988). Rebellion and Political Crime in America. Review: N.N. Kittrie and E. Wedlock, *The Tree of Liberty. A Documentary History of Rebellion and Political Crime in America*. *Social Justice*, 15(3/4), 197–203.

(1988). Steven Box and Ken Pryce. *Contemporary Crises*, 12, 181.

(1988). Introducción a la edición española. In: S. Cohen, *Visiones de control social. Delitos, castigos y clasificaciones*. Barcelona: Promociones y Publicaciones Universitarias (PPU), I–V.

(1989). The Critical Discourse on 'Social Control': Notes on the Concept as a Hammer. *International Journal of the Sociology of Law*, 17, 347–357.

(1989). Criminological Theory: From Inside Out or Outside in? *Annales internationales de criminologie*, 27(1/2), 57–64.

(1989). The Myth of 'the Rule of Law'. *Jerusalem Post*, 23 January.

(1989). Education as Crime. *Jerusalem Post*, 18 May.

(1989). Killings by Any Other Name. *Jerusalem Post*, 31 May.

(1989). Foolproof Scheme. *Jerusalem Post*, 23 June.

(1989). Words and Pictures. *Jerusalem Post*, 21 September.

(1989). The Brutalization of Israeli Soldiers. *Jerusalem Post*, 25 December.

(1989). The Psychology and Politics of Denial: The Case of Israeli Liberals. In: *Psychological Barriers to Peace*. Jerusalem: Mental Health Workers for the Advancement of Peace, 10–23.

(1990). Politics and Crime in Israel: Reactions from the Home Front. *Social Justice*, 17(1), 5–24.

(1990). The Intifada in Israel: Portents and Precarious Balance. *Middle East Report*, 164/165, 16–20, 78.

(1990). *Intellectual Scepticism and Political Commitment: The Case of Radical Criminology*. Amsterdam: Stichting W.A. Bonger-Lezingen.

(1990). Review: D. Weisburd, *Jewish Settler Violence: Deviance as Social Reaction*. *International Journal of the Sociology of Law*, 18(4), 502–506.

(1990). Preface. In: W. de Haan, *The Politics of Redress: Crime, Punishment and Penal Abolition*. London: Unwin Hyman, xiii–xiv.

(1990). Torture in Israel: Defining the Issues. *New Outlook*, 33(9), 45–48.

(1991). Talking about Torture in Israel. *Tikkun*, 6(6), 23–30, 89–90.

(1991). Alternatives to Punishment – The Abolitionist Case. *Israel Law Review*, 25(3), 729–739.

(1991). Review: C. Dandeker, *Surveillance, Power and Modernity: Bureaucracy and Discipline from 1700 to the Present Day*. *Contemporary Sociology*, 20(3), 427–429.

(1991). *The Human Rights Movement in Israel and South Africa: Some Paradoxical Comparisons. Lecture in Memory of Professor Michael Wade*. The Truman Institute. Occasional Papers No. 1. The Hebrew University of Jerusalem, 12 November.

(1991). Prólogo. In: E. Larrauri (ed.), *La herencia de la criminología crítica*. Madrid: Siglo, xi–xiv.

(with D. Golan) (1991). *The Interrogation of Palestinians during the Intifada: Ill-Treatment, 'Moderate Physical Pressure' or Torture?* Jerusalem: B'Tselem, The Israeli Information Center for Human Rights in the Occupied Territories.

(1992). Moral Boundaries Have Vanished: The 'Only Democracy in the Middle East' has Given Up Any Semblance of Following Democratic Rule. *Los Angeles Times*, 24 December.

(1992). From the Sealed Room: Israel's Peace Movement during the Gulf War. In: P. Bennis and M. Moushabeck (eds), *Beyond the Storm: A Gulf Crisis Reader*. New York: Olive Branch Press, 205–214.

(with D. Golan) (1992). *The Interrogation of Palestinians during the Intifada: Follow-up to March 1991 B'Tselem Report*. Jerusalem: B'Tselem, The Israeli Information Center for Human Rights in the Occupied Territories.

(with L. Taylor) (1992). *Escape Attempts: The Theory and Practice of Resistance to Everyday Life. Second Edition.* London: Routledge

(with L. Taylor) (1992). Have We Got to Get Out of this Place? *The Guardian*, 25 August.

(with L. Taylor) (1992). The Supermarket of the Self. *The Guardian*, 26 August.

(1993). Human Rights and Crimes of The State: The Culture of Denial. *Australian & New Zealand Journal of Criminology*, 26, 97–115.

(1993). Intellectual Skepticism and Political Commitment: The Case of Radical Criminology. *Studies in Law, Politics, and Society*, 13, 187–209.
(1993). Fear and Violence in Israel. *Tikkun*, 8(3), 31–32.
(1993). Reacting to Torture in Israel. Talk Given at the Conference 'The International Struggle against Torture and the Case of Israel', Tel Aviv, 13 June 1993. *Torture: Quarterly Journal on Rehabilitation of Torture Victims and Prevention of Torture*. 3(4), 122–124.
(1994). Social Control and the Politics of Reconstruction. In: D. Nelken (ed.), *The Futures of Criminology*. London: Sage, 63–88.
(1994). Postscript: If Nothing Works, What Is Our Work? *Australian & New Zealand Journal of Criminology*, 27(1), 104–107.
(1995). *Denial and Acknowledgement: The Impact of Information about Human Rights Violations*. Jerusalem: The Hebrew University of Jerusalem, Center for Human Rights.
(1995). State Crimes of Previous Regimes: Knowledge, Accountability, and the Policing of the Past. *Law & Social Inquiry*, 20(1), 7–50.
(1995). Justice in Transition? Prospects for a Palestinian-Israeli Truth Commission. *Middle East Report*, 194/195, 2–5.
(1995). Review: M. Maguire, R. Morgan and R. Reiner (eds), *The Oxford Handbook of Criminology*. *British Journal of Criminology*, 35(1), 146–149.
(1995). Conference Life: The Rough Guide. *The Scottish Journal of Criminal Justice Studies*, 1 (June), 33–50.
(1995). Outline of Report 'Denial and Acknowledgment: The Impact of Information about Human Rights Violations'. In: *Human Rights Violations: Communicating the Information*. International Workshop. Oxford, 24–29.
(with T.G. Blomberg) (eds) (1995). *Punishment and Social Control. Essays in Honor of Sheldon L. Messinger*. New York: Aldine de Gruyter.
(with T.G. Blomberg) (1995). Editorial Introduction: Punishment and Social Control. In: T.G. Blomberg and S. Cohen (eds), *Punishment and Social Control. Essays in Honor of Sheldon L. Messinger*. New York: Aldine de Gruyter, 3–14.
(1996). Government Responses to Human Rights Reports: Claims, Denials, and Counterclaims. *Human Rights Quarterly*, 18(3), 517–543.
(1996). Crime and Politics: Spot the Difference. *British Journal of Sociology*, 47(1), 1–21.
(1996). The Kitsch of Death and Peace. *Index on Censorship*, 25(1), 22–27.
(1996). Witnessing the Truth. *Index on Censorship*, 25(1), 36–45.
(1996). No Time for Reconciliation. *Index on Censorship*, 25(5), 162–169.
(1996). Review, J.I. Ross, *Controlling State Crime: An Introduction*. *British Journal of Sociology*, 47(4), 733–734.
(1996). Review: J. Simon, *Poor Discipline: Parole and the Social Control of the Underclass, 1890–1990*. *British Journal of Sociology*, 47(4), 735–736.
(1996). Review: J. Ferrell and C.R. Sanders (eds), *Cultural Criminology*. *Justice Quarterly*, 13(4), 737–740.
(1996). The Political Question in Criminology; The Criminal Question in Politics. In: T. von Trotha (ed.), *Politischer Wandel, Gesellschaft und Kriminalitätsdiskurse. Beiträge zur interdisziplinären wissenschaftlichen Kriminologie. Festschrift für Fritz Sack zum 65. Geburtstag*. Baden-Baden: Nomos Verlagsgesellschaft, 77–91.
(1996). Criminology. In: A. Kuper and J. Kuper (eds), *The Social Science Encyclopedia (Second Edition)*. London: Routledge, 151–154.
(1997). Conference Life: The Rough Guide. *The American Sociologist*, Fall, 69–84.
(1997). The Revenge of the Null Hypothesis: Evaluating Crime Control Policies. *Critical Criminologist*, 8(1), 21–25.

(1998). Intellectual Scepticism and Political Commitment: The Case of Radical Criminology. In: P. Walton and J. Young (eds), *The New Criminology Revisited*. Houndmills: Macmillan Press, 98–129.

(1998). Review: J. Borneman, *Settling Accounts: Violence, Justice, and Accountability in Postsocialist Europe*. *American Journal of Sociology*, 104(3), 927–929.

(1999). Moral Panics and Folk Concepts. *Paedagogica Historica*, 35(3), 585–591.

(2000). Some Thoroughly Modern Monsters. *Index on Censorship*, 29(5), 35–43.

(2000). Preface. In: C. Banks (ed.), *Developing Cultural Criminology: Theory and Practice in Papua New Guinea*. Sydney: Sydney Institute of Criminology Monograph Series No. 13, 1–4.

(2001). *States of Denial. Knowing about Atrocities and Suffering*. Cambridge: Polity Press.

(2001). Memory Wars and Peace Commissions. *Index on Censorship*, 30(1), 40–48.

(2002). Moral Panics as Cultural Politics. Introduction to the Third Edition. In: S. Cohen, *Folk Devils and Moral Panics: The Creation of the Mods and Rockers. Third Edition*. London: Routledge, vii–xxxvii.

(with B. Seu) (2002). Knowing Enough Not to Feel Too Much: Emotional Thinking about Human Rights Appeals. In: M.P. Bradley and P. Petro (eds), *Truth Claims. Representation and Human Rights*. New Brunswick: Rutgers University Press, 187–201.

(2003). Review: J. Steinberg, *Crime Wave: The South African Underworld and its Foes*; M. Shaw, *Crime and Policing in Post-Apartheid South Africa: Transforming under Fire*. *Journal of Southern African Studies*, 29(2), 576–578.

(2003). Review: E. Klinenberg, *Heat Wave: A Social Autopsy of Disaster in Chicago*. *British Journal of Sociology*, 54(3), 420–421.

(2003). The Real World. *Sociology Research News*, 2(1), 3–4.

(with T.G. Blomberg) (eds) (2003). *Punishment and Social Control. Enlarged Second Edition*. New York: Aldine de Gruyter.

(2004). The Lies We Tell. *Index on Censorship*, 33(2), 42–47.

(2004). The Photo Never Lies. *Index on Censorship*, 33(2), 48–53.

(with J. Young) (2004). Comments on Simon Cottee's 'Folk Devils and Moral Panics: "Left Idealism" reconsidered'. *Theoretical Criminology*, 8(1), 93–97.

(ed.) (2005). Torture: A User's Manual. *Index on Censorship*, 34(1).

(2005). Post-Moral Torture: From Guantanamo to Abu Ghraib. *Index on Censorship*, 34(1), 24–30.

(2005). Prólogo a la edición en español. In: S. Cohen, *Estados de negación. Esayo sobre atrocidades y sufrimiento*. Buenos Aires: Departamento de Publicaciones. Facultad de Derecho. Universidad de Buenos Aires. 11–12.

(2006). Neither Honesty nor Hypocrisy: The Legal Reconstruction of Torture. In: T. Newburn and P. Rock (eds), *The Politics of Crime Control: Essays in Honour of David Downes*. Oxford: Oxford University Press, 297–318.

(2006). Review: J. Torpey, *Making Whole What Has Been Smashed: On Reparations Politics*. *Contemporary Sociology*. 35(6), 600–602.

(2007). Downloading Evil. *Index on Censorship*. 36(4), 111–115.

(2007). Don't Look Back. *New Humanist*, 31 May, https://newhumanist.org.uk/articles/1005/dont-look-back.

(2007). What is Genocide? *New Humanist*, 31 May, https://newhumanist.org.uk/articles/922/what-is-genocide.

(2007). Utopian Rallying Call. *New Humanist*, 31 May, https://newhumanist.org.uk/articles/793/utopian-rallying-call.

(2007). Auschwitz Report by Primo Levi with Leonardo de Benedetti. *New Humanist*, 23 July, https://newhumanist.org.uk/articles/1560/auschwitz-report-by-primo-levi-with-leonardo-de-benedetti.

(2007). Diary of a Bad Year by J.M. Coetzee. *New Humanist*, 7 September, https://newhumanist.org.uk/articles/1593/diary-of-a-bad-year-by-jm-coetzee.

(2008). The Virtual Reality of Israeli Universities In: A. Karpf, B. Klug, J. Rose and B. Rosenbaum (eds), *A Time to Speak Out: Independent Jewish Voices on Israel, Zionism and Jewish Identity*. London: Verso, 36–46.

(2008). American Barbarity. *New Humanist*, 8 January https://newhumanist.org.uk/articles/1693/american-barbarity.

(2009). Carry on Panicking. Address on receiving the Award for 'Outstanding Achievement' from the British Society of Criminology at its Annual Conference, Cardiff, 29 June 2009. *British Society of Criminology Newsletter*, 64, 5–10.

(2009). Unspeakable Memories and Commensurable Laws. In: S. Karstedt (ed.), *Legal Institutions and Collective Memories.* Oxford: Hart, 27–38.

(2010). Ideology? What Ideology? *Criminology & Criminal Justice*, 10(4), 387–391.

(2010). Diary: The Gradual Anarchist. *New Humanist*, 29 March. https://newhumanist.org.uk/articles/2269/diary-the-gradual-anarchist.

(2011). Whose Side Were We On? The Undeclared Politics of Moral Panic Theory. *Crime, Media, Culture*, 7(3), 237–243.

(2013). Panic or Denial. On Whether to Take Crime Seriously. In: J. Gilmore, J.M. Moore and D. Scott (eds), *Critique and Dissent: An Anthology to Mark 40 Years of the European Group for the Study of Deviance and Social Control.* Ottawa: Red Quill Books, 101–108.

(2014). Remembering Harold Wolpe. Memorial Speech (23rd March 1996). In: K. Plummer (ed.), *Imaginations: Fifty Years of Essex Sociology*. Wivenhoe: Wivenhoe Books, 76.

STANLEY COHEN

Stanley Cohen, 1942–2013

I. Introduction

I WAS ONE OF THE CO-AUTHORS of the biographical introduction to a Festschrift, *Crime, Social Control and Human Rights*, that was published in 2007 to mark Stan Cohen's retirement two years before from the Martin White Chair of Sociology at the London School of Economics.[1] This memoir is intended to complement and extend that biography and other chapters in the Festschrift rather than merely duplicate them, although it is inevitable that there will be some small acts of cannibalism. Whilst the introduction was largely literary in content and exegetical in method, this memoir will be more of an intellectual portrait or mosaic based on interviews and discussion with those who knew him well, and in writing it I shall try to trace a number of broad themes which gave contour to his life and his views of the world, sociology, politics and human rights. Unless there is a statement to the contrary, it should be assumed that any quotation is taken from those conversations. It should also be said that I have been mindful throughout that it is all too easy to impose an artificial coherence on what was a long, contradictory and complicated life, but a measure of simplification cannot be avoided.

---

[1] D. Downes, P. Rock, C. Chinkin and C. Gearty (eds.), *Crime, Social Control and Human Rights* (Cullompton, 2007).

II. A brief résumé

Stan Cohen was the eldest of three brothers born into a comfortable Jewish family in Johannesburg, South Africa, on 23 February 1942, the son of Ray and Sie Cohen,[2] themselves part of a larger family originating in Lithuania but dispersed through emigration and flight from the oppressive regimes of Europe in the 1930s and 1940s. He attended Parktown Boys' High School in Johannesburg, took a BA degree in social work at the University of the Witwatersrand, worked briefly as a psychiatric social worker in England between 1963 and 1964, and then studied for a Ph.D. on *Hooligans, Vandals and the Community: a Study of Social Reaction to Juvenile Delinquency*, in the fledgling field of criminology, under the supervision of Terence Morris and, for a while, David Downes, at the London School of Economics (LSE). David Downes remembered that he was 'enormously vital, buoyant and creative, full of ideas but with a clear sense of what he wanted to achieve ... it gave me a false idea of what it was like to supervise Ph.D.s because he never had any doubt really as to what he wanted to do. But he was open all the time to learning new things.' The doctorate, awarded in 1969, was published in part three years later as *Folk Devils and Moral Panics*,[3] and then again with new prefaces in 1987, 1999 and 2003.

A 'moral panic', Stan Cohen said, was 'A condition, episode, person or group of persons [that] emerges to become defined as a threat to societal values and interests; its nature is presented in a stylized and stereotypical fashion by the mass media; the moral barricades are manned by editors, bishops, politicians and other right-thinking people; socially-accredited experts pronounce their diagnoses and solutions; ways of coping are evolved or (more often) resorted to; the condition then disappears, submerges or deteriorates and becomes more visible.'[4] The notion condensed ideas about the capacity of powerful groups to shape social phenomena; the ineluctably political complexion of law and order; the processual and interactive character of social problems; the ever-present potential for irrational, ephemeral, distorting and punitive traits to colour reactions to rule-breaking; and the frequent helplessness of deviants and others effectively to counter what was done to them. It was not the first

---

[2] A fuller account of his boyhood is given by Adam Kuper in 'Growing up with Stan', in *Crime, Social Control and Human Rights*, pp. 3–6.
[3] S. Cohen, *Folk Devils and Moral Panics* (London, 1972).
[4] Ibid., p. 9.

time anyone had written on and around that theme.⁵ It was not the first time that Stan Cohen himself had published a piece on that topic. He and I had produced a chapter employing very similar ideas in a short history of the Teddy Boy that had appeared three years before,⁶ but we had not used the term *moral panic*, a more colourful and elaborated concept that was to become celebrated in the academic literature,⁷ and one of the very few sociological phrases to enter common currency (there were 2,750,000 'results' in response to a search on Google in the autumn of 2013). Moral panic was a powerful and seductive concept. It seemed to capture important truths about the condition of England in the 1970s and beyond, and it established Stan Cohen as a public intellectual at a very young age.

Stan Cohen married Ruth Kretzmer in 1963, and they had two daughters, one of whom, Judith, became a Reader in the Philosophy of Education at the Institute of Education, University of London, and the other, Jessica, living in the United States since 1997, was to become a translator from Hebrew into English of books by David Grossman, Yael Hedaya, Ronit Matalon, Amir Gutfreund and Tom Segev. Ruth Cohen, a delightful and highly principled woman, and a ceramic artist, died in 2003. He and Ruth were doting grandparents, taking great pride and pleasure in their grandchildren in London and America.

Stan Cohen's career took him from place to place and country to country. It was not always smooth. He was appointed lecturer in sociology at Enfield College (later Middlesex University) in 1965, but the patronage system of British criminology in the 1960s then blocked him from leaving to take a post at Bedford College, at the time part of the University of

---

⁵ See, for instance, R. Fuller and R. Myers, 'The natural history of a social problem', *American Sociological Review*, 6 (1941), 320–9; E. Lemert; 'Is there a natural history of social problems?', *American Sociological Review*, 16 (1951), 217–23; and E. Sutherland, 'The diffusion of sexual psychopath laws', *American Journal of Sociology*, 56 (1950), 142–8.

⁶ S. Cohen and P. Rock, 'The Teddy Boy', in V. Bogdanor and R. Skidelsky (eds.), *The Age of Affluence* (London, 1970), pp. 288–319.

⁷ See, for example, the 35 references to books and articles on moral panics in the British Library catalogue <http://explore.bl.uk/primo_library/libweb/action/search.do?dscnt=0&vl(174399379UI0) =any&frbg=&scp.scps=scope%3A%28BLCONTENT%29&tab=local_tab&dstmp= 1382087986360&srt=rank&ct=search&mode=Basic&dum=true&tb=t&indx=1&vl(free Text0)=Folk+Devils+and+Moral+Panics&vid=BLVU1&fn=search>; the 214,000 'results' on Google Scholar <http://scholar.google.co.uk/ scholar?hl=en&q=moral+panic&btnG=&as_sdt= 1%2C5&as_sdtp=>; and the 1,413 citations on JSTOR <http://www.jstor.org.gate2.library.lse. ac.uk/action/doBasicSearch?Query=moral%2Bpanic&Search=Search&gw=jtx&prq= moral+panic&hp=25&acc=on&aori=a&wc=on&fc=off> (all searches conducted on 18 Oct. 2013). And see D. Garland, 'On the concept of moral panic', *Crime Media Culture*, 4 (2008), 9–30.

London, and it engendered some justified resentment against the professoriate of the London School of Economics. He did however eventually move in 1967 to become lecturer and then senior lecturer at the University of Durham; senior lecturer in 1972 and then Professor of Sociology in 1974 at the University of Essex; Professor at the Hebrew University, Jerusalem, in 1981; and then, on his return to England, Centennial Professor in 1994 and finally Martin White Professor of Sociology at the London School of Economics two years later, retiring in 2005.

If his first career was in criminology sociologically conceived, his second was in the linked field of human rights, epitomised by his *States of Denial: Knowing about Atrocities and Suffering*,[8] an exploration of how torture became socially and psychologically possible, which was awarded the 2002 British Academy Book Prize that had been instituted to 'celebrate books that significant [*sic*] contributed to scholarly understanding and, by being lucidly written, appeal to the general reader'.[9] It was a book described by Dame Gillian Beer, the Chair of the Judging Panel, as 'a powerful analysis of an extraordinarily important topic. How is it possible for witnesses—or participants—in atrocities to deny what has, incontrovertibly, occurred? Can one speak of a culture of denial? In exploring these questions Stanley Cohen has carved out a whole new field of enquiry relating sociology, psychology, philosophy, political theory and personal experience.'[10]

Amongst the other honours he received were the Sellin–Glueck Award ('given in order to call attention to criminological scholarship that considers problems of crime and justice as they are manifested outside the United States; internationally or comparatively'[11]) from the American Society of Criminology in 1985; his Fellowship of the British Academy in 1997; an honorary doctorate from the University of Essex in 2003; and the newly established Award for Outstanding Achievement from the British Society of Criminology ('intended to celebrate outstanding contributions made to the discipline by members of the BSC'[12]) in 2009. He died on 7 January 2013 after a long and harrowing illness bravely borne. The British Society of Criminology elected in that year to affix his name to the opening, plenary addresses that would be delivered thereafter at its annual conferences.

---

[8] S. Cohen, *States of Denial: Knowing about Atrocities and Suffering* (Cambridge, 2001).
[9] <http://www.britac.ac.uk/about/medals/book-prize.cfm>.
[10] <http://www.britac.ac.uk/news/news.cfm/newsid/115>.
[11] <http://www.asc41.com/awards/SellinGlueckAward.html>.
[12] <http://www.britsoccrim.org/prizes.htm>.

III. South Africa

Stan Cohen grew up in the South Africa of apartheid, and, although he was not politically active there, it did reinforce in him an abiding scepticism about the benevolence of the State, its ideology and its institutions. After all, his relatives had long known the cruelty of States (Robin Cohen headed part of an account of the family's history 'Beware the State', and had then moved on to allude to the 'Family's experience of the Russian, Nazi and Lithuanian States'[13]).

Stan Cohen once remarked to me that he was puzzled by the propensity of lawyers to look upon formal social control as benign. He took it to be malign. The social anthropologist, Adam Kuper, his oldest friend and a fellow South African, observed that 'that anti-authoritarian thing was very strong among us'. It instilled in Stan Cohen a restless, lively, questioning intelligence that would take nothing on trust, and certainly not the utterances of those in political power. He once talked of what he called the 'three voracious gods' that faced the sociologist, and, of those, one was 'an overriding obligation to pursue honest intellectual enquiry (however sceptical, irrelevant and unrealistic)'.[14] It led not only to systematic doubt but also to a rugged political and intellectual integrity, what Thomas Hammarburg called a 'stubborn search for honest answers',[15] that emboldened him publicly to confront atrocities in Israel, despite the calumny that could follow;[16] and to defend academic freedom against assault from even quite influential figures.[17]

If Stan Cohen had a political ideology at all, it was probably a liberal or humanist variant of the anarchism, not of Mikhail Bakunin or Sergey

---

[13] In the meeting held at the LSE on 10 Dec. 2013: 'From *Moral Panics* to *States of Denial*: a celebration of the life and work of Stan Cohen'.

[14] S. Cohen, 'Intellectual scepticism and political commitment', in P. Walton and J. Young (eds.), *The New Criminology Revisited* (London, 1998), p. 122.

[15] At the meeting, 'From *Moral Panics* to *States of Denial*'. Thomas Hammarburg was until recently the Council of Europe Commissioner for Human Rights.

[16] His erstwhile colleague at Hebrew University, Daphna Golan, talked at the LSE meeting of 10 Dec. 2013 about Stan Cohen's exceptional courage in talking about the occupation and torture in a university where 'lectures took place as usual as if there were no intifada'.

[17] See the reporting in *The Times Higher Education Supplement* of Stan Cohen's handling of the aftermath of Conor Gearty's critical article on Michael Ignatieff's *The Lesser Evil*, in the *Index on Censorship* ('Ignatieff ducks debate with critics in torture row', *The Times Higher Education Supplement*, 9 Sept. 2005). Ignatieff had attempted to ensure that the article would not be published but Stan Cohen, as guest editor, refused to comply. Conor Gearty commented that 'Stan behaved magnificently throughout—fending off telephone calls from the furious Ignatieff pleading friendship as a reason to help him handle "Mr Gearty"'.

Nechayev, but of William Godwin, that embraced a mistrust of the State, the millenarian[18] and big ideas. It was an allegiance that he had contracted very early in life. His brother Robin remembered that 'at our family dining table [in South Africa] we sometimes formally took positions on issues of the day—Stan anarchist, me socialist, Clive capitalist. This is relevant to ... Stan's close engagement with anarchism. And truth to tell the three positions—which were adolescent self-ascriptions—were not far from our final positions.'[19]

Stan Cohen particularly admired the British anarchist Colin Ward,[20] a family friend until his death, of whom it was said that he 'saw all distant goals as a form of tyranny and believed that anarchist principles could be discerned in everyday human relations and impulses'.[21] He was at one with Colin Ward in being particularly distrustful of the apocalyptic and the absolutist. It was no accident that what may have been Stan Cohen's very first publication[22] appeared (like those of some of his criminological contemporaries on the British Left[23]) in *Anarchy*, the journal which Ward edited between 1961 and 1970. And one of the later concomitants of that antipathy to the State and its institutions was his publication with Laurie Taylor in 1972 of a clandestine study of long-term prisoners' strategies of survival in Durham Prison[24] that was based on a remarkable empathy with the lot of the incarcerated (Paul Wiles called it 'one of the most sensitive accounts of prison life ever published'[25]) but which also led to protracted antagonism between the authors and the Home Office[26] and a wider and enduring souring of relations between criminologists and government.

---

[18] See S. Cohen, 'Criminology and the sociology of deviance in Britain', in P. Rock and M. McIntosh (eds.), *Deviance and Social Control* (London, 1974), p. 30.

[19] Email, 13 Nov. 2013.

[20] Colin Ward, 1924–2010, was the author of some 30 books and edited the journals *Freedom* and *Anarchy* between 1961 and 1970.

[21] K. Worpole, Colin Ward Obituary, *The Guardian*, 22 Feb. 2010 <http://www.theguardian.com/society/2010/feb/22/colin-ward-obituary>.

[22] The first was S. Cohen, 'Vandalism and the social structure', *Anarchy*, 64 (1966), 181–7.

[23] See D. Downes, 'What will happen to Jones and Robinson?', *Anarchy*, 53 (1965), 195–201; D. Downes, 'One boy's story', *Anarchy*, 64 (1966), 173–5; J. Young, 'The zookeepers of deviancy', *Anarchy*, 98 (1969), 101–8; L. Taylor, 'The criminologist and the criminal', *Anarchy*, 98 (1969), 114–21.

[24] S. Cohen and L. Taylor, *Psychological Survival: the Experience of Long-Term Imprisonment* (Harmondsworth, 1972).

[25] Review in *The British Journal of Sociology*, 24 (1973), p. 255.

[26] See S. Cohen and L. Taylor, *Prison Secrets*, Radical Alternatives to Prison and National Council for Civil Liberties (London, 1976).

Authority at large was ever problematic for him. He chafed when baulked by senior staff, officials and bureaucracies, in Israel, in London and elsewhere. He was not to be confined by rules. He was to be something of an innocent abroad in the highly regulated labyrinth of English higher education. One of his research students, Olga Jubany, recalled, quite spontaneously:

> He had no idea about the practicalities of the PhD, registrations or any other issue. In fact, I didn't even realise that I wasn't actually registered for a PhD (but formally for an MPhil) until almost a year on, when my colleagues told me so. He would not bother with any of the admin machinery (you would not expect him to do so anyway). If at the very beginning I ever asked him something about how I should submit the Aims and Methods paper,[27] or how the bursary system was for PhDs, or what was the research seminar timing; he would look at me like: 'you seriously expect me to know that? surely not!'. What's more, he would not follow up on what courses I registered for and would certainly not make me choose specific ones over others (except for the wonderful Criminology seminar, where he participated too and was really the best course of the whole PhD years).

If Stan Cohen was an anarchistically minded sceptic, he was also a sceptic about some of the forms adopted by anarchism itself, observing in one of those pieces in *Anarchy* that 'Anarchists, whose intellectual roots go deeper back than any other group fighting the horrors of today's society should be the first to see that a committed and passionate position is not incompatible with an orderly argument ... antagonism needs to be documented as much as acceptance.'[28] Jessica, his daughter, said 'he disliked the idea of hard-line ideological positions and movements.... I think it just came from his suspicion of dogma and structure. He could never have been a member of a political party.' It was a scepticism that could even turn in on itself, serving reflexively, in Harvey Molotch's words, as a 'loyal nag that what he was thinking might be wrong'[29] and that those with whom he disagreed might be right. It even led him eventually to distance himself from criminology itself, the discipline that had suckled him, when he was living in Israel (although there are some, like David Downes, who believed that the title of his matricidal book, *Against Criminology*,[30] was ironically intended).

---

[27] The 'Aims and Methods Paper' was intended to serve as a test of the research student's competence to proceed to the second year of the Ph.D. course.
[28] S. Cohen, 'Notes on Detention Centres', *Anarchy*, 101 (no date), 210.
[29] At 'From *Moral Panics* to *States of Denial*'.
[30] S. Cohen, *Against Criminology* (New Brunswick, NJ, 1988).

Growing up in South Africa also instilled in Stan Cohen a desire to leave what he conceived to be a malevolent country for one more admirable, Israel. His adolescent world was permeated by Zionism. The Students Jewish Association at Parktown Boys' High School was steeped in it. The November 1961 issue of the school magazine, *The Parktonian*, recorded, for instance, how the Association's:

> ... first few meetings of the year were addressed by members of the Zionist Youth Movement, who spoke on different aspects of life on Communal Settlements. As usual films were shown at various times of the year. Their topics ranged from Communal Settlements to Jewish holidays.... Dr. H. Michel returned to the school and gave an awe-inspiring talk on 'The Tide of the New Immigration' concerning the emigration of Jews from Arab and Communist dominated countries.[31]

As an adolescent, Stan Cohen had travelled with his family to Israel, visiting relatives and the tourist sites, and he had spent brief periods of time with *Habonim* at the South African-affiliated Kibbutz Tsora and Kibbutz Yizrael in the winter of 1958–9. It was to Israel that he determined he would return. Adam Kuper remembered:

> He wasn't that radical in South Africa. Of course he was anti-apartheid ... and he had black friends and so on but he was not politically active in South Africa in the way that a number of us were. Because he belonged to this group which said, 'okay, you know, the situation is terrible, we're against it, we're going to go to Israel.' So for a number of his friends, not for me, but for a number of his friends who then went to Israel, the great issue was 'why didn't Stan ... get further qualifications and then he would join us'.

The lure of *aliyah* was strong, and it was thought to demand particular talents from those who chose to emigrate. Robin Cohen said: 'Stan was much more committed than either Clive or myself to a sort of Zionist dream. By dream I mean ... something that was ... idealistic and he had some idea that he needed some skills that he would be able to apply in that context. And I think he sort of stumbled into social work.' It was an unusual course to take. Stan Cohen acknowledged that he was something of a disappointment and *Luftmensch* in the eyes of his parents[32] (all three brothers had 'said "no" to my father's increasingly despairing pleas to take over his retail clothing business' said Robin Cohen). Social work was not the common aspiration of young Jewish men growing up in the South Africa of the 1950s and 1960s, but 'each of his cohort were supposed to

---

[31] R.D.W., 'Students Jewish Association', *The Parktonian*, LVII (1961), 18.
[32] A. Kuper, 'Growing up with Stan', p. 6.

have a specialism that would be particularly useful in Israel'.[33] Stan Cohen's daughter, Judith, reflected that he and Robin, who would also become a Professor of Sociology, 'were regarded as the mad ones. The younger brother [Clive] stayed in South Africa, went into finance and insurance and that was regarded as the sensible, reasonable thing to do. Whereas Stan and Robin were always ... just a bit mystifying to our grandparents ... as to how they could possibly have chosen that ... and they never understood why he left South Africa.'

Leaving South Africa was Stan Cohen's first displacement. He had felt uncomfortable there and he departed, although he always retained an ambivalent affection for the country. Judith Cohen said 'he loved it. He always felt that that was his home and yet whenever he was there ... every visit that we went on when we were little, there was horrible tension always in the background.' But, at the age of 21, Stan Cohen was to go first, not back to Israel, but to England. Robin Cohen said 'I think his idea was that he would get some practical experience as a psychiatric social worker. He would perhaps do an MA and then he would go to Israel. And then somehow the lure of LSE and the entrance to the things he was doing took him away from that.'

IV. England

By contrast with South Africa, London was a free and febrile place in the mid-1960s. David Downes recalled that 'he always said that he got an enormous amount just out of being here. Don't forget, South Africa was then such a closed society in almost every way ... he came here and he could go to all the things that he and Ruth had seen in smuggled back copies of *The New Statesman*. You know, meetings about politics in Red Lion Square and so on. [He] just loved to go to all those things [and the] debate and discussion.' The sociological criminology practised with his fellow-students, Jock Young and others, at the London School of Economics, and indeed in the United Kingdom at large, was itself febrile at the time. I have described elsewhere[34] how the great university expansion that took place in the wake of the 1963 Robbins Report[35] created a

---

[33] Email 13 Nov. 2013.
[34] P. Rock, 'The present state of British criminology', *British Journal of Criminology*, 28 (1988), 188–99.
[35] *Higher Education: Report of the Committee appointed by the Prime Minister under the Chairmanship of Lord Robbins 1961–63* Cmnd 2154 (London, 1963).

substantial cohort of youthful scholars who formed an intellectually tumultuous and self-referential critical mass that set itself against what was seen as the orthodoxies, postures, politics and authority of a fusty older generation.

Stan Cohen was at the centre of it all. He had arrived in England just as that ferment began, and his thesis captured what was in effect the minor intellectual revolt that was in progress around him. The Young Turks of the so-called new criminologies[36] rejected what they conceived to be the atheoretical positivism and subservience to the State of criminology proper, and celebrated in its place a blend of the symbolic interactionism and phenomenology personified by the Americans, Howard S. Becker, Edwin Lemert and David Matza; a sociology from below that reported the world-views of those who had hitherto lacked credit and a voice;[37] and, a little later, the radical Europeans, Karl Marx, Nicos Poulantzas, Evgenii Pashukanis, Louis Althusser and others.

The arguments which Stan Cohen collated and examined in his Ph.D. *Hooligans, Vandals and the Community* presented a particularly prescient and articulate opening statement of a number of those 'recent developments in the sociology of deviance',[38] and they served as a platform on which he would build almost all his subsequent theorising, and, indeed, as something of a platform for much of British criminology itself.[39] He talked there about how what he called transactionalism was a loose approach rather than 'a fully fledged theory' (p. 10); an approach that was best 'understood as a reaction against traditional ways of looking at one's subject matter' (p. 11) and against the theoretical insulation of criminology. In his exegesis of the work of Howard Becker, Erving Goffman, Kai Erikson, Ronald Laing, Edwin Lemert, David Matza, George Herbert Mead and others, he sought to bring sociology back into criminology; reject what he believed to be the essentialising, static and dehumanising definitions current in the thought of those working in social control agencies and the orthodox criminology that was their handmaiden; acknowledge the diversity of deviants and deviant phenomena; and subscribe to an imagery of deviance that was centred on social and psychological process. Rule-breaking was said to be rooted in identities that were negotiated, step by

---

[36] See, for instance, I. Taylor, P. Walton and J. Young, *The New Criminology* (London, 1973).
[37] See H. Becker; 'Whose side are we on?', *Social Problems*, 14 (1967), 239–47.
[38] He was not then, or afterwards, much influenced by Marx and the Marxists.
[39] As our biographical entry in the Festschrift argued, Stan Cohen 'made his mark *before* the new criminologies forked, and he continued to exercise influence thereafter as an ancestral father figure over all the criminological lineages ...', *Crime, Social Control and Human Rights*, p. xxiii.

step and reflexively, in an unequal conversation with others, often more powerful, in a sequence of transformations which Erving Goffman represented as a moral career. Critical to that processual model, Stan Cohen said, is 'the use of concepts such as meaning, mind and self [which] moves us far away from the tenets of positivism; ... alerts us not only to seeing the reactions of others ... but also to seeing the interaction process *from the point of view of the deviant*' (p. 29, emphasis in the original). There was in all this a part of him that toyed with the deviant and the risqué himself (and in the jointly written introduction to one work he celebrated taking drugs with students, watching pornography and organising street protests[40]) but one suspects that much of it was more vicarious than practised, however much it may have been eulogised by his collaborator, Laurie Taylor, who often reminisced in public about their daring exploits together.

In affirming his position, Stan Cohen could be quite perfunctory and scathing about the failings of those who differed from him. He opened a review of Irvin Waller's *Men Released from Prison* with the dismissal 'Standard criminological stuff';[41] called John Williams's *Narcotics and Drug Dependence* 'lunacy';[42] and noted how 'sad' it was that Richard Sparks had spent time 'on this sort of stuff [the mathematical modelling of penal systems]. Mathematical models might well have their place—but perhaps not in a book subtitled: "The Crisis in the English Penal System".'[43] In so doing, he made it clear how much he disliked positivism, grand theory, descriptions grounded in the workings of impersonal social systems,[44] and what David Matza called 'correctionalism',[45] the pursuit of criminology to punish or change the deviant. He disliked dogmatics, even the dogmatics of his friends and colleagues on the Left (although, as Adam Kuper observed, he was outwardly tolerant of a politics that was 'so much the orthodoxy in the circles he moved in'). He was certainly not persuaded that revolution would answer the problems of crime and criminology: it might conduce only to the substitution of one form of oppression by another, to a 'model of social control in which offenders wearing

---

[40] See S. Cohen and L. Taylor; *Escape Attempts: the Theory and Practice of Resistance in Everyday Life* (London, 1976), p. 2.
[41] S. Cohen, Review, *New Society* (30 May 1974), 526.
[42] S. Cohen, Review, *New Society* (5 Sept. 1974), 624.
[43] S. Cohen, Review of R. Sparks, *Local Prisons: the Crisis in the English Penal System, New Society* (23 Sept. 1971), 579
[44] Robin Cohen said 'He wasn't keen on ... structuralism as in Marx, or structuralism as in Levi-Strauss, as in Parsonian [theory], I mean none of that really resonated.'
[45] D. Matza, *Becoming Deviant* (Englewood Cliffs, NJ, 1969), pp. 15–24.

sandwich boards listing their crimes before a crowd which shouts "Down with the counter-revolutionaries!" are then led away to be publicly shot'.[46]

He was driven by extension to the biographical and the intimate in the micro-sociology of everyday life. That is why he followed Terence Morris and turned to the work of the so-called Chicagoans and their heirs with their focus on the sociology of everyday life (and that emphasis was to be reinforced by semesters spent at the University of California, Santa Barbara, in the company of scholars such as Harvey Molotch, himself a product of the University of Chicago). Robert Park, the founder of the Department of Sociology at the University of Chicago and one of the progenitors of the 'Chicago School', once remarked that William James had taught him that 'the real world was the experience of actual men and women and not abbreviated and shorthand descriptions of it that we call knowledge'.[47] Stan Cohen would have approved. He once told me that of all the books he would keep, it would be those that had been published by the University of Chicago Press. Adam Kuper remarked he had been 'terrifically influenced by that stuff ... the study of the pool halls. Those were very important to him.' In his review of that study, *Hustlers, Beats and Others*, Stan Cohen said that he 'was grateful to Ned Polsky [its author] for reminding us that sociology could be interesting and even entertaining'.[48]

The new sociology was to be institutionalised in the form of the National Deviancy Conference that met for the first time at the University of York in 1968. Stan Cohen was in the van (David Downes claimed that 'the anchor-men of the NDC were Stan Cohen and Laurie Taylor'[49]). He edited the very first collection of papers from the Conference, *Images of Deviance*, as a *de facto* group manifesto, and it was there that he announced, in an echo of his preamble to *Hooligans, Vandals and the Community*, that 'Our feelings towards official criminology ranged from distrust at its orientation towards administrative needs and impatience with its highly empirical, anti-theoretical bias, to simply a mild lack of interest in the sort of studies that were being conducted.'[50]

---

[46] S. Cohen, 'Guilt, justice and tolerance', in D. Downes and P. Rock (eds.), *Deviant Interpretations* (Oxford, 1979), p. 44.
[47] In P. Baker, 'The life histories of W. I. Thomas and Robert E. Park', *American Journal of Sociology*, 79 (1973), 255.
[48] S. Cohen, Review, *New Society* (3 June 1971), 969.
[49] D. Downes, 'The sociology of crime and social control in Britain, 1960–1987', *British Journal of Criminology*, 28 (1988), 46.
[50] S. Cohen, 'Introduction', in S. Cohen (ed.), *Images of Deviance* (Harmondsworth, 1971), p. 15.

But, if he was averse to positivism and all its works, to abstracted empiricism, to grand theory and to structuralism—to dogmas, ideologies and systems—his scepticism about orthodoxy encouraged him to be otherwise eclectic, not accepting any single theory *tout court*. He was an intellectual in love with ideas. His daughter, Jessica, said 'I think that he had difficulty relating closely to adults who were not academics or not intellectual. He ... wasn't comfortable, I think, with people who were not intellectual because they would not find a common language.' And his other daughter, Judith, agreed: 'that's right, that's how he related to people. That was the only way he related to people, to discuss ideas. You couldn't talk about just everyday stuff.'

Stan Cohen had a great liking for conversation, teaching and students, and his students were fond of him in their turn. In Israel and England, he was ever in their midst. Judith Cohen said 'he was always encouraging students to come and talk to him and ... he would spend hours talking to people ... but it was only if they had a shared intellectual language'. His was a teaching rooted in discussion, story-telling and anecdote. Olga Jubany recalled that 'His supervision relied almost entirely on our regular conversations that would focus on discussing the development and approach of the investigation. Later these would develop into personal chats ... but certainly never, ever, about any administrative or bureaucratic proceedings.'

Stan Cohen's thought was grounded in what he called transactionalism. He flirted with the ideas of Michel Foucault, Ronald Laing, ethnomethodology and anarchism. He was intrigued by the psychology of the self, being, as his brother Robin said, 'much more self-reflective, much more personally aware than ... either Clive or myself'. He had studied psychoanalysis, practised briefly as a psychiatric social worker, and received therapy in California. At the very opening of his intellectual career he had talked scathingly about the 'sort of philistine distrust ... which greeted the work of Durkheim and Freud.... How [some said] can the intrapsychic conflicts of middle-class Viennese Jews explain how the normal mind works?'[51] His answer was that they could do so pretty well. Indeed, just as Sigmund Freud's study was littered with small carvings of gods and idols from ancient Greece, Rome, Egypt and the Orient,[52] so Stan Cohen kept a plastic manikin of Freud on his desk at work. Malcolm Feeley, Claire Sanders Clements Dean's Professor of Law at the University

---

[51] Cohen, *Hooligans, Vandals and the Community*, p. 13.
[52] See <http://www.freud.org.uk/about/house/>.

of California, Berkeley, who used from time to time to occupy Stan Cohen's office at the Hebrew University, recalled that 'the books of psychoanalysis took up a big part of his library collection.... I do think that underlying a lot of his work is some sort of implicit psychology.... Think of moral panics as something that creates anxieties in people.... *States of Denial* is implicit there.' Indeed, Stan Cohen was to talk often and at length to Irene Bruna Seu, an academic and a psychoanalytical psychotherapist, whilst he was writing the book.

Stan Cohen was, in short, something of a polymath and an eclectic. One of his students, Megan Comfort, later a research sociologist working in San Francisco,[53] remembered the diversity and breadth of his thought as a teacher: 'it felt like he brought in a lot of different perspectives and different theoretical ideas into our thinking through all of these different issues'. He thought on a large, panoptic scale. His colleague at the LSE, Claire Moon, put it that 'Typically, Cohen took an unsettling approach to ... problems [of the denial of human rights], what might be called a 360 degree approach ...,'[54] and by that she meant that he looked 'not just [at] the state, but also the bystanders (the consumers of humanitarian campaigns and appeals), and the humanitarian entrepreneurs, the human rights NGOs themselves. All of these were, he argued, complicit in denial and "bystander passivity".'[55]

Perhaps Stan Cohen was above all *playful*. He enjoyed the life of the mind. He had an abiding sense of humour, irony and the absurd (and the transactionalism which he espoused had at times itself veered into a sociology of the absurd[56]). A reflexive sociologist who looked continually at the interplay between biography and the social world, he loved anecdote and narrative, teaching through stories, and funny stories above all (one of his students, Sharon Shalev, said 'he was a wonderful gossip. There were few things I enjoyed as much as sitting and just gossiping about people with him.') His LSE colleague Conor Gearty said too that 'The other memory I have is of course how funny he was. And that, to some

---

[53] Her full title was senior research sociologist with the Urban Health Program and an adjunct assistant professor of medicine at the Center for AIDS Prevention Studies at the University of California.

[54] C. Moon, '"Looking without seeing, listening without hearing": Cohen, denial and human rights', *Crime, Media, Culture*, 9 (2013), p. 194.

[55] C. Moon, keynote lecture delivered to the Moral Panic, Society and Rights Conference in Honour of Stan Cohen, University of Athens, Greece, 7 Dec. 2013.

[56] See, for instance, S. Lyman and M. Scott, *A Sociology of the Absurd* (New York, 1989); P. Carlen, *Magistrates' Courts: an Ethnography in the Sociology of the Absurd*, Ph.D. dissertation, University of London, 1974.

extent, comes through in the writing but the fun was rooted in such a strong sociological understanding of the self you know. I mean he was so aware that he was part of something. It was incredible.'

Stan Cohen had a great store of Jewish jokes, and he told them very well, often to poke fun at authority, the staid, the conventional and himself. Stan Cohen's colleague, Tim Newburn, said 'one of the things that's an overriding memory for me of Stan is [that he] had extraordinarily twinkly eyes which betrayed, I thought, a really important bit of his character which was, Stan was just a little bit naughty, I thought. And that naughtiness probably displayed itself in a variety of ways but I think that as a scholar, that naughtiness presented itself at least in part, as a desire in some small way, always to subvert.'

V. Israel

England in the 1960s and 1970s may have been intellectually exciting, Stan Cohen may have come into his own and prospered there professionally, but he was never quite at home. He liked individual Britons, and he and Ruth made close friendships, mostly through work, some of which endured for the rest of their lives. They did talk fondly about their life in Durham. Yet Judith, his daughter, reflected they had 'a sense of aloofness from "the Brits" as a nation'. He did not talk about 'us' but about 'the British' as if they were foreign to him. A political animal, he never became involved in British politics. ('I was', he said, 'acutely aware that [my] original commitments could never find a home in English politics. I couldn't read about what was happening in South Africa and Israel and then connect with the striking British trades unionists or university Trotskyists.'[57]) In the whole of England there was but one little area for which he had come strongly to care, Belsize Park, in North London. But the Cohens were living in Colchester in Essex in the 1970s, and that was another matter altogether. Robin Cohen said 'it was very grey and bleak and even within Wivenhoe or Colchester, wherever they were, they seemed to somehow pick out the greyest stucco and drabbest walls'.

Disengaged and rather rootless, Stan Cohen and his family quit England for Israel in 1981. Many were taken aback at their decision. David Downes said 'it took me completely by surprise ..., his going to Israel. I mean I hadn't been in on that, as it were. So it came as a bolt from

---

[57] L. Taylor, 'The other side of the street', *New Humanist*, 119 (2004), 4.

the blue ... that he found British society so boring. I mean that did surprise me 'cause I don't find British society boring. I find it really endlessly fascinating. But then, from his perspective, I could see how that could be. You know, there was no really powerful fundamental challenge going on to the powers that be.' It should be reported that Stan and Ruth Cohen also told Malcolm Feeley, their friend from Berkeley, that their emigration had been prompted by the anti-Semitism of the Left in England, although they seem to have said that to no one else, and certainly not to their daughters.

Other forces were in play. There was the residual influence of Zionism (Stan Cohen said afterwards that 'So strong was the brainwashing I'd received from the Zionist youth movement that I'd managed to avoid facing the full reality'[58]). Jessica Cohen claimed that there was a quest for the *frisson* of political commitment, what David Downes had called a 'really powerful fundamental challenge'. 'For obvious reasons', she said, they 'couldn't go back to South Africa ... before apartheid ended, so I think Israel was a place for them to feel involved in.' And her sister, Judith, concurred: 'They needed to be in a struggle ... there was the political thing, that they wanted to feel part of something, there was a connection ... at that point in Israel, there was a sense that there was a real political struggle that was going in a positive direction. There was Camp David and there was a sense that if you joined this swell of people who were you know, progressive and moving towards peace, then you could be part of this.' There were family links. Ruth's parents lived in Jerusalem. So did David, her brother, at that time the Bruce W. Wayne Professor of International Law at the Hebrew University. And thus it was that the family left.

It was not to be a wholly happy experience. Stan Cohen said it had been 'complete madness'.[59] Judith Cohen called it 'a complete fiasco'. Instead of a vibrant politics, they found, in the words of Jessica Cohen, that 'the South African friends they had who had moved to Israel ... most of them, the vast majority of them were just not involved in any kind of political activity. They were just living *bourgeois* lives.' Stan Cohen was not to be at home intellectually or socially in the Department of Sociology at the Hebrew University. He had been lauded in England but, Jessica Cohen continued, 'he felt under-appreciated in Israel, right from the

---

[58] L. Taylor, 'The other side of the street: an interview with Stan Cohen', in Downes *et al.*, *Crime, Social Control and Human Rights*, p. 20.
[59] Ibid., p. 20.

beginning, professionally'. He found Shmuel Noah Eisenstadt,[60] a powerful baronial figure in the department, a grand theorist in the tradition of structural-functionalism, to be a difficult colleague. In turn, Shmuel Eisenstadt and another colleague, Joseph Ben-David,[61] dismissed Stan Cohen's work as not properly sociological, rejected his wish to remain in the department,[62] and obliged him to move into the Institute of Criminology where, again, he was to be ill at ease professionally. Malcolm Feeley, who knew him in Israel and the United States, said 'Stan was just head and shoulders above them ... [he] was not happy there and he got increasingly unhappy ... he did not have a comfortable intellectual home.' Adam Kuper put it even more pithily, 'he hated the Hebrew University, hated the sociologists. He thought the university was not a very good university.' *Aliyah* had become something of an illusion. Robin Cohen said 'Israel he regarded as a pretty big mistake you know, he was living out that interrupted adolescent dream ... he had friends, he had significant ... achievements in the UK and in the United States. Israel was very much a sort of backwards move.' He and Ruth began to question whether their daughters could ever have a future in the country.

Some members of his immediate family did somewhat temper that narrative of alienation and deracination. Jessica Cohen certainly did so—her memories of life in Israel were more affectionate. But Stan Cohen had undoubtedly become estranged from large portions of Israeli society, sociology and criminology and, finding the 'Israeli military occupation of the West Bank an ongoing source of pain',[63] he moved into the politics and study of human rights, focusing especially on torture.[64] Adam Kuper recalled too that 'he'd got a bit bored with sociology and criminology as well ... in Israel, the most interesting people in any case were often

---

[60] Shmuel Eisenstadt (1923–2010) taught at the University from 1946 to 1990 and was head of the Department of Sociology between 1949 and 1969. He was said to have 'developed comparative knowledge of exceptional quality and originality concerning social change and modernization, and concerning relations between culture, belief systems and political institutions. His work combines sociological theory with historical and empirical research in the study of modernities and civilizations' (citation for the Holberg Prize, 2006, <http://www.holbergprisen.no/en/shmuel-n-eisenstadt/shmuel-noah-eisenstadt-1923-2010.html>).

[61] Joseph Ben-David (1920–86), the George Wise Professor of Sociology, a committed anti-relativist, was a sociologist of science who had taught at the Hebrew University from 1950. See R. Westrum; 'Obituary: Joseph Ben-David (1920–86): sociologist of science and of higher education', *Social Studies of Science*, 16 (1986), 565–7.

[62] See N. Ben-Yehuda, 'Stan', *Crime, Media, Culture*, 9 (2013), 188.

[63] Ibid., p. 188.

[64] See B. Hudson; 'Professor Stanley Cohen: an appreciation', *Criminal Justice Matters*, 92 (2013), <http://www.tandfonline.com/doi/full/10.1080/09627251.2013.805380#.Upd0wNJSiS8>.

82   *Paul Rock*

involved in these human rights things'. So it was that he moved to work with others 'to expose the torture of Palestinian political figures. And Stan published not only key papers on it,[65] he was very involved with the pressure group which ... got the Supreme Court to see what could be done.'[66] Robin Cohen added, 'he had to find some space for himself which allowed him to live in this place that he clearly hated. And I think that's probably where the human rights stuff came from. Again, the biographical angle, the personal and the political connecting.' It was in the vigorous intellectual and political world centred on human rights in Israel that Ruth and Stan Cohen then came to find a new anchorage. Judith Cohen remembered:

> ... he did find himself—largely through political activity—connecting to a small group of intellectuals and activists on the Left, where he and Ruth were instrumental in founding and organizing groups and activities within the anti-occupation movement ... during their time in Israel, despite the problems, they were very involved politically—Ruth perhaps more than Stan—and the friendships they formed through this activity were hugely significant and provided them with a support network, a rich social life that, I think ... encouraged them to stay on even when things got difficult.

The Professor of International Law, Christine Chinkin, Stan Cohen's future colleague at the London School of Economics, met him first at a conference in Gaza organised by the Palestine Human Rights Association, and found in his work a complementarity with her own legal interest in genocide. But what Stan Cohen introduced analytically into what was then a largely legal and activist field was a sociological inflection unusual at the time. He began by transposing the psychoanalytic vocabulary of denial, sociological ideas about good people and dirty work,[67] and the criminological language of techniques of neutralisation[68] to a new empirical terrain:

> Human rights were colonised by law. There's no doubt about that at all.... I don't think other people have done the sort of sociological roots of human rights in the way he did, how issues emerge through a language and then through being identified in such a way that they can ... explor[e] that sociological root.

---

[65] See S. Cohen, *Denial and Acknowledgement: the Impact of Information about Human Rights Violations* (Jerusalem, 1995); and S. Cohen, 'Government responses to human rights reports: claims, denials and counterclaims', *Human Rights Quarterly*, 18 (1996), 517–43.

[66] He was referring to the consequences of the 1991 B'Tselem Report, co-authored by Stan Cohen, and discussed by Stan Cohen's brother-in-law, David Kretzmer, in 'The torture debate: Israel and beyond', in Downes *et al.*, *Crime, Social Control and Human Rights*, pp. 120–35.

[67] E. Hughes, 'Good people and dirty work', *Social Problems*, 10 (1962), 3–11.

[68] See G. Sykes and D. Matza, 'Techniques of neutralization: a theory of delinquency', *American Sociological Review*, 22 (1957), 664–70; and D. Matza, *Delinquency and Drift* (New York, 1964).

> *The States of Denial* stuff.... Nobody else ... has really looked at this concept of what is the complicity of people with respect to human rights violations of those who are in some sense peripheral or on the margins or watching.

Another colleague in the same area, Claire Moon, would add that Stan Cohen then proceeded to apply a further idea integral to criminology, that of the politics of social control, to the comparative analysis of transitional justice, examining how societies policed the past by opening up and closing down access to discreditable and dangerous knowledge. The idea raised ancillary questions about how such knowledge should be acted on—about lustration and punishment—and about how (if at all) those who received that knowledge responded to what they were told[69] ('the assumption that drives a lot of human rights NGO work is, of course, if only people knew, they would act [but there are] defence mechanisms that prevent us from acting on information about suffering'[70] she said). And, moving even further down that spiral of actions and reactions, the idea invited an exploration of how states such as Israel responded to those selfsame responses by 'contest[ing] and rebuff[ing] claims by human rights organizations, such as those made by PCATI [the Public Committee Against Torture in Israel], Human Rights Watch or Amnesty International in their reports?'[71] Their official rejoinder, it seemed, was typically to redefine the victim, the perpetrator and the act in ways that softened the impact of knowledge about torture, restored a measure of legitimacy, distance and necessity to what was done and allayed the bystander's disquiet—accomplishing, in effect, the very antithesis of a moral panic. In short, Stan Cohen's criminology of human rights posed very big sociological questions of truth, acknowledgement, catharsis and reparation:

> [T]he control by opening and the control by closing was a really interesting way of looking at it because he was pointing right early on to the political dimensions ... looking at the State institutions and at how people were made to speak, who was allowed to speak, who could speak, what kind of truths were being generated and so on.

In Israel, Stan Cohen had encountered what he considered to be an oppressive polity and his antipathy to Leviathan had grown. Robin Cohen

---

[69] S. Cohen; 'State crimes of previous regimes: knowledge, accountability, and the policing of the past', *Law and Social Inquiry*, 20 (1995), 7–50.

[70] See S. Cohen and B. Seu; 'Knowing enough not to feel too much: emotional thinking about human rights appeals', in M. Bradley and P. Petro (eds.), *Truth Claims* (Piscataway, NJ, 2002), pp. 187–228.

[71] C. Moon, keynote lecture delivered to the Moral Panic, Society and Rights Conference in Honour of Stan Cohen, University of Athens, Greece, 7 Dec. 2013.

said: 'I think part of what happened to him there was "it's every bit as bleak as I feared, the State is immutable, the populace is completely behind the State. This looks to me like I can't believe in any meaningful sense".' It is perhaps unremarkable then that one of the few intellectual positions he came to accept almost without cavil for a while was to be the work of Michel Foucault, because Foucault wrote allusively and polemically about the diffuse and overweening tyranny of the State. Foucault's *Discipline and Punish* was an especially graphic, almost poetic, account of the way in which the controls imposed by the State insidiously and systemically permeated every fibre of the body social.[72] Adam Kuper reflected that 'there was a stage where Foucault was really terrific' for him. Stan Cohen himself enthused in 1974 about 'the marvellously rich French school around Foucault [that] has built up an impressive theoretical edifice ...',[73] calling it 'wonderful' to Nachman Ben-Yehuda, his colleague at the Hebrew University. The consonance between the thoughts of the two men was especially pronounced in Stan Cohen's paper 'The punitive city',[74] published in 1979, and the influential book, *Visions of Social Control,* published in 1985 whilst he was in Israel, a book replete with references to Foucault, in which he explored how the apparent attenuation of State power perversely only extended State power through what he called boundary-blurring, 'net-widening' and 'mesh-thinning'. But they were references made at a later stage, and by then Stan Cohen had come to be somewhat dubious even about 'the marvellously rich French school',[75] wondering, Nachman Ben-Yehuda recalled, about its meagre empirical foundations.

VI. England Again

Belsize Park in North London was where Stan and Ruth Cohen had first stayed when he was a research student, and it was to become the *Heimat*

---

[72] M. Foucault, *Discipline and Punish* (English translation) (Harmondsworth, 1979).
[73] S. Cohen, Review of D. Rothman, *The Discovery of the Asylum, New Society* (7 Feb. 1974), 332.
[74] S. Cohen. 'The punitive city: notes on the dispersal of social control', *Social Crises*, 3 (1979), 341–63.
[75] He was to say that 'I am altogether unsympathetic to the intellectual climate in which his work flourishes and (being exactly the type of "humanist" he is always attacking) totally opposed to his structuralist denial of human agency. But to write today about punishment and classification without Foucault, is like talking about the unconscious without Freud': S. Cohen, *Visions of Social Control* (Cambridge, 1985), p. 10.

to which they returned on his appointment to the London School of Economics. His brother said 'he fixed on one place which was Belsize Park and he never really felt comfortable in any other space. By that I mean to say, did he feel comfortable in South Africa? No. In Israel? No. In the UK at large? No. In American space? No. It was just that little zone ... he needed a certain sense of buzz and activity, eating with friends, meeting interesting people.' The grand houses of Belsize Park are physically elegant and many of its inhabitants are intellectually animated and urbane. Judith Cohen described it as 'the hub of this ... political, cosmopolitan environment'. In that last decade or so of his life, working at the LSE and living in North London, he seemed to have become much more content with his lot. Jessica Cohen said 'I think by the time [the family had] sort of come to terms with all the turmoil of moving back and forth and just accepted that they were now in London.'

VII. The Marginal Man

Judith Cohen said 'in spite of all their moving around, [my parents] sustained close friendships, often for over fifty years, with individuals from all over world. Friends were hugely important in their lives and it was their close network of friends, both those that went back to the early days in South Africa or England, and more recent ones, that made them feel at home and rooted, especially here in London.' The family could never simply be described as homeless cosmopolitans. Yet there was, at the same time, a sense in which they were perennial outsiders. Jessica Cohen said they felt that they never completely belonged anywhere. Stan Cohen himself was frequently described by friends and colleagues as a wandering Jew, a marginal man, who had never quite settled. His friend and student, Sharon Shalev, called it 'the curse of the Jew ... we belong everywhere, we don't belong anywhere ... we look at the big ugly parts of the societies we live in and ... you belong but you don't really belong.' His brother reflected in like vein that Stan Cohen 'did have that habit of looking past you and that's what I'm calling displacement and you can put some other label to it which may be more slightly psychoanalytical, but it was a sense of unease with where he was'. And that was an engrained part of his background. At the LSE celebration on 10 December 2013, Robin Cohen further reflected that 'Identities are made on the move' and theirs had long been a family in motion.

Marginality has its consequences. It may inhibit a full taking of the role of the other, of empathy and *Verstehen*. Allied to the Young Turks' preoccupation with the deviant actor, it can bring about a descriptive neglect of the sensibilities of everyone else involved in volume crime—the victims, witnesses, bystanders, police, judges and others who are all too readily forgotten or reduced to stereotype—only when roles are reversed and the perpetrator is the state or corporate business do they merit attention. It can in its turn render almost all formal social control incomprehensible, futile or sinister. But marginality can also be propitious intellectually.[76] It leads to the attainment of an anthropological distance in which the familiar may become strange and problematic; and where, in Alfred Schutz's terminology, one can attain the *epoché* of the natural attitude.[77] The stranger can question what others accept.[78] He or she can be sensitive to what Robin Cohen called 'people out of place'. That was probably at the root of Stan Cohen's endemic scepticism and of his analytical strength. He was somewhat outside the taken for granted social and political world (Sharon Shalev said 'he was able, which very few of us are able to do, ... to look at what's happening in his own society and analyse it'). And he was also outside the very analytic frameworks, such as criminology, that examined it. His daughter, Judith, remembered 'I did discuss the kind of general idea of being on the outside of a discipline. And I remember once having a discussion in which he said he thought you were better placed to be critical of a discipline or an ideological position if you were on the outside. And that was a position that he'd adopted.'

Stan Cohen had as a consequence an extraordinary ability to interrogate apparently banal and commonplace problems anew, to say interesting things about them as if encountering them for the very first time. It was a trait commonly cited. Megan Comfort, a former student, captured it when she talked of how 'he suddenly ... turned everything on its head from what you had just been thinking ... you're ... thinking of this one lens and then, where you suddenly apply another lens into the picture, you realise that you have to rethink everything you had just been considering'. He had, she said, a flair for 'getting right in there and turning everything

---

[76] See E. Stonequist, 'The problem of the marginal man', *American Journal of Sociology*, 41 (1935), 1–12.

[77] A. Schutz, 'Common-sense and scientific interpretation of human action', in M. Natanson (ed.), *Alfred Schutz: Collected Papers*, Vol. 1 (The Hague, 1967), pp. 4–47.

[78] See G. Simmel; 'The stranger', in D. Levine (ed.), *Georg Simmel on Individuality and Social Forms* (Chicago, IL, 1971), pp. 143–9.

upside down and making you laugh and making you question'. Conor Gearty, Professor of Human Rights Law at the London School of Economics, captured it too:

> He had this incredible freshness. I mean to be able to pick up and run with ideas which were foreign to his area of academic life ... the problematising of it, the uncertainty about it, the awareness that the [ideas] which we supported were not obvious and needed to be understood and were multi-layered, was really quite new. And getting behind the term and understanding that it stands for something and could easily stand for something else in the hands and in the mouths of somebody else was important.

VIII. Conclusion

Originality, marginality, scepticism, moral purpose and a sense of the absurd encapsulate the defining contradictoriness of the man. He was a sociological relativist committed politically to the enlightenment project of universal human rights. He may have called himself 'a pessimist, a "miserabilist," even a depressive',[79] but his occasional gloominess about the world and a consciousness of its cruelty were leavened always by a besetting sense of the ludicrous. He was *homo ludens*. Even when he was very ill, *in extremis*, he joked to me that he felt he was, like Job, being punished by God for not believing in Him. He was the only person, his colleague, Claire Moon, remarked, 'who could shoehorn the odd genocide joke into a lecture'.[80] Laurie Taylor alluded in his obituary to 'his happy readiness to undermine anything too serious with a joke'.[81] And that sensibility occasionally surfaced in his writing. Frances Heidensohn reminded me about what she called 'some endearingly quirky pieces which show his sense of humour and maybe his anarchism', and she cited his 'Conference life: the rough guide'[82] and 'The last seminar',[83] 'a darker paper but also subversive', with its imagery of the university as a madhouse populated by the lost and the damned wandering around mouthing 'Commentaries on

---

[79] Response to Public Orator by Professor Stanley Cohen, University of Essex, 9 July 2003, p. 5.
[80] Moon, 'Looking without seeing, listening without hearing', p. 193.
[81] L. Taylor, Stanley Cohen obituary, *The Guardian*, 23 Jan. 2013.
[82] S. Cohen, 'Conference life: the rough guide', *Scottish Journal of Criminal Justice Studies*, 1 (1995), 33–59 (also published in *The American Sociologist*, 28(3) (1997), 69–84).
[83] S. Cohen, 'The last seminar', *The Sociological Review*, 27 (1979), 1–27.

commentaries. All sense of the world gone, washed away with the excreta of the Left Bank.'[84]

An intellectual, enamoured of ideas, he was nevertheless uninterested in history, the natural world and the physical sciences; he could not understand how campaigners could become involved in the preservation of animal species; and he did not go to the theatre (although he loved the opera). He was also far from being unremittingly bookish, having been fascinated by boxing and boxers, and especially Muhammad Ali, since boyhood; he gambled on the horses; and he adored watching old videos of the comedian and magician, Tommy Cooper, who died in 1984, and *Il Bacio di Tosca*, a 1986 film about the operatic denizens of the *Casa di Riposo per Musicisti*, a home founded in 1896 by Giuseppe Verdi for retired opera singers.

His quirkiness was a strength. Stan Cohen's prime achievement was not to be an ethnographer in the mould of Ned Polsky (he did none of that kind of work after *Folk Devils and Moral Panics* and *Psychological Survival*); nor a grand theorist, for he had emphatically eschewed that role; but as a theorist of what might be called the lower middle range,[85] injecting a number of illuminating, unusual, beautifully phrased and always enticing ideas into the analysis of the misuses of power in societies purporting to be benign. Tim Newburn put it well:

> my sense of Stan was that he was quite an unpredictable scholar, an imaginative, unpredictable scholar. So I would have said that there have been many people working as it were, in the field of criminology broadly defined, sociology, deviance and so forth, who have done great things. But I, having read one or two of their great things, I would sort of know what was coming next ... and that's not meant in any disparaging way ... I was never quite sure what he was going to do next and where he was going to come from other than a sort of overriding concern with justice in some broad form.

PAUL ROCK
Fellow of the Academy

Note. I am most grateful to Nachman Ben-Yehuda, Christine Chinkin, Jessica Cohen, Judith Cohen, Robin Cohen, David Downes, Malcolm Feely, Conor Gearty, Frances Heidensohn, Adam Kuper, Claire Moon, Tim Newburn and Sharon Shalev for their often detailed comments on an earlier draft of this memoir and to Joyce Lorinstein for transcribing the interviews.

---

[84] S. Cohen, 'The last seminar', *The Sociological Review*, 27 (1979), 12.
[85] See R. Merton, *Social Theory and Social Structure* (Glencoe, IL, 1957).

[1]
Mods, Rockers and the Rest:
Community Reactions to Juvenile Delinquency*

THIS paper deals with one part of a research project being carried out within a certain theoretical framework in criminology and the broader field of the sociology of deviance. To understand why certain aspects of the subject matter—the Mods and Rockers phenomenon—are being considered rather than others, it is necessary to provide a brief statement of this framework.

Theoretical Framework

The main purpose of the research project is to investigate social reaction to deviant behaviour. The rationale behind this approach was first set out in a strangely neglected textbook by Lemert[1] and systematized more recently by Becker[2]. This approach views deviance as a transactional process, the result of interaction between the person who commits an act and those who respond to it. Social reaction to deviance, the crucial variable in this approach, is largely ignored in conventional research in criminology and social deviance. In the field of juvenile delinquency, for example, the bulk of research is directed towards the taxonomic tabulation of the delinquents' traits (or attitudes, or values) in an attempt to see how delinquents differ from non-delinquents.[3] On this basis causal theories are constructed. But the deviant act is not, or not only, deviant *per se*, it has to be defined and treated as such by the community. Social problems are what people think they are—there is an objective and verifiable situation, but also a subjective awareness of it and a definition by certain people that the situation is inimical to their interests and that something should be done about it[4]. The damage to art treasures by floods is a 'problem' to those whose commercial or aesthetic values are tied up with the preservation of art treasures. If this group of people didn't exist, there would be no problem. In the same way, the delinquent is a problem, but a problem *for someone*.

So when Becker writes that society creates deviance, he does not mean this in the conventional sense of there being social factors in the individual's situation which prompt his action, but that '... social groups create deviance by making the rules whose infractions constitute deviance, and by applying these rules to particular persons and labelling them as outsiders.' From this point of view, deviance is not a quality of the act the person commits, but rather a consequence of the application by others of rules and sanctions to an 'offender'.[5] The audience, not the actor, is the crucial variable.

One effect of community reaction is to confirm the deviant in his self-identity. When the community reacts negatively to a person's deviation from valued norms, he tends to define his situation largely in terms of the reaction. He takes on a

* Lecture given to Howard League, 6th December, 1966.

new self-concept, identifies himself in a new light and even begins to act like the stereotype of him. James Baldwin has vividly described the position of many Negroes in these terms: he notes how his father '. . was defeated long before he died because . . . . he really believed what white people said about him' and warned his nephew: 'You can only be destroyed by believing that you really are what the white world calls a nigger'.[6]

This reaction sequence sets into operation what Wilkins calls a 'deviation-amplifying system'[7] and the present research is aimed at observing the workings of this sort of system. The sequence would run something like this:
1. Initial deviation from valued norms, leading to:
2. Punitive reaction by the community (which may lead to the segregation of groups and marking them as deviant):
3. Development of a deviant self-identity and behaviour appropriate to this identity:
4. Further punitive reaction, etc.

Although it is not within the scope of this lecture to develop the theme, it should be pointed out that this sort of analysis is not just a manipulation of theoretical models. As Wilkins himself has made very clear, the implications for social policy, in the fields of both treatment and prevention, are considerable. Schur has recently used this type of model to examine the impact of public policy on abortion, homosexuality and drug addiction.[8] He shows, for example, how policy based often upon vital misconceptions about the nature of the deviant behaviour, may be expressed in legal prescriptions. This 'criminalization' of deviance then forces the individual into reinforcing a criminal self-image that creates problems for himself and society at large. The classic example, of course, is the creation of the addict sub-culture as partly at least a consequence of the public stereotype (the 'dope fiend') and repressive legislation. In the context of compulsory hospitalization, treatment may just reinforce the self-image.

The Present Study

Deviance is not a 'thing' which can be observed and studied. The term is a conceptual category and all we have are types of behaviour that have been classified as deviant. For research purposes we have to choose one of these types and juvenile delinquency is simply one such type that can be studied. Again though, juvenile delinquency is not a concrete enough category for this type of study—the term is a legal definition and not a behavioural syndrome. So, for reasons including its topical importance as a subject in its own right, the unit of study for this section of the project was narrowed down to what is classifiable (for want of a less emotive word) as 'hooliganism'. The Mods and Rockers phenomenon of the last three years, particularly in the form it took of disturbances and so-called riots at English seaside resorts over bank holiday weekends, provides an archetypal example of this behaviour.

Because we are using the transactional framework to explore certain aspects of the community reaction, the study is necessarily self limiting. It does not attempt to provide a comprehensive account of the whole phenomenon e.g. in historical terms or in terms of sub-cultural theory.

Method

In an exploratory study of this nature there are few guidelines on which method to use for collecting data. In the event almost all possible methods were tried. These included:—content analysis of all press cuttings covering the period Easter 1963—August 1966 (national as well as relevant local press); 65 interviews carried out with a quota sample of spectators on the Brighton seafront during Whitsun 1965; various other interviews with local figures, e.g. newspaper editors, local government officials, hotel proprietors, M.P.'s etc., and personal observation of crowd behaviour, police action and court hearings. (The final research report will also use data from 140 intensive interviews carried out in a London Borough on the more general topic of attitudes to delinquency.)

The Initial Deviation

Clacton is an East Coast resort not particularly well known for the range of amusements it provides for its younger visitors. Easter 1963 was worse than usual—it was cold and wet, in fact the coldest Easter Sunday for eighty years. The shopkeepers and the stall-owners were irritated by the lack of business and the young people milling around had their own irritation fanned by rumours of cafe owners and barmen refusing to serve some of them. A few groups started roughing around and for the first time the Mods and Rockers factions, a division at that time only vaguely in the air, started separating out. Those on bikes and scooters roared up and down, windows were broken, some beach huts were wrecked, one boy fired a starting pistol in the air. The vast number of young people crowding the streets, the noise, everyone's general irritation and the often panicky actions of an unprepared and undermanned police force, made the two days seem rather frightening.

One of the most significant features about Clacton is that there appear to have been present a number of what the police would call 'troublemakers'— mainly Rockers from the East End or small East Anglian villages. Contrasted with the fringe supporters, these are the same hard core who in race riots and other crowd situations are predisposed to take the initiative and to respond violently to what is perceived as police provocation. All the 24 boys charged in the Clacton court claimed that they had been the unlucky ones, that they had been picked out at random. Yet 23 out of the 24 had previous convictions— the police's chances of picking out 23 previous offenders at random out of a crowd of say a thousand, is one in a couple of million.

As we shall show, many aspects of the Mods and Rockers have parallels in the class of phenomena known as mass delusion. These studies[9] show that the first stage is invariably a real event—the delusion or hysteria is created because the initial event is reported in such a way as to set in motion a cumulative sequence which serves to fulfill the expectations created by the earlier events. In terms of our model this is an amplifying process.

The Process of Amplification

One of the most important elements in the reaction to deviance is the growth of a generalised set of beliefs to explain the behaviour. Once the first stage of reporting is past, the community feels the need to make sense of what has occurred—this is especially the case when the event is perceived as a dislocation of the smooth running of things: the killing of a policeman, a political assassination, a natural disaster. People look for explanations, self-styled experts proclaim favourite theories, stereotypes are confirmed or new ones are created, words acquire a symbolic meaning—'Aberfan', 'Dallas', 'Braybrook Street', 'Clacton'.

In the case of deviancy, these generalised beliefs invariably involve spurious attribution; all sorts of traits are attributed to the deviant and, on the basis of little or no evidence, a whole set of misconceptions arise. Let us give a few examples of some of these elements.

'Violence and Damage'—it was widely believed that the Mods and Rockers caused widespread damage and were involved in violent assaults on each other or 'innocent holidaymakers'. In fact the amount of damage done was not excessive—in the three year period there were less than ten cases of malicious damage—in Hastings, August 1964, for example, one of the 'big' events, there were only four charges of malicious damage out of 64 arrests.

During Whitsun 1964, although there were 54 arrests in Bournemouth the damage was £100, in Brighton with 76 arrests the damage was £400, in Margate with 64 arrests the damage was £250. Compare these figures to the *real* cost to the resorts which was in extra police charges: the four successive bank holidays between Easter 1965 and Easter 1966 cost the Brighton Council an extra £13,000. The amount of serious violence similarly was negligible—only one tenth of the original Clacton offenders were charged with offences involving violence. In Margate, Whitsun 1964, supposedly the most violent week-end, where according to the *Daily Express* (19/5/64) 'The 1964 boys smeared the traditional postcard scene with blood and violence', there were two not very serious stabbings and one man dropped onto a flower bed. The typical offence was using threatening behaviour or obstructing the police. Leaving aside the obvious inconvenience caused to adults by crowds of youths milling about on the pavements and beach, few innocent holidaymakers were the victims of violence—the targets were members of a rival group or, more often, the police.

'Loss of trade'—it was widely believed that the troubles scared potential visitors away and the resorts suffered financially. The evidence for this is at best dubious. Papers quoted figures from Brighton for Whitsun 1964 showing that the number of deck-chairs hired had dropped by 8,000 on the previous year's week-end. This drop was attributed to the effects of the Mods and Rockers. Analyses of other figures, however, show that the total number of visitors was probably more—the reason why fewer deckchairs were hired was that Whit Monday was one of the coldest for decades—the temperature had dropped overnight by 14º F. and the beaches were virtually deserted. Interviews and observation suggest that if anything, the Mods and Rockers attracted some visitors and by the end of 1965 certainly, the happenings were part of the Brighton scene—the pier, whelks and the Mods and Rockers could all be taken in on a day trip.

'Affluent Youth'—attitudes and opinions are often shaped and bolstered up by legends and myths. One of the most recurrent of the Mods and Rockers myths was the one about the boy who told the Margate magistrates that he would pay his £75 fine with a cheque. This myth was frequently used to justify the image of the Mods and Rockers as classless, affluent, and scooter or motor-bike owners. The story was in itself true enough—what few papers bothered to publish and what they all knew, was that the boy's offer was a pathetic gesture of bravado. He later admitted that not only did he not have the £75 cheque but did not even have a bank account and had never signed a cheque in his life. The affluence image has very little factual basis. The Clacton offenders had on them an average of 15/- for the whole bank holiday week-end. The best off was a window cleaner earning £15 a week, but more typical were a market assistant earning £7 10s. and a 17-year-old clerk earning £5 14s. The average take home pay in a sample of offenders from Margate, Whitsun 1964, was £11 per week. The classless image is also none too accurate—the typical Rocker was an unskilled manual worker, the typical Mod a semi-skilled manual worker[10]. In all cases, the majority of young people present hitched or came down by train or coach. The scooter and motor-bike riders were a minority, albeit a noisy and ubiquitous minority.

A detailed analysis of a number of other such images, shows that a large component of the deviation is, in Lemert's term, 'putative': 'The putative deviation is that portion of the societal definition of the deviant which has no foundation in his objective behaviour.'[11] Why is this sort of belief system important?

In the first place the stereotypes implied in the putative deviation serve to sensitize the community to any sign of incipient deviance. A previously ambiguous situation which may have been 'written off' as a Saturday night brawl now becomes re-interpreted as a 'Mods and Rockers clash'. In the weeks following the first two or three major happenings, a number of such incidents were reported from widely scattered localities. Minor scuffles and fights and increased police vigilance were reported by the Press under such headings as 'Mods and Rockers Strike Again'. There were also numerous false alarms—after Whitsun 1964 for example, the police in Stamford Hill after answering a false alarm stated that 'people are a bit jumpy after the trouble on the coast'. This type of sensitization which turns non-events into events, is exactly the same process noted by students of mass delusion. In a state of hypersuggestibility following the reporting of a 'Mad Bomber' or a 'Phantom Anaesthetist' or a 'Sex Fiend On The Loose' ambiguous events are re-interpreted to fit into the belief. This is made easier when there is a composite stereotype available with readily identifiable symbols such as clothes. To the residents of Brighton, any boy between fourteen and twenty wearing a fur-collared anorak was a Mod. At the end of one Bank Holiday the police stood at the station putting back on the trains all 'suspicious looking' arrivals who could not prove that they were local residents.

Another way in which beliefs are important in amplifying deviance is that they serve to legitimate the action of society's agents of control. *If* you are dealing with a group that is vicious, destructive, causing your community a financial loss, and symbolically repudiating your cherished values, then you are justified to respond punitively. *If*, moreover, this is an affluent horde of scooter-riders, then 'fines won't touch them' and you have to propose confiscation of their scooters, forced labour camps, corporal punishment, turning the fire hoses on them. By the logic of their own definitions, the agents of control have to escalate the measures they take and propose to take to deal with the problem. So by Easter 1965 the magistrates in Brighton were employing the highly dubious practice of remanding young people in custody as a form of extra-legal punishment. Bail was refused not on the merits of the individual case but as a matter of principle—the ostensible reason given by the magistrates for remand as being to enable the police to make enquiries, was not in fact the reason given in court when bail was opposed. The police opposed bail on the grounds that if the boys were allowed to go free justice would not be done and that the public would not be protected. On the flimsiest evidence a boy, who by the police's own account had done nothing more than refuse to 'move along', would be certified as an 'unruly person', refused bail and remanded in custody in an adult prison—in some cases for up to three weeks. A test case of this sort when taken before a Judge in Chambers resulted in the immediate release of a 16-year-old boy from prison on bail. Although precise data is difficult to obtain, at least 20 cases have been traced of successful appeals on the grounds of wrongful arrests or disproportionately high sentences. There is no doubt that in certain cases, admittedly under conditions of extreme physical and psychological strain and under direct provocation, arrests were made quite arbitrarily and with unnecessary violence. In one instance, arrested youths were observed being pushed through a gauntlet of police punches before literally being thrown into the van.

Informal agents of social control also took up extreme positions. On the initiative of a group of senior aldermen and councillors, the Brighton Council overwhelmingly passed a resolution calling for the setting up of compulsory labour camps for Mods and Rockers. A group of Great Yarmouth businessmen and hotel-keepers set up a Safeguard Committee which seriously debated a scheme of setting up road blocks outside the town to prevent any invasion.

We have discussed three types of processes indentifiable in the reaction: the growth of generalised beliefs, which contain a putative element, the sensitization to deviance and the escalation of methods of social control. To evaluate the effects of the reaction on the self image we would need a more complicated type of research design than has been used here—a longitudinal study of the impact of community reaction on young people's self concepts. At present we can only use the overt behaviour as the dependent variable and assume that this behaviour is consonant with the actors' self image.

In the first place, as we have seen, the behaviour was often 'created' because of community sensitization. The atmosphere of expectancy present at the seaside resorts resulted in incidents being created out of nothing.

> Two boys stopped to watch a very drunk old tramp dancing about on the beach. They started throwing pennies at his feet. Within 45 seconds there were at least a hundred people gathered round and in 60 seconds the police were there. I turned my back on the crowd to watch the spectators gathering on the promenade above and by the time I turned back, two policemen were leading a boy away from the crowd.
> (*Notes*, Brighton, Easter 1965).

Incidents such as these were created by sensitivity on the part of both audience and actors. There was a sense among the young people that they had to play to the gallery; the literal gallery of the adults lining the railing as at a bullfight, and the photographers running around from one event to the other; and the metaphorical gallery of the consumers of the mass media who had read in their morning papers 'Seaside Resorts Prepare for the Hooligans' Invasion'. The control agents, especially the police, created deviance not only in the sense of provoking the more labile members of the crowd into losing their tempers, but in Becker's sense of making the rules whose infraction constituted deviance. So, for example, certain areas were designated in advance as 'trouble spots'. If a number of youths were congregating in one of these trouble spots even for legitimate reasons (such as sheltering from the rain) they could be moved along, because policy was to keep these spots free. If one refused to move along he could be arrested and charged with wilful obstruction. (Under Sec. 51(3) Police Act 1964.)

Another significant effect of the reaction was, in Tannenbaum's phrase, the 'dramatization of evil'. The adult reaction was not only negative—it could hardly have been otherwise—but it was hostile in the melodramatic sense. There was the famous speech by a Margate magistrate about his town being

'... polluted by hordes of hooligans... these long-haired mentally unstable petty little hoodlums, these sawdust Caesars who can only find courage like rats hunting in packs'; there were the newspaper headlines about 'vermin'; there was the show of force on the spot—police dogs, horses, walkie talkies, water board vans converted into squad cars; there were scenes like the police ceremoniously marching a group of youths through a street lined with spectators.

One way in which this hostility was reacted to was by returning it in kind. In the first series of events, the crowd, with the exception of the hard core referred to earlier, maintained fairly good humoured relations with the police. Attacks were disrespectful gestures such as knocking off helmets rather than malicious. In the 1966 incidents, the atmosphere was more tense. The lines had hardened:

> A policeman walked quite peacefully between two rows of boys near the aquarium. Some of them started whistling the Z-car theme and one shouted out 'Sprachen the Deutsch Constable'?
> —(*Notes*, Brighton, Easter 1966).

Another way in which the conflict was hardened was between the two groups themselves. Although the Mods and Rockers represent two very different consumer styles—the Mods the more glossy fashion-conscious teenager, the Rockers the tougher, reactionary tradition—the antagonism between the two groups is not very deep, they have much more in common, particularly their working class membership. There was initially nothing like the gang rivalry supposed to characterise the American type of conflict gang caricatured in West Side Story, in fact there was nothing like a gang. Commercial and media exploitation of the Mod-Rocker difference, and misguided attempts to explain the whole situation of unrest in terms of this difference, hardened the barriers. The groups were merely loose collectivities or crowds within which there was occasionally some more structured grouping based on territorial loyalty. e.g. 'The Walthamstow Boys', 'The Lot From Eltham'. Constant repetition of the gang image made these collectivities see themselves as gangs and behave in a gang fashion. Yablonsky has noted the same process in his study of delinquent gangs as near groups.[12]

The Role of the Mass Media

Without being able to consider here all the mechanisms through which the reaction was amplified, it is necessary to comment on the most important of these, the mass media. One must remember that in mass society one's view of deviance is usually second hand. In the hypothetical village community one might have been able to react to the village idiot in terms of first-hand impressions. In mass society images arrive already processed—policymakers can and do make decisions about say delinquents or drug addicts on the basis of the most crude and misleading images. In the case of the Mods and Rockers the media were responsible to a large extent for the putative deviance. An analysis, for example, of the House of Commons debate on 'Juvenile Delinquency and Hooliganism' (27th April 1964) shows the extent to which the images and stereotypes provided by the media were the basis for theories and policy proposals.

It is not just that the newspapers exaggerated the amount of behaviour—this is more or less inevitable. Estimates in any crowd situation such as a political rally or sporting event are notoriously inaccurate. What was more important was the manner of presentation—the sensational headlines, the interviews with dramatic characters and subtle techniques well known to war correspondents, such as reporting the same incident twice. Another effective technique was the misleading juxtaposition of headlines—on at least three occasions headlines such as 'Mod Found Dead in Sea', 'Boy Falls to Death from Cliff' were used as sub-headings in Mods and Rockers reports. In every case the deaths had no connection at all with the disturbances and were pure accidents.

The chief rôle of the media seem to have been in transmitting the stereotypes and creating an expectancy before each event that something was going to happen. This last rôle was particularly taken by the local press which highlighted reports about local traders arming themselves with tear gas, citizens forming vigilante patrols, etc.

Differential Reaction

It is, of course, a fallacy to think of the mass media influencing a purely passive audience. Communication is responded to selectively, and the sort of questions we would like to answer are:—To what extent were the stereotypes and images absorbed by the community? How did the reaction crystallize into attitudes and opinions (e.g. about causes and solutions)? How were these attitudes affected by variables such as social class, education, political membership? Why did the reaction take the form it did?

The final research report will attempt to answer these questions. A preliminary analysis of the data from the Brighton sample only, suggest that the following type of generalisations might emerge:—

    1. The reaction of the general public is less intense and less stereotypical than the reaction reflected in the mass media.

    2. Local residents in the areas affected are more punitive than out of town visitors and the public in general.

    3. Little difference between the Labour and Conservative groups were found. Except at the extreme of authoritarianism, political preference does not correlate with attitudes to delinquency.

    4. The two most frequent single causes given for the Mods and Rockers events are 'boredom' and 'too much money'.

    5. A dimension such as 'punitiveness' is too gross to measure attitudes to deviant behaviour. Certain groups, particularly working class and upper

class, can at the same time be 'tolerant' of the behaviour and also devise the most punitive solutions for dealing with the behaviour when it is perceived as 'going too far'. The middle class less often make this distinction.

Conclusion

It must be emphasised again that as this is an analysis of the ways in which social reaction impinges upon the genesis and amplification of deviance, little has been said about the behaviour itself. This does not mean that one is trying to deny an objective reality or even less trying to present the Mods and Rockers as innocent victims of conspiracy and discrimination. Social forces work in far more subtle ways. Although people *were* inconvenienced or hurt, and there were fights and vandalism, there is at the very least enough evidence to suggest that the development of this behaviour was not independent of the reaction it provoked. Can one go further and say that the transactional theory is proved?

Clearly the present study is not a complete validation. For one thing, the crucial variable of the deviant self identity has not been measured and it might be a defect of the theory that this type of variable is peculiarly difficult to operationalise. There are problems in the model immediately apparent—for example why does the Wilkins-type of amplification sequence ever stop? Theoretically something like the Teddy Boy movement should have carried on growing. We know that this did not happen and there are already signs that the Mods and Rockers are going the same way. There are obviously factors 'outside' the model to account for these changes. Another problem is why not everybody exposed to the same definitions develops the appropriate self-image.

Until such questions are answered, we can only conclude that transactional theory provides a potentially useful framework for studying deviance. In the case of the Mods and Rockers at least, it gives an additional dimension to any other causal explanation.

REFERENCES

[1] Lemert, E. M.: *Social Pathology*, (London: McGraw Hill 1951).
[2] Becker, H. S.: *Outsiders, Studies in the Sociology of Deviance.* (New York: Free Press, 1963).
[3] Deutcher, I.: 'Some Relevant Directions for Research in Juvenile Delinquency', in Rose, A. R. (Ed.). *Human Behaviour and Social Processes.* (London: Routledge and Kegan Paul, 1962) pp. 468-481.
[4] Fuller, R. C., and Meyers, R. R.: 'Some Aspects of a Theory of Social Problems', *Amer. Sociol. Rev.* 6, (February 1941), pp. 24-32.
[5] Becker: op. cit. p. 9.
[6] Baldwin, J.: *The Fire Next Time*. (Penguin, 1964) p. 13.
[7] Wilkins, L.: *Social Deviance*, (London, Tavistock, 1964).
[8] Schur, E. M.: *Crimes Without Victims, Deviant Behaviour and Public Policy*, (New Jersey: Prentice Hall, 1965).
[9] Johnson, D. M.: 'The Phantom Anaesthetist of Mattoon', *Journal of Abnormal and Social Psychology*, 40, (1945) pp. 175-186 etc.
[10] Barker, P. and Little, A.: 'The Margate Offenders: A Survey', *New Society*, Vol. 4, No. 96, (30th July 1964), pp. 6-10.
[11] Lemert: op. cit. p. 56.
[12] Yablonsky, L.: *The Violent Gang*, (New York: Collier MacMillan, 1962).

[2]
The Politics of Vandalism

We're well into the season of smashed football specials and headlines about vandalism. Vandalism seems one of the more mysterious crimes – but is it "one" crime or many? Indeed, is it always a crime? Any prescription relies on diagnosis. In these three articles, Stanley Cohen draws on his research work to provide one.

All disciplines tend to have an underground of theory which challenges the traditional ways of studying their subject matter, the ways that are ensconced in undergraduate courses, textbooks, journal articles and reach their apex in the formalised PhD thesis. This underground – similar to underground movements in art and literature – eventually becomes fashionable, goes through a period of vulgarisation and eventually ends up by being absorbed into the traditions of the discipline.

Such a process can be observed in the fields of criminology and the sociology of deviance, with the gradual emergence from the underground of what has been called "transactional" or "labelling" theory. This approach, which owes much to the work of Edwin Lemert and Howard Becker, has its starting point in the assumption that deviant behaviour is a transaction between the deviant and the community. Deviance is not a static category: an act has to be defined and labelled as deviant by others.

This means that the sociologist must question, and not take for granted, the labelling by society (or powerful groups in society) of certain behaviour as problematic or deviant. In regard to certain forms of mental illness for example, psychiatrists such as R. D. Laing have suggested that the labelling can be seen to involve a *political* decision: somebody (who has, or is seen to have, power, influence or status) acts in such a way that somebody else is defined as mad.

In discussing vandalism, I want to use this term "political" in the very broad sense that Laing and Becker have used it. In its narrower sense, it is perfectly clear that the label one attaches to certain forms of behaviour is affected by one's political position: to some, members of an African nationalist group who sabotage a power station in Rhodesia are "freedom fighters", to others, including the Rhodesian police, they are "terrorists."

This then is the first point I want to make about vandalism: the term is an emotive label, which is attached only to certain forms of behaviour and only under certain conditions. The term itself, of course, has its origins in the behaviour of the Vandals, an east Germanic tribe who invaded western Europe in the 4th and 5th centuries and eventually sacked Rome in 455.

They were regarded as the great destroyers of Roman art, civilisation and literature and the term "vandal" was used in a broader sense in the 17th century to refer to anyone who ruthlessly and recklessly destroyed property, particularly works of art.

Vandalism is currently defined by dictionaries as "ruthless destruction or spoiling of anything beautiful or venerable." The vandalism that criminologists study (for example, a group of youths smashing the windows of a school), or the vandalism defined more as "political" than "criminal" and which carries clear ideological overtones (for example, breaking shop windows during racial disturbances, or stoning embassy windows during a demonstration), seems far removed from the etymological origins of the term. Nevertheless, these origins should not be lost sight of: the adjectives which the behaviour of the original Vandals conjure up – barbarous, wilful, ignorant, reckless, ruthless – remain part of the stereotype of contemporary vandalism. They are still commonly used in a political context to justify action against the deviant.

In many cases, naturally, the deviant himself does not accept this description. To him, his acts are not reckless and barbarous but eminently sensible. As was the case with the Luddites of the early 18th century, property destruction – in their case machine breaking – may be a deliberate act of protest. Economic historians, such as E. J. Hobsbawm, have done much to dispel the stereotype of Luddism as being "pointless" and "frenzied" or a mere "overflow of high spirits."

Hobsbawm's distinction between two types of machine breaking ("collective bargaining by riot," which under some conditions was a normal way of putting pressure on employers; and the type of destruction which expressed working class hostility to the new machines of the industrial revolution) is more relevant to contemporary forms of vandalism than it first appears. Research on racial disturbances in American cities over the past few years suggests that most of the property destruction was patterned and, in a sense, "rational." The targets chosen were not arbitrary: I quote, for instance, from the 1968 US Report of the National Advisory Commission on Civil Disorders:

"In at least nine of the cities studied, the damage seems to have been, at least in part, the result of deliberate attacks on white-owned businesses, characterised in the Negro community as unfair or disrespectful toward Negroes."

Even if the targets were arbitrary, there is no denying a peculiar logic, in a society dominated by consumption, for those who are denied access to the goodies, to destroy whatever they can get their hands on. As the International Situationists' analysis of the 1965 Watts riots expressed it: "The man who destroys commodities, shows his human superiority over commodities."

One does not have to accept this statement, with its somewhat dangerous implications, to make the simple point that to describe property destruction – whether it is pulling up the paving stones of Paris, breaking embassy windows in Manila, or wrecking a department store in Los Angeles – with a phrase like "reckless, ignorant vandalism" is a political act. It means that one denies the legitimacy of the motives behind the behaviour and also justifies punitive measures, which themselves might be "reckless" and "ignorant".

Why should the sociologist of deviance spend his time on what might be thought to be historical and political issues? The answer is simply that the very act of defining one's subject matter is a highly problematic process. Sociologists who are interested in, say, violence, will generalise from data on criminal homicide which, using most "objective" criteria (such as statistical incidence), is of minor significance. They might give painstaking attention to a study of the electro-encephalograms of three Italian murderers; meanwhile in Vietnam and Biafra thousands are being killed and in Chicago demonstrators are being clubbed on the head.

Where is the violence? In the case of vandalism, we come up very starkly against the problem of problems: what we call a social problem has objective elements (people are killed, property is damaged, the air is contaminated, the streets are congested, children are dying of malnutrition) but also a subjective element: the perception and definition by certain people that "something should be done" about the situation.

There are many forms of illegal property destruction which are not defined as problematic. Certain groups, such as students, have often been given some sort of collective licence to engage in violence and vandalism; for example after sporting fixtures, during initiation rites, "hazing" ceremonies and so on. Some months ago, students at Keble College, Oxford, taking part in a traditional celebration after boat races, caused about £1000 damage. Not only was a boat worth £600 burnt, but the blaze was supplemented by property such as chairs, tables and books, including some looted from the rooms of students opposed to the whole ritual.

Only *Private Eye* reported this.

Much of such tolerance and licence has recently been withdrawn; this again illustrates a political process: painting "Fink College is the Best" on a wall is not vandalism, painting "Stop Making Bombs" is. Destroying property during rags is "youthful exuberance" and after all "for a good cause," but destroying property during a political demonstration is "thoughtless hooliganism."

Many forms of vandalism never become defined as problematic, simply because they are invisible: they might occur within the confines of an institution such as a factory, hospital or school. Other forms are, similarly, in Edwin Lemert's term "normalised"; they occur with a certain regularity and individually are quite trivial. An example would be the defacement of walls of public toilets with various forms of graffiti: (one would be extremely surprised to find bare walls in the toilets of a pub, park or railway station.) These forms of vandalism only get defined as problematic when somebody says "Look, it's getting beyond a joke" or "Things are going too far."

If we turn to the more conventional forms of vandalism, it is again interesting to note that the behaviour is conceived – by social scientists and the public alike – in terms of stereotypical labels that from the start obscure any attempts to understand the phenomenon. The most commonly used labels are "wanton," "aimless," "pointless," "senseless," "malicious" or "meaningless". These labels are part of a stereotype which again serves to justify particular forms of social control. Society is saying in effect "If you do such meaningless things, don't ask us to be meaningful in what we say or do about you."

Conventional vandalism is not as meaningless or wanton as these labels imply. The acts both make sense to the actor (for example, to settle a grudge or gain revenge) and possess a distinguishable pattern (for example, the property damaged has certain physical and social characteristics). Vandalism by teenage gangs, which attracts all the labels the original Vandals conjure up, is often far removed from this imagery.

In his study of gangs in "Midcity," Walter Miller has shown not only that vandalism is a small part of gang activity, but also that much damage, instead of being a wanton outpouring of accumulated aggression against arbitrary objects, is often specific and directed. The damage might be inflicted on the property of a person who had angered the gang. An example he gives is defacing the automobile of a mother responsible for having a gang member committed to a correctional institution.

On the other hand, one should be wary of reading into certain types of vandalism, which look to be obviously ideologically motivated, motives which don't exist.

Studies of the 1960 swastika daubings in America show that a fair proportion of the offenders were not particularly anti-semitic and were carried away by the wave of publicity and hysteria which surrounded the incidents.

Incidents of vandalism which occur at the same time but are otherwise totally unrelated are sometimes given a degree of organisation and a centralised planning which never existed. Politicians are particularly prone to advancing conspiratorial theories for such incident: this leads to scapegoating, victimisation and other such manoeuvres.

The label of mental disturbance is often erroneously pinned on acts of vandalism, particularly when the form of damage appears to be somewhat bizarre or the target is a particularly emotive one. Writing or chipping names on the walls of public buildings is a form of vandalism that dates back for centuries: it is recorded that on the walls of Pompeii slogans were written, such as "Good Luck to Comrade Proculus" and "Vibius Restitus Slept Here."

When, however, in 1965 the names "Andy" and "Dell" were scratched on the Kennedy memorial at Runnymede, there was a vast public outcry, in which the offenders were thought to be part of some obscure political plot, or else simply "mad." The bomb, planted at the memorial at the time of the 27 October anti-Vietnam demonstration this year, was also called vandalism, though clearly political in intention. When the word "Peace" was daubed in Canterbury cathedral, following a speech by the Archbishop in 1965 supporting the use of force by Britain if Rhodesia were to declare independence unilaterally, the action was described as "the work of a lunatic."

Another point about vandalism needs to be made. When society defines certain people as outsiders, it needs to emphasise the ways in which these people are different from the insiders, those who are normal. Thus, criminals are not just people who have broken the law, but are also generally dangerous and not to be trusted.

People who habitually take drugs don't just take drugs, but are also "dope fiends" who are vicious, degenerate and dirty. To stress the discontinuity between deviance and normality gives a feeling of security: the custodians of our morality can be clear about the difference between good and bad (or, to be more up to date, between "healthy" and "sick"). It is more disturbing to consider a view such as that advanced by David Matza that much adolescent behaviour – and vandalism would seem to me a good example – is a caricature rather than an inversion or repudiation of middle class conformist culture. There is a dialectic between the conventional and deviant traditions of society, as shown, for example, in the ambivalence of most adults (in private) to many forms of youthful misconduct.

Similarly, the values associated with juvenile vandalism and thought to be peculiar to delinquents – such as the search for excitement and kicks, the high valuation of toughness and aggression – might reflect values running through the whole society. These values might come out into the open on ritual occasions, or else they may be left to the delinquent to express.

The adolescent is easily stigmatised as a violent yob, or an irresponsible hedonist, and – as Edgar Friedenberg has pointed out – many American adults almost use the terms "adolescent" and "delinquent" interchangeably. But there is, after all, nothing peculiarly adolescent in the violence and vandalism of James Bond movies, or for that matter, of real life.

In conclusion, I would like to make two points clear.

The first is that I have not tried here to explain vandalism. This does not mean that I consider attempts at such explanations irrelevant; rather, I am suggesting that one must first be sure of *what* one is explaining. The usual terms used to describe various forms of vandalism obscure and discredit what may be the real explanations: if a boy breaks into his school one weekend and smashes up the classrooms because he has a grievance against the teachers, it is no help to call his behaviour "wanton" and "pointless."

The only problems that these labels solve are the teachers' problems in trying to preserve the image that they are blameless. If one looks at this example – school vandalism – most research, in fact, indicates that there *is* something wrong with the school that is damaged. The highest rates of school vandalism tend to occur in schools with obsolete facilities and equipment, low staff morale and high dissatisfaction and boredom among the pupils.

The final point I want to make is that, in using the labelling perspective, I am not saying that vandalism only exists "in the mind of the beholder." This would be a patently ridiculous position, especially to anyone who has seen the figures for the cost of damage from conventional vandalism in its many forms: street lamps broken, windows smashed, public buildings defaced, fixtures on trains and buses broken, and so on.

Such damage does not only entail a financial loss, but is a symbolic threat to a society which places high value on property.

Particular forms of vandalism also threaten accepted values about the resolution of political, racial and religious conflict. Yet other forms of vandalism may lead to loss of life as well as property: for example, trains have been derailed by obstacles placed on the railway lines, often by very young children; calls for medical help have been delayed because public phone boxes have been damaged.

We must be careful of the vulgarisation that I referred to earlier; this leads people to assert, for example, that nobody is really mentally ill, they are just passive victims of conspiracies organised by their families and abetted by wicked psychiatrists. Such a view not only ignores the fact that the potential deviant himself may resist the labels forced on him, but it also romanticises him: it discredits the subjective feelings of suffering, guilt and unhappiness he might have.

The view I have illustrated in regard to vandalism must simply alert us to the point that Edwin Lemert makes: that while traditional sociology rests on the idea that deviance leads to social control, the reverse idea – ie, social control leads to deviance – "is equally tenable and the potentially richer premise for studying deviance in modern society." One must aim at a truly transactional view of deviance and social problems, in which the political processes whereby certain forms of behaviour and certain people become defined as deviant, are considered along with the ways in which the person responds to these labels and social problems are shaped because of these labels.

[3]
The Nature of Vandalism

In about 1962, vandalism was perceived in Britain as being an emerging social problem: this was the time when people began to define it as a threat, a menace, something which had to be "clamped down on" before it "spread." Each succeeding wave of vandalism – on railway lines, public telephone boxes, after football matches – was hailed as part of a national malaise. Vandalism was defined as something new, ever-increasing and a phenomenon of the sixties.

By 1967–68, however, together with the mods and rockers phenomenon, with which it was often associated, vandalism was no longer such news. Drugs, Grosvenor Square, student militancy had occupied the arenas of public debate on the "youth problem" in the same way as the teddy boys had a decade earlier.

What are the facts about the problem during its peak period 1962–67? It can be said with some certainty that the extent of its increase and seriousness was grossly exaggerated. The percentage increase in the amount of vandalism recorded in the criminal statistics since the beginning of the sixties was not excessive and certainly not disproportionate compared with other juvenile and adult offences. The following table shows the increase in the main category of vandalism covered by the law, the non-indictable offence of "malicious damage to property."

Malicious Damage to Property: Number of Persons Dealt with by Magistrates Courts 1960–67

1960	15,866
1961	16,399
1962	16,852
1963	17,003
1964	16,857
1965	19,192
1966	18,522
1967	18,014

A large proportion of the 1965 increase was an artefact of a change in the law: under the Malicious Damage Act, 1964, certain provisions of the Criminal Justice Act, 1914, were amended so that magistrates courts could deal summarily with some offences where the damage did not exceed £100 (instead of £20). The following table, showing persons found guilty of both main legal categories of vandalism, does not indicate any dramatic increase and shows how the very small contribution of vandalism to the total crime picture in fact *decreased* during the relevant period.

Persons Found Guilty of "Malicious Injuries to Property" and "Malicious Damage" 1961–67

	Number found guilty	% of all offenders
1961	18,018	1.6
1962	18,952	1.5
1963	18,779	1.4
1964	17,971	1.3
1965	18,397	1.3
1966	17,668	1.2
1967	17,297	1.1

Of course these figures – like all criminal statistics – leave a great deal unsaid. Vandalism has a very low detection rate: it is a safe and anonymous offence, there is no property to dispose of and data from organisations affected by the problem show a much higher incidence. Figures I have obtained from British Rail, the GPO, local government authorities and other sources indicate an increase in vandalism in about 1963.

This was the year when most of these organisations started keeping detailed figures for the first time, so exact comparisons with previous periods are very difficult to make. Nothing in these figures contradicts the point that the mass media inflated the increase in vandalism during these years, although taken in themselves, the statistics do show a pervasive problem. The following are some illustrative figures of the total amount of vandalism reported in what was probably the peak year for this, 1965:

Railways: about 4,000 incidents of wilful damage.

Public telephone boxes: about 110,000 incidents, about 2,600 phones out of order (out of a total of 57,000 in England).

In 1965 the total cost of vandalism to the main targets – the railways, the GPO and local government authorities – was about £1.5 million. This is a substantial amount, but small when compared with the loss from theft (nearly £50 million) or arson (at least £10 million). A city like Birmingham – which I quote only because of the accurate records it keeps – lost £50,000 from the routine sort of vandalism that all local authorities have to face but which the mass media seldom pay attention to: damage to school windows, traffic signs, street name plates, public conveniences, street lamps or parks.

There are some significant patterns behind these increases which are not at first apparent. For example, the dramatic increase in telephone vandalism from 1964–66 was partly attributable to the introduction of the STD system. There was now more money to steal from the coin boxes which were also easier to force open. This is an offence which caused the largest proportion of phones to be put out of order and is strictly speaking an ordinary theft offence and not "wanton damage for its own sake."

We cannot begin to understand vandalism unless we are clear that this is not a homogenous type of behaviour. In the same way that cliched phrases like the "age of violence" do no justice at all to the many manifestations of violent behaviour, so is vandalism a term which tells us very little beyond the fact of property being damaged or destroyed.

Adapting somewhat a typology used by John Martin in a study of vandalism in New York, I would distinguish the following main types of vandalism. The main criterion for a typology such as this should be the subjective meaning that the behaviour has for the individual.

1. Acquisitive vandalism. Damage done in order to acquire money or property: breaking open telephone coin boxes, electric or gas meters, slot machines, stripping lead and wire from buildings.
2. Tactical vandalism. The damage is a conscious tactic employed to advance some other end: breaking a window in order to be arrested and get a bed in prison, jamming a machine in a factory to ensure an enforced rest period, drawing attention to grievance.
3. Ideological vandalism. Similar to the last example of tactical vandalism, but carried out to further an explicit ideological cause or to deliver a message: breaking embassy windows during a demonstration, chalking slogans on walls.
4. Vindictive vandalism. The damage is done in order to gain revenge: for example, windows of a youth club or school are broken to settle a grudge against the club leader or head teacher.
5. Play vandalism. The damage is done in the context of a game: who can break the most windows of a house, who can shoot out the most street lamps?
6. Malicious vandalism. The damage is an expression of rage or frustration and is often directed at symbolic middle class property. It is this type that has the vicious and apparently senseless façade which people find so difficult to understand. Many types of juvenile vandalism have the elements of both play and malice: defecating in lifts (usually in council flats), urinating in public telephone receivers, cutting boats loose from their moorings, breaking lights in railway carriages.

In addition, one might have to distinguish the type of vandalism committed in large group situations for example, in streets after football matches, in British Rail "football specials," or during 5 November celebrations.

Clearly, acquisitive, tactical, vindictive and most types of ideological vandalism are directed against specific targets. Even in play and malicious vandalism, however, the property destroyed has certain distinguishable characteristics. In the first place, it is mostly public rather than private property. It is also more likely to be derelict, unused or in a state of half completion. In the case of council estates, the estates most likely to be damaged are large flatted ones as opposed to the older cottage estates and are more likely to be in deteriorating areas of the city.

If there are types of vandalism, there are also types of vandals. Clearly not all of them will correspond to the stereotype of the adolescent yob or hooligan which is held by most people. Nearly two thirds of telephone vandals are adults, while most railway vandalism (of the type involving placing objects on the railway lines) is carried out by young children, between ten and twelve years old.

Research on hard core juvenile vandalism, using data on convicted offenders, indicates that vandals are very much like other juvenile delinquents. Both groups come from the same lower socio-economic classes; they both live in the same sort of urban areas. Vandals differ slightly from other delinquents in that they are even more likely to be male and to commit their offences in groups of three or more and that they are somewhat likely to be younger.

In John Martin's group of convicted New York vandals, the mean age was 12.9 while the mean for other delinquents was 14.5. Studies in the East End of London indicate that most vandalism occurs at a younger stage of the life cycle than the peak age for property offences (14) but some also occurs in the context of general rowdyism offences in late adolescence. There is no evidence that vandalism is – as is often believed – the first stage of a delinquent career.

Although each type of vandalism has its own peculiar causal antecedents, the hard core of juvenile vandalism is not very different from most juvenile delinquency and should be conceptualised and explained within the same framework. This framework should include – as it has not done sufficiently up to now – an account of the stages that ease the individuals' drift into delinquency, the processes which enable him to rationalise his activity and the nature of the community reaction his activity evokes.

Explanations should take into account the fact that much vandalism can be rationalised: "nothing was stolen," "they had it coming to them," "a few broken windows won't make any difference to them." Vandalism is often – as Andrew Wade has recently described – spontaneous activity arising out of group interaction and situational factors, rather than deliberate planned action. As such, it is pretty far removed from the image of hordes of Vandals descending on our cities bent on pillage and destruction.

[4]
Can it be Controlled?

The type of vandalism which society wants to prevent and control – what I describe as being the "hardcore" or "conventional" juvenile vandalism – is so much like other delinquency that it is difficult to describe or evaluate measures specific to it.

Broadly speaking, however, four approaches to the prevention of vandalism can be distinguished: (a) primary prevention, (b) technical prevention, (c) deterrence and (d) publicity. Let me look at each of these four in turn.

Primary prevention would be measures based on an understanding of the causes of vandalism and delinquency. They are usually aimed not at what sociologists would regard as the "real" primary causes (factors in the wider social structure of society) but at the local neighbourhood level.

For example, the quite justified assumption is made that much vandalism among younger children arises out of a combination of the desire for adventure and excitement, and the opportunity presented in certain neighbourhoods by the presence of property (such as derelict houses, old bomb sites, large panes of glass in council flats, street lamps) which is regarded as fair game. If one further assumes that such damage cannot be tolerated but that the need for excitement is an acceptable motive and is blocked by the absence of adequate facilities, schemes such as the building of adventure playgrounds suggest themselves to prevent vandalism.

There is no clear evidence for the success of such schemes. There does tend to be a correlation between the absence of adequate play facilities and the amount of minor vandalism by young children, but building adventure playgrounds and similar schemes (although, I would argue, desirable in themselves) is not the panacea for preventing vandalism. On some large housing estates, the opposite effect occurs: new schemes attract the attention (often of children from other areas) and the equipment gets damaged. It is the very illegality of the play situation which gives it more excitement.

One approach that recommends itself is simply the provision of *better* facilities. Virtually all organisations affected by vandalism tend to agree that it is the better kept property which attracts less damage in the first place. There is a sort of coals-in-the-bath attitude among many local authorities which leads them to the belief that "if you give them new things, they just destroy them."

Often it is true that new, attention-attracting and sometimes alien property, such as a water feature or abstract statue on a council estate is destroyed. This initial effect, however, eventually dies down. The more important effect is the tendency to regard badly maintained and dirty property as fair game for destruction, in the same way as streets already dirty attract the most litter.

Among the older age group responsible for vandalism, the element of hostility and malice cannot be neutralised simply by the provision of recreational facilities. The most plausible analysis of such delinquency in Britain – that suggested by David Downes and given added weight by David Hargreaves's recent analysis of the relationship between streaming and the delinquent subculture in a secondary modern – lays stress on the deficiencies of the educational and employment situations for the working class adolescent.

The tension resulting from these deficiencies may occur in the realm of leisure, where vandalism – and delinquency in general – might provide the satisfaction and excitement that a dead-end education and an ever deader job-market patently do not offer. But the drift to delinquency cannot be counteracted simply by laying on more leisure facilities.

David Cooper has referred in the context of mental hospitals (New Society, 11 March, 1965) to "the ancient myth that tells us that Satan makes work (destructiveness, masturbation, promiscuity) for idle hands." One can free oneself from this myth by trying to understand what sort of realistic alternative to delinquency is possible and by realising the implications of arguments such as Downes's and Hargreaves's: that solutions (if any) lie further back than the field of leisure.

Another frequently suggested preventive measure is the use of psychiatric treatment. This is more often mentioned in regard to vandalism than delinquency as a whole, because the equation is made between "senseless" action and psychological disturbance: "nobody in their right mind would do something like vandalism."

To the extent that this equation is fundamentally wrong, psychiatric approaches to vandalism do not offer much. A very small proportion of vandalism is associated with psychological disturbance and there is no evidence that vandalism in childhood is correlated with later disturbance. (On the contrary, a recent 30 year follow-up study of children referred to a child guidance clinic showed that vandalism was one of the few offences initially recorded at referral which had no relation at all to later "sociopathic personality traits.")

Technical prevention (the second of the possible approaches) means the various protective devices which have been employed to cut down the chances of the property being destroyed at all or increase the chances of detecting the offender. These devices have included: burglar alarms in telephone boxes, guard dogs and security patrols on parks and building sites, bus shelters bugged with hidden microphones and an extensive range of other conventional security devices.

The measures obviously have their place, and local authorities and other public bodies see their duty in terms of using these methods if they save the ratepayer or taxpayer money. Sometimes, however, they are unnecessarily melodramatic and often have the effect of attracting the opposite sort of attention that was intended: warning signs for example are often destroyed themselves. More important, perhaps, is the fact that these measures often cost far more than the damage they were originally intended to prevent.

What, then, about the third approach – *deterrence*? The most frequent public reaction to vandalism is "hit them hard": all that is needed to deter vandalism is better detection by the police and stiffer sentences handed out by the courts. It is impossible in a few lines to evaluate this claim or to set it in its proper context, which is the general effectiveness of various penal measures for delinquency as a whole. There is nothing to suggest that cautions, fines, probation and the usual range of measures employed against the younger group of juvenile offenders are more or less effective for vandalism than they are for other offences.

One point specific to vandalism should, however, be made. This is overwhelmingly a group offence and an offence which is situational in character: it arises spontaneously out of group interaction and – except in specific forms such as "tactical" and "acquisitive" vandalism (defined the previous article) – it is not deliberately planned. Consequently, general deterrent measures, and the publicity given to them, are less likely to be effective. Among young children especially, who easily rationalise vandalism as play, warnings of punitive sentences will not be very successful.

One example that is often quoted to show the effectiveness of harsher sentences (and the publicity given to them) in preventing vandalism was the apparently successful campaign against telephone vandalism in Birmingham in 1965–66. The Recorder of Birmingham was hailed as "the iron man in Britain's fight against crime" when it was announced that telephone vandalism in the city had been drastically reduced because of his policy of handing out sentences of up to three years' imprisonment for the offence.

There are two points to be made about this claim. A major proportion of the reduction was due to preventive measures introduced by the GPO in Birmingham. The new STD coin boxes (which were almost the sole target for the damage) were strengthened and in some cases completely replaced. Other items of equipment were strengthened and in the case of some telephones burglar alarms were introduced.

The other point is that, even if the deterrent effect is provable (which it is not), this is a very specific offence. Thefts from coin boxes were committed mostly by adults who in some cases had been involved in anything up to 40 similar offences. Any deterrent for such an offence and such an offender cannot be generalised – as it widely was – to cover *all* types of vandalism.

The final approach is greater *publicity*. The guiding principle behind many campaigns to prevent vandalism is to expose the problem in the hope that this will lead to a greater awareness of its seriousness. It is assumed that this awareness will have some sort of preventive effect – for example in increasing community responsibility or in "instilling in parents more responsibility for their children" (or some other favourite slogan). These campaigns have taken the form of exhibitions showing the effects of vandalism, publishing statistics showing the cost of vandalism to the community or publicising horror stories about the dangers of vandalism: trains being derailed, calls for medical help being delayed by damaged public telephone boxes and so on.

Some of these campaigns have been very ingenious. In Chertsey, for example, a lorry loaded with examples of vandalism toured the streets of the town. But their effects are almost impossible to assess. In Birmingham – whose "Stop Vandalism Week" in 1966 was the best organised of these campaigns – the effect certainly was to increase community awareness of the problem, but the figures suggest that there was virtually no impact in decreasing the amount of vandalism a year later.

Publicity almost invariably works in the opposite direction to that intended. Vandalism often occurs in waves, much like waves of fashion, and the initial reporting of an incident often has the effect of triggering off incidents of a similar kind. At football matches, appeals over the public address system not to let off firecrackers or throw bottles onto the field are immediately followed by an explosion of firecrackers and a barrage of bottles. This, in microcosm, is what often occurs in group phenomena such as waves of vandalism.

The relationship between publicity and vandalism is nothing like a straight causal one. Vandalism occurs at times and in contexts where there is no publicity at all.

Publicity is not the primary "cause" of vandalism, any more than the cause of a man barricading himself and his family in a house with a shotgun is the fact that he had been informed of similar incidents by the mass media. It would be difficult, however, to say that the event and the information were unrelated.

I have surveyed only the mainstream of measures to prevent vandalism. There have been many others suggested in the past few years – ranging from getting children to plant their own trees so that they will develop a pride in property, to placing offenders in stocks and pelting them with rotten tomatoes. In the face of everyone's certainty that they have "the" solution, it is tempting to analyse the public's responses to vandalism in the same way as one would their responses to a Rorschach ink blot. The solutions tell us interesting things about the person who formulates them.

This is not particularly helpful, though, to people who want to know "the answer" to the social rather than sociological problems of vandalism. To such people, one can perhaps only offer research insights and techniques to evaluate proposed solutions. More important – because such techniques are not peculiarly sociological – one should argue for a clarification of just what the problem is and a removal of the images and mythologies which obscure an understanding of vandalism.

[5]
Criminology and the Sociology of Deviance in Britain: A Recent History and a Current Report

A danger that faces the sociologist who indulges in the current vogue for 'sociologies of sociology' or 'self-reflexive sociology' is that he will end up playing what Goffman (1959: 149) describes as the 'discrepant role' of go-between or mediator. In this role, he 'learns the secrets of each side and gives each side the true impression that he will keep its secrets; but he tends to give each side the false impression that he is more loyal to it than to the other.' The sociologist, as a member of many more than two teams, is continually doing this sort of thing: telling society all the sordid secrets of his discipline, its inconsistencies, dishonesties, evasiveness, and then telling his colleagues how unreasonable, reactionary, irrational this society is. He goes continually backwards and forwards to employers, students, the profession, making sincere noises about responsibility, truth, relevance, or whatever the appropriate demand is.

Such manœuvres can be exciting; but we live dangerously when we publish or give conference papers, because then we are always and inevitably in the simultaneous presence of all our teams. Goffman suggests what may then happen: 'When a go-between operates in the actual presence of the two teams of which he is a member, we then obtain a wonderful display, not unlike a man desperately trying to play tenis with himself.' Papers of the 'current report' type are particularly prone to such displays, especially if the writer is, however insignificantly, part of what he is supposed to be reporting on.

I have tried where possible to avoid these problems, but it would be disingenuous to claim that the paper is a detached report from a spectator with no team loyalties. Let me indicate three further but more mundane limitations of this paper, which arise primarily from the brief that was given to me:

(1) I have concentrated on the *recent* history of criminology and the sociology of deviance; this implies for criminology going back not much further than the immediate pre-war years and for sociology the post-war expansion of the subject in its academic settings. This does not mean that a proper chronology (which could be a rewarding sociological exercise) would not have to go much further back, at least, for example, to Booth, Rowntree, Mayhew, and others.[1]

(2) A full scale treatment of the subject would have to deal first with the ideas involved in all the disciplines under review, secondly with the institutional contexts in which they arose and were diffused, and thirdly with the wider ideological and structural contexts in which they manifested themselves. This three level distinction corresponds more or less to the one made by Horowitz (1968) between 'the inner life of sociology', 'the academic life of sociology' and 'the political life of sociology'. This paper deals more fully, if still selectively, with the second of these levels, about which Horowitz's remarks apply even more forcibly if one substitutes 'criminology' for 'sociology':

> 'Without an appreciation for the institutional setting for sociology – the place after all where most sociologists make their living and legitimize their careers – the analysis of theory appears a formalistic exercise in the passage of novel ideas from great man to great man ... sociological history is embodied in the educational agencies and research bureaucracies from which sociologists issue forth their proclamations and projections.' (Horowitz 1969: Preface)

Only at a few points do I try to make explicit the wider political contexts in which such education and research must be located.

(3) I have chosen to deal with a number of aspects of the subject superficially, rather than concentrating on a few in any depth. Questions of values and methodology, for example, need a much more sustained treatment than is given here, nor can I pretend to do full justice to the individuals or institutions whose work is reviewed.

The paper is divided into five sections. The first identifies a number of rudimentary signposts pointing to the directions in which the sociology of deviance seems currently to be going. Then a selective review of British criminology is presented which partly uses these

Criminology and the sociology of deviance in Britain 3

signposts as evaluative criteria and partly analyses further related characteristics which acted as an impetus for the 'new' sociology of deviance to develop in this country. A third section deals briefly with the response of British sociology to the substance and theory of studying crime and deviance – again, only in so far as this response stimulated new developments in the sociology of deviance. The origins and impact of the National Deviancy Conference are then sketched and in the final section the traditional criminological institutions and the newer sociology of deviance are polarized and assessed.

IDENTIFYING A SOCIOLOGY OF DEVIANCE

In this brief section, I would like to list four signposts by which most self-styled 'genuine' sociologists of deviance would probably identify the ways they are moving. To repeat, this is not meant to be a sociology-of-knowledge exercise on how this subject has evolved; such an exercise is in any event partly redundant after Matza's analysis of criminological positivism (1964) and his subsequent chronicle and recommendation (1969) of the naturalist perspective on deviance. On a more parochial level and for a general public, I have tried elsewhere (1971) to identify how what I called the 'sceptical' approach to deviance differs from more established positions.

The term 'genuine' is, of course, tendentious and the distinction between 'new' and 'old' is also not particularly satisfactory. To make the polarizations on which the paper depends, I will refer simply to *mainstream criminology* and the *sociology of deviance*. In a somewhat religious vein, I use texts from four influential American contributors – Becker, Lemert, Matza, and Skolnick – to point to my four signposts:

(1) *Continuity with sociology*

It would seem absurd to insist on the self-evident, but one of the characteristic features of the study of crime, delinquency, and social problems has been its non-sociological or even anti-sociological nature. It is therefore the first and minimal criterion of the field that its connexions, if not continuity, with sociology should be recognized. Becker is justified in claiming that whatever 'labelling theory' is (and this claim is not of course peculiar to it) it fulfils this criterion:

4   *Stanley Cohen*

' "Labelling theory" so called, is a way of looking at deviance which actually represents a complete continuity with the rest of sociology. In other words, if a sociologist were going to study any topic, he would probably take such an approach, unless there were reasons not to. But there have been reasons not to approach criminology and the study of crime in the same way we might approach some more neutral topic. In studying most kinds of social organization, we will more likely understand that we have to study the actions of all the people involved in that organization... But somehow when sociologists studied crime, they didn't understand the problem that way. Instead they accepted the commonsense notion that there must be something wrong with criminals, otherwise they wouldn't act that way... The study of crime lost its connections with the mainstream of sociological development and became a very bizarre deformation of sociology.' (Becker, in Debro, 1970: 165–6)

(2) *The significance of social control*

It is not necessary for a sociologist of deviance to accept all the implications of labelling theory, the societal reaction perspective or its variants. What is necessary is to recognize the problematic nature of social control. Lemert presents one perspective on this problem with typical restraint:

> '... older sociology tended to rest heavily upon the idea that deviance leads to social control. I have come to believe that the reverse idea, i.e. that social control leads to deviance, is equally tenable and the potentially richer premise for studying deviance in modern society.' (Lemert 1967: v)

There are many levels at which such a proposition can be approached, and sociologists might find any or all of these levels weak. But at least they would concede that the problem of deviance and control is a real one.

(3) *Appreciation*

I take from Matza the crucial contrast between 'correction' and 'appreciation' (Matza 1969: Chapter 2). The correctional stance takes for granted the objective of getting rid of the deviant phenomenon under question – and in so doing it 'systematically interferes with the

Criminology and the sociology of deviance in Britain 5

capacity to empathize and thus comprehend the subject of enquiry'. Mainstream criminology has refused to go beyond the correctional stance: a weak demand from sociologists is to question the applicability of this ideology; a stronger demand would be to accept appreciation and the subjective view as the only defensible one. This acceptance, as Matza indicates, is a 'fateful decision': it entails a commitment to render the phenomenon with fidelity and without violating its integrity. In a more fundamental way:

> 'It delivers the analyst into the arms of the subject who renders the phenomenon, and commits him, though not without regrets or qualifications, to the subject's definition of the situation. This does not mean that the analyst alway. concurs with the subject's definition of the situation; rather that his aim is to comprehend and to illuminate the subject's view and to interpret the world *as it appears to him.*' (Matza 1969: 24, 25)[2]

(4) *The political implications of studying deviance*

It follows from my second and third criteria and it *should* follow from the first that the very categories of crime and deviance and hence how one studies them, are problematic in specifically political ways. That is, the field has something to do with control, power, legitimacy, ideology. Skolnick points to two cases: 'it's becoming increasingly apparent to a whole generation of criminologists and sociologists, that it is increasingly difficult to distinguish between crime and political and moral dissent' (Skolnick, in Carte 1969: 115). Then, in connexion with drug legislation, if one asks questions such as how the political structure ever allowed laws like this to be passed, '... as a criminologist or sociologist you necessarily come into the field of political science' (117). Leaving aside disciplinary demarcations, the problem is the structural and political *loci* of definitions of deviance, a problem that has been accentuated rather than created by recent convergences between the 'ideological' and the 'criminal'.[3]

I have listed these four signposts as ones that would be recognized by the current generation of adherents to the sociology of deviance 'institution' but have been largely ignored or by-passed by mainstream criminology. I am not setting these up as articles of faith to be demanded by some new orthodoxy, still less as criteria for evaluating research, methodology or theory. They do however, singly or together, serve to demarcate significantly one set of collective self-conceptions from another.

The drift of my argument in the next section is that the history and, to a large extent, the current state of British criminology, are antithetical to the sociology of deviance as conceived above – as well as containing intrinsic limitations many of which are peculiarly British. It has not moved out of its paradigm, and even its uncomfortable recognition that 'where it's happening' is elsewhere cannot change the position much. It tries to graft on new bodies of thought, concepts, models, leaving the basic structure intact. Because this structure has an integrity of its own, a certain impressive weight and an umbrella-like quality which is able to embrace so much, I do not believe that our task as sociologists should be to reform it. To a large extent we will have to remain partly parasitic on it while improving our critique of it. Although the analogy is not exact, the relationship might be similar to that between the sociology of industry on one hand, and industrial relations on the other.[4]

MAINSTREAM BRITISH CRIMINOLOGY

In many respects, Charles Goring, author of *The English Convict* (1913) and perhaps the first recognized major figure in British criminology, epitomizes the whole tradition which followed him. It is not just that as an archetypal representative of positivism he survived in the spirit of criminology long after the substance of his contribution was repudiated (though this is so and what Matza says about positivist criminology in general is doubly true in Britain). I am not dealing with the 'inner life' of criminology in this way. My point is that Goring's contribution can be characterized in further ways that found themselves mirrored in the history of mainstream British criminology in the sixty years after his work.[5] I have picked out four such characteristics, only the last of which relates to Matza's evaluation of positivism: these are (1) *pragmatism*; (2) criminology as *interdisciplinary science, insulated from sociology*; (3) the *correctional and reformative* positions and (4) the *positivist trap*.

Goring's approach was totally pragmatic. He belonged to no criminological school and, starting from his day to day experience as a prison doctor, simply set out more systematically to test the claims of Lombroso. (This pragmatism carried with it another quality, a certain amateur, whimsical spirit which at one stage I thought of tracing in later criminology; the parallels are not always clear though and in the case of, say, the Cambridge Institute of Criminology, hardly apply. Goring did combine an odd mixture of what was at the time a fairly sophisticated control group technique with a rather bizarre notion of where to select his controls. His choice of Scottish, Oxford and Cambridge undergraduates, University of London professors, inmates of a general hospital, British Royal Engineers and German army recruits did, though, enable him to indulge in the following: 'From a knowledge only of an undergraduate's cephalic measurement, a better judgement could be given as to whether he were studying at an English or Scottish University than a prediction could be made as to whether he would eventually become a university professor or a convicted felon.' When this tone appears in later British criminology, one finds it – depending on aesthetic preferences – either disarming or wholly irritating.)

Goring was not just pragmatic, but in his combination of disciplines – some background in philosophy, a training as a doctor, a bit of psychological speculation, a familiarity with statistical techniques – he exhibited one of the most characteristic features of British criminology, its inter-disciplinary approach, which as I will show was more than usually catholic and indiscriminate. And, although the same may be said for most national criminologies excluding the American, this mixture never really allowed for a sociological perspective. As Mannheim correctly states, this applied even more to Goring than Lombroso (Mannheim 1965: 227). Goring wrote: 'Crime is only to a trifling extent (if to any) the product of social inequalities of adverse environment and of other manifestations of ... the force of circumstances.' And, as a prison doctor, Goring's interests in doing research were fairly clear-cut: one had to find better ways of dealing with convicted criminals, presumably by treating them on the basis of their supposed psychological characteristics.

Finally, Goring seemed caught in the positivist trap in a way which keeps recurring in British criminology. His statistical analysis disproved Lombroso, but instead of stopping at this point, he went on to develop a causal account as predictable and as misleading as Lombroso's and pointing in a specifically clinical direction. I will try to show that later British criminologists, even with an intellectual awareness which Goring could never have had of the paradoxes of this model, fall into the same trap.

I have chosen these four characteristics to organize my review of

British criminology because they are the ones which provide the main impetus for the new sociology of deviance to take root in the middle 1960s. The main institutions under review are: (1) the Home Office and particularly the Home Office Research Unit, set up in 1957 to carry out a long term research programme, mainly concerned with the treatment of offenders and to act as 'a centre of discussion with universities and other interested organizations'; (2) the Institute for the Study and Treatment of Delinquency (ISTD), set up in 1931, and crucial in that it directly produced the British Society of Criminology (BSC) and the only criminological journal in the country, the *British Journal of Criminology* (*BJC*); (3) the Institute of Criminology at Cambridge, set up under Home Office sponsorship in 1958 and (4) the teaching of criminology in London, particularly the work of Hermann Mannheim. These institutions and individuals by no means represent a monolithic establishment, and there are many cross links, for example, the Cambridge Institute has close links with the Home Office, but not with the *British Journal of Criminology* group.

(1) *Pragmatism*

The pragmatic approach has become an indisputable feature of British criminology. This is not a characterization made in retrospect by current observers (see, for example, Carson and Wiles, 1971: 7) but one that has been proudly proclaimed by the leading representatives of the indigenous British criminological tradition. Thus Radzinowicz (1966) after surveying what he calls the 'liberal' and 'deterministic' theories of crime, ends up by endorsing what he himself terms the 'pragmatic position'. This he sees as a 'new realism': there is no single purpose of punishment, there is no single causal theory of crime, therefore any or all perspectives, from Burt to Merton, have something to recommend themselves and in this 'lies the strength and promise of the pragmatic position' (1966: 128).

The pragmatic frame of reference is the one that shapes the few general textbook-type works produced by British criminologists (e.g. Walker 1965; Jones 1965; Mannheim 1965; West 1967) as well as the organization of research and teaching. One finds an overall distrust for theory or for some master conception into which various subjects can be fitted.

The impediments to a theoretical criminology are easier to find than account for. One major reason has been alluded to at several points by Radzinowicz (1961, 1966): that the fact that the whole idea of 'schools' of criminal law and criminology in the Continental sense is quite alien to the British legal tradition. On the Continent, major schools of criminal law – liberal, classical determinist, positivist, social defence – flourished for decades, partly because of the powerful position of professors of criminal law in the legal system. In England such positions of influence were the prerogative of the judiciary, the makers and interpreters of the law, 'to them the formulation of an all-embracing doctrine and the emergence of a school was something quite alien' (Radzinowicz 1966: 21). Criminology had to take root in this pragmatic legal tradition.

In making the contrast with America, the significant point is that although an autonomous criminology, as in Britain, also developed, it was from the outset located among the social sciences (in the broadest sense). As Radinowicz (1961: 119) among others has suggested, this location was partly due to the American ideology of optimism in which crime could be seen as the product of remediable social forces. There has also been something different about American legal training: quite unlike Britain, lawyers have for a long time been exposed to the social sciences in their undergraduate training. The strong American legal-sociological tradition has been virtually absent in Britain.

There was little opportunity then for either a legally or a sociologically based theoretical criminology to emerge.

In a wider sense, the pragmatic tradition is part of the national culture. I am referring not just to the amateur, muddling-along air which foreigners detect about British life but, for example, to the Fabian type of pragmatism in which disciplines such as criminology with obvious practical implications are located. The attitude behind many enterprises in such fields has been more or less one of finding out the facts, and letting the well-meaning chaps (say, in the Home Office) make the obvious inferences and do the rest. Contrasted to America, the collection of information for policy making is very different; compare say the composition of the National Commission on the Causes and Prevention of Violence, with its impressive range of experts, the professionalism with which it could produce about fifteen massively documented volumes in less than two years, to the typical Royal Commission with its motley collection of peers, bishops, judges, very part-time experts, and 'informed laymen', and its unbelievably slow rate of productivity.[6]

Although I do not accept the drift of much of his argument, all these points need to be put into a broader context such as the one suggested by Anderson (1968). His argument is that there is not just an absence of a tradition of revolutionary thought in Britain, but an absence of major intellectual traditions at all. Thus the weakness of sociology (which he overstates) is diagnosed in terms of its failure to produce any classical tradition and its historical dependence on the charity, social work, and Fabian institutions. Significantly, from the point of this paper, Anderson finds one reason for the absence of a separate intelligentsia in the factor I have already mentioned – the absence of Roman Law in England and the blocking of an intelligentsia based on legal faculties, teaching abstract principles of jurisprudence (Anderson 1968: 15). Another – somewhat less secure – plank of his argument is the influence of European *émigrés* (Popper, Wittgenstein, Berlin, Eysenck, *et al.*). These were '... intellectuals with an elective affinity to English modes of thought and political outlook' who found British empiricism and conservatism – the way it shunned theories and systems even in its rejection of them – quite congenial (18–19).

It is (aesthetically at least) appealing to apply much of this analysis to British criminology. To give a specific parallel, the careers of the major founders of contemporary British criminology – Mannheim, Radzinowicz, Grünhut – are not too far removed from those of the *émigrés* Anderson considers. Mannheim, for example, after a distinguished judicial career in Germany, came to London in 1934, where – according to all his biographers and ex-students – his natural empiricism and tendency to relate his teaching to practical work in the courts found an affinity in 'the ideas of English social reformers, the work of the probation service and expedients in the after care of prisoners' (Croft 1965: xvi).[7] To point to this pragmatic frame of mind does not, of course, detract from the contributions, for example in teaching or reform, of figures such as these – indeed, this might be their strength – but it does provide a necessary lens through which to view their work.

(2) *The interdisciplinary conception*

Pragmatism and empiricism are perspectives which often go hand in hand with the interdisciplinary ideology. Criminology cannot, I believe, be other than interdisciplinary in the sense that it has to draw on the findings of what Morris (1966: 62) refers to as the 'strange motley of investigators who have at some time or another borne the title of criminologist' – doctors, lawyers, statisticians, psychiatrists, clinical psychologists, and others more bizarre than these. It would be a waste of time then to labour this point, if not for two additional turns this feature has taken in British criminology – the first has been to make a religion out of the necessity of drawing on different disciplines and the second has been the playing down of the sociological contribution to this pantheon, pushing criminology either in the legalistic direction or (more frequently and more unfortunately) towards the clinical/psychological/forensic ideology.

Again, let me start with an assertion from Radzinowicz (1961: 177) to the effect that progress in criminology can only be made by the interdisciplinary approach: 'a psychiatrist, a social psychologist, a penologist, a lawyer, a statistician joining together on a combined research operation'. In the British context, the fact that a sociologist is not even mentioned is predictable. By the end of the 1950s the major figures in teaching and research were Radzinowicz (legal), Grünhut (legal), Mannheim (legal training and later psychiatric and especially sociological interest). The major institutions directly or marginally contributing – the Maudsley Hospital, the Tavistock Institute, the ISTD, the BSC, and the *BJC* – heavily weighted the field towards psychology and psychiatry. This weighting remained despite the later contribution by sociologists such as Mays, Morris, and later Downes.

This multidisciplinary image was reflected at a number of levels. It was part of the criminologist's presentation of self to the public.[8] It could be found in criminological conferences in textbooks and in lecture courses. Thus in Walker's (1965) text, out of fifty-seven pages devoted to the topic of explaining crime, seven are given to 'constitutional theories', fifteen to 'mental subnormality and illness', twenty to psychological theories of 'maladjustment, the normal offender, and psychopathy' and fifteen to 'environmental theories' (including 'economic theories', 'topographical aspects' and 'the human environment'). Mannheim's work is more difficult to characterize in this way because, although he clearly sees criminology as multi-disciplinary and his own training was legal,[9] he made significant sociological contributions in such books as *Social Aspects of Crime in England between the Wars* and his treatment of most sociological theories (with exceptions such as differential association) is as comprehensive as the rest of his 1965 text.

12   *Stanley Cohen*

A very clear statement in favour of criminology remaining exceptionally wide in scope was provided by another leading British criminologist, Gibbens, at a recent Council of Europe Criminological Conference:

> '... most of the important ideas and research hypotheses in criminology still come from the parent disciplines of law, social science, psychology and psychiatry... major contributions to criminology continue to come from studies which are not originally designed to come within its scope. Geneticists stumbled upon the significance of the XYY syndrome, the Danish twin study was a by-product of medical study, the English study of a sample of the population born on the same day was originally designed to study midwifery and infant mortality...' (Gibbens 1970: 5)

Other institutions reveal much the same, with an even more striking weighting towards the legal or clinical disciplines. The twelve research reports published to date by the Home Office Research Unit contain mainly topics of a statistical, social administrative type, together with highly technical psychological research (e.g. on the Hewitt and Jenkins hypothesis, and the use of the Jesness Inventory).

The character of British criminology is seen very distinctively in the ISTD, BSC, *BJC* axis. The Institute for the Scientific Treatment of Delinquency, set up in 1931, was the only one of its kind until the establishment of the Cambridge Institute. Its original objects included 'to initiate and promote scientific research into the causes and prevention of crime', to provide educational and training facilities and 'to establish observation centres or other auxiliary services for the study and treatment of delinquency'.

The essentially clinical nature of its approach was not altogether removed after its 'Psychopathic Clinic' was taken over by the National Health Service in 1948 and the phrase 'Scientific Treatment' was changed to 'Study and Treatment'. Thus in its 1957-8 *Annual Report* the case against handling crime from the penal end of the system and just using outside scientific information was stated and the case made for moving from the outside towards 'extending the principle of treating offences whenever possible as behaviour disorders calling for appropriate psycho-social measures' (p. 4). Clinical positivism was stressed as the scientific ideal; in the following year's *Report* the phrase '... the root problem of delinquency, viz. the condition of "pre-delinquency"' (p. 3) occurred.

Criminology and the sociology of deviance in Britain 13

The possibility of predicting delinquency – an obsession in British criminology – was always stressed and the 1960-1 *Report* complained that there were still resistances to dealing with crime as a 'behaviour problem with characteristic antecedents... Judging by comparative study of *other* forms of mental disorder, it is in the highest degree probable that in all cases the existence of a "predelinquent" stage can be established...' (p. 3, emphasis mine).

It is of course true that the ISTD was uniquely dominated by the psychiatrists (Edward Glover and Emmanuel Miller being the most notable) but Mannheim was a leading member from the outset and a scrutiny of the Annual Reports from 1950 onwards shows that virtually every leading British criminologist (with the exception of Radzinowicz) held some office in it. The parent organization had considerable import through its educational activities, but also through its offshoots, the *BJC*, started in July 1950 as the *British Journal of Delinquency*, with Glover, Miller, and Mannheim as its editors[10] (the name was changed in July 1960), and the BSC, which started off life within the ISTD in 1953 as the Scientific Group for the Discussion of Delinquency Problems.

The contents of the *BJC* over its twenty years have fairly accurately reflected the concerns of the discipline. Considerable attention is given to penology, to abnormal psychology, to delinquency and institutions for delinquents, and there is consistent interest in matters of legal and penal reform. A detailed classification of the contents (Wright 1970) contains the following frequencies of articles etc. appearing between 1950 and 1970: penology (including institutions, probation, capital punishment) 205; criminology (including delinquency classification, special types of offences) 379; social work 28; law 33; administration of justice 67; psychology 24; abnormal psychology 80; psychiatry 37; social sciences (including 'social factors', education) 79. This classification does not reveal disciplinary origins (for example, under criminology and penology) very clearly, nor does it convey the characteristic flavour of the journal. The attention given to very practical issues and the reprinting of addresses such as those given by a Commissioner of Police of the Metropolis (April 1968) clearly moves the journal away from a strictly academic format. And despite what to an outsider might look as a fair proportion of space given to clinical material, one of the editors recently complained: 'Where, we may ask, are the brave, resourceful, and imaginative clinical papers of yesterday?' (Glover 1970: 315)

The BSC reveals a more or less similar pattern. The make-up of its original Organizing Committee in 1961 (the year after it changed its name) included one representative each from the following: biology; criminal law and justice; organic medicine; psychiatry; psychoanalysis; psychology; social work; criminology; statistics; treatment of offenders; education and ethics, and moral philosophy. (Currently the Committee is made up of four representatives each from criminal law and the administration of justice; criminological medicine and psychology; treatment of offenders; criminological treatment of research; 'other persons'.)

One of its first meetings (in November 1953) was addressed by the two physiological psychologists, while its seventieth meeting (in February 1971) was addressed by a forensic psychiatrist on the subject of epileptics in prison. Out of 96 guest speakers at its meetings (some conferences or meetings had more than one speaker), there were 16 sociological criminologists, 16 psychologists (7 from the Home Office Research Unit, 2 from prisons), 12 psychiatrists, 12 lawyers, 5 Home Office administrators, 5 'criminologists', 4 Home Office statisticians, 6 social workers, 6 social administrators, 5 police officers, and a miscellaneous group of 10 including historians, geneticists, prison officers, prison doctors, and prison governors.

This rapid analysis of the disciplinary content and preoccupations in British criminology is not meant to give the impression that sociologists were somehow wilfully excluded due to some conspiracy. The imbalance is there partly because sociological criminology has not demonstrated its practical pay-off, but more simply, in Britain, because there was just so little of it available. As the editors of a recent collection on the sociology of crime and delinquency point out:

> 'Our reliance upon theories developed in other countries and particularly the United States is sometimes so pronounced in the teaching context, that students gain the impression of an almost complete hiatus in British research. Erroneous as such an impression may be the fact remains that the heavy traffic in ideas about delinquency has tended to flow almost exclusively in one direction.' (Carson and Wiles 1971: 48)

As I will show in the next section, the impression of a hiatus in sociological attention on crime is not all that erroneous. With the notable exceptions of Morris's ecological study and its predecessors (Mays, Sprott, Jephcott, Carter, and Kerr) the Morrises' sociological studies of prison, and some work on sentencing, there was virtually nothing before the post-1965 wave following Downes' book (Hargreaves, Willmott and others). Two of the most frequently cited works of sociological relevance before the 1960s – Sainsbury's study of the ecological patterns of suicide in London and Scott's description of delinquent gangs – were in fact both done by psychiatrists. An index of the paucity of indigenous sociology – and of the fact that one does not have to invoke conspiracy theories – is that the Institute of Criminology has often 'imported' leading American sociological criminologists such as Cressey and Wolfgang.

While it is difficult altogether to blame British sociology for paying so little attention to indigenous sociology, it cannot be exonerated easily from two further charges: a certain *parochialism* which wilfully excluded American sociology of crime and deviance for so long and, then, a clear *misunderstanding* as to what sociology is about. Mannheim is partly guilty on the first charge, with his apparent policy of selecting for his textbook American work only when British or European work could not be found; while the work of West is a clear example on both these counts. Curious notions about sociology being concerned with 'area' or 'environmental' factors appear, sociology is identified with statistics, and concepts such as anomie, subculture, or deprivation are distorted.[11]

In summary, the off-putting features of the interdisciplinary approach are the rigidity with which it is defended, the way it is skewed to exclude sociology and lean in the clinical direction, its parochialism, and its misunderstanding of sociology. These features may be illustrated by the following anecdote: during a visit two years ago David Matza was introduced to a body of British criminologists by a leading British criminologist, who said that although he hadn't actually read any of Professor Matza's work, he'd been told it was very interesting...

(3) *Correction, reform, and the problem of values*

British criminology has always been tied to two interests: the first, the administrative interest of making the correctional system more efficient and the second the humanitarian interest in reforming the system. These interests are not, of course, necessarily incompatible especially in their recent appearance under the psychiatric ideology which rationalizes the treatment approach as being both more efficient and more humane.

The problems these interests raise are complex and although it is easy enough to find instances in British criminology where investigators have compromised themselves by their institutional connexions or their open espousal of correctional interests, the charge against criminology is that it has simply not even realized the complexity of the issue. Correctional aims are apparently taken for granted:

> 'Criminology, in its narrow sense, is concerned with the study of the phenomenon of crime and of the factors or circumstances... which may have an influence on or be associated with criminal behaviour and the state of crime in general. But this does not and should not exhaust the whole subject matter of criminology. There remains the vitally important problem of combating crime... To rob it of this practical function, is to divorce criminology from reality and render it sterile.' (Radzinowicz 1961: 168)

Or attempts are made to divorce criminology from such 'practical functions'. Walker, for example, states that 'Perhaps the hardest impression to eradicate is that the criminologist is a penal reformer' and concedes that although his findings might form the basis of reform campaigns such campaigns are humanitarian not scientific in nature:

> 'It is no more his [the criminologist's] function to attack or defend the death penalty than it is the function of the political scientist to take part in an election campaign. The confusion, however, between criminologists and penal reformers has been encouraged by criminologists themselves, many of whom have also been penal reformers. Strictly speaking, penal reform is a spare time occupation for criminologists just as canvassing for votes would be for political scientists. The difference is that the criminologists' spare time occupation is more likely to take this form, and when it does so it is more likely to interfere with what should be purely criminological thoughts.' (Walker 1965: preface)

It is to Walker's credit that he states his resolution of the problem so clearly. In contrast, the major institutions of British criminology have apparently quite unselfconsciously accepted the goals of social control taking up, within these, various correctional or reformative stances. Contributions are made by those (like Goring) who are part of the system, those who are sponsored by the system (e.g. doing research financed by the Home Office) or by the numerous institutions part of whose policy is to encourage cooperation between so-called 'scientific' and so called 'practical' objectives. These styles appear in various guises in the ISTD, the *BJC*, the BSC, and the Cambridge Institute. Thus, for example, when the BSC held a conference four years ago on 'The Role of the Prison Officer' the speakers were the Secretary of the Prison Officers Association, a Chief Prison Officer, the Principal of the Officers Training School, a prison psychiatrist, and the Assistant Secretary of State in the Home Office Prison Department. When such styles appear in the work of bodies as the Cambridge Institute, they are more sophisticated and it would be insulting to suggest that the individuals involved in such research or communication are unaware of potential tensions and conflicts of interests. But I would repeat that if any such self awareness is there, it has not – with few exceptions – been manifested in any public way.

Now, while Walker's solution is clear, it is both over-simplified and untenable. One cannot believe that what has been problematic to social scientists for generations – for Weber, Myrdal, and Mills no less than in the special deviancy context for Becker, Polsky, Gouldner, and others – can be resolved by asserting that there are such things as 'purely criminological thoughts'. The constraints that operate in the very selection of certain subjects as worthy of research, the methods one chooses, the way one is funded and sponsored, how one's results will be used ... these and numerous other problems cannot be brushed under the carpet. Unless and until the private doubts that most criminologists express – what to do, for example, if the Home Office refuses to let one's research assistant look at records because he is a security risk – are made public, these criminologists should not complain that the outsider believes that they do not have these doubts.

This is not, of course, a problem peculiar to criminology. There are many parallels, for example, in contemporary research on race relations, where there is the continual conflict between accepting official goals, taking a reformist position, siding with particular interest groups, or showing an allegiance to some professional ethic. In studying crime and deviance, where what Becker (1967) terms the hierarchies of credibility and morality are so much taken for granted, the problems are heightened. It is not enough for the Social Science Research Council to comment as follows on its policy in regard to criminological research:

'the great grant-giving foundations do not appear to have any place in the present quasi-official arrangements between the Home Office, the Cambridge Institute and the Advisory Council on the Treatment of Offenders and this again might well be a matter for consideration by the SSRC which could well accept responsibility for co-ordination in the allocation of funds and maintain a balance between the interests involved.' (SSRC 1968)

It must be made clear just whose 'interests' are being 'balanced'.

(4) *The positivist trap*

The heavy dominance of clinical positivism within the interdisciplinary rubric of British criminology is one of many indices that support my contention that the basic model which shaped Goring's thought has not really been transcended. It should be made clear that this is not an objection to explanations at the psychological level *per se* (unlike most of my sociological colleagues, I believe that such objections are theoretically indefensible) but to demonistic psychology of the Eysenck type. As this is not the level of analysis the paper is primarily concerned with, let me just give two brief examples of the trap.

The first surrounds the concept of determinism, which has been so controversial an issue in legal, psychiatric and recently sociological discussions of crime. Jones (1965: 70), a sociological criminologist, in discussing the implications of the treatment model in imputing criminal responsibility, cites a distinction made by a philosopher between the kleptomaniac and the thief: the former is not responsible for his behaviour while the latter is to be treated as a rational person. 'But', Jones comments, 'current psychological and sociological research gives us reason to question the validity of such a distinction.' Good, one thinks, even if he is not referring to the general problem about responsibility as Matza does, he is going to make the specific point that Cressey makes in his well-known paper (1954, revised 1962) that so-called compulsive crimes such as kleptomania in fact lack the characteristics imputed to them by psychiatrists, and if re-examined in terms of sociological theories of motivation, identification, role-playing etc. are similar to other motivated, rational behaviour. But no, Jones is making *exactly the opposite* point, the trap has been well laid:

'The ability to resist temptation, for example, depends upon a person's character structure and this in turn arises out of personal relationships within the family during earliest years of life – experience over which the individual has no control.'

My other example is less specific and will serve to epitomize – as much as Goring did – all the characteristics of mainstream British criminology I have highlighted in this review. It is a recent book by West (1969), the first Report (after seven years work) of the Cambridge Study in Delinquent Development. It is one of the largest single pieces of criminological research ever carried out in this country, financed by the Home Office (£70,000 to March 1968, now under annual review, the project still having some years to go) and with an eminent Consultative and Advisory Committee (including only two out of eleven with more or less sociological backgrounds). In his preface to this report, Radzinowicz hails the research as being '... in the great tradition of explorations of the springs of delinquency. Although on a smaller scale it will ultimately claim a place alongside such classics as the work of Robins, the Gluecks and the McCords. All too little of this sort has been attempted in England' (p. vii).

This assertion is correct: in methodology and conception this research goes no further than the extraordinary jumble of eclectic positivism that rendered the work of the Gluecks such an anachronism. Sociologists cannot be expected to be very impressed with a study which states that although it is more concerned with individual characteristics, it is also interested in the 'demonstration' of the extent to which troublesome boys and other family problems are concentrated among the very poorest: 'It may be that the next stage of the inquiry will go some way to answering the question of whether these problems spring from poverty or whether poverty itself merely reflects an underlying individual inadequacy' [sic] (p. vii).

The design involves an eight-year follow-up of some 400 boys selected at the age of eight or nine. Did some overall conception inform the selection of dimensions to be studied? West answers: 'The aim was to collect information on a large number of items, all of them said to have relevance to the development of juvenile delinquency and to see in the event which items or which combination of items would prove to be the clearest determinants of future delinquency' (p. 2). Social factors such as television were excluded because these were too 'universal' and of course – as the Gluecks also argued – neighbourhood influences could be excluded because these were constant. Besides such indices as teachers' ratings and psychological dimensions of the family, items used includes ones such as height, weight, body-type and various tests of psychomotor habits.[12]

The preliminary findings suggest that the social level of the family was the most important single factor in discriminating poorly behaved boys from the rest. From an actuarial point of view, the most efficient prediction might be based on a few easily registered and objective social facts. The index 'family income inadequate' was 'remarkably effective' in identifying the 'problem prone minority'. If this is so (and of course such a finding was the basis of Toby's devastating critique of the Gluecks six years ago) then what is the point of a study like this? Why use the opportunities provided by a long scale longitudinal design in such a way? Leaving aside any theoretical pay-off (which the researchers might want to say does not concern them) the practical advantages of such individualistic prediction studies – as numerous critics have shown – are highly dubious.

If this is the sort of research which is to command prestige and credibility in the future, then British criminology cannot be said to have advanced a great deal and, more particularly, it cannot be expected to command much positive sociological interest.

Let me conclude this review with three important footnotes, without which the point of the exercise could be misunderstood:

(1) These four distinguishing features were chosen not only because they were in some ways characteristic, but because they were ones which were reacted against by the new sociology of deviance. In only the last of these can the reaction be said to be a partial resolution. Pragmatism – if not in the form it takes in British criminology – is partially unavoidable and in some instances can be recommended. Then, it is difficult to see criminology not being inter-disciplinary – although again the particular form it has taken (the advocacy of 'teamwork' for example) is intellectually facile and when it has no theoretical edifice to support it, it is extraordinarily vulnerable to attack from faddishness, not to say charlatanism. The advances of the XYY 'explanation',[13] Eysenck's excursions into criminology, and the onslaught which is just gathering momentum, the ethology kick, do not give one much faith in the subject's integrity. Finally, while sociologists have seemed more aware – at times perhaps obsessed – by the value problem, they can hardly have said to have solved it. Self-images stressing styles such as appreciating, muckraking, cynically commenting, reflecting, might all have their aesthetic appeals, but they do not constitute solutions to doing research, say, on prisons. Such

research cannot but resemble that by orthodox criminologists in being reformist, in laying itself open to be used for other ends, in having to compromise itself at various points.

(2) Talking about 'mainstream' criminology has meant leaving out those few attempts which cannot be characterized by at least all of these features. In sociological criminology the work, say, of Morris and Downes has already been mentioned and the same applies in psychology to that of Trasler: although his 'explanation of criminality' has severe limitations, it at least constitutes a theory. The work of Tony Parker, too often disparaged as being 'just a few good stories', must also be singled out.

(3) There are a number of current developments in the sociology of law, which already has one base in the contributions by Radzinowicz (in his history of the English criminal law) and Walker (in his histories of the use of psychiatric concepts in the legal system). This field has received recent theoretical interest and empirical contributions such as those from the Legal Research Unit at Bedford College, recent studies of the legal profession and allied subjects (by Abel-Smith, Zander, and others), and the current development of a Legal Advice Research Unit (financed by Nuffield) could vitalize the whole field, relating it, for example, to wider sociological interests in social control and the legal order. A second development has been research in the sociology of the police. There have already been a few isolated projects in this field over the last few years and attempts are currently being made – although one has some misgivings about the directions some of these might go – by Banton and others (again with Nuffield Foundation assistance) to 'evaluate recent research and define future priorities'. Finally, an interest in deviance has been shown by students of mass media and mass culture; these are shown in different ways in Stuart Hall's paper to this conference and in the work of the Centre for Mass Communication Research at Leicester (see Halloran, *et al.*, 1970).

THE RESPONSE FROM SOCIOLOGY

That the study of deviant behaviour, crime, and social problems has become insulated from sociology is, I think, self-evident and I have tried to show the form this insulation took in Britain. What, though, was the response from the 'other side', from the mainstream of sociology? No one has considered this problem, although Morris, in his review of Mannheim's text, points out that even if British criminology has not moved in a neo-Lombrosian direction away from the concerns of such Victorian amateurs as Mayhew, it '... would still not have been able to gain much from association with the social sciences in British Universities' (Morris 1966: 61). Without pioneers such as Mannheim, he suggests, criminology would still be where it was in the thirties. But what have sociologists been doing all this time? The answer to this question is important, because there is little doubt that at an intellectual level the new deviance theories are responses to the insulation from sociology and at a personal level, as I will suggest, their adherents see themselves as stigmatized outsiders trying to get back into the respectable, i.e. sociological, community. (Although, as I will also suggest, this is a partially serious passing rather than repentant attempt at full re-socialization.)

One index of the insulation has been the relative lack of interest admitted by sociologists in the pre-occupations of criminology. Few would show a comparable unfamiliarity with other sub-fields – say, educational or industrial sociology. For the most part this indifference is justified, but even potentially important issues in sociological criminology (e.g. white collar crime) have been ignored. On the surface, this state of affairs is all the more surprising as the study of deviance was rooted in the central concerns of sociological theory. As Becker, among others, has pointed out, to theorists like Durkheim 'problems of deviance were problems of general sociology' (Becker 1964: 1). This is no more true for the obvious case of *Suicide* than it is for *Rules* and *Division of Labour*, both works having produced themes explicitly taken up later, for example, by Erikson in the sceptical sociology of deviance.

The reasons for severing these connexions are complex and beyond my scope in this paper. On the side of sociology, they include a sophisticated version of the sort of philistine distrust which greets, say, Durkheim's *Suicide* and the whole work of Freud. How can looking at suicide explain how societies work 'normally'? How can the interpsychic conflicts of a few middle class Viennese Jews explain how the 'normal' mind works? Studying deviance is seen as an esoteric and marginal occupation. Crucial too, has been the development of consensual theories in sociology, in the more mechanistic versions of which crime and deviance are simply the results of the machine going wrong. It is precisely this sort of conception that recent theorists of deviance have reacted against.

The major barriers, though, have been created on the other side: the moralistic, non-abstract ways in which deviance has been studied and the early identification of this field with social work, reformative or correctional concerns.[14] As Polsky has noted, criminology has been the least successful of all subfields of sociology in freeing itself from these concerns. He comments on Merton's condemnation of the 'slum encouraged provincialism of thinking that the primary subject matter of sociology was centred on such peripheral problems of social life as divorce and delinquency' that:

'Given the perspectives within which delinquency and crime are always studied it is obvious why Merton might regard them as peripheral problems of social life rather than fundamental processes of central concern to sociology.' (Polsky 1967: 142)

Polsky is guilty here of caricaturing criminology and is certainly wrong if the old Chicago School studies of crime and deviance are considered. But clearly the development of criminology has little to recommend itself to sociology.

Returning to the institutional level, would one not expect the reverse in Britain, that the pragmatic Fabian stream in sociology would find criminology and related fields highly congruent with its self-image? To some extent, this *has* been true, but this stream is running dry. On the one hand, sociology is developing scientific, academic, or professional self-images into which certain topics are not respectable enough to be fitted and on the other, soft, liberal attitudes are becoming anathema to the hard radicals of sociology who don't consider deviants as 'really' political. Both these developments, but particularly the first which is the more dominant, lead to those common room sniggerings about 'girls who want to do sociology because they like people'.

Elsewhere (Cohen 1971) in trying to describe the sort of attitudes that were prevalent in the profession, I wrote:

'In terms of having congenial people to discuss our work with, we found some of our sociological colleagues equally unhelpful. They were either mandarins who were hostile towards a committed sociology and found subjects such as delinquency nasty, distasteful or simply boring, or else they were self-proclaimed radicals, whose political interests went only as far as their own definition of "political" and were happy to consign deviants to social welfare or psychiatry. For different reasons, both groups found our subject matter too messy and devoid of significance. They shared with official criminology a depersonalized, dehumanized picture of the deviant: he was simply part of the waste products of the system, the reject from the conveyor belt.'

In an earlier draft I hadn't included 'some of' before 'our sociological colleagues'; the alteration was partly in response to a sociological colleague who had written 'who are these nasties?' next to this passage. I took his point that not all sociologists were like this caricature, but I remain convinced that the mandarin attitude exists.

This attitude is buttressed by the erroneous conception that sociology is being swamped by hordes of deviance researchers while the really important subjects, such as education, industry, and stratification are being neglected. In fact, even a superficial examination of the market will show that this is not the case. A comparison of the three major British sociological journals with, say, the *American Sociological Review* and the *American Journal of Sociology* shows a low proportion of articles even remotely connected with criminology or deviance. Whole substantive areas such as sexual deviance, drug taking, mental illness, are virtually completely missing, and there are no journals like *Social Problems* to cover these areas. In the one – admittedly inadequate – survey of research from the early 1950s to the 1960s (Krausz 1969) nothing much emerges from the five pages on deviance, aside from a few studies of penal institutions and the ecological-subcultural traditions from Mays, Morris, Downes, and Willmott (this, incidentally, being most misleadingly summarized).

More substantial information can be found from the 1966 survey of British sociologists undertaken by the Social Science Research Council in collaboration with the British Sociological Association.[15] In the context of the 'sociological explosion' in Britain (one university chair before the war and over forty in 1967) sociological attention given to crime and deviance is insignificant. The replies from the 416 BSA members whose questionnaires were 'usable' (this included about three-quarters of teachers of the subject) indicated that crime ranked low on each of the separate criteria of 'main interests', 'other special interests', 'research completed 1945–1960', 'research completed 1961–1966', and 'current research'. In terms of 'main interests' for example (excluding 'basic theory', 'methodology', and 'methods') criminology (30) ranked well behind sociology of education (102), industrial sociology/sociology of work (96), social stratification (66), and community studies (46). Out of the 340 projects listed under 'current research', industrial sociology maintains the lead it had in earlier periods with 74, sociology of education next with 51 and, after a big drop to community studies (34), criminology only registered 10. (One might add to this a few of the 25 classified under 'sociology of social services/policy/problems.)

Using these indices at least, it would not appear that British sociology has nurtured much of an interest in crime and deviance. Although the mandarin characterization may be an overstatement I believe there has been and is likely to remain a basic divide between those who, to use Horowitz's terms (1969: 92-3), think that sociology should be *impeccable* and those who think it should be *important*: 'The aesthetic vision of the impeccable sociologist... preserves him from the worst infections of "helping people".' The gap is more than a matter of aesthetic styles, though '... it demands a specific decision on the part of scholars and researchers as to where they will place their intellectual bets: on scientific autonomy or on social relevance' (1969: 99).[16]

Leaving aside for the moment the complication that much conflict exists *within* the sociology of deviance between impeccability and importance, the obvious political question remains as to what is 'socially relevant' and, more to the point, relevant to whom? This leads me to the stream of political radicalism within and on the margins of sociology that is indifferent, if not hostile, to the field of deviance. The Left have simply followed the liberal rhetoric and consigned deviants to the welfare category while orthodox Marxists (whose sole contribution to the field was that of the Dutch criminologist Bonger some fifty years ago) have written criminals off as the *Lumpen*, or the 'rabble' who, as Marx described to Engels, gathered to jeer at him when he was evicted from his Soho flat. The only stream of radical political thought which is sympathetic is anarchism and it is no accident (!) that five out of the seven founder members of the National Deviancy Conference (although not all anarchists themselves) have published articles about deviance at one time or another in the British journal, *Anarchy*.

The various sources of insulation that I have sketched are, I believe, becoming less potent. Much of the above analysis would not apply to the current younger cohort of British sociologists and, even among the others, an ideology which rejects deviance as a topic of interest is hardly dominant. The present potential of research and theory on deviance is on balance more likely to convince mainstream sociology of its centrality rather than its marginality. But the relationship between deviance and the rest of sociology must always remain strained: the interests of its students, the peculiar institutional constraints it has to operate in, the umbrella-like nature of areas like criminology, are features which cannot be glossed over in the name of some professional consensus. I will refer to more of these strains in the next section.

THE EVOLUTION OF THE NATIONAL DEVIANCY CONFERENCE

At this point in the paper I experience my discrepant role of mediator most acutely, having to describe in a supposedly detached way a development I have been closely concerned with. The greatest danger lies in exaggerating the importance of this development and I would like to stress that I do not consider it (or the sociology of deviance as a whole) worthy of extensive self-reflection. The development is also not unique and has some parallels with the emergence in America of the Society For the Study of Social Problems (in 1951!) although the Society is more closely tied to bodies such as the ASA and is undoubtedly more professional.

I have indicated implicitly throughout the paper the constellation of intellectual reasons which created the 'need' for such a development. By the middle 1960s there were a number of young sociologists attracted to the wholly American field of the sociology of deviance. (I suspect they were turned on first by *Outsiders* and then *Delinquency and Drift*.) These ideas seemed to relate to what they were either teaching or doing research on (subjects including drugs, homosexuality, approved schools, vandalism, youth culture, mental illness, etc.). For reasons I have indicated, official criminology was regarded with attitudes ranging from ideological condemnation to a certain boredom (and I suspect that the latter was more dominant than many would admit). One had to get away from that scene, but being a sociologist wasn't enough, one had to find a separate subculture within the sociological world. The sheer physical isolation of many of us in small departments, teaching a subject with no colleagues in the field and few graduate students, was another contributory pressure.

So, ostensibly for these reasons (although this account sounds suspiciously like colour supplement history), seven of us met in July

1968, fittingly enough in Cambridge in the middle of the Third National Conference of Teaching and Research on Criminology, organized by the Institute and opened by the Home Secretary. We decided to form a group to provide some sort of intellectual support for each other and to cope with collective problems of identity, not to mention the problems of reaction formation and the absence of a legitimate opportunity structure. Friends and colleagues were to be sounded out, ideas about circulating reading lists and research plans were discussed and it was proposed to arrange a symposium. Before taking up the subsequent progress of the group, let me speculate on some further reasons for its formation and subsequent rapid growth: it would be dishonest as well as sociologically naïve to suggest that the ostensible intellectual reasons I have given were the only ones.

The first is that we all sensed something in the sceptical, labelling, and societal reaction perspectives, the anti-psychiatry school and similar currents, which struck a responsive political chord. The stress on labelling, injustice, scapegoating, stigmatizing, the implicit underdog sympathy, the whole 'central irony' (as Matza calls it) of the neo-Chicago School and its recognition of Leviathan, the implications of Laing's work – these were all sympathetic ideas. It is precisely the limitations of this sympathy (which I don't believe was ever expressed that simply anyway) which has provoked indiscriminate attacks (such as those by Gouldner 1968) as well as the more discerning remarks such as those of Lemert in the course of his re-examination of the secondary deviance concept: ' "Secondary deviance" may be a convenient vehicle for civil libertarians or young men of sociology to voice angry critiques of social institutions' (Lemert 1967: 59).

Both such interests were present in the original group and these ideas were found appealing for reasons strongly related to the personal background of the group's members. Without exception they had all been involved in orthodox political movements with degrees of commitment ranging through Anarchists, CND, Young Communists and International Socialists. In common with many of their contemporaries they were going through various degrees of disillusionment with such activities. They had all been through the generational experience which only a few commentators such as Jeff Nuttall (1968) have tried to comprehend. Talking or doing something about deviance seemed to offer – however misguided this might now look to an outsider – a form of commitment, a way of staying in, without on the one hand selling out or on the other playing the drab game of orthodox politics, whose simplicities were becoming increasingly irritating.

Such commitment was easier because the historical period was one of growing and visible militancy of deviant groups working outside the political structure. The hope for real social change (or any event, where the action was) seemed to be with the hippies, druggies, squatters and, above all, everything that was happening in the American campuses and ghettoes. These identifications were facilitated by personal involvement in some of these marginal groups. Some of the original members and even more of the later members of the Deviancy Conference were on the fringes of what Jock Young has nicely called 'the Middle Underground'. Involved as participants, they couldn't resist the lure to be observers and make a decent living from it. The romantic, voyeur-like appeal of the subject matter was thus important; one doubts whether a similar group could have sprung up around, say, industrial sociology, educational sociology, or community studies.

I have speculated at some length on this sort of reason because it would seem implausible to suggest that some sort of disinterested quest for knowledge was drawing people to the field. These reasons are complex to unravel and have meant more or less to different people at different stages of their involvement: the organization has become all things to all members. Such a background contains intrinsic tensions, which I will comment on later, but despite such tensions – or because of them? – the sheer numerical strength of the group has increased dramatically, although it has possibly reached some sort of plateau now. The original group of seven increased at the first Conference at York in November 1968 to about twenty (most of them friends) and this number rose to 130 by the seventh Conference in October 1970 (about twenty more having to be turned away for lack of accommodation). The paid-up membership of the organization is now 230.

At a minimal level, the fact that the group has kept going and attracted so many new people shows that it is filling some obvious need. It has tried, not altogether successfully, to involve groups other than sociologists, the largest of these being social workers. Other 'lay' activists or commentators on the scene have also been drawn in as speakers: a crime reporter, the leader of a squatters' group, a detached youth worker. A forum and some support have also been given to groups such as tenants' associations, claimants' unions, Case Con (the militant social work organization), and RAP (Radical Alternatives to Prison). Plans are in hand to formalize contacts with these groups and perhaps in the long run provide them with some sort of umbrella organization. It is possible that a journal might be published and there are plans to publish policy oriented pamphlets on such subjects as aversion therapy of homosexuals, restrictions on prison visiting, invasions of privacy, and drug legislation. Another achievement is presumably to have played the major role in organizing and manning this BSA Conference.

Papers at the seven York conferences have been mainly in the four categories: ethnographies of deviant types, studies of social control, theories of deviance, and critiques; plus attempts to connect with institutions such as social work, psychiatry, and the mass media. There is no shortage of topics, but a semi-conscious colonialism seems to be operating in which whole new territories (for example education and the mass media) are taken over and planted with a sociology-of-deviance flag. Interests listed in the research register range from homosexual prostitutes, crime in the USSR, physical handicap as deviance, to tenants' associations, false consciousness(!), and the sociology of soccer.

As the group has expanded, so its conception of itself has changed and clearly new tensions are introduced in simply coping with the range of interests and involvements. The original circular of invitation to the first Conference simply said '... A group of social scientists who are currently concerned with problems of crime and deviancy have decided to hold a one day symposium related to these areas.' The subjects were described as being a 'mixed bag' but, continued the circular, 'the aim of the symposium is not to create an artificial academic consensus, but rather to bring together a group of people who appear to share certain common perspectives.' A year later, in August 1969, one member of the committee 'at the risk of accusations of Leninism' as he put it, circulated a letter to his fellow members which included the following:

'The most important worry is perhaps over the total nature of the project we're involved in. At the moment, it does seem that we are on the way towards being a "left wing" value committed "social problems" sociology, reinforcing each other periodically in our institutional isolation, revivifying our lecture courses with ideas culled from the symposium – but never really moving outside our chosen...occupational roles. Perhaps we might also be helping to create a new (rather ill-defined, libertarian) sociological culture among our students and friends. But there are other activities we should be involved in.'

The 'other activities' he suggested included being a pressure group, acting as a corrective to official definitions of deviance and social problems, and the setting up of a kind of anti-sociology. It has become transparent subsequently – and was so all along to anyone aware of the group's diversity – that there are different and partially irreconcilable ways ahead. Let me end this section by just listing some differences which have become manifest so far:

(1) Should the group just drift along, amplifying and if need be changing, or should some attempt be made at tightening up?

(2) Should one tighten up in the direction of demanding greater commitment to social action?

(3) Should one tighten up in the direction of demanding greater theoretical sophistication, making everything more impeccable? As a corollary, does this mean excluding or limiting the numbers of non-sociologists?

(4) To what extent should the perceived limitations of the theories which originally looked so attractive lead to an immersion in 'harder' and ostensibly more political theories?

My personal inclination, because of an aversion to the apocalyptic, is to avoid a tightening up in any of these directions; this does not mean that the tensions which result from these differing conceptions can always be coped with. One other tension is worth noting, the one with sociology. I have made much of the desire to get the subject back into sociology, but my impression is that the commitment to sociology among many in the Conference is somewhat weak. Mainstream sociologists are not wholly unjustified in seeing the group as marginals, with loyalties elsewhere, who would prefer, for example, to teach a group of social workers than a group of honours sociology students and whose avowed interests in making theoretical links with the sociological tradition are not always very convincing. Again, although this might be an important issue to some, I do not personally see it as a priority.

SOME CURRENT COMPARISONS

In this last, highly speculative, section, I would like to make some assessment of the current position, particularly by comparing mainstream criminology and the sociology of deviance with each other and the world outside. I have used the three criteria of *impact*, *relevance*, and *commitment*.

(1) *Impact*

There is little question that the institutional position of mainstream criminology is powerful and fairly concentrated. The Institute of Criminology at Cambridge, with its close links to the Home Office, commands prestige and support and in the public eye virtually *is* criminology. Its educational impact has been made through its highly successful diploma course (as well as other short courses) and is strong in a number of law faculties. It has certain high level connexions with bodies such as the Advisory Council on the Treatment of Offenders. The BSC – ISTD – *BJC* axis is perhaps less powerful and its direct influence is more on middle range professionals (probation officers, clinicians) or through the institutional positions of its non-academic members. In terms of access to the mass media, potential influences on policy through official inquiries, reports, commissions etc., these groups are fairly well placed.

In contrast, the sociology of deviance group – although just as inbred as mainstream criminology – has a much more diffuse power base, mainly confined to academic sociology departments. In so far as part of its original aim was to spread to this area, it has been fairly successful. There are about twelve university or polytechnic courses in criminology or deviance run by persons closely associated with the group and perhaps an equal number by those with some ties. Strength with professionals lies more with social workers and others. Many members of the group spend time talking to magistrates, probation officers, prison officers, and others, but I doubt whether this is a very distinctive contribution.

Describing the position in this way does not imply that many members of either group would see themselves as engaging in some sort of power struggle. Also, having prestige or running undergraduate courses hardly means the same as having any impact. Clearly criminologists do have some impact and are in positions which ensure that their definitions are given credibility. I suspect though that both groups, not to mention sociologists as a whole, are given to exaggerating any such influence they may have. Introducing his collection on *The Impact of Sociology* Douglas (1970: 1) speculates on the 'profound' and 'rapidly accelerating' effects the social sciences are having on everyday lives. 'While it may still be too prophetic to be accorded much credibility, I believe that many of us will live to see the social sciences become the primary means by which we seek to determine social policies which will rationally order our everyday lives.'

One doubts it. Matza's passing remarks about functionalism are relevant here '... the functionalist perspective has had little public consequence. It has neither bolstered the social order nor subverted it. Except among a few thousand sociologists it has passed unnoticed' (Matza 1969: 58). This argument can be used against some of Matza's own theories: some research and much impressionistic evidence indicates that – in this country at any rate – control agents have simply not been won over to the positivist ideology and in their day to day work and reflections about delinquency use a much more common sense model, which is hardly deterministic at all. In the same light, one might note Radzinowicz's conclusion that there has not been much of a connexion between criminological research and penal reform:

> 'Treatment by probation, the borstal system, the juvenile courts and several other innovations were not devised on the strength of fresh and precise criminological knowledge. They can be shown to have evolved on the whole under the influence of growing social consciousness, of religious movements and philanthropic stimulus, from some temporary measure, or just from straightforward common sense, supported by experience.' (Radzinowicz 1961: 178–9)

Research is needed on just how much, and in what form, the criminological belief system percolates through to policy makers and becomes part of the common sense rhetoric.

Finally, in terms of mutual impact, clearly the sociology of deviance is too mistrustful of British criminology to admit to being influenced in other than a negative direction. In fact though, as I have suggested, it will remain somewhat parasitic on criminological knowledge, partially dependent on the same resources and subject to some of the same pressures. It is beginning to look more on the legal – as opposed to the psychiatric side – of the discipline. One might speculate that the sociology of deviance as a whole, and the way it has appeared in this country, is having some impact on criminology. A number of the York group have taught on the Cambridge post-graduate course and gave papers at the Fourth National Conference on Teaching and Research in Criminology. The more cynical talk about power politics, being lured by the Establishment and so on. I do not agree that such contacts should be avoided, although I do think that the 'Establishment' sees the newer perspective as being simply a fashion which will eventually pass over or (more mistakenly) simply consisting of a few interesting ideas which can be swallowed up without changing the existing paradigm at all.

A more plausible reception to some of the criticism levelled by sociologists can be seen at some points of a recent text by Hood and Sparks (1970), both Assistant Directors of Research at the Institute of Criminology. Not only does their book contain a pronounced sociological content – subcultural delinquency and the sociology of the prison are included among the 'key issues in criminology' – and a nearly complete exclusion of clinical interests, but 'traditional' interests are raised in such a way that their relationship to sociology is made fairly explicit. Thus, attention on self-report studies and hidden delinquency – which in Britain has seemed to be related to a desire to root out all those recalcitrant contributors to the 'dark figure' who refuse to become detected – is justified in terms of the light it may shed on problems of discretion, control, and labelling.

The book is still somewhat pragmatic: as the authors admit, no single theme or theory underlines the subject and the justification for singling out the eight 'key issues' is that a lot of research has been done on them in recent years, in most of them some progress has been made and important questions remain. There are other subjects, they state, '... in particular so called labelling or transactional theory in which too little empirical research has been done. Work in this area ... seems likely to develop rapidly in the future.' As far as policy matters go, Hood and Sparks submit that while most of the subjects they have chosen have implications for penal policy, this is not the reason for their inclusion. They disagree that criminology is the study of the ways of preventing crime and is professionally interested in reforming offenders. Criminology is not a kind of social work and there is scope for 'disinterested and purely scientific research' on such matters as the operation of the penal system:

> 'This is not, of course, to say that criminology cannot make any contribution to penal policy. What it cannot do is decide what the *aims* of penal policy should be. But by discovering how much crime is committed and by showing how and why it was committed, criminology can help to show what policy goals are reasonable; and if given certain aims, they can try to discover by research the best means of accomplishing them. It is unfortunately true, however, that at the present time much too little is known ... to permit us to draw definite practical conclusions concerning questions of penal policy.' (1970: 9)

The uncharitable might call such a line defensive, and its model of finding out the facts in a 'disinterested' way, drawing the 'definite practical conclusions' and showing what policy goals are 'reasonable', while attractive, does not confront the fact-value-interest problems that have bedevilled sociology. But at least it is a form of self-consciousness which criminology has not shown very conspicuously in the past.

(2) *Relevance*

Criminology has often chosen to deal with areas which society – or its elected representatives or mass media – have defined as most relevant. This is a theoretically indefensible basis of choice, but it does give criminology its strength: it is *seen* to be relevant.

In contrast, sociologists of deviance, while making a lot of pious noises about 'other' criteria of relevance, have often opted for the esoteric, the catchy, the hip – precisely those areas which seem less relevant. This is due partly to personal preference, but more importantly due to the fact that the interactionist type of approach seems better able to cope with forms of deviance such as homosexuality, drugtaking, certain kinds of behaviour defined as mental illness, which are ambiguous, marginal and already subject to widespread normative dissensus. Until attention is focused on what to the public seem more relevant areas such as violence *or* a coherent case is made for choosing these other areas, this type of sociology will always be at a disadvantage.

(3) Commitment

I have probably said more than enough on the problem of values and a whole session in this Conference was devoted to the 'political and ethical implications of deviance theory'. Let me repeat that mainstream criminology has compromised itself too far and too much because of its close connexions with the institutions and ideology of the correctional system. It has complacently thought that there are no problems of competing values and interests. At worst, this has led to an unquestioning acceptance of official goals and policies; at best it has led to sustained and well informed criticism of these policies if not the goals.

The sociology of deviance has been complacent in another way, though, by sometimes giving the impression that it has solved these problems. At worst this has led to a self-indulgent romanticism, at best it has been simply good sociology.

I started off this paper by noting one danger in self-reflective social science; let me end with another: the danger of tilting at windmills. This is not to say that the divisions I have indicated are not real; students who had accused me of exaggerating have come back from occasions such as Institute of Criminology conferences reproaching me for *underplaying* such divisions. The point is that the impact (of the theories at least – as opposed to that of powerful groups) is not as massive and monolithic as some attacks on it credit it with being. This is the same point that Bottomore (1971) makes against Gouldner's *The Coming Crisis of Western Sociology*: why the excessive attention to functionalism when it is very doubtful that it enjoyed the pre-eminence attached to it?

This would all be unimportant if not for the further argument that Bottomore levels against reflexive sociology in general and Gouldner in particular:

> 'In the end, it achieves the opposite of what Wright Mills advocated at the beginning of the radical revival: instead of turning personal troubles into public issues, it turns public issues into personal troubles, by exhorting the sociologist to give his attention narcissistically to the problem of the relationship "between being a sociologist and being a person" and to worry about his relation to his work. I do not believe that such pre-occupations have ever in-

spired a critical analysis of society or ever will. They are a symptom of an intellectual malaise, not a remedy.'

They can be both symptom and partial remedy though, in areas and contexts where they have hardly ever appeared. It is in these terms that papers of this sort can be justified – if only very slightly.

Notes

1. See the Introduction and Readings in Section A 'The Development of a Sociological Perspective on Crime in Britain' in Carson and Wiles (1971). For an evaluation of nineteenth-century ecological studies see Chapter 3 of Morris (1957) and for a particularly interesting perspective on Mayhew, see Yeo and Thompson (1971).
2. For parallel defences of an appreciation see 'The Defence of Meaning' (Cohen, 1971: Introduction) and Young (1969). For comments on the subjective viewpoint in the context of the Becker-Gouldner debate, see Taylor and Walton (1970).
3. For an important general argument about these convergences, see Horowitz and Liebowitz (1968) and a specific application to the study of violence, Cohen (1969 and 1971).
4. Thus, our criticisms of criminology might be something like those of industrial sociologists writing about a specific institution such as the Human Relations school – see, for example, Brown (1967).
5. The accounts of Goring's work I am mainly relying upon are those by Mannheim (1965: 227-8) and Driver (1960).
6. This is not to say that such bodies ultimately get different treatment from the political structure. Compare President Nixon's reaction to the Report of the Commission on Obscenity and Pornography with the Home Office's reaction to the 'Wootton Report' on cannabis when both came up with the 'wrong' results.
7. For fuller accounts of Mannheim's work see Chorley (1970), Grygier et al. (1965) and Morris (1966).
8. See, for example, the collections of papers published in connexion with the centenary of the Howard League for Penal Reform (Klare 1966; Klare and Haxby 1967).
9. Some indication of his approach to the subject is given in his note in the Twentieth Anniversary Number of the *BJC*. See Mannheim (1970).
10. When it added a group of assistant editors, one was a clinical psychologist, one a psychiatrist, one a lawyer and one a sociologist.
11. See Wootton (1959: 69) for a misuse of the concept of anomie.

12 Such as the Gibson Maze Test; the Body Sway Test (most of the boys apparently hardly swayed at all, while others found this test unpleasant and anxiety provoking); and the Tapping Test (tapping a pencil on a blank piece of paper for 10 seconds; this apparently reveals extra-punitive personality types and it could be expected that 'boys with delinquent personalities would tend to scatter their dots more widely'. Sceptics will note that the scores did reveal a slight but significant positive correlation with bad conduct as rated by teachers: $r = 0.17$).
13 For a convincing treatment of this explanation as a form of demonism, see Sarbin and Miller (1970).
14 The classic documentation is still to be found in C. Wright Mills (1945).
15 I am relying on three versions of the report of this survey: one is circulated by its author, M. P. Carter, to members of the BSA in 1967, a longer version reproduced by the SSRC at about the same time and a re-draft of this a year later. Another version is in preparation. See also Carter (1968).
16 I would strongly recommend Horowitz's whole essay 'The Sociology of Social Problems: A Study in the Americanization of Ideas' (Horowitz 1969: 80–100), particularly the section entitled 'The metaphysical predispositions of sociologists of social problems'. This is not a simple argument in favour of 'importance'; he points to the considerable dangers of applied sociology and the central contradictions involved in the 'God-like' role of sociologists as therapist. I need hardly add that much deviance research is quite unimportant anyway, compared to, say, the sociology of development.

References

ANDERSON, P. 1968. Components of the National Culture. *New Left Review* 50: 3–57.
BECKER, H. S. (ed.) 1964. *The Other Side: Perspectives on Deviance*. New York: Crowell Collier Macmillan.
—— 1967. Whose Side Are We On? *Social Problems* 14: 239–47.
BOTTOMORE, T. 1971. Has Sociology a Future? *New York Review of Books* 16 (4): 37–40.
BROWN, R. K. 1967. Research and Consultancy in Industrial Enterprises: A Review of the Contribution of the Tavistock Institute of Human Relations to the Development of Industrial Sociology. *Sociology* 1: 33–60.
CARSON, W. G. & WILES, P. (eds.) 1971. *Crime and Delinquency in Britain: Sociological Readings*. London: Robinson.

CARTE, G. E. 1969. Dialogue with Jerome H. Skolnick. *Issues in Criminology* **4**: 109–22.
CARTER, M. P. 1968. Report on a Survey of Sociological Research in Britain. *Sociological Review* **16**: 5–40.
CHORLEY, Rt Hon. Lord. 1970. Hermann Mannheim: A Biographical Appreciation. *British Journal of Criminology* **10**: 324–47.
COHEN, S. 1969. Ideological and Criminal Violence: Convergences in Labels or Behaviour? Paper given at British Sociological Association Conference (Teachers' Section).
—— (ed.) 1971. *Images of Deviance*. Harmondsworth: Penguin.
—— 1971. Directions for Research on Adolescent Group Violence and Vandalism. *British Journal of Criminology*: 319–40.
CRESSEY, D. R. 1954. The Differential Association Theory and Compulsive Crimes. *Journal of Criminal Law, Criminology and Police Science* **45**: 29–40.
—— 1962. Role Theory, Differential Association and Compulsive Crimes. In A. Rose (ed.) *Human Behaviour and Social Processes: An Interactionist Approach*. London: Routledge and Kegan Paul.
CROFT, J. 1965. Hermann Mannheim – A Biographical Note. In T. Grygier *et al.* (eds.) *Criminology in Transition: Essays in Honour of Hermann Mannheim*. London: Tavistock Publications.
DEBRO, J. 1970. Dialogue with Howard S. Becker. *Issues in Criminology* **5**: 159–79.
DOUGLAS, J. D. (ed.) 1970. *The Impact of Sociology: Readings in the Social Sciences*. New York: Appleton Century Crofts.
DRIVER, E. D. 1960. Charles B. Goring. In H. Mannheim (ed.) *Pioneers in Criminology*. London: Stevens.
GIBBENS, T. C. N. 1970. *Identification of Key Problems of Criminological Research*. Strasbourg: Council of Europe.
GLOVER, E. 1970. 1950–1970 – Retrospects and Reflections. *British Journal of Criminology* **10**: 313–16.
GOFFMAN, E. 1959. *The Presentation of Self in Everyday Life*. New York: Doubleday Anchor.
GOULDNER, A. 1968. The Sociologist as Partisan: Sociology and the Welfare States. *American Sociologist* **3**: 103–16.
GORING, C. 1913. *The English Convict*. London: HMSO.
GRYGIER, T. J. H., JONES, H. & SPENCER, J. C. (eds.) 1965. *Criminology in Transition: Essays in Honour of Hermann Mannheim*. London: Tavistock Publications.
HALLORAN, J. D. *et al.* 1970. *Television and Delinquency*. Leicester: Leicester University Press.
HOME OFFICE RESEARCH UNIT AND STATISTICAL DIVISION. 1969. Summary of Research and of Research Supported by Grants.

HOOD, R. & SPARKS, R. 1970. *Key Issues in Criminology*. London: Weidenfeld & Nicolson.

HOROWITZ, I. L. 1969. *Professing Sociology: Studies in the Life Cycle of Social Science*. Chicago: Aldine.

HOROWITZ, I. L. & LIEBOWITZ, M. 1968. Social Deviance and Political Marginality: Toward a Redefinition of the Relationship Between Sociology and Politics. *Social Problems* **15**: 280–96.

JONES, H. 1965. *Crime and the Penal System*. London: University Tutorial Press.

KLARE, H. J. (ed.) 1966. *Changing Concepts of Crime and Its Treatment*. Oxford: Pergamon.

KLARE, H. J. & HAXBY, D. (eds.) 1967. *Frontiers of Criminology*. Oxford: Pergamon.

KRAUSZ, E. 1969. *Sociology in Britain: A Survey of Research*. London: Batsford.

LEMERT, E. M. 1967. *Human Deviance, Social Problems and Social Control*. Englewood Cliffs, N.J.: Prentice Hall.

MANNHEIM, H. 1965. *Comparative Criminology*. London: Routledge and Kegan Paul.

—— 1970. 1950–1970: Retrospects and Reflections. *British Journal of Criminology* **10**: 317–20.

MATZA, D. 1964. *Delinquency and Drift*. New York: Wiley.

—— 1969. *Becoming Deviant*. Englewood Cliffs, N.J.: Prentice Hall.

MILLS, C. WRIGHT 1945. The Professional Ideology of Social Pathologists. *American Journal of Sociology* **49**: 165–80.

MORRIS, T. P. 1957. *The Criminal Area: A Study in Social Ecology*. London: Routledge & Kegan Paul.

—— 1965. The Sociology of the Prison. In T. Grygier *et al.* (eds.) *Criminology in Transition*. London: Tavistock Publications.

—— 1966. Comparative Criminology: A Text Book. *Howard Journal* **XII**: 61–4.

NUTTAL, J. 1968. *Bomb Culture*. London: MacGibbon and Kee.

POLSKY, N. 1967. Research Method, Morality and Criminology. In *Hustlers, Beats and Others*. Chicago: Aldine.

RADZINOWICZ, L. 1962. *In Search of Criminology*. London: Heinemann.

—— 1966. *Ideology and Crime: A Study of Crime in its Social and Historical Context*. London: Heinemann.

SARBIN, T. R. & MILLER, J. E. 1970. Demonism Revisited: The XYY Chromosomal Anomaly. *Issues in Criminology* **5**: 195–207.

SOCIAL SCIENCE RESEARCH COUNCIL. 1968. Review of Research in Sociology. Unpublished.

TAYLOR, I. & WALTON, P. 1970. Values in Deviancy Theory and Society. *British Journal of Sociology* **21**: 362–74.

WALKER, N. 1965. *Crime and Punishment in Britain.* Edinburgh: Edinburgh University Press.
WEST, D. J. 1967. *The Young Offender.* Harmondsworth: Penguin.
—— 1969. *Present Conduct and Future Delinquency.* London: Heinemann.
WOOTTON, B. 1959. *Social Science and Social Pathology.* London: Allen and Unwin.
WRIGHT, M. 1970. Twenty Years of the British Journal of Delinquency/Criminology. *British Journal of Criminology* **10**: 372–82.
YEO, E. & THOMPSON, E. P. 1971. *The Unknown Mayhew.* London: Merlin Press.
YOUNG, J. 1969. The Zookeepers of Deviancy. *Anarchy* **98**: 101–8.

[6]
How Can We Balance Justice, Guilt and Tolerance?

In the first of three articles **Stanley Cohen** *asks why criminologists shun the question: What is to be done?*

These articles deal – in one way or another – with the relationship between a body of ideas (criminology), the supposed object of these ideas (crime), and the way society deals with this object (crime control policy). This set of relationships are, and always have been, tenuous.

Hannah Arendt once argued that thinking only ceases to be politically marginal when special emergencies arise. Then, thinkers are drawn out of hiding and become relevant. Criminologists – old or new, conservative or radical – have always assigned to themselves a more ambitious role than this.

They have believed that by dealing with something as intrinsically messy as crime, they have retained contact with a reality somehow "more real" than that portrayed in other areas of social science. In the first of these articles, I want to suggest that in one sphere at least – the connected issues of morality, guilt, justice and responsibility – this belief is illusory and that many current theories have drifted too far from public conceptions of crime.

Of course, the strength of the "new" or "radical" criminologies which developed in Britain and America in the mid-sixties, lay precisely in their refusal to be bound by the orthodoxies of official or public definitions. What was being attacked was a powerful form of *absolutism*: the theoretical notion that the definition of crime was morally fixed and unquestionable, and the political notion that the role of the "expert" was to advise the state in its war against crime by identifying the causes and cures of criminality. The basic rationale for this attack remains – but something went wrong in the way it became elaborated.

I find an illuminating (if pretentious) historical parallel to what went wrong in Isaiah Berlin's wonderfully sympathetic studies of the 19th century Russian intelligentsia. These thinkers were torn between a suspicion of absolutism – and a yearning to discover another absolute, monolithic idea. Many drifted towards new forms of absolutism, because of what Berlin describes as a Russian habit of taking ideas to their extreme, even absurd conclusions – as if not to do so, was a sign of moral cowardice.

In criminology, one of the potentially extreme doctrines to emerge in those heady years of the mid-sixties – that period of cultural relativism, in which doing your own thing became elevated into a moral virtue – was the notion of "appreciation." This doctrine suggested – with a considerable theoretical and methodological soundness that still applies – that the adoption of conventional moral positions systematically interferes with our ability to comprehend crime and deviance. Consequently, such judgments (these people have done bad things, and deserve to be punished for them) should be suspended. This would result not only in richer sociological understanding, but also a political bonus: a challenge to the dominant value system – particularly the "hierarchy of credibility" which accepts only the definition of the powerful.

To most of us, the problems, even absurdities of carrying the conventional doctrine to its extreme were evident enough – evident at least in the world of seminar rooms and journals which we inhabited. But they could not be readily translated into the public world of social policy.

If – so one of the public's questions ran – deviants were not pathological beings driven by forces beyond their control, then surely as rational, responsible beings they should be punished *more* severely? Ah no, that's not *quite* what we meant.

And when we talked about being on the side of the deviant, did this mean we were actually in favour of what he did? Here, our answers were really tortuous. Faced with behaviour like vandalism, mugging or football hooliganism, which we couldn't openly approve (in the sense of advocating tolerance or non-punishment), then our main message was that actually there was much *less* of this than the public thought (because of moral panics, selective perception, stereotyping, scapegoating and suchlike). Simultaneously, of course, to other audiences, we welcomed such behaviour, and pointed to the evidence which showed that if society didn't radically change, then indeed the public's fears would materialise and more of the behaviour occur.

With other forms of deviance easier to support openly within the liberal consensus – abortion, the gay movement, smoking dope – we happily advocated tolerance, even in public. And this time we would say that there was not less, but far far *more* of such behaviour than anyone could even imagine through their stereotypes. Confusion indeed.

In the undiluted pre-19th century classical doctrine – which said that criminals are responsible for their actions, and should be punished accordingly – there was little room for such confusion. The moral fit between theories of crime and models of crime control was reasonably close. But then the 19th century positivists introduced the doctrine of determinism – that criminals were forced into crime for reasons beyond their control and should be rehabilitated accordingly. The fit between image and policy now became extremely uneven.

Theoretically, things looked tidy enough. But in the world of policy, all that happened was that different and incompatible sets of rhetoric were used simultaneously in the same courts, agencies and institutions. Running around the fields of a borstal became both "treatment" and "punishment."

A massive exposure of the con job in criminological positivism – paralleled by the anti-psychiatry movement and the Illich-inspired attack on medicine – then took place. One of the ostensible points of this exercise was to defrock the spurious expertise of professionals and technologists; to lay bare the morality underneath their scientific pretentions. Deviance was to be revealed as a moral matter, a matter about what sort of society we want.

But the potential effect of this defrocking and undermining was lost, because the implicit substitute – the Emperor under the tacky clothes of positivism – was revealed not in his full moral nakedness, but in his new garb of appreciation. For a time the deviant was the mismanaged, stigmatised, labelled underdog and then – with a bewildering switch – he became the "fully social," rational, crypto-political hero.

A peculiar moral agenda – peculiar, because it was never acknowledged as such – was constructed. Towards most forms of deviance, an exceedingly low-minded moral nihilism seemed the order of the day among academic criminologists. Either moral judgments were no business of ours or else, when appropriate, we went along with the well-charted J. S. Mill/Wolfenden argument that the interfering states should never criminalise actions where there was neither victim nor harm.

But towards other forms of deviance, the crimes of the powerful, a high-minded moral absolutism prevailed. These crimes were condemned with puritanical zeal. Appreciative studies of polluters, exploiters, manipulators, frauds (all highly morally loaded words), were not, to my knowledge, ever advocated. And who today would dare to embark on an "appreciative" study of rapists in the face of the feminist-inspired consensus that these are sub-human monsters who should be quietly garotted?

How volatile this agenda has turned out to be, also. Pornography, studied only a few years ago through the libertarian lens of "crimes without victims," is now denounced not just by the old enemies from the right – the Mary Whitehouse lobby – but by the left and by radical feminists, who see in it the exploitation of women.

In truth, the new moral nihilism was not only volatile, but largely bogus. Taking a recognisable stance against conservative values, the theories would not admit to any substitute beyond a vague and quite inconsistent underdog sympathy. Replacing this vagueness by marxism – the direction taken by one influential strand in British criminology – hardly helped. It only disguised the moral agenda of criminology under a new form of absolutism. It refused, anyway, to occupy the terrain of middle-range political questions, such as *what is to be done?*

Now, of course, I am caricaturing all this imagery. It was always presented with many reservations, and it has since been modified. But its echoes remain – and are partly responsible for criminologists' inability to mount a serious alternative to dominant conservative crime-control policies.

Such policies are just as firmly entrenched as ever. So, too (more amazingly), are the illusions of conventional, positivist criminology. The latter retains its reputation for combining scientific neutrality with humanitarianism. And it retains its credibility as a science, despite the fact that in terms of its success in explaining, identifying or treating criminals, it should long ago have been relegated to the status of alchemy, astrology or phrenology.

The survival of conventional criminology cannot be explained in pragmatic terms alone. It has simply not produced theories or policies which "work". But, at least, it has kept itself within the frame of conventional political debate. By criticising the very ground rules of that debate, the new theories slipped right out of this frame. It would be consistent (from a revolutionary, rather than reformist position) to argue that we should continue staying out in the cold. But we wanted it both ways: to be devastatingly critical, *and* to intervene in the messy world of crime control.

There are, perhaps, some strategies for having it both ways. One would be to translate our elegant pirouettes about the ideas of freedom and determinism into the old questions which have always been at the heart of crime-control politics: what actions should the state punish, and how should blame be allocated to some actors?

Social scientists often complain about not being understood by their audience. Our problem was that we never quite understood what our audience made of us. The influential American theorist, David Matza, tells a revealing story. After publishing *Delinquency and Drift*, his critique of positivism in the juvenile court, he received enthusiastic letters from the likes of police chiefs. At last, they said, someone is coming out clearly in favour of tough punishment, and against soft liberal treatment.

We never understood the point of such stories – mainly because we had never really abandoned either underdog sympathy, or deterministic theories, in the first place. The constant sociological impulse is to shift accountability for crime onto higher and higher levels of the social structure. Not just family, school, neighbourhood, social class, but the whole society is to blame. And final irony: the very system of social control itself is fatefully implicated in the causal path to crime.

Criminals started looking like very peculiar creatures, indeed. They made rational choices in the morning, drifted into crime at lunchtime, were brutalised by the social structure in the afternoon, and then faded away in the dusk as mere shadows created by the mass media.

Leaving aside any internal theoretical inconsistencies in all this, the point is that causal theories, however aesthetically pleasing or even morally worthy, have to be translated into the real social settings in which blame is allocated. Before I go on to look at some promising developments which have – at last – moved in this direction, let me illustrate the whole problem with the unusual but instructive case of "war crime."

Even the most cursory examination of this subject shows how problematic are the connections between theories ("they were just carrying out orders," "they were part of the system") and assessments of responsibility, culpability, blameworthiness or guilt. One of the best recent examples of the mess which we can get into because of not thinking through these problems, is the reaction of part of the American left to the series of trials of Calley, Medina and others for their alleged part in the My Lai massacres in Vietnam.

Mary McCarthy's superb account of Medina's trial should be required reading for criminologists. Her argument is that the deliberate massacre of over a hundred innocent villagers at My Lai was morally different – and seen to be so – from, on the one hand, the "ordinary" prosecution of the war and, on the other, the haphazard rapes and killings practised by ordinary soldiers. The earlier attempts by President Nixon and the American right to whitewash Calley coincided with attempts by the left to denounce the Calley prosecutions as "scapegoating" (Calley was innocent, the army was the real criminal). Though, by most accounts, Medina (Calley's company commander) knew pretty well what was happening in the village, it was argued that it was liberal hypocrisy to blame such intermediary figures.

Mary McCarthy's point is that, from the North Vietnamese and Vietcong positions, it did not follow that if Lyndon Johnson and General Westmoreland were war criminals, then Calley, Medina and others directly responsible for the massacre were "choiceless victims of the war machine." The North Vietnamese could draw a distinction between the ordinary soldier shooting at troops, and an infantry company butchering women, old men and children.

Some of the left and the counter-culture in America not only would not concede this distinction, but also seemed to hold to a theory which denied all freedom of action. The notion was that those like Calley were pawns moved around from birth by "the system."

But if Calley's social conditioning left him no option as to whether to "open up" or not on the people of My Lai, how did other (presumably similarly conditioned) ordinary soldiers keep their rifles to the ground? And how did others express disbelief and shock and eventually denounce the massacre to the authorities?

Without some notion of individual responsibility, no credit of blame could be assigned to anybody. Masochistic indictments of the whole culture of being "guilty" – everyone is a war criminal – sound virtuous, but are politically sterile. They helped in producing the visibly devastating result that Mary McCarthy described: "Medina and Henderson off the hook, Calley's sentence reduced, others not tried, several identified and unidentified mass murderers welcomed back into the population. Now any member of the armed forces in Indochina can, if he so desires, slaughter a reasonable number of babies, confident that the public will acquit him, (a) because they support the war or (b) because they don't."

The position is, perhaps, more complicated than she allows in that it should be possible to theorise about the "ultimate" or "real" cause of the massacre – and still hold that individual participants exercised some real choices at a particular moment. I have, nevertheless, singled out this case because there are some parallels between the dissidents who championed Calley and Medina against the army, and criminologists who champion "their" criminals against society.

Few, if any, areas in the social sciences have to confront problems like these. We criminologists are doomed by our subject matter to steer carefully away from being police informers only to become amoral hipsters; from being sociologists to being ideologues, and then back again. But the last few years have seen some interesting responses to these problems.

One line has been to pay close attention to how theories are negotiated in day-to-day social-control settings. Probation officer records and social inquiry reports, for example, might be studied as "accounting systems." They provide images of the delinquent (as "deprived," "disturbed" or "depraved"), which are used to justify particular control decisions. But as social workers know, their actual model of intervention usually reverses the positivist sequence of diagnosis-then-treatment. The *first* stage is to decide on the best treatment (and by "best" I mean the "most just"). The reports and case histories are constructed accordingly.

This leads to another crucial new debate – or rather the oldest of debates under a new guise. This is the "back to justice" movement – whose most recent statement (Andrew von Hirsh's *Doing Justice*) I reviewed in NEW SOCIETY last year (16 February 1978) as marking a major milestone in criminal justice policy. It represents a profound liberal disenchantment with the treatment ideal, and the whole baggage of progressive 20th century penology.

The state should take a minimalist position: a commitment to do less harm, rather than more good. Sentencing should be justified not by prevention, deterrence, protection, or – least of all – rehabilitation, but by the notion that certain things are wrong and deserve to be punished. Past action only, and not predicted future action, should be the criterion.

There are considerable flaws in this "just deserts" model. Not the least of these is the illusion that justice can be achieved by a penal system which in fact helps maintain an unjust, unfair social order. But at least this approach is a convenient springboard for confronting policy questions which had earlier been submerged.

The final debate I would like to mention is the revival of interest in the question of tolerance. The claim – not always well supported – that capitalism as such causes crime, leads on to the axiom that it is at least possible to conceive of a crime-free society. For some, this utopia is to be found (rather unconvincingly) under conditions of "socialist legality." But the idea at least connects criminology with general social and political theory about what a good society might look like.

It also leads to a consideration of middle-range social-control alternatives: de-centralised community schemes, such as factory and community courts; the dispute and conciliation mechanisms used in non-western societies; the control systems in "miniature societies" like communes.

Such models have their problems, too – and in my next article I look at the particular illusions of the community control movement. But whichever direction the debates on justice and tolerance take, they are at least reconnecting criminology with its subject matter.

In some fashionable circles – notably Althusserian and Left Bank – it is precisely this reconnection which is suspect. The more congruent a discipline becomes with society's definitions of its subject, the more it degenerates into mere ideology.

But this position traps radical criminologies in their own pretentions. They originally emerged because the spurious scientific claims of conventional criminology had served to de-politicise crime, to cut it off from the study of the state. They can hardly now allow themselves to drift away from these very same political and common-sense considerations.

[7]
Community Control – a New Utopia

In his second article on penal policy, **Professor Cohen** *underlines the sceptical lessons that history should teach all optimists.*

Some four years ago in NEW SOCIETY I attempted to predict what the inside of our prison system will look like, given the apparent consensus in most western societies that imprisonment should only be used as a punishment of last resort ("Human warehouses: the future of our prisons?", 14 November 1974). Here, I want to speculate on what this same development might be leading to *outside* the walls of the prison and juvenile institution. What are the implications of the new ideology of "community treatment" or "community control" for crime and delinquency?

We need to start from some historical base. Our current system of deviancy control originated in those great transformations which took place at the end of the 18th and the beginning of the 19th centuries. A centralised state apparatus was developed to control crime and take care of people in need of help. The deviants and dependants were segregated into "asylums" – mental hospitals, prisons, reformatories and other such closed, purpose-built institutions, for treatment and punishment.

The most extraordinary of these features to explain is the growth of the prison and its subsequent survival, despite one and a half centuries of failure. "Failure" in the sense that if a factory regularly produced some 40 to 60 per cent of products that didn't work, then it would surely be closed. But prisons with the same failure rate (measured by re-conviction) still keep going.

Of course, prisons – like the network of community control which is now supposed to be replacing them – are not evaluated in these terms. Social control is an enterprise which largely justifies itself. "Success" is not the object of the exercise. As Foucault argues about the foundation of the late 18th century prison system – when the object of punishment was transferred from the body to the mind – the point of the system is to classify, order, regulate, compartmentalise.

The new network of social control is doing little more than this, either. It is reproducing outside the walls of the prison those astonishingly complicated systems of classification – the atlases of vice – which were erected within the walls of the 19th century penitentiaries.

These historical continuities have been lost in the drama of what *appears* to be a reversal of the great victories of incarceration, won nearly 200 years ago. At the end of the 18th century, asylums and prisons were places of the *last* resort. By the mid-19th century they became places of the *first* resort, the preferred solution to problems of deviancy and dependency. By the end of the 1960s, they looked like once again becoming places of the *last* resort. The extraordinary notion of abolition, rather than mere reform, became common talk. With varying degrees of enthusiasm and actual measurable consequences, officials in Britain, the United States and some western European countries, became committed to the policy labelled "de-carceration": the state-sponsored closing down of asylums, prisons and reformatories.

This apparent reversal of the great incarcerations of the 19th century was hailed as the beginning of a golden age – a form of utopianism whose ironies cannot escape anyone with an eye on history. The millenial expectations aroused by the prospect of abolishing prison are the same as those which greeted its adoption.

The irony goes further. For just at the historical moment when every commonplace critique of "technological," "post-industrial" or "mass" society mourns the irreplaceable loss of the traditional community, so a new mode of deviancy control is advocated which depends on this same lost community being present. The new movement is profoundly romantic. The ideal form of social control has to reproduce the features of a pre-industrial village.

This arcadian vision is backed up by two sets of pragmatic assumptions, each of which is ritualistically stated. The first set is seen either as a matter of common sense, "what everybody knows" or the irrefutable result of empirical research: (a) prisons and juvenile institutions are (in the weak version) simply ineffective: they neither successfully deter nor rehabilitate (in the strong version, they actually make things worse by strengthening criminal commitment); (b) community alternatives are much less costly; and (c) they are more humane than any institution can be: prisons are cruel, brutalising and beyond reform. Their time has come. Therefore: community alternatives "must obviously be better."

Some custodial and non-custodial sentences for juveniles, 1966–77

	1967	1971	1972	1973	1974	1975	1976	1977
imprisonment	1,864	1,202	1,161	1,041	1,148	1,484	1,756	2,239
detention centre	5,789	8,109	8,151	7,087	8,414	8,502	8,945	9,404
borstal	896	1,152	995	803	741	717	711	721
supervision order	–	18,025	17,111	18,038	20,226	18,877	17,561	17,990
care order	–	7,326	6,953	7,456	8,077	7,473	6,336	5,875
community service order	–	–	–	226	462	1,313	3,638	4,443
Total	8,549	35,814	34,371	34,651	39,068	38,366	38,947	40,672

The second set of assumptions appeals to a number of sociological and political beliefs which are not as self-evident as the previous set, but is taken by the believer to be just as well-established: (a) theories of stigma and labelling have demonstrated that the further the deviant is processed into the system, the harder it is to return him to normal life – "therefore" measures designed to minimise penetration into the formal system and keep the deviant in the community as long as possible are desirable; (b) the causes of most forms of deviance are in society (family, community, school, economic system) – "therefore" prevention and cure must lie in the community and not in artificially created agencies constructed on a model of individual intervention; (c) liberal measures, such as reformatories, the juvenile court and the whole rehabilitative model are politically suspect, whatever the benevolent motives behind them. The state should be committed to be doing less harm rather than more good – "therefore" policies such as decriminalisation, diversion and de-carceration should be supported.

It is the last of these beliefs which must be used to scrutinise them all. Why should community control itself not be subjected to the very same suspicion about benevolent reform? A large dose of such scepticism should lead us to the following doubts:

1. It is by no means clear that de-carceration has been taking place as rapidly as the ideology would have us believe. The establishment of various supposed alternatives to incarceration does not necessarily decrease imprisonment rates, nor have beneficial effects on the rest of the system.
2. It has not been established that any community alternative is more effective in reducing crime (through preventing recidivism) than traditional imprisonment.
3. Nor are these new methods always dramatically cheaper.
4. The humanitarian rationale for the move from imprisonment may be unfounded in two entirely opposite ways. Either it may indeed lead to something like a non-interventionist policy – and this ends up as a form of benign neglect, with groups like the old, the mentally ill, the inadequate dumped back into communities unable to look after them. For fiscal and other pragmatic reasons welfare state services are withdrawn from those who need them most. Or alternatively – the more likely route for criminals and delinquents – new and more extensive forms of intervention result. These may be hard to distinguish from the old institutions and may produce in the community the very practices they were designed to replace.

I want to expand on these problems of community control under three headings: *blurring, widening* and *masking.*

Blurring

Blurring refers to the increasing invisibility of the boundaries of the social control apparatus. The segregated and insulated institution made the boundaries of control obvious enough. Whether prisons were built in the middle of cities, out in the remote countryside or on deserted islands, they had clear spatial boundaries which were reinforced by ceremonies of social exclusion, such as the criminal trial. Those outside could wonder what went on behind the walls; those inside could think about the "outside world." Inside/outside, guilty/innocent, freedom/captivity, imprisoned/released, voluntary/coercive, formal/informal: these distinctions made more or less sense.

In today's world of community control, such boundaries are no longer as clear. There is, we are told, a "correctional continuum" or a "correctional spectrum": criminals and delinquents may be found anywhere in these spaces. So fine – and, at the same time, so indistinct – are the graduations along the continuum that it is by no means easy to know where the prison ends, and the community begins, or why anybody is to be found at any particular point.

So tricky has the community/prison boundary become, for example, that criminologists are actually spending a great deal of time, money and ingenuity in the ludicrous task of devising quantitative scales to measure how a new programme fits the "institutionalisation-normalisation continuum."

But, alas, these are not just untidy loose ends which scientific research will one day tie up. The ideology of the new movement quite deliberately and explicitly demands that boundaries should not be made too clear. The metaphor of "crumbling walls" implies a vague open space.

New diversion agencies become attached to the court, without supposedly being part of the legal system. Very open prisons become indistinguishable from secure "community correctional centres." Intermediate treatment is supposed to be somewhere between sending a child away from home and leaving him in his normal home environment.

The same treatment is used for those who have actually committed an offence and those who are thought "at risk" of committing an offence. A halfway house (or "residential treatment centre" or "re-integration residence") may be halfway *in* – for those too serious to be left at home, but not serious enough for the institution and hence a form of "diversion" – or halfway *out* for those who can be released from the institution but are not yet "ready" for the open community, hence a form of "aftercare." To confuse the matter even further, the same centre is sometimes used for both these purposes, with different rules for the half-way in and the half-way out inmates.

We are seeing, then, not just a proliferation of agencies and services, finely calibrated in terms of their degree of coercion, intrusion or unpleasantness. The uncertainties and blurrings are more profound than this and perhaps beckon to a future where it will be impossible to determine who is emeshed in the social control machine at any one time.

Widening

The second process – *widening* – is even more at variance with its stated rationale. On the surface, one of the ideological thrusts behind the new movements towards "community," "alternatives" and "diversion" was that the state should do less, rather than more. It is ironical then, that the major results of the new network of social control have been to increase, rather than decrease, the amount of intervention directed at many groups of offenders; and to increase, rather than decrease, the total number of offenders who get into the system in the first place.

In other words, "alternatives" become not alternatives at all, but new programmes which supplement the existing system or else expand the system by attracting new populations – the net of social control is widened. Or else something like "diversion" becomes not movement out of the system, but movement into a programme in another part of the system. The mesh of social control is thinned.

Neither of these possible effects is easy to demonstrate. But it is already quite clear that despite the proliferation of "alternatives," the overall rates of incarceration in Britain and America – particularly of juveniles – are not declining as rapidly as one might expect. As one devastating American assessment of national statistics said: "In general, as the number of community-based facilities increases, the total number of youths incarcerated increases."

One way this happens is that the new alternatives are on the whole not being used for juveniles who are at the *deep end* of the system – i.e., those who definitely would have been sent to institutions before. The strategy rather is being used for *shallow end offenders* – i.e. minor or first offenders, whose chances of receiving a custodial sentence would have been slight.

The exact proportions of these types are difficult to estimate. One English study of community service orders shows that only half of the offenders sent would otherwise have received custodial sentences. Leaving aside the question of the exact effects on the rest of the system, there is little doubt that a substantial number of those in the new programmes will receive a degree of intervention higher than under previous non-custodial options like fines, conditional discharge or ordinary probation. The paradox is that the more benign, attractive and "successful" the programme is defined, the more it will be used.

Something similar happens with so-called diversion. The theory here is to restrict the full weight of the law to more serious offences – and either to eliminate or substantially minimise penetration for all others by screening them right out of the system.

Of course, such screening has always existed. Police discretion has traditionally been widely used (especially for juveniles) to "divert" offenders – either by simply dropping charges, by cautioning or informally reprimanding, or else by referral to social service agencies. What has now happened is that many of these discretionary and screening powers have been formalised, extended and organised into programmes.

The effect has been quite the reverse of diversion theory. New populations are brought into the system who would otherwise not have been processed at all, or would have been placed on traditional options like probation. Whereas the police used to have two options – screen right out (the route for by far the *majority* of encounters) or process formally – they now have the third option of diversion into a programme. Diversion can then be used as an alternative to screening (doing nothing), and not an alternative to processing.

The proportions so selected will vary. Research on such schemes as police juvenile liaison shows that something like a half of the referrals are there as an alternative to screening. There are some genuine forms of diversion. But in more cases diversion takes place *into* the system rather than *from* the system. Hence there is more intervention.

Masking

The final process I want to list – *masking* – concerns the way in which the benevolently intentioned move to the community may sometimes disguise the intrusiveness of the new programmes. In the first place, the contrast between the brutality of the institution and the alleged humanitarianism of the community programme is wholly spurious if the one is not actually an alternative to the other. Sometimes, offenders will be exposed to both. Even when this does not happen, some community schemes – like the much vaunted Californian Community Treatment project – may use a degree of more or less traditional custody. When clients fail to comply with the programme, they may be locked up. And because the new programmes often have low visibility or accountability, and are organised along welfare or psychiatric rather than legal principles, traditional legal protection disappears. Clients may only be accepted if they agree to plead guilty.

The more the alternative does take "deep-end" offenders, the more it will come to resemble the traditional institution. Some half-way houses, for example, and the community correctional centres now being set up in America, have rules about security, curfew, surveillance and treatment, which are just as oppressive than conventional prisons, or more so. Some community programmes are using a behavioural contracting model. Juveniles agree to perform certain tasks at home and school for financial rewards, or to avoid punishments like having their hair cut or being sent away. The humanitarianism of such programmes is by no means self-evident.

The expansion of control

These processes, then – *blurring, widening, masking* – point to some dangers in the new movement. To be aware of these dangers is not to defend the old system. Nor – even less – is it to argue that no reforms should ever be contemplated on the grounds that they will inevitably lead to disaster. This is a recipe for political nihilism, and there is no inexorable logic in society to support the assumption that things always get worse.

Undoubtedly, some programmes of community treatment or diversion are genuine alternatives, and in addition are more humane and less intrusive. Such programmes might indeed succeed in avoiding the harsh effects of early stigmatisation and brutalisation. And in addition, all these terrible-sounding "agents of social control" might be able to deploy vastly improved opportunities and resources to offer help and service to groups which need them.

These possibilities must not be ignored for a minute. Nor should the possibility that, from the delinquent or criminal's own subjective personal experience, these new programmes might indeed be preferable. And finally, many of these reforms are worth supporting as they expose the contradictions and absurdities in the old system.

But such encouraging possibilities should not lead to the type of naïve utopianism which obscures what social control is all about. And here the continuities rather than the discontinuities with the system which established the state control of crime two centuries ago, are striking.

The move to community entails merely more subtle calibrations of care, control, welfare, punishment and treatment. New categories and subcategories are being created under our eyes. All these wonderful new agencies and programmes are re-processing the same old group of deviants (with a few new ones thrown in). Each set of experts produces its own "scientific" knowledge: screening devices, treatment modalities and evaluation scales.

All this creates new categories, and the people to fill them. Where there was once talk about the "typical" prisoner, first offender or hardened recidivist, now there will be typical "clients" of half-way houses, or intermediate treatment programmes. These creatures are then fleshed out – in papers, research proposals, official reports – with sub-systems of knowledge and new vocabularies: locking up becomes "intensive placement"; dossiers become "anecdotal records"; rewards and punishments become "behavioural contracts," guards become "correctional counsellors" and prisons "residential centres" or "milieu therapy."

And "community" only exists for middle class, white, healthy, middle-aged socially powerful males. The rest have all been classified by them.

The concluding article will attempt to answer the question raised in the first article: What is to be done?

[8]
Some Modest and Unrealistic Proposals

In his concluding article, **Professor Cohen** *tackles the question, 'What is to be done?' He looks at the prison issue especially.*

In the first of my articles in this series on crime and its punishment (1 March), I drew attention to a certain fuzzy evasiveness about the way in which recent academic criminology relates to middle-range policy and political questions. NEW SOCIETY's editor called the bluff – and now I have to address myself to these same questions.

This is not too easy. Academic social scientists are always much better at debunking than at making "constructive" proposals – a task anyway which many (inside and outside our ranks) would judge to be quite improper. Certainly, we have a trained incapacity to even think at this level. And crime and punishment issues are particularly difficult to contemplate. Far from being marginal to the working of society, they are absolutely central. Conservative and reactionary interests have always understood this. But they have then reversed this understanding by advocating policies which assume that crime can be magically "cured," "controlled" or "solved."

It is especially tricky to know where to pitch any proposals. Most short-term reforms are easily absorbed and coopted into the system and end up by strengthening it; I illustrated this process in my second article (15 March) with reference to community control. On the other hand, the advocate of genuinely radical or revolutionary changes, changes that assume different values, is defined out of the system as an irrelevant or utopian. One also has to balance some degree of enthusiasm for what sounds like a "good idea," with the near-certain research knowledge that nothing works much better than anything else.

In any event, what I have tried to do is provide a *sample* of the sort of proposals which might follow from my previous articles. I have concentrated on issues surrounding adult rather than juvenile crime, and on the prison rather than any other form of punishment. Entire crucial areas such as law reform, police and the courts are ignored. In no way is this a package policy on crime and punishment, and I am claiming no more than a certain consistency with my earlier criticisms of other people's proposals.

The proposals are modest in the sense that (while not subscribing to the nihilistic nothing-can-be-done position) they recognise that reforms of the machinery of crime control are only of incidental relevance to the nature of the "crime problem." This truth cannot be repeated too often. Most of the proposals are also quite unrealistic in that their acceptance depends on broader shift of interests and priorities elsewhere in society.

Nevertheless, these are the sort of things we academics might say if our collective bluffs were called:

1. Repeating the obvious

Education is just as much a policy as mindless activism and sloganeering. The syllabus is not a particularly evangelical one; but politicians, those who run the crime control system, and the general public, need reminding of the few obvious criminological truths.

The main one I have already stated. Crime is rooted in the overall social system: political structure, economy and values. There is no evidence that the rate of crime rises or falls with such changes in penal policy as the intensity of punishment. The total crime picture remains much the same, whatever we may do to *individual* criminals.

There is an analogy from the history of medicine and public health. Such 19th century killer diseases as TB, whooping cough and scarlet fever were not conquered because of a dramatic advance in medical science. The decline of these diseases was a response more to overall social change than to any scientific discoveries. Similarly, rates of crime and delinquency are totally unaffected by "advances" in criminology, penology, forensic psychiatry or whatever. The whole notion of a "war against crime" is totally misconceived. Crime is an event. You can't fight events.

It is, of course, possible to isolate factors which have more or less something to do with conventionally defined crime and delinquency – overcrowding, slums, poverty, racism, deprivation, degrading education, unhappy family life. But the eradication of such conditions should not have to depend on their supposed association with crime. We find such conditions intolerable because of our values – not because this is a way of reducing crime. And we have to recognise also the "evil causes evil" fallacy. Crime is connected not just to these evils, but to society's most cherished values like individualism, competitiveness, masculinity.

2. Towards prison 'attrition'

I take for granted the need for an educational campaign about the futility, ineffectiveness and injustice of prisons for nearly everyone sent there. I also take it for granted that convincing people of all this is not the whole point. The system survives despite this knowledge, and this is why my proposals here are "unrealistic." But the eventual long-term objective of abolishing prisons is the only consistent aim. "Reforming the system" is as bizarre an objective as it would have sounded to 19th century opponents of slavery.

I would recommend that abolition follows a strategy like the *attrition model*, advocated in that excellent and practical publication, *Instead of Prisons*. This handbook for abolitionists was published two years ago by the New York group, PREAP (Prison Research Education Project). Attrition, as they say, means the rubbing away or wearing down by friction. It reflects the persistent and continuing strategy necessary to diminish the function and power of prisons in our society.

The first component in the model is a *total moratorium* on all new prison construction. No money at all should be spent on building any prison, under any name. I would also suggest that when the existing prisons have to be blown up or closed down, this should be done on the well established principle of "last in, first out."

That is, all the shiny model prisons built since the war should be phased out first.

Constructions like the £14 million Lancashire prison opened earlier this year should be converted (if it is indeed so much *unlike* a prison as its advocates claim) into a residential conference centre for social workers or Home Office civil servants. The splendid old early 19th century prisons – half-empty; cleaned up, and with decent facilities – will serve the diminished social function of imprisonment much better.

The second component in the attrition model is *de-carceration*. As many prisoners should be let out of their cells as possible. A "release timeline" might be needed – with something like 70 or 80 per cent going out immediately, and most of the rest phased out according to schemes worked out by PREAP and other such groups. The figure of "70–80 per cent immediately" is no figment of radical rhetoric. It is simply the sort of figure cited time and time again even by prison staff as the proportion of prisoners who could be released "safely."

If the public insists that prisons "protect" them, then this bluff must be called. There is no evidence at all that releasing proportions like this tomorrow will be dangerous, or would affect rates of re-conviction. It would make little difference either way. One often-quoted American study of 1,252 felons (serious criminals) released early because of a legal technicality, shows that two years later their reconviction rate (13.6 per cent) was actually *lower* than a group with similar records who had to serve out their full sentences (25 per cent).

The final element in the attrition model in *exarceration* – that is, stop putting people in prison in the first place. This, of course, is contingent on other policies, some of which I will consider later: the complete de-criminalisation of crimes without victims (abortion, drug taking, consensual sex, vagrancy); virtual abolition of pre-trial detention; the establishment of genuine alternatives; and – most critically – a major overhaul of how the courts allocate punishment, moving it towards the principle of justice (as outlined in my next proposal).

Prison sentences that remain will be allocated on a fixed-time basis. Then sentences will vary only in time, not in the nature of the regime. The hardness or softness of the regime will be entirely irrelevant. Institutions which try to be harder than the norm of decent containment, such as detention centres (which should have disappeared years ago on humanitarian and pragmatic grounds), should be demolished at once.

3. Giving priority to justice

I have severe reservations about the back-to-justice movement as a whole. Nevertheless, as a strategy towards reducing and questioning the legitimacy of imprisonment, the "just deserts" programme could be an expedient starting point for policy.

The principle of just (or commensurate) deserts demands this: the severity of a sentence should depend primarily on the seriousness of the crime, on what the offender *did*, rather than what the sentencer *expects* he will do if treated in a certain fashion.

All those criteria which look forward rather than backward should be secondary: individual deterrence, general deterrence, rehabilitation, protection of society. All these are to be subservient to the principle that punishment should be allocated in proportion to the perceived seriousness of the act.

There are other important elements in this new version of the (obviously very old) "just deserts" package. The standard requirements about culpability and liability will still have to be met, and limited variation is permitted for aggravating and mitigating circumstances. But sentencing disparities must be severely reduced – which means the introduction of standard penalties and a cutting down of discretion.

The model must also (and this distinguishes it from its conservative antecedents) be tied up with something like the attrition programme I outlined earlier. There must be a stringent limitation to the use of incarceration as a punishment. Only those convicted of the most serious offences will be so confined. Even then, the duration would be strictly rationed. Very few sentences would exceed, say, three years.

Some prisoners *may* be reformed as a result of imprisonment. But there is no evidence that any particular system can do this better than any other. More to the point, this contingent outcome should not be the reason for locking people up in the first place.

4. Negative reforms only

The attrition model is a long-term one, and the justice model will still leave some people in prison. Immediate short-term and humanitarian interests demand that something should be done meanwhile. So some prison reforms must be considered.

These reforms should, however, never be positive reforms – that is, reforms which strengthen the system. The history of such reforms has coincided with the history of prisons. The 19th century reform literature contains all the baggage of what is seen as today's progressive penology. Prison always ends up as the solution to its own problem.

Such reforms, then, as replacing old with new prisons; better training for prison staff; more professionals and experts; more money; more therapy; better diagnostic and classification techniques – should all be strongly resisted. In another context, all these measures would be seen as "neo-colonialism": disguised increase of power.

Only those reforms which have been variously termed "negative," "negating" or "abolishing" should be implemented. These will satisfy the humanitarian criterion, because genuine humane reforms will not strengthen the prison bureaucracy. And at the same time they should also be reforms which unmask or unveil the system's attempt to hide its true nature.

Two examples of such humane and negating reforms might be the ending of all prison secrecy and censorship, and the complete banning of any sort of drug treatment in prison. A more complete package would include: (obviously) a vast reduction in the length of sentences; and reasonable educational, medical, welfare, psychiatric, vocational and other such services, completely independent of the prison, with prisoners free to take advantage of them if they desire, with no coercion attached, and no connection made with the length of time served. A crucial negating reform would be the complete abolition of the parole system or anything like it.

5. Restraining the few

Those of us who have spent many years talking about prisons to general audiences, refer among ourselves to the one question that *always* comes up, as "What about Jack the Ripper?" What is to be done about the "few" that are too "dangerous" to be let out of prison? In the absence of the death penalty, it would be naïve not to recognise that there will be some criminals for whom nothing other than long-term imprisonment is conceivable. But, before leaving things at this point, let us address a few myths.

A myth – as the philosopher, Gilbert Ryle, reminds us – is, "of course, not a fairy story. It is the presentation of facts which belong in one category, in the idioms belonging to another. To explode a myth is accordingly not to deny the facts but to re-allocate them." Some facts that need re-allocating are these: violent or predatory street crime is only a very small proportion of the total crime picture; the amount of such crime is greatly exaggerated by the media and by law and order campaigns; there are crimes such as drunken driving which are just as physically harmful as conventionally defined violent crime.

This is *not* to deny the fact (and, in some instances, real increase) of armed robbery, rape, assault, mugging; or the fact that many people are unhappy, devastated, bereaved, frightened or insecure because of (or in anticipation of) these crimes.

It is a myth to think that *individuals* can be accurately or reliably classified as "dangerous" or "not dangerous." Their *acts* can certainly be classified in this way – and, I believe, the debate about the "few" should concentrate on defining as specifically as possible the nature of the offences (not offenders) which might call for a policy of restraint for a period of time.

Any other policy would be misguided and unjust – in particular the policy of using either subjective judgments or psychological/psychiatric tests (or both) to predict which offenders are dangerous and hence should be kept out of circulation. No reliable predictions have been found.

We return to the justice principle: incarceration will remain for people who commit dangerous, or harmful actions. No other equally severe and ethically acceptable punishment has been devised. Only if this principle undermines the need to protect or reassure the public, should it be modified.

6. Supporting real alternatives

My second article in this series – on the idea of "community control" – was sceptical about most attempts to provide alternatives to, or diversions from, the penal system. I argued that many such attempts result not in genuine alternatives, but supplements to the existing system. The machine of social control enlarges itself by sweeping more groups into its reach.

To put the attrition model into effect, however, some forms of intervention will still be needed. The choice is not the meaningless "control versus no control," but between different modes of control.

There are two main strategies. The one is to work within the already wide range of punishments offered as official alternatives to imprisonment: warnings, unconditional release, conditional discharge, fines, temporary deprivation of liberty, restitution. There is no reason why these options should not be expanded or experimented with.

Another quite different and more radical strategy is to encourage modes of social control and conflict resolution which are right outside the system. There are numerous models here: community dispute and mediation centres, based on analogies with moot and tort; restitution or reconciliation programmes organised by victim organisations; self-help projects, of which the rape crisis centre would be an excellent example. There are major problems in implementing these models: the danger of cooption into the official system; the inevitable cashing in by professionals who will see these agencies as just another gravy train in the people-processing industry; the profound, not to say ludicrous, problem of setting up in complex urban settings models of intervention based on a romantic vision of pre-industrial or tribal society. But the sheer inventiveness and imagination behind many of these schemes (which have received virtually no attention in this country) must surely recommend at least a trial.

7. The limits of benevolence

"Soft" and "hard"; "humane" and "punitive"; "tender-hearted" and "realistic" – no informed history of the social control of crime and delinquency will sustain such simple dichotomies. The story is, alas, more complicated. Benevolence has often been inextricably linked with coercion, the best of intentions have often led to the most disastrous results.

The liberal mood about crime control is now one of a profound disenchantment with anything smacking of paternalism and benevolence. The new slogan is "Less harm rather than more good." When extended towards other areas of welfare, this liberalism-gone-sour is uncomfortably difficult to distinguish from conservative policies of benign neglect and self-reliance.

But in the sphere of crime and delinquency control, the commitment to do less harm rather than more good might be a welcome balance. Lionel Trilling's warning (originally against marxists rather than liberals) needs attention: "Some paradox in our nature leads us once we have made our fellow-men the objects of our enlightened interest, to go on to make them the objects of our pity, then of our wisdom, ultimately of our coercion."

In immediate policy terms, where this leads is: a much greater stress on legal protection and due process in areas such as the juvenile court; a massive cutting down of administrative, bureaucratic and professional discretion; a replacement (along the lines recommended by liberation groups such as gays and prisoners' organisations) of the rhetoric of "needs to be fulfilled" by "rights that should be immune from interference."

The juvenile court and delinquency laws would be prime candidates for this sort of reform. The bland acceptance of labels such as "being in need of care and protection"; the way prevention and early intervention programmes deliberately blur the question of whether an offence has actually been committed – all this is potentially suspect.

Much research (for example, the Philadelphia cohort study) suggests pretty clearly that early processing either has no effect on later behaviour, or else fixes and perpetuates later delinquency. Children appearing in the juvenile court may commit more crimes later, and this *may* not be because they were the more serious offenders to begin with.

It is a brutal criterion; but I would suggest then that, for a few years at least, every proposed programme to deal with delinquency (intermediate treatment, community service orders and so on) should be judged not just on the basis of its supposed good, but whether it might make things worse. If punishment is intended, intervention of course is justified on different grounds, and it should not be called anything else. Benevolence is a value to be justified on its own terms. If the ideal of the welfare state is taken seriously, there needs to be a massive *expansion* in provision for health, education, personal welfare, housing, but an expansion not justified as a form of delinquency control.

There will be, of course, major exceptions. A social worker who judges that a baby is at risk of being injured by its parents is justified in intervening without having to wait around for an offence to be committed. But such cases are not the norm, and should be used to define limits.

I have used juvenile delinquency prevention as an example. There are other major areas where benevolently rationalised legislation needs also to be restricted – notably in the whole range of crimes without victims. Such matters as public drunkeness and vagrancy, abortion and the purchase or possession of any drug should be taken right out of the scope of the criminal law.

From the point of view of the "new realists" of crime control, the massive enforcement resources thus freed, could be re-deployed to fight "crime on the streets." From quite another point of view, there could be a tightening-up on the regulation of traffic, food, housing, dangerous drugs, industrial safety, employment, racial discrimination or the control of corporate crime: the plunder of the community by graft, corruption, restrictive practices, tax evasion.

8. De-frocking the professional

Allied to the caution about benevolence is a newfound scepticism about the role of expert, professional knowledge. The definition in medical terms of what are political, social or moral problems is particularly insidious. This is obviously part of a broader issue. But let me give three simple examples of what might be done now.

First, there should be a concerted campaign to use words properly. Language confers power on its users. One has to fight that particular twist in what Michel Foucault calls the "power-knowledge spiral," which allows prisoners to be called inmates; punishment to be called treatment, withdrawal of privileges or negative reinforcement; truancy to be called school phobia; and unruly children to be called hyperkinetic.

Secondly, most *specialist* professionals should be cleared out of the system immediately. There should be no such designations as "prison psychiatrist" or "prison psychologist." These functions should be performed by a rotating corps of professionals who, instead of specialising in crime, spend most of their working lives in other parts of society. This might prevent the growth of delusions about the existence of crime experts. More important, it will allow the helping and healing professions to operate properly without their functions being undermined by organisational goals.

The move by professionals into the new community settings should also be actively resisted by self-help victim organisations or rights groups. Current attempts, for example, by zealous probation officers to jump onto the bandwagon of "an integrated community treatment service" should be seen for what they are: professional self-aggrandisement.

Finally, there should be a moratorium on nearly all types of standard criminological research and publication. Absolutely prohibited should be any research about the "causes" of crime and delinquency or the personal characteristics of criminals and delinquents. For three years, say, no public money should be given to anyone proposing such research, and articles of this sort should be rejected immediately by any journal.

Instead, thought and research should be devoted to such questions as: differential perceptions of the seriousness of various crimes and the level of appropriate punishment; the degree to which certain forms of deviance can be tolerated without invoking the criminal sanction; the extent and nature of harm, victimisation and damage by crime; the feasibility of decentralising the justice system; the viability of forms of social control right outside the system ... and so on.

Lest anyone cry about intellectual freedom, let me add that such a moratorium should be entirely voluntary. And it would protect academic criminology from the ridicule to which it must surely be subject for doing the same research and writing the same articles over and over again. The posture of ivory tower academic independence anyway, ill-becomes a group who more than most social scientists have followed what Raymond Mack nicely calls the "reverse Midas principle": whatever turns to gold, you touch. If we have to dirty our minds and hands with the label of "applied," we might as well do some work which could have practical results.

9. Raising doubts

Criminology – applied or pure – is just one branch of sociology. To retain any sort of intellectual credibility, we must be sociologists first. This means that we must not be seduced too far away from the particular mode of thinking that makes for good sociology.

This mode of thinking is often – and quite rightly – irrelevant or subversive to the enterprise of solving practical problems. Good sociology renders the world strange. After we have been exposed to it, things shouldn't look quite the way they looked before. The study of crime and deviance is particularly subversive of accepted reality. The very step of taking seriously behaviour or people seen as deviant, dishonoured, discredited, disreputable, degraded, leads to a questioning of these definitions.

Hierarchies of credibility are challenged. Labels are not seen as fixed, but the product of political action. What seemed like knowledge, turns out to be vested interest: what seemed like benevolence, coercion.

Our own ideas, of course, should be subject to the same ruthless scrutiny and doubt. The very notion of justice – which runs like a constant thread through all these proposals – is highly suspect. A return to the undiluted classicism of the "punishment fits the crime" principle loses sight of humane and compassionate victories of the last century. Once it was "radical" to attack law, now it is radical to attack psychiatry. Before we rush back to the bewildered embrace of lawyers who always thought we were their enemies, we should remind ourselves how tyrannous and *unjust* the literal rule of law can be.

We must remember also that using the "back to justice" slogan as part of a pious campaign to protect victims against street crime, can be entirely hypocritical. There is, indeed, a genuine desire for justice; but it might be focused on spurious targets. The enemy in the war against crime becomes not property speculators, but squatters; not unemployment, but social security scroungers; not irresponsible drug companies, but recreational dope smoking.

It is – and should be – subversive to raise awkward doubts like these. The theme of my first article in this series was, of course, the silliness we sometimes get into if we are perverse enough *only* to raise such doubts and to lose sight of the everyday social, as contrasted to sociological, problems at issue. But the price paid for occasional silliness, inconsistency and self-indulgent speculation is less than the price paid for becoming a hired hand.

Criminology is successful not to the extent that it solves the state's problems but to the extent that it becomes a vehicle for understanding society. This is itself a moral goal in so far as crime and punishment are ultimately only markers to what sort of society we live in, and want to live in.

[9]
The Punitive City
Notes on the Dispersal of Social Control

> This, then, is how one must imagine the punitive city. At the crossroads, in the gardens, at the side of roads being repaired or bridges built, in workshops open to all, in the depths of mines that may be visited, will be hundreds of tiny theatres of punishment.
>
> Michel Foucault, *Discipline and Punish*

The study of social control must be one of the more dramatic examples in sociology of the gap between our private sense of what is going on around us and our professional writings about the social world. Our private terrain is inhabited by premonitions of *1984, Clockwork Orange* and *Brave New World*, by fears of the increasing intrusion of the state into private lives and by a general unease that more and more of our actions and thoughts are under surveillance and subject to record. Our professional formulations about social control though, reveal little of such nightmares and science-fiction projections. They tend to repeat bland structural-functional explanations about the necessity of social control or else simplistic comparisons of pre-industrial and industrial societies. There are, to be sure, powerful macro theories, especially Marxist, about the apparatus and ideology of state control and a great deal of Marcusean-like rhetoric left over from the sixties about "repression". And then there are those exquisite interactional studies about the social control dimensions in talk, gaze and gesture.

But for an overall sense of what the formal social control apparatus of society is actually getting up to, we have surprisingly little information. Those sub-fields of sociology most explicitly concerned with all this — criminology and the sociology of deviance — are not as much help as they should be, especially when trying to understand the major shifts in the ideology and apparatus of control over the last few decades. Thus writings about community control — the subject of this paper and, if my argument is correct, the key area in which to find transformations in social control — are usually of a very low level. They are either blandly descriptive or else "evaluative" only in the sense of using the pseudo scientific language of process, feedback, goals, inputs, systems etc., to decide whether this or that program "works" or is cost productive. Little of this helps towards understanding basic structural and ideological trends.

Some connecting bridges have, of course, been made somewhere here between private nightmare and sociological work. This is most evident in the current wave of disenchantment about benevolent state intervention in the name of welfare or rehabilitation [1]. The historical work by David Rothman on the origins of the asylum and (from a quite different tradition) Michel Foucault's series of great works on the history of deviance control have marked a major intellectual breakthrough. The extension of this work into the contemporary scene in Scull's analysis of the decarceration movement and in the less theoretically penetrating but polemically equally compelling formulations about the "Therapeutic State" (Kittrie), "Psychiatric Despotism" (Szasz) and the "Psychological Society" (Gross) are also important. But this work is surprisingly sparse and tends anyway to concentrate on psychiatry, only one limited system of social control.

On the whole, the promise of the new sociology of deviance to deal with the "control" side of the "deviance and control" equation, has not been fulfilled. Certainly there are enough good studies of specific control agencies such as courts, prisons, police departments, abortion clinics, mental hospitals, and so on. But the problem with this ethnographic work is not so much (as the familiar criticism runs) that a pre-occupation with labelling, stigma and interaction may leave the analysis at the microscopic level. The problem is more that such studies are often curiously fragmented, abstracted from the density of urban life in which social control is embedded. It is not so much that these agencies often have no history: they also have little sense of place. They need locating in the physical space of the city, but more important in the overall social space: the master patterns of social control, the network of other institutions such as school and family, and broader trends in welfare and social services, bureaucracies and professions. This paper is a preface to a grander project of this sort.

What I want to do — largely for a sociological audience outside crime and justice professionals — is sort out some of the implications of the apparent changes in the formal social control apparatus over the last decade or so. I will concentrate on crime and juvenile delinquency though there are important tendencies — some parallel and some quite different — in such areas as drug abuse and mental illness which require altogether separate comment. I will be drawing material mainly from the United States and Britain — countries which have developed a centralized crime control apparatus

341

embedded in a more (Britain) or less (United States) highly developed commitment to welfare and more (United States) or less (Britain) sophisticated ideologies and techniques of treatment and rehabilitation.

This paper, then, is an exercise in classification and projection, rather than explanation.

From Prison to Community

Our current system of deviancy control originated in those great transformations which took place from the end of the 18th to the beginning of the 19th centuries: firstly the development of a centralized state apparatus for the control of crime and the care of dependency; secondly the increasing differentiation of the deviant and dependent into separate types each with its own attendant corpus of "scientific" knowledge and accredited experts; and finally the increased segregation of deviants and dependents into "asylums": mental hospitals, prisons, reformatories and other such closed, purpose-built institutions for treatment and punishment. The theorists of these transformations each place a somewhat different emphasis on just what happened and just why it happened, but all are agreed on its essentials [2].

The most extraordinary of these three features to explain — the other two being, in a sense, self evident in the development of the modern state — is the growth of the asylum and its subsequent survival despite one and a half centuries of failure. Any account of the current and future place of incarceration, must come to terms with that original historical transformation [3].

We are now living through what *appears* to be a reversal of this first Great Transformation. The ideological consensus about the desirability and necessity of the segregative asylum — questioned before but never really undermined [4] — has been broken. The attack on prisons (and more dramatically and with more obvious results on mental hospitals) became widespread from the mid nineteen-sixties, was found throughout the political spectrum and was partially reflected in such indices as declining rates of imprisonment. At the end of the eighteenth century, asylums and prisons were places of the *last* resort; by the mid-19th century they became places of the *first* resort, the preferred solution to problems of deviancy and dependency. By the end of the 1960s they looked like once again becoming places of the *last* resort. The extraordinary notion of abolition, rather than mere reform became common talk. With varying degrees of enthusiasm and actual measurable consequences, officials in Britain, the United States and some Western European countries, became committed to the policy labelled "decarceration": the state-sponsored closing down of asylums, prisons and reformatories. This apparent reversal of the Great Incarcerations of the nineteenth century was hailed as the beginning of a golden age — a form of utopianism whose ironies cannot escape anyone with an eye on history: "There is a curious historical irony here, for the *adoption* of the asylum, whose *abolition* is now supposed to be attended with such universally beneficent consequences, aroused an almost precisely parallel set of millenial expectations among its advocates" [5].

The irony goes even further. For just at the historical moment when every commonplace critique of "technological" or "post-industrial" or "mass" society mourned the irreplaceable loss of the traditional *Gemeinschaft* community, so a new mode of deviancy control was advocated whose success rested on this very same notion of community. Indeed the decarceration movement derives its rhetoric from a much wider constituency than is implied by limited questions of how far should imprisonment be used. It touches on issues about centralization, professionalization, the rehabilitative ideal, and the limits of state intervention. The current (variously labelled) "pessimism", "scepticism", or "nihilism" about prisons, draws on all these wider themes [6].

In the literature on community treatment itself [7], two sets of assumptions are repeated with the regularity of a religious catechism. The first set is seen either as a matter of common sense, "what everybody knows" or the irrefutable result of empirical research: 1) prisons and juvenile institutions are (in the weak version) simply ineffective: they neither successfully deter nor rehabilitate. In the strong version, they actually make things worse by strengthening criminal commitment; 2) community alternatives are much less costly and 3) they are more humane than any institution can be — prisons are cruel, brutalizing and beyond reform. Their time has come. Therefore: community alternatives "must obviously be better", "should at least be given a chance" or "can't be worse".

The second set of assumptions appeal to a number of sociological and political beliefs not as self evident as the previous set, but taken by the believer to be just as well established: 1) theories of stigma and labelling have demonstrated that the further the deviant is processed into the system, the harder it is to return him to normal life — "therefore" measures designed to minimize penetration into the formal system and keep the deviant in the community as long as possible are desirable; 2) the causal processes leading to most forms of deviance originate in society (family, community, school, economic system) — "therefore" prevention and cure must lie in the community and not in artificially created agencies constructed on a model of individual intervention; 3) liberal measures, such as reformatories, the juvenile court and the whole rehabilitative model are politically suspect, whatever the benevolent motives which lie behind them. The state should be committed to be doing less harm rather than more good — "therefore" policies such as decriminalization, diversion and decarceration should be supported.

It is the last of these beliefs which must be used to scrutinize them all — for why should community corrections itself, not be subjected to the very same suspicion about benevolent reform? A large dose of such scepticism, together with a much firmer location of the new movement in overall structural and political changes, is needed for a full scale critique of community corrections. Such a critique — not the object of this paper — would have to note at least the following doubts [8]: 1) it is by no means clear, in regard to crime and delinquency at least, that decarceration has been taking place as rapidly as the ideology would have us believe; 2) it has not been established that any community alternative is more effective in reducing crime (through preventing recidivism) than traditional imprisonment; 3) nor are these new methods always dramatically cheaper and 4) the humanitarian rationale for the move from imprisonment may be unfounded for two (opposite) reasons: a) decarceration may indeed lead to something like non-intervention or benign neglect: services are withdrawn and deviants are left neglected or exploited by private operators; b) alternatively, new forms of intervention result, which are often difficult to distinguish from the old institutions and reproduce in the community the very same coercive features of the system they were designed to replace.

However cogent this emergent critique might be, though, it comes from the margins of contemporary "corrections". Perhaps more than in any other area of social policy, crime and delinquency control has always allowed such doubts to be neutralized in the tidal wave of enthusiasm for any new "reform". There is little doubt that the rhetoric and ideology of community control is quite secure. And — whatever may be happening to overall rates of incarceration — most industrialized countries will continue to see a proliferation of various schemes in line with this ideology.

I shall take the term "community control" to cover almost any form of formal social control outside the walls of traditional adult and juvenile institutions. There are two separate, but overlapping strategies: firstly, those various forms of intensive intervention located "in the community": sentencing options which serve as intermediate alternatives to being sent to an institution or later options to release from institutions and secondly, those programs set up at some preventive, policing or pre-trial stage to divert offenders from initial or further processing by the conventional systems of justice. Behind these specific policies lies an overall commitment to almost anything which sounds like increasing community responsibility for the control of crime and delinquency.

344

Blurring the Boundaries

The segregated and insulated institution made the actual business of deviancy control invisible, but it did make its boundaries obvious enough. Whether prisons were built in the middle of cities, out in the remote countryside or on deserted islands, they had clear spatial boundaries to mark off the normal from the deviant. These spatial boundaries were reinforced by ceremonies of social exclusion. Those outside could wonder what went on behind the walls, those inside could think about the "outside world". Inside/outside, guilty/innocent, freedom/captivity, imprisoned/released — these were all meaningful distinctions.

In today's world of community corrections, these boundaries are no longer as clear. There is, we are told, a "correctional continuum" or a "correctional spectrum": criminals and delinquents might be found anywhere in these spaces. So fine — and at the same time so indistinct — are the gradations along the continuum, that it is by no means easy to answer such questions as where the prison ends and the community begins or just why any deviant is to be found at any particular point. Even the most dedicated spokesmen for the community treatment have some difficulty in specifying just what "the community" is; one N.I.M.H. Report confessed that the term community treatment: "... has lost all descriptive usefulness except as a code word with connotations of 'advanced correctional thinking' and implied value judgements against the 'locking up' and isolation of offenders" [9].

Even the most cursory examination of the new programs, reveals that many varieties of the more or less intensive and structured "alternatives" are virtually indistinguishable from the real thing. A great deal of energy and ingenuity is being devoted to this problem of definition: just how isolated and confining does an institution have to be before it is a prison rather than, say a residential community facility? Luckily for us all, criminologists have got this matter well in hand and are spending a great deal of time and money on such questions. They are busy devising quantitative measures of indices such as degree of control, linkages, relationships, support — and we can soon look forward to standardized scales for assigning programs along an institutionalization-normalization continuum [10].

But, alas, there are not just untidy loose ends which scientific research will one day tie up. The ideology of the new movement quite deliberately and explicitly demands that boundaries should not be made too clear. The metaphor of "crumbling walls" implies an undifferentiated open space. The main British prison reform group, the Howard League, once called for steps to "... restore the prison to the community and the community to the prison" and less rhetorically, here is an early enthusiast for a model

345

"Community Correction Centre":

> The line between being 'locked up' and 'free' is purposely indistinct because it must be drawn differently for each individual. Once the client is out of Phase I, where all clients enter and where they are all under essentially custodial control, he may be 'free' for some activities but still 'locked up' for others [11].

There is no irony intended in using inverted commas for such words as "free" and "locked up" or in using such euphemisms as "essentially custodial control". This sort of blurring — deliberate or unintentional — may be found throughout the complicated networks of "diversion" and "alternatives" which are now being set up. The half-way house might serve as a good example. These agencies called variously, "residential treatment centers", "rehabilitation residences", "reintegration centers" or (with the less flowery language preferred in Britain) simply "hostels", invariably become special institutional domains themselves. They might be located in a whole range of odd settings — private houses, converted motels, the grounds of hospitals, the dormitories of university campuses or even within the walls of prisons themselves. Their programs [12] reproduce rules — for example about security, curfew, permitted visitors, drugs — which are close to those of the institution itself. Indeed it becomes difficult to distinguish a very "open" prison — with liberal provisions for work release, home release, outside educational programs — from a very "closed" half-way house. The house may be half-way *in* — for those too serious to be left at home, but not serious enough for the institution and hence a form of "diversion" — or half-way *out* — for those who can be released from the institution but are not yet "ready" for the open community, hence a form of "after care". To confuse the matter even further, the same center is sometimes used for both these purposes, with different rules for the half way in inmates and the half way out inmates.

Even this blurring and confusion is not enough: one advocate [13] draws attention to the advantages of *quarter-way* houses and *three-quarter* way houses. These "concepts" we are told are already being used in the mental health field, but are not labelled as such in corrections. The quarter-way house deals with people who need supervision on a near permanent basis, while the three-quarter way house is designed to care for persons in an "acute temporary crisis needing short term residential care and little supervision". Then — taking the opposite tack from devising finer and finer classification schemes — other innovators argue for a multi-purpose center: some half-way houses already serve as a parolee residence, a drop-in center, a drug treatment program and a non-residential walk in center for after-care.

The fact that many of these multi-purpose centers are directed not just at convicted offenders, but are preventive, diagnostic or screening enterprises aimed at potential, pre-delinquents, or high risk populations, should alert us to the more important forms of blurring behind this administrative surrealism. The ideology of community treatment allows for a facile evasion of the delinquent/non-delinquent distinction. The British system of "intermediate treatment" for example provides not just an intermediate possibility between sending the child away from home and leaving him in his normal home environment, but also a new way "... to make use of facilities available to children who have not been before the courts, and so to secure the treatment of 'children in trouble' in the company of other children through the sharing of activities and experiences within the community" [14]. There is a deliberate attempt to evade the question of whether a rule has been actually broken. While the traditional screening mechanism of the criminal justice system have always been influenced to a greater or lesser degree by non-offense related criteria (race, class, demeanour) the offense was at least considered. Except in the case of wrongful conviction, some law must have been broken. This is no longer clear: a delinquent may find himself in custody ("short term intensive treatment") simply because of program failure: he has violated the norms of some other agency in the continuum — for example, by not turning up to his therapy group, "acting out", or being uncooperative.

We are seeing, then, not just the proliferation of agencies and services, finely calibrated in terms of degree of coerciveness or intrusion or unpleasantness. The uncertainties are more profound than this: voluntary or coercive, formal or informal, locked up or free, guilty or innocent. Those apparently absurd administrative and research questions — when is a prison a prison or a community a community? is the alternative an alternative? who is half-way in and who is three-quarter way out? — beckon to a future when it will be impossible to determine who exactly is emeshed in the social control system — and hence subject to its jurisdiction and surveillance — at any one time.

Thinning the Mesh and Widening the Net

On the surface, a major ideological thrust in the move against institutions derives from a desire to limit state intervention. Whether arising from the supposed failures of the treatment model, or the legal argument about the over-reach of the law and the necessity to limit the criminal sanction, or the implicit non-interventionism of labelling theory, or a general disenchantment with paternalism, or simply the pragmatic case for easing the burdens on the system — the eventual message looked the same: the state should do less rather than more. It is ironical then — though surely the irony is too obvious even to be called this — that the major results of the new movements towards "community" and "diversion" have been to increase rather than decrease the *amount* of intervention directed at many groups of deviants in the system and, probably, to increase rather than decrease the total *number* who get into the system in the first place. In other words: "alternatives" become not alternatives at all but new progams which supplement the existing system or else expand it by attracting new populations.

I will refer to these two overlapping possibilities as "thinning the mesh" and "widening the net" respectively. No one who has studied the results of such historical innovations as probation and parole should be surprised by either of these effects. As Rothman, for example, comments about the early twentieth century impact of the psychiatric ideology on the criminal justice system: "... rationales and practices that initially promised to be less onerous nevertheless served to encourage the extension of state authority. The impact of the ideology was to expand intervention, not to restrict it" [15].

The detailed processes through which the new community agencies are generating such expansion are not my concern here [16]. I will merely use the two strategies of "alternatives" and "diversion" to suggest how illusory is the notion that the new movement will lead to a lesser degree of formal social control.

Let us first examine community alternatives to incarceration. The key index of "success" is not simply the proliferation of such programs, but the question of whether they are replacing or merely providing supplementary appendages to the conventional system of incarceration. The statistical evidence is by no means easy to decipher but it is clear, both from Britain and America, that rates of incarceration — particularly in regard to juveniles — are not at all declining as rapidly as one might expect and in some spheres are even increasing. Critically — as one evaluation suggests [17] the "alternatives" are not, on the whole, being used for juveniles at the "deep end" of the system, i.e. those who really would have been sent to institutions before. When the strategy is used for "shallow end" offenders — minor or first offenders whose chances of incarceration would have been slight — then the incarceration rates will not be affected.

The exact proportions of these types are difficult to estimate: one English study of community service orders shows that only half the offenders sent would otherwise have received custodial sentences [18]. Leaving aside the question of the exact effects on the rest of the system, there is little doubt that a substantial number — perhaps the majority — of those subjected to the new programs, will be subjected to a degree of intervention higher than they would have received under previous non-custodial options like fines, conditional discharge or ordinary probation.

348

What all this means is that as long as the shallow end principle is used and as long as institutions are not literally closed down (as in the much publicized Massachusetts example) there is no guarantee either than incarceration will decrease dramatically or that the system will be less interventionist overall. The conclusion of the recent National Assessment of Juvenile Corrections holds true generally: although there are exceptions, "in general as the number of community based facilities increases, the total number of youths incarcerated increases" [19].

The paradox throughout all this that the more benign, attractive and successful the program is defined — especially if it uses the shallow end principle, as most do — the more it will be used and the wider it will cast its net:

> Developing and administering community programs can be a source of gratification to sincere correctional administrators and lay volunteers who believe they are 'doing good' by keeping people out of dungeons and helping them obtain social services. Judges, reluctant to send difficult children to a reformatory and equally reluctant to release them without an assurance that something will be done to prevent them from returning may be especially enthusiastic about the development of alternative dispositions [20].

Turning now to the more explicit forms of diversion, it is once again clear that the term, like the term "alternatives" is not quite what it implies. Diversion has been hailed as the most radical application of the non-intervention principle short of complete decriminalization. The grand rationale is to restrict the full force of the criminal justice process to more serious offences and to either eliminate or substantially minimize penetration for all others [21]. The strategy has received the greatest attention in the juvenile field: a remarkable development, because the central agency here, the juvenile court, was *itself* the product of a reform movement aimed at "diversion".

Clearly, all justice systems — particularly juvenile — have always contained a substantial amount of diversion. Police discretion has been widely used to screen juveniles: either right out of the system by dropping charges, informally reprimanding or cautioning, or else informal referral to social services agencies. What has now happened, to a large degree, is that these discretionary and screening powers have been formalized and extended — and in the process, quite transformed. The net widens to include those who, if the program had not been available would either not have been processed at all or would have been placed on options such as traditional probation. Again, the more benevolent the new agencies appear, the more will be diverted there by encouragement or coercion. And — through the blurring provided by the welfare net — this will happen to many not officially adjudicated as delinquent as well. There will be great pressure to work with parts of the population not previously "reached".

All this can be most clearly observed in the area of police diversion of juveniles. Where the police used to have two options — screen right out (the route for by far the *majority* of encounters) or process formally — they now have the third option of diversion into a program. Diversion can then be used as an alternative to screening and not an alternative to processing [22]. The proportion selected will vary. British research on police juvenile liaison schemes and similar measures [23] shows a clear widening of the net and one survey of eleven Californian diversion projects suggests that only 51 percent of clients were actually diverted from the system, with the rest receiving more processing than they would have received otherwise [24]. Another evaluation of 35 police departments running diversion programs concludes:

> ... the meaning of 'diversion' has been shifted from 'diversion from' to 'referral to'. Ironically, one of the ramifications of this is that in contrast to some earlier cited rationales for diversion as reducing costs, caseload and the purview of the criminal justice system, diversion may in fact be extending the costs, caseload and system purview even further than had previously been the case [25].

The key to understanding this state of affairs lies in the distinction between *traditional* or *true* diversion — removing the juvenile from the system altogether by screening out (no further treatment, no service, no follow up) — and the *new* diversion which entails screening plus program: formal penetration is minimized by referral to programs in the system or related to it [26]. Only traditional diversion is true diversion in the sense of diverting *from*. The new diversion diverts — for better or worse — *into* the system. Cressey and McDermott's laconic conclusion from their evaluation of one such set of programs might apply more generally.

> If 'true' diversion occurs, the juvenile is safely out of the official realm of the juvenile justice system and he is immune from incurring the delinquent label or any of its variations — pre-delinquent, delinquent tendencies, bad guy, hard core, unreachable. Further, when he walks out of the door from the person diverting him, he is technically free to tell the diverter to go to hell. We found very little 'true' diversion in the communities studied [27].

To conclude this section: whatever the eventual pattern of the emergent social control system, it should be clear that such policies as "alternatives" in no way represent a victory for the anti-treatment lobby or an "application" of labelling theory. Traditional deviant populations are being processed in a different way or else new populations are being caught up in the machine. For some observers [28] all this is an index of how good theory produces bad practise: each level diverts to the next and at each level vested interests (like job security) ensures that few are diverted right out. And so the justice machine enlarges itself. This looks "successful" in terms of the machine's own operational definition of success, but is a failure when compared to the theory from which the policy (supposedly) was derived.

Be this as it may, the new movement — in the case of crime and delinquency at least — has led to a more voracious processing of deviant populations, albeit in new settings and by professionals with different names. The machine might in some respects be getting softer, but it is not getting smaller (and probably not more efficient — but that's another story).

Masking and Disguising

The softness of the machine might also be more apparent than real. It became common place in historical analyses to suggest that the more benign parts of the system such as the juvenile court [29] masked their most coercive intentions and consequences. This conclusion might apply with equal force to the current strategies of diversion and alternatives. Even more than their historical antecedents, they employ a social work rather than legalistic rationale; they are committed to the principle of blurring the boundaries of social control and they use the all-purpose slogan of 'community' which cannot but sound benign.

There can be little doubt that the intentions behind the new movement and — more to the point — its end results, are often humane, compassionate and helpful. Most clients, deviants or offenders would probably prefer this new variety to the stark option of the prison. But this argument is only valid if the alternatives are real ones. The net-thinning and mesh-widening effects, though indicate that the notion of alternatives can be misleading and mystifying. Note, for example, the curious claim that agencies like half-way houses are justified because they are just as successful in preventing crime as direct release into the community. As Greenberg notes, however, when such alternatives are presented as a condition of release from prison, "... the contrast between the brutality of the prison and the alleged humanitarianism of community corrections is besides the point, because the community institution is not used to replace the prison; instead the offender is exposed to both the prison and the community 'alternatives'" [30].

Even when the alternatives *are* real ones, it is not self evident that they are always more humane and less stigmatizing just because, in some sense they are "in the community". Community agencies, for example, might use a considerable amount of more or less traditional custody and often without legal justification. As the assessment of one experiment revealed:

> When subjects failed to comply with the norms of the intensive treatment regime, or even when a program agent believes subjects might fail to comply, then, as they say in the intensive treatment circles, detention may be indicated. Both these features, and the extensive use of

home placements as well, suggest that the term 'community' like the term 'intensive treatment' may come to have a very special meaning in programs designed to deliver 'intensive treatment in the community' [31].

Such disguised detention, though, is probably not a major overall source of masking. More important is the bureaucratic generation of new treatment criteria which might allow for more unchecked coercion than at first appears. In a system with low visibility and low accountability, there is less room for such niceties as due process and legal rights. Very often, for example, "new diversion" (minimization of penetration) occurs by deliberately avoiding due process: the client proceeds through the system on the assumption or admission of guilt. Indeed the deliberate conceptual blurring between "diversion" and "prevention" explicitly calls for an increase in this sort of non-legal discretion.

All this, of course, still leaves open the question of whether the end result — however mystifying some of the routes that led to it — is actually experienced as more humane and helpful by the offender. There is little evidence either way on this, beyond the rather bland common sense assumption that most offenders would prefer not to be "locked up". What is likely, is that deep end projects — those that are genuine alternatives to incarceration — have to make a trade-off between treatment goals (which favour the integrated community setting) and security goals which favour isolation. The trade-off under these conditions will tend to favour security — resulting in programs which simulate or mimic the very features of the institution they set out to replace. Let us consider two somewhat different examples.

The first is Fort Des Moines, a "Community Correctional Facility" which is part of a wider Community Corrections Program [32]. This is a 50 bed non-secure unit, housed in an ex-army base. The clients work in ordinary jobs outside and there is minimal physical security in the shape of bars or fences.

Here, though, are some of the security trade offs: 1) the low "client-counsellor" ratio — one staff person for every two clients — allows for intensive "informal observation" of the clients for security purposes. There is, for example, a "staff desk person" who signs clients in and out, recording their attitudes and activities. There is also a "floating staff person" who circulates throughout the institution, observing client behaviour, taking a count of all clients each hour (called the 'eye check') and recording the count in the log; 2) the client has to "contract" to behave well and participate actively in his rehabilitation: the sanction of being returned to prison is always present. From the beginning of his stay (when he has to sign a waiver of privacy granting the program access to information in confidential agency files) he is closely scrutinized. Besides the obvious offences like using drugs, fighting or trying to escape the failure to maintain "a

352

significant level of performance" is one of the most serious offenses a client can commit and results in immediate return to jail [33]; 3) the court retains jurisdiction over the client, receiving detailed rosters and program reports and having to authorize internal requests for work, schooling or furloughs. In addition, the local police and sheriffs departments receive weekly listings of the residents, indicating where each has to be at specified hours of each day. This information is available to patrol officers who may see inmates in the community.

These features — especially the complicated compulsory treatment process itself — suggests an intensity of intervention at least as great as that in most maximum security prisons. The commitment to a behaviourist conditioning program — a feature of many American versions of community treatment — is particularly insidious and is illustrated well in my second example, the Urbana-Champaign Adolescent Diversion Project [34]. This — unlike the first example — is genuinely enough in the community: juveniles considered as "beyond lecture and release and clearly headed for court" are referred by the police to a program of behavioural contracting organized by a university psychology department. The volunteer staff monitor and mediate contractual agreements between the youth and his parents and teachers: privileges in return for complying with curfew, house chores and personal appearance. Here are extracts from a typical day in the life of Joe, a sixteen year old who had come to the attention of the juvenile division for possession of marijuana and violation of the municipal curfew laws:

Joe agrees to:

1. Call home by 4:00 p.m. each afternoon and tell his parents his whereabouts and return home by 5:00 p.m.

2. Return home by 12:00 midnight on weekend nights.

3. Make his bed daily and clean his room daily (spread neat; clothes hung up).

4. Set table for dinner daily.

Joe's parents agree to:

1. Allow Joe to go out from 7:30 to 9:30 Monday through Thursday evening and ask about his companions without negative comment.

2. Allow Joe to go out the subsequent weekend night.

3. Check his room each day and pay him 75 cents when cleaned.

4. Deposit 75 cents per day in a savings account for Joe.

Bonus
If Joe performs at 80 percent or above of 1 through 4 above, his parents will deposit an additional 3 dollars in his account for each consecutive seven day period.

Sanction
If Joe falls below 60 percent in 1 and 2 above in any consecutive seven day period, he will cut two inches off his hair.

353

Comments about the alleged "humanitarianism" of this program are redundant.

Merging Public and Private

The notion that the state should be solely responsible for crime control only developed in England and America in the later part of the nineteenth century. The key changes then – the removal of prisons from private to public control and the creation of a uniformed public police force – are taken as the beginning of the continued and voracious absorption of deviancy control into the centralized apparatus of the state. Certainly the political and economic demands of industrial society have led to increasing state control in the form of laws, regulations, administrative and enforcement agencies.

At a somewhat different level, though, there are other developments – in line with the move from concentration to dispersal traced in this paper – which are going in a somewhat different direction. Indeed some observers – particularly in the case of the police, have gone as far as noting a tendency to the "privatization of social control" [35]. While this might be an exaggeration, it is apparent that along with the other types of blurring, there has been some merging of the obviously public and formal apparatus of control with the private and less formal. The ideology of community implies this: on the one hand, the repressive, interventionist reach of the state should be blunted, on the other, the "community" should become more involved in the day to day business of prevention and control.

It would be tempting – but too simple – to see this interpenetration of the public and private as going back full circle to its earlier historical forms. The connections between crime control and contractual or other forms of profit making which emerged at the end of the seventeenth century, are not quite the same as today's versions of private control – nor can they ever be in the rationalized centralized state.

The increasing involvement, though – particularly in the United States – of private enterprise in the public service sector, is noteworthy enough. Indeed in Scull's analysis decarceration itself is attributed to a fiscal crisis: the state divests itself of expensive crime control functions allowing private enterprise to process deviant populations for profit. This is readily observable in the case of private clinics, hospitals or welfare hotels for the old and mentally ill, where private agencies either serve their "own" clientele or function under licence or contract from the state.

In the areas of crime and delinquency it is not quite as clear how ". . . the spheres of public and private actually have become progressively less dis-

354

tinct" [36]. The term privatization does not fully cover the complicated ways in which the new community alternatives relate to the system from which they are supposedly diverting. In some cases, there *is* clear privatization in the form of half-way houses, hostels, group homes or fostering schemes being run for private profit. But the fate of most private agencies in this area — especially if they prove successful — is to become co-opted and absorbed into the formal state apparatus. This has happened even to radical self-help organizations which originated in an antagonistic relationship to the system. In the case of diversion, the ideal non-legal agency (free from system control, client oriented, with voluntary participation, independent of sponsor's pressure) often becomes like the various "para-legal" agencies closely connected to the system and dependent on it for space, referrals, accountability and sponsorship [37]. Various compromises on procedure are made as temporary tactics to deflect suspicion and criticism, but are then institutionalized. The private agency expands, for example, by asking for public funding and in turn might change its screening criteria to fit the official system's demands. It becomes increasingly difficult to assign the status of private or public to these agencies.

At the same time as private agencies find it difficult not to be co-opted, the public sector responds to pressures (some fiscal and some sincerely deriving from the community ideology) by using more private resources, especially in the form of volunteers. Ex-offenders treat offenders, indigenous community residents are recruited to probation or voluntary "big brother" type schemes, family members and teachers are used in behavioural contracting programs or university students take on counselling functions as part of their course work.

All this is a fairly long way removed from the pre-nineteenth century forms of privatization. The closest parallels to this might be in the area of policing. In both Britain and the United States private policing has become a massive industry. In the United States, private police outnumber their counterparts in the public sector — a growth attributed to the increasing involvement of the ordinary police in human services "dirty work", leaving large corporations dependent on private protective and investigative services in areas such as pilferage, security checks, industrial espionage and credit card scrutiny.

Alongside all this, there have been changes in police methods which have some other curious historical parallels — to the time when the dividing lines between the civilian population and a uniformed, centralized police force were not at all clear. There has been considerable expansion in the use of informers, secret agents, undercover work, agents provocateurs — all those disguised operations in which the police are made to look more like citizens and citizens more like the police. There is a great deal of evidence about the infiltration of social movements by informers and agents provocateurs [38] while undercover work and entrapment in the field of victimless crime or vice (drugs, gambling, prostitution) has become — if this is not a contradiction — open knowledge. Here, police work is less re-active than pro-active: aimed at anticipating and preventing crimes not yet committed through such methods as police posing as criminals (prostitutes, fences, pornographic book dealers) or as victims (for example, as elderly citizens to attract mugging).

Leaving aside the surrealistic possibilities this opens up (agents who are themselves under surveillance selling drugs to and arresting other agents), and the implications for civil liberties and conceptions of trust and privacy [39] it directs attention to further twists and ambiguities in the already complex relationship between deviance and social control. While some parts of police work are becoming more underground and secretive, others are trying to reach out more openly into the wider community. Schemes for "community based preventive policing" are now well established in Britain and America. Community relations officers, juvenile liaison bureaus, school-linked officers are all involved in establishing closer links with the community, humanizing the face of police work and encouraging early reporting and surveillance. Official law enforcement agencies also actively support various projects aimed at encouraging early reporting of crime through such methods as building up neighbourhood "whistle alert networks" or citizen band radio reporting. A more obvious form of privatization is the development of unofficial residents patrols to maintain surveillance over neighbourhoods as well as mediating between the police and residents [40].

It might be premature to cite these developments as heralding a quite new mode of law enforcement. The appeal of the ideology of citizen involvement in crime prevention, though, is strong and shares the very same roots as the broader movement to the community. Here is an official version:

> ... Crime prevention as each citizen's duty is not a new idea. In the early days of law enforcement well over a thousand years ago (sic) the peacekeeping system encouraged the conceopt of mutual responsibility. Each individual was responsible not only for his actions but for those of his neighbours. A citizen observing a crime had the duty to rouse his neighbours and pursue the criminal. Peace was kept for the most part, not by officials but by the whole community [41].

Needless to say, today's forms of peacekeeping by the community are not quite the same as those golden days of "mutual responsibility". Closed circuit television, two way radios, vigilante patrols and police decoys hardly simulate life in a pre-industrial village. This is not for want of trying. In some large stores, private security police are posing as employees. They conspicuously steal and are then conspicuously "discovered" by the management and ceremonially disciplined, thus deterring the real employees. They

356

then presumably move on to stage somewhere else another such Durkheimian ceremony of social control.

Absorption, Penetration, Re-integration

The asylum represented not just isolation and confinement — like quarantining the infected — but a ritual of physical exclusion. Without the possibility of actual banishment to another society, the asylum had to serve the classic social function of scapegoating. The scapegoat of ancient legend was an animal driven to the wilderness, bearing away the sins of the community.

In the new ideology of corrections, there is no real or symbolic wilderness — just the omnipresent community into which the deviant has to be unobtrusively "integrated" or "reintegrated". The blurring of social control implies both the deeper penetration of social control into the social body and the easing of any measures of exclusion, or status degradation. For the apologists of the new corrections, the word "re-integration" has a magic ring. Thus Empey [42] argues that we are in the middle of a third revolution in corrections: the first from Revenge to Restraint (in the first part of the nineteenth century), the second from Restraint to Reformation (from the late nineteenth to the early twentieth century) — and now from Reformation to Re-integration. Leaving aside the historical inaccuracy of this sequence, it does not actually tell us what this new utopia will look like.

In the most immediate sense, what is being proposed is a greater direct involvement of the family, the school and various community agencies in the day to day business of prevention, treatment, and resocialization. This implies something more profound than simply using more volunteers or increasing reporting rates. It implies some sort of reversal of the presumption in positivist criminology that the delinquent is a different and alien being. Deviance rather is with us, woven into the fabric of social life and it must be "brought back home". Parents, peers, schools, the neighbourhood, even the police should dedicate themselves to keeping the deviant out of the formal system. He must be absorbed back into the community and not processed by official agencies [43].

The central role allocated to the family — part of the broader movement of the rediscovery of the family in sociology and social policy — is a good example of the integration ideology. Well established methods such as foster care, substitute homes and family placements are being extended and one enthusiast looks forward to "... the day when middle class American families actually wanted in large numbers to bring juvenile and predelinquent youths into their homes as a service commitment" [44]. The family having a delinquent living with them is seen as a "remarkable correctional resource" for the future. In Britain and Scandinavia a number of alternative systems of family placement besides salaried foster parents have been tried — for example "together at home", the system of intensive help in Sweden in which social workers spend hours sharing the family's life and tasks. Alongside these diversionary alternatives, parents and schools are also encouraged to react sooner to early signs of trouble.

Going beyond the family setting, the stress on community absorption has found one of its most attractive possibilities in the system of community service orders developed in England. Under this system, offenders are sentenced to useful supervised work in the community: helping in geriatric wards, driving disabled people around, painting and decorating the houses of various handicapped groups, building children's playground etc. This is a particularly attractive scheme because it appeals not just to the soft ideology of community absorption, but the more punitive objectives of restitution and compensation.

Needless to say, there are profound limits to the whole ideology of integration — as indeed there are to all such similar patterns I have described. The "community" — as indicated by the standard local reaction to say, half-way houses or day centers being located in their own neighbourhood — is not entirely enthusiastic about such "integration". In the immediate future the segregation of the deviant will remain as the central part of the control apparatus. The established professionals, agencies and service bureaucracies are not going to give up so easily their hard won empires of "expertise" and identity in the name of some vague notion of integration. Nevertheless at the rhetorical and ideological levels, the move to a new model of deviancy control has been signalled. On this level at least, it may not be too dramatic to envisage the distinction between cannibalism and anthropemy becoming less relevant:

> If we studied societies from the outside, it would be tempting to distinguish two contrasting types: those which practise cannibalism — that is which regard the absorption of certain individuals possessing dangerous powers as the only means of neutralising those powers and even of turning them to advantage — and those which, like our own society, adopt what might be called the practice of anthropemy (from the Greek èmai', to vomit); faced with the same problem the latter type of society has chosen the opposite solution, which consists of ejecting dangerous individuals from the social body and keeping them temporarily or permanently in isolation, away from all contact with their fellows, in establishments especially intended for this purpose [45].

Conclusion — Towards the Punitive City

These emerging patterns of social control — dispersal, penetration, blurring, absorption, widening — must be seen as no more than patterns: repre-

358

sentations or models of what is yet to be fully constructed. Historians of social policy can use the emergent final system to validate their reading of such early, tentative patterns; the student of contemporary policy has no such luxury. The largest question mark must hang over the future role of the prison itself in the total system. The rhetoric of community control is now unassailable, but it is not yet clear how *far* the prison will be supplemented and complemented by these new forms of control.

It is, eventually, the sheer proliferation and elaboration of these other systems of control — rather than the attack on prison itself — which impresses. What is happening is a literal reproduction on a wider societal level of those astonishingly complicated systems of classification — the "atlases of vice" — inside the nineteenth century prison. New categories and sub-categories of deviance and control are being created under our eyes. All these agencies — legal and quasi-legal, administrative and professional — are marking out their own territories of jurisdiction, competence and referral. Each set of experts produces its own "scientific" knowledge: screening devices, diagnostic tests, treatment modalities, evaluation scales. All this creates new categories and the typifications which fill them: where there was once talk about the "typical" prisoner, first offender or hardened recidivist, now there will be typical "clients" of half-way houses, or community correctional centers, typical divertees or predelinquents. These creatures are then fleshed out — in papers, research proposals, official reports — with sub-systems of knowledge and new vocabularies: locking up becomes "intensive placement", dossiers become "anecdotal records", rewards and punishments become "behavioural contracts".

The enterprise justifies itself: there is hardly any point in asking about "success — this is not the object of the exercise. Research is done on the classification system *itself* — working out a "continuum of community basedness", prediction tables, screening devices — and one does not ask for a classification system to "work". In one massive American enterprise [46] some 10 Federal agencies, 31 task forces and 93 experts got together simply to study the ways of classifying various problem groups of children.

The overwhelming impression is one of bustling, almost *frenzied* activity: all these wonderful new things are being done to this same old group of troublemakers (with a few new ones allowed in). It might not be too far fetched to imagine an urban ethnographer of the future, that proverbial Martian anthropologist studying a day in the life of this strange new tribe, filing in a report something like this [47]:

> Mr. and Mrs. Citizen, their son Joe and daughter Linda, leave their suburban home after breakfast, saying goodbye to Ron, a fifteen year pre-delinquent who is living with them under the LAK (Look After a Kid) scheme. Ron will later take a bus downtown to the Community Correctional Center, where he is to be given two hours of Vocational Guidance and later tested

on the Interpersonal Maturity Level Scale. Mr. C. drops Joe off at the School Problems Evaluation Center from where Joe will walk to school. In his class are five children who are bussed from a local Community Home, four from a Pre-Release Facility and three, who, like Ron live with families in the neighbourhood. Linda gets off next — at the GUIDE Center (Girls Unit for Intensive Daytime Education) where she works as a Behavioural Contract Mediator. They drive past a Threequarter-way House, a Rape Crisis Center and then a Drug Addict Cottage, where Mrs. C. waves to a group of boys working in the garden. She knows them from some volunteer work she does in RODEO (Reduction of Delinquency Through Expansion of Opportunities). She gets off at a building which houses the Special Intensive Parole Unit, where she is in charge of a five year evaluation research project on the use of the HIM (Hill Interaction Matrix) in matching group treatment to client. Mr. C. finally arrives at work, but will spend his lunch hour driving around the car again as this is his duty week on patrol with TIPS (Turn in a Pusher).

Meantime, back in the ghetto . . . .

The logic of this master pattern — dispersal, penetration, spreading out — as opposed to its particular current forms, is not at all new. Its antecedents can be traced though, not to the model which its apologists cite — the idyllic pre-industrial rural community — but to a somewhat later version of social control, a version which *in theory* was an alternative to the prison. When, from the end of the eighteenth century, punishment started entering deeper into the social body, the alternative vision to the previous great concentrated spectacles of public torture, was of the dispersal of control through "hundreds of tiny theatres of punishment" [48]. The eighteenth century reformers dreamed of dispersal and diversity but this vision of the punitive city was never to be fully realized. Instead punishment became concentrated in the coercive institution, a single uniform penalty to be varied only in length. The earlier "projects of docility" which Foucault describes — the techniques of order, discipline and regulation developed in schools, monasteries, workshops, the army — could only serve as models. Panopticism (surveillance, discipline) began to spread: as disciplinary establishments increased, ". . . their mechanisms have a certain tendency to become 'de-institutionalized', to emerge from the closed fortresses in which they once functioned and to circulate in a 'free' state; the massive compact disciplines are broken down into flexible methods of control, which may be transferred and adapted" [49].

This principle of "indefinite discipline" — judgements, examinations and observations which would never end — represented the new mode of control as much as the public execution had represented the old. Only in the prison, though, could this utopia be realized in a pure, physical form. The "new" move into the community is merely a continuation of the overall pattern established in the nineteenth century. The proliferation of new experts and professionals, the generation of specialized domains of scientific knowledge, the creation of complicated classification systems, the establishment of a

360

network of agencies surrounding the court and the prison – all these developments marked the beginning a century ago of the widening of the "carceral circle" or "carceral archipelago".

The continuous gradation of institutions then – the "correctional" continuum" – is not new. What is new is the scale of the operation and the technologies (drugs, surveillance and information gathering techniques) which facilitate the blurring and penetration which I described. Systems of medicine, social work, education, welfare take on supervisory and judicial functions, while the penal apparatus itself becomes more influenced by medicine, education, psychology [50]. This new system of subtle gradations in care, control, punishment and treatment is indeed far from the days of public execution and torture – but it is perhaps not quite as far as Foucault suggests from that early reform vision of the punitive city. The ideology of community is trying once more to increase the visibility – if not the theatricality – of social control. True, we must not know quite what is happening – treatment or punishment, public or private, locked up or free, inside or outside, voluntary or coercive – but we must know that something is happening, here, in our very own community.

An obvious question: is all this good or bad? Most of us – consciously or not – probably hold a rather bleak view of social change. Things must be getting worse. My argument has obviously tilted towards this view of the world by dwelling on the undesirable consequences – some unintended and others not too unintended – of the emerging social control system. The consequent series of all-purpose radical assumptions, though – that things must always be getting worse; that all reforms, however well intentioned ultimately lead to more repression and coercion; that industrial capitalism contains the seeds of its own destruction – need some correction. Undoubtedly some programs of community treatment or diversion are genuine alternatives to incarceration and in addition are more humane and less intrusive. Sometimes the programs might succeed in avoiding the harsh effects of early stigmatization and brutalization. In addition, all these terrible sounding "agents of social control" instead of being disguised paratroopers of the state, might be able to deploy vastly improved opportunities and resources to offer help and service to groups which desperately need them. These possibilities must not be ignored for a minute, nor should the possibility that from the delinquent or criminal's own subjective personal experience, these new programs might indeed be preferable – whatever the overall consequences as depicted by any outside sociologist.

Many of these possibilities are yet to be resolved by more or less empirical evidence. But in the long run – as they say – social control is in the interests of the collective, not the individual. It could hardly be otherwise.

Notes

1. In the United States, some recent and explicit versions of this disenchantment — framed in the language of embittered liberalism — may be found in the various essays in Gaylin, W. et al (1978). *Doing Good: The Limits of Benevolence*, New York: Pantheon Books. In Britain, despite the fact that substantial cuts in welfare services have occurred, the commitment to the welfare state is more entrenched and consequently a liberal disenchantment with "doing good" has not yet surfaced.
2. Rusche, G. and Kircheimer, O. (1938). *Punishment and Social Structure*, New York: Russell and Russell; Foucault, M. (1967). *Madness and Civilisation*, London: Tavistock and (1977). *Discipline and Punish: The Birth of the Prison*, London: Allen Lane; Rothman, D. J. (1971). *The Discovery of the Asylum*, Boston: Little Brown.
3. For various relevant attempts, see Cohen, S. (1977). "Prisons and the Future of Control Systems" in M. Fitzgerald et al (eds.) *Welfare in Action*, London: Routledge, pp. 217–228; Scull, A. (1977). *Decarceration: Community Treatment and the Deviant*, London: Prentice Hall; and Rothman, D. "Behavioural Modification in Total Institutions: A Historical Overview", *Hastings Centre Report*, 5: 17–24.
4. Scull, op. cit., documents both the presence at the end of the nineteenth century of the equivalent of today's liberal/social scientific critique of institutions and the reasons for the failure of this earlier attack. For him, the origins of current policy lie in certain changing features of welfare capitalism. Crudely expressed: it no longer "suits" the state to maintain segregative modes of control based on the asylum. In relative terms (and hence the appeal to fiscal conservatives) such modes become costly, while the alternative of welfare payments allowing subsistence in the community, is easier to justify and can be sold on humanitarian and scientific grounds. Scull's argument is a useful corrective to accounts purely at the level of ideas, but it places too much importance on the supposed fiscal crisis, it is less relevant to Britain and America and far less relevant for crime and delinquency than mental illness. In regard to crime and delinquency the picture is not the non-interventionist one Scull implies but — as this paper suggests — the development of parallel systems of control.
5. Scull, op. cit., p. 42.
6. See Gaylin et al, op. cit. and Von Hirsh, A. (1976). *Doing Justice: The Choice of Punishments*, New York: Hill and Wang.
7. The most informative sources in the United States would be journals such as *Crime and Delinquency* and *Federal Probation* from the mid-sixties onwards and the various publications from bodies such as the National Institute of Mental Health and, later, the Law Enforcement Assistance Administration. A representative collection of such material is Perlstein, G. R. and Phelps, T. R. (eds.) (1975). *Alternatives to Prison: Community Based Corrections*, Pacific Palisades, Calif: Goodyear Publishing Co., In Britain the ideology of community control has been slower and less obvious in its development, though it can be traced in various Home Office publications from the end of the nineteen sixties. See also Blom-Cooper, L. (ed.) (1974). *Progress in Penal Reform*, Oxford: Oxford University Press and Tutt, N. (ed.) (1978). *Alternative Strategies for Coping with Crime*, Oxford: Basil Blackwell.
8. Some of these may be found in Scull, op. cit. and Greenberg, D. F. (1975). "Problems in Community Corrections", *Issues in Criminology*, 10: 1–33.
9. National Institute of Mental Health (1971). *Community Based Correctional Programs: Models and Practices*, Washington, D.C.: U.S. Government Printing Office, p.1.
10. Coates, R. B., et al (1976). "Social Climate, Extent of Community Linkages and Quality of Community Linkages: The Institutionalisation Normalisation Continuum" unpublished Ms., Centre for Criminal Justice, Harvard Law School.
11. Bradley, H. B. (1969). "Community Based Treatment for Young Adult Offenders", *Crime and Delinquency*, 15 (3): 369.
12. For a survey, see Seiter, R. P. et al (1977). *Halfway House*, Washington, D.C.: National Institute of Law Enforcement and Criminal Justice, L.E.A.A.

13 Fox, V. (1977). *Community Based Corrections*, Englewood Cliffs: Prentice Hall, pp. 62–63.
14 Hinton, N. (1974). "Intermediate Treatment" in Blom Cooper (ed.) op. cit., p. 239.
15 Rothman (1975), op. cit., p. 19.
16 The most exhaustive research here deals with the two Californian projects – Community Treatment and Probation Subsidy – widely hailed as exemplars of the new strategy. See, especially Lerman, P. (1975). *Community Treatment and Social Control: A Critical Analysis of Juvenile Correctional Policy*, Chicago: University of Chicago Press and Messinger, S. (1976). "Confinement in the Community: A Selective Assessment of Paul Lerman's 'Community Treatment and Social Control'", *Journal of Research in Crime and Delinquency*, 13 (1): 82–92. Another standard Californian study of the diversion strategy is Cressey, D. and McDermott (1974). *Diversion from the Juvenile Justice System*, Washington, D.C.: National Institute of Law Enforcement and Criminal Justice. L.E.A.A. For two useful general evaluations of the field, see Rutherford, A. and Bengur, O. (1976). *Community Based Alternatives to Juvenile Incarceration*, Washington, D.C.: National Institute of Law Enforcement and Criminal Justice, L.E.A.A.; Rutherford, A. and McDermott, R. (1976). *Juvenile Diversion*, Washington, D.C.: National Institute of Law Enforcement and Criminal Justice, L.E.A.A.
17 Rutherford and Bengur, op. cit.,
18 Pease, K. (1977). *Community Service Assessed in 1976*, Home Office Research Unit Study No. 39, London: H.M.S.O.
19 Quoted in Rutherford and Bengur, op. cit., p. 30.
20 Greenberg, op. cit., p. 23.
21 A clear statement of this rationale and the legal problems in implementing it, is to be found in Law Reform Commission of Canada (1975). *Working Paper No. 7: Diversion*, Ottawa: Law Reform Commission of Canada.
22 Dunford, F. W. (1977). "Police Diversion – An Illusion?", *Criminology*, 15 (3): 335–352.
23 Morris, A. (1978). "Diversion of Juvenile Offenders from the Criminal Justice System" in Tutt (ed.), op. cit., pp. 50–54.
24 Bohnstedt, M. (1978). "Answers to Three Questions about Juvenile Diversion", *Journal of Research in Crime and Delinquency*, 15 (1): 10.
25 Klein, M. W. et al (1976). "The Explosion in Police Diversion Programmes: Evaluating the Structural Dimensions of a Social Fad", in M. W. Klein (ed.) *The Juvenile Justice System*, Beverly Hills: Sage, p. 10.
26 Rutherford and McDermott, op. cit.
27 Cressey and McDermott, op. cit., pp. 3–4.
28 Rutherford and McDermott, op. cit., pp. 25–26.
29 See, especially, Platt, A. M. (1969). *The Child Savers: The Invention of Delinquency*, Chicago: Chicago University Press.
30 Greenberg, op. cit., p. 8.
31 Messinger, op. cit., pp. 84–85.
32 Boorkman, D. et al (1976). *An Exemplary Project: Community Based Corrections in Des Moines*, Washington, D.C.: National Institute of Law Enforcement and Criminal Justice, L.E.A.A.
33 Ibid., pp. 35–36.
34 Ku, R. and Blew, C. (1977). *A University's Approach to Delinquency Prevention: The Adolescent Diversion Project*, Washington, D.C.: National Institute of Law Enforcement and Criminal Justice, L.E.A.A.
35 Spitzer, S. and A. T. Scull (1977a). "Social Control in Historical Perspective: From Private to Public Responses to Crime" in D.F. Greenberg (ed.) *Corrections and Punishment*, Beverley Hills: Sage, pp. 265–286 and Spitzer, S. and A. T. Scull (1977b), "Privatisation and Capitalist Development: The Case of the Private Police", *Social Problems*, 25 (1): 18–29.
36 Spitzer and Scull (1977a) op. cit., p. 265.
37 For a description of this process, see Rutherford and McDermott, op. cit.
38 Marx, G. T. (1974), "Thoughts on a Neglected Category of Social Movement Participant: The agent provocateur and informant", *American Journal of Sociology*, 80 (2): 402–442.
39 Marx, G. T. (1977). "Undercover Cops: Creative Policing or Constitutional Threat?", *Civil Liberties Review*, pp. 34–44.

40 For approved examples of these new forms of policing, see Bickman, L. et al (1977). *Citizen Crime Reporting Projects*, Washington, D.C.: National Institute of Law Enforcement and Administration of Justice and Yin, R. K. et al (1977). *Citizen Patrol Projects*, Washington, D.C.: National Institute of Law Enforcement and Criminal Justice, L.E.A.A.
41 National Advisory Commission on Criminal Justice Standards and Goals (1973). *Community Crime Prevention*, Washington, D.C.: U.S. Government Printing Office, p. 7.
42 Empey, L. T. (1967). *Alternatives to Incarceration*, Washington, D.C.: U.S. Government Printing Office.
43 For typical statements about absorption, see Carter, R. M. (1972). "The Diversion of Offenders", *Federal Probation* 36 (4): 31–36.
44 Skoler, D. (1975). "Future Trends in Juvenile and Adult Community Based Corrections" in Perlstein and Phelps (eds.), op. cit., p. 11.
45 Levi Strauss, C. (1977). *Tristes Tropiques*, Harmondsworth: Penguin, p. 508.
46 Hobbs, N. (1975). *Issues in the Classification of Children*, San Francisco: Jossey Bass Publishers.
47 Strangers to the world of community corrections should be informed that all the projects named in this imaginary report are *real* and current.
48 Foucault (1977), op. cit., p. 113.
49 Ibid., p. 211.
50 Ibid., p. 306.

[10]
Social-Control Talk:
Telling Stories about Correctional Change

This is a paper about stories, words and talk: what do the people who run the social-control system say about what they are doing? Of course, these are not just ordinary 'people', but politicians, reformers, social workers, psychiatrists, custodians, researchers, official committee members, professionals and experts of all sorts. And they may not be 'running' or 'doing' very much at all. Most of their words are produced to describe, explain, justify, rationalise, condone, apologise for, criticise, theorise about or otherwise interpret things which have been done, are being done or will be done by others. And all these words might bear only the most oblique relationship to what is actually happening in the cells, buildings, corridors, offices and encounters of the social-control apparatus.

This vexed question about the relationship between words and action is obviously not just a problem for students of social control. It appears in any interesting psychological inquiry about an individual human being or any interesting sociological inquiry about a whole society. This is what is meant in the debates, respectively, about 'motive' and 'ideology'. What is perennially at issue is how surface reasons can differ from 'real' reasons, or how people can say one thing, yet be doing something which appears radically different. Perhaps such gaps between appearance and reality, or between words and action, exist because people cannot ever comprehend the real reasons for their actions. Alternatively, they may understand these reasons only too well, but use words to disguise or mystify their real intentions. Or perhaps the stated verbal reasons are indeed the real ones, but because of the obdurate nature of the world, things somehow turn out differently.

We will be returning later to such different theories about words and actions, intentions and consequences, but first we must define the subject-matter of social-control talk. The term 'social control' has lately become a Mickey Mouse concept, used to include all social

102   Stanley Cohen

processes ranging from infant socialisation to public execution, all social policies whether called health, education or welfare. This vagueness in historical studies of social control has already been commented on (Stedman-Jones, 1977), as well as the problems in seeing all state social policy as social control (Higgins, 1980). In the absence of a more satisfactory term, however, I will continue to use 'social control' to refer to something narrower and more specific than the standard sociological and anthropological concept, yet something wider and more general than the formal legal apparatus for the control of crime. This in-between territory belongs to all organised responses to crime, delinquency and allied forms of deviance – whether sponsored directly by the state or by institutions such as social work and psychiatry, and whether designated as treatment, prevention, punishment or whatever.

This is the conception of social control which I adopt in the larger project from which this paper derives. Here, I am concerned with a more restricted part of the topic: the working ideologies which inform current changes and apparent future directions in the control of crime and delinquency. The American textbook notion of 'correctional change' covers this subject-matter well enough; one useful recent version refers to:

> (1) A transformation of the structural arrangements employed to deal with convicted offenders (for example, the establishment of the penitentiary system); (2) a change in the severity of punishment dispensed to offenders (for example, an increase in the average length of time offenders spend in confinement); (3) a change in either the numbers of the proportion of convicted offenders dealt with by various components of the correctional system (for example, an increase in prison population or assignment of an increasing number of convicted offenders to pre-trial diversion programmes); and (4) a change in the prevailing ideologies employed to 'explain' or make sense of offenders and their involvement in criminology. (Shover, 1980: 36)

Such definitions, however, pick up too many minor and ephemeral fluctuations. There is general agreement that, behind such fluctuations, two master correctional changes in western industrialised societies can be detected. The first, which took place between the end of the eighteenth and the beginning of the nineteenth centuries, laid the foundations of all subsequent deviancy-control systems. The second, which is supposed to be happening now, is thought to represent a questioning and a partial reversal of that earlier transformation.

The original change was marked by the following key elements: (1) the decline of punishment involving the public infliction of physical pain – the mind replaces the body as the object of penal repression; (2) the development of a centralised state apparatus for the control and

Social-Control Talk: Correctional Change   103

punishment of crime and delinquency and the care or cure of other types of deviants; (3) the increasing differentiation of these groups into separate types, each with its own body of scientific knowledge and eventually accredited experts and professionals; (4) the increased segregation of deviants in asylums, penitentiaries and other closed purpose-built institutions: the prison emerges as the dominant instrument of behaviour modification and as the favoured form of punishment.

The recent revisionist historians of this transition are all agreed on the reality and clarity of these momentous changes (Rothman, 1971; Foucault, 1977a; Scull, 1977a, ch. 2; Ignatieff, 1978). The point where there is disagreement, is just *why* these changes occurred. The second master correctional change (the subject of this paper) is considerably more opaque. The very essence of the transformation – just *what* is happening – is open to dispute as well as its supposed causes. For some of us (Scull, 1977a; Cohen, 1979b; Mathiesen, Chapter 6 of this volume), there have indeed been real changes – the increasing extension, widening, dispersal and invisibility of the social-control apparatus – but these have been continuous, rather than discontinuous, with the original nineteenth-century transformation. Moreover, these changes run in almost every respect diametrically opposite to the ideological justifications – the words – from which they are supposed to be derived.

If we listen just to the words, today's social-control talk tells us something quite profound: no less than a reversal of the direction taken by the system in the late eighteenth century. A great destructuring and abolitionist impulse seems to be at work. The move from body to mind (the first of those original four changes) is not alleged to have been reversed, but each of the other three has been the object of well-defined destructuring movements – movements with slogans of deep resonance for today's apostles of correctional change. First, under such slogans as 'decentralisation', 'diversion', 'deformalisation' and 'decriminalisation', there appears the notion of dismantling or bypassing the central state apparatus; then under 'delegalisation', 'deprofessionalisation' or 'demedicalisation', a widespread distrust of the monopoly and presumptions of experts; and finally, under 'decarceration', 'deinstitutionalisation' and 'community control', a move against the dominance of the traditional closed custodial institution.

So patently are these slogans at odds with the reality of contemporary crime control, that it is hardly surprising to find them already subject to much sociological debunking and demythologising. But such exercises are really a little more complicated than first appearances would suggest. For one thing, the task of accounting for the gap between rhetoric and reality still remains. So does the problem of making sense of the rhetoric and of explaining the real changes which have occurred. And there is a curious ambivalence in all this debunking. Those of us who have participated in the exercise seem to be saying simultaneously that the desired changes we have always fought for (such as prison abolition, weakening professional power, informalism) are not after all as desirable as we thought; but also that these changes have not been taking place anyway.

A first step towards confronting these complications might be to listen a bit more carefully to current social-control tales than the notion of 'demythologising' implies. What I propose to do is to analyse the internal logic, background appeal and obvious paradoxes of three such representative tales. First, though, I will look backwards to the first transformation, for sociological scepticism about current change very much draws on the revisionist rewritings of this history.

Some historical tales
The justification for beginning with the past is not just the simple empirical one that current changes must be understood in terms of the system's original foundations. Equally important are the conceptual analogies with the present, thrown up by the extraordinarily interesting current debates about eighteenth and nineteehth-century structures of punishment and justice. For these are not just competing versions of what may or may not have happened in history, but are informed by fundamentally different views about the nature of ideology and hence quite different ways of making sense of current correctional changes. Because the lines of these historical debates have been drawn so sharply, we can use them as some sort of template on which to mark current ideologies of control.

Three putative models of correctional change emerge from the historical debate. These I will caricature as 'uneven progress', 'benevolence gone wrong' and 'mystification'.

Uneven progress
The conventional view of correctional change in general, and prison history in particular, presents all change as a record of progress. The birth of the prison in the late eighteenth century, as well as concurrent and subsequent changes, is seen in terms of a victory of humanitarianism over barbarity, of scientific knowledge over prejudice and irrationality. Early forms of punishment, based on vengeance, cruelty and ignorance give way to informed, professional and expert intervention.

The vision is not altogether complacent. The system is seen as practically and even morally imperfect. There are abuses such as overcrowding in prisons, police brutality and other remnants of irrationality, but in the course of time, with goodwill and enough resources (more money, better trained staff, newer buildings) the system is capable of being humanised by good intentions and made more efficient by the application of scientific principles. Failures, even tragedies, are interpreted in terms of sad tales about successive generations of dedicated administrators and reformers being frustrated by poor co-ordination or problems of communication (McKelvey, 1977: i). Intentions are radically separated from outcome. It is not the system's professed aims which are at fault, but their imperfect realisation. The solution is 'more of the same'.

A modern version of Enlightenment beliefs in progress, this vision represents the mainstream of penal-reform rhetoric. Its believers are the genuine heirs of the nineteenth-century reform tradition.

Benevolence gone wrong
The second model (which might also be called the 'we blew it' version of history) is a more recent, more complicated and more interesting heir to this tradition. Roughly from the mid-1960s onwards, a sour voice of disillusionment, disenchantment and cynicism – at first hesitant, now strident – appeared within the liberal reform camp. The message was that the reform vision itself is potentially suspect. The record is not just one of good intentions going wrong now and then, but of continual and disastrous failure. The gap between rhetoric and reality is so large, that it can only be understood by crucial flaws in the rhetoric itself and by problems in reality which are not merely technical ones.

Good intentions must still be taken seriously, but an appreciation of their historical origins, the political interests behind them, their internal paradoxes and the nature of their appeal shows that the reform vision was far more complicated than terms such as 'reform', 'progress', 'doing good', 'benevolence' and 'humanitarianism' imply. An appreciation of how reforms are implemented shows that the original design can be systematically – not incidentally – undermined by managerial and other pragmatic goals. In the terms used by Rothman, the most important and convincing exponent of this model, the continual tension is between 'conscience' and 'convenience'. This is the model he uses for analysing the original establishment of the prison and asylum in post-Jacksonian America (Rothman, 1971), the later setting up of probation and other alternatives during the 'Progressive Era' (Rothman, 1980), and much current social welfare and control policy in general (Rothman, 1978).

Informed by a particular ideology about the desirable limits of state intervention and by the same intellectual currents as labelling theory's

106 Stanley Cohen

ironical view about social institutions, the lesson extracted from history is that benevolence itself must be distrusted. A guide to future policy might be 'do less harm', rather than 'do more good' – or anyway 'do less altogether', rather than 'do more of the same'. But if the reform enterprise is to be distrusted, it is certainly not to be dismissed as being foolhardy or deceptive. No inevitable historical forces determine correctional change: 'Choices were made, decisions reached; and to appreciate the dynamic is to be able to recognise the opportunity to affect it' (Rothman, 1980: 11). There is an implicit identification between the analyst and the historical reformers being analysed – hence '*we* blew it'. A new type of liberalism, unencumbered by the naive optimism of its historical predecessors, still allows room for manoeuvre.

Mystification
The third and most radical model may be called the 'it's all a con' view of correctional change. Its departure point is the question of the supposed 'failure' of the reformed nineteenth-century prison. In the stream of revisionist history gathering momentum over the past few years, the explicit argument is that the prison was not a failure, but a success (Ignatieff, 1978).

Drawing upon Marxist theories of history and ideology, this model assigns a quite different significance to the matter of state intent. The problem is neither one of uneven realisation of the reform vision, nor of a tragic cycle of failure arising from the historical tension between 'conscience' and 'convenience'. In this view, everything has occurred as ordained by the needs of the capitalist social order. Intentions and ideologies cannot change the story much. Stated intentions are assumed a priori to conceal the real interests and motives behind the system. They constitute a façade to make acceptable the exercise of otherwise unacceptable power, domination or class interests which, in turn, are the product of particular politico-economic imperatives. Ideology is important only in so far as it succeeds at passing off as fair, natural, acceptable or even just a system which is basically coercive. Unlike either of the first two models, the analyst can have little in common with the reformer or manager. Those who run the system are either knaves who are deliberately hiding their true intentions, or else fools who are sheltered from full knowledge by the vantage point of their class interests. Only the outside (Marxist) observer, uncontaminated by false consciousness, can really know what is going on.

This model appears in a number of somewhat different versions. The first is actually quite close to Rothman's in its close scrutiny of stated intentions. Thus Ignatieff (1978) acknowledges the reformers' motives to be very complex. Driven by a perceived disintegration of society as they knew and valued it, they yearned for a return to what they imagined to be a more stable, orderly and coherent society. They acted out of political self-interest, but also religious belief and a sense of guilt: an understanding that the wealthy had some responsibility for crime. These motives are, of course, very similar to those attributed by Rothman to his reformers, but the changes are conceived more directly as the product of economic and material interests – and, moreover, as being successful.

A second, tougher, version of the story shades into this, but stresses more starkly the eventual irrelevance, or at least derivative status, of stated intention. The control system continued to replicate and perpetuate the forms needed to serve its original purpose: ensuring the survival of the capitalist social order. The only real changes are those required by the evolving exigencies of capitalism: changes in the mode of production, fiscal crises, phases of unemployment, the requirements of capital. The theory of change is unambiguously materialist: knowledge, theory and ideology are generated as instruments to serve ruling-class interests (for various versions, see Rusche and Kirchheimer, 1939; Scull, 1977a; Spitzer, 1979a and 1979b; Melossi and Pavarini, 1981).

In a third version (Foucault, 1977a and 1980d), and to my mind the most complex and useful, power and knowledge are inseparable. Humanism, good intentions, professional knowledge and reform rhetoric are neither in the idealist sense the producers of change, nor in the materialist sense the mere product of changes in the political economy. They are inevitably linked in a 'power–knowledge spiral': 'We should not be content to say that power has a need for such-and-such a discovery, such-and-such a form of knowledge, but we should add that the exercise of power itself creates and causes to emerge new objects of knowledge and accumulates new bodies of information' (Foucault, 1980d: 51; see Smart, Chapter 3 of this volume).

I will use something of this view later. Let me just make a final contrast between idealist and materialist views about crime-control talk by drawing an analogy from the field of literary criticism. In the liberal humanist tradition, the text is a matter of interpretation in which the author's intentions and motives are taken seriously. The question is: what does it mean? The new criticism – Marxist and/or structuralist inspired – approaches the 'text' in a quite different fashion. A 'reading' has little to do with matters of surface meaning and interpretation, and even less to do with the author's stated intent. It is a matter of decoding, demystification, unmasking. There is always a deeper reality behind the texts surface appearance.

This is hardly the place to arbitrate between these great meta-theories of human history. For, as I have said, the more parochial debate about how to interpret correctional change derives from just such grand differences — rival theories of social change, epistemology, sociology of knowledge, materialist versus idealist versions of history. Let me merely extract from this debate a few points which might help us make sense of current control talk.

What must first be said is that the 'distrust of benevolence' model has great potential in understanding correctional change. To the extent that we can simultaneously take intentions seriously and also grasp their structural context, we can indeed detect and be warned against good intentions going wrong. Critics have done less than justice to Rothman's histories by taking his view of intentions as being a simple-minded one. Such critics might be more justified in pointing to the incompleteness of the model's account of the structural conditions under which the original transformation took place, and to its implicit identification with the reform enterprise itself. As reviewers of Rothman's most recent book claim, his own criticism of Progressive penology is launched from a point of view well within the Progressive consensus: he is 'a Progressive in spite of himself' (Davis, 1980; Lasch, 1980b; Scull, 1981). The demonstration that custodial, pragmatic and managerial goals ('convenience') have undermined treatment, reform and rehabilitation ('conscience') might leave other questions unexamined. For Lasch (1980b: 30): 'Only by transforming the terms of the debate can we explain why an institution that has consistently failed and whose failure has been criticised in the same words from the very beginning of its history, has nevertheless survived essentially unchanged for more than a century and a half.'

To these critics, Rothman's model is fixated with ideas: 'Ideas remain free-floating and change remains the product of the "power of the rhetoric" the reformers invent' (Scull, 1981: 308). Their complaint — not always, I think, a fair one — repeats Marx's famous warning against taking words too seriously: 'Whilst in ordinary life every shopkeeper is very well able to distinguish between what someone professes to be and what he really is, our historians have not yet won this trivial insight. They take every epoch at its word and believe that everything it says and imagines about itself is true' (Marx and Engels, 1970: 67).

But to let the matter rest here and to 'transform the terms of the debate' into a simple materialism would also be mistaken. To reduce ideology to epiphenomenal status, a mere mirage, or to dismiss stated intent as an index of confusion, delusion, partiality, class interest or whatever is to ignore why institutions like the prison were seen as solutions to lived-through problems. It would be to underestimate what Berlin refers to as 'the terrible power over human lives of ideological abstractions' (1978: 193). Ideas, of course, do not exist in some numinous realm of their own, abstracted from political and material interests, but they do vary over time and one must argue seriously about why they take particular and successive forms. Even independent of any supposed influence they might have, even if they are wholly spurious, they are still of sociological interest. The structure might indeed only 'allow' certain ideas to dominate at any one time, but once this facilitation occurs, the ideas take on something of a life of their own – a life which generates its own social facts. Not often do these facts take the form of conscious and intentional falsification and distortion.

Knowledge is its own form of power – whether or not the knowledge is self-deceptive. In the hands of the state intelligentsia, ideas obviously serve purposes other than those stated or accessible. But they must still be seen as lived-through solutions to certain moral demands. And as Berlin suggests, our judgements of these solutions – past or present – cannot be made simply in terms of an a priori epistemology nor even by an appeal to how things actually turned out, but in terms of dilemmas and contradictions actually seen and theorised at the time. Even if apologists for the system are *only* apologists, they cannot be consigned to represent abstract historical forces.

In practice, just as few liberal historians of social control 'take every epoch at its word', so do most Marxist alternatives pay attention to these words. And although the fundamental division between these positions remains, they might both want to ground the study of social-control talk in terms of its actual working functions. This is a less grand way of stating Foucault's view that control ideologies or theories are forms of knowledge which are wholly utilitarian: they serve as 'alibis' for certain measures.

What I propose to do now is to discuss three exemplary themes from the type of social-control talk which has been heard – mainly in Britain and North America – over the last two decades. In each case I give a fairly literal summary of the story, then consider its appeal and, finally, its ramifications, anomalies and paradoxes. My first two examples – 'community' and 'minimal statism' – appeal to a partly mythical past and signal falsely a future which has not come. The third example – 'new behaviourism' – signals a partial, but real, change which has not been registered fully.

Community
All of today's destructuring ideologies (decarceration, diversion, decentralisation) and their implied or actual preferences (substantive justice, informalism, community control) are sustained by and owe their public appeal to the rhetoric of community. It would be difficult

110 Stanley Cohen

to exaggerate how this ideology -- or, more accurately, this single word -- has come to dominate western crime-control discourse in the last few decades.

What 'community control' (or 'treatment' or 'alternatives' or 'placement' or 'correction') actually means is difficult to know. The surface ideal is clear enough: to replace, wherever possible, the individualistic mode of intervention symbolised by cellular confinement behind the walls of the classic penitentiary. This replacement is described, theorised about or idealised primarily in negative or abolitionist terms. Community control is not individualistic, not segregative, not behind walls, not in a specially created institution. In the hagiology and demonology of crime-control talk, the contrast is between the good community -- open, benevolent, accepting -- and the bad institution -- damaging, rejecting, stigmatising.

The surface -- and just below the surface -- reasons for the successful appeal of this ideology from the mid-1960s onwards, have already been described in detail elsewhere (Greenberg, 1975; Scull, 1977a and this volume; Cohen, 1979b). It is not difficult now to categorise these appeals: pragmatic arguments about the system not working; humanitarian and civil-liberties critiques; labelling and stigma theory; cost-benefit and fiscal-crises pressures. The positive message from these various sources was that methods outside the institution would be more effective, more humane, less stigmatising and cheaper. The community was self-evidently good or at least could not be worse than the institution.

There was another element in the appeal which has received much less notice and which gives an important clue to the shape taken by community control. The causes of deviance, so the theory runs, lie in the community, especially in the form of weak or defective social control exercised by the family, school, religion, neighbourhood and other such institutions. The state therefore has to compensate by creating new external controls (see Chapter 6). The founders of the nineteenth-century asylum had similarly and correctly diagnosed the causes of deviance in community breakdown (anomie, disorganisation), but had incorrectly located the solution in a simulated, artificial setting. The compensatory controls which the state now has to create are 'external' only in the sense that they could hardly emerge organically from the very institutions which have caused the problem. They would have to be 'internal', though by being physically located back in the community.

To trace the ideological anomalies in this story, we might start with the word 'community' itself. This is not only a word rich in symbolic power, but it lacks any negative connotations. This is true of its everyday usage, its political appeal to left and right, and also -- more

Social-Control Talk: Correctional Change   111

remarkably – of its social-scientific connotations.

Much of this symbolic power derives from a powerful sense of nostalgia, which is, as we know, a rather more complicated phenomenon than first appears (Davis, 1979). The form it takes in crime-control ideology is a look backwards to a real or imagined past community as providing the ideal and desirable form of social control. This impulse is reactionary and conservative – not in the literal political sense, but in always locating the desired state of affairs in a past which has now been eclipsed by something undesirable. As in all forms of nostalgia, the past might not really have existed. But its mythical qualities are profound. The iconography is that of the small rural village in pre-industrial society in contrast to the abstract, bureaucratic, impersonal city of the contemporary technological state.

This iconography is, of course, as old as sociology itself. Conventional histories of the sociological tradition have regarded community not only as 'the most fundamental and far-reaching' of sociological ideas, but have also seen the 'rediscovery of community' as 'unquestionably the most distinctive development in nineteenth century social thought' (Nisbet, 1962 and 1966: 44–96).[1] Community continued in classical theory both as fact and value (Plant, 1974): not just a concept but a quest, not just a classificatory term to designate how life is led in a particular geographical or social space, but how life should be led.

This idealisation of community was already apparent in the late eighteenth century, the point when contemporary deviance-control systems took their shape. The original inspiration might have been something like the Greek *polis*, the homogeneous participatory democracy of Periclean Athens. Both conservative and radical critics of industrialism were to draw on this ideal: to the conservative, the image was of a lost stability, hierarchy, sense of order; to the radical, the image was participation, devolution of power, emotional involvement. Even when this polarisation became more complicated in sociological theory proper, its traces remained.

In community lay everything the opposite of alienation, estrangement, rootlessness, loss of attachment, disintegration of the social bond. These were the products of the city, of mass society, of technology, of industrialism. As one observer notes, 'Community is often defined in much the same way as God was in medieval Jewish theology – that is to say by the *via negativa* that is, saying what God is not rather than describing his particular attributes' (Plant, 1974: 47–8). But there was also a positive picture available – not so much Periclean Athens, but the small rural village, whose traces still existed in living memory (or at least in the pages of the *National Geographic*). Here, there could be a sense of belonging, shared values and rules, commitment to the group, mutual aid, intimacy, stability.

112 Stanley Cohen

Such a rich iconography depended on an equally rich image of urban confusion and degradation. The intellectual distaste for the city was to combine in American sociology with the classical European tradition to create a particularly powerful influence on social-control theory. This was what Mills called 'the professional ideology of social pathologists': a view of social problems in which 'all the world should be an enlarged Christian democratic version of a rural village' (Mills, 1943).

By the 1960s, of course, this vision had been largely disowned in sociology itself. The ascendancy of abstract structural functionalist theory and then the fragmentation of the sociological enterprise, caused by interactionism, phenomenology, Marxism and feminism, all replaced that naive moralism with more complicated theories and values. Social workers, criminologists and other 'social pathologists' might indeed have continued being influenced by the older, more 'primitive' nostalgia, but the theorists around them were responding to more sophisticated chords.

Sophisticated, but not radically different in their underlying vision of the good society. For the 1960s witnessed yet another renewal of the quest for community. The diffusion throughout the educated middle class of bohemian, underground, radical and counter-cultural values took the form of a great destructuring impulse. Traditional forms of authority were questioned and utopian alternatives were evoked from a lost past or from societies as yet untainted by industrialism. This demodernisation movement sanctioned the powerful emotional appeals behind communes, people's parks, 'free' or 'community' schools, hospitals, clinics, universities.

In social-control talk, this destructuring impulse took the form of what Beck (1979) calls an 'anti-institutional sentimentality'. Anarchist and other such ideologically consistent critiques were lifted, and vulgarised by otherwise unsympathetic people. Sentimental anarchist ideas – bureaucracies are impersonal, the state is evil, small is beautiful – could be relied upon to win support for any policy which appeared to create free, collective living space, liberated zones where you could do your own thing apart from the state.

The appeal of deinstitutionalisation, Beck argues, lay in invoking this ideal not on behalf of the self,[2] but some other oppressed or disadvantaged group, especially those behind the walls of the closed institution (Beck, 1979: 5). For many middle-class radicals, the message from the counter-cultural heroes of the time – Illich, Kesey, Marcuse, Laing, Szasz, Goffman – was that the benign terminology and pretensions of all these places (helping, nurturing, healing) was a fraud and had to be exposed. These places could only be brutalising

Social-Control Talk: Correctional Change 113

and degrading. Beck is aware, of course, that the appeal of these sentiments depended on certain objective changes: the institutions were under strain from overcrowding, administrative difficulties, fiscal pressures, periodic scandals. Just as anarchist sentimentality could be genuinely subscribed to by liberals and radicals, so it could be used as an alibi by the new cadre of foundation directors, managerial consultants and professionals at the forefront of correctional change. But we must be careful of being too cynical about motives and of underestimating the deep resonances of the image: not just tearing down the walls, but also re-creating the community for those let free and those not yet locked away.

The place where a dose of cynicism might be required is in comprehending the results: not why the reality is so unlike the vision, but how could anyone expect it to be at all like it. I will suggest four overlapping lines of inquiry.

(1) The first line of inquiry is the idealistic flaw of trying to base a social-control ideology on a vision derived from another society. Leaving aside the fact that these visions (the pre-industrial rural village, the tribal or folk society) are often historical and anthropological nonsense, even the authentic or ideal typical features of the vision cannot simply be re-created mimetically – like exhibits in a folklore museum. The overall societal conditions which made 'community control' possible – fixed hierarchies, the pervasiveness of ritual and traditional – are simply absent in industrial society.[3]

(2) We must note particularly that the essence of community, when it appeared as an ideal in classical political philosophy, was of something apart from the state. The eighteenth and nineteenth-century defenders of the community ideal saw well enough how the modern industrial state was antithetical to community life. The quest for true community would have to take place on a voluntary basis, it would be a retreat from the all-embracing state.

But the most obvious and incontrovertible feature of current correctional policies is that they are the creatures of the state: they are sponsored, financed, rationalised, staffed and evaluated by state-employed personnel. There are indeed 'community workers' – but they are usually people employed to tell other people that they do, after all, have a community. The notion that the very same interests and forces which destroyed the traditional community (bureaucracy, professionalisation, centralisation, rationalisation) can now be used to reverse the process is bizarre. Under the guise of destructuring, the movement is really one of colonisation: from the established 'closed' institutional domains to new territories in the 'open' institutions of society.

None of this is new, surprising or particularly subtle. It is difficult

114 Stanley Cohen

to think of the historical evolution of social control in terms other than a decline in private space and an increase in public regulation. It is not that institutions like the family, eduation and the community lost their social-control functions – the metaphor of 'emptying' – but that state agencies entered their space (Foucault, 1977a; Lasch, 1977 and 1980a; Donzelot, 1980).

(3) In other words, the destructuring and abolitionist elements in community ideology are largely illusory. The gates are not being altogether opened and the community agencies are enlarging their reach by processing new populations. Deinstitutionalisation hardly affects the original problem of how to control deviant populations. As Beck reminds us, these are populations already certified inadmissible for one or other reason (unwillingness, incompetence, disability, moral blemish) to the world of work. They are marginal, residual, embarrassing groups; the development of alternative control strategies neither eliminates these populations nor the processes whereby they were initially identified and classified (Beck, 1979: 7–8).

(4) Moreover, although they may perhaps be 'in' the community, these new institutional arrangements can hardly be described as providing compensatory communities in any recognisable sense. For many offenders, of course, such compensation is hardly needed; they were perfectly well integrated into communities before their offences. For many more offenders, though, there is simply no community to which they can return: 'The fact that they have fallen among state officials is eloquent testimony to the lack of social, political and economic resources that support the kind of household and community life that protects the individual from the hard edge of the state' (Beck, 1979: 9).

Few of the new programmes even begin to provide such resources. Deviants are transferred from the case-load of one agency to another, or on to public welfare rolls or into the private sector. They find themselves physically in the wastelands of the inner city and in communities quite unable to look after them or tolerate their behaviour (Scull 1977a and this volume). Furthermore, the type of help they actually receive, though justified (as we shall see) in terms of 'reintegration' rather than 'rehabilitation', often looks suspiciously like the old one-to-one treatment encounters. Although the notion of 'internal' individual pathology appears to have been discredited, the offender is still someone with a defect to be corrected: not his psyche, but his ties to the external social world, his social and vocational skills, his role competence, his presentation of self.

Minimal statism

The segregative mode of control, signalled by the 'Great Incarcerations' of the early nineteenth century, was the object of reform and criticism from its very inception. In a sense, there have always been 'alternatives' – conceptual and actual – to the prison and asylum. But the master correctional change in which the victory of the asylum was embedded, the development of a centralised-state monopoly for the control of crime and delinquency, has only recently been explicitly questioned. In the last few decades, and in response to the same ideological currents which inform current talk about community, a new story is being told which blames the failure of crime control on an over-zealous extension of state power. The post-welfare, liberal democratic state, we are told, has over-reached itself. It must pull back or withdraw from selected areas of deviancy control.

This movement has appeared in many diverse (and sometimes disguised) forms. The notion of 'delegalisation' alone (Abel, 1979) covers major substantive changes (such as the decriminalisation of crimes without victims and radical non-intervention) and even more momentous formal changes: decentralisation, deformalisation, removal of professional power, diversion outside the system. But even more diverse than these forms are the extraordinary collections of ideological bedfellows grouped around the minimal state slogan. I have space merely to list some and comment briefly on others.

Pragmatism
Parallel to the 'nothing works' critique of prison and rehabilitation, the whole centralised-state apparatus has been attacked on pragmatic grounds. The system is inefficient, clogged up with minor cases, incapable of using discretion rationally. Justice is being discredited. The answer is new forms of control somehow 'outside' the law.

Disillusioned liberalism
The historical model of the 'distrust of benevolence' both draws upon and amplifies a particular ideology about the desirable limits of state intervention. We must be wary of good intentions; organised benevolence might do more harm than good; the zeal of liberal reformers and moral entrepreneurs of all sorts must be curbed; the welfare state must pull back. But aside from these specific morals drawn from the history of deviancy control, there is a much wider ideological current here: the mood of revisionism, self-doubt and retrenchment about the basic premises of the liberal tradition. Its shifting perspectives on crime and punishment can be used to illustrate the shattering of the post-war American liberal consensus that programmes for a better society can be devised (Bayer, 1981). The vigorous and self-confident strain in liberalism, which dismissed conservative and pessimistic formulations as backward or stupid, has given way to an altogether more

116 Stanley Cohen

uncertain and pessimistic mood about crime and punishment, about changing people or the world.

Neo-conservatism
With this pessimism, a strain in liberal thought now increasingly resembles the conservatism to which it was originally opposed. From the Second World War onwards, most capitalist societies took for granted a Keynesian state interventionism in the economy. The socialisation of production was associated with a belief in reformism, amelioration and benevolent state intervention which even most conservatives shared. During the 1970s, though, this tendency came under severe attack by a loose consensus labelled 'neo-conservatism' or the 'new Right'. The drift to the right evidenced by the 1979 British and 1980 American elections was taken to reflect populist support both for 'law and order' and for welfare-state retrenchment. Neoconservatives played on both these strains, with the more traditional, 'genuine' conservative crime-control ideologues attacking liberal solutions as played out and hopelessly optimistic. This was the tone of the 'new realists' of crime control (Platt and Takagi, 1977).

Anti-professionalism
At the level of ideas, at least, the 1960s marked the start of a radical questioning of professional monopolies and claims to expertise. Slogans such as 'deschooling', 'demedicalisation' and 'anti-psychiatry' moved from the counter-culture and the universities into the rhetoric of the very state professionals being attacked. Moreover, at the soft edge of the system, groups like social workers had their moral licence to be doing good severely questioned and found themselves charged with being policemen in disguise.

Sentimental anarchism
The same sentimental anarchism that was invoked against the closed institution was extended more generally to other forms of state interventionism. A popularisation (and usually distortion) of such philosophical writings as those of Rawls and Nozick found its way into both left and right versions of libertarianism. The state must limit itself.

Given the diversity of these inputs, it must clearly be expected that all sorts of paradoxes, contradictions and anomalies appear in the ideology of minimal statism. Indeed, even if we stayed at the surface level of all these 'texts' – without venturing into the political economy – we should be not at all surprised to find that current correctional change is occurring in precisely the opposite direction to the story. We are

Social-Control Talk: Correctional Change 117

seeing an increase rather than a decrease in the level and degree of state intervention, an increase rather than a decrease in professional and bureaucratic power. I will explore three different tensions within the minimal-state ideology which might, in themselves, contribute to these apparently paradoxical results.

First, there is the complicated nature of the terrain shared by neo-conservatives and disenchanted liberals. On one level, this reflects the real move over the twentieth century against the enlightenment faith in reason and progress. Utopias become displaced by dystopias: a sense that industrialism is played out, that the machine will devour us, that we must conserve and retract rather than expand. But a closer examination of neo-conservatism (Steinfels, 1979; Waltzer, 1980) shows not just a simple conservative impulse to retreat into the past out of a sense of crisis, apocalypse, imminent or actual loss. True, in the voices of Bell, Glazer, Kristol, Moynihan *et al.* (and their less articulate counterparts in Britain) one does detect a sense of crisis: the collapse of authority, the disintegration of community ties, the erosion of traditional values. True also, there is a simple conservative backlash against the undercurrent of 1960s radicalism. But in other respects, these intellectuals are not at all real conservatives. They take for granted most features of the interventionist state; they seldom propose a *laissez-faire* social policy to solve any legitimacy crisis; they eventually remain committed to the very political and economic arrangements which cause the transformation they so bewail.

The tension in modern liberalism is between freedom, individual rights, the pursuit of human happiness, on the one hand, and the requirements of community, traditional authority and morality, on the other. As Waltzer (1980) points out, the neo-conservative answer to the problem of fostering moral habits and communal ties that could check an unbridled individualism and hedonism is to shore up the 'non-political' attachments of society: church, family, school, welfare, neighbourhood. By another route we return to the state, having to compensate for weak social control. Whether this takes the form of heightening the visibility of the hard edge of the system (law and order) and/or decreasing the visibility of the soft edge, the end result can only be increased intervention. One need only pause for a minute to see that although in areas like mental illness the private sector might genuinely displace the state, this would be an impossible outcome in crime control. For the state to give up here would be to undercut its very claim to legitimacy (see Chapter 7).

If this is the neo-conservative answer, there is little in Waltzer's 'democratic socialist' alternative – politicising society from the grass roots upwards – to reverse this trend:

politics can be opened up, rates of participation significantly increased, decision-making really shared, without a full scale attack on private life and liberal values, without a religious revival or a cultural revolution. What is necessary is an expansion of the public sphere. I don't mean by that the growing of state power – which will come anyway, for a strong state is the necessary and natural antidote to liberal disintegration – but a new politicising of the state, a devolution of state power into the hands of ordinary citizens. (Waltzer, 1980)

This mention of public and private leads on to the second of my two contradictions in minimal statism. In the classic political philosophies of western political democracies, the state is seen as creating and managing the public sphere. The emergence of the idea of civil society in the modern state strongly depends on a separation of politics from private and social life. The public and the private emerge as clear categories (Sennet, 1978). Intermediary agencies like the school are buffers to the private realm or mediators with it. This vision is usually contrasted with totalitarianism or fascism, where the ideological function of the state is to unify public and private. The nightmare of fascism (and of all science-fiction dystopias) is the total fusion of public and private: the child informing on his parents.

Whether the modern bourgeois state ever achieved a radical separation of public from private is another matter. Certainly, in the sphere of crime control, once the separations insisted upon in classical criminology broke down (act from actor, the rule of law as a 'protection' from the state), the public and private spheres began to overlap. Positivism merges act with actor: judgements about private life (family, personality, toilet training, even dreams) become part of the public sphere. Those who have followed Foucault's method – notably Donzelot (1980) in his analysis of the juvenile court – have shown vividly how social control in fact creates a separate realm which is neither public nor private – a hybrid domain. In Donzelot's metaphors, the family is 'encircled', 'suffocated' or 'invaded' by the juvenile court, social workers, psychiatrists. And with a different method, but a similar metaphor, this is what Lasch describes as the family 'besieged'. The bourgeois family of liberal capitalism – a privatised refuge from the harsh economy – becomes increasingly subject to professional judgement and surveillance (Lasch, 1977 and 1980a).

The image of these same state professionals, experts, bureaucrats and managers rallying around the libertarian, non-interventionist flag strains credulity. And the possibility that they will support policies which will result in anything other than more work, prestige and power for people like themselves is even more incredible. The same result might also stem from the more genuinely radical pressure in the 1960s to legislate or otherwise control previously unpatrolled areas of private and social life. Some radical feminists, for example, are beginning to warn that the unintended consequence of increased state regulation and surveillance of private and domestic life is to substitute one patriarchal authority for another (Stang and Snare, 1978).

Thus, although much of the critique of benevolent state intervention — the 'state as parent' (Gaylin *et al.*, 1978) — was genuine enough, it was curiously beside the point. There is no need for the state to act as parent and teacher, if parent and teacher can be made to act as state.

My third and final example of the problems in the minimal-state story is more concrete. When they are being less grandiose, the new movements present their objective not as a total destructuring of the apparatus, but as a dismantling of the soft bits which have attached themselves like leeches to the core. If one could only dislodge these soft bits (status offences, crimes without victims, minor disputes and conflicts), then the apparatus could concentrate on the real hard stuff of dangerous crime. This dislodging is the main guiding principle of movements towards diversion, delegalisation, extra-judicial dispute processing and so on.

This is a logically consistent argument and follows from the bifurcation policy now dominant in most western crime-control systems: the soft offenders are to be removed from the system, the hard core are to be the target for the full (and now concentrated) weight of the state. The fundamental flaw in this model, though, is that the dislodged soft bits are hardly being left to move in a free-floating voluntaristic realm, far away from the scrutiny of the state. The new agencies responsible for the dislodged bits, first, are dependent on the selection procedures, discretion, patronage and back-up authority of the core parts of the system; secondly, they create new managerial and professional groups with their own vested interests; thirdly, they sweep into their orbit not simply the cast-offs from the old system, but new populations who might otherwise never have found themselves in contact with the official system at all. These processes might apply not just to crime control, but the whole ideology of informalism (Abel, 1981).

New behaviourism
By the end of the eighteenth century, the move from Body to Mind was well under way. The 'social' had been constituted as a special domain in which people could be scrutinised, supervised and changed. This transformation incorporated and facilitated the victory of positivism: as the mind rather than the body became the object of penal repression, so the actor rather than the act became the object of criminological attention. Those developments, seen as specific

products of the twentieth century – rehabilitation, the treatment ideal, the 'therapeutic state', the medical model, the whole baggage of Progressive penology – are all fully continuous and consistent with that original transformation.

In the last few decades, though, the story becomes a little more complicated than either the 'Progressive' defenders of this heritage or its 'radical' critics allow. Rather than talk being more dramatic than actual change, there have been changes too complex for the talk to register. The move towards mind has been seen as a unilinear process. Much post-war intellectual commentary – for different reasons, from liberal/humanist, radical/socialist and conservative directions – saw grave dangers in the psychiatrisation of social control. The nightmare was total thought control. Constructed from the instant pop iconography of *Brave New World, Nineteen Eighty-Four, Clockwork Orange,* the elements in the scenario could be purchased in every intellectual supermarket over the last few decades: electronic surveillance, data banks, informers and agents, drugs and psychosurgery. We have learnt to fear that our innermost private thoughts will be open to scrutiny and will be made to conform to the political dictates of the state.

Orwell's vision captured all these elements. Big Brother is watching you through the telescreen which receives and transmits. There is no way of knowing whether you are being watched. The Thought Police are in total control. Not only can they penetrate beyond behaviour to thought, but 'thought crime' is 'the essential crime that contained all others in itself'. The State is well on the way to mastering the secret of finding out what another human being is thinking. The great aim of the Party is to extinguish the possibility of independent thought, to achieve not just external compliance but uniformity of inner thought. There is that famous chilling moment in Winston's interrogation when he is informed that a simple punishment is not the point. Neither passive obedience, nor even abject submission is enough: he must be made to think in a particular way. As O'Brien tells him: 'We are not interested in those stupid crimes that you have committed. The Party is not interested in the overt act: the thought is all we care about' (Orwell, 1949: 254).

This is not the place to contemplate our proximity to 1984. What is worth pointing out here, though, is that the facile way in which many intellectuals have incorporated this vision into their private nightmares derives from their own contact (or fear of contact) with the political edge of the machine. Telephone tapping, informers, censorship of political journals and interference with academic freedom are not, after all, part of the everyday experience and concerns of the vast bulk of the population in western democracies. The daily business of

Social-Control Talk: Correctional Change 121

the social-control machine does not consist of processing thoughts rather than overt acts. It is indeed 'stupid crimes' that matter and those who commit them — and always have — are not treated as traitors or thought-criminals.

With characteristic prescience, but in a part of his vision often forgotten, Orwell saw this. To control the proles — the 80 per cent of the population outside the Party and the Inner Party — the State did not really need Thought Police or telescreens. The proles could be segregated within ghettos 'the whole world-within-a-world of thieves, bandits, prostitutes, drug peddlars and racketeers of every description' (Orwell, 1949: 73), subjected like animals by a few simple rules. They had no political significance at all and left to themselves they could continue 'working, breeding and dying'. Their thoughts did not matter.

I do not want to argue that a split of precisely this type might be developing within western crime-control systems: deviant thoughts of the Party members being monitored and changed; deviant behaviour of the proles being punished or segregated away. Rather, we must look for some subtle manifestations of this split and also understand that in some respects, current correctional changes are moving in the direction of body rather than mind. Tales — sad or glad — about the inexorable victory of positivism are simply wrong.

Current versions of the body–mind/behaviour–thought/act–actor dichotomies are hardly novel. Indeed they were prefigured exactly by the early-nineteenth-century battle between different prison systems. The Philadelphia system, we remember, stressed change through internal spiritual insight and rebirth. The object of change was mind, thought, actor. In the twentieth century, this was the vision to be captured in the Freudian model of rehabilitation. The Auburn system, on the other hand, stressed change through external compliance. The object of change was body, behaviour, act. And in the twentieth century, this became the Skinnerian model of behaviour control. The system has always contained these two different visions, and my argument here is that although there are contradictory tendencies strengthening each, a crucial move at the core of the crime-control system is towards the behaviourist vision. Let me first deal with this change.

The most readily observable reaction against the rehabilitative ethic was within the prison system itself. Here, the 'nothing works' debate, the anti-treatment lobby, liberal retrenchment and the 'back to justice' emphasis on procedural safeguards all combined to allow for a gradual replacement of Freudian by behaviourist methods. Not that behaviour modification is any less a form of 'treatment', nor that it provides better safeguards to civil liberties. But the rejection of an

122 Stanley Cohen

'inner states' model in favour of one stressing 'behaviour patterns' was more congruent both with internal (managerial) and external (ideological) demands. Compared to psychoanalytically derived models, behaviour modification is simply the better technology; it is uniquely suited to settings like the prison. You can observe behaviour in a way that you cannot observe insights; you do not have to rely on verbal skills or indeed any form of talk at all; the theory tells you how to modify the regime.

As we move outside the prison walls to other control settings and strategies, the appeal of the behaviourist paradigm remains. Rehabilitation was always attempting something quite extraordinarily difficult: to change attitudes or even the whole person. The ideology which informs community agencies, such as diversion centres, hostels or half-way houses, is much more modest and limited. The criminal is not asked to change, but to show an ability to maintain the overt demands of a conforming life. One evaluation of half-way houses, for example, describes a move from rehabilitation to 'reintegration' in which the programme's objective becomes redefined as 'no serious behavioural incidents' (Seiter et al., 1977). This is a long way from insight or attitude change.

When extended to the whole criminal justice system, the current fashion for 'applied behavioural analysis' sanctions a new way of evaluating correctional changes. Behaviour is the problem – not words, motives, attitudes or personality: 'The focus of the approach is not on what people report they do, but on how they actually behave and the conditions under which that occurs' (Morris, 1980: 135). The target for attack is 'behaviours' in daily living: the offence pattern, but also social, vocational and learning skills. The weapon is an applied technology, with procedures consistently replicable by other similarly trained personnel.[4]

When attention is shifted from individual 'behavioural sequences' to the wider society, this does not take the form of traditional, liberal, social reforms in the education, employment or community structure. Intervention is directed more at the physical environment (Jeffrey, 1976). The talk is about the 'spatial' and 'temporal' aspects of crime, about systems, ecology, defensible space, environmental psychology, feedbacks, situations, target hardening, design, opportunities. Crime is something which can be 'designed out' (Clarke and Mayhew, 1980) by changing the planning and management of the physical environment.

Even the most sacrosanct of the discourses of positivist criminology, the search for the criminal personality, has been touched by the new behaviourism. Indeed, current versions of the search (for example, Yochelson and Samenow, 1976) are only credible in terms of a revival of interest in the behavioural ideas of social defence and dangerousness. Screening and surveillance depend on the identification of certain wrong behaviours which are then tied to particular people. The treatment to be directed at this hard core has little to do with traditional rehabilitative change through insight. The whole point of the exercise is to identify those intractable offenders who are beyond change. The 'renaissance of the concept of dangerousness' in contemporary penology (Bottoms, 1977) depends on the decline of the rehabilitative ideal, together with the acceptance of a policy of hard–soft bifurcation. Although the old treatment modalities are discredited, new experts are to be given more power to perform the crucial role of separating out the dangerous from the rest of the system and devising suitable technologies to contain their behaviour ('predictive restraint') or change it through 'last ditch' treatment modalities (drugs, electronic control, psychosurgery).

These, then, are some manifestations of what I term 'new behaviourism': mentalistic concepts such as mind, thought, intention and insight are edged out of the discourse. The success of the change depends, as I have said, not just on its appeal to managerial goals, but its potential fit with wider ideological currents. In that common zone of pessimism shared by embittered liberalism and neo-conservatism, ambitions are to be limited and scaled down. As Rothman (1971) showed originally, the belief that deviants could be changed was essential to the initial victory of the asylum and depended on a switch from the pessimistic Calvinist view of human nature to the optimistic Enlightenment view that the psyche could be changed. The decline in fatalistic world views such as innate depravity removed the conceptual obstacles to intervention. The helping professions received their licence from this faith in change, reform, treatment, perfectability. This licence has now been questioned by the new realism of contemporary corrections. Failure rather than success must be assumed:

> Heretofore, at the heart of the penal system or of parole and probation was a 'success' model: we could reform the deviant. As an alternative I believe that we could accomplish more by frankly adopting a 'failure' model by recognising our inability to achieve such heady and grandiose goals as eliminating crime and remaking offenders. Let us accept failure and pursue its implications. (Rothman, 1974: 647)

Not only does rehabilitation not work, but root causes – psychological or social – are too difficult to deal with altogether. In Wilson's influential attack on liberal social policy: 'Ultimate causes cannot be the object of policy efforts, precisely because being ultimate they cannot be changed' (Wilson, 1974).

The 'unjoyful message' in the attack on liberal treatment and social reform comes from 'confronting the uncomfortable possibility that human beings are not very easily changed after all' (Etzioni, 1972a). For those bringing this message, the lesson of the optimistic 1960s was that solving social problems by changing people is simply unproductive. Accept them as they are or modify their circumstances.

Here is where the new behaviourism appears: it offers the modest prospect of changing behaviours rather than people, of altering situations and physical environments rather than the social order. To be sure, the pure Skinnerian model was a highly ambitious one: a totally synchronised and predictable environment. But the realists of crime control will settle for a derivative pragmatic version, sharing with the original a refusal to accept consciousness as a variable. As long as people behave themselves, something will be achieved. The vision is quite happy to settle for sullen citizens performing their duties and not having any insights.

These directions are, of course, also congruent with the neo-classical, back-to-justice movement. The initial victory of positivism was to admit questions of mental states into the discourse about crime: action could be interpreted, motives imputed, complex debates allowed about responsibility and culpability. Positivism, although later to be criticised for its inhumane scientism, in fact allowed room for the human. The conservative neo-classical movement, now dominant, looks forward to a return to an undiluted behaviourism – a view obviously much more conducive to the just deserts, modified Kantian, social defence and deterrence models now being canvassed.

The conservative model – as one of its leading ideologues (Wilson, 1981) has recently made clear – does not rule out the idea of treatment as such. 'Amenables' must be sorted out from those who cannot be changed; treatment must be devised on the basis of research, which (supposedly) shows that the strictness of supervision of delinquents (and not the treatment programme) has the greatest effect on arrest rates. 'Treatment', in the sense of any planned intervention, then becomes the same as special deterrence: 'Behaviourally, it is not clear that a criminal can tell the difference between rehabilitation and special deterrence if each involves a comparable degree of restriction' (Wilson, 1981: 13). Thus, if eighteenth-century crime as infraction became reconstituted in the nineteenth century by the invention of the delinquent actor, we are now moving back to a revised version of crime as infraction, 'pure' illegality.

Behaviourism, realism, justice – these are some of the tendencies which run counter to the simple body-to-mind story. But there are contradictory tendencies as well. For one thing, the burial of the old treatment model is somewhat premature. To be sure, the new behaviourism is less ambitious, but the old paradigm of one person doing something to another person has hardly been altered. Reality therapy, behaviour modification, transactional analysis have all introduced new vocabularies, but much the same groups of experts are doing much the same business as usual. The basic rituals incorporated in the move to the mind – taking case histories, writing social-inquiry reports, constructing files, talking at case conferences – are still being enacted.

However, it is outside the hard core of the criminal justice system – either in the softer community and diversion agencies, or in the more or less voluntary counselling and therapy business – that the treatment-through-insight model remains intact. The mass-therapy movement of the 1960s shows no sign of being resisted. And here, the question of 'who you are' is certainly still more important than 'what you do': behaviour is not the stuff of discourse, but insight, identity, fulfilment, self-actualisation, growth. The post-Freudian health movement – that whole army of psychiatrists, clinical psychologists, social workers, counsellors, sensitivity group leaders, mystics, EST operators and recycled Dale Carnegie and encyclopaedia salesmen which gathered force over the 1960s – are now concentrating on healthy neurotics. The business is more lucrative, the clients are only too willing to 'refer' themselves and they are quite satisfied with talking and being talked to, massaged or stroked in other ways. Outside these enclaves of narcissism, the 'community' can be left to work out its own model – using behaviour modification, drugs, cybernetics, environmental planning – to deal with those old deviants who will not voluntarily submit themselves to change. The up-to-date version, then, of Orwell's division is thus: the middle class (the Party members) obtain neo-Freudian self-scrutiny; the old deviants (the proles) are contained in their defensible spaces or, if they offend, have their behaviour patterns altered through negative conditioning, drugs, environmental design or token economies. Each side has its own 'community of interests' (Newman, 1980).

We are, I believe, only at the most rudimentary stage of understanding the three-part relationship between causal models of deviance, technologies of control, and the form taken by the dominant social order. What might turn out to be an important shift, for example, in current control models, is the lack of interest in any causal theory. A feature of behaviourism is its insistence that causes are unimportant (Beit Hallahmi, 1976): the result is what matters and causal theories are either contradicted by the programme or quite irrelevant to it. For conservatives particularly, trying to figure out why people commit crimes is futile: the point is to design a system of deterrence which will work without knowing what factors would promote crime in the absence of deterrence.

126 Stanley Cohen

Conclusion: telling stories about change

Community, minimal statism, behaviourism – these are three of the more common stories about social control which are being heard today. Having retold and interpreted them, what now can be said about our opening debate regarding words and reality, ideology and practice?

Remember those three contrasting positions: first, all is going more or less well and according to plan; secondly, there is a radical, but unintended gap between rhetoric and reality; thirdly, the words are mere camouflage, behind which another plan is unfolding. There is no denying the radical theoretical differences between these positions. But, in one sense, the debate is phoney because each side is obsessed with the same quixotic search for fit, congruence and consistency. Everything we know about the way social-control ideologies originate and function should warn us about the delusion of ever expecting a synchronisation of words with deeds. If one side is like the child who believes that fairy stories are actually true and those who tell them always good, the other side is like the adult who laboriously tries to prove that fairy stories are not really true and that those who tell them are always bad.

No doubt there are some tellers of social-control tales who are either well-intentioned fools or ill-intentioned knaves. Let us imagine someone running a community-control project who actually believes that everything he does is fostering values of personal intimacy, emotional depth, social cohesion or whatever – and simply cannot understand suggestions to the contrary. Or a private management consultant drafting a crime-control programme in which he cynically inserts the word 'community' on every second page. But the social world is not always like this, and my contact with these story-tellers conjures up a much more opaque set of images: the same people sometimes knowing what they are doing, sometimes not; believing in what they are doing, yet also being sceptical about the whole enterprise; succeeding in some ways, totally failing in others.

An informed sociology of social-control talk can afford neither to be deceived by appearances nor to be obsessed by debunking. The notion of demystification is based on an inadequate understanding of the contexts, sources and functions of control talk. The point is that abstract ideologies of the type we have analysed only make sense when grounded in the day-to-day operating philosophies of control agencies. They constitute working or practice languages. For the most part, the workers and managers – who are simultaneously the apostles and architects of the new order – cannot explain very well what they are doing or what is happening. Therefore they improvise a vocabulary – drawing on those abstractions – which invests and dignifies their daily organisational imperatives and contingencies with the status of a theory.

Social-Control Talk: Correctional Change   127

What we might ask, then, is less whether these theories are correct or not, or whether they came before or after the policy, but how they can be made to work. We must begin neither with a simple congruence (whose presence or absence then has to be demonstrated) between words and deeds, nor with the existence of abstract forces which will render any such congruence illusory. The best working strategy is to assume, for perfectly concrete sociological reasons, that most of the time there will be incongruence, lack of fit, contradictions, paradoxes.

There are a reasonable number of good theories which might help us here. We can range from Mao's conception of the contradictory nature of ideology to Becker's more simple assumption that officials who run institutions like schools, hospitals and prisons will always be lying and covering up because these places hardly ever perform in the way they are supposed to (Becker, 1967). Interactionist studies teach us how these officials organise their talk (denying failures, explaining failure which cannot be hidden, saying what they would really like to do); Marxist theories guide us to the external conditions under which such talk — however internally implausible — gains acceptability in a certain social order.

In both cases we will be dealing with the symbolic language of politics, which invariably tries to convey choice, change, progress, rational decisions (Edelman, 1964). Even if things stay much the same, social-control talk has to convey a dramatic picture of breakthroughs, departures, innovations, milestones, turning-points: continually changing strategies in the war against crime. Professionals, politicians, agencies, fund raisers, researchers and the mass media are all mounting a complex socio-drama for each other and their respective publics. This takes the form of shamanism (Etzioni, 1972b): a series of conjuring tricks in which agencies are shuffled; new names invented; incantations recited; commissions, committees, laws, programmes and campaigns announced. All this is to give the impression that social problems (crime, mental illness, pollution, alcoholism or whatever) are somehow not totally out of control. Promises and gestures can be made, anxieties can vanish away or be exorcised, people can be reassured or mesmerised. So magical is the power of the new languages of systems theory, applied behaviour analysis and psycho-babble, that they can convey (even to their users) an effect opposite to the truth.

It might be that we need a model of correctional change much 'looser' than any of those we have considered: not the simple idealist, nor the simple materialist, nor even Foucault's complex power–knowledge spiral. The complications we have observed seem to elude these frameworks: consequences so different from intentions; policies carried out for reasons opposite to their stated ideologies; the same ideologies supporting quite different policies; the same policy supported for quite different ideological reasons. Any possible correspondence between ideas and policies will become even harder to locate as the system announces its own 'end of ideology'. Previous phases of crime control also exhibited ideological inconsistencies (classicism allowed some determinism, positivism allowed punishment), but then there was at least a dominant set of ideas from which departures could be noticed. Now, anything goes and policies need have nothing to do with causal theories.

On the principle that metaphors and analogies are often more helpful than substantive models themselves, let me conclude with stories about a quite different type of social change. In his classic analysis of Kachin social structure, Leach (1970) presents a highly suggestive analysis of how mythology can be said to justify changes in the social structure. Structure is usually seen as being 'represented' in certain rituals, and myths are the verbal statements which accompany and sanction ritual action. But this neat complementarity, Leach argues, hardly ever exists. Indeed, in Kachin mythology, contradictions and inconsistencies are fundamental: they are more significant than the uniformities. Inconsistencies are not occasions to select one version as being more correct than another. Even the 'simple' Kachin society is more complex than this: particular structures can assume a variety of interpretations, different structures can be represented by the same symbols.

As Leach makes clear, the explanations given by certain members of society about how particular institutions actually function necessarily constitute a fiction. Moreover, these fictions are quite different from the language used by outside anthropological observers. Members do not use such scientific verbal tools: they become aware of structure only through performance of ritual acts and reciting tales of ritual implications. Leach shows empirically that actual crucial changes within particular communities are not all reflected in the stories these communities tell about themselves. Kachin mythology is not a simple kind of history: the same characters and symbols are used, but the tale differs according to who is telling it, and justifies the attitude adopted at the moment of the telling:

> Kachins recount their traditions on set occasions, to justify a quarrel, to validate a social custom, to accompany a religious performance. The storytelling therefore has a purpose; it serves to validate the status of the individual who hires a bard to tell the story, for among Kachins the telling of traditional tales is a professional occupation carried out by priests and bards of various grades... But if the status of one individual is validated, that almost always means that the status of someone else is denigrated. One might then almost infer from first principles that every traditional tale will occur in several different versions, each tending to uphold the claims of a different vested interest. (Leach, 1970: 265-6)

Social-Control Talk: Correctional Change 129

Analogously, we must study not just the content of social-control talk, but the particular set occasions (inquiries, reports, evaluations) for which it is produced and the interests of the professional priests and bards who do the telling. Further, we must expect the tales to be 'unrealistic'. As Leach (1970: 281) comments on one example: 'At the back of the ritual, there stood not the political structure of a real state, but the "as if" structure of an ideal state.' When pushed, participants themselves will understand quite well that they are not talking about an actual society. Nobody running a community dispute-mediation centre in New York actually believes that this re-creates the conditions of a Tanzanian village court any more than 'house-parents' in a 'community home' believe that they are living in a family with their own children. And criminologists who mount research projects to determine whether an agency is in the community or not in the community are busy with theology, not science.

But this 'as if' quality of control talk (which renders it so vague, ambiguous or contradictory) derives from the ideal rather than the idealistic nature of ritual.

> Ritual and mythology 'represents' an ideal version of the social structure. It is a model of how people suppose their society to be organised, but it is not necessarily the goal to which they strive. It is a simplified description of what is, not a fantasy of what might be. (Leach, 1970: 286–7)

This means that the mythology of crime-control talk – even at its most fantastic and utopian moments – is very much grounded in the real world. The next stage is to study one part of this world: the 'new class' of salaried mental workers. We must look at the tellers – their distinctive structural position, vested interests, preferred language – and not the tales.

Notes

1. Nisbet (1962) interestingly quotes Marx as the only dissenting voice among the founding fathers who warned against the romanticism of the community ideal. Writing in 1853 about the village community in India, Marx (while deploring the 'sickening loss' of the traditional community as a consequence of English colonialism) noted also: 'we must not forget that these idyllic village communities, inoffensive though they must appear, had always been the solid foundation of Oriental despotism, that they restrained the human mind within the smallest possible compass, making it the unwitting tool of superstition, enslaving it beneath traditional rules, depriving it of all grandeur and historical energies'. Despite this warning, though, it does not seem to me that many contemporary heirs to the Marxist traditions have really questioned the idealisation of community. For a notable exception, see Sennet *et al.* (1977).
2. On such attempts to establish free enclaves of the self, see Cohen and Taylor (1977).
3. I deal elsewhere (Cohen, 1981) with the problems of transferring crime-control models back and forth between industrialised and developing societies.
4. Some recent reviews include Burchard and Harig (1976), Richard (1977) and Stumphauzer (1979).

References

Abel, R. L. (1979), 'Delegalization: a critical review of its ideology, manifestations and social consequences', in E. Blankenburg et al. (eds.), *Alternative Rechtsformen und Alternative zum Reche* (Jahrbuch für Rechtssoziologie Bund G), Opladen.

Abel, R. L. (1981), 'Conservative conflict and the reproduction of capitalism: the role of informal justice', *International Journal of the Sociology of Law*, vol. 9, pp. 245–67.

Bayer, R. (1981), 'Crime, punishment and the decline of liberal optimism', *Crime and Delinquency*, vol. 27, no. 2, pp. 169–90.

Beck, B. (1979), 'The limits of deinstitutionalization', in M. Lewis (ed.), *Research in Social Problems and Public Policy*, vol. 1, Greenwich, JAI Press.

Becker, H. S. (1967), 'Whose side are we on?', *Social Problems*, vol. 14, no. 3, pp. 239–47.

Beit-Hallahmi, B. (1976), 'Psychological theories and correctional practise: a historical note'. *Corrective and Social Psychiatry*, vol. 22, no. 4, pp. 38–9.

Bottoms, A. E. (1977), 'Reflections on the renaissance of dangerousness', *Howard Journal of Penology and Crime Prevention*, vol. 16, no. 2, pp. 70–96.

Burchard, J. D. and Harig, R. T. (1976), 'Behaviour modification and juvenile delinquency', In H. Leitenberg (ed.), *Handbook of Behavior Modification and Behavior Therapy*, Englewood Cliffs, NJ, Prentice-Hall.

Clarke, R. V. G. and Mayhew, P. (eds.) (1980), *Designing Out Crime*, London, HMSO.

Cohen, S. (1979b), 'The punitive city: notes on the dispersal of social control', *Contemporary Crises*, vol. 3, pp. 339–63.

Cohen, S. (1981), 'Western crime control models on the third world: benign or malignant?', in R. Simon and S. Spitzer (eds.), *Research in Law, Deviance and Social Control*, vol. 4, Greenwich, JAI Press.

Cohen, S. and Taylor, L. (1977), *Escape Attempts: The Theory and Practice of Resistance to Everyday Life*, London, Allen Lane.

Davis, D. B. (1980), 'The crime of reform', *New York Review of Books* (26 June), pp. 14–17.

Davis, F. (1979), *Yearning for Yesterday: A Sociology of Nostalgia*, London, Collier Macmillan.

Donzelot, J. (1980), *The Policing of Families*, London, Hutchinson.

Edelman, M. (1964), *The Symbolic Uses of Politics*, Urbana, University of Illinois Press.

Etzioni, A. (1972a), 'Human beings are not very easy to change after all', in *Saturday Review* (3 June) (reprinted in *Annual Editions: Readings in Social Problems*, Dushkin, 1973).

Etzioni, A. (1972b), 'The grant shaman', *Psychology Today* (November).

Foucault, M. (1977a), *Discipline and Punish: the Birth of the Prison*, London, Allen Lane.

Foucault. M. (1980d), in C. Gordon (ed.), *Michel Foucault: Power/Knowledge, Selected Interviews and Other Writings 1972–1977*, Brighton, Harvester Press.

Gaylin, W. et al. (1978), *Doing Good: The Limits of Benevolence*, New York, Pantheon.

Greenberg, D. (1975), 'Problems in community corrections', *Issues in Criminology*, vol. 19, pp. 1–34.

References

Higgins, J. (1980), 'Social control theories of social policy', *Journal of Social Policy*, vol. 9, no. 1.

Ignatieff, M. (1978), *A Just Measure of Pain: The Penitentiary in the Industrial Revolution,* London, Macmillan.

Jeffrey, C. R. (ed.), (1976), 'Criminal behaviour and the physical environment', *American Behavioral Scientist*, vol. 20, no. 2 (November–December).

Lasch, C. (1977), *Haven in a Heartless World: The Family Besieged,* New York, Basic Books.

Lasch, C. (1980a), 'Life in the therapeutic state', *New York Review of Books,* vol. xxvii, no. 10, pp. 24–32 (12 June).

Lasch, C. (1980b), 'Review of Rothman', Conscience and Convenience, *The Nation,* pp. 29–30 (14 June).

Leach, E. R. (1970), *Political Systems of Highland Burma: A Study of Kachin Social Structure,* London, Athlone Press (1st edn, 1954).

McKelvey, B. (1977), *American Prisons: A History of Good Intentions,* Montclair, NJ, Patterson Smith.

Marx, K. and Engels, F. (1970), *The German Ideology,* Lawrence and Wishart.

Melossi, D. and Pavarini, M. (1981), *The Prison and the Factory: Origins of the Penitentiary System,* London, Macmillan.

Mills, C. W. (1943), 'The professional ideology of social pathologists', *American Journal of Sociology,* vol. 46, no. 2 (September), pp. 165–80.

Morris, E. K. (1980), 'Applied behavior analysis for criminal justice practise: some current dimensions', *Criminal Justice and Behavior,* vol. 7, no. 2 (June), pp. 131–47.

Newman, O. (1980), *Community of Interest,* New York, Anchor Press.

Nisbet, R. A. (1962), *The Quest for Community,* New York, OUP.

Nisbet, R. A. (1966), *The Sociological Tradition,* New York, Basic Books.

Orwell, G. (1949), *Nineteen Eighty-Four,* London, Secker & Warburg.

Plant, R. (1974), *Community and Ideology: An Essay in Applied Social Philosophy,* London, Routledge & Kegan Paul.

Platt, A. and Takagi, P. (1977), 'Intellectuals for law and order: a critique of the new "Realists"', *Crime and Social Justice,* vol. 8, pp. 1–6.

Richard, H. C. (ed.) (1977), *Behavioural Intervention in Human Problems,* New York, Pergamon.

Rothman, D. J. (1971), *The Discovery of the Asylum,* Boston, Mass., Little Brown.

Rothman, D. J. (1974), 'Prisons: the failure model', *Nation* (21 December).

Rothman, D. J. (1978), 'Introduction' and 'The State as Parent', in W. Gaylin *et al., Doing Good: The Limits of Benevolence,* New York, Pantheon.

Rothman, D. J. (1980), *Conscience and Convenience: The Asylum and its Alternatives in Progressive America,* Boston, Mass., Little Brown.

Rusche, G., and Kirchheimer, O. (1939), *Punishment and Social Structure,* New York, Columbia University Press (reissued by Russell & Russell, New York, 1968).

Scull, A. T. (1977a). *Decarceration: Community Treatment and the Deviant – A Radical View,* Englewood Cliffs, NJ, Prentice-Hall.

Scull, A. (1981), 'Progressive dreams, progressive nightmares: social control in twentieth century America', *Stanford Law Review,* vol. 33, pp. 301–16.

Seiter, R. P. *et al.* (1977), *Halfway Houses,* Washington, DC, National Institute of Law Enforcement and Criminal Justice, LEAA.

Sennet, R. (1978), *The Fall of Public Man,* London, OUP.

References

Sennet, R. *et al.* (1977), 'Destructive Gemeinschaft', in N. Birnbaum (ed.), *Beyond the Crisis,* New York, OUP.

Shover, N. (1980), *A Sociology of American Corrections,* Homewood, Ill., Dorsey Press.

Spitzer, S, (1979a), 'Notes towards a theory of punishment and social change', in S. Spitzer (ed.), *Research in Law and Sociology,* Greenwich, JAI Press, pp. 201–29.

Spitzer, S. (1979b), 'The rationalization of crime control in capitalist society', *Contemporary Crises,* vol. 3, pp. 187–206.

Stang, D. T. and Snare, A. (1978), 'The coercion of privacy', in C. Smart and B. Smart (eds.), *Women, Sexuality and Social Control,* London, Routledge &. Kegan Paul.

Stedman-Jones, G. (1977), 'Class expression versus social control?', *History Workshop Journal,* vol. IV, pp. 163–71.

Steinfels, P. (1979), *The Neo-Conservatives: The Men who are Changing American Politics,* New York, Simon & Schuster.

Stumphauzer, J. S. (ed.) (1979), *Progress in Behaviour Therapy with Delinquents,* Springfield, Ill., Charles C, Thomas.

Waltzer, M. (1980), *Radical Principles,* New York, Basic Books.

Wilson, J. Q. (1974), 'Crime and the criminologists', *Commentary,* (July), p. 49.

Wilson, J. Q. (1981), 'What works? revisited: new findings on criminal rehabilitation', *The Public Interest,* no. 61, pp. 3–17.

Yochelson, S. and Samenow, S. E. (1976), *The Criminal Personality,* Vol. 1, New York, Aronson.

[11]
The Critical Discourse on "Social Control": Notes on the Concept as a Hammer*

Introduction

Children (invariably boys) are sometimes given a toy hammer for a present. At first they learn the many good uses of the instrument, like hitting nails into wood; then they discover some other uses and delights like banging on the floor, attacking a baby sibling, enjoying the sound of breaking glass. This is when parents regret buying the present.

In sociology—as elsewhere—concepts are used like hammers. A formless and recalcitrant reality is banged into shape, rendering it manageable and comprehensible. This is both necessary and inevitable; otherwise there would be no need for "science". Sometimes, though (like small children with their hammers) the project gets a little out of hand. The concept/hammer is wielded with much imagination and inventiveness, but without much attention to consequences.

In this paper, I consider some such features of the concept of social control as they appear in various radical, critical or revisionist writings about crime, deviance, and law over the past two decades. There are considerable differences within this literature—between early labeling theory, the Marxist phase of critical criminology, the European abolitionist stream, the emergent left realism—but for the purpose of this exercise, I will stay with the consensus. This is to be found in the eventual emergence in the 1980s of a quite distinctive discourse of "revisionist" or "critical" social control theory—a discourse in which common theoretical assumptions are brought to bear on a wide range of substantive areas (crime, mental illness, sexuality etc.) and social processes (decarceration, medicalisation, privatisation, net-widening etc.). [1]

---

* This is a revised version of a paper that originally appeared in Dutch in R. van Swaaningen *et al* (eds.) *A Tort et à Travers: Liber Americorum Herman Bianchi* (Amsterdam: Free University Press, 1988).

348 *Stanley Cohen*

My aim is not to lay down some correct usage for the concept and then reprimand others for not following the epistemological party line. This is rather a stock-taking exercise, which singles out those features of this literature which have become common wisdom and distinguish it from anything that went before. These tendencies seem to me to have been mostly inevitable, neither the cause for celebration nor condemnation, but rather as markers that show which routes were taken. After listing these tendencies, I then single out a few problems worthy of future attention that are already beginning to be acknowledged within the critical discourse itself.

I will not say much about "what went before" critical social control theory, though I do accept the argument (being worked out most explicitly by Melossi, 1989) that many of the confusions in this literature are derived from the concept's erratic genealogy. To trace this genealogy seriously, we would have to move through three phases: first, the original meaning of the problem of "social control" as it appeared to pre-20th century social thought; second, the domestication of the concept in American sociology, particularly in the Chicago School and Parsonian functionalism; and finally (the point where my story begins) the emergence of social control as being more or less synonymous with "reactions to deviance" in the interactionist and labelling theories of the mid-60s followed then by the radicalisation of the concept in New Left or Marxist formulations about repression, coercion, criminalisation and "law and the state". We are left with traces from all these periods: the classic political question of how social order is possible; the social psychological problems of socialisation, conformity and internalisation; the dialectic between deviance and control as it appears in concepts such as labeling, stigma and amplification; and then the attempt to "bring the state back in" through a historically informed analysis of such structures and ideologies as the prison and the rule of law.

Tendencies

Ten Features of the Critical Discourse

1. The first and most noteworthy tendency in the revisionist literature is the use of the concept of social control to refer to a single, essentialist "thing". Whether the project is historical, theoretical, descriptive or policy directed, the concept appears as unitary and unifying. Something called social control happens in all societies; it takes many forms and appears in many places but is always a manifestation of the same essence.

At the immediate linguistic level this means invoking the concept as the common denominator for a wide variety of social processes: the operation of state security systems, the hospitalisation of schizophrenics, the streaming of unruly school children, the normative power of gender or whatever. At a more ambitious empirical level, the project is to unravel the increasing interdepend-

The Critical Discourse on "Social Control"

ency between various structures and ideologies of control. Otherwise (to the naive observer) separate institutions, mechanisms, strategies, professionals and beliefs are alleged to be overlapping, to be blurring into each other. Thus various "complexes"—penal, welfare, judicial, therapeutic—become united. At an even more ambitious level, the concept becomes imperialist. It is extended to go beyond the obvious coercive control functions of the state (military, police, judicial) beyond the regulation and care of "soft" deviance (through social work, psychiatry, clinical psychology), to the entire institutional apparatus of the modern state, whether formally designated as education, health or welfare.

All this is done by pointing to: overlaps in clientele (the same population is relabeled); interchangability of personnel (the same professionals move shop from one target group to another); the growth of common ideologies or knowledge systems (medicalisation, behaviourism); the same developments which affect different groups (privatisation, decentralisation or centralisation; in-, de- or trans-carceration); the presence of similar causal patterns (fiscal crisis, rationalisation) and an assumed identity of objectives (education or psychiatry or welfare "as" social control).

2. Social control is conceived as an active, autonomous force that has to be explained, not with reference to the character of the "deviance" but by its own internal properties or its relationship with the wider social order. Social control, that is, is not merely reactive nor does it ever show any rational correspondence to the amount, intensity or nature of the deviance to which it is supposedly addressed.

The project is to elevate the sociology of social control (or of punishment or "penality") into a subject with its own internal trajectory. This can be done (as in labeling theory) by depicting the content of control cultures, doing ethnographies of control agencies or watching control agents at work. In later structural and historical models, the strategy is to explain the origins and transformations of control mechanisms (such as the prison) or ideologies (such as the rule of law). Thus in one of the most sophisticated examples in the current literature, the historical and sociological questions become, respectively, "how is penal change possible and how does it come about?" and "what is the relationship which holds between punishment and social structure or rather between forms of penality and the forms of social organization within which they operate" (Garland, 1985 p. vii).

Depending on the favoured theory, the answers to such questions lie in: humanitarianism; moral enterprise; rationalisation and bureaucracy; the fiscal crisis of the state; the perpetuation of capitalism; the power-knowledge complex; the interests of professionals . . . and so on. In each case the tendency is to see the object of social control (whom or what is being controlled) as a *tabula rasa*, a blank space which is given identity and form only through the operation of social control. Deviance is an artifact of social control, virtually a reflection of this active and autonomous force which has a life of its own. In this respect, despite their obvious other theoretical differences, there is something similar between the interactionist/labelling model, of, for example, sexual deviance (or sexuality in general) and Foucault's account of the normalising power which constructs the domain of sexuality and gives it differential meanings.

3. There is a concomitant refusal to analyse the ideologies and structures of social control in their own terms (justice, deterrence, treatment, welfare, reform), rather, they are traced back to wider social contexts and interests. The "taken for granted" constructs of social control (whether physical constructs such as the juvenile court, or social constructs such as normal sexuality) are pulled out of their nominal systems of power and knowledge (criminology, criminal justice, counselling, social work, psychiatry) and re-located instead as different forms of the essentialist phenomenon of social control. This in turn becomes located in terms of whatever master force is alleged to lie behind the common sense appearance (mode of production, inchoate sense of social disorder or reproduction of class relationships).

Alternatively, deconstructionism leads not to the identification of any one of these hidden master forces, but to the conclusion that the deconstructed fragments defy any reassembly at all. This debate appeared less in the early phase of revisionism (where essentialism was assumed) than in current versions such as critical legal studies. Here, to deconstruct law as a repository of noble liberal principles may be to reveal not a "ruling class game plan" but a "plastic medium of discourse" (Gordon, 1988, p. 15).

4. This refusal to take ideology, claims, pretentions, intentions and programmes wholly in their own terms, leads to a characteristic "hermeneutics of suspicion". Social control talk (penal philosophies, medical ethics, reforming ideals, humanitarianism) is demystified (exposed as fairy stories, myths, rationalisations) and reduced to matters of self-serving professional rhetoric, economic interest or the will to power. Liberals thus tend to be somewhat suspicious of intentions (the mistrust of benevolence) and wholly sceptical of consequences (disasterous, counter-productive); radicals are either uninterested in questions of success or failure (dismissed as "correctionalism") or assume failure to be inevitable (the function of the prison is to create delinquents).

5. The results of this demystificatory, debunking exercise invariably opens up the dark side of the dialectic. Social control is seen in sinister, negative and pejorative terms. The concept is gradually stripped of any benign or even neutral meaning. Consequences are invariably malignant.

6. There is an overall trend to favour historical, not to say historicist theories and research strategies. The original revisionist social histories about the transformation of social control in early European capitalism (the birth of the prison, the codification of the criminal law, the origins of public policing, the growth of professional monopolies) have not only become influential in their own terms (not to be historical is now a cause for embarrassment) but are widely taken to be models which explain contemporary reality. These are

"histories of the present". More particularly (and somewhat peculiarly) the history of incarceration is widely used as a model for analysing other transformations in social control practices.

Even if not explicitly sharing Foucault's "genealogy of morals", these demonstrations of historical contingency tend to "debunk grand values by pointing to their lowly origins", notably their "parochial and non-edifying character" (Minson, 1985 p. 18).

7. Throughout the revisionist literature, a privileged role is given to the working of the modern state—identified with the public and formal realm, the polity. The explanatory question "who controls the controllers?" is invariably referred back to the powers of the centralised, panopticonal and omnipotent state.

The modes and sites of "primary" or "informal" social control (family, peer group, religion, morality, public opinion, community) are taken as given or ignored or (as in the paradigm derived from the history of incarceration) assumed to be disintegrating. The state somehow has to "compensate" for weak primary social control. Those modes of social control which are non-primary but formal (in the sense of being organised responses to deviance and social problems) and non-statist (derived from various voluntary, self-help or community models) do receive attention, but usually as modes that only function in the shadow of the state system. They are seen, that is, as compromised, liable to co-option and dependent on the largesse of the state. Finally, the social control functions performed by market forces, receive little attention at all when they are "primary" (mass media, popular culture, advertising). The market enters the discourse only when it takes over existing state systems ("privatization"), works for them (e.g. manufacturing surveillance technologies) or mimics them (e.g. private policing).

8. There is a tendency to identify the eventual rationality of organised systems of social control: to assume the existence of a game plan that "works". Despite the apparent absurdities, ironies and failures which the demystification project unveils, there must surely be some logic, some hidden pattern behind the exercise of state power. Somewhere there is a master (state, capital) or master pattern (social order, functional pre-requisites, class hierarchy) which ultimately makes sense of all the confusion.

9. It is assumed that there is an overarching trend in modern societies (all? just capitalist?) towards *more* social control. To the extent that it is capable of measurement—using such indicators as capital expenditure on criminal justice, number of psychiatrists, proportionate rates of the population in prison—social control is becoming more intensive, intrusive and extensive. There is a relentless and voracious move towards the processing of more people and actions. In the familiar metaphor: the net is widening.

10. Finally, the literature both celebrates and is part of, the growth of various social movements which were aimed at changing or replacing the original taken for granted structures and ideologies of social control. Critical social

control theory did not originate in any sort of detached, disinterested scholarly enterprise. It was and is partisan and political in proclaiming its commitment to alternative values, visions and policies. Such commitment takes the form of: support for specific destructuring movements (decarceration, decriminalisation, deprofessionalisation, informal justice, anti-psychiatry etc); allegiance to some visionary alternative (justice without law, diversity without criminalisation, reduction of pain, abolition of punishment, socialist legality, etc.) and preference for styles of work and presentations of self which are simultaneously analytical and normative. The support for alternatives is today much more qualified, ranging from cautious re-affirmation (Cohen, 1987) to an even more guarded re-assessment (Mathews, 1988), but there is seldom an outright rejection.

Problems

The caricatured style in which I listed those 10 features of critical social control discourse obviously invites a reconsideration of each one—proof that the hammer is being wielded too enthusiastically. No, social control is not the same thing everywhere; yes, it sometimes is directly reactive and responsible; yes, intentions and claims deserve often to be taken at their face value... This humourless exercise is however, beyond my scope here. No doubt it can and should be done (and this, of course, is just the type of revision of revisionism that we are now witnessing). The self-referential nature of post-modernity ensures that any critical discourse is soon subject to its own deconstruction, not from the old orthodoxies (which now become increasingly difficult to identify) but from sympathetic fellow "radicals". Each one of those 10 features could be described in the past tense, or at least as being already subject to dispute.

Thus, for example: the unmasking of the supposed control functions of law, medicine, welfare, and especially psychiatry, have been denounced as "tedious repetitions" (Adlam & Rose, 1981; Miller & Rose, 1986): many critics of state-centred theory have returned to contemplating the market, consumerism and the commercialisation of desire; yet other radicals have been re-reading Foucault to derive an image of power and resistance quite different from the monolith of repressive social control. Then, of course, there is left realist criminology which comes close to asserting that the whole deconstructionist focus on social control (rather than criminals and their victims) was a self-indulgent, idealistic evasion from "confronting" the real problems of crime. [2]

Feminist theory has been particularly important in this current phase: reviewing the standard distinctions between formal and informal control; questioning the inevitable pairing between deviance and control; criticising the "law as social control" equation in regard to the regulation of women, family and sexuality (Brophy & Smart, 1985) in order to argue for abandoning the whole concept of social control (Chunn & Gavigan, 1988) and—

The Critical Discourse on "Social Control" 353

increasingly in "friendship" with Foucault (Diamond & Quinby, 1988)—looking for strategies of resistance.

This entire package needs careful attention. What I will do instead, is select out of a few of the more obvious now emerging. These are all directly or obliquely related to those original 10 features of the original revisionist enterprise.

1. Demystification produces its own form of mystification. The dismissal of ideology and intention as merely epiphenomenal, the search for a unifying causal nexus, the reluctance to concede proclaimed success to existing policy; these conceptual temptations call for caution and common sense. This applies no less to the accepted historical wisdoms than it does to the evaluation of current social control practices. Indeed, the accounts of the "how" and "what" of social control changes given in most revisionist history (in its original and current phase) are far too layered and textured to allow for such glib sociological generalisations. The "trick"—as Garland notes in his review of Spierenburg's history of the development and decline of public executions (Garland, 1987)—is the old one: to do justice both to the "integrity" of the form and its "relatedness". Thus, in this example, the changing "moral sensibility" about public executions and the "punitive mentality" are both social facts with an internal integrity as well as external referents.

2. Then there is the question of the privileged status given to the formal state apparatus of social control. Afraid of the ghost of Parsons, ashamed to be heard talking "merely" of culture, interactions, micro-structures and situations we have bullied ourselves (and others) into thinking that social control is synonymous with state control. This is to ignore the dominant roles played by the family, gender, mass culture and the market in the regulation and control of social life. It is embarrassing to repeat this, for it is no more than a cliche from any "Introduction to Sociology" course. The really difficult problem is to integrate this general notion of "social control" with the more restricted notion of "organized reactions to deviance" which still informs our literature.

There are enough helpful guides in critical theory. One (more obliquely) comes from something like the Frankfurt School's analysis of mass culture. However fashionable it is now to denounce the 60s version of this tradition (via Marcuse and the old New Left), it provides a residue of ideas—about the regulation of fear, desire and need, the power of commodities and consumption—that were prematurely dropped from the social control literature. These ideas provide not just a radical alternative to the conventional way of linking social control to subjective states (consciousness, memory, internalisation, socialisation) but also (as Spitzer notes) might be more relevant in advanced capitalist societies based less on centralised political control of the Orwellian type, than a more diffuse economic regulation of need and gratification (Spitzer, 1987, pp. 56–57).

Another guide (this time more directly and explicitly) comes from feminism.

More important (in this context) than the general work on the role of the state in transforming patriarchal and family relations (the alleged shift from familial to state patriarchy, Boris and Bordaglio, 1983) has been the formidable deconstruction of all those standard dichotomies between political and personal, public and private, formal and informal, state and civil. This critique is now well-established in its own terms. Even the barest summary of its main lines—the private realm is not natural, but socially constructed; these constructs are used to legitimate control by men over women and non-intervention by the law—will expose the flaws in works such as *Visions of Social Control*. Others (Rose, 1987) go beyond these terms: instead of showing the falsity of those dichotomies (private/public etc) by revealing their essential functions for reproducing patriachy, we need a more fragmented view of power and law. This, suggests Rose, allows for a diversity of practises, a shifting and pluralistic network of agencies, decisions, bodies of knowledge and expertise which cannot in any simple sense be seen as the products of a centralised and voraciously expanding state power.

It goes without saying that only Foucault provides the master narrative to understand this alternative image of power and social control.

3. Besides the more general issues suggested by feminism, such as the question of the public and private realms, there is the more particular question of gender. The argument that gender is a normative system with its own set of rules and sanctions, through which female (and male) behaviour is controlled, calls for a new understanding of many standard issues in the social control literature. The question is not just how gender rules and roles may produce or inhibit deviance, but what are the structures and ideologies of control over women's labour, identity and sexuality. Such controls—leading to invisibility, marginality or powerlessness—are not naturally located in the terrain of crime and deviance.

Recent feminist work in such areas as divorce and family law, prostitution, abortion and birth control, pronography, adoption, family and sexualised violence suggest quite different ways of mapping this terrain. Two striking current examples might be cited: Bartky's (1988) account of how modern versions of femininity render women's bodies docile in a way distinct from the disciplinary practises addressed to men and Bordo's (1988) demonstration of how anorexia nervosa is a pathology that crystalises the cultural discourse of femininity. Such work not only questions state-centred theories of power, but dissolves the deviance/control coupling into the wider "anthropoligical" meaning of social control.

4. A further set of problems stems not from the dominance of the state-centred paradigm as such, but from the particular instrumental view of social control operations. The assumption of rationality implies not only that the state is always acting in its best interests but also that the results (however ineffective they look on the surface) actually do serve these interests. This assumption tends to support an image of the objects of social control as being passive

(docile bodies and trained souls) and receptive (the dependent variable rather than the initiator of social change).

The problem here is that totality of the vision. There is too little room for cracks in the system, irrationalities, random innovations, trial and error. And there is even less room for seeing deviants as subjects rather than objects, for allowing resistance by human agency or collective reforms which advance the interests of the powerless.

5. The final problem—the one that really subsumes all the others—is the question of specificity. In the understandable aim of uniting all those diverse fields into one rubric, a level of generality was achieved which is sometimes too diffuse, too top heavy. Many of the generalisations *have* stood up; for example, about common historical origins, relabelling of deviant populations, the connections between knowledge and power, the nature of professional interests and the changing contours of social welfare. There is still potential for conceptually colonising other areas; for example, using "state social control" framework, to understand the transformation of civil law, especially tort, contract, negligence theories, liability, workers compensation, at the end of the 19th century (Messinger & Weston, 1987). And while social control is more (and other) than "state organized reactions to deviance and crime" this meaning surely is worth contemplating in itself.

Finer distinctions have to be made, however, within these general lines. This is a banal enough suggestion, and is already being followed. For example: the concession by students of decarceration that mental health poses different questions from criminal justice, or (a much more complex issue because of the poverty of all comparative frameworks) the realisation that Western capitalist democracies are poor models for understanding social control in state socialist or third world countries.

How though to register the specific and yet be alert to the general? The standard solution to such problems is to call for conceptual rigour. And indeed one way to tidy up the conceptual waste in the social control field may be to try to formulate some rules: this, and only this, is when and how to use the hammer. Such a solution has always struck me as a ritualistic gesture of pedantry, as well as a misunderstanding of how concepts are used in the social sciences. My suggestion is something quite different: to follow the inductive and pragmatic method of simply taking as given the diverse contexts in which the concept of social control is already invoked, and then posing the appropriate empirical questions. We might construct thus, a checklist of what we should ask about whatever it is we call "social control". Cryptically, this is what such a list might contain:

1. *Agent*: Who is doing the social control? (state, market or voluntary; type of institution; bureaucratic or professional organisation).
2. *Domain*: Where is this being done? (public or private space; visible or invisible).

3. *Ideology*: What is the belief system used to justify and explain the intervention? (justice, education, therapy, welfare).
4. *Purpose*: What is the supposed aim of doing this? (re-education, deterrence, psychic change, prevention).
5. *Outcome*: What is the actual result? (consequences in line or not with the original intentions; the criteria for success or failure).
6. *Method*: How is it being done? (techniques, instruments).
7. *Target*: What are the characteristics of the populations to whom the social control is being directed? (age, gender, class . . .).
8. *Object*: What exactly is being controlled? (thoughts or behaviour; predispositions or consequences or action).
9. *Extent*: Can we measure and compare the amount and intensity of forms of intervention? (costs, numbers of agents, numbers and rates in target populations).
10. *Alternatives*: Finally (the question that only abolitionists have continued asking with such persistance) is it possible to imagine and then construct alternative ways to deal with the same problem? (This is the question that reveals the delightful paradox of critical social science: to inquire about what may be, is the best way to understand what is.)

To work with such a checklist of specificities is not to give up the possibility of generalisation; it is rather to recognise that to hammer reality with the concept of "social control" will produce neither the coherent social essence nor the unambiguous political messages that were once promised. It will reveal fragments—shifting strategies and alliances, unconnected zones of power, changing vocabularies of intervention—which cannot be reassembled by conventional means. As interpreters of post-modernity have suggested (Bauman, 1988) the project is not so much a rectification of the blunders of previous theory, but a recognition of new forms of social life.

Notes

1 My own book, (Cohen, 1985) reflected the first wave of this literature. For the current prototype of critical social control theory, see Lowman *et al.*, (1987).
2 For a commentary on this aspect of realism, see Cohen (1988), Chapter 2.

References

Adlam, D. & Rose, N. (1981) The Politics of Psychiatry. *Politics and Power* 4, 165–202.
Bartky, S. L. (1988) Foucault, feminity and the modernization of patriachal power. In *Feminism and Foucault* (Diamond I, and Quinby, L., Eds) Northeastern University Press: Boston, pp. 61–86.
Bauman, Z. (1988) Viewpoint: sociology and postmodernity. *Sociological Review* 36 pp. 790–813.
Bordo, S. (1988) Anorexia Nervosa: Psychopathology as the Crystallization of Culture.

In *Feminism and Foucault* (Diamond I. and Quinby L. eds) Northeastern University Press: Boston, pp. 87–118.

Brophy J. & Smart C. (1985) *Women in Law* London: Routledge & Kegan Paul.

Chunn, D. E. & Gavigan, S. A. M. (1988) Social Control: analytical tool or analytical quagmire? *Contemporary Crises* **12, 2**, pp. 107–124.

Cohen, S. (1985) *Visions of Social Control: Crime, Punishment and Classification.* Polity Press: Cambridge.

Cohen, S. (1987) Taking decentralization seriously: values, victims and policies. In *Transcarceration* (Lowman, J. et al., Eds) Gower, Aldershot pp. 358–379.

Cohen, S. (1988) *Against Criminology.* Transaction: New Brunswick N.J.

Diamond, I. & Quinby, L. (1988) *Feminism and Foucault: Reflections on Resistance.* Northeastern University Press: Boston.

Garland, D. (1985) *Punishment and Welfare: A History of Penal Strategies.* Gower: Aldershot.

Garland, D. (1987) The punitive mentality: its socio-historic development and decline. *Contemporary Crises* **10, 3**, 305–320.

Gordon, R. W. (1988) Law and ideology. *Tikkun* **3**, pp. 14–18.

Lowman, J., Menzies, R. J. & Palys T. S. (1987) Eds: *Transcarceration: Essays in the Sociology of Social Control* Gower: Aldershot.

Mathews, R. (Ed.) (1988) *Informal Justice* Sage: London.

Melossi, D. (1989) *The State of Social Control* Polity: Cambridge.

Messinger, S. L. and Weston, N. A. (1987) Social Control in Industrial Society: Garland's *Punishment and Welfare. American Bar Foundation Research Journal* 1987, **4** 791–807.

Miller, P. and Rose, N. (Eds) (1986) *The Power of Psychiatry.* Polity: Cambridge.

Minson, J. (1985) *Genealogies of Morals.* Macmillan: London.

Rose, N. (1987) Beyond the Public/Private Division: Law Power and the Family. *Journal of Law and Society* **14, 1**, 61–76.

Spitzer, S. (1987) Security and control in capitalist societies: the fetishism of security and the secret thereof. In *Transcarceration* (Lowman et al., Ed.) Gower: Aldershot, pp. 43–58.

[12]
Alternatives to Punishment – The Abolitionist Case

Heinz Steinert[1] and Louk Hulsman[2] represent "abolitionism" — a stream of critical thinking about criminology, crime, criminal law and punishment that has been developing in Western Europe (mainly Holland, Germany, Austria and Norway) over the past two decades. Given that the participants to this Conference are mainly Anglo-American and Israeli academics or lawyers who have been quite insulated from this intellectual movement, it seemed to me that my most useful task as commentator would be to place these ideas in their wider intellectual context. After this, I will select a few general themes from these papers and compare them to the papers by Abel[3] and Galanter[4] in the related session on "Alternatives to Punishment".

My own position towards abolitionism is that of a sympathetic, but critical fellow traveller: I agree with much, want to believe more but am skeptical about some.

Abolitionism as "Deconstruction"

In the mid to late 1960s, a number of areas in the humanities and social sciences were seized by a deconstructionist impulse. This initially took the form of a radical questioning of dominant theories, categories and methods of enquiry — for example, by the various "anti-positivist"

---

1 Heinz Steinert, "Is There Justice? No — Just Us", in this issue, at p. 710.
2 Louk Hulsman, "The Abolitionist Case: Alternative Crime Policies", in this issue, at p. 681.
3 Richard Abel, "The Failure of Punishment as Social Control", in this issue, at p. 740.
4 Marc Galanter, "Punishment: Civil Style", in this issue, at p. 759.

tendencies in the social sciences. At the same time, these intellectual and academic exercises were complemented by the growth of social movements aimed at "liberation" from various structures of domination. These two levels of attack — knowledge and power — were eventually drawn together by Foucault in the most uncompromising possible way: an undermining, no less, of the whole base of liberal enquiry about the nature of the human subject. We are only now beginning to absorb and revise the products of this intellectual revolution.

In the small (and still largely unknown) sector of this movement which is relevant to this Conference, the old subjects of crime and punishment, deviance and control, also came under critical scrutiny. The results were: (i) the formation within criminology, law, sociology, social work and psychiatry of various radical, critical or counter cultures dedicated to reconstituting their disciplines and professions; (ii) the establishment of social movements aimed at weakening, by-passing or abolishing conventional structures of legality, punishment, control and treatment, and setting up alternatives; and (iii) struggles by various deviant groups themselves for liberation from the techniques of control and the dominant modes of thinking which they saw as oppressive.

These attacks were expressed at the level of *power* — an attempt to change actual policy and practice — and *knowledge* — an attempt to change cognition, theory and disciplinary paradigms. Thus:

(1) *Power* — the growth of movements and ideologies directed against the basic structures and techniques of the modern crime control system as laid down from the end of the 18th to the beginning of the 19th centuries. (The consolidation and centralization of the state's crime control monopoly through the criminal law; the categorization of deviant, criminal and dependent groups into separate types, each with its own system of accredited knowledge and professional power; the segregation and incarceration of these criminal and deviant populations into closed-purpose-built institutions of care, treatment and custody).

(2) *Knowledge* — the development of counter theories and paradigms directed against positivist criminology (and allied disciplines). The object of attack becomes those "normalizing" sciences which — in Foucault's terms — emerge as "alibis" for the exercise of power, embodiments of the replacement of the body by the "soul" as the object of penal power. Thus in criminology and the sociology of deviance: labelling theory, abolitionism and critical criminology; in psychiatry: anti-psychiatry; in law: critical legal studies.

At both these levels, these counter-ideologies assumed political forms — sometimes implicitly and sometimes stridently. Both conservative and liberal assumptions were attacked in the name of various permutations of Marxism, anarchism and critical theory.

The following Table gives a caricatured summary of the varied mid-sixties destructuring movements that operated in the areas of crime, punishment and social control.

Base: 19th Century Transformations	1960's Counter Ideologies/ Destructuring Movements
Power	
(1) Centralized State Control	Decentralization; Deformalization; Decriminalization; Diversion; Divestment; Informalism; Non-intervention
(2) Categorization; Separate knowledge sytems; Expertise; Professionalization	Decategorization; Deprofessionalization; Demedicalization; Delegalization; Anti-psychiatry; Self-help; Removal of stigma and labels; Abolitionism
(3) Segregation: Victory of the asylum	Decarceration; De-institutionalization; Community control; Prison Abolition
Knowledge	
(1) Positivist Theory: Move from "Body" to "Mind"	(a) New deviancy theory — interactionism-labelling theory (b) Critical/new/radical criminology (left idealist) (c) Abolitionism
(2) From Classical to Positivist Criminology	Back to Justice; Neo-classicism; Behaviourism
Politics	
"Conservative" practice Liberal hegemony over theory	(1) Neo-liberal scepticism (2) Variations of Marxist, anarchist and libertarian "New Leftism" (3) Neo-conservative

This is not the place for a detailed commentary on these developments nor for an account of their subsequent fate.[5] I simply wanted to set the context for an understanding of Hulsman's and Steinert's versions of abolitionism — which have turned out to be the most radical and durable of the original deconstructionist impulses. "Radical" because they operate both at the levels of knowledge and power, and insist throughout on an uncompromising and literal reading of the deconstructionist project; "durable" because most of the other sixties movements have, in the name of "realism", retreated from their original positions.

Let me now summarize the way in which abolitionists present their case.[6] Taking their geneology from the movements for the abolition of *slavery*, then *imprisonment* (but not, strangely, the death penalty), they argue that *punishment* itself — at least as it appears in the conventional criminal/penal law model — should and can be abolished. To arrive at this point, we are invited to move through this five-part sequence:

(1) Events that are criminalized — and hence candidates for state regulated punishment — make up only a minute part of events that *can* be so criminalized. These events have nothing in common other than the fact that they have been usurped by the criminal justice system. The criminal justice system has been given or taken authority over them.

(2) Crime, as Hulsman says, thus has no "ontologicical reality" independent of the definitional activities of the criminal justice system. Crime is not the *object* but the *product* of criminal justice policy.

(3) Only inertia, habit, bad faith, vested interest, ideological hegemony — an unreflexive commitment to what Hulsman calls the "penal dialect" (something like Foucault's discourse) — prevents us from finding other ways of dealing with those events. That is, other cognitive ways (knowledge — the way we see these events) and other policy ways (power — what we do about them).

---

5   I provide this in *Visions of Social Control* (Cambridge, Polity Press, 1985) and *Against Criminology* (New Jersey, Transaction, 1988).
6   In addition to Hulsman's and Steinert's papers at this Conference, I draw here on other writings by them and other European abolitionists (Christie, Bianchi, Mathiesen, Scheerer et al). For an introduction to this literature, see the Special Issue (1986) 10 Contemporary Crises: Law, Crime and Social Policy.

(4) We *should* look for these other ways. Why? Because the criminal justice system as we know it (the mode of identifying, blaming and punishing individuals) is: *unjust* (see the critique of domination in Steinert's paper); *ineffective* (allocating blame to individuals has little effect on the "crime problem" — and to think otherwise is to confuse the two quite separate questions of what to do with individuals identified as perpetrators, and events which are classified as criminal); and *counter-productive* or *damaging*. These three criticisms are, as abolitionists note, conventional criminological wisdom. Only they, however, take them seriously.

(5) These alternative ways not only should, but can be found. In *cognitive* terms: by re-classifying events (as they are done "naturally" anyway) into the language of "conflicts", "troubles", "disputes", "problems", "undesirable behaviour", etc. As in the pristine version of labelling theory, this is epistemological politics, the politics of the inverted comma. What had happened in classifying these events as "crime" (as in classifying madness as "mental illness") was a gigantic error of categorization. And in *policy* terms: by seeking or devising alternative forms of social control outside the criminal law model. Thus the abolitionist emphasis on dispute mediation, conflict resolution, technical prevention, models drawn from civil law and tort, etc. Their historical and philosophical concerns are thus combined — most unusually — with a very practical involvement in real-life experiments in alternative living.

Punishment as the Problem

For abolitionists, then, punishment is not a solution to be justified by philosophers, allocated by lawyers and measured by criminologists. It is a problem to be solved by an imaginative quest for alternatives.

This claim, I believe, is based primarily on ideological and normative grounds. In the conventional criminological discourse, however — to which abolitionists, despite themselves, belong — the claim appears in instrumental terms. The assertion, that is, is that punishment by means of criminal law is a particularly ineffective form of social control. As Abel puts it: state imposed sanctions are "unacceptably ineffective". He gives two plausible reasons for this: that behaviour punished by the state is encouraged by other social institutions and that the threat of punishment is empty because its likelihood is so slight. The abolitionist, as well as conventional research literature, suggests many other good reasons. It is a bizarre tribute to criminology that its major industry for nearly two decades has been to prove that "nothing works".

This finding (or assumption or allegation — depending on your reading of the literature) generates an equally significant theoretical question: why, despite failure, does punishment remain? The answer for abolitionists, for Abel, for most social control theorists and, most elegantly for Foucault, is that punishment does not "fail" because it was never intended to succeed. It functions less as an instrumental mechanism to produce conformity than as an ideological or symbolic construction designed to empower the state and to exclude its social enemies — in Steinert's words: "a show of energetic state action that does not do harm to important social interests while at the same time eliminating single persons who have no social backing".

I want to concentrate my comments, though, on neither of these dual assumptions of instrumental failure and ideological success, but on a series of related claims made by Steinert and Hulsman (and referred to by Abel and Galanter). The issue is what we should *do* with the slogan "legitimation despite failure". Join the abolitionist cause? Keep up the eternal quest for something that "works"? Or take the path of compromise — the "accretionist" attempt to give the punitive-legal model only the minimum possible power?

Much depends on how we evaluate these three claims: (1) that the actual willingness or desire of citizens in modern society to evoke the punishment response is less than it might appear; (2) that, outside the criminal law, there is very little punishment and that systems of regulation such as the civil law offer alternative models of non-punitive control; and (3) that the social control of undesirable behaviour by non-punitive methods is thus altogether feasible. A few words about each of these claims.

(1) *A "naturally" low punishment response?*

The question is not even deceptively simple: what status has punishment (via the criminal justice system) in the entire repertoire of responses to conflict, damage, normative deviation, victimization, trouble, etc.?

In historical (or geneological) terms, the abolitionist answer here is quite straightforward and unobjectionable. Clearly, they are right to note that the punishment/criminal law model is highly relative and historically specific. Whether this means that we should seek for alternatives is, of course, more problematic — as is any appeal to historical and cultural variability.

The empirical, contemporary issue — what happens in any one society — is more complicated. Steinert and Hulsman argue that in the whole repertoire of social control, punishment through the criminal law is (variously):

- a relatively unimportant measure: non-legal approaches are statistically and normatively the rule, rather than the exception (not only has this always been so, but is so now);
- something that only comes very late in the reaction sequence: that is, well after other responses have been tried;
- only of secondary, tactical concern in dealing with problems and conflicts. (Similarly justice — and here Steinert seems to me wrong — is also only of tactical concern). People are not interested in justice via punishment; they actually want less punishment (victims, for example, will settle for compensation and care — and not seek revenge).

In other words, abolitionists don't have to preach their message — people are "naturally" abolitionist. Instead, for example, of devoting so much energy to root out the famous "dark figure" of crime (the favourite enterprise of criminologists/police throughout the world) we should be *celebrating* the fact that so few criminalizable events ever get reported as such. Abolitionists are not utopians saying what should be, but pointing to what already is part of daily life.

How do we evaluate these claims? One form of evidence is clearly on the abolitionist side: that most criminalizable events are never punished. In Abel's summary: "Americans actually are very reluctant to mobilize both criminal and civil processes with the result that the vast majority of normative violations go unpunished" (p. 744). The literature documents many good reasons for this: the nature of urban life, perceptions of the police and criminal justice, the tendency of social institutions to shield their members from the state, the interest in material compensation rather than vindictiveness, etc. All this may indeed make people "natural abolitionists".

On the other hand, though, the notion that society is non-punitive is, as Abel says, wholly counter-intuitive and against common sense. The overwhelming trend in modern society is to increase the range of behaviour that the state will punish, to increase the number of people drawn into the criminal justice system and to increase the severity of punishment. In all Western societies, the net of formal state social control is becoming more complex, extensive and intensive. And — to the extent that opinion surveys measure anything — intense public punitiveness towards crime is a constant component of most such societies.

There are, of course, plausible ways of reconciling these two opposing forms of evidence. For example: although people sense that the law and punishment are ineffective, they can still be seduced by the false promise of instrumentalism; the punitive apparatus will always draw on its symbolic and ideological power; public opinion surveys about "punitiveness" create reifications which bear no relationship to how people live; people use the criminal justice system for strategic reasons only (e.g., to report losses for insurance); professional and state monopolies have disempowered people, making them feel weak and helpless.

Plausible as these arguments might sound, however, it does not seem to me that abolitionists have clearly demonstrated (rather than merely assumed) that the reluctance to seek punishment is somehow a "natural" human response. Nor is it sufficient for them to dismiss as misguided the extraordinary trend today for those "radical" groups, previously the most suspicious of the criminalizing power of the state, to be supporting campaigns for "heavy" criminalization in areas such as rape, domestic violence, pornography and ecology.

(2) *Non-punitive forms of regulation outside the criminal law?*

Most of the abolitionist enterprise is devoted to discovering, encouraging and expanding forms of regulation and control outside the penal law model. This has been an altogether rewarding exercise — but it has raised some awkward problems for the overall abolitionist vision. For example:

(i) As Galanter's paper suggests, many "indigenous" forms of ordering and control outside the criminal law do contain elements of punishment. His claim, indeed, is that a large part of punishment as a social institution lies outside the law. True, these extra-legal forms of punishment often exist "in the shadow of the law" (law delegates the power to punish to codes, tribunals, professional associations, etc). Still, this does not make it obvious that these can be taken as functioning models of non-punitive regulation.

(ii) Similarly — as Galanter again argues — the civil law itself (a much favoured abolitionist model) contains strong elements of punishment: not just in the notion of "punitive damages" but in its overall language and strategies.

(iii) Then there are the dual problems of *transfer* and *co-option* (as revealed in the critical social control literature). Once the non-punitive ideal is found, can it be transferred from one cultural or historical setting to another? And can it then remain free from being penetrated and exploited by the state's punitive system?

(iv) There is also the problem that there are forms of regulation outside the criminal law which may indeed be "non-punitive", but are otherwise quite undesirable in terms of the overall abolitionist vision. Examples include private security systems and the panopticon control over public space.[7]

These and similar problems do not negate the abolitionist enterprise, but they call for some caution.

(3) *The abolition of punishment as desirable and feasible?*

The strongest appeal of abolitionism derives from its uncompromising normative basis. Steinert, for example, tries to convince us that state-inflicted punishment in immoral, illegitimate and inadmissible. It results in the infliction of pain on people who are already disadvantaged; it replicates rather redresses injustice; it is a show of domination with no instrumental value except for the state apparatus; it is a bad model for morally legitimate social censure, etc. The abolitionist call is to mount a moral crusade to reduce the amount of deliberately inflicted pain.[8]

But how feasible is this in any complex modern society? It is interesting to note Abel's grounds for pessimism about realizing even the "minimalist", compromise vision which he does find morally desirable (that is: reducing the severity of state-imposed punishment and in-

---

[7] See C. D. Shearing and P. L. Stenning, eds., *Private Policing* (Beverly Hills, Sage, 1987).

[8] N. Christie, *Limits to Pain* (Oxford, Martin Robertson, 1982).

creasing the frequency by which victims mobilize resources outside the official system). The global social changes he sees as unlikely — more responsibility by private citizens, a displacement of professional and bureaucratic monopolies, sacrifice of values of privacy and mobility, levelling off of power differentials, etc. — are, of course, precisely those which abolitionists think can be achieved.

We cannot decide this issue without reviewing the entire history of sociology! This is just the direction being taken by abolitionists such as de Haan who are trying to place the programme in more general theories of progress, modernization and evolution.[9]

In more immediate terms, all we can do is list specific questions of desirability and feasibility: how can areas such as corporate crime possibly be controlled by non-punitive means? Is it not obvious that non-statist, informal means of control will leave the powerful untouched, and the powerless and minorities even less protected? How can the vision be realized outside its origins in the smaller, more homogenous societies of Western Europe? Why should the ideology of the whole person and the total situation (as revealed in the elaborate tapestry of Hulsman's case study) always be preferable to the simple classicism of the "act" — and where could there ever be time and space for these fine confrontations? . . . and so on.

Conclusion

I cannot obviously offer a full scale evaluation of the abolitionist package. Most of the problems that I have mentioned are familiar enough to Steinert and Hulsman. They would not be dismayed by charges of being visionaries or utopians.

The main point is this: the historical and sociological evidence that "crime" and "punishment" are not absolute, fixed and natural responses to certain damaging events, nor particularly efficient responses, should have a liberatory effect on thinking and policy. Instead of supporting the increasingly desperate attempts to save the punitive law model — compensating for infrequency by severity of punishment, widening the control net, developing technical gadgetry for surveillance and enforce-

---

[9] W. de Haan, *The Politics of Redress: Crime, Punishment and Penal Abolition* .(London, Unwin Hyman, 1990).

ment, moving to pro-active policing — we *should* be looking for alternatives.

There are normative and pragmatic reasons for this. The abolitionist case, however, does not eventually rest on matters of feasibility, effectiveness or efficiency any more than the objection to slavery rested on such grounds. Its value is that it proclaims an absolute value. Not a better system of slavery, but no slavery. Further, abolitionism is a "thought experiment": the type of critical opposition to accepted modes of thinking that intellectuals should provide instead of the corrupted technicism of such disciplines as criminology.

Instead of assuming as natural social facts that there are some things called "crimes" and some people called "criminals" — and that these facts call for a conference like this about the justification and allocation of punishment — we might convert these assumptions into problems. Abolitionism then, with all its problems, would be a good subject for opening rather than closing such a conference.

[13]
Talking about Torture in Israel

In *The Body in Pain*, her dense meditation on the vulnerability of the human body, Elaine Scarry keeps returning to the political consequences of the "rigidity" of pain, its sheer inexpressibility. "Physical pain does not simply resist language," she writes, "but actively destroys it, bringing about an immediate reversion to a state anterior to language, to the sounds and cries a human being makes before language is learned."

There are many situations in which the experience of pain has to be rendered into words: patients talking to doctors, artists depicting suffering, human-rights organizations reporting on torture, injured parties claiming legal damages. Of all these contexts, torture is perhaps the most problematic, and the consequences of even using this word are the most profound. Torture is the calculated infliction of pain, but it is also an emblem of state power. To talk about torture is not just to talk about pain, but to enter a complex discourse of morality, legality and politics. As Scarry notes, the very structure by which pain is produced within the body of the prisoner entails denial, "a perceptual shift which converts the vision of suffering into the wholly illusory but, to the torturers and the regime they represent, wholly convincing spectacle of power." All talk about torture becomes a contest between different observers—the victim, the state, human-rights organizations—over how to reproduce this vision. Indeed, even to attempt any reproduction can be a way of subverting the spectacle of power.

The event itself should be simple enough to describe. For all the different contexts (religious inquisition, nationalist conflict, political thought control), for all the different techniques (crude blows, burning rods, psychotropic drugs), the primal scene is simple, and sickeningly identical from case to case. There is a room in which one or more persons (the "interrogators") deliberately inflict pain on another (the detainee, suspect, enemy of the state). But the technical problems inherent in representing this scene—how the experience is memorized, conveyed to others, corroborated, translated into a public language—are only compounded by its political context. There is always a struggle to define reality, an epistemological politics. On the one side, there are the forces to whom torture is real, to be denounced, to be abolished: the victim, international prohibitions and laws, human-rights organizations. On the other, there is the organized power of the state, denying that "it" happens, calling it something else, or justifying it as necessary, or even as something that serves a higher moral good. A history of torture is a history of talking about torture.

In the higher reaches of postmodernist theory (which, in this case, serves the interests of the powerful very nicely), no common, universal definition of torture is possible. It all depends. It depends, postmodernists tell us, on context, on the observer's values, on the truth-rules of the prevailing discourse. It depends, the powerful tell us, on context, on the interests of the state, on how you interpret those universal definitions. But in the struggle for social justice and human rights—however tarnished we are told these master-narratives are—some pragmatic, commonsense definition of the word must be attempted. The historian Edward Peters is surely right to say that if we reject the purely moralistic or sentimental uses of the term, then "the longest and surest definition is a legal—or at least a public—one." The common historical thread, "torment inflicted by a public authority ostensibly for public purposes," is captured in the standard 1975 United Nations Declaration Against Torture definition:

> Any act by which severe pain or suffering, whether physical or mental, is intentionally inflicted by or at the instigation of a public official on a person for such purposes as obtaining from him or a third person information or a confession, punishing him for an act he has committed or intimidating him or other persons.

But what is meant by "severe"? What is meant by excluding (as the UN definition goes on to do) pain and suffering "inherent in ... lawful sanctions"? Is the mere threat of inflicting pain to be included? What does it mean to declare oneself to be "against" torture? How can information or confession be obtained from unwilling persons if not by causing them some suffering? There is a massive discourse—human-rights reports, judicial rulings, government commissions, philosophical tracts—that depends on the continued salience of these questions. And if there ever was a call for a shared public language, this is the place for it. However indeterminate the boundaries—between moderate and severe pain, between permissible and impermissible sanctions—the notion of boundaries assumes that there is an area that can be talked about.

TALK AS EXPOSURE

Talking about torture is difficult enough in general; it is even more so in Israel. In the depressing global league of torture drawn up by organizations like Amnesty International, Israel ranks far below Syria, Iraq, Turkey, and dozens of other countries all over the world. The methods of torture used in Israel are less elaborate, less systematic, and less intense than those favored by more brutal authoritarian regimes. But there are deep-seated ideological barriers to talking openly about the cases that do exist. Within the tiny (and diminishing) liberal enclaves of Israeli society, there is the self-serving myth that "things like this can't happen here"—and if they do, they are isolated abuses that will be dealt with properly. The ideological Right, as we shall see, perceives any attempt to expose gross human-rights violations as anti-Israel propaganda. The rest of the society—the majority of which has no moral unease about what happens to Palestinians and will justify anything in the name of national security—pays no attention to any such talk.

Just what is the record? In the first decade after the Occupation began in 1967, some allegations surfaced about the ill-treatment of Palestinian political detainees. These stories circulated mainly among political activists and a few lawyers, and were not given wider exposure or deeper credibility. In 1977, a number of well-grounded claims were published in the *London Sunday Times*. In the late 1970s, immediately after the first Begin government, torture clearly declined—apparently because of restraints ordered personally by the prime minister, to whom the General Security Service (Shin Bet or Shabak) is formally accountable.

By the mid-1980s, though, new reports were surfacing. From that period on, Israel has possessed the basic requirements for making the question of torture an official public problem: first, the objective record of events; and second, the subjective awareness on the part of a growing human-rights community and an increasingly brave Israeli media that there is something to be talked about. By 1990, even the U.S. State Department review of human rights in the Occupied Territories could record that "physical and psychological pressures are particularly severe during incommunicado detention in investigation." Note, though, the inhibition about using the taboo word "torture" in writing about Israel (an inhibition that even Amnesty International overcame only in its 1990 report). The political causes of this inhibition are obvious. In very few other country-entries does the State Department identify the sources of claims merely as "critics" and make no attempt to evaluate them.

The crucial year for the construction of torture as a public problem was 1987. One dramatic case triggered the discussion. Izzat Nafsu, an Israeli Circassian army officer, had been sentenced in 1982 to an eighteen-year prison term for espionage and treason. He continued to claim that he was innocent and that his confession had been extracted by force during a Shin Bet interrogation. In May 1987, the High Court accepted his claim, along with the corollary charge that the investigators had lied to the court, and ordered his release. A government commission, chaired by former Supreme Court president Justice Moshe Landau, was set up in June and issued its report four months later.

> *This is not "really" torture; there is no permanent damage; what is a couple of days without sleep, or being spat at, or being tied up and beaten compared with what happens "elsewhere"?*

It is impossible to talk about torture in Israel without referring to the Landau Commission report. Indeed, this text is so rich and resonant that even a superficial reading reveals every major contradiction of Israeli society. The report arrived at three main formal conclusions. First, it concluded that since 1971, Shin Bet agents had systematically lied to the courts by denying that they had used force to extract confessions. Second, it ruled that the officials responsible for these sixteen years of torture and perjury should be exempt from any prosecution, on the grounds that they were "ideological criminals" doing their sacred national duty, and that too many criminal cases would disrupt the agency's normal work. Finally, the commission decided that although perjury was to be utterly condemned, the actual methods of interrogation used in the past were "largely to be defended, both morally and legally." According to the Landau report, not only are methods of "nonviolent psychological pressure" justified to extract information, but "when these do not attain their purpose, the exertion of a moderate amount of physical pressure cannot be avoided." A secret second part of the report lays out the precise "operational guidelines" for permissible "moderate physical pressure."

This is not the place to consider the legal and moral reasoning by which the commission arrived at these extraordinary conclusions, nor to review the deluge of criticism that they have aroused. This has already been done in a special issue of the *Israel Law Review* and in the report on torture in the Occupied Territories published recently by B'tselem (the Israel Information Center for Human Rights in the Occupied Territories; see "The Wrong Arm of the Law," *Tikkun*, September/October 1991). The main lines of criticism cover the spurious adaptation from criminal law of the "necessity defense" to authorize in advance the use of force by government officials; the lack of distinction between preventing possible future harm and testifying about supposed past offenses; and the elastic and wholly political definition of the enemies of the state against whom "special means" are permissible (the commission's definition of "hostile terrorist activity" or "subversion," which could include flying a PLO flag). For the purposes of this discussion, however, we need to focus on the clear prospect that the advance licensing of physical pressure—that is, lifting the absolute moral and legal taboo on the sanctity of the body—will open the door to the routine resort to other, graver abuses. This was indeed the peril that the Landau Commission professed itself so eager to avoid: "the danger of sliding toward methods practiced in regimes that we abhor."

Throughout the report, the commission avoids the word "torture" except in references to international conventions and methods used by the British in Northern Ireland. The less vivid and emotive phrase "moderate physical pressure" (or a set of similarly euphemistic equivalents) has to be used as long as Israel continues to hold on to a democratic self-image. In order to circumvent international prohibitions and the provisions against torture in Israeli law, the commission had to work within, rather than outside, the discourse of legal liberalism. We could see this not as a deliberate attempt to deceive, but as either self-deception or deception of the commission by the Shin Bet. In any event, whatever the Landau Commission's intentions (and let us read them as benevolent: to avoid excesses, to regulate, to place limits and restrictions, indeed *not* to allow torture), what follows from its recommendations is the institutionalization of abuse. The Shin Bet received the stamp of kashrut it requested. This is hardly surprising, given the commission's definition of its "principal function": to "guide the essential process of rehabilitation and healing" of the GSS, thus restoring to its agents "inner conviction in the rightness of their way which they require for their work."

The Israeli legal community, not usually given to public moral indignation, received the report with dismay. Mordechai Kremnitzer, dean of the Hebrew University Law School, summed up this reaction at the end of a sixty-two-page legal critique published in the *Israel Law Review*:

> It is difficult to live with the Landau report. One is tempted to shake oneself free of it, to awaken as if from a bad dream and say: perhaps it never was, perhaps the confidential part of the report does not contain a license for physical pressure in interrogation.

The shock that torture can indeed be justified in apparently democratic language is, as Kremnitzer is aware, not unique to Israel. Totalitarian states, military dictatorships—"regimes that we abhor," in Landau's words—don't have to talk about torture in any complicated way. They do it, deny it, and need not lay down any limits. George Orwell anticipated the awful truth fifty years ago, when he predicted that our century would be the time when practices like torture "which had long been abandoned, in some cases for hundreds of years ... not only became common again, but were tolerated and even defended by people who considered themselves enlightened and progressive."

The emblematic case was France during the Algerian War. As Rita Maran shows in her recent book *Torture: The Role of Ideology in the French-Algerian War* (Praeger, 1989), France's colonial government defended the use of brutal, systematic torture—much worse than anything practiced in Israel—as part of its historical mission to maintain the French presence, to uplift and civilize native Algerians. France's 1955 Wuillaume Report (an investigation into allegations about torture in Algeria) could have been copied by the Landau Commission: Yes, torture ("excesses," "violence") had been used in Algeria; no, responsibility should not be fixed on individuals; in the future, "less brutal methods" or "special procedures" should be used under careful supervision; and it is important to "restore confidence in the police." Maran stresses the importance of democratic discourse in the Wuillaume Report:

A state that acknowledged itself or any of its agents as torturers would stand discredited before its citizenry and the world. And so its agents spoke not of "torture" but of "abuses" and when arguing either for or against torture, did so in the lexicon of colonialism's civilizing mission.

Some two months after the Landau Commission issued its report, the intifada began, creating a political context that, of course, the commission could not have anticipated. Initial waves of mass arrests were followed by batch trials, which convicted prisoners on the basis of "evidence" no more substantial than the testimony of the soldiers who had arrested them. Court cases became (and remain) cruel parodies of judicial norms. At least twenty-five thousand Palestinians were arrested during each of the first three years of the intifada. Either the army or the Shin Bet has subjected at least eight thousand of these detainees to some form of formal interrogation, and at least a quarter of these eight thousand to what professional jargon euphemistically refers to as "intensive methods."

The untalkable has to be talked about because in all societies at all times (and Israel is no exception), and for the vast majority of the population, the contours of daily life depend on ignorance, silence, and passive collusion.

Repeated allegations circulated about gross ill-treatment of Palestinians during detention and interrogation: severe beatings, various forms of verbal and physical humiliation, being tied up in painful positions, long confinement in "closets," "coffins," or "refrigerators." In 1988 and 1989, eighteen Palestinians died during detention; in five of these cases, death apparently resulted from interrogation methods. In December 1989, Khaled al-Sheikh Ali was beaten to death by his interrogators in Gaza Central Prison. (His family's attorney was informed that Ali died of a heart attack.) Two Shin Bet agents were eventually sentenced to six months' imprisonment for causing death by negligence.

Against this background, the Public Committee Against Torture in Israel was established at the beginning of 1990; it continues to work on publicity and education and take up individual complaints. In the summer of 1990, B'tselem also decided to investigate the subject. Research director Dr. Daphna Golan and I began to investigate methods of interrogation used against Palestinian political detainees since the beginning of the intifada. We worked for six months; in March 1991, B'tselem published our report, entitled "The Interrogation of Palestinians During the Intifada: Ill-Treatment, 'Moderate Physical Pressure,' or Torture?"

In talking about torture, we immediately faced intertwined technical and political problems. Torture is a unique form of human-rights violation in two respects. First, the international prohibition is absolute. No contingencies can be invoked to justify the use of torture: neither superior orders nor exceptional circumstances, such as war or a perceived threat to national security. This absolute ban creates strong requirements of proof. Allegations cannot be thrown around carelessly. Torture is too potent, too special a word to be debased by rhetorical use. But this leads to the second problem: Indisputable proof is difficult to obtain. Torture represents the public—in the sense that it is perpetrated by the state, which claims to protect the public—but it does not occur in public, as it did in the spectacle of torture that prevailed in the premodern era. Modern torture is invisible. There is the victim and the interrogator in that closed room. The victim very rarely makes a formal complaint and if he does, he is seldom believed. The interrogator remains silent and unaccountable—except in those rare cases when the regime gives way to a more democratic successor.

As a result, great care has to be taken in checking stories. The moment the word "torture" is used, rather than pressure, force, ill-treatment, abuse, even violence, the talk takes on a dimension absent in standard human-rights documentation. Other human-rights abuses at least can be submitted to common criteria of observable fact: house demolitions, shootings, teargassing, deportation, land confiscation, administrative detention. In each case, the event can be documented as a matter of public record and its semantics are not disputed. A house is blown up—and the issue is not whether this happened, but whether this is justified or not. In the case of torture, however, the value position is preceded by first-order questions: Is this happening? Can it be happening here? Is torture the proper word to use?

These questions appeared even before the report was published. The B'tselem board (lawyers, law professors, politicians, human-rights experts) read various drafts of the report more intensely than any of the organization's previous reports and scrutinized its language, sources, and methodology. By all standards of the genre, the B'tselem report is a conventional human-rights document: We review international definitions and prohibitions, Israeli law, the status of the GSS, the Landau report, and previous allegations. We then describe each of the eleven methods of interrogation reported by our forty-one interviewees; this is followed by longer stories from seven individual detainees. Some common methods of torture are illustrated with drawings—like the "banana tie," in which the suspect's legs are bound to the front and his hands to the back legs of a stool, the body bent over like a banana, to be beaten. These drawings were our main departure from the normal genre. We wanted to undermine the function of political language ("moderate physical pressure") that Orwell pointed to: "Such phraseology is needed if one wants to name things without calling up mental pictures of them."

But even the drawings, even the vivid testimonies of deliberate abuse, humiliation, and violence over periods as long as forty-five days, even the medical documentation on six detainees injured so badly by their interrogators that they needed hospital treatment—all this knowledge enters a discourse in which nothing can be taken for granted.

Here is Mohammed Jit, in the Shati Detention Camp in Gaza: "They put a sack over my head, choked me with their hands around my throat, let go, put my head in a pail of water up to my neck. The sack was stuck to my face. They did this six or seven times.... When they took my head out of the pail of water, they beat my head with their fists." Here is "Hassan," with the interrogator known as "Maradona" in Dahariya Detention Center: "He began to hit me on the head with the pole [a bolt about twenty centimeters long with a rubber handle]. He hit me twice and I fell down. When I came to, they were still beating and kicking me. I tried to get up and got more beatings on the head. I fell down. While I was lying down they continued to beat me all over my body.... I thought that I was going to die then and there—I couldn't move. Two stood over me and began to spit all over me, again and again without stopping. They stepped on my face with their shoes." And here is "Barakat," in the Russian compound off Jaffa Road, which every tourist in Jerusalem passes: "Someone held a pipe of Tippex [correction fluid]. Another grabbed me by the hair and poured Tippex into my mouth. I immediately spat up everything and his face was covered all over with spit and Tippex.... Then they really got mad and beat me harder. They continued beating me and because of all the beating I lost control and began urinating in my clothes and I noticed that my urine was full of blood. I saw blood on my pants and blood and urine on the floor. They wiped up the blood with my beard and hair."

Ill-treatment, "moderate physical pressure," or torture? Our subtitle recognized the liguistic ambiguities that attended these descriptions.

Talk as Self-Correction

Of the many contradictions in Israeli society, one of the strangest for the outsider to understand is that the same political space is shared by brutal repression and democratic institutions. As much as the denial of Palestinian rights is total, as much as racism and militarism penetrate civil society, so—for Israeli Jews, that is—the terrain of democracy, legality, and civil rights remains more or less open.

This means that the work needed to expose human-rights violations can be done in relative freedom and that there are open arenas for talking about this work, such as the media, universities, and political meetings. Human-rights organizations—Israeli, international, and to a lesser extent, Palestinian—can do the sort of documentation impossible in societies where gross human-rights violations take place under a regime of total state control with no access or accountability. In Israel, the formal mechanisms of liberal legality are intact, if vulnerable. There are special sections in the Foreign Ministry and the Ministry of Justice that painstakingly handle complaints from bodies such as Amnesty International and the International Committee of the Red Cross. There are officials whose entire working lives are spent meeting with endless delegations from all over the world. And the press is restrained more by its own sense of the national consensus than by direct state censorship.

None of this freedom, of course, is enjoyed by the Palestinians—and this, in itself, corrupts and compromises the heart of Israeli democracy. It also means that these officials are engaged in ritual denials, accusations of worldwide bias against Israel, uncheckable promises to "investigate each allegation," or appeals to preposterous legalistic sophistry to explain why, for example, the Geneva Convention does not apply to the Occupied Territories. It means that allegations coming from Palestinian, or international, or suspect Israeli sources are easily discredited—while exactly the same information from a mainstream Israeli organization like B'tselem has to be taken seriously. Despite all these limitations, though, the freedom to talk is real and should not be taken for granted.

The consequence of this freedom is to create the impression of a self-correcting social system. The image is of a society where departures from democratic norms are exposed, recognized only *as* departures, and then automatically corrected by built-in mechanisms of restraint and regulation. There are reports, complaints, investigations of allegations, commissions of inquiry, routine procedures, questions in the Knesset, an independent state-comptroller office, and prosecutions of individual officials who go too far. During the first two weeks after the B'tselem report was published, we saw extensive reaction from the liberal bloc of Israeli society. The Hebrew papers—particularly *Ha'aretz* and the influential mass-circulation weeklies—gave detailed coverage to our report; they printed extracts of testimonies, descriptions of interrogations, and the drawings (which made a special impact). Editorials and articles carried demands for an inquiry into the allegations. Sixteen Knesset members—all from RATZ, MAPAM, Shinui, and Labor—appealed to the prime minister either to deny or confirm the conclusions of the report.

This coverage was generally sympathetic and fair. The impression was that people were genuinely perturbed. This, remember, was the period after the Gulf War, when there was hardly any sympathy for the Palestinians even among liberals. But the question "Can this be happening here?" drew forth the liberal anxiety about how these patterns of violence might spread to Israeli society itself. Even a right-wing journalist, Dov Goldstein, joined the front and demanded: "Is it or is it not true that the Shabak, or the police, or the army ... is breaking the arms of Palestinian prisoners by torture ... as happens in South America, Africa, and Asia?"

How did the official system respond? At first, there were standard techniques of official-talk: The Israel Defense Forces (IDF) criticized B'tselem for releasing the report without prior notice; the Ministry of Justice claimed (falsely) that it had not been sent allegations to check; assurances were given that individual complaints were always followed up. But clearly the subject was not going to be buried. Two powerful Knesset committees (Foreign Affairs–Defense and State Comptroller) demanded and planned debates. A vivid testimony by Ari Shavit, an Israeli reservist who had served in Ansar 2 (the army detention facility at Gaza Beach), was published in *Ha'aretz* (an English translation later appeared in the *New York Review of Books*). The sounds of pain that Shavit recorded—the "hair-raising human screams" from the interrogation block—could not be easily shut out.

A week later, no fewer than three separate official inquiries were announced: one by the IDF (to cover allegations about ill-treatment in army prisons), one within the GSS itself, and another coordinated by the Ministry of Justice. As I write, we are still waiting for the results of these investigations. A press release in August that reproduced part of the IDF report suggested that the report's authors at least took our allegations seriously: They recommended that some interrogators be prosecuted but also (curiously) that all interrogations be transferred from the army to the Shabak. The other investigations are totally secret. Overall, there is likely to be some discrediting of our evidence and criticism of our refusal to identify informants whose anonymity we guaranteed. Our careful reservations about not being able to vouch for every detail might backfire. And the limitation of all such official inquiries is that they remain within a legal model of checking individual testimonies, rather than looking for general patterns.

To what extent can the system correct itself through such mechanisms? Clearly there are major limits to what the "watchdog" mode of human-rights work can achieve when it is running against the dominant political current. In fact, the conditions that allow ill-treatment and torture are endemic rather than incidental. These conditions are, first of all, political: a perceived threat to national security; the need to process large numbers of suspects; dehumanization of the out-group; high-level authorization (provided formally by the Landau Commission) to violate normal moral principles; the invocation of a sacred mission to justify anything. Second, there is a set of legal conditions: a prolonged period of incommunicado detention without access to a lawyer (two weeks is the norm, a month common, three months possible); the fact that detainees cannot identify their interrogators by name or number; trials under military regulations rather than in regular courts; the absence of independent medical examinations; procedural rules that do not automatically exclude evidence obtained by force.

The political will needed to eradicate such conditions does not exist in Israel today. I don't want to sound too cynical about self-correction. The traditional rationales for human-rights intervention remain valid: humanitarian help for individuals; the possibility of redress; the inhibiting effect produced by the knowledge that one is being watched; the chance to make violations more (and hopefully, unbearably) costly for the authorities. Even on general principles, the Israeli legal system still retains some flexibility. In June 1991, for example, attorney Avigdor Feldman (acting on behalf of the Public Committee Against Torture) won a notable case in the High Court by obtaining a restraining order calling on the government to justify the legality of the Landau recommendations. There have been limited victories on limited terrain; law can be a shield if not a sword.

A more depressing event, on wider political terrain, took place in April. At the annual Independence Day ceremony, Landau was awarded the prestigious Israel

Prize. The citation noted that, as president of the Supreme Court, Justice Landau had written decisions that translated "basic values of freedom, equality, and fairness into a way of life"; it extolled his role in advancing the "principles and values of an enlightened society ... and human rights." The citation was signed by the two leading Israeli liberal figures, former attorney general Yitzhak Zamir and Justice Aharon Barak. The citation made no reference to the Landau Commission—only to Landau's previous distinguished record. (A newspaper advertisement by the Public Committee drawing attention to this was denounced as "bad taste.")

TALK AS TREACHERY

For the Right—who claim, quite correctly, to speak for the national consensus—there is nothing to correct. Indeed, in their view, the problem with Israeli society is that too many concessions are made to universal principles such as legality and civil liberties. This is just the Hellenism that Kahane used to denounce in every speech. To respond to internal and external criticism is to be too sensitive to a "foreign" ideology, to worry too much about what the goyim think. And for those on the Right who genuinely understand human-rights principles, the doctrine of national security overrides other considerations.

A graphic statement of this position came not from the Right but from a political journalist identified with the liberal center. In an article in *Ha'aretz*, Dan Margalit told his own atrocity story. His daughter and her friends were walking along a Jerusalem street. Some Palestinians in a Mercedes drove toward the girls and kept stopping near them; when they started getting out of the car, the girls ran and screamed for help from a soldier. The Palestinians drove away and the girls complained to the police. What was Margalit's message? "One of these young girls is my daughter and as far as I'm concerned, the Shabak can use as much 'moderate physical pressure' as the Landau Commission says in order to find the gang. I don't care what the B'tselem report will write about it." Yes, there must be some controls; yes, deviations must be punished; but a democracy cannot deal with its violent political enemies as it does with ordinary delinquents.

The range of explicitly right-wing opinion was revealed in a series of interviews published in *Ha'aretz*. Only three of the eleven right-wingers interviewed had read the report, but all tried to discredit information based on Palestinian sources and disseminated by an organization like B'tselem. More fundamentally, right-wing critics saw the whole enterprise of talking about human-rights violations as suspect. For Limor Livnat, member of the Likud Central Committee, even to read the report would mean being contaminated by the "moral obscenity" of its source. Those who talk about human rights are denounced as traitors, enemy agents, or self-hating Jews. In a letter I received from one "Blanche Tannenbaum, New York" after talking about the report on WBAI radio, the exact description of me was a "Jewish anti-Semitic piece of shit."

But the most extraordinary of all such terms of abuse is "informer" (the Hebrew word *malshin*). Can there be another country in the world where whistle-blowers—those who expose not just human-rights abuses but also fraud, corruption, and malpractice in government agencies—are routinely branded as "informers"? The dovish Knesset members who toured the United States in June to draw attention to the government's expansionist settlement plans were also denounced by Arik Sharon and the Right as a "commando of informers." According to this rhetoric, talk is treachery. ("Careless talk costs lives" was the wartime slogan in Britain.) An important subtext is "Don't let the goyim know." Even if the picture is true, it should not be allowed to circulate. A peculiarly Israeli theme, articulated clearly by former Chief Rabbi Goren, is that Jews (and particularly the "holy and pure" Jews who work for the GSS) are simply incapable of doing anything bad. Right-wingers and centrists have also questioned the accuracy of the allegations or assigned them the status of "exceptions," departures from the norm. These objections have to be responded to seriously by human-rights organizations anywhere, especially if they are presented in an open-minded way, rather than as a technique of denial.

All these statements, however, express a single, if internally contradictory, message: "It can't be happening here, but if it is, it must be all right." Let us call the two elements in this message denial and justification.

A common form of denial finds expression in self-protective homilies, such as "You can never believe what Palestinians say." An extreme racist version of this position appears in an interview reprinted in our report, in which two retired Shabak agents claim that Arabs have a "mental problem," a "genetic difference" that prevents them from telling the truth: "A Bedouin cannot pass a polygraph because his moral level is different from yours." A more sophisticated version says that because Palestinians are the enemy, they deliberately lie and exaggerate for the purpose of political propaganda. Critics have also discredited B'tselem as politically biased and gullible, or else downplayed the seriousness of the injuries: This is not "really" torture; there is no permanent damage; what is a couple of days without sleep, or being spat at, or being tied up and beaten compared with what happens "elsewhere"? And after all, they don't really feel it; look at the violence they inflict on each other.

Justifications of torture draw first on the idea of "necessity," which appears in a sophisticated form in the Landau report. There is no other way, this argument goes; national security requires these methods. A second, more elevated version, appeals to a sacred mission, a higher set of values that transcend the rule of law. (As Livnat argues, "Zionism is above all. If a group like B'tselem had existed when Israel was being established, a Jewish state would not have come into being.") A third appeal—deeply ingrained in the collective Israeli psyche—is to the Darwinian struggle for survival: It's us or them; it's our fate to be locked into a cycle of violence that has no end. And finally, a fourth line of defense is to reproduce wholesale the self-image of the security services: good people doing their job as best they can under difficult conditions. Somebody has to do the dirty work; "you can't chop wood without splinters flying"; every palace has its dirty corners.

Many of these reactions were publicly expressed not by the far Right, but by no less than Justice Landau, the bastion of Israeli liberal legalism. In response to a private (but admittedly provocative) letter from the director of B'tselem asking if he saw any connection between the methods revealed by our inquiry and those permitted by the commission, Landau published an open letter in the mass-circulation daily paper *Yediot Achronot*. Understandably sensitive to what he saw as unfair criticism, Landau took two main lines of defense. The first was to repeat the commission's argument that international definitions of torture cover only methods that cause "severe" pain and suffering. These were not approved; "moderate physical pressure" is obviously something different, since it does not destroy the subject's dignity. The second was to requote the commission's conclusion that "false claims" and "wild exaggerations" are "part of the systematic campaign conducted by terrorist organizations against the GSS, with the aim of weakening it in its war against Hostile Terrorist Activity, and tarnishing its image in the eyes of well-wishing individuals and organizations by presenting it as a ruthless organization engaged in torture and maltreatment of innocent 'freedom fighters.'" He poured scorn on our methods of checking sources for internal consistency and validating them through external evidence such as medical reports.

Lest his political subtext remain unclear, Landau went on to accuse B'tselem of having caused prejudice and animosity toward the Shin Bet investigators, "as if the torture of people under interrogations was their daily bread. The B'tselem report viciously maligned a service whose function is to defend the residents of the state and the Territories (Jews and Arabs) against mass and individual terror. Ultimately you therefore assisted—unintentionally, I assume—those evil-mongers of the State who conduct psychological warfare against it, in addition to other kinds of warfare, with the purpose of undermining its existence."

The question of terrorism is, in fact, irrelevant: Not a single one of our forty-one subjects was charged with or even suspected of committing or planning an act of terrorism. But the real irrelevance of Landau's letter, as we noted in our reply (which *Yediot Achronot* refused to publish), is that nowhere does he decide between two possible alternatives: either that these practices (or something like them) occur—but they fall within the commission's secret approved guidelines—or else that such practices (or something like them) lie outside the approved guidelines, and therefore should be condemned as torture. Neither alternative, of course, can be publicly confirmed unless the secret guidelines are disclosed.

Talk as Discursive Practice

The public criticism we least expected came from our own side. In a series of articles in the weekly supplement to *Davar*, Adi Ophir, a philosopher from Tel Aviv University and a founder of the anti-Occupation group the Twenty-First Year, launched a sardonic attack on the B'tselem report. His thesis is complex and became qualified in response to counter-criticism, but its essence is clear enough to anyone immersed in current postmodernist theory and anti-positivist philosophy.

Ophir argues that radical intellectuals should know better than to work within the standard genre of human-rights documentation. The B'tselem report, for Ophir, is just another text—a text with a pretense to representation that it cannot sustain. Ophir sees any claim to objectivity—checking the facts ("I was tied up for twelve hours") or their representativeness ("Most detainees are tied up...")—as merely a "rhetorical strategy" designed to give the document legitimacy. Behind this strategy, he writes, lies a

> worldview, liberal and positivist, according to which facts exist on their own and one can really distinguish between facts and values, description and interpretation and, above all, one can disconnect a description of social reality from the power struggle that attempts to shape this reality. In a postmodern world, in a culture that rejects the

(Continued on p. 89)

TORTURE
(Continued from p. 30)

possibility of a transparent descriptive language or an objective spokesperson, this worldview appears naive, if not ridiculous.

Intelligent radicals such as the writers of the report, Ophir allows, could hardly be so naive. Their strategy surely must have been different, more complex, less ridiculous; we must rather have assumed that torture is such an obvious case of evil that there is no need to differentiate (or pretend to) between description and interpretation; that all we have to do is say that the events happened—and invite the authorities to confirm or deny that. The facts would speak for themselves and every reasonable and sensitive person would find them shocking. But if this worldview is more epistemologically sophisticated than the first, it is just as politically wrong. For there is no general consensus about the evil of torture.

In any event, Ophir argues, whatever our rhetorical strategy, the results are devastatingly the same: We simply reproduce and thereby strengthen the culture of the Occupation. The report by necessity "joins the hegemonic political discourse that the regime of the Occupation creates as if this were the natural order of things, a discourse whose function it is to normalize relations between the occupier and the occupied." The very attention that the report generated—the official inquiries, questions in the Knesset (talk as self-correction)—only proves that it posed no serious challenge. Although organizations like B'tselem aim to provide alternative knowledge, the genre they are forced to use is far too limited; it shuts out too much and compromises too much in trying to adapt itself to the dominant discourse.

To emphasize the limits of the genre—and the costs paid by radicals for using it—Ophir compares the report unfavorably with the recently published volume *Poets Will Not Write Poetry,* edited by Ilana Hammerman and Roly Rosen (Am Oved, 1990). This is a collection of texts (soldiers' testimonies, legal protocols) that makes up a collage of impressions, a montage that abandons any pseudoscientific pretense to objectivity as a way to challenge the hegemonic culture. Such a montage invites the reader to make an active choice (resist or collaborate) rather than—like the B'tselem report—merely placing responsibility on the regime and leaving the reader as a passive observer. The fact that *Poets Will Not Write Poetry* did not sell and received little media coverage compared with the report, needless to say, vindicates its radical status.

In a later response to his critics, Ophir notes that he is just making a division of labor; each genre has its place. His dividing line, however, is clearly between the mere liberalism of RATZ or Peace Now—the discourse into which he claims the B'tselem report is locked—and the true radicalism of the montage. Moreover, the report is not even authentic liberalism, but the work of fellow subversives who, out of despair with radical politics in Israel, have deflected their energy and talents into an inherently defective strategy.

No one exposed to the astonishing twists in critical theory over the last two decades can afford to ignore the intellectual sources from which Ophir's critique derives. Anyone who works in a field such as human rights must share some of his theoretical doubts. Yes, we make compromises and pay prices. No, such reports will not end the Occupation. But a critique that aspires to this type of translation or "application" of theory to the case in question, torture in Israel, is just too facile and self-indulgent. It is victim of two ironies (that favorite postmodern attribute): At the theoretical level, it uses a perspective that rejects any totalizing metanarratives precisely to construct a totalizing critique that lacks any openings, that offers no possibility of multiple meanings other than the fixed hegemonic structure into which all attacks are gobbled up. And at the political level, it is symptomatic of the very despair of which he accuses us.

The genre, the rhetorical strategy, is seen as limiting and restrictive. There is no sense of its possible advantages or effects. First, there is the immediate humanitarian possibility: As long as the terrain of democracy, legality, and accountability continues to exist in Israeli society, it has to be exploited to its absolute limit. Every such strategy of intervention—prevention of individual suffering, redress, tightening legal controls, holding officials accountable—depends on a mode of knowledge that must use the language of facts and universal human-rights standards. An autopsy report shows whether a prisoner died from a beating rather than a heart attack; there is no question here of another "genre" being more effective. As Hammerman and Rosen would be the first to concede, if they had included such an autopsy report in their collage, it would only have been because a human-rights organization had struggled (with the only rhetorical strategy possible) to obtain an independent inquiry to discredit official lies.

Second, there is the admittedly more remote but genuine prospect of delegitimization. People, especially political elites, can be persuaded to change if they pay too much of a price for staying the same—not only a material price (standard of living, loss of life) but a moral price, a sense that what is being done in their name is no longer legitimate. No doubt, material damage is more threatening than moral damage. But as a case like South Africa shows, the combination of external pressure (sanctions, isolation, disinvestment) and internal fragmentation, which finally led to political change, was informed by decades of "liberal positivist" exposure of the evils of apartheid. Or take a closer case, the French withdrawal from Algeria—in which the intellectual campaign against torture was decisive.

The exquisite aesthetics by which politics becomes text and pain becomes semiotics leaves us with a bitter taste. The problem is not that we are too ready to place our theoretical doubts aside because of political expediency and despair. Nor are we saying that these intellectual worlds—whether those of Quine, Davidson, and Rorty, or of Derrida and Foucault—do not belong in the Middle East (that the Left Bank is not the same as the West Bank, as one of Ophir's critics suggested). The problem lies in sorting out which strands in these theories make any sort of political sense in general and in our local situation in particular. The solution is not to use so inherently (and intentionally) ambiguous a body of ideas to prescribe some "correct" rhetorical strategy. Deconstruction itself does not necessarily undermine the utility of any discourse, nor its truth value, nor the desirability of any political practice, nor the power of the master narratives from which it draws its value.

These master narratives—social justice, national liberation, human rights, the struggles against racism and sexism—have not sunk into some historical black hole. A scene that I often like to think about is Michel Foucault at a press conference in Geneva in 1981, joining activists from "humanitarian" organizations to announce a new human-rights initiative in defense of Vietnamese boat people. Here stands that most profound archaeologist of the link between knowledge and power, that most skeptical critic of liberal humanism, talking about "facts," "rights," and the "duty of international citizenry." Foucault uses the opportunity to theorize about political action itself: how organizations like Amnesty International are trying to create a new right (the right to speak about the unspeakable), a will of individuals "to inscribe itself in a reality over which governments have wanted to reserve a monopoly for themselves—a monopoly that we must uproot little by little every day." I don't see any inconsistency here between theory and practice—or at least no more than is inherent in all life.

Silence

There were moments—when we were collecting testimonies, writing the report, dealing with our critics, or giving evidence to the investigating committees—when we felt that all these words were superfluous. This feeling of hopelessness came not from the avant-garde conceit that the only role for the progressive intellectual is a dignified silence, a refusal to enter the dominant discourse. My inclination to silence came rather from the sense that all the empirical, legal, and moral niceties we were trying to convey added little to the moral issue at stake. Here we were—in company with thousands all over the world who face risks we do not face and expose still worse horrors—still trying to convince our fellow citizens about the importance of *torture?* At the end of the twentieth century, why should anyone still have to explain all this? As a Salinger character says of the Gettysburg Address: Lincoln should just have stood in front of the crowd, shaken his fist at them and walked away.

As with slavery, the only morally defensible position about torture is abolitionist. It simply is not the task of human-rights organizations to talk about alternatives, even to begin to ask, "What would you do if you were in our place?" But even abolitionism needs words. The untalkable has to be talked about because in all societies at all times (and Israel is no exception), and for the vast majority of the population, the contours of daily life depend on ignorance, silence, and passive collusion. Most people exercise what Daniel Ellsberg nicely calls "the right not to know."

There is another very special obstacle to talking about torture, and not just in Israel: the pervasive myth that while such practices are undesirable and unfortunate, they are, alas, necessary. This is the classic utilitarian justification, as old as torture itself: that it is only a method (and the only possible method) of obtaining information, intelligence, testimony, confessions, or evidence. If our findings or those of any other investigation leave only one memory behind, it should be this: Whether the utilitarian defense is morally justifiable or not is not what torture is about.

Orwell saw this in *1984*. No one can ever forget O'Brien's terrible explanation of why Winston must be tortured rather than simply killed: "The object of persecution is persecution. The object of torture is torture. The object of power is power. Now do you begin to understand me?" ☐

[14]
Intellectual Skepticism and Political Commitment: The case of Radical Criminology

INTRODUCTION: DOUBT AND ACTION

My subject derives from a theme in the life and work of Willem Bonger, the Dutch criminologist who killed himself on the day the Nazis occupied Holland in May 1940. Bonger's biographer describes the integrity with which he confronted the tension between intellectual honesty and political commitment, his "double loyalty"—as sociologist and socialist. I have chosen to illustrate the tension between intellectual skepticism and political action by retelling the recent story of radical criminology.

In general, this is how the problem presents itself. Intellectual and academic life in general and in the social sciences in particular, thrives best and depends on a spirit of skepticism, doubt and uncertainty. Answers are provisional; thought is ambiguous; irony is deliberate. All this can best be achieved when one is free from pressures of everyday demands—especially those to be "relevant" and to fit and tailor your ideas to serve the managers of society.

Uncompromising intellectual honesty does not usually please politicians and civil servants.

Political life, on the other hand—and in this context I include social policy, welfare, social work, social control, criminal justice—calls for some immediate commitments. Decisions have to be made, clear public statements made, bets placed, budgets drawn up, doubts temporarily laid aside. You have to respond to values that are binding and encourage neither skepticism nor irony: social justice, humanitarianism, doing good, equality, citizenship, public safety, or the needs of victims.

All this is familiar. But the familiar is always with us.

THE CASE INTRODUCED: "RADICAL" CRIMINOLOGY

My case is the story of the development of "critical," "alternative," or "radical" theories about crime, law and social control over the last twenty-five years. Various stages and many versions of this story have been chronicled before (Cohen 1989; cf. Young 1988)—so there are no hidden plots, unknown heroes, or surprise endings. My interest here lies less in the story's details than its wider lessons.

Whether such narratives are called the history of ideas, the sociology of knowledge or (more fashionably these days) "archeologies" or "genealogies," they tend eventually to degenerate into self-serving defenses of present intentions and claims. The narrative takes on a triumphalist note: mistakes are rectified, false paths abandoned, excesses moderated, new directions sighted, the final metaphysical goal achieved: "correct" theory and practice. This is not going to be my reading. I will leave you with vague directions rather than achieved destinations.

This is how the story might be told in a three-part Walt Disney serial:

EPISODE ONE: DECONSTRUCTION

After the middle of the 1960s—well before Foucault made these subjects intellectually respectable and a long way from the Left Bank—our little corner of the human sciences was seized by a deconstructionist impulse. What does this pretentious term mean?

First, there is the everyday sense of "deconstruction" as a breaking up of something that has been built. Second, this is the metaphor that best captures the spirit of those movements which tried to undermine dominant theories of crime and structures of social control. Third, there is the sense in which these movements either explicitly or (more often) unknowingly, parallel the formal theory of deconstructionism in literary criticism, cultural studies and feminism.

Pretentious as this sounds, it is this last sense which connects the insular (and insulated) world of criminology with the wider debates of post modernism.

The connection appeared the moment that criminologists began constructing a counter discourse—known variously as "alternative," "critical," "new," or "radical" criminology. Similar stories can also be told about psychiatry (with its counter discourse of anti- or critical psychiatry) and law (with its counter discourse of critical legal studies). In all these areas, deconstruction took (and still takes) place in the everyday, metaphorical and formal senses.

The initial impulse drew on a heady intellectual mixture—soon to disintegrate under its weight and internal inconsistency—of critical theory, romantic utopianism, new-left Marxism, phenomenology, interactionism and something like deconstructionism proper. It took the form of radical skepticism about accepted disciplinary paradigms, cognitive categories, and methods of enquiry (positivist criminology, the very concept of crime, the medical model of mental illness, liberal legal theory). This is the level of theory or—in Foucault's term—knowledge. At the same time, the critique was directed at the dominant structures and ideologies for the control of crime and deviance— the physical apparatus and visible mechanism of the system (prisons, criminal justice agencies, mental hospitals). This is the level of policy or power.

Social movements were directed at weakening, by-passing or even abolishing conventional structures of legality, punishment, control and treatment; innovative and radical alternatives were advocated or actually set up; deviant groups themselves struggled against "oppression" and for "liberation" from techniques of control and categorization; social theory and political ideologies were advanced to rationalize these movements; counter cultures appeared in criminology, law, sociology, social work and psychiatry aimed—no less—at reconstituting their disciplines and professions.

I've described elsewhere the content of these movements (Cohen 1985). At the level of power: decentralization and decriminalization (against state power and monopoly); deprofessionalization, informal justice, de-labeling (against bureaucratic classification and professional power); decarceration, prison abolition, community control (against segregation and isolation in the closed, total institution). Behind all this, a common vision of inclusion rather than exclusion: decentralized community control, somewhere out of the reach of the state criminal justice system.

At the level of knowledge, counter theories were directed against positivist criminology (and other such "normalizing sciences"). You are all acquainted with the main streams in the anti-criminology discourse: labelling theory, critical criminology and (best known in Holland) abolitionism.

Sometimes these maneuvers were relatively modest. At the level of power— traditional liberal reformism; at the level of knowledge—new concepts, concerns and methods. Often, the message was more ambitious and utopian: the very systems of power and knowledge identified with the modern state were to be broken up and returned to the people. The 1960s gave courage to attack Big Enemies: scientism, dehumanization, determinism, reification, fake neutrality, the denial of politics.

So (with crucial internal differences that must be explained in any detailed telling of this tale), the counter-criminology discourse began to deconstruct the very concept of crime. Version One was skeptical labelling theory; the reified categories of positivism disappear in the shifting sands of labelling, social reaction, definition, relativism, normalization, tolerance, diversity, moral panics...

In Version Two—original radical criminology—the sands are shaped by the political economy and the needs of capitalism. The essence behind the facade of legality and justice is a system to protect an unjust, unequal and repressive social order. The main object of criminology—conventional street crime—is ideologically constructed and exploited by the powerful to divide the working class and justify repressive law-and-order campaigns. "Real" crime lay elsewhere, the crimes committed by the powerful themselves: corporate crime, state crime, the unnamed "crimes" of exploitation, racism, sexism and the abuse of power.

Version Three, abolitionism, took the most uncompromising and literal reading of the deconstructionist project. The object of abolition is not just prisons, not just punishment but the whole apparatus of criminal justice and the very concept of crime itself. The vision is a society without punishment, where human inflicted pain is reduced to the minimum. You are familiar with the abolitionist case for finding alternatives to the rituals of punishment organized by penal law. That is: cognitive (knowledge) alternatives (in a language of "problem," "conflict," and "trouble" more congruent with ordinary people's experience) and policy (power) alternatives (in systems of mediation, conciliation, reparation and other ways to resolve conflict).

My caricature does little justice to the textures of the emerging discourse. Nor does it credit its contribution in turning criminology into a subject of intellectual richness. And it makes us sound much dumber than we really were. I draw these crude lines only to extract the three meta-problems that will become crucial in the later episodes of the story. These I will call essentialism, idealism, and negative skepticism. The last is the most relevant to my subject here.

1. *Essentialism:* The mystery posed by deconstructionism is this: underneath the surface (progressive penology, liberal legalism or whatever) is there an essence to be revealed—or just an infinite series of multiple meanings? In the early phase of critical criminology, this was the (submerged) conflict between on the one hand, more libertarian and subjectivist theories such as labelling, interactionism, phenomenology, ethnomethodology and on the other, versions of sociological positivism—including Marxism—that depended

on some notion of a fixed reality, a hidden master narrative behind the surface appearance.

2. *Idealism:* What is the relationship between the intellectual exercise of deconstruction—unmasking, breaking down categories, ruthless skepticism—and what is going on or what can be changed in the real world? As we will see, the main criticism of early critical criminology was that it was mere "left idealism"—a facile intellectual inversion of the categories of positivist criminology, a word game that would not affect policy and politics.

3. *Negative Skepticism:* This is our question here: Does the deconstructionist, post-modernist project—"de," "anti," "counter"—carry with it any moral, intellectual or political obligation to suggest actual alternatives? Or is radical skepticism (the critique) or negativity (refusal, "abolitionism" in the ordinary sense of the word) justified in its own terms?

This is to run ahead of the story. We now have to return to anti-criminology somewhere at the end of the Nineteen Seventies.

EPISODE TWO: RECONSTRUCTION

If the mid-1960s saw the dawning of the Age of Aquarius—idealism, optimism, utopianism, the sense that everything was possible—then the mid-Seventies heralded a bleaker, more pessimistic time: the Age of Realism. Again, I've described in detail elsewhere the manifestations which this spirit took in our area. First, in the sphere of policy:

—*Among liberals:* disenchantment, disengagement, a sense of lowered horizons and expectations. Good intentions lead to disastrous consequences, benevolence ends up as coercion, less harm is better than more good, everything costs too much and anyway nothing works.

—*Among radicals:* a wearier cynicism. Reforms had not been implemented at all, but if so, only for the wrong reasons or else co-opted and absorbed in such a way as to blunt their radical edge. The old structures (prisons, professions, state bureaucracies) had turned out not only more resilient than we supposed, but even more powerful (despite community control, rates of incarceration increase; despite decentralization, the reach of the centralized state widens). The new alternatives were not manifestly more humane, just or effective. And worse; all sorts of previously unimagined problems and dangers had been created: the net of social control widened, coercion disguised.

As I've also described, there were different ways to make sense of the news. Conservatives said: we told you so. Liberals thought that the ideas had been taken too seriously. Abolitionists continued saying that the original ideas had not been taken seriously enough.

Other members of the original radical cohort began a more profound stocktaking—leading eventually to what is now called "left realist criminology." Again, a caricature:[1] the original deconstructionism of the 1960s, is dismissed as romantic, utopian and politically irresponsible because of its negativity. "Left idealism" was theoretically misconceived—in its simplistic attempt to reverse the discourse of criminological positivism by mere word magic. Its content was also misconceived:

1. It was wrong to gloss over the significance of street crime. Instead of demystifying the crime problem as a product of media myths, moral panics, faulty categorization or false consciousness, crime must be acknowledged as a real problem for the powerless. The weak and the marginal are the targets of crime. There is a rational core to their fear and insecurity. Victimization studies have re-discovered old victims (the working class, the elderly, ethnic minorities) and discovered some "new" ones—notably women victims of male sexualized violence. Indeed it was the feminist critique of the "romantic" strain in original deconstructionism that presented the model with its most serious anomalies. The result, in any event, is that the damaging, brutalizing and demoralizing consequences of conventional crime must be confronted rather than glossed over.

2. It was wrong to see the origins and functions of the criminal justice system in repressive terms or as mere reflections of class interest. This crude instrumentalism must be replaced by a more nuanced appreciation of the rule of law as a historical victory of democratic legality over arbitrary power.

3. It was wrong also to abandon the traditional causal questions of positivism. This does not mean reviving psychological determinism, but it does mean restating the causal connection in which crime emerges in modern capitalist societies such as Britain and the United States. That is: poverty, deprivation, racism, social disorganization, unemployment, the loss of community, the power of gender.

4. Above all, it was wrong to try to abandon the discourse of the old criminology and try to construct an alternative with its own problematic. Radical criminology must make itself politically relevant by operating on the same terrain that conservatives and technocrats have appropriated. "Law and order" is not naturally a conservative issue; a socialist vision of law and order can also be constructed. But not by taking the risks of the 1960s: at worst, being marginalized as freaky, at best, as "interesting—but not leading anywhere." The point is to be relevant. This leads:

1. To a renewed appreciation of certain aspects of the old system. The criminal law model must be affirmed to deal with street crime and expanded

to control the crimes of the powerful—corporate crime, environmental crime and (especially) crimes of men against women: rape, sexual harassment, pornography. The police, instead of being attacked as oppressors, must be democratized and made more accountable. Similarly, the formal judicial system is defended as a strategy to protect the weak against the powerful.

2. The soft parts of the system (welfare, social work, treatment, rehabilitation), instead of being attacked as they used to be as disguised forms of social control, should now be defended in the face of the conservative onslaught on the welfare state.

3. The overall policy/political message supports reformism: the pursuit of immediately achievable political goals rather than long-term, utopian or revolutionary alternatives.

In Britain in particular, left realism has emerged as the dominant voice in the radical movement and is already creating its own theoretical discourse that contains: the claim to have developed a new paradigm; a complex intellectual autobiography to justify realism as being faithful to the spirit of critical criminology rather than (as abolitionists charge) a betrayal; even an appeal to "realist" (that is, anti-relativist and anti-nominalist) philosophy.

This entire self critique is interesting and important. I will comment, though, only on the elements relevant to my subject of intellectual doubt and political action. Here, the self critique overlaps (and indeed has been constructed in response to) the more hostile external criticisms of the 1960s package. I'm referring not to conservatives nor to disenchanted liberals, but to those traditional liberals who are upset that the original radical attack so undermined the ideology of progress and rationality. This—it is claimed—has lent strength to the enemy— with disastrous consequences to the progressive "civilizing" reform project.

I could give many examples of such criticism, but I will take one from a source familiar to you in Holland. This is an address (at the last International Society of Criminology Conference in Hamburg in 1989) given by Dr. Jan van Dijk, the Director of Research and Information in the Dutch Ministry of Justice (van Dijk 1989).

Dr. van Dijk accuses criminological criticism itself of contributing to a mood of despair and disillusionment in which the commitment is abandoned to humanize the prisons and criminal justice system. Such criticism, he notes, is "post modernist in the derogatory sense;" it undermines the utilitarian and humanistic traditions that inform penal reform.

So, for example, he claims that the liberal case against rehabilitation and for "just desserts" leads to warehousing; that the abolitionist case that prisons are beyond redemption, inhibits the drive for prison reform; that the "hostile skepticism" towards community alternatives (on the grounds of "net-widening," etc.) unwittingly lends political support (as he alleges has happened in The Netherlands) for re-expanding the prison system.

So (in van Dijk's works) criminologists—lured by abstract notions like "just desserts" or "abolitionism," and "fellow travelling with post-modernist or radical ideas,"—have deserted their traditional cause: finding a rational and humanitarian approach towards the problem of crime. Such abstract notions are "not very helpful for those who seek to reform the criminal justice system."

Now of course, Dr. van Dijk is right about that. But is this the end of the story—a joyous reproachment between academics and Ministry of Justice officials to reform prisons? Hang on; I would say as a fellow traveller.

First, haven't we heard this message before? Perhaps a century ago—when academic criminology originally became joined to the penal reform project. Is the whole task of constructing an intellectually respectable subject now to be abandoned to bolster the platitudes of progressive penal reform?

Second, is this really the way ideas affect social policy? Or isn't this rather like saying that functionalist sociology causes inequality and that Freudian psychology causes human unhappiness? Are prisons like they are now because their managers read post modernist theory—or rather because they are doing what they've always done (for more than a hundred years); that is, "reforming" the penal system. And surely prisons have expanded over the Eighties (in low-imprisonment countries like Holland and high-imprisonment countries like Britain and the United States) in response to realities (such as the drug problem) and political contingencies that have nothing to do with the critical discourse.

And third, why should "abolitionism," "labelling" (and so on) be merely "abstract notions," while "rationality," "humanitarianism" and the "civilizing process" are not? We need a better theory of the complex relationship between ideas/knowledge and policy/power than Dr. van Dijk even hints at.[2] But his bitter attempt to blame the messenger for causing the news, points directly to the wider lessons we might extract from the curious story of radical criminology.

EPISODE THREE: INSTRUCTION

We could, of course, agree with the realist case—and that of "progressive" critics like van Dijk—against the original radical impulse. The counter-theories were modified in the light of experience, new findings, anomalies and a recommitment to rationality. Re-construction was thus perfectly natural and signals the maturation of radical theory rather than any dramatic mutation or reversal. In response to the "aetiological crisis" (the failure to explain rising crime rates) and "radical" victimology, the new paradigm emerged. Left realism is, in Jock Young's terms, simply "critical criminology come of age."

But we cannot, I believe, end the triumphalist narrative at this point. In addition to (or instead of, as some philosophers urge us) asking "Is it right?" we might ask "Why do you say something like that?" This might mean speculating on: the supposed biographical (rather than logical) maturation and sense of responsibility and "realism" alleged to come from middle age and getting tenure; or the generational transformation from the culture of the 1960s—the joys of "trashing," attacking the old order, the sense of alternative realities, the unbounded optimism—to the lowered horizons and defensiveness of the next decade; or the revisions through which the Western radical tradition is passing—confronted by feminism, the ecological movement, the dramatic transformations in State Socialism. The legitimacy of "conservative" concerns is acknowledged and there is more receptiveness to reformist politics (what used to be dismissed as "working within the system").

The political context is crucial to my subject here. At first sight at least, this looks like a clear case where the tension between sociological skepticism and socialist commitment is resolved by abandoning an intellectual route that offered no immediate political relevance. In Britain at least—where the realist course has been most dramatic—this is clear enough; left realism is social democratic or Labor Party criminology, produced by socialists appalled by the long years of Thatcherite conservativism and convinced that the original "left-idealist" paradigm offered nothing to counter this.

Besides these sociology of knowledge explanations ("why are you talking like that?") we must also confront the realist message in its own right. Here, the debate with abolitionism still remains instructive and by no means settled. Aside from the bitter question (of limited interest to the outsider) about which side is the "true" heir to the critical legacy, many of the abolitionist/realist differences remain important. Abolitionism is an anomaly: although sharing the original deconstructionist impulse, it can hardly be accused of negative skepticism; far from being nihilist, most abolitionists are seen as quaintly optimistic. Quixotically—according to their realist critics—they remain: committed to "thought experiments" about a future society; skeptical about purely instrumental and utilitarian justifications of the criminal law; reluctant to support means which are incongruent with the desired end state; insistent that there is no simple congruence between everyday cognitive categories and the discourse of penal law; reluctant to take crime or criminology seriously... and so on.

But the instruction for which I'm searching lies not in the details of the debate between abolitionists and left realists. The question is not who is being more "realistic"—but rather what is the point of intellectual work that seems to lead to skepticism, irony and self-doubt. After all the "trashing" (the term used in Critical Legal Studies for the negative critique) is there some essence to be revealed, which tells us how to act—or just another set of meanings, another text to be decoded and so endlessly on? Is negative skepticism good in itself even if no well-grounded proposals for institutional change are offered? Does its value lie precisely in its ability to distance itself from the professed aims of progressive crime control policy (or liberal legal ideology)? Is the refusal even to suggest "constructive" alternatives something of which to be proud?

If the answers to all these questions are an unqualified "yes," then no wonder liberal supporters of progress and rationality are so unhappy. They hardly want to hear this news about their own (as well as the conservative) project: "Whatever it looks like, that's not it. And whatever it is, it's bad." Nor too, can socialists be happy about an epistemology which offers them only this non-connection between theory and practice. Therefore, left realist criminology.

Now, as someone whose values come from the same socialist or communitarian liberal vision, I should be satisfied with the realist solution. And indeed I respect their political stance and their attempt to stake out a clearly radical opposition to today's grim coalition between enterprise capitalism and neutered administrative criminology. Unlike their harsh critics from the Left, I see no reason to question their continued commitment to socialist theory and practice. But why does their sociology leave me uneasy? With a sense that this is a premature closure of the debate, a denial of the tension between intellectual doubt and political action? Have not some important theoretical problems and insights been forgotten in order to respond to a particular set of political contingencies?

Before returning both to criminology and to our general problem, let us look for instruction elsewhere.

FURTHER INSTRUCTION

Moving from the immediately relevant to the apparently irrelevant, there are three areas that might illuminate our original problem of "double loyalty": critical legal studies; feminism; and deconstruction "proper" (in literature, philosophy, cultural criticism).

Critical Legal Studies

Critical legal studies (CLS) is something of an intellectual anomaly. Though it formally appeared at a time—the late Seventies—when the first wave of critical criminology was already under drastic self-revision, its spirit is that of the 1960s. It draws on the same mixture of New Left and critical theory; appeals to the same project of "advancing human liberation"; shares the commitment to attacking dominant orthodoxies (in this case, the paradigm of liberal legalism); rewrites history to show the contingent and transitory nature of current arrangements; is hostile to rules, formalism and bureaucracy in the name of visionary alternatives (such as "society without law").

But precisely because CLS appeared later on the scene, it registered more clearly the meta-problems behind the deconstructionist enterprise.[3] Also, unlike criminology, it explicitly works with texts. Thus, the issue of essentialism becomes clear: if law is "unmasked" not as a repository of noble liberal principles then what is it? In essence, an instrumental ruling class plot, a mask for domination? A set of multiple meanings liable to further and further deconstruction? Or (an intermediate position recommended in such moderate expositions as Gordon's), a more "plastic medium of discourse that conditions how we experience social life?"

Just as in radical criminology, this debate results from grafting onto the original critical project (demystifying the law as an instrument of domination) those strands in post modernist thought that resist any idea of fixed meaning, order or essence. And hostile outsiders are correct to note that any claim to decode the discourse according to a master narrative (whether of progress, rationality or historicism) is quite incompatible with pure deconstructionism. I'll return to this question—but just want to note here the sharpness of this theoretical debate in CLS compared to its premature burial in radical criminology.

The same can be said about the question of idealism. Its version in critical legal studies is this: what is the connection between decoding legal consciousness—exposing its inconsistencies, anomalies and "foolishness"—and any recognizable political agenda? However elegantly one unmasks the contradictions of liberal legalism or takes apart its concepts ("contract," "property," "consent") or breaks up its dichotomies (substance/process, public/private, voluntary/involuntary)—so what? The "crits" answers to this question are—to say the least—elliptic. At least, though, they do not merely denounce "left idealism" as self indulgence.

This leads onto the problem of negative skepticism. In its most outrageous declarations, CLS proclaimed trashing to be good in itself, even if no well-grounded proposals for institutional change were offered. Its virtue lies precisely in its negativity. This, of course, was the same message in the original attempt by anti-criminology to distance itself from "correctional" concerns. And this is the literal meaning of abolitionism (as defended by Mathiesen, though quite contradicted by the fact than most abolitionists are very busy working out practical alternatives).

This negativity worries both realists and critics (internal and external) of CLS. These worries are justified—without them, my lecture would have no subject. They are only partially confronted by the critique (and, in my view, this is as much as we should expect). In CLS, taking legal discourse apart, seeing how it works and then re-interpreting it, is supposed to give you the energy and motivation to look for alternatives. You then pose the question—as abolitionists do—what would society look like if these were implemented? From a common hostility to formalism, professions and state monopolies, emerges the communitarian vision of decentralized, informal social control.

Realists, as we have seen, are not only unhappy with "pure" skepticism, but less sympathetic now to the content of this type of negative critique. The trashed values of liberal democracy must be re-confirmed; legal reforms supported. CLS is more ambivalent (and hence in my mind, more realistic!) than either realists (with their new-born faith in formalism) or abolitionists (with their absolute rejection of anything to do with the criminal justice apparatus). They allow that justice, legality, the rule of law and rights are shorthand symbols for desired values that hide latent utopian possibilities. And they also recognize that under certain conditions it is useful to maintain the pretense that laws have an objective fixed set of meanings that can be invoked in the struggle against arbitrary power. For those involved in this struggle—whether in Third World military dictatorship or the current upheavals in East Europe—the critique must indeed look at best a distraction, at worst, counter productive. What can the progressive struggle mean, if its goal is dismissed by the intellectual avant garde as illusory?

I agree wholly with this way of defending legal formalism; all of us know the derision which greets the pristine critique in societies like these. This, however, is a point about the political specificity of the critique and not the skeptical enterprise itself.

Feminism

The few words I want to say about feminism derive not so much from the large substantive overlap between feminist work and the fields of law, crime and social control: abortion, birth control, family law, pornography, divorce, rape, sexuality, prostitution, labor law, and so on. My interest is more theoretical (how feminist theory has used deconstructionism) and political (how feminist resolutions of the tension between theory and practice, are more convincing than those in general critical theory).

Both in the loose sense of the 1960s "de" movements and the particular area of literary theory, feminist work has been "deconstructionist" in spirit. Take the three central subjects of gender roles, sexuality and the differences between public/private or market/family. In each case, standard categories are questioned, fixed dichotomies broken down, the natural exposed as ideological, hidden forms of power revealed, self-serving legitimations unmasked. In each case, the truth lies either in an essence ("patriarchy") or in a set of contingent and infinitely variable meanings. This is the issue of essentialism. And then there is the problem of idealism: the presentation of alternative, liberating possibilities, either in the realm of the practical (e.g., legal reform) or the imaginary (androgeny, de-sexualization, the dissolution of categories).

The "strong" version of radical feminism goes along the whole deconstructionist path. In the radical discourse on rape, for example, the legal categories of "will," "spheres of consent," "relationships," and "exemptions" all dissolve and, eventually, it is difficult to even tell the difference between normal heterosexual intercourse and rape. For radical feminists such as MacKinnon, rape becomes merely the paradigmatic case of male power (MacKinnon 1982, 1983). Or—for Olson—the dichotomy between market and family is exposed as false, as impoverishing, as inhibiting the possibilities of change (Olson 1983).

The weaker—in this context, "realist" case—argues the opposite. All the talk about the "dissolution" of categories, the "reconstruction" of social life, the creation of a new "referential system" is irrelevant to the political agenda. Policy lies in the spheres of legal reform, protection through formal legality, and so on. This, of course, is to oversimplify the debate within feminist theory. But even in this form, its resonance for critical criminology should be obvious.

Deconstructionism

Finally—before returning to criminology—something about formal deconstructionism in literary and philosophical theory. This now-fashionable way of contemplating texts and language sounds totally remote from criminology. It is not by chance, however, that critics of critical criminology (like van Dijk) have spotted the connection with post modernism. As I've argued elsewhere, the highly specific message of critical criminology must be seen not just in terms of the 1960s' cultural idealism nor even of general critical theory, but the long and powerful line of Western intellectual thought which Steiner calls the "dissent from reason."

The original moment of critical criminology was part of the wider postmodern skepticism about the faith that with good will, scientific knowledge and rationality, human and social problems could be solved. At the heart of this attack on objectivity and reason, the language revolution was critical: the breaking of the relationship between the word and the world. No longer could we assume this connection, no longer could there be an observation that was theory-free. The truth value of any claim was either up for grabs (wholly relativist) or mere ideology (hiding a hidden essence).

In the 1960s, these ideas were torn from their complex theoretical origins and translated into guides for action—guides that led (without us being aware) in quite opposed directions. When we took the essentialist path, the language of others was depicted as mystifying while ours was liberatory. We knew what were people's "real needs." With pessimism, we discovered repression everywhere; with optimism we proclaimed that we could transform reality. When we took the relativist, subjectivist path, then reality was negotiated meaning, a variable language game. The accepted language (of "crime" or "mental illness") was only one way of making sense of the world, the particular language game that had achieved currency for entirely contingent reasons. And throughout, we confused demolition—taking the elements apart to make the structure collapse ("left idealism") with deconstruction: showing that despite its anomalies and inconsistencies, the building goes on standing.

Twenty years ago, we had never heard the word "deconstruction." But now we know. Deconstructionism proper is the culmination of this challenge to the Enlightenment faith in reason, progress and objective knowledge. It denies the possibility of rational discourse. In a disciplined and rigorous form and by reading texts (therefore its appeal to students of law) it poses the same questions that appeared so inchoately in the 1960s: is there an objective access to reality? Do our discourses correspond to a reality independent of consciousness?

Precisely because pure literary deconstructionism—Derrida's relentless break with the instituted wisdom of language—is so bizarre and irrelevant to a subject like criminology, this is why it is so instructive.[4]

The realist case becomes obviously correct: a libertarian textual theory which equates radical politics with the free play of an infinitely pluralized meaning, offers little more than an impotent gesture of defiance. It becomes impossible to defend this version of "skeptical theory" (the term I used twenty years ago to describe the "Great Refusal" by criminologists to accept the commonsense, the obvious, the surface).

We could hardly have imagined, however, the wild directions that philosophical skepticism were to take. Literary deconstructionism, is an extreme form of the skeptical tradition that "...makes manifest the fact that any radical shift of interpretative thought must always come up against the limits of its seeming absurdity" (Norris 1986, p. xii). The particular absurdity in life, if not literature, lies in knowing that this line of thought cannot be followed through into action. As Norris goes on, such philosophers have long recognized that "...thinking may lead them inescapably into regions of skepticism such that life could hardly carry on if people were to act on their own conclusions."

Deconstructionism works at a "giddy limit" that suspends all we take for granted about language and experience. It is "...an activity of thought which cannot be consistently acted on—that way madness lies—but which yet possesses an inescapable rigor of its own" (Norris 1986, p. xiii). Without actually appealing to this philosophical debate, this is just the objection to critical theory that comes from realists and liberals. As one such critic notes about the "excessive" or "radical" skepticism in critical legal studies that insists on pushing any premise to its furthest level of justification, this "...is less appropriate to practical matters such as law than it is to, say, philosophy" (Brosnan 1986, p. 267). This simple point is surely irrefutable: however rigorous might be the work of skeptical deconstructionism (in fact, the more rigorous it is)—the critique, trashing, genealogy or whatever—no moral, political, practical or policy lines follow.

To me, however, this does not mean that we should abandon these intellectual journeys. It does mean that we should abandon the silly idea that they will tell us "what is to be done." As Norris remarks about literary deconstructionism: "Its proponents have never pretended that life could be conducted in a practical way if everyone acted consistently on skeptical assumptions" (Norris 1986, p. 128). Language continues more or less to communicate; life goes on. Norris again: "Deconstructionism neither denies nor really affects the commonsense view that language exists to convey meaning. It suspends that view for its own specific purpose of seeing what happens when the writs of convention no longer run" (1986, p. xiii).

This type of "suspension" is precisely what critical theory and movements like CLS and abolitionism (at their best) encourage. This, of course, is neither an immediately practical nor a very appealing political strategy. And, at their worst and silliest, abolitionism and CLS do indeed pretend that life could be conducted in a practical way by acting on skeptical assumptions. This is one reason why realist and other critics have lost patience with radical skepticism. They are altogether correct in saying that no amount of talk about the contingency of categories, the historical specificity of the punishment response, or the vision of reconciliation will help city dwellers protect themselves from mugging, drug abuse, rape or pollution. To travel the subways of New York, I need more help than a deconstructed map of the category of "mugging."

So the call for a politically relevant form of "help" is justified. But this can be done by suspending, not junking, some hard-won theoretical insights. Otherwise we forget that language is not a simple representation of social reality, that metaphors (like the "war against crime") compete with each other rather than being self evident. Otherwise we forget that the public discourse of crime control reflects the interests of the powerful; that it is saturated with images that justify the social order as natural, necessary, and even just. To claim that this discourse serves "everyone's" interest in protection is to lose any critical reading of "texts" like official criminal statistics, public opinion polls, or victim surveys.[5]

And to say that people want justice and legality is to agree that of course the discourse of legality draws its legitimacy from a widely held, if inchoate, sense of the ideal. But this hardly tells us how to reach this ideal.

For this project, the point is not to choose between skepticism and realism but to show in concrete situations just where intellectual subversion might (or might not) lead. Take the skeptical (and wholly idealist) project of "dissolving" categories. However soluble are the categories of, say, positivist criminology or legal liberalism, they might still provide the best (or only) way of improving services, achieving social justice, compensating the victim, empowering the weak—or whatever. As one feminist commentator on projects such as "desexualization" notes: "Having achieved a position from which to enter the struggle over definition, we are confronted with the avant garde's observations that sexual difference, sexual identity, sexuality itself are fictions, and that the perpetuation of these categories can only further enhance the workings of power"(Martin 1988, p. 17). Women might then not be able to speak as women: "...our oppression may easily be lost among the pluralities of new theories of ideologies and power."

But this is a political point; it raises questions of strategy, tactics, alliances. Deconstructionism itself does not necessarily undermine the utility of any discourse, still less the importance of any values or the desirability of any practice. This is clear when we look not at Derrida-like extravaganzas, but the position advanced by pragmatic philosophers like Richard Rorty. The message is more moderate—but is also firmly opposed to any sort of realism. Yes, language is contingent—all we have are different language games for making sense of what interests us. None has any privileged status. Rorty presents not an alternative epistemology, but denies the need for epistemology at all. This does not mean that any language game is as "good" as another. It does mean that the choice depends on what works, not what is true.

Even if we concede, that is, that an infinite number of meanings are possible—we are still left with two old questions: first, the traditional sociological question: why does one meaning system become dominant? And second, the political and value question: by exactly what pragmatic criterion does one meaning system work better than another? This last question is crucial for those of us working in "practical" areas such as law and crime control as opposed to deconstructing literary texts: what are the implications of these theories for concrete social policy choices and political actions?

BACK TO CRIMINOLOGY

My answer to that question is less an answer than a partial evasion. For the critique of knowledge/power in criminology and similar subjects—our meta-debates, our histories or genealogies, our persistent skepticism—takes place at a different level from our policy choices.

On a "realist" level—the "thing" itself (crime, victims, control)—we do research, construct theories and suggest policies about what is to be done. On a "skeptical" level, we ask why some subjects are studied rather than others and how they are studied—and then comment on this choice in the name of some explicit political ideology, some vision of how the world should be, or (if so inclined) a pure philosophical skepticism.

It is easy enough to "see" the difference between these different levels. On one level, for example, we might describe an act of rape, explain why it happened, document the extent of women's fear of victimization and propose viable social policy. This is different from claiming that rape is a logical extension of male power or that a male-centered epistemology cannot comprehend the phenomenon.

How to connect these levels? Some of this task is phoney: a prison manager in Holland should not be expected to produce a Foucault-type analysis of social control any more than a Foucault analysis of knowledge/power tells us how to judge whether a theory of delinquency "works" or whether a social worker is doing a good job. Some of the task, however, is real, because claims at one level turn out to inform what happens at another. This is no more than any self-respecting sociologist knows anyway. If we have consistently looked at rape from a male world view (a meta-point, an ultra theoretical claim) then how can we begin to construct a just social policy?

The second (or third, or fourth...) level critique can tell us neither what to do nor what is good; it can only give us the ground rules for what Foucault calls "making facile gestures difficult." Thus if there are no easy solutions to the cliched problem of "integration between theory and practice," the task is even harder for "meta-theory and practice." I am uneasy about the triumphalist narrative of realism—with its impatient dismissal of skeptical questions as a romantic hangover from the past, a distraction from the demands of "confronting crime." Nor have I argues for a pure deconstructionism that leads nowhere except to the paralysis of infinite philosophical redress. Both these solutions are legacies from the confused politics of the 1960s: the urge on the one hand to be "relevant" and on the other, to detach ourselves from what others defines as "relevant."

There must always be a tension between these demands and it is all too easy either to respond only to one or to look for false integration. Studying criminological knowledge and power can indeed only be achieved by skepticism, by detachment, by not being the slightest bit interested in "relevance." This work is superior because it tries to transcend the discourse itself. On the other hand, realists (from left, right, or center) must surely be right in asserting that there is something "out there" independent of our closed circuit of knowledge/power. This is the "superior" reality that demands immediate reaction: fear, damage, loss of life, injury, suffering, victimization, massive investment of money, skill and energy.[6] To dismiss these matters as ancillary to the business of meta-theorizing, is something like dismissing the traditional concerns of literature—imagination, creativity, moral worth, literary value—as irrelevant. What Frank Kermode calls the "flight from literature" might indeed have its echo in the realist slogans about denying the grim facts of urban life.

We all "know" this—because inside every relativist, skepticist and deconstructionist, there is a little realist, a closet positivist, struggling to get out. He or she, however, should not feel obliged to retreat from the insights derived from critical and deconstructionist thinking. It is an act of bad faith to bracket off this knowledge—deriving as it does from the best of the 1960s message, the sense of "unravelling, rethinking, refusing to take for granted—thinking without limits" (Gitlin 1987, p. 7).

The problem of deconstruction is that it took up only one half of this message—the reflexive, skeptical, sociology of knowledge question—and pushed it to its giddy limits. This is the impulse that culminates in today's paradigm of post modernity: in which there are no dominant schools, no sense of evolution or progress, no authoritative aesthetic discourse, only pastiche, plagiarism, collage and endless self referentiality.[7]

The other half of the 1960s message was the drive to make moral and political positions explicit, a commitment to reshape our theoretical and policy agenda to meet the needs of people and the demands for social justice. It is here—and neither by "being realistic" nor by "thinking without limits"—that we find the criteria to know whether what we are doing is "right." It is here that realist criminologists are working—justifiably, in my view—to create an anthropology that better fits the demands of a reconstituted socialism or social democracy.

But does this political stance demand all the new epistemological fervor of realism? Surely it is possible to be skeptical and ironical at the level of theory—yet at the level of policy and politics to be firmly committed. This is just the position that anti-realist philosophers like Rorty are trying to defend. His ideal is the "liberal ironist" (1989; cf. Williams 1989) who is a liberal (in his version), a person who thinks that cruelty is the worst thing we can do, that human suffering and humiliation should be diminished.[8] Someone who is an ironist is a person who faces up to the contingency of his or her central beliefs and desires—someone sufficiently historicist and nominalist to have abandoned the idea that these beliefs and desires refer back to something "real," "essential," beyond the reach of time and chance. The opposite of irony is not just realist metaphysics ("real interests," "true desires," the "quest for truth," "progress"), but also the appeal to common sense ("...the watchword of those who unselfconsciously describe everything important in terms of the final vocabulary to which they and those around them are habituated") (Rorty 1989, p. 74).

I personally agree more with Rorty's irony than with his political position, which looks much like a triumphalist defense of liberal capitalism. My point here though, is that liberal (or any other) irony is not mindlessly relativist, nihilist or irresponsible. It is quite possible to recognize the contingency of your values, language and conscience—yet remain wholly faithful to them.

DOUBT AND ACTION: AGAIN

This returns us, by a long route, to where we started: the problem of double loyalty to sociology (intellectual) and to socialism (political). I have argued elsewhere (Cohen 1987) that this is really a triple loyalty—first, an overriding obligation to honest intellectual enquiry itself (however skeptical, provisional, irrelevant and unrealistic), second, a political commitment to social justice, but also (and potentially conflicting with both) the pressing and immediate demands for short term humanitarian help. We have to appease these three voracious gods.

How? Not, I have argued here, by giving into one to the exclusion of others. Each strongly tempts. We have seen the appeal of "detached" radical skepticism—but we are fooling nobody if we think that this stance can be sustained, not in our subjects (justice, suffering, violence, guilt, punishment) and not in our time. And as for political systems built on essentialism and teleology, they have turned out poor intellectual guides and even worse when translated into practice. Nor can we return to the Garden of Eden of intuition, common sense, kindness and compassion. Such sentiments need to be framed by a theory and informed by a political strategy.

But if there is more than one God to appease, this does not mean that we should be using all our precious time searching for false symmetry, for the modern alchemist' stone of "integration." Both the liberal, idealist theory of knowledge and the materialist metaphysics that dismisses such knowledge as ideology share the illusory commitment to "getting it right," finding the correct fit between theory and practice. We don't have to surrender to the pretentious charms of post modernist fragmentation to be able to live without such integration. Although much of this article is a defense of the spirit of the 1960s, here surely is one part of that legacy too flawed to revive: our hope that somewhere integration was possible, not only between the intellectual and political but also between this gestalt and our innermost personal lives, our true selves.

Allow me a personal example. I work now in the field of human rights violations by Israelis against Palestinians in the Occupied Territories. Despite my deep theoretical skepticism about the discourse of pure legality (the apolitical model of civil rights), I accept this as the only "realistic" weapon to ensure moral accountability (e.g., of soldiers guilty of atrocities). Despite my sympathy with some abolitionist ideas, I have no doubt that such accountability requires punishment. At the same time, I don't feel inhibited about writing critiques of this model (which are then criticized by my liberal colleagues for giving ammunition to the Right). Despite our commitment to particular long-term political goals, I spend more time working (help, solidarity) with individual victims. Despite my conflicts with colleagues who think that the university should be "free of politics," I feel (willingly) obliged to teach courses ("Introduction to Criminological Theory" or "Crime and Politics") in as wholly detached and objective way as possible.

And so on. I am simplifying these examples—but the lack of easy "integration" is typical rather than unusual or (at least I would like to think) a product of my own cognitive defects. These worlds are split. All we can do, is find the best guide to each one—then confront the tension that results. This is hard going. In the end, the only guides are first, our sense of social justice and second, whatever time we have in the twenty-four-hour day.

Others, of course, have laid down more sophisticated instructions. Of the critics of our century, it is peculiarly Foucault whom I find most helpful and even inspiring. "Peculiarly" because his post modernist disengagement is seen by many as entirely unhelpful. This, for example, is Waltzer's (1989) reading in his recent study of social criticism and political commitment in the Twentieth Century. He sees Foucault as the supreme example of the critic—someone who specializes in complaint—who cannot be a social critic, because of his deliberate attempt to step back, to distance himself from his own "community," to make no virtue of "connectedness," to refuse engagement with all reform projects. My guess is that left realist criminology would agree with Waltzer's dismissal of Foucault. Note, for example, Taylor's sense of the political task, along with his "friends in the developing tradition of realist criminology:" "...sociology should not remain content with the task of critique, but it must be involved in the project of reform and social construction organized around a coherent, specific conception of the public interest" (Taylor 1989).

Foucault is seen as negative, pessimistic, hostile to any such project of social reconstruction—the pure, nihilistic critic. This is not my reading. I take literally his model of the specific intellectual who does not make too many general injunctions but works in his or her own field, eternally questioning the self-evident, dissipating what is accepted and familiar. It is this reproblematization in the role of the intellectual which allows him "...to participate in the formation of a political will (in which he has his role as citizen to play)" (Foucault 1988, p. 265).

True: Foucault does not supply us with the guiding values for knowing what is good, for knowing (as he prefers it) "whether the revolution is worthwhile." But we don't need him for this. We need him for his sense of wonder, the intellectual ethics that demands: "...to make oneself permanently capable of detaching oneself from oneself (which is the opposite of the attitude of conversion)" (Foucault 1988, p. 262). This means that: "There are times in life when the question of knowing if one can think differently than one thinks, and perceive differently than one sees, is absolutely necessary if one is to go on looking and reflecting at all" (Foucault 1984, p. 8).

There is an apocryphal story about a British sociology professor thirty years ago who was criticized for teaching totally untheoretical courses year after year. His reply was: "I give then the facts—and then let their Marxist intuition do the rest." We live in more complicated times. We have been taught to be skeptical about what constitutes "facts" and even more skeptical about systems like "Marxism" to arbitrate our intuitions. But a post-modern version of that old certainty might still, oddly, apply: an honest deconstruction (which is not a denial) of the facts plus an intuitive sense of the values.

To resolve the conflicting demands of honesty and relevance is facile but false. Ideally, though, these demands should be informed by similar values. The ruthless skepticism needed for good intellectual work need be only a little less ruthless for honest politics and even for the ordinary human solidarity and decency that motivates help for our fellows—whether offender or victim.

The problem of skeptical, post modernist thought is not so much that it is politically "unrealistic" but that its slogans (such as "the end of history" or "the death of rationality") are so intellectually naive. For most of the world, the old truths of racism, naked injustice, mass starvation and brutal physical repression still apply. In these parts of the world, just to be a sociologist, to state these old truths openly and honestly, is an act of courage and consequence. In the January 1990 Newsletter of the American Sociological Association, an obituary appeared for two sociologists murdered in November 1989 in El Salvador—just for using their research skills to expose their country's social injustice. As one of their colleagues writes: "It is not a coincidence that all the professors had their brains blasted out of their skulls. It is not a coincidence that all the tools of the social scientists—their computers and typewriters— were physically destroyed in the attack. This massacre was not only an attack on these individuals, but an attack on reason itself" (*Footnotes* 1990, p. 2).

If there is an inconsistency in sometimes speaking out for reason and humanitarianism but sometimes questioning this faith—this inconsistency is a product of intellectual honesty. If the old ways of connecting facts and intuition make little sense, neither do the detachments of post modernism.

Our task is seemingly impossible: to combine detachment with commitment. There is only one universal guide for this: not to use intellectual skepticism as an alibi for political inaction. I'll give the last word to a poet rather than a sociologist. In his famous poem "In Praise of Doubt," Brecht harshly condemns, remember, "...the thoughtless who never doubt." But just as harshly, he condemns "...the thoughtful who never act."

> They doubt not in order to come to a decision but
> to avoid a decision.
> Therefore if you praise doubt/
> Do not praise/
> The doubt which is a form of despair.

We, the living, can know nothing of Bonger's last moments of despair. We can only decide at what point to stop praising doubt.

ACKNOWLEDGMENTS

This article is a shortened version of my inaugural lecture of the annual W.A. Bonger Memorial Lectures at the University of Amsterdam on May 14 1990. I am deeply grateful to Professor Elisabeth Lissenberg and her colleagues at the Willem Bonger Institute of Criminology for inviting me to give this lecture. I received many helpful comments from them and my other friends in The Netherlands. An earlier version was given at the Amherst Seminar on Legal Ideology and Legal Process; I am grateful to members of the Seminar for the opportunity to discuss these ideas.

NOTES

1. I list only the realist claims relevant to our theme of intellectual skepticism. For full statements, see Young (1986) and subsequent publications by Young and his colleagues at the Middlesex Polytechnic Centre of Criminology, England (listed in "Realism: A Selected Bibliography," December 1988).

2. A depressingly relevant example of just how problematic is this relationship is to be found in Dirk Van Zyl Smit's fascinating study of criminology and Afrikaner nationalism in South Africa. Geoff Cronje, one of the two founders of criminology in South Africa, studied criminology in Amsterdam with Professor Bonger in 1933 and was awarded his doctoral degree by the University of Amsterdam. From Bonger he picked up—"correctly" or not—the determinist thread of Marxism. Cronje returned to South Africa to deploy this—not to advance social justice and democracy, but to justify the inevitable emergence of the Afrikaner volk—threatened by the British, by communism and by liberalism. From this, there emerged an elaborate "scientific" justification for racism in criminology and apartheid in society. See Van Zyl Smit (1989).

3. I do not provide detailed citations of the key writings (by Kennedy, Kelman, Gabel et al) in the C.L.S. canon. A good source remains the various articles in *Stanford Law Review*, Vol. 36 (1984). See also Fitzpatrick and Hunt (1987). An accessible summary is Gordon (1988).

4. I suggest "instruction" about our skepticism/action problem only. Literary theory is even more instructive on the essentialist problem—especially if we accept the claim that the methods for reading a text can be used to "read" social reality. Once (in opposition to liberal humanist inquiry) the text is interrogated, broken up, unpacked, we can move in two different directions: either the quest for the secret sub-text (of power, class or gender) or the exposure of another set of meanings, an infinite contextualization. On this conflict (in its early stages!), see Jameson (1982).

5. Sophisticated statements of the realist position do not, of course, forget such critical readings. Thus Young explicitly lists one political advantage of radical criminology over its conservative competitors: "It is sensitized to the fact that crime statistics are social constructs and that their reality is not something 'out there' as positivism and administrative criminology would have it, but a product of behavior and evaluation." (Young 1988, p. 175). Realists also acknowledge that "fear of crime" is often a convenient semiotic shorthand, a metaphor to capture a sense of urban decay, displacement and marginality.

6. For a vivid sense of the consequences of criminal victimization, see standard research on crime injuries. A current report, for example, estimates that between 1979 and 1986, 2.2 million people were injured by violent crime each year in the United States, one million of whom received medical care, with an average hospital stay of 9 days. See *Injuries From Crime* (Bureau of Justice Statistics 1989). This made up 30 percent of the hospitalization days caused by traffic accidents. No one would deny the sickening details of such crime injuries; to say that these could be called something other than "crime" looks strangely beside the point. But to say that more injuries result from hidden abuses of power remains an important point. And why haven't the remaining 70 percent of hospitalization days not produced a discipline of "traffic accidentology" that commands the same resources as criminology?

7. For some commentators, however, sociologists have little choice but to follow the directions of post modernity. The post 1960s deconstructionist movements, rather than being rectifications

of previous blunders, "...can best be understood as a mimetic representation of the postmodern condition." (Bauman 1988, p. 806).

8. Philosophers do not read criminology. So there is little reason for Rorty to cite the striking similarity between this version of liberalism—placing a supreme value on preventing cruelty, humiliation and pain—and Christie's defense of abolitionism: (Christie 1981).

REFERENCES

Bauman, Z. 1988. "Sociology and Postmodernity." *Sociological Review* 36: 804-830.
Brosnan, D. 1986. "Serious But Not Critical." *Southern California Law Review* 60:
Christie, N. 1981. *Limits to Pain*. Oxford: Martin Robertson.
Cohen, S. 1985. *Visions of Social Control*. Cambridge: Polity Press.
———. 1987. "Appeasing Voracious Gods." *Canadian Criminology Forum* 8: 132-148.
———. 1989. *Against Criminology*. New Jersey: Transaction.
Fitzpatrick, P. and A. Hunt. (Eds.). 1987. *Critical Legal Studies*. Oxford: Blackwell.
Footnotes. (American Sociological Association). 1990. "In Memoriam," p. 2.
Foucault, M. 1984. *The Uses of Pleasure*. London: Penguin.
———. 1988. "The Concern for Truth." In *Michel Foucault: Politics, Philosophy and Culture*, edited by L.D. Kritzman. London: Routledge.
Gitlin, T. 1987. *The Sixties: Years of Hope, Days of Rage*. New York: Bantam Books.
Gordon, R.W. 1988. "Law and Ideology." *Tikkun* 3: 14-19, 83-86.
Jameson, F. 1982. *The Political Unconsciousness*. Ithaca: Cornell University Press.
MacKinnon, C. 1982. "Feminism, Marxism, Method and the State" (Part 1). *Signs* 7: 215-241.
———. 1983. "Feminism, Marxism, Method and the State" (Part 2) *Signs* 8: 635-683.
Martin, B. 1988. "Feminism, Criticism and Foucault." In *Feminism and Foucault: Reflections on Resistance*, edited by I. Diamond and L. Quigley. Boston: Northeastern University Press.
Norris, C. 1986. *Deconstructionism: Theory and Practise*. London: Methuen.
Olson, F. 1982. "The Family and the Market: A Study of Ideology and Legal Reform." *Harvard Law Review* 96:000-000.
Rorty, R. 1989. *Contingency, Irony and Solidarity*. Cambridge: Cambridge University Press.
Taylor, I. 1989. "Sociology and the Condition of the English City." Inaugural Lecture, Department of Sociology, University of Salford.
van Dijk, J. 1989. "Penal Sanctions and the Process of Civilization." *International Annals of Criminology* 27: 191-204.
van Zyl Smit, D. 1989. "Adapting and Adopting Criminological Ideas: Criminology and Afrikaner Nationalism in South Africa." *Contemporary Crises* 13: 227-251.
Waltzer, M. 1989. *The Company of Critics*. London: Peter Halban.
Williams, B. 1989. "Getting It Right." *London Review of Books* 11: 1-3.
Young, Jock 1986. "The Failure of Criminology: The Need for a Radical Realism." In *Confronting Crime*, edited by J. Young and R. Mathews. London: Sage.
———. 1988. "Radical Criminology in Britain: The Emergence of a Competing Paradigm." *British Journal of Criminology* 28: 159-183.

[15]
State Crimes of Previous Regimes: Knowledge, Accountability, and the Policing of the Past

> *The policy of lustration is set in the context of responses to abuses of power by previous regimes. Using examples from three recent forms of social reconstruction (in Latin America, the former communist states, and South Africa), the author reviews the "justice in transition" debate. How do societies going through democratization confront the human rights violations committed by the previous regime? Five aspects of this debate are reviewed: (1) truth: establishing and confronting the knowledge of what happened in the past; (2) justice: making offenders accountable for their past violations through three possible methods: punishment through the criminal law, compensation and restitution, and mass disqualification such as lustration; (3) impunity: giving amnesty to previous offenders; (4) expiation; and (5) reconciliation and reconstruction. A concluding discussion raises the implications of the subject for the study of time and social control.*

"We are not going to be able to investigate the past. We would have to put the entire army in jail."

—Newly elected President Cerezo Arevalo of Guatemala, November 1985

My contribution to this symposium does not concentrate on the specific topic of lustration. I choose rather to view lustration as only one response available to societies confronting human rights abuses committed by previous regimes. I will classify these varied responses, concentrating on

A. Context

The current debate about lustration should be set in the wider context of those extraordinary and diverse political transitions of the past decade covered by the all-encompassing term "democratization." One of the fateful questions faced by these new governments during and after social reconstruction is how to deal with gross human rights violations committed by previous regimes. Three quite different sets of events have entered this debate: first, the collapse and dismantlement of the Soviet Union and state communist regimes in Eastern Europe; second, the transition in parts of Third World—in Africa, Asia, but most especially Central and South America (Brazil, Argentina, Chile, Uruguay, El Salvador, Paraguay)—from variants of dictatorships and military juntas to formal democracies; and third, the collapse of apartheid and the emergence of a multiracial democratic society in South Africa.[1]

Each of these sets of events requires quite separate attention—what happened in Chile is not at all what happened in Czechoslovakia—and there is no substitute for either a detailed consideration of each case or a systematic comparison between them. Any such comparison would have to examine such variants as the extent of collusion with the old regime, the specificity of its victims, the seriousness of the abuses, the degree to which the transition was willing and nonviolent, the residual strength of the military, and the existing traditions of democracy.

Nor, of course, is this the first time such issues have been raised. Other comparisons could be made with the earlier wave of democratization in Spain, Portugal, and Greece. And, needless to say, virtually all these issues were prefigured by the end of Nazi period, the Nuremberg Trials, and the beginning of the massive and surely endless process of coming to terms with the Holocaust and the Nazi extermination machine. Although the Nuremberg precedent (and the Japanese War Crimes judgments) followed defeat in an international war, an imposed peace, and then an externally constituted political-judicial authority, this remains the template on which all similar issues—moral, legal, jurisprudential—are judged.

---

1. These three sets of transitions have been explicitly linked in the work of the New York-based Project on Justice in Times of Transition. The lessons from the Eastern European and Latin American cases for South Africa were the subject of a conference "Justice in Transition: Dealing with the Past," held in Cape Town in February 1994. I am grateful to the organizers, IDASA (Institute for Democracy in South Africa), for their invitation to participate. The edited discussion of this conference is an excellent introduction to all the themes of my paper. See Alex Boraine et al., eds., *Dealing with the Past: Truth and Reconciliation in South Africa* (Cape Town: IDASA, 1994) ("Boraine, *Dealing*").

My immediate concern lies with those recent cases in which the democratic transition—although sometimes caused or precipitated by outside events (e.g., the Argentinian defeat in the Falklands)—takes place within the country itself. The following has been the familiar sequence: (1) A military regime—reluctantly or willingly, in good or bad faith—hands over power to a civilian government. Or a dictatorship dissolves itself and gives way to a multiparty democracy. Or a communist state collapses from within and is replaced by a more democratic government. (2) The new government proclaims its allegiance to human rights, civil liberties, and the rule of law. It pledges itself to "confront the past" and to prevent it from happening again. (*Nunca Mas*—Never Again—was the name of the famous Argentinian Commission.) A debate opens about whether to exhume this past. (3) The international human rights community calls upon the government to deal with the grave violations—genocide, arbitrary, summary or extrajudicial executions (death squads), disappearances, torture—that took place under the previous regime.

Lustration is one of the many choices near the end of this sequence. Although this specific policy (and the term itself) has been confined to certain countries in Eastern Europe, it is merely a variant in the general repertoire of responses to past abuses. Each country going through the democratization process has to decide what should be done with the secret police, torturers, death squads, informers, and collaborators from the old regime and their political superiors. Should their deeds be investigated and should they themselves be hunted down, exposed, made accountable, and punished? Or—to let old wounds heal, to achieve national reconciliation, to preserve a fragile democracy—should the past be allowed to recede and its offenders benefit from amnesty, impunity, forgiveness, and reintegration into the new social order?

B. Issues

This wider context in which I have chosen to set the lustration debate raises many complex issues. These range from the historiography about how the past is recovered and reconstructed; moral debates about accountability for actions that were once legalized government policy; jurisprudential and legal issues about due process, retrospective justiciability, and enforcement; questions about the scope of international law. I will restrict myself to two sets of interests: first, those coming from criminology and the sociology of crime, punishment, and social control and, second, those from the international human rights community. These two interests are linked—not as explicitly as they should be—by the concept of "crimes of the state."

10 LAW AND SOCIAL INQUIRY

1. Criminology

There are obvious problems in simply "applying" criminology to this debate. First, with a few isolated exceptions, Western-dominated criminology has paid little attention to crimes of the state or even the broader category of "political crime"—this despite the acceptance of corporate crime, environmental crime, etc., as belonging to the broader rubric of "crimes of the powerful" or "abuses of power" and despite the influence of a radical victimology that identified the victims of such abuses. Second, even the wider fields of the sociologies of punishment and social control have confined themselves to stable Western democracies and not dealt with the type of societies where these radical transitions are taking place.[2] This is true even of revisionist or critical social control theory, in its state-centered or Foucault-inspired variants. Third, standard debates about criminal justice assume that society faces damaging, disruptive, or normatively unacceptable behavior against its own current rules and norms. The relevance of such debates is not clear when the current authority is not the same that existed when the offense was committed and, moreover, when the offenders were empowered by the very authority that existed at that time.

Despite these problems, I will try to suggest some points of contact between conventional debates about criminal justice and the more political debates about justice during democratic transitions. Rather than first setting out a list of these points, I will introduce them into my substantive discussion. The phrase "policing the past" in my title is meant to convey no more than a loose analogy between the ways in which these societies confront previous state crimes and the more familiar ways in which all societies confront their "ordinary" crime problems. In my final section I will return to the uses of this analogy.

2. Human Rights

If the criminological route to these questions is somewhat opaque, the human rights literature is very obviously and directly connected with the issue of accountability for past state crimes. Indeed, this has always preoccupied the human rights movement and has acquired a new urgency because of the dramatic transitions in the last decade. Organizations like Amnesty International and Human Rights Watch have a clear formal position: Those who commit gross abuses of human rights should be held accountable for their crimes.

---

2. For speculation on how this revisionist literature might be relevant to societies under transition, see Stanley Cohen, "Social Control and the Politics of Reconstruction," *in* D. Nelken, ed., *The Futures of Criminology* (London: Sage, 1994).

This means, first, setting up independent and public judicial inquiries to establish individual or collective responsibility and, because violations were endemic, to investigate patterns of abuses as well as individual cases. Second, it means bringing offenders to justice, through a trial conducted according to the rule of law and with appropriate penalties. Third, it involves an opposition to amnesty laws and all other such policies that immunize those who have committed gross abuses from exposure, criminal procedures, or civil suits for damages.

Behind this formal consensus, though, there are, as we will see, striking differences within the human rights community, even on the most divisive of all the relevant issues: a strict policy of criminal accountability against a preference for reconciliation.

C. Outline

Recent as these transitions have been, they have already raised a set of rich and dense debates within each society facing state crimes of the previous regime, dismantling an apparatus of repression, and creating or restoring what is variously referred to as the rule of law, democracy, or civil society. I will classify five overlapping debates, illustrating also how some of them have been resolved in practice. Sometimes, when these debates appear in sequence, I will refer to them as "phases." Sometimes I will refer to each group of debates as a "discourse," not to convey any meta-theoretical commitment to "discourse analysis," but because this term has entered into everyday usage to cover distinguishable groupings of theoretical knowledge and its associated practice.

First, there is the debate about *knowledge*. This, in the human rights community, is known as the "truth phase" of accountability. In a more complex sense than merely uncovering factual evidence, this means confronting or coming to terms with the past. Sometimes doing so is seen as an objective in itself ("facing the truth") to be achieved by something like a "Truth Commission." Sometimes it is intrinsically tied to deciding what to do with individual offenders or wider social goals such as reconciliation. I will devote disproportionate space to this debate because it raises so many resonant issues.

Second—the more obviously relevant discourse to criminology and legalistic human rights work—there is *accountability*: what actually to do with the state criminals at various levels of responsibility in the old regime. This is what is called the "justice phase."[3] The strong pressure for justice, to do

---

3. There is some inconsistency in the terminology. Sometimes "accountability" is used as a broad term to cover all modes of dealing with the past. Thus "truth" and "justice" are forms of accountability. Sometimes, "accountability" is used only in the narrower legal sense as synonymous with justice. My typology is based on this second, more restricted, notion.

something, takes three forms: (*a*) *punishment* according to the traditional criminal law model; (*b*) *compensation* for victims and/or their families, and (*c*) *lustration*, the term that has been used, mainly in Eastern Europe, to described mass purification, especially by removal or disqualification from government jobs.

Third, there is *impunity*. This is the opposite of all forms of accountability. Under the heading of various legal and quasi-legal terms such as "amnesty," "immunity," and "indemnity," the argument and practice here is to cancel previous legal sanctions and/or not to initiate any new ones against offenses committed during the previous regime. The reasons offered, as we will see, range from the wholly expedient to the mostly principled.

Fourth, there is *expiation*, the inchoate sense that the enormity of what happened in the old regime requires more radical responses than merely appointing a commission of inquiry, punishing a few selected offenders or demoting them from their jobs. Some kind of ritual cleansing is needed—lustration is one such method—to remove impure elements or ways of thinking so that they will lose their power.

Finally, there are the dual political objectives of *reconciliation* and *reconstruction*. These seek to deal with the problems of transition outside legal frameworks of accountability. They look forward rather than backward. They try to reconcile previous enemies to each other and unite them in the rebuilding (or new building) of democracy.

At the risk of some overgeneralization, I will attempt to identify common conceptual divisions and policy dilemmas. My concluding section speculates on the relevance of the "justice in transition" debate for the wider study of social control.

COMING TO TERMS WITH STATE CRIMES

A. Knowledge: The "Truth Phase"

To come to terms with the past is to know exactly what happened, to tell the truth, to face the facts. There are many old and well-known obstacles to this enterprise, as well as a rather new one in the slippage of the "past," "truth," and "facts" down the postmodernist black hole.

At the *individual* level lie the complex psychic mechanisms which allow us to "forget" unpleasant, threatening, or terrible information. Memories of what we have done or what has been done to us, what we have seen or been told about, are selected out and filtered. Such forgetting is a denial of the past, a personal amnesia which prevents the individual from recalling disturbing incidents or feelings.[4]

Here, we are more interested in the *collective* level, what is sometimes called "social amnesia"—the mode of forgetting by which a whole society separates itself from its discreditable past record. This might happen at an organized, official, and conscious level—the deliberate coverup, the rewriting of history—or through the type of cultural slippage that occurs when information disappears. Let me comment briefly on these two types of collective denial.

First, there are the organized attempts to cover up the record of past atrocities. The nearest successful example in the modern era is the 80 years of official denial by successive Turkish governments of the 1915–17 genocide against the Armenians in which some 1.5 million people lost their lives.[5] This denial has been sustained by deliberate propaganda, lying and coverups, forging documents, suppression of archives, and bribing scholars. The West, especially the United States, has colluded by not referring to the massacres in the United Nations, ignoring memorial ceremonies, and surrendering to Turkish pressure in NATO and other strategic arenas of cooperation.

The less successful example, of course, is the so-called revisionist history of the annihilation of European Jews, which dismisses the entire event as a "hoax" or a "myth." Fanatic, marginal, and simply insane as this literature might be, it merits attention because the techniques of this particular historical denial draw on a standard repertoire used elsewhere. Indeed the partial success of the "revisionists" in provoking a counter-response and in giving even formal respectability to the rhetoric of denial[6] suggests how

---

4. In our context, this is what may be called the "Kurt Waldheim Syndrome." There are two symptoms: (1) "At the time, I didn't know what was happening," and/or (2) "I might have known at the time, but afterwards I forgot it all." The syndrome appeared in the March 1994 Versailles trial of the French wartime collaborator, Paul Touvier. Asked whether he was aware of the Vichy government's anti-Jewish decrees, he replied, "No, I missed that." Did he know of the mass deportations to Germany? "We didn't have television then. I didn't know about it" or "I don't remember. It was all too complicated for me." Andrew Gumbel, "Touvier Retreats into Forgetfulness," *Guardian*, March 3, 1994.

5. For introductions to this literature, see Richard G. Hovanissian, "The Armenian Genocide," in Israel Charny, ed., 1 *Genocide: A Critical Bibliographic Review* (London: Mansell, 1988), and Roger W. Smith, "Denial of the Armenian Genocide," in Israel Charny, ed., 2 *Genocide: A Critical Bibliographic Review* (London: Mansell, 1991) ("Charny, *Genocide*").

6. Much attention was given to the astonishing finding of an April 1993 Roper Poll that some 22% of a U.S. public opinion sample thought it was possible that the Holocaust never happened and a further 12% did not know whether it had. Later critics have shown that the questions were badly worded (through a double negative) and grossly overestimated the extent of actual denial. A later 1993 Gallup Poll found that 83% thought that the Holocaust definitely happened, 13% that it probably happened, and 4% that it did not or had no opinion. A March 1994 Roper Poll found that 1.1% of the population thought it was possible that it never happened, with 7.7% not knowing. Any denial seemed more a result of ignorance than an ideological commitment to the denial movement. On these data and interpretations, see Deborah Lipstadt's "Preface to the Paperback Edition" of her *Denying the Holocaust: The*

much easier it is for other, more obscure cases to be forgotten and denied. Long before the 1994 atrocities in Rwanda received media attention, Lamarchand referred to the Western forgetting of previous genocidal massacres in Rwanda and Burundi as "the politics of ethnic amnesia."[7]

Such forgetting belongs to the second type of collective denial, which is less the result of a planned and conscious campaign than a process of slippage in which uncomfortable knowledge is repressed. Here we enter the gray area sketched out by psychoanalysis and cognitive theory. In what senses can we be said to "know" about something we profess not to know about? If we do shut something out of knowledge, is this done consciously or unconsciously? Under what conditions (for example, information overload or desensitization) is such denial likely to take place?

It is difficult to know when denial and forgetting about your own society's past are wholly individual, when they are reinforced by the massive resources of the state, or when they result from a less conscious collective amnesia. In each case, their expressions are similar: "We didn't know," "We didn't see anything," "It couldn't have happened without us knowing" (or "It could have happened without us knowing"). Or "Things like this can't happen here." Or "You can't believe the source of your information" (victims, political sympathizers, human rights monitors, historians, journalists are all biased, partially informed, or ignorant).

Recovering the past records of atrocities presents varied degrees of difficulty in our three sets of current transitions. These are the differences that serious comparative research should examine. Either the current regime has some collusive interest in suppressing the past (that is, encouraging cultural amnesia) or, on the contrary, it might have a strong interest in differentiating itself against the past and reaping some of the benefits of truth-telling as a way of maximizing its legitimacy. In some cases, events are readily recoverable because they were meticulously recorded at the time. In other cases, even with the best political will, past events are unrecoverable because their traces were obliterated at the time. Sometimes the previous regime knew that it was only temporary and would later have its record examined. In other well-known historical episodes, the authorities never anticipated that there would be an "afterwards" when their actions might be judged from a vantage point different from their own.

These important differences determine how emerging democracies confront three common forms of denial. First, the essence of violations such as disappearances and death-squad killings is to give them maximum deniability at the time and afterward. Second, there is a psychological sense

---

Growing Assault on Truth and Memory (New York: Penguin, 1994), and "New Poll Shows Only 1.1% of Americans Doubt Holocaust," *Jewish Bull.*, 15 July 1994.

7. Rene Lamarchand, "Burundi," *in* Helen Fein, ed., *Genocide Watch* (New Haven, Conn.: Yale University Press, 1992).

in which perpetrators can deny atrocities even as they commit them.[8] Third, there is a standard rhetoric of official government responses to allegations of human rights violations. This rhetoric contains three elements, which sometimes appear in sequence, more often simultaneously:

1. "Nothing happened": There was no massacre; no one was tortured; people like us don't do things like that; they are all lying.
2. Usually in response to evidence from journalists, human rights organizations, victims, and historians (exhumed graves, eye-witness testimonies, video footage, autopsy reports), "Yes, something happened, but this was not what you call it, not what it looks to be, but really something else." (There was a "transfer of population," not genocide; "collateral damage," not killing civilians; "moderate physical pressure," not torture;[9] "an isolated incident," not a systematic pattern.)
3. The crucial subtext—"What happened anyway was justified." That is, we acted for morally good, even noble reasons: in defense of national security, part of the war against terrorism, for the revolution, to protect democracy, in the name of Islam (or Zionism or socialism or the Free World or whatever).

In the *truth phase* of social transitions, the recovery or uncovering of the past is an onslaught on all these forms of denial—personal and collective, the conscious coverup and the convenient forgetting, the euphemistic renaming. This process can be as painful as its common metaphors imply: digging up graves, opening wounds. Much depends on the relationship between current and past regime. Because there are no historical cases of total regime change—a complete displacement of every agent of power and influence—the knowledge phase is always compromised by the fact that many people in power in the transitional or final democratic regime were involved in crimes of the past or (more commonly) colluded in them by their silence. Revelations might prove politically embarrassing for those with something to hide and open a past too dangerous to acknowledge today.[10]

This is even more true when the change is not dramatic, sudden, or revolutionary but the result of a gradual unfreezing or the slow buildup, then sudden collapse, of state communist regimes. In the former Soviet Union, for example, the terrible legacy of the past is being explored only gradually and grudgingly. There have been admissions of the official lies about individual incidents (for example, the Katyn Massacre) but no formal overall

---

8. See Israel Charny, "The Psychology of Denial of Known Genocide," in Charney, 2 *Genocide*.

9. "Moderate physical pressure" is the term used in Israeli legal discourse to deny the use of torture against Palestinian political detainees; see Stanley Cohen, "Talking about Torture in Israel," 6 *Tikkun*, Nov. 1991, at 23-30.

10. An unforgettable example of this process is depicted in Michael Verhoven's 1990 film *Nasty Girl*, which is based on a true story of a girl, Anna Rosmus, who relentlessly digs up the Nazi links of prominent citizens in her small German town, Passau.

government investigation and disclosure of state crimes. This has been left to private organizations such as Memorial, set up in 1989 to assemble documents and testimonies. This organization evolved from a popular movement to reveal the truth about the Stalinist repression and to commemorate the victims, into an educational project linked to current human rights advocacy.[11] But, unlike in other societies where human rights activists have emerged from the opposition into the mainstream and also because of the long distance from worst horrors, the truth phase has not been tied to demands for justice.

In East Germany, the former Czechoslovakia, and Romania, knowledge was, initially at least, more tied to demands for individual punishment or the purgative policy of lustration. The truth phase took the dramatic form of "opening files." The best-known events took place in East Germany. Angry crowds stormed the Stasi (former communist secret police headquarters) early in 1990; files were seized, exposed, and publicized; the former Ministry of Security office was opened as a "Stasi Museum." A January 1992 law granted all citizens access to the dossiers. Controlled revelations are still continuing about one of the most spied-on societies ever: some 100,000 full-time agents, some 300,000 informal informers; betrayal by friends, colleagues, and close family; 6 million dossiers in the archives.

Most of the Latin American cases in which military juntas handed over to civilian rule resulted in more organized, ritualistic, and institutionalized searches after knowledge. Official and highly publicized investigations were set up, with appropriate names such as the "Commission of Truth." Each has its own fascinating story.

In Brazil, for example, there was the underground project, kept totally secret for five years, to document every single abuse of the military regime between 1964 and 1979.[12] This was carried out by a volunteer team under the direction of church organizations and culminated in the publication *Brazil: Nunca Mias* (Never Again) in 1985. All information was derived from official records of the regime itself, verbatim transcripts of military trials never intended to be read by public. With the true arrogance of power, the old regime took for granted that it would never change.

The amount of documentation in Brazil—the stories of 17,000 victims, details of 1,800 torture episodes, all gathered on a million pages—raises an issue revealed again by the recent end of President Stroessner's brutal 34-year regime in Paraguay. When human rights groups and lawyers broke into central police headquarters in 1992, they found records of every torture and disappearance. Foucault should know that the "dossier society" has its pro-

---

11. Theodora Lurie, "Making Rights Real," Ford Foundation Report, Summer 1993.
12. The story is dramatically told by Lawrence Weschler in *A Miracle, a Universe: Settling Accounts with Torturers* (New York: Penguin, 1990) ("Weschler, *Miracle*").

gressive uses: without this compulsive bureaucratic urge to record every detail, however loathsome, full knowledge would never be possible.

Argentina and Chile are the two cases most cited in the internal human rights debate about accountability. In Argentina, immediately on assuming office in 1983 after the collapse of the military junta, President Raoul Alfonsín set up a civilian commission (CONADEP—the "National Commission on Disappeared Persons") to investigate the "disappearances" during the junta's preceding 8 years—when some 9,000 people were abducted, tortured, murdered, and their bodies secretly disposed of. The Commission's report (subsequently published as a best-selling book, *Nunca Mas*, named after the Brazil case) analyzes the entire machinery of state terror that operated during the years of the junta, describing every detail about the abductions, torture, clandestine imprisonment, and murder.

The Argentinian report shows that a new democratic government, working with human rights organizations, can establish the painful truth about repression that took place a few years earlier. The enterprise was also unique in being initially tied to accountability: that is, truth should lead to justice. Prosecutions in fact immediately began. But, as we will see, something went wrong. The story became—in the title of Americas Watch's chronicle—"Truth and Partial Justice."[13]

In Chile, the National Commission on Truth and Reconciliation set up by President Aylwin's new democratic government in April 1990 was no less thorough but, as its title indicates, was not linked to questions of judicial punishment. Its massive report[14] documented 4,000 cases and accounted in detail for each of the 2,000 killings and disappearances committed by the previous government. All victims, though not any perpetrators, were named. The report also described the precise political context and methods of repression used by the military regime. The findings were widely publicized and presented individually to all the victims' families.

In El Salvador, a Truth Commission was set up under the U.N.-brokered peace accords in 1992 to investigate past abuses by the government and opposition. A characteristic incident it investigated was the 1981 El Mozote massacre—the largest single massacre in modern Latin American history—where members of the U.S.-trained Atlacatl Brigade systematically murdered some 794 people, many of them small children.[15] Both the El

---

13. "Truth and Partial Justice in Argentina: An Update," *Americas Watch Report*, New York, April 1991.

14. The two-volume English version has now been published, an essential document in the chronicles of state crime: *Report of the Chilean National Commission on Truth and Reconciliation* (South Bend, Ind.: University of Notre Dame Press, 1993) ("*Report of the Chilean Commission*"). Note the "Introduction" by Jose Zalaquett, a member of the commission and a central figure in the human rights debate about justice in transition.

15. The entire story of the El Mozote massacre—how it happened, how exactly it was covered up by the Salvadoran and U.S. governments and how it became uncovered—is recounted by Mark Danner, "The Truth of El Mozote," *New Yorker*, 6 Dec. 1993. Danner takes

Salvadoran and U.S. governments officially denied this massacre for 10 years; the *New York Times* journalist who broke the story was pulled out of Central America under State Department pressure. Now, the mass graves have been exhumed—but with little prospect of accountability.[16]

Let me end this section on the "truth phase" with two questions. First, why is truth-telling seen as so important? Second, what is the relationship between the projects of knowledge (truth) and accountability (justice)?.

i) For survivors of the old regime, whether active agents in bringing about its collapse or mere historical observers, the primary drive behind truth-telling (difficult as it these days to retain this belief) lies in the value of truth in itself. After generations of denials, lies, coverups, and evasions, many people have a powerful, almost obsessive desire to know exactly what happened. Writing particularly about victims of torture, Weschler notes that the demand for truth is often more urgently felt than the demand for justice. People do not necessarily want their former torturers to go to jail, but they do want to see the truth established. This is "a mysterious, powerful, almost magical notion, because often everyone already knows the truth—everyone knows who the torturers were and what they did, the torturers know that everyone knows, and everyone knows that they know. Why, then, this need to risk everything to render that knowledge explicit?"[17]

I agree with Weschler that the best answer to this question was given by the philosopher Thomas Nagel at a recent conference about the punishment of state crimes.[18] It lies in the distinction between *knowledge* and *acknowledgment*. Acknowledgment is what happens to knowledge when it becomes officially sanctioned and enters the public realm. As Havel and others have so eloquently shown, there is less need in the European state socialist societies for "new" historical revelations. Most people at the time knew what had happened in the past and retained this information in private memory and consciousness; no one really believed the official lies. The desire—for some at least—was to convert this private knowledge into official and public acknowledgment.

Lustration is one way of doing this. But besides its moral and legal flaws, it is technically rather unsuitable as a method of truth-telling. Truth

---

the whole episode as a parable of the Cold War. See also "El Salvador: The Massacre at El Mozote: The Need to Remember," *Americas Watch Newsletter*, 4 March 1992.

16. As of this writing (August 1994) it is still too early to know the exact terms of reference of the proposed Truth Commission in South Africa. The likelihood is that there will be a full investigation into patterns of serious abuse but that indemnity will be given to all perpetrators who disclose and admit crimes committed in apartheid's name.

17. Weschler, *Miracle* at 4.

18. *State Crimes: Punishment or Pardon?* (Papers & Report of Conference organized by Justice and Society Program of Aspen Institute (Wye Center, Colo.: Aspen Institute, 1989) ("Aspen Institute, *State Crimes*").

lies in accumulation of individual details—who did what to whom—not in a blanket disqualification of anyone tainted by the old system.

ii) A more specific drive behind truth-telling is the special sensitivity of victims. This is particularly acute for families and friends of people who were "disappeared." Even if you have entirely given up hope of finding your loved ones alive, you desperately want to know what happened to them. For victims of torture, the need is equally dramatic. Part of the official rhetoric surrounding torture is to deny its existence. The victim is often told by his or her interrogator: "Scream all you like. . . . No one will ever know." Ariel Dorfman, in his study of Latin American testimonial literature,[19] describes the devastating double problem of such victims: first, they are accused of being liars; second, they have to confront the official rhetoric that what was done to them was justified because they were guilty of terrible crimes. Even if truth-telling might be more important to some victims than retribution, any kind of amnesty to torturers allows, in a horrible way, this double problem to persist.[20]

iii) A final justification for truth-telling lies in the sentiment "never again," embodying the eternal hope that an exposure of the past is enough to prevent its repetition in the future. The debate here touches the familiar terrain of deterrence theory. The claim is that if unpunished offenders are likely to repeat their past crimes (impunity), then they will be even more likely to repeat them if no one bothers even to find out and record what they did. Perhaps more plausibly, the deterrent case may be that truth-telling will weaken potential support for any future repetition of the same abuses.

But criminological-type deterrence theory is ill-equipped to deal with the more profound issues of "learning from history" that are raised by these particular cases of social reconstruction. Leaving aside today's postmodern skepticism about the Enlightenment faith that such learning is even possible, there is the more brutal political reality that despite all the knowledge about the past, the same institutions of repression reproduce themselves in a different social order. In addition, as I have already noted, there is much evidence to suggest that at the moment of planning and action, some perpetrators "anticipate" the techniques of denial and coverup that will be used

---

19. Ariel Dorfman, "Political Code and Literary Code: The Testimonial Genre in Chile Today," in *Some Write to the Future* 141 (Durham, N.C.: Duke University Press, 1991).

20. Although there is agreement among those who work with victims of torture on the therapeutic value of testimony—the need to let survivors tell their story fully and without disbelief—there is less agreement about whether this should be done in the purely therapeutic setting or in public inquiries or through the judicial process. For a summary of the victims' perspective in dealing with past state crimes, see Ronald D. Crelinsten, "After the Fall: Prosecuting Perpetrators of Gross Human Rights Violations," *PIOOM Report*, Summer 1993, at 4–7. See also such practical handbooks as G. R. Randall & E. Lutz, *Serving Survivors of Torture: A Practical Manual for Health Professionals and Other Service Providers* (Washington, D.C.: American Association for the Advancement of Science, 1991).

later. This dark possibility should restore rather than weaken our faith in the preventive potential of truth-telling. "Who, after all," asked Adolf Hitler in August 1939, "speaks today of the annihilation of the Armenians?"

For all these reasons, then, we have truth commissions, government investigations, human rights reports, academic research, and teams of forensic experts now traveling the world, exploring the dark secrets of mass graves. These enterprises are obviously not always welcomed. And they face profound obstacles: technical problems of memory; political opposition by those who have something to hide; and the sometimes genuine but sometimes disingenuous sentiment that old graves should stay unopened, that wounds should be allowed to heal, that we should forget and forgive.

I will return to these sentiments when discussing the issue of accountability. For even those who do not want to forget might prefer to forgive. Should the truth phase inevitably lead to justice? To convert private knowledge to public acknowledgment, are the rituals of accusation, proof, attribution of blame and shaming, or punishment necessary? In formal human rights terms, the driving rationale to investigate and generate knowledge is indeed only to identify those responsible and bring them to account.[21]

In practice, this seldom happens. There has probably been no historical instance where anything remotely like a full policy of criminal accountability has been implemented. In our current cases of regime change, investigations into the past are seldom empowered to go anywhere beyond recording knowledge. The pursuit of knowledge is not the first phase in coming to terms with the past but the only phase. This is where the matter ends. The latent function of the investigation is to abort any sense of accountability: There is no political will to go further, the inquiry is endlessly dragged on (evidence is destroyed, witnesses somehow lose their memory), the investigators turn out to be corrupt, intimidated, or connected to the security forces, the criminal justice system is hopelessly weak and inefficient. Variations on this theme are part of standard human rights reporting.[22]

There is another relationship between knowledge and accountability worth exploring: not whether the uncovering of the past "should" lead to accountability but whether the conventional rituals of evidence according to the criminal law model offer an effective way of obtaining knowledge. After all, this is what the ordinary criminal trial, whether in its investigative or accusatory form, tries to do. And in the political realm, this function has

---

21. On the legal obligations of governments to investigate and prosecute human rights violations, see Naomi Roht-Arriaza, "State Responsibility to Investigate and Prosecute Human Rights Violations in International Law," 78 *Cal. L. Rev.* 449 (1990), and Jose Zalaquett, "Confronting Human Rights Violations Committed by Previous Governments," 13 *Hamline L. Rev.* 623 (1990).

22. See International Human Rights Law Group, *Maximizing Deniability: The Justice System and Human Rights in Guatemala* (Washington, D.C., July 1989), and Americas Watch & Physicians for Human Rights, *Guatemala: Getting Away with Murder* (New York, August 1991).

a well-known history: whether in staged Stalinist show trials or the many famous Durkheimian boundary-setting trials of history—from the trial of Jesus to those of Dreyfus, Sacco and Vanzetti, the Rosenbergs, Nuremberg, Eichmann.

The debate here is whether legal strategy serves or only obliterates and distorts the cause of truth-telling. A recent controversial example that raised these issues was the trial of Klaus Barbie. Here, as in the regime changes in Eastern Europe,[23] the justification for the trial was explicitly pedagogic: an opportunity for self-improvement, a history lesson for the new generation. Critics of the Barbie trial[24] all point (on very different grounds) to the trial's failure as a method of generating relevant knowledge. Finkielkraut persuasively argues, for example, that the baggage from the long-distant past was too heavy. Because of the particular strategy used by the defense, too many historical issue became confused: the meaning of Nazism; anti-Semitism and racism; the uniqueness of the Holocaust; the character of the Occupation of France; collaboration and resistance; the French record in Algeria and Vietnam. The result was a postmodernist trial—a text from which no one could learn very much.

The Barbie trial and the wider phenomenon of revisionism raise a final footnote to this section that is of very direct interest to criminologists. Precisely in response to the conscious attempt to deny and obliterate the past by the "revisionist historians" of the Holocaust, there is now a strong moral enterprise to make denial of the Holocaust a punishable criminal offense. This has already happened in France and there are similar moves throughout the Western world. The debate has been couched in familiar legal terms: on the one side, the symbolic functions of law, the possibility of deterrence, and the feelings of the victims; on the other side, the civil liberties case for freedom of speech.

The renaissance of fascist, racist, and neo-Nazi groups has given this debate a revived political relevance. Could these phenomena have been prevented by a more rigorous (and even legally enforced) attempt to know about the past? The use of the criminalization model for the social control of what should be known—and made known—about history raises other more theoretical issues to which I will return at the end of the article.

It is too early to know which of the current transitions will sustain or abandon its interest in the past, or whether any of these countries will gen-

---

23. Julian Barnes's satirical version of the trial of "Stoyo Petkanov" (*The Porcupine* (London: Picador, 1992)) (based loosely on Todor Zhivkov, the former ruler of Bulgaria) is a fine account of the ambiguities of the "truth" revealed by trials in the former communist states.

24. Alain Finkielkraut, *Remembering in Vain: The Klaus Barbie Trial and Crimes against Humanity* (New York: Columbia University Press, 1992) ("Finkielkraut, *Remembering in Vain*"). For a more eccentric critique of the Barbie trial, see Guyora Bindner, "Representing Nazism: Advocacy and Identity at the Trial of Klaus Barbie," 98 *Yale L.J.* 1321 (1989).

erate its own equivalent of the Holocaust discourse, which has long moved to meta-questions of representation: Not whether or what to know, but how to know, to remember, to construct memorials, literature, oral history, testimonies, documentaries.[25] Our theoretical literature deals mainly with these emblematic cases engraved on Western consciousness and not with those remote places whose histories slip so quickly out of knowledge.

B. Accountability: The "Justice Phase"

The current human rights debate about accountability refers most immediately to the Nuremberg precedent and the subsequent construction of new categories of state crime such as crimes against humanity, gross human rights violations, war crimes, and genocide. The creation of human rights and humanitarian law (and the universal criminalization of acts like torture) provides the formal international context for this debate.

Most literature on this subject invokes the traditional rationale for penal law. The state has a moral and legal responsibility not to ignore the violations of the past, and it must also prevent crude revenge, settling of accounts, lynching, the Robespierre justice of summary trials and executions. In some cases, of course, "accountability" is still translated—as it has been throughout history—into a traditional tool to purge the country of supporters of the old regime and legitimate further repression. This is not exactly the accountability that the human rights community has in mind.

Justice, whether justified as retribution or just deserts, individual or general deterrence, or symbolic denunciation, must be done and seen to be done by giving the accused all the benefits of due process and legality that they never allowed their victims. Zalaquett (the most eloquent advocate within the human rights community for reconciliation *against* strict justice)[26] argues well for the utilitarian objectives of accountability: to prevent the reoccurrence of abuses and to repair the damage they caused. The nonutilitarian case rests on establishing and upholding the rule of law as a value in itself. In neither case is punishment legitimate for retribution and revenge, or to discipline the political opposition, or to produce scapegoats.

There is a formal consensus in the human rights community about these demands. In the case of regime change, international organizations consistently press new governments and their patrons (usually the United States which, in every noncommunist case, invariably supported the repres-

---

25. For a recent fascinating study of the iconography of monuments—how we remember the past, for what reasons, to what ends, in whose name—see James E. Young, *The Texture of Memory: Holocaust Memorials and Meanings* (New Haven, Conn.: Yale University Press, 1993) ("Young, *Texture of Memory*").

26. Jose Zalaquett, "Confronting Human Rights Violations Committed by Former Governments: Principles Applicable and Political Constraints," in Aspen Institute, *State Crimes* 23–70 (cited in note 18) ("Zalaquett, 'Confronting Human Rights Violations' ").

sions of the old regime) to bring to justice those responsible for past abuses. In each of those dramatic transformations of the 1980s (though not for the earlier cases of Spain, Portugal, and Greece), accountability for dealing with the perpetrators of gross human rights violations is seen as a sign of good faith, almost the most important test of the viability of the emerging democracy.[27]

The more tangled political question is what to do if the sovereign state will not or cannot undertake such responsibility. This leads to the call, long on the human rights agenda, for establishing some form of International Criminal Jurisdiction. Thus, the appeals to the United Nations to set up a war crimes or "crimes against humanity" tribunal to prosecute those with high-level responsibility for the atrocities in the former Yugoslavia.

But leaving aside the vexing question of international jurisdiction, there are enough complex problems in implementing the demand for justice within the emerging new regime. I will first set out the three somewhat different forms this demand may take—legal punishment, compensation, and lustration—and then consider the various obstacles and objections to implementing *any* of these strategies.

1. *Legal Punishment*

The most common form of accountability demanded by the human rights community is the adaptation or adoption of the standard criminal law model. That is, identifying those with individual or collective responsibility; assembling the evidence; organizing a civilian trial conducted by standard legal procedures; the implementation of suitable punishment (short of the death penalty, which is uniformly opposed). This has been the dominant normative model, and the Nuremberg version is the most often cited. Its appropriateness, though, for current regime transitions is more often assumed than argued,[28] and its implementation has been inconsistent at best, a travesty at worst.

The early years of the Argentinian transition provided perhaps the closest approximation to this model. Parallel to the quest for truth, the new president immediately ordered the prosecution of the junta leaders. The na-

---

27. This criterion was also often cited to judge the new Clinton administration's foreign policy. See, e.g., *Human Rights Watch World Report 1993* (New York: Human Rights Watch, 1993).

28. The Greek, Spanish, and Portuguese experiences are less often cited. So, too, are the useful studies of how countries in Nazi-occupied Europe implemented various forms of accountability for collaboration. The Scandinavian histories are particularly interesting on the question of "degrees" of collaboration and how much collaborators knew about the special fate that awaited Jews whose deportation they aided. On Norway, see Per Ole Johansen, "Norway and the Holocaust," and on Denmark, Ditliv Tamm, "The Trial of Collaborators in Denmark after the Second World War," in H. Takala & H. Tham, eds., 10 *Scandinavian Studies in Criminology* (Oslo: Norwegian University Press, 1989).

ture and extent of their crimes were investigated; the legal rights of the accused were protected; guilt was properly assessed; the five main leaders were convicted and sentenced to prison terms ranging from four and a half years to life. And the judicial process seemed to satisfy the demand for public knowledge about what had taken place. We will soon see what "went wrong" after this initial phase.

It should be noted that in both the human rights community and the wider public debate, forms of punishment have been proposed or accepted that assume due process but differ from standard criminal law measures like imprisonment. These include removal or demotion from office for convicted police, soldiers, judges, or civil servants; loss of pension rights; impeachment or public censure; and deprivation of voting rights.

2. *Compensation*

Debates on current social transitions give far less attention to various forms of compensation, reparation, and restitution despite the importance of the original German policy of mass reparations to victims of Nazism. The strategy here is to use variants on the civil law model to give material compensation and restore dignity to victims and their families.[29] Financial reparations can be given to families. Torture victims can be helped to receive treatment and rehabilitation.

There may be fewer political obstacles to this policy if the current government assumes strict liability for the offenses of its predecessor, without having to identify or prosecute individual perpetrators. The act of reparation is symbolically extremely important—and may be more effective than individual punishment in meeting the victims' need for recognition of their dignity. In some circumstances, though, mass reparations might become a substitute for truth-telling or a payoff to keep people quiet.

The notion of collective restitution has become particularly influential in South Africa: advocating social and economic policies to "compensate" blacks for centuries of injustice. In general, though, compensation is seldom raised as an alternative to the criminal law model.

3. *Lustration*

In some Latin American countries, part of the formal transitional agreement is that military officials responsible for gross human rights violations will be removed from their position or demoted. If implemented—and

---

29. For a useful summary of victim compensation methods available for both regular and state crimes, see Joanna Shapland, *Guide for Practitioners Regarding the Implementation of the Declaration of Basic Principles of Justice for Victims of Crime and Abuses of Power* (United Nations, A/Conf. 144/20 June 1990).

in most case, like El Salvador, these agreements have been ignored—this would be a form of collective sanction not dependent on the conventional criminal law model. And such mass purging of the guilty has its major precedent in the denazification process initiated by the Allies and the purification of collaborators in Occupied Europe.

But despite other precedents, this whole policy, and the term "lustration" itself, has taken on its special connotation in the postcommunist regimes of Eastern Europe. The question of policing the past is very different here from the Latin American transitions. With a few exceptions—such as the criminal prosecutions of former East German officials for killing people trying to cross the Berlin Wall or the prosecutions of the Romanian leadership—the issue is mass collusion (silence, informing, collaborating) rather than individual crimes or gross human rights violations. There are no recent allegations of massacres or disappearances; practices like torture have a long bureaucratic history rather than appearing as a new instrument of state terror.

Czechoslovakia, Poland, East Germany, and Hungary have each followed different paths. But the common strategy has been some combination of unmasking ("outing") and denouncing individually named agents and informers of the previous regime or else identifying whole categories of people (e.g., former high-level Communist Party officials) and removing them from any government jobs.

Czechoslovakia has been the most familiar and best documented case.[30] Immediately after the transition, Havel (and others) called for an explicit acknowledgment of the collective responsibility which kept the old system going. He warned against vindictiveness and the impulse to find easy scapegoats. Within a short time, though, people who suffered under the old system were dismayed by the impunity enjoyed by the worst collaborators from the regime. These former official servants were not only going unpunished but were benefiting from the new order. They could also sabotage any democratic gains. Many saw the new leadership as being too magnanimous. And there was also a suspicion that the transition had been too peaceful to have been genuine—and must have been faked by the StB (the former secret services). A campaign to "do something" began, coming from very different political forces.

The Right wanted broad legislation to prohibit all former Communists above a certain level, all officers above a certain rank, all security agents and their collaborators, from holding any position of authority. Havel and his supporters objected to this notion of collective punishment and called

---

30. Many Western observers were introduced to the lustration issue by Lawrence Weschler's article on the Jan Kavan case: "The Velvet Purge: The Trials of Jan Kavan," *New Yorker*, 19 Oct. 1992, at 66–96. See also Jerri Laber, "Witch Hunt in Prague," *N.Y. Rev. Bks.*, 23 April 1992, at 5–8. My account of the Czech story is a paraphrase of these sources.

for purging to be limited to those actually responsible for suppressing human rights—with the burden on the legal system to prove this and allowing reasonable defense, due process, and the right to appeal.

In the end, the right-wing version won out and the October 1991 Lustration Law banned whole categories of people with various degrees of involvement from specific kinds of employment. "Lustration" derives from the Latin word *lustratio*, which means purification by sacrifice. The law set out the rules for mass purifications that soon led to the leaked publication of lists of nearly 200,000 names: former secret police agents and their informers; former Communists who were in positions of authority from district level up; members of the voluntary Peoples Militia, etc. The law barred, for a five-year period, former members of these groups from any high-level government position and required job applicants to produce an Interior Ministry document declaring that they are "clean"—that is, did not belong to any of the listed categories.

The detailed story of how the lustration policy was implemented in Czechoslovakia is still being told: the attempts to modify the law; the actual process whereby people were lustrated by an Interior Ministry panel naming people as "StB positive" or "StB negative"; the mechanism of selection from the police archives, which contained the names of no less than 140,000 secret police agents, collaborators, and contacts; the inclusion of names on these lists even of people who refused to collaborate or who were blackmailed; the resulting mistakes, abuses, and injustices.

Critics of the policy have pointed out that although a small number of dissidents themselves (including those severely persecuted) supported lustration, much support came from those who had no claim on self-righteous purity. Relatively few people had actively opposed the regime (Charter 77 only had 1,864 signatures). Most people benefited from the old system—and after the changes, they began sheepishly asking themselves, "Why didn't we say anything earlier?" The answer: the all-powerful Secret Services with its network of agents who must now be expunged! Those who hardly dissented against the old regime—people who belonged to the "gray zone," neither Communists nor dissidents, who kept quiet—became the most vehement in supporting the purges and the publication of lists.

Of course, this is not the whole story. There was a real desire for truth and justice, a need to hear some admission of shame from the worst of the former officials. But there was no public shame, no apologies, no confessions, no accountability at all. Havel, in this reading of the events, might have been too advanced and too quick in his forgiveness and reconciliation. Therefore, the obsession with naming, publishing lists, and purging.

From the strictly legalistic human rights position, the lustration policy is clearly an unsatisfactory way of policing the past: a collective witch-hunt rather than the pursuit of individual responsibility through some variant of the criminal law. People are punished for association, however tenuous, rather than for any specific infraction. All forms of collective punishment reproduce features of the worst state crimes (e.g., whole communities being punished for the actions of one member). The human rights community has severely criticized the policy of lustration (or "decommunization," as it sometimes called). First, it violates the right of freedom of expression: a new law defined it a crime to propagate such ideologies as fascism and communism. Second, it contravenes all standards of due process:[31] no independent tribunal, no opportunity to know and confront evidence, no right to legal counsel, no appellate review.

This critique is understandable but sometimes "legalistic" in the pejorative sense. Given the mass collaboration, it is difficult to see how the standard individual legal model could work. The nuances of "collaboration" in regimes like this are too devious, complex, and ambiguous to be slotted into any known version of individual legal culpability. Assuming that the process of identification itself could be fair, it seems quite reasonable and just to be satisfied with removal from public office as a minimal form of accountability rather than demanding punishments such as imprisonment. Lustration is a more morally ambiguous process than either its supporters or its critics concede. On the one hand, disqualification—this person should not hold this public office for some time—is a less moralistic form of social control than legal punishment. On the other hand, its application (in Eastern Europe at least) has been directed at supposed informers and collaborators—those categories of offenders who pose a special threat to the moral purity of a society by blurring the boundaries between good and bad.

The objections to lustration should be directed at the process rather than at the sanction. In their repugnance with the poisonous way in which lustration was implemented—the leaks, rumors, suspicion, false information, witch-hunting—many critics have not conceded the suitability of nonpenal measures such as removal from official position. I do not know whether Laber is correct in asserting that the lustration law is "a symptom of a swing to the right in Czech political life."[32] But it does mimic the tactics and mentality of the old regime. Indeed "lustration" was the term used by the StB for conducting checks on citizens loyalty to the Communist Party during its 40-year rule. Now it becomes a tool to deal with current potential political opposition, as well as a rather crude way of screening knowledge

---

31. "Czechoslovakia: 'Decommunization' Measures Violate Freedom of Expression and Due Process Standards," *News from Helsinki Watch*, April 1992. While the standard critique of lustration is that too many people are being swept into its net, the problem with denazification in postwar Germany was that too few people were made accountable: "What had begun as a rather foolish incrimination of the entire population turned into wholesale exemptions and finally wholesale exoneration. Denazification in the end meant not purge but rehabilitation." John H. Herz, "An Historical Perspective," in Aspen Institute, *State Crimes* 18 (cited in note 18).

32. Jerri Laber, *N.Y. Rev. Bks.*, 23 April 1992, at 7.

about the past. As the Czechoslovakia Helsinki Committee wrote in a letter to President Havel, with only slight exaggeration: "The law puts on the same level the young man who cooperated with the police because he could not hold out during a beating after one of the Prague demonstrations and the policeman who beat the young man into signing."[33]

Despite—or because of—such obvious defects, the lustration controversy did open up a wider public debate about accountability. It was not a deliberate evasion of the past. This debate, however, now seems to have lost its urgency. In most of the postcommunist societies, even the former East Germany, which seemed so preoccupied with the Stasi record and dramatic individual cases like Christa Wolf, public interest in lustration or any other form of policing the past has waned. Economic problems, unemployment, and political instability all seem far more important than digging back into history. There is no popular demand on the current leadership to track down offenders from the past. Many progressives argue that the obsession with the past is a way of evading current problems.

C. Impunity

The same issues raised in talking about accountability also appear, by definition, in what is conceived as its opposite, "impunity." The meaning of this term is often elusive. The literal definition of impunity as "exemption from punishment" applies most clearly when referring to crimes of current governments. Impunity here is the normal state of affairs and the major object of human rights concern. Repression occurs precisely because the state allows its officials to act without accountability.

When talking about atrocities committed by the previous government (or by armed oppositional forces that have taken power), impunity might refer to a gradual historical indifference or be the result of a conscious policy. Sometimes this policy anticipates the regime change: either formal legislation or secret political agreements that guarantee impunity (or amnesty, immunity, indemnity) for current members of the government or security forces. Sometimes this happens only after the transition through amnesty laws which gives retrospective immunity or an official pardon to the offenders of the old regime. Sometimes the new regime starts with the rhetoric of accountability but then, through weakness or lack of political will, creates a de facto state of impunity.

All these variations have occurred during the current transitions. But what complicates the story is not so much the timing or form of the policy but the ongoing debate between those who insist on strict accountability and those who see "impunity" as not necessarily a pejorative alternative or

---

33. Cited in *News from Helsinki Watch*, April 1992, at 7.

failure, but part of a desirable strategy to achieve reconciliation and to advance the prospects of a genuine democratic reconstruction.

We will return to some versions of this debate. But even proponents of reconciliation have to concede that in most cases of transition, impunity for the "wrong" reasons is virtually the norm. Attempts to enforce accountability—through punishment, compensation, or removal from office—are politically neutered or blocked. Investigations lead nowhere; even if judicial proceedings start, they fade away through inefficiency and pressure from other branches of government; punishments are ludicrously mild; cases are referred to military or other administrative tribunals, resulting in acquittals or even promotions; amnesty laws suddenly halt the prosecution.

The recent Central and South American cases provide familiar variations of this impunity story. In Brazil the armed forces granted themselves a self-amnesty in 1979, six years before permitting civilian government to be restored. In Chile the Pinochet handover was conditional on the promise not to prosecute members of the armed forces, thus limiting the scope of the later National Commission on Truth and Reconciliation. In El Salvador the president ratified a general retrospective amnesty immediately after the U.N.-sponsored Truth Commission announced its finding in 1992.

Uruguay is a particularly interesting story because of the decisive role played by public opinion. The civilian government which took power in 1983 adopted a total amnesty law in 1986, apparently making good a secret agreement with the armed forces that permitted the transition in the first place. Unlike every other case, however, this decision met with mass political opposition, culminating in a successful petition by a quarter of the population to force a national referendum on the amnesty law. After a bitter campaign,[34] only just a majority of voters upheld the amnesty.

Argentina provides a different, and well-documented, story of something "going wrong" with the punishment model.[35] If Uruguay is a good case to study the groundswells of public sentiment about policing the past, then Argentina is a good case to study the legal and political constraints on implementing the principle of accountability.

Despite a serious commitment to truth-telling and even the initiation of successful criminal prosecutions, the Argentinian story is one of a gradually unfolding process of impunity. There were three stages—each in the context of successive attempted revolts by low-ranking military officers. First, there was the Punto Final law of 1986, that established a time limit beyond which more prosecutions could not be initiated. ("Punto final" means literally "full stop"). Second, and more important, was the Due Obe-

---

34. Described in detail by Weschler, *Miracle* 83–236 (cited in note 12).
35. See "Truth and Partial Justice in Argentina" (cited in note 13). On the different forces impinging on the political and legal systems, see Mark Osiel, "The Making of Human Rights Policy in Argentina," 18 *J. Latin Am. Stud.* 235 (1986).

dience Law of 1987. This accepted the principle that certain ranks of officers, during a certain period (1973-76)—even those already found guilty—could be deemed to have acted under orders.[36] There should be a presumption of innocence indicating that subordinates were acting in error about the legitimacy of the orders they received. The effect of this, of course, was a de facto amnesty. Finally, in 1990, under Alfonsín's successor, Carlos Menem, formal pardons were given to the 5 senior junta leaders already sentenced and covering a further 280 members of the armed forces. Everyone whose prosecutions were left standing after the Punto Final and Due Process laws was now pardoned.

For some, the "backtracking" in Argentina was a failure resulting from basic flaws in the strict accountability model. Either the system tried to achieve too much or should have looked for goals other than punishment. For others, the story was neither a failure nor evidence of a flaw in the accountability model: the system did not try to achieve enough and lost its nerve at the critical moment.[37]

Why are these chronicles of impunity so frequent? Why—as in El Salvador—was the appalling knowledge about a decade of 75,000 political killings not followed by a single legal consequence? Poor peasants arrived in truckloads to testify to the Truth Commission—perhaps knowing in their hearts that no one would be made accountable for the horrors. People are being asked to settle for a measure of truth, rather than the measure of justice offered by the criminal law, civil compensation, or lustration-type measures.

At the structural level, the reasons for impunity are often pretty straightforward.[38] There is no political will or resources to do anything about the past; the army or security forces still retain enough power, openly or behind the scenes, to threaten any attempt to render them accountable; the current machinery of law enforcement is intimidated, politically unwilling, corrupt, or technically inept. Furthermore, the events of the past immunized themselves from later accountability: there was special legislation (for example, "state of emergency" laws) which gave elaborate legal justifications for just about anything; there were multiple command structures which made responsibility difficult to identify; some crimes were committed by paramilitary groups whose relations to the authorities were unknown.

---

36. Kathryn Lee Crawford, "Due Obedience and the Rights of Victims: Argentina's Transition to Democracy," 12 *Hum. Rts. Q.* 17 (1990).

37. Various sides of this debate are well presented by Juan Mendez, Aryeh Neier, and Jose Zalaquett in Boraine, *Dealing* 35-40 (cited in note 1).

38. Note Zalaquett's typology of how different forms of transition determine the political constraints on current human rights policy: (1) the defeated forces have lost legitimacy but retained armed power; (2) there is a gradual transition and popular forgiveness; (3) the new government represents a realignment of political forces in a situation of unresolved armed conflict, etc. Zalaquett, "Confronting Human Rights Violations," at 45-47 (cited in note 26).

At first glance these structural conditions constitute a set of wholly undesirable impediments to accountability. And so they are. But some of these constraints pose more morally nuanced problems about accountability after regime change. Five such problems are particularly salient to the lustration debate—and versions of all of them have been advanced even within the human rights community to argue against implementing full "Nuremberg-model" accountability.

1. *Time Lag*

I am not concerned here with the legal complications about the relationship between long past crimes and current jurisdiction. These matters (statutes of limitation, double jeopardy, and retrospective liability) are familiar to scholars in more conventional legal areas. They have also figured prominently in the debates about Nazi war criminals, for example, in regard to demands for extradition.

A less strictly legal question concerns the nature of political responsibility for the actions of a previous regime. A current government could, of course, plausibly assert that it has no moral responsibility for its predecessor's actions. But, curiously, it is when talking about *current* human rights violations that the demand for accountability is so quixotic. The demand is rhetorical (designed to expose the government's obvious unwillingness) or utopian (why should a brutal government act against its own agents?).[39] These objections should not apply to the past. In theory, the new government should be eager to demonstrate its good faith and its distance from the previous regime. What better method than pursuing some form of accountability?

But there are two other temporal problems. The first is the obvious one: How far back to go in looking for accountability (truth or justice)? For a military junta which lasted, say, 5 to 10 years after a previously democratic regime, this is less of a problem. But how far back will the proposed Truth Commission in South Africa have to go? To the gross violations of the 1980s? To the formal legal origins of apartheid in 1948? Or even further back in history?

There is a second, more emotionally charged issue of time to which I will return in my conclusion. For many people, there is something faintly repellent, even unjust, in the relentless judicial pursuit of fugitive monsters from a decade or even a generation ago. Should we really be hunting down an 80-year-old Ukrainian living peacefully in Scotland, Canada, or Australia because he might have worked as a concentration camp guard? Should

---

39. This is well explained in regard to African cases such as Uganda by Richard Carver, "Called to Account: How African Governments Investigate Human Rights Violations," *Africa Watch* (New York, 1991).

80-year-old Britons who were prisoners of war in Japan still be insisting on compensation for the atrocities they suffered 50 years ago?

My own personal opinion is that no amount of time can be "too long" to satisfy the needs for truth and some measure of accountability, nor can some arbitrary legal time limit be set. The argument that some wounds are too old to be exposed has little moral integrity. And this argument cannot be applied to most of our current cases, certainly in neither South Africa nor the Latin American transitions. The wounds are still there for all to see; the parents of the disappeared are still wandering around trying to trace their children's fate; the torturer and his (nearly always his) victim literally pass each other in the street. Indeed in these societies, we often hear the entirely disingenuous argument that the wounds are too *recent* to be exposed.

2. Authority and Obedience

The most profound and genuine obstacle to accountability is raised by issues of authority, responsibility, and obedience to orders. Obviously the Nuremberg judgments, the Eichmann trial, and the entire edifice of international human rights law sets the context for this familiar debate. More recently, the legalistic-moral discussion about the defense of "just following orders" has been supplemented by a sustained social-psychological examination of how "crimes of obedience" occur.[40]

Among our case studies, the Argentinian story is again instructive. At all levels—the balance of political forces, the legal proceedings, and public debate—the issue of obedience was critical. The prosecution of the high-level command was initially widely approved or at least tolerated. But when mid-level officers were indicted as well, army revolts took place and popular support weakened. Although these officers clearly and directly presided over tortures and killings, this was justified by the claim that they were only following higher orders. The Due Obedience Law accepted this justification.

The Eastern European settings in which the lustration policy has been implemented is more complex and morally ambiguous. Leaving aside the carrying out of individual orders to kidnap, kill, or torture, the recent record is more one of collusion, silence, and complicity in the institutional denial of everyday democratic rights. The notion of "obedience" is somewhat different—and so is the line between perpetrator and bystander.

The controversy about prosecuting the East German border guards while allowing their political master Erich Honecker to go free has become a contemporary focus of this dense debate. It is facile to take a simple posi-

---

40. Herbert C. Kelman & V. Lee Hamilton, *Crimes of Obedience: Toward a Social Psychology of Authority and Responsibility* (New Haven, Conn.: Yale University Press, 1989).

tion. The strongest case is to prosecute those with the highest level of political responsible; it is just as persuasive to argue that this should not exonerate their underlings. Finkielkraut derives a paradoxical lesson from the Klaus Barbie trial: it is important to bring to justice such low-level figures, precisely *because* they were so unimportant in the hierarchy.[41] In combating a system that dehumanized humanity, it is vital to restore individual responsibility to each cog in the inhuman machine.

3. Degrees of Involvement

"Temporal contamination" raises the question of time lag: How far back in time should we look for accountability? The question of "spatial contamination" is even more sensitive. How deeply into social space do we attribute responsibility for the past? This is a wider version of the debate about obedience and authority because it does not refer only to the actual perpetration of atrocities. Again, the experience of the Third Reich and Nazi-occupied Europe is the standard historical precedent for questions of collective responsibility, a precedent that has shaped 50 years of debate on the differences between passive and active collusion, between deliberate silence and willful ignorance. Individual guilt is difficult to establish; collective guilt is morally repellent.

These debates take different forms in each of the current transitions. The range shifts from the relatively restricted number of criminals involved in most of the Latin American military regimes, through the moral ambiguities of involvement, collusion, and silence which characterized, in different ways, both the former state communist regimes and apartheid South Africa. In South Africa—one of the most complex cases imaginable because of the near-total corruption of the white community in benefiting from the crimes of apartheid—attempts to "draw the line" are particularly difficult. It is certainly obvious to all that there is a moral distinction between police officers carrying out death-squad executions and low-level government clerks signing a "pass" which restricted blacks' freedom of movement. But how should this distinction be applied?

The human rights community follows this commonsense distinction by drawing three related (but not identical) lines. On the one side of the line are the routine deeds of an immoral system that would be unfair or impossible to prosecute, and on the other (the side of legal accountability) are three categories: (i) those who directly carried out or ordered human rights violations that lay within their domain of responsibility; (ii) those actions categorized as gross violations and prohibited by international law such as

---

41. Finkielkraut, *Remembering in Vain* (cited in note 24).

genocide and "crimes against humanity"; (iii) those actions that were also illegal by the state's own law at the time.

In abstract, such distinctions are all plausible enough. With the exceptions, however, of the clearest cases, their implementation is so open to dispute that impunity might result by default. The unfolding South African transition is instructive for its distinctive combination of individual crimes that meet all three criteria for legal culpability (similar, crudely, to the Latin American cases) together with an extensive web of bureaucratic offenses more like the recent communist record. Whether or not the death squads will be prosecuted, the problem is that the deepest grievances of most people are untranslatable into the criminal model.

4. Regime Stability and Preserving Democracy

Equally complex is the question of the political risk posed by pursuing accountability to its logical and legal conclusions. In most cases, this has been *the* dominant issue in transitions to democracy. And it constitutes, depending on your position, either the major political constraint *against* the principle of accountability or one of the best political reasons *for* abandoning this principle in favor of the more desirable objectives of reconciliation and reconstruction.

The obvious risk in a highly polarized society, often with a weak new regime, is that prosecution and punishment of the security, police, or armed forces—often not yet completely neutralized—will provoke a coup and reverse all the gains of the fragile democracy. This debate often appears during periods of prolonged negotiation toward a transitional government or constitution. This was the South African case: the democratic opposition negotiating a power-sharing arrangement with the same forces (indeed the very same people) responsible for the worst oppression. In response to a comment that the danger in many Latin American societies was "the dragons on the patio," a South African noted that "in our case, the dragons will be right inside the living room."[42] At this point (arranging the April 1994 elections), the opposition could hardly have said to the security forces: "Let the elections go ahead, then we'll lock you up."

The debate is sometimes presented as a morally absolutist position on accountability against a pragmatic political assessment of what is possible. But the paradox is that some measure of impunity might be the best way to create the political conditions under which the rule of law is eventually attainable. Discretion and prudence might call for clemency and reduction of sentences—or the pursuit of controls outside the criminal law such as

---

42. Mary Burton, in Boraine, *Dealing* 122 (cited in note 1).

purges of the military and police, civil law compensation, public shaming, and censure.

These compromises are all feasible and defensible. But the pragmatic decision to sacrifice the past for the sake of the future in order to live to fight the next battle can never be easy. Even those closer to the strict accountability position, such as Aryeh Neier, the former Director of Human Rights Watch, are obviously all too aware of the dilemma: "Permitting the armed forces to make themselves immune to prosecution for terrible crimes seems intolerable; yet it also seems irrational to insist that an elected civilian government should commit suicide by provoking its armed forces."[43] In these circumstances, you may feel that punishment should happen but also agree that it is politically expedient and in the national interest that it should not.

A particular form of political expediency is the provision (usually during the period of negotiations leading up to the transition) of a guaranteed future immunity from prosecution for all government officials, together with an immediate retrospective amnesty (usually meaning release from prison) for members of the opposition. Because of its long duration—transitions within transitions—the South African case is particularly instructive here. The amnesty chronicle began soon after the release of Nelson Mandela and the unbanning of the ANC in February 1990. Then came the negotiated release of other (oppositional) political prisoners through the 1990 Indemnity Act. Then the government attempted (in the 1992 Further Indemnity Act) to extend the definition of "political prisoners" to include a general amnesty not just for members of the democratic black opposition (ANC and others) and right-wing political prisoners, but also state officials after the impending transition.[44] This was initially opposed by the ANC, but later negotiations leading to the 1993 Constitution opened up yet further permutations.

These arrangements, of course, raise some awkward moral comparisons—which I have ignored so far—between the atrocities committed by government officials and by armed oppositional groups (liberation movements, guerrillas, terrorists). The mutual amnesty provides—as the legal system so often does—a convenient symmetry to disguise very different social realities. The same effect can be obtained by just the opposite legal strategy—that is, by refusing any form of impunity for either side and insisting on strictly comparable punishments for state and oppositional offenders.

---

43. Aryeh Neier, "What Should be Done about the Guilty?" *N.Y. Rev. Bks.*, 1 Feb. 1990, at 34.

44. For a study of how the first stage of indemnity was actually implemented and particularly on the tricky question of how to define a "political prisoner," see Raylene Keightley, "Political Offences and Indemnity in South Africa," 9 *S. Afr. J. Hum. Rts.* 334 (1993).

5. *Reconciliation and Reconstruction*

If there is an expedient and pragmatic case against absolute accountability, there are also far more principled arguments, many emerging from the human rights community itself. The two main versions, "reconciliation" and "reconstruction," have been translated into a powerful case to which I will return in a separate section.

When raised in the call for amnesty and impunity, the slogan of "national reconciliation" can, of course, be entirely bogus and self-serving. The spectacle of people who have physically destroyed entire parts of a society and set neighbors, friends, colleagues, and families against each other as informers now preaching national reconciliation is pretty sickening. No wonder that the same liberals and radicals who might be abolitionists or minimalists about the application of the penal law to ordinary crime and deviance now find themselves demanding strict and maximum punishment.

At other times, the rhetoric of reconciliation is genuine enough. It comes from the belief that punishment is not a productive way to solve social conflicts. Where civil society has been fractured by a tyrannical regime and must be reconstructed, some degree of tolerance might achieve more for human rights in the long run than an insistence on punishment and risking further political instability and divisiveness.[45] Although the consensus is that such discretion and prudence should never be extended to genocide and crimes against humanity, the difference remains between this type of political calculation and a more absolute affirmation of the rule of law. A particular question is whether the values of reconciliation and accountability are reconcilable.

One of the few examples where criminological theory might be applied to this type of political debate is provided by Braithwaite's model of reintegrative shaming.[46] It is surely not beyond political imagination to devise ritual ceremonies of public shaming and denunciation that would answer the demand for "acknowledgment" (official recognition by perpetrators and their political masters that what they did was wrong) without depending on the criminal justice system or the vagaries of "proportionate" punishment.

Both shaming theory and the abolitionist movement in criminology (which seeks to eliminate legal punishment) would sympathize with Nadezhda Mandelstam's reaction to a confrontation with a woman who had been a paid informer during the Stalin years. People she had denounced came to get revenge, but on seeing her pitiful reaction to the confrontation, they lost interest in revenge. But still, Mandelstam reflects, something must be done to make it more difficult to recruit people for such jobs in the

---

45. Zalaquett, "Confronting Human Rights Violations," at 38 (cited in note 26).
46. John Braithwaite, *Crime, Shame and Reintegration* (Cambridge: Cambridge University Press, 1989).

future: "They need not be imprisoned or killed, but a finger should be pointed at them, and they should be named."[47]

Criminologists are familiar enough with the problems here: Will shaming be enough to satisfy all victims and survivors? Is this really a deterrent? How exactly is "reintegration" to take place? But at least the prospect of shaming is a low-risk form of accountability that might answer the human rights demand for full truth and as much justice as possible. This is implied even by those human rights advocates who take the strict accountability view:

> By knowing what happened, a nation is able to debate honestly why and how dreadful crimes came to be committed. To identify those responsible and to show what they did, is to mark them with a public stigma that it is a punishment in itself, and to identify the victims, and recall how they were tortured and killed, is a way of acknowledging their worth and dignity.[48]

This assertion of the symbolic value of punishment as a sign of respect for the rule of law and for the victims' suffering emerges, though, from a Kantian, just deserts position. It does not make the utilitarian, preventive claims of the reintegrative shaming model. It might seem plausible enough that the cycle of political violence will never be broken under a regime of impunity. But the actual deterrent value of individual punishment in this political context remains even more uncertain than it is for conventional crime. In fact, everything we know about the political conditions under which crimes of obedience occur makes it extremely unlikely that the risk of future punishment has even the remotest deterrent effect. The same, of course, can be said about the presumed utilitarian value of pardons and amnesties: We simply do not know whether these promote reconciliation.

D. Expiation

In a realm beyond knowledge and accountability lies a more profound way of coming to terms with the past. It is no accident (as we used to say) that this way is conceived in religious rather than secular terms: *expiation*—making amends for previous sins; *exorcism*—expelling evil forces by invocation of the good; *expurgation*—purification by removing objectionable matter; and the many variations of *contrition, confession, atonement,* and *repentance.* This religious vocabulary does not rest easily in the modern discourse of "rights." The only remotely similar secular vocabulary comes from

---

47. Nadezhda Mandelstam, *Hope Abandoned* 572 (New York: Athenaeum, 1972).
48. Neier, *N.Y. Rev. Bks,* 1 Feb. 1990, at 43.

psychoanalysis:[49] "working through," "catharsis," "confrontation." We could still describe the Nazi record in the terminology of sin and evil. Now, the injunction "thou shalt not kill" has been replaced by "thou shalt not commit gross human rights violations."

As we have seen, though, traces of the old vocabulary remain—the policy of lustration is an explicit example. The notion of shaming also hints at some of these sentiments. It would be worthwhile to examine how these ideas might be translated into methods for dealing with crimes of the previous regime. The desire for a more satisfying way of confronting the past can best be understood by the profound sense of dissatisfaction with the current repertoire of methods.

This dissatisfaction is a recurrent theme of Holocaust literature. Everyone who writes on this subject writes to express frustration—with how knowledge was represented, how the offenders were judged, how German society became accountable. No reaction ever looks "right." Without knowing exactly what to propose instead, something fake is sensed about all attempts to achieve truth or justice.

Though nowhere as dense and dramatic, much of the debate about lustration, aside from its purely legal or human rights aspects, raises similar issues. Critics of lustration routinely use the religiously derived terminology of "witch-hunting" and "scapegoating." At first sight, the policy looks to be an appropriate solution to the demand for purification. But if the impulse was real, the form it took was ersatz, a fake substitute for what people might have wanted: some gesture of sorrow, contrition, shame, confession. History reveals shades of collusion, not identifiable groups of deviants. As the Czech opposition journalist Jan Urban wrote: "The silence was what mattered, not any individual bastards. . . . And all the current noise surrounding lustration is simply a way of keeping silent about the silence. . . . We are not looking for facts but hunting for ghosts."[50]

This is not to say that some real forms of expiation are impossible. We can imagine "repentance laws" where offenders who publicly repent are not punished. And, in addition to dealing with perpetrators, individual rituals can be arranged to cleanse the identities of those who were unfairly blamed. Political prisoners can be rehabilitated by simple public declarations. Victims' names can be cleared by searching the police and secret service files to find the falsely accused, the arbitrarily arrested, the tortured, and then publicly reminding people of what was done to them. "Freeze-dried" stigmas can thus be unfrozen, a invaluable way of making reparation to living victims as well as their surviving families and friends.

---

49. As Amos Elon notes, the subject of dealing with the recent past in East Germany is referred to as *Aufarbeitung*—a term derived from psychoanalysis and meaning coping or coming to terms with. Amos Elon, "East Germany: Crime and Punishment," *N.Y. Rev. Bks.*, 14 May 1992, at 6.

50. Cited in Weschler, *New Yorker*, 19 Oct. 1992, at 82 (cited in note 30).

In a sense, all these responses are forms of acknowledgment. The demand is not just for a public recording of the facts but for a deeper sense of remorse about the past. As South Africans have made especially clear,[51] this means asking the old regime to make two rather difficult acknowledgments: (1) It can admit that apartheid (or its equivalent elsewhere) was not just a "mistake," "irrelevant," "a dead end," a "closed book" (all terms actually used) nor what former President de Klerk referred to (as late as March 1992) as something that "started in idealism in the quest for justice." These are wholly inadequate expressions of regret for the deliberate suffering that was caused. (2) It can concede that opposition's cause was justified: that is, people were victimized not because they wrong or bad but because they were right and good.

Few of those fallen from power can be expected to make such acknowledgments. Instead of expressing regret, they are more likely to see themselves as forced by circumstances ("history") to accommodate to change. South African commentators are particularly cynical about the apparent ease with which some of the worst offenders of the old regime have adopted the rhetoric of the "new South Africa," even asserting that they suffered from private remorse in the past. In some transitions, though, the new constellations of power allow genuine acknowledgment. In Chile, for example, when President Aylwin presented the National Commission's report on television, he "atoned" publicly on behalf of the state (for actions which, as part of the opposition, he bore no responsibility).

Some of our case studies—especially those where the transition is being made with relative good will and over a long period—provide moving stories of voluntary expiation. An example is the simple public letter written in 1991 by the South African doctor, Dr. Benjamin Tucker.[52]

In 1977, Dr. Tucker had behaved in a negligent and unethical way by failing to properly treat the black-consciousness leader Steve Biko in prison. He also credulously accepted the Security Police version of Biko's injuries. The truth came out about Biko's killing, and in 1985 Dr. Tucker was made accountable and shamed by being barred from practice for "disgraceful conduct" by the disciplinary committee of the South African Medical Council. He was then reintegrated: his medical license reinstated after he sent a letter of apology to the Council. His subsequent public letter does not just admit negligence, plead unthinking obedience, or claim that he was only doing his job. He gets to the heart of the matter by admitting that he had become too closely identified with the state's security interests rather than being faithful to medical and personal ethics.

---

51. Kadar Asmal, "Victims, Survivors and Citizens—Human Rights, Reparations and Reconciliation," Inaugural Lecture, University of the Western Cape (University of the Western Cape, Pub. Series A, No. 64) ("Asmal, 'Victims' ").

52. Reprinted in *N.Y. Times*, 10 Oct. 1991.

Dr. Tucker's letter is, simply, an apology, the secular version of the expiation trope. It corresponds to Goffman's fine definition of apology as a reparative and remedial device:

> In its fullest form, the apology has several elements: expression of embarrassment and chagrin; clarification that one knows what conduct has been expected and sympathizes with the application of negative sanction; verbal rejection, repudiation and disavowal of the wrong way of behaving along with vilification of the self that so behaved; espousal of the right way and an avowal henceforth to pursue that course; performance of penance and the volunteering of restitution.[53]

It should be noted that while this definition draws clearly on notions of guilt ("penance"), it can also be adapted to Braithwaite's theory of reintegrative shaming. This is what happened to Dr. Tucker. Many South Africans have been particularly sensitive to the nuances of the distinction between guilt and shame. One well-known activist and human rights advocate, Albie Sachs, whose arm was amputated as a result of a bomb sent by the security services, recounts a later encounter with an Afrikaner who said to him, "Forgive me."[54] Sachs recalls being uncomfortable with this apology on two grounds: first, there was no need for this man to accept collective responsibility merely because he was an Afrikaner; second, any apology should be directed not toward white activists who made knowing choices in joining the democratic struggle but toward the millions of blacks who suffered without choice. But perhaps, as Sachs might agree, this man was expressing not an inappropriate guilt but a quite appropriate shame.

Admirable though rare as these individual expressions might be, as well as their collective manifestations (commemorations, reparations), neither they nor truth commissions nor any forms of accountability match up to the political demands of major social transformations. Indeed some have argued that much of the religious-psychological rhetoric of expiation is redundant. Repentance—or whatever spiritual change "in the head" is called for—does not matter as long as people change their external behavior. Perhaps the villains should be swept away by history, left to live with their own consciences. Why should survivors worry too much about purging the souls of their victimizers?

And even if rituals of expiation are initiated and completed, this will not necessarily eradicate the political conditions which gave rise to gross abuses in the past. For this reason, the wider process of democratization has

---

53. Erving Goffman, *Relations in Public* 113 (London: Allen Lane, 1971). I am grateful to Tom Scheff for drawing my attention to the ways in which rituals of apology appear in political conflicts as forms of acknowledgment. Some of these ideas appear in Thomas J. Scheff, *Bloody Revenge: Nationalism, Emotion and War* (Boulder, Colo.: Westview Press, 1993).

54. Albie Sachs, "Personal Accounts," in Boraine, *Dealing* 20–25 (cited in note 1).

to be more forward-looking, to address the whole base of the emerging government and civil society.

E. Reconciliation and Reconstruction

The two resonant themes of reconciliation and reconstruction are rhetorically presented as the opposite of "backward-looking" forms of accountability. Instead of punishment and retribution, offenders and victims should be reconciled to each other and learn to live together. Instead of dwelling on the past, we should get on with the business of repairing and reconstructing the social fabric. The best way of acknowledging the past is to look toward the future.

This debate is far more complex than such polemical opposites suggest. As I have already noted, the "forget the past" rhetoric can be entirely self-serving. When used by the old regime, it is an attempt to avoid accountability by using these liberal slogans in bad faith. Cliches about "turning a new page," "letting bygones be bygones," and "no one has clean hands" must be placed in their political context. The distinction is perhaps a little self-righteous, but there is a difference between a "tactical" and a "principled" use of the appeals to reconciliation and reconstruction. One sign of a bogus appeal is when offenders pardon themselves, give themselves the right to be magnanimous, and take the prerogative on closing the book on the past.

The more principled appeals for reconciliation or reconstruction do not call for any denial of the past. On the contrary, they depend on a full acknowledgment of what happened. This is particularly true when reconciliation involves some element of forgiveness. Victims and survivors cannot forgive if they do not know what it is they are forgiving. The truth phase needs completion before such pardoning and reconciliation can be attempted: "Father, I am ready to forgive, but I need to know whom to forgive and for what."[55] Again, this is not just a matter of factual knowledge. Political repair is seldom needed for the symmetrical infliction of damage. As one human rights organization wrote to President de Klerk in 1992 when the South Africa government was planning a general amnesty: "It is impossible to expect 'reconciliation' if part of the population refuses to accept that anything was ever wrong, and the other part has never received an acknowledgment of the suffering it has undergone or of the ultimate responsibility for that suffering."[56] This means that if reconciliation is used as the opposite of punishment, doing so does not mean "doing nothing." Positive

---

55. Response by a woman being counseled by a priest in Uruguay about the disappearance of her child; *quoted in* Boraine, *Dealing* 121.
56. "South Africa: Accounting for the Past," *Hum. Rts. Watch Africa* (Newsletter), 23 Oct. 1992, at 2. Asmal ("Victims") makes a comprehensive case for reconstruction based on accountability.

reconciliation—for example, the methods used by the Chilean Commission such as compensation to victims, direct information to families, commemorations—does not leave the past behind.

Unlike, however, the practice of reconciliation as an "alternative" to criminal justice, there have few attempts after regime transitions to arrange actual encounters of reconciliation—for example, between torturers and their victims. The strategy is more often used in the wider social sense. Students of torture, though, have applied the idea of reconstruction to the dismantling of the entire "torture regime."[57] For a practice like torture to have occurred for a long period in any society, it must develop its own laws, jurisprudence, government bureaucracy, language (such as the specialized jargon used by torturers and transmitted to their victims), and political justifications. This regime cannot be replaced by the rituals of legal or quasi-legal accountability. There must be reeducation, not just on the bland "value" of human rights, but on the limits of obedience, the virtues of whistle-blowing, the duty to intervene, the permissible limits of dissent. Professional associations, such as those of doctors and lawyers, have to understand how they were drawn into the regime. The challenge is to identify and reverse the social conditions under which crimes of obedience were perpetrated.

Such radical reeducation must also allow the possibility that "victims" are really "survivors" and, further, might have been "heroes." Indeed, a political version of a normally individualistic victimology might offer an instructive guide to the entire process of policing the past of repressive regimes. Instead of a dubiously relevant deterrent theory or a rigid retributionism, the politics of reconstruction could be based on the survivors and the interests they represented. The damages inflicted by the old regime—the loss of human dignity, the destruction of solidarity, the poison of distrust—surely cannot be repaired by traditional legal means. The victims' demand for acknowledgment calls not simply for factual or legal recording but for replacing their physical pain and loss with political dignity.[58]

Victim-centered guides, however, are seldom internally consistent. In some circumstances, some survivors may indeed be content with truth-telling, shaming, and political testimony. Others can hardly be expected to acquiesce in a policy which lets known offenders go completely unpunished if they fully confess their crimes. At points like this, the difference between the "strict justice" and "principled reconciliation" positions reveals itself

---

57. Ronald D. Crelinsten, "The World of Torture: A Constructed Reality" (presented at Workshop on the Crime of Torture, International Congress of Criminology, Budapest, Oct. 1993).

58. Id. at 19. On the notion of replacing physical pain with political dignity, see Inger Agger & Soren Buus Jensen, *Trauma and Healing under State Terrorism: Human Rights and Mental Health in Chile during the Military Dictatorship* (Report to Council for Developmental Research, Danish Ministry of Foreign Affairs, 1993).

most starkly. Drawing as it does on the retributionist rationale, those in favor of accountability will support punishment even if victims and the democratic will of the wider public are against it. Their point is precisely that the abstract value of law cannot be determined by the vagaries of public opinion.

F. Summary

Setting out these issues as five separate "discourses" is a rather facile exercise. The really difficult questions concern the links between them. What is the point of knowledge without justice? Should justice or truth be the guiding aim of accountability? Is punishment through the criminal justice system a suitable means of arriving at knowledge? When are wounds "too recent" to heal and when are they "too distant" to contemplate? Is justice compatible with reconciliation? Can even the most rigorous policy of accountability remove the political conditions which allowed for the initial abuses?

Within the human rights community, there is both a wide area of agreement and a single deep thread of disagreement about these issues. The agreement is expressed in the slogans "amnesty, but not amnesia" (attributed to Adam Michnik) and "all the truth and as much justice as possible" (attributed to Jose Zalaquett). The disagreement lies between the "strict justice" position, informed by Kantian principles and the "principled reconciliation" position informed by a more utilitarian sense of wider political interests.

I have not set out this disagreement in any systematic way, because it has been so well rehearsed in the literature. For one side, represented by Neier, the rule of law is a value in itself which must determine our actions without being dependent on democratic consensus. For the other side, represented by Zalaquett, "*all things being equal*, forgiveness and reconciliation are preferable to punishment."[59] All things, of course, never being equal, Zalaquett's guide becomes a sense of the politically viable. In this context, he specifically cites Weber's famous distinction between the ethic of conviction (which favors acting by ethical precepts regardless of outcome) and the ethic of responsibility (which is guided by the predictable consequences of action).[60]

This disagreement is not always as sharp as it appears. The strict justice position is sensitive to political constraints, and the principled reconciliation position supports prosecution under certain circumstances. And both

---

59. Zalaquett, in Boraine, *Dealing* 11 (cited in note 18). Neier's position is set out in the same conference proceedings at 1-3 and 99-102.

60. Zalaquett, Introduction to English edition of *Report of the Chilean Commission* at xxx (cited in note 14).

oppose forgetting, both support compensation, both oppose witch-hunting, and both support the due process model.

Even though the terminology and context differ, these debates might look familiar to criminologists. The values behind reconciliation are similar to abolitionism, minimalism, or peacemaking. Where the debate is unfamiliar is in its obsessive emphasis on the value of knowledge. "All the truth and nothing but the truth" is less of pious formula here than in the everyday courtroom. Each strategy, whether justice, restitution, expiation, or reconciliation, assumes that truth-telling has to take place first.

TIME AND SOCIAL CONTROL

Why should any of these questions interest students of crime, punishment, and social control?

There is an obvious sense in which most modes of formal social control and all forms of punishment are responses to the past. Yes, there are preventive and proactive forms of social control—surveillance, intelligence gathering, preventive detention, risk assessment, psychological screening, clinical and statistical prediction, situational crime prevention—that are directed only to the present or to unknown future events. The deviant or criminal act has not yet happened. And these future-directed forms might indeed be characteristic of the "new penology."[61]

But punishment through the criminal law model remains at the core of all state-sponsored systems of justice and social control. By definition the model is directed toward the past, to what has already happened. Even forms of social control outside the punitive model—restitution, compensation, dispute resolution, reconciliation, therapy—imply some coming to terms with a past event.

But this obvious sense of past direction—the criminal act occurs in the biographical past of the individual—is not especially helpful in talking about political history. Nor does the concept of "social control" appear particularly relevant to policy decisions about state crimes of the previous regime—except in classic Orwellian sense: "Who controls the past, controls the future. Who controls the present, controls the past."

The temporal dimensions of social control have been altogether less observed than its spatial dimensions. Under Foucault's influence, we have studied how social regulation is deployed over space. Thus the contrast between concentrated, hierarchical, and state-centered models as against various forms of dispersed, panoptic, or destructured models. This literature is

---

61. Malcolm M. Feeley & Jonathan Simon, "The New Penology: Notes on the Emerging Strategy of Corrections and Its Implications," 30 *Criminology* 449 (1992).

full of spatial metaphors: concentration, penetration, dispersal, control over space, bodily space, private and public space.

But how might we think of time in the allocation of social control in the modern state? Only a few sociologists, such as Spitzer, have explicitly raised the question of how states create and enforce a sense of continuity over time and how this continuity influences public order.[62]

The problem of escaping state-centered social control is to establish a break between present and past. For the individual, to become free from social control means to become a permanent fugitive, fleeing from one's own past.[63] All over the world people sit with their dreadful memories—as victim, survivor, perpetrator, bystander. They see themselves trapped in the past, they talk of escaping the past or living in the past. Or else they try to deny or forget a painful past; through some complex form of amnesia, they seem actually unable to remember. Like Oliver Sach's patients, they need the psychological equivalent of L-DOPA to be awakened.

In the political context at least, individuals are not subject to such unitary, neurological processes. There is more than one perception of the past; perception is always distorted to meet the agenda of the present. For state crimes—much more than for any nonideological crime—personal memory is profoundly contaminated by the passing of political time. Memory is a social product—a product that reflects the agenda and social location of those who invoke it and the political struggle to suppress or resurrect what has been or what potentially might be forgotten. When you say that you were "just doing your duty" or were "only a cog in the machine" or that "others have done much worse," was this "true" at the time, or fabricated in the light of later political history?

Of course, this is also a central issue in theorizing about ordinary crime. This is precisely what the "techniques of neutralization" debate is about: Are the typical accounts, denials, and vocabularies of motives offered by delinquents merely ex post facto rationalizations or were they causally significant when the offense was originally committed? The theoretical problem is similar[64]—but obviously the subject of past state crimes raises far more fateful and dramatic issues. The "real time" of the offender who robbed a bank last year is not very different from the time of his criminal trial today. But the torturer from last year's military junta does not always seem to quite belong to today's time.

---

62. Steven Spitzer, "Policing the Past" (presented at Law & Society Association annual meeting, Amsterdam, June 1991) ("Spitzer, 'Policing the Past' ").

63. Martin Amis's novel *Time's Arrow* (New York: Vintage, 1991) is a original meditation on this subject: a escaped Nazi war criminal now in the United States lives his life backward till the moment he became an Auschwitz doctor.

64. Elsewhere, I apply Sykes and Matza's well-known theory of neutralization to analyzing government denials of complicity in state crimes: Stanley Cohen, "Human Rights and Crimes of the State: The Culture of Denial," 26 *Australian & New Zealand J. Criminology* 97 (1993).

Harold Rosenberg, writing about Marcel Ophul's film *The Memory of Justice*, meditates on the profound discontinuity resulting from the fact that the accused is always tried for an act he has committed in the past. At the time of his trial, he is a different person. "In some degree, punishment is always meted out to a stranger who bears the criminal's name."[65] This, again, is true for all criminals. But the state criminal appears before a tribunal far more profound than a district court: no less than the "judgment of history." On these occasions we might project time from the offense backward. Rosenberg notes that during the early trials of the French collaborators, Sartre and de Beauvoir were troubled by the question of identity: they had known this fellow in school, a bright friendly boy. What did he have to do with this nasty informer in the dock? Or—more relevantly—we project time from the offense forward: would this harmless-looking bumbler in court—Eichmann peering through his spectacles—be capable of committing these atrocities *now*? A survivor of Auschwitz walks past the Nuremberg prisoners' box and suddenly sees the accused as human beings:

> A metamorphosis had taken place. The real criminals have been carried off by history and will never return. In their place has been left a group of aging stand-ins, sick and trembling with fear. Judgement will be pronounced on a round-up of impersonators, a collection of dummies borrowed from the wax-works museum. At worst, these feeble mediocre fellows, "just like other people," could only have been, as they claim, cogs in the death machine somehow fashioned by history.[66]

Of course, not all state criminals present themselves as pathetic mediocrities. Depending on circumstances, they can just as easily be arrogant, bullying, and self-righteous. Like the Argentinian generals, like Ceausescu in Romania, they can proudly justify every act, condemn their judges, not recognize the court's legitimacy. They might even assert that no amount of information recorded by truth commissions, no details revealed in criminal trials, will detract from the historical justice of their cause. This is what the convicted Argentinian former junta commander Emilio Masseru meant by his chilling words, "My critics may have the chronicle, but History belongs to me."

These appeals to higher loyalties (the sacred cause) or denials of responsibility (just following orders) are attempts to deny history, to become fugitives from time, to be judged not by standards of today (legality, human rights, justice) but by the standards of the past. More than the bank robber, the delinquent, or the corporate criminal, these offenders are saying, "If you

---

65. Harold Rosenberg, "The Shadow of the Furies," *N.Y. Rev. Bks.*, 20 Jan. 1977, at 47.
66. *Id.* at 48.

were there then, you would have done the same." So set me free, cut me loose from history.

The voice of the present—truth, accountability, compensation, expiation—struggles against this appeal. Whatever form this struggle takes—whether legal punishment or mass lustration—and however just or unjust the process, the new society refuses to accept these pleas for historical relativity. It repeats what Rosenberg says was cried out from the balcony during the Eichmann trial: "But ah! You should have seen him in his colonel's uniform." The trial is about that other: the creature empowered to dispatch millions to death, not the balding old man wearing headphones; about the doctor who raped and tortured, not this pleasant man running a clinic in Montevideo.

So much for the individual. But what refuge is there for the collective, for the whole society? To be free from social control means to be totally without any repository of historical knowledge. There is no need for collective rituals of expiation or reparation, because nothing has happened, there is nothing to be sorry about. Whole societies slip into such mass denial, with terrible consequences, especially for victims and survivors who find themselves, like the Armenians, literally dislocated from historical time. Given the pace of events, this slippage is normal.[67]

Social control may be achieved not only in the ways that I have discussed here and that are assumed in the discussions of criminologists, lawyers, and human rights workers: that is, by relentlessly pursuing and confronting the past—opening the last archive, digging up the last grave, exposing the last informer, punishing the last offender, compensating the last victim. The individual punishment model which so dominates criminology and legalistic human rights work assumes that control is inextricably tied up with accountability. You discover the truth about the past in order to achieve justice in the present.

But social control—as Spitzer notes[68]—is also possible by transforming or obliterating the past, especially by weakening or redefining the relationship between what has gone before and what currently exists. Social control can be achieved not by opening the past to scrutiny but by closing it, by deliberately setting up barriers to memory. This mode of policing the past calls not for the recovery of memory but its eradication.

All societies use both strategies—recovery and eradication. But perhaps particular societies, at particular times, slip into one or the other mode—control by opening, control by closing. And both opening and closing are, of course, highly selective. Spitzer suggests a difference between

---

67. Note, though, that at the same time as events like the Holocaust recede in time and become unretrievable, so the contemporary landscape of commemoration become more dense. The result is a kitsch memorial industry being consumed by crowds of what James Young nicely calls "memory tourists." See Young, *Texture of Memory* (cited in note 25).

68. Spitzer, "Policing the Past" at 3.

regimes of continuity and *regimes of discontinuity*. In *regimes of continuity*, selective amnesia is induced by eliminating special elements of the past and preserving others. The past has to conform with the present to establish a version of history (a master narrative) to legitimate current policy. The Stalinist form of controlling the past—the deliberate suppression and distortion of history—is the classic example of this type of regime.[69] On the other hand, there is the selective forgetting of *regimes of discontinuity*—where the multiple narratives of the market dominate. Here, forgetting is the byproduct of rapid social change, a postmodern Disneyland "history," an inability to assimilate the present. The past is not deliberately obliterated and rewritten in the Orwellian sense, but it literally evaporates in the cacophony of the present.

Regimes of continuity, as Spitzer notes, tend to be centripetal. In state communist or classic totalitarian societies, the truth is shaped toward a single center, a homogeneous core of beliefs not to be questioned or disturbed. The past is continuously adapted and revised to reflect shifts in belief and current political agenda. Some events are, in Kundera's memorable phrase, "airbrushed" out of history—but they might also be restored when previously unacceptable ideas or persons are rehabilitated. This experience explains precisely why lustration is so characteristic of such societies. This is just the type of policy to be expected in regimes familiar with the business of rewriting history—and which have gone through previous sequences of upheaval, followed by purges, followed by rewriting history. One day someone is in power and favor; the next day, someone else.[70]

The process is different and more subtle in the postmodern market societies. In these regimes of discontinuity, knowledge disintegrates and is subject to skepticism, revision, and irony. The truth dissolves in an implosion of too much information or quasi-information, facts or factoids, documentaries or dramatic reconstructions. The movement is centrifugal rather than centripetal. Information and memory simply fall away. It becomes difficult to establish the connection between what is and what has gone

---

69. Many commentators on the current phase of unblocking the past in totalitarian societies have celebrated the failure of the original rewriting of history. As Havel notes: "It is truly astonishing to discover how, after decades of falsified history and ideological manipulation, nothing has been forgotten." Vaclav Havel, "The Post-Communist Nightmare," *N.Y. Rev. Bks.*, 27 May 1993, at 10. Future students of political violence will have to explain how current recoveries and inventions of these "memories" are used to justify nationalist and ethnic hatred.

70. Thus in Romania, the trial and execution of the Ceausescus and the first trials of their henchmen were more reminiscent of Stalinist show trials than the Nuremberg precedent to which they appealed. Some have claimed that the death sentences were imposed on the day before the putative trial started and that variously edited videotapes of the trial were shown. Indeed, some cynical commentators have gone as far as to claim that the whole transition was faked. See Andrei Codresco, *The Hole in the Flag: Smoke and Mirrors in the Romanian Revolution* (New York: Morrow Press, 1992).

before. The past is erased without need for censorship, propaganda, or Orwell's Ministry of Truth.

Unlike Spitzer, I doubt that these are two completely distinct types of society or that this is a critical difference between communist and market societies. And the global movement to the free market (that other face of democratization) will allow postmodern forms of forgetting to supplement the older, more ideological forms. For example, the very traditional (continuous, linear, centripetal) Turkish denial of the Armenian genocide has now been supplemented by a contemporary, postmodern version. The discourse now is one of mindless relativism, a mechanical repetition of the stupid idea that there must always be another point of view.[71] In the name of "looking at both sides," the massive historical record of the massacres now becomes "allegations," "feelings, "claims," or "rumors."

It would be difficult to classify, let alone predict, the various methods of policing the past that follow from these different forms of collective remembering and forgetting. In each of the very different current transitions that concern us, only one common point appears: the need to assert discontinuity between past and present. History was ruptured; something happened; it no longer happens; there is no point in talking about it too much for too long.

Critics of the current failures of various shades of totalitarian regimes to come to terms with their past should remember that very few nations anywhere have fully acknowledged their own historical victims. The international record on indigenous people—the treatment of Native Americans or the Australian aborigines—is an obvious case where the "West" has hardly provided an ideal. The current resurgence of interest in these long-distant histories also reveals how strategies of policing the past are continually revised. We can understand how the nature of the present determines how the past is viewed—but without colluding in the postmodernist denial of the status of truth claims independent of time and place.

Let me conclude with three vignettes that illustrate the worrying subjects this essay has covered.

The first comes from Uruguay—in a television documentary made with the help of organizations that treat torture victims.[72] A victim of the horrible torture during the Uruguayan military rule (his one hand is permanently damaged) visits the small town in which he lived before and during the regime. He cannot bear living there permanently because in the same town lives a doctor who was—and is known to be—this man's torturer. The doctor was neither punished nor expelled from the medical association and

---

71. Terence de Pres, "On Governing Narratives: The Turkish-Armenian Case," 75 *Yale Rev.* 517 (1986), and Gregory F. Goekjian, "Genocide and Historical Desire," 83 *Semiotica* 211 (1991).

72. "Doctors and Torture," BBC 1, Broadcast, 1 Sept. 1990.

continues his medical practice. In one frame of the film, the victim points to the doctor's office. The two men might see each other in the streets.

Should the torturer have been punished, forbidden to practice as a doctor, ordered to pay compensation? Or is this a desirable form of "reintegrative shaming?"

My second image comes from Zimbabwe. After the start of majority rule, the new black government effectively amnestied officials of the previous white regime who had committed human rights violations. Not only were they not brought to justice, but they sometimes retained their positions in the lower levels of the police and intelligence services. There was a reluctance to prosecute in order not to lose white confidence. So these white officials continued their same work for their new political masters. The story is told that the current minister of state responsible for security routinely introduces visiting journalist and human right workers to the man who had been his torturer when he himself was a political detainee before independence. This official now plays the same role as before on the minister's staff.

Healthy national reconciliation? Or a dreadful example of the continuity of state power despite political differences?

My third image comes from Morocco. Tazmanant was a secret fortress detention center in Southern Morocco. For the 18 years from 1971 to 1993, 58 political prisoners were detained there in appalling conditions. Half died from their treatment; all suffered terribly. All along, despite frequent allegations by human rights organizations, the Moroccan government denied the prison's existence. As late as July 1991, King Hassan said in a public statement that "Tazmanant existed only in the minds and imaginations of ill-intentioned people." At about this time, the last inmates died or were released; their families were never notified of their fates; the place that never existed was closed.

In July 1992, King Hassan stated: "It was a place used to keep persons administratively assigned there... it has no further reason to exist. The chapter is closed. It existed. It no longer does. That's all."[73]

Knowledge without acknowledgment; suffering without compensation; violation without accountability; horrors that are not exorcised; history without continuity. A perfect postmodern event.

---

73. See Amnesty International, "Morocco: Tazmanant: Official Silence and Impunity" (London: Amnesty International, Nov. 1992).

[16]
Government Responses to Human Rights Reports: Claims, Denials, and Counterclaims

I. INTRODUCTION

A major part of human rights work is the production of written reports. The report is usually seen as a means to an end. Information is collected, checked, standardized, and disseminated as part of a wider strategy to prevent violations and implement universal standards. Reporting also may become an end in itself: The belief that even without results there is an absolute duty to convey the truth, to bear witness.

There are many types of human rights reports. The major international nongovernmental organizations (such as Human Rights Watch and Amnesty International) produce regular and detailed book-length reports. These are the equivalent of social science research projects, giving a comprehensive account of a particular country's current human rights record. Then there are the simplest reports—legal or journalistic, rather than social scientific—giving information only on a single case or problem. Other variants include entries in annual world-wide atlases of human rights violations, press releases, regular documentation by regional and national organizations, results of fact-finding missions, publications of academic human rights centers, and official documents from intergovernmental organizations within the UN orbit.

These reports have generated an extraordinary volume of information over the last twenty-five years. This coverage is obviously neither completely comprehensive nor evenly distributed. There are clear reasons for this—both rational (human rights problems are objectively worse in some countries than in others) and contingent (some countries are closed to outside scrutiny, more obscure and less politically interesting to international, especially US-based, organizations). Some countries are more highly scrutinized than others, especially those with a combination of visible violations and open access to media and human rights observers.

Because of such contingencies in reporting, it would be impossible to claim that the human rights problem is "objectively" constructed, in the sense of there being an exact correspondence between the severity, duration, and extent of violations and the amount of attention any particular country receives. For this reason, some government responses to international criticism are justified, even if usually disingenuous or a distraction from the issue: Yes, human rights organizations do report more about Israel than Syria.

Despite this selectivity, though, the cumulative picture produced by all human rights scrutiny is impressive. It would be difficult to find a country or issue which has not been the object of substantial attention. Despite occasional legendary cases of misreporting (such as the dubious incubator babies in Kuwait) and other less dramatic mistakes, this reporting is generally fair and reliable.

What happens to these reports when they are "released?" The resources that organizations devote to compiling all this information are not matched by attention to how reports are disseminated or what impact they might have on target audiences. Much information hardly gets off the shelves. Or it flows only within a closed circuit of other human rights organizations, governments, or intergovernmental bodies. When it does reach the wider public—either directly (through appeals, publicity, campaigns) or through the mass media—its effects remain unknown and unmonitored. Recent refinements in techniques of information collecting, standardized recording, and data-retrieval do not address this issue at all.

I have just completed an enquiry into how human rights information is communicated.[1] Focusing on international organizations, my research considered three target audiences: (1) the official circuit of perpetrator and observer governments; (2) the mass media; and (3) direct appeals to the general public. This article deals only with the first audience—reactions by perpetrator governments. These reactions arise in three settings: (1) within their own country in response to criticism from domestic organizations; (2) within their country in response to international organizations; and (3) in the international arena in response to international organizations. This article concentrates on this third arena.

Perpetrator governments, however, when framing their replies to allegations by human rights organizations have to address other audiences as well—domestic public opinion and media, international public opinion and

---

1. STANLEY COHEN, DENIAL AND ACKNOWLEDGEMENT: THE IMPACT OF INFORMATION ABOUT HUMAN RIGHTS VIOLATIONS (1995).

media, allied or friendly governments, and international bodies. Official reactions, therefore, resonate far beyond the restricted channels of a government press release in response to a critical report. The vocabulary of official reactions draws from the acceptable pool of accounts available in the wider public culture. The official ideology, in turn, is the most powerful producer of these accounts.

Government reaction may be public (briefings, press releases, official statements) or carried through more restricted channels (direct letters and meetings with delegations, communications in UN agencies, etc.). The material used in this article—the circuit of report (claims) followed by government reaction (counterclaims), often followed by further rounds of exchanges—derives from records of major international organizations over the last two years. This article cites examples from Israel and the Occupied Territories, because I am most familiar with this case and because these texts are particularly dense.

These responses obviously belong to the standard repertoire of government reaction to any criticism. Although the issues might be different in other domains—domestic or foreign policy, corruption or personal scandals—the rhetoric draws on the same methods of disinformation, propaganda, political persuasion, and ideological legitimation. These are ways of "putting a spin" on information—one corner in the wider terrain of "thought control" and the "manufacture of consent" so well documented by Noam Chomsky.[2]

Although most of this rhetoric derives from what Chomsky calls "the sacred right to lie in the service of the state," some government responses to human rights reports might be perfectly accurate and truthful. Allegations are sometimes exaggerated, details may be inaccurate, some violations might indeed occur without official knowledge or responsibility. As the conclusion suggests, the truth games by which these claims are contested are becoming more volatile.

II. THE ORIGINAL REPORT

There are no mandatory guidelines about how to write a human rights report. Nevertheless, the genre has developed a recognizable standard style and format of its own. Most organizations feel constrained to follow certain rules, cover certain subjects and use a particular terminology. We find a

---

2. All of Noam Chomsky's writings on the political economy of atrocities are relevant. See especially NOAM CHOMSKY, THE CULTURE OF TERRORISM (1988) and NOAM CHOMSKY, NECESSARY ILLUSIONS: THOUGHT CONTROL IN DEMOCRATIC SOCIETIES (1989).

language of objectivity, references to how sources are checked, standard ways of documentation and citation of testimonies, obligatory references to appropriate international human rights standards, avoidance of taking sides in the conflict or expressing political views, and references to previous reports.

These traditional self-imposed rules have good justifications. Adherence to a standard format, however, allows for a predictable set of government responses. There is a ritualistic pattern to the sequence of claim, counter-claim, and repeated claim.

There are variations by subject, scope, and type of organization, but the basic report contains the following seven fixed elements:

1. Expressing Concern

The first paragraph, introduction, briefing, executive summary, or press release states the organization's position about the situation (for example, torture in Turkey or political killings in Colombia). The organization "is concerned," "remains concerned," "is deeply troubled," "strongly condemns," "has grounds to believe that. . . ."

2. Stating the Problem

Then follows an introductory statement about the problem—either the overall human rights position in the country or the specific abuse in question (press censorship, unfair trials, prison conditions, etc.).

3. Setting the Context

Some attempt is made to set out the context of the alleged abuses with the length and detail varying between book-length reports to ten page briefings. A brief political history gives the background to the conflict.

4. Sources and Methods

There is an account (usually rather inadequate) of where, when, from whom, and how the organization obtained its information.

5. Detailed Allegations

The largest section of the report is devoted to a detailed description of the violations in question. Statistics are given where appropriate. More often, individual cases are presented: conditions in a particular prison, testimonies of ex-detainees alleging torture, eyewitness accounts, and affidavits given to lawyers.

6. International and Domestic Law

The contents and applicability of relevant international legal provisions—covenants, conventions, standards—are set out. The target country's obligations according to international law, as well as details of domestic laws and enforcement procedures, are explained.

7. Required Action

The report ends by "calling on," "urging," or "demanding" the government to do something. The required action might be: (1) intervention on a particular case (release this political prisoner, reopen this newspaper, unban this organization); (2) changing a policy (repeal this law, end deportations, ensure fair trials); (3) conformity to international law; (4) implementing accountability (prosecutions or disciplinary actions against those responsible for violations); (5) investigation (an independent inquiry, access to human rights observers); (6) merely asking the government to condemn the violations in question.

III. THE REPERTOIRE OF OFFICIAL RESPONSES

The obvious differences between government responses to reports derive from the country's particular human rights situation; its political history and current status in the international arena; and the source, nature, and timing of the criticism. In this sense, every country—or at least type of country—should be studied separately.

Here I look more for similarities and common themes—the ideal type that allows variations and differences to be observed. What follows are composites of three forms of reaction. These are sometimes deployed simultaneously; sometimes one form becomes dominant. The first form is what I call the "classic" discourse of official denial. The second form is the strategy of turning a defensive position into an attack on the critic. The third form is the disarming type of response, characteristic of more democratic societies, which partially acknowledges the criticism. These are all more or less active reactions. Many countries—including and especially those with the most appalling human rights records—pay no attention to outside criticism. They shut their shells and withdraw from any engagement. Because of pressures from outside (stigmatization, sanctions, boycotts, isolation) and their own internal ideology (everyone is against us, no one understands us), they simply do not react at all. They see no political necessity to engage in dialogue with the rest of the world; nor do they have to contend with internal criticism. In this sense, their silence is the most radical form of denial possible.

Fewer countries of this type remain in the "new world order." However, versions of this withdrawal appear even in countries who have to respond more actively. In Israel, for example, where exquisite legalistic rationalizations are produced in response to all allegations (Amnesty International officials report that they receive more detailed replies from the Israeli government than from any other country in the world), there are also resonant political themes of isolation, unfair attention, and dismissal of outside criticism as biased.

These internal political variations must be understood in applying my rather abstract typology to any particular country.

A. The Classic Discourse of Official Denial

Three forms of denial appear in the discourse of official responses to allegations about human rights violations: *literal denial* (nothing happened); *interpretive denial* (what happened is really something else); and *implicatory denial* (what happened is justified).

Sometimes, these forms appear in a visible sequence: If one strategy does not "work," then the next is tried. Thus, if literal denial is countered by producing irrefutable evidence that something indeed happened—video footage of passive demonstrators being shot, corpses in mass graves, autopsy reports—then the strategy switches: for example, to legalistic reinterpretations or political justifications of what happened. However, these forms do not always run in sequence. More often, they appear simultaneously, even within the same one-page press release.

Whether they appear in sequence or at the same time, it is hardly worthwhile to look for contradictions: How can one say that a massacre did not take place, but also that "they got what they deserved?" These three elements form a deep structure of official denial; their relationship to each other is ideological rather than logical. Students of torture, for example, note the characteristic ways in which the literal denial that any torture took place is accompanied immediately by reinterpretations and justifications for the act.[3] Torture victims who hear their interrogators' words "scream as loud as you like, no one will believe you" face a double problem when they are released. They are indeed not believed, but are also confronted with the response that they "must have done something." The ideology of state terror justifies action whose existence is never officially admitted: "On the one

---

3. *See* Elaine Scarry, The Body in Pain (1985); The Politics of Pain (Ronald D. Crelinston & Alex P. Schmid eds., 1995).

hand . . . the repression is justified, and on the other, those who have suffered at its hands are accused of being liars."[4]

1. "Nothing is Happening": Literal Denial

Literal denials assert simply that "nothing happened" or "nothing is happening": There was no massacre, no one was tortured, there are no political prisoners in our country. For many authoritarian and repressive regimes, this is the only "technique" needed; this is as far as the matter goes. A laconic denial of this type is the most that appears. More often, the allegations are simply ignored or brushed aside. Lacking any internal accountability and insulated from outside scrutiny, such countries have no need to elaborate any response. Their control over internal information, the absence of free media, and the ban on human rights monitoring does not allow their denials to be countered.

In certain circumstances, though, literal denial can be used by any government, not just totalitarian regimes that dismiss the relevance of human rights criticism. Indeed, precisely those governments paying the strongest formal allegiance to human rights rhetoric may choose to contest allegations at the literal, factual level. "We would never allow something like that to happen, so it could not have happened." These claims are especially prevalent in the international diplomatic arena where financial aid or strategic alliances are dependent on an image of conformity to human rights standards. Mark Danner's account of the US government's active collusion in the cover-up of the 1981 El Mozote massacre in El Salvador is a classic case study of this process.[5] At the same time as claiming that its El Salvadoran ally was making every effort to improve its human rights record (and therefore was eligible for aid to be certified by Congress), US Embassy officials in El Salvador and the State Department were involved in baroque maneuvers to deny what they knew about the massacre.

There are no limits to the astonishing methods that are used to deny, cover-up, explain away, or lie about the most obvious realities. This is clear in the well-known episodes of historical denial: the intense efforts by the Turkish government to deny the genocide of the Armenians, the Holocaust denial movement, the Soviet denials of the atrocities against its own citizens. As soon as events become assigned to "history," powerful denial techniques become available: it happened too long ago, memory is unreliable, the records have been lost, no one will ever know what took

---

4. Ariel Dorfman, *Political Code and Literary Code: The Testimonial Genre in Chile Today*, in SOME WRITE TO THE FUTURE 141 (George Shivers trans., 1991).
5. MARK DANNER, THE MASSACRE AT EL MOZOTE: A PARABLE OF THE COLD WAR (1993).

place. Because of the proliferation of human rights-type monitoring, the greater spread of international reporting, and advances in information technology with instant global television coverage, the literal denial of current events is more desperate. For example, the Serb government response to the February 1993 market massacres in Sarajevo—either there was no massacre (the Bosnians had faked it by substituting dummies or corpses from previous incidents) or the Bosnians cynically had shelled their own citizens to obtain political advantage by blaming the Serbs.

Responses to visual evidence usually have to be more subtle than this. Thus, journalists may be accused of slanting their reports, selecting pictures to fit an already predicted scenario, or—more dramatically—staging the incident in collusion with the victims. Or the event is conceded, but knowledge about it denied. Not "it couldn't have happened without us knowing" but "it must have happened without us knowing." Or responsibility is displaced onto third parties ("unknown forces"). These denials are prominent in attempts to achieve truth, justice, and accountability during and after transitions to democracy.[6] "Maximum deniability" is often built into the judicial system.[7]

The most common way to imply, rather that assert, literal denial is to attack the reliability, objectivity, and credibility of the observer. Victims are lying and cannot be believed because they have a political interest in discrediting the government. Witnesses are untrustworthy or drawn from the political opposition. Journalists and human rights organization are selective, biased, working from a hidden political agenda or else naive, gullible, and easily manipulated. If the source of the evidence can be shown to be suspect in any of these ways, then the violations obviously did not take place or are being exaggerated.

A somewhat different counterresponse is to "prove" the denial by asserting that because the action in question is prohibited by the government (which has even ratified the appropriate international conventions) then, by definition, the action could not have occurred. The legalistic version of this magical syllogism follows: Torture is illegal in our country, this means that we don't allow it, this means that it cannot be happening.

One particular violation, "disappearances," takes its very definition from the government's ability to deny that it happened. A study of the official rhetoric surrounding Argentina's "Dirty War," notes that the essence of disappearance is that the physical acts of abduction, torture, and execution are complemented by the speech act of denial; otherwise terms

---

6. Stanley Cohen, *State Crimes of Previous Regimes: Knowledge, Accountability and the Policing of the Past*, 20 Law & Soc. Inquiry 7 (1995).
7. *See, e.g.*, Kenneth Anderson, International Human Rights Law Group, Maximizing Deniability: The Justice System and Human Rights in Guatemala (1989).

such as "arrest" or "detention" could have been used.[8] For a disappearance to be a disappearance it has to be denied. At the same time, the junta's official denials were framed by ideologies—"divine violence," radical Christianity, and security—which justified everything that the government had done.

Events such as disappearances or political massacres raise an obvious difference between reports by international and domestic organizations. Literal denial to foreign audiences often seems credible: the sources of information can be discredited easily, the situation is too complicated for an outsider to understand, patron governments can participate in the cover-up. In the domestic setting, though, it is harder to get away with such denial. Everybody knows what is happening. The essence of state terror is that everyone should know.

2. "What is Happening is Really Something Else": Interpretive Denial

Greater international visibility and transparency have made the more radical forms of literal denial more difficult to sustain. Even the most repressive governments—more dependent on global economic controls and exposed by the collapse of Cold War alliances—are less likely to ignore all criticism completely or to issue crude denials.

The most common alternative is to admit the "raw" facts—yes, something did happen: people were killed, injured, or detained without trial—but to deny the interpretive framework that is placed on these events. No, what happened was not really torture, genocide, or extra-judicial killing, but something else. The harmful behavior is cognitively reframed and then reallocated to a different, less pejorative class of events.

This strategy is complex and subtle to study, precisely because the process of interpretation is inherent in the naming of all social events. Many current forms of radical social constructionism or epistemological relativism would assert, of course, that there can be no objective, universally agreed definition of any social event. However, the human rights ethos assumes that such definitions can be made in good faith and with some degree of consensus. Without some idea of what constitutes torture, a fair trial, or freedom of speech, human rights work becomes impossible. A human rights report must be able to assign a mutually acceptable definition to an event. This definition might have some ambiguities, but it should be able to exclude those official reinterpretations that are deliberate evasions not made in good faith.

---

8. Frank Graziano, Divine Violence: Spectacle, Psychosexuality, and Radical Christianity in the Argentine "Dirty War" (1992).

Such evasions are deployed because some categorizations are so pejorative, stigmatic, and universally condemned that they cannot be openly admitted or defended. Assuming that it cannot resort to literal denial, no government will concede publicly that it is responsible for systematic torture, political massacres, and genocide. Even those governments advancing the strongest possible moral justifications for their actions will not normally acknowledge that what they are justifying belongs to these extreme categories. They have to reframe and rename in order to contest the imputed meaning of their policy—what it looks like to the outside observer—and replace this with another meaning.

This process, of course, is often entirely plausible. There is an arena of legitimate controversy—claims and counterclaims—between human rights organizations and governments. These definitional disputes arise not because of the sociological truism that all actions are interpreted, but because the dominant language of interpretation is legal. The common sense meanings of terms such as genocide, political killings, or torture have all been superseded by the legal definitions that frame international standards and prohibitions. Concepts such as "genocide," "crimes against humanity," or "war crimes" are notoriously difficult to define, even in good faith—a condition hardly evident in the rhetoric of official denial. International prohibitions are always subject to the politics of definition. What degree of intent, for example, is needed to fit the definition of genocide and hence make the action eligible for charges under the Genocide Convention? Governments have an obvious interest in applying the most restrictive formal definition.

The resulting disputes become legitimate because law is a "plastic medium of discourse," capable of varied, though certainly not infinite, interpretations. In this sense a protracted debate between a human rights organization and a government about whether a particular method of interrogation is "acceptable" rather than "ill-treatment," or is "ill-treatment" rather than "torture," is no different from a defendant in an ordinary criminal trial trying to argue "justifiable homicide" or "manslaughter" rather than "first degree murder." Without these legalistic games of truth, the institutions of international human rights enforcement would collapse and return to the older moralistic language that they replaced.

Reinterpretation is a compromise form of response. Sometimes it contains elements of literal denial: The "denial of injury" technique allows that something happened, but so disregards or minimizes the effects of any harmful behavior that the accuser is cast in the wrong for exaggerating what happened ("blowing things out of proportion"). Sometimes, the acknowledgement of harm is more realistic, but particular formal, legalistic definitions are contested. Yes, these people were killed, injured, mistreated, or detained, but the definitions of the relevant convention do not fit. The following four techniques tend to be used in combination:

a. *Euphemism*: The most familiar form of reinterpretation is the use of euphemistic labels and jargon. These are everyday devices for masking, sanitizing, and conferring respectability by using palliative terms that deny or misrepresent cruelty or harm, giving them neutral or respectable status.

Orwell's original account of the anaesthetic function of political language—how words insulate their users and listeners from experiencing fully the meaning of what they are doing—remains the classic source on the subject.[9] His original examples have become only too banal: "pacification," "transfer of population," "elimination of unreliable elements." In each instance, "[s]uch phraseology is needed if one wants to name things without calling up mental pictures of them."[10] In the half century since Orwell listed his examples, the language of euphemism has been enriched in directions he might have anticipated (such as "collateral damage" and "ethnic cleansing"), but also through the specialized jargon, convoluted verbiage, and techno-babble of modern warfare.[11]

The area of torture is a rich source of euphemisms: the "intensive interrogations" used by the British in Northern Ireland, the "special procedures" used by the French in Algeria,[12] the "moderate physical pressure" that the Israeli legal system permits and insists does not constitute torture.[13] From 1987 onwards, there has been a prolonged definitional dispute—generating a massive volume of paper work—between the Israeli government and every human rights organization (domestic and international) that has reported on the subject. How "moderate" is the permitted pressure? When is the resultant pain "severe" enough to fit legal definitions of torture?

b. *Legalism*: Euphemism derives from everyday language or technology, psychology and other professional discourses. But most forms of interpretive denial are supplied by the language of legalism. Countries that are proud of their democratic credentials and sensitive to their international image cannot easily issue crude literal denials. Their standard response is to embark on a legal defense—often scholarly and protracted. These claims

---

9. George Orwell, Nineteen Eighty-Four (1949); George Orwell, *Politics and the English Language*, in The Penguin Essays of George Orwell (1984). On euphemism and other techniques of "control-talk," see Stanley Cohen, Visions of Social Control 273–81 (1985).
10. Orwell, *Politics and the English Language*, supra note 9, at 362.
11. See Robert Jay Lifton & Eric Markusen, The Genocidal Mentality: Nazi Holocaust and Nuclear Threat 214–23 (1990).
12. On the French use of terms such as "special procedures" in response to allegations of torture during the French-Algerian conflict, see Rita Maran, Torture: The Role of Ideology in the French-Algerian War (1989).
13. The term "moderate physical pressure" originated in a 1987 report (the "Landau Commission") constructed to permit the Israeli security services to use interrogation practices against Palestinian detainees that were not "really" torture. On the debate and evidence, see B'tselem (Israeli Information Center for Human Rights in the Occupied Territories), The Interrogation of Palestinians During the Intifada: Ill-treatment, "Moderate Physical Pressure" or Torture? (Mar. 1991).

and counterclaims take place on a legal-diplomatic terrain, mainly invisible to the public.

It would be superfluous to summarize these familiar legal defenses or cite particular examples. This is the bread and butter work of the formal international human rights apparatus. There are two legitimate and one more disingenuous variations on the theme. One more legitimate strategy is the legalistic claim that while the event in question took place, it does not fit the appropriate category (right, law, article, convention). Yes, this demonstrator was arrested, but this was not a violation of freedom of expression. A second strategy denies that the provisions of a particular prohibition or convention are applicable in the circumstances in question. Yes, this might have been a violation of the Fourth Geneva Convention, but the Convention does not apply.

A third strategy is fair only up to a point, but then becomes more propagandistic. This is to respond to an allegation by "proving" that it could not possibly have the meaning imputed to it, because this type of action is illegal in the country. The government gives detailed lists of domestic laws and precedents, ratifications of international conventions, appeals mechanisms, and provisions for disciplining or punishing violators. Remember the syllogism used for literal denial: Torture is strictly forbidden in our country; we have ratified the Convention Against Torture; therefore what we are doing cannot be torture.

Such defenses are more difficult for human rights organizations to counter than crude denials of fact. They are plausible precisely because they appear to recognize the legitimacy of human rights concerns. It becomes very demanding to reveal the pictorial reality (Orwell's "mental pictures") that lies beneath the intricate facade of legalism. Instead of countering patent lies or evasions, the task of human rights reporting becomes more subtle and looks more polemical: to expose the gap between noble rhetoric and actual reality.[14]

c. *Denial of Responsibility*: The technique of "denial of responsibility" has many functions in the vocabulary of human rights violations. One use is

---

14. For a nice example, see AMNESTY INTERNATIONAL, TUNISIA: RHETORIC VERSUS REALITY: THE FAILURE OF A HUMAN RIGHTS BUREAUCRACY (1994). This report notes that few governments have been more eager to use the language of human rights than Tunisia. It has ratified nearly every UN human rights instrument, there is an ombudsman, there are human rights offices in several ministries and departments. Yet over the last three years, violations have continued unabatedly and even taken new forms. The report notes that Tunisia's "growing mastery in deploying the vocabulary and diplomacy of human rights abroad serves to mask a practice of serious and systematic human rights violations at home." *Id.* at 2. Amnesty International concludes that it "now feels unable to recommend that the Tunisian Government set up any new human rights bodies since those in place so signally fail to achieve their purpose." *Id.* at 42.

as a justification that deflects ultimate responsibility onto the victim. Three other variations are closer to reinterpretations than to active moral justifications.

The first variation acknowledges that the act occurred, but attributes responsibility to forces—named or unknown—that supposedly have nothing to do with the government and are beyond its control. Something bad happened, but this something cannot have the status of a human rights violation because the government is not directly responsible and, therefore, not accountable. Responsibility lies with shadowy armed groups, vigilantes, rogue psychopaths, proxy armies (such as the Israeli-controlled SLA in South Lebanon), vague "third forces" (such as those in South Africa), or death squads (such as those in El Salvador, Peru, Colombia, and Brazil). Or these matters are "endemic," resulting from communal violence, civil war, ethnic tensions, or drug wars.

The second and similar variation—most plausible under the anarchic conditions caused by a breakdown of state authority—is to assert that no responsibility can be found anywhere. Lines of political authority have collapsed, things happen with no identifiable ordering force.

A third variation draws on the standard euphemism of the "agentless passive form." This linguistic device creates the impression that atrocities just happen, resulting from nameless forces rather than human action: thus "Four Palestinians were killed yesterday in Gaza."

d. *Isolation*: An important form of reframing accepts that a particular act has occurred, accepts the imputed legal interpretation, even accepts responsibility, but denies the systematic, routine, or repeated quality attributed to the act. This was an "isolated incident," quite atypical of the overall pattern. It did not happen before; it has not happened since. It was isolated in space (untypical of what normally happens) and time (nothing like this happened before or after). Hence it is unfair and tendentious to accuse our government of any serious violations or to imply that we belong in the same category as other governments that systematically do this.

3. "What's Happening is Justified": Implicatory Denial

A full list of the justifications and rationalizations for human rights violations would constitute no less than a catalogue of all the causes and ideologies behind conflict, war, and repression throughout history. These are the standard denials that conventional moral codes apply in particular situations or towards particular groups. The literature on atrocities such as genocide, political massacre, mass rape, or torture distinguishes between the justifications offered by perpetrators themselves (at the time or afterwards) and the underlying structural causes, which may not correspond to those verbal accounts.

The following is a list of typical justifications found in the official responses to human rights criticism. Some of these may have causal status (that is, they do explain why the violations occurred); some are merely retrospective inventions. Some are sincere and offered in good faith; some are blatant and knowing lies. Some are closer to classic "justifications" in that they accept responsibility for the act, but deny its pejorative quality; others are closer to classic "excuses" in that they deny full responsibility, but accept the pejorative quality of the act;[15] yet others are intermediate neutralizations that appeal to common values to make the action more acceptable. Some need decoding; others are openly stated. Some are confined to perpetrator governments; others are offered on their behalf by their allies and supporters. Sometimes these justifications (for example, racism) are quite visible in the state's internal ideology, but not admitted in the international setting.

Two matters should be noted. First, although this list is drawn from government responses, equivalent justifications also appear in the ideological defenses used by armed oppositional groups—national liberation movements, political factions, ethnic separatists, terrorists, guerilla armies, or underground forces. Second, although these justifications are evoked for actions that are denied in the literal or interpretive sense, they will also be used to justify actions that governments openly and publicly admit—the death penalty, violations of women's rights, or restrictions on religious or press freedom.

a. *Righteousness*: The most radical forms of justification—"appeals to higher loyalty"—make two types of claims about the universal values supposedly enshrined in international human rights standards. One claim is that there are no such universal values at all and, therefore, any society can act according to its own morality. The other claim asserts that there are alternative sets of values that under certain circumstances (or in regard to certain people) take precedence over any universals. The strongest versions of such justification invoke a transcendent ideology, righteous cause, or sacred mission. One's own group (nation, class, religion) is seen as exalted, extraordinary, and possessed of a higher wisdom and morality that permits even harmful behavior for a higher good. A slightly weaker, but more common version, appeals to less transcendent, but equally binding ideologies—the fight against communism, the revolutionary struggle, nationalism, ethnic purity, the survival of Western civilization, the free world. Loyalty to any of these causes provides a temporary or permanent release from the moral claims behind human rights prohibitions.

---

15. This common distinction between excuses and justifications derives from Marvin Scott & Stanford Lyman, *Accounts*, 33 Am. Soc. Rev. 46 (1968).

b. *Necessity*: A less stridently ideological justification is utilitarian, pragmatic, and expedient: "we had to do it," "there was no alternative." This is a dominant theme in virtually every official government response. There is no principled attempt to deny human rights values nor appeal to an alternative value system. The claim is that the government, reluctantly, had to act out of necessity: self-defense, national survival, prevention of greater harm, anticipation of danger, protection of its citizens.

This claim can be backed up in different ways. The most effective is to demonstrate immediate physical danger and the absolute necessity of self-defense. Demonstrators, for example, turned violent and soldiers opened fire purely to save their own lives. Less immediate versions of the necessity defense appear in standard justifications for torture, administrative detention, states of emergency, and restrictions on freedom of movement and expression. Rather than the imminent self-defense of a soldier faced by a violent mob, this is a calculated prevention of a long term foreseeable danger. An even more distant justification is to neutralize political opposition before it can pose such a danger.

A more ideological version of the necessity/security defense might appear in the notion of a Darwinian struggle for survival: The conflict has gone on for centuries, only one side can win, no compromises are possible, it's either them or us.

c. *Denial of the Victim*: There are complex ways of displacing blame onto those who are harmed. Governments will exonerate themselves by attributing all the blame to others. As in the necessity defense, harm is presented as the result of circumstances rather than of choice.

The most common forms of victim blaming are variations on the themes of "they started it," or "they got what they deserved." As with the doctrine of necessity, these justifications appear either in the current situation (reacting to immediate resistance, provocation, and violence) or the long-term historical context in which the current victim is alleged to have been the original perpetrator. As we know from the atrocities of the last few decades—whether in Northern Ireland, Rwanda, the former Yugoslavia, or the Middle East—there is virtually no end to the historical spiral of conflicting claims about which group is the original, "real," or ultimate victim.

Other forms of "denial of the victim" are less explicit (though decodable) in the official response presented to the outside world but clearer in the internal ideology through which governments ensure that their own citizens are cooperative perpetrators or complicit bystanders.

These include: First, *dehumanization*: disparagement of the victim groups by repudiating their humanity. They become a lower form of being with less right to comparison with other humans, less ability to feel and less entitlement to compassion or empathy. They are savages, gooks, slits, vermin, animals, two-legged monsters. Violence is "the only language they understand." Second, *condescension*: the other is regarded not so much as evil or subhuman but is to be patronized as inferior, childlike, uncivilized, and irrational. Third, *distancing*: the dominant group ceases to feel the presence of others; they virtually do not exist. Because their very presence is not acknowledged, they cannot be seen as victims.

These three variations differ from standard victim-blaming rhetoric by not needing to identify or impute either immediate provocation or long-term responsibility to the victim. They get what they deserve, not because of what they did, but because of whom they are. These justifications, remember, are seldom openly used in the international arena, but are sufficient for internal consumption. These also might imply a fourth sub-text of *double standards*—a different set of moral rule and obligation applies to different categories of people. We would never behave like this to our own people.

Under certain circumstances, a fifth variation might be *expanding the target*—the "legitimate" enemy is redefined to include a wider category of "sympathizers" or "passive supporters." This expansion justifies, for example, collective punishments such as restricting freedom of movement for whole classes of people, placing curfews on whole villages, expelling or even "eradicating" community inhabitants.

Many such forms of denying or blaming the victim are justified by an appeal to "Just World Thinking."[16] In a just world, there can be no such thing as random and unpredictable suffering. You deserve to suffer because of what you must have done. Your suffering then becomes a source of further devaluation.

d. *Contextualization and Uniqueness*: In a sense, all justifications such as "necessity" and "victim-blaming" are forms of contextualization. Governments typically respond to human rights organizations by accusing them of not knowing, understanding, or mentioning the context in which the alleged violations take place. They say, in effect: "If only you really understood our history, politics, the nature of the conflict, then [the weak version] your judgement would not be so harsh or [the strong version] you would support what we are doing." Many government responses consist of a review of the historical background to the conflict.

A strong form of contextualization is to assert that the particular circumstances in which this country finds itself are so special that normal standards of judgement cannot apply. There are unique features of the situation—the military threat, the methods used by terrorists, the balance of forces—that make it wholly specific. This is not to reject universal standards: We only wish we could observe them, but alas, the situation does not allow us to be like everyone else.

---

16. Melvin J. Lerner, The Belief in a Just World: A Fundamental Delusion (1980).

Another variation on the uniqueness theme is to assert that a level of violence is normal, acceptable, and ordinary in this particular situation. What is happening may look bad elsewhere, but here everyone is used to it: Look how they always have behaved toward each other. Prison conditions, thus, might look bad by universal standards, but are better than the way these people live in their own homes.

e. *Advantageous Comparisons*: Another oblique form of justification is the self-righteous comparison of your own record with that of your critics.[17] The language of comparison has a series of different functions: literal denial (by discrediting the credibility of the source), justification (by the common appeal "everyone is doing it, so why not me?"), and deflection (by counterattacking the critic's record). There are three common sets of comparisons:

— First, you can praise or justify your own harmful acts by contrasting them with morally reprehensible atrocities committed by your adversary. This might allow the act to look righteous by contrast to their more flagrant inhumanities. Governments will give long, detailed (and often credible) lists of the atrocities perpetrated by armed oppositional groups. Large sections of replies to human rights criticism consist of such lists. Whatever we do is nothing compared with what they do. Moreover, not only is our response legitimate, but it is carried out according to the rule of law.

— Second, there is "condemning of the condemners": the comparison is made not with your adversary, but with your outside critics. Such critics are accused of hypocrisy (their own hands are not clean) or selectivity (why do they keep picking on us?). They are themselves too morally compromised to have the right to judge us. The Israeli version of this tactic is especially resonant: When Jews were slaughtered during the Holocaust, the very countries now condemning us either colluded or stood by in silence; the international community, therefore, has lost its right to criticize us now.[18] Particular contempt is reserved in Israel for the International Committee of the Red Cross because of its dubious record during World War II. Another example of such historical appeals can be found in former colonies: Their own (or any other) former colonists have no right to judge them. More generally: All democracies were born out of violence, slavery, occupation, and the extermination of indigenous people; what right do they have to judge us now?

---

17. The technique of "advantageous comparison" and others in my list are well analyzed by Albert Bandura, *Selective Activation and Disengagement of Moral Control*, 46 J. Soc. Issues 27 (1990).
18. In response to international criticism after the 1982 invasion of Lebanon and bombing of Beirut, the Prime Minister, Menachem Begin said in the Knesset: "No one, anywhere in the world, can preach morality to our people."

— Third, comparisons are made not with your adversary or critics, but with other countries with supposedly similar problems. Other governments faced with the same provocations and dangers would have acted and do act worse—without any of the self-imposed restraints we show. In fact, other governments with far less serious problems are acting worse all the time.

Usually these three sets of comparisons are combined in a single discourse of righteous indignation: our adversaries behave terribly (and you don't condemn them); your own moral record is flawed (so you have no right to judge); other countries with even lesser problems behave worse than us (and you say nothing about them). Thus, you are using double standards.

f. *Rejection of Universal Standards*: The "higher loyalty" defense appeals to an ideology that temporarily or permanently supersedes universal human rights standards; the "specificity" defense depicts a situation so unique that universal values do not apply. A more radical version of these justifications—worth separate attention because of its current prominence in the human rights debate—is the principled rejection of any universality.

Some versions of this defense are highly sophisticated, but the crude core goes something like this: The values enshrined in international human rights declarations originated historically in the West (notably in the Anglo-American and Western European dominated United Nations after World War II); they were then imposed, in classic imperialist and colonialist fashion on the third world and on other unique cultures with an integrity of their own (such as Islam); these so-called "universal values" are not universal at all, but highly ethnocentric and alien to local cultures; they have, therefore, no relevance or status as a universal measuring rod.

Parts of the argument are more plausible than others—for example, the thesis that individualistic Western conceptions of rights differ from the collective notions of more traditional societies or the claim that social and economic rights for basic subsistence should take priority over the finer principles of civil rights. However, the crude public form of this defense to human rights criticism simply allows any country to do what it likes because that's the way it does things.

B. Counteroffensive

We have already seen the "shoot the messenger" strategy at work: Attack the source of the information by casting doubt on the truth of allegations and questioning the right to criticize. This government strategy is so prevalent and powerful that it is worth listing separately.

Its most radical form rejects the whole report as lies: "communist propaganda," "Western ideology," "disinformation," "anti-Arab prejudice." More subtle and specific forms of discrediting include: (1) citing mistakes or distortions in this organization's previous and current reports (this detainee was interrogated in March not May, this witness was mistaken, this prisoner later withdrew his allegations of ill-treatment); (2) making allegations about the suspect sources of the organization's financing or the political affiliations of its informants, fieldworkers, or board members; and (3) attacking the organization for releasing the report at a particular time calculated to embarrass the government.

The common strategy is to prove (or just to assert) that the report is biased, untrustworthy, tendentious, prejudiced, unreliable, part of a campaign of vilification, and evidence of an undeclared political agenda. These claims vary according to whether the source of criticism is internal or external.

1. *Internal Sources*: Claims by local human rights organizations or media are simply responded to within the society's political culture. A more accountable government defends its legitimacy; a more authoritarian government declares all criticism as illegitimate. Thus, internal critics of the Peruvian government are "pro-Sendero," of the Sri Lankan government, "pro-Tamil," of the Israeli government "PLO sympathizers." Human rights organizations are presented as mouthpieces or fronts of the opposition—terrorists, national liberation movements, or ethnic separatists.

Given the nature of these conflicts and the political location of human rights advocates, it is both easy and plausible to identify all criticism with political opposition. Every organization is forced into this debate: How to distinguish a strict human rights position from a political position?

A variation on the theme of political bias is to accuse internal critics of being terrorists, unpatriotic, or irresponsible.[19] Sometimes their bona fide human rights status is conceded—they have good intentions, they are not merely taking political sides—but they are depicted as "useful idiots." They have been manipulated by a cunning enemy or been naive in not realizing that their reports will be exploited by extremist and antinational forces. Closing of ranks in the face of external hostility is an especially potent theme in some countries. Internal critics, especially those who allow their allegations to be disseminated abroad (by writing in a foreign language or talking to the international media or other organizations), are "irresponsible" and traitors to their country. Israeli human rights activists are denounced as *malshinim*—which literally means "informers"; they are playing into the hands of anti-Zionist or even anti-Semitic forces. Internal critics of Arab regimes are accused of washing their dirty linen in public and reinforcing anti-Arab or anti-Islamic forces.[20]

---

19. On such recent attacks against human rights workers in India, see Ravi Nair, *Activists in India Are Confronting a "State-Sponsored Hate Campaign,"* 1 HUM. RTS. TRIB. 5 (1992).
20. *See generally* KANAN MAKIYA, CRUELTY AND SILENCE: WAR, TYRANNY, UPRISING AND THE ARAB WORLD (1993).

2. *External Sources*: Accusations of treachery and lack of patriotism cannot be appropriately applied to international sources, but the rest of the rhetoric is similar.

External organizations are lined up in a familiar demonology of hostile sources: Communist-inspired, anti-Islam, anti-Zionist, racist, or imperialist. Sometimes particular organizations are singled out: "Amnesty International is known for its anti-India record." This might be followed by a list of the far worse depredations carried out by other countries—either in general or in the region—which the organization allegedly has ignored or downplayed. A standard attack by the Israeli government and its supporters is to point (with justification) to the record of worse violations by Arab states in the Middle East and the fact that organizations like the United Nations Commission on Human Rights have paid undue attention to Israel. More polemically, this record is seen as proof of a concerted attempt to delegitimize Israel.

If such images of deliberate bias and lack of credibility do not sound convincing, then variations on the "naive, ignorant and gullible" theme are put forward. The organization simply does not understand the complexities of the historical and political context (a charge obviously not easily made against internal sources) or has been duped.

The rhetorical question posed in both the domestic and international arenas is this: If human rights organizations were genuinely concerned with the rights of all people, then why would they just concentrate on the government and ignore the victims of armed oppositional groups? This means that they are not bona fide human rights groups at all, but rather—in the terms of President Fujimori of Peru—"the legal arm of subversion," "accomplices of terror," and "part of an international campaign to discredit the government."[21]

C. Partial Acknowledgement

On the continuum between full denial and full acknowledgement, the responses I have listed so far are closer to the denial side. In certain circumstances, though, governments appear to acknowledge at least some claims and criticisms. Without attacking its sources or evading its contents, they give every appearance of taking the report's allegations seriously.

This is often the response of observer governments. Either because of changed political alliances or because the evidence is too embarrassing to explain away, they will abandon their ally or client and demand that it

---

21. Letter from Ian Martin, then Secretary-General of Amnesty International to President Fujimori (21 Nov. 1991) (on file with author).

makes the full acknowledgement requested. Yes, this was definitely an extra-judicial killing; it cannot be justified; it must be stopped; we will cut off your aid unless something is done.

Such acknowledgement is rare from the perpetrator government itself. However, most countries with a democratic image to maintain must make an effort to move in this direction. The strategies of ignoring allegations completely, crude denial, ideological justification, or aggressive counterattack are difficult to sustain indefinitely. One line of response goes like this: "We welcome constructive criticism, in fact we are the only democracy in the region and we allow human rights organizations to do their job without restrictions. We met with your delegation and will meet with them again. The human rights situation is not perfect and we are doing what we can to improve things. But the situation is difficult; things can't change overnight; you must be patient."

A recent example of this was the response of the Indian government and media to the 1993 Amnesty International campaign.[22] The campaign and report were denounced as hostile and provocative, but India's democratic tradition ("the world's largest democracy") and open media were reaffirmed: We are willing to permit scrutiny; we have shown restraint in facing violent threats to our citizens; look at our judicial safeguards.

Such generalizations hardly add up to full acknowledgment because they invariably avoid the specific details of the violations alleged to have taken place. If these details are conceded, then they are qualified by three devices:

1. *Spatial Isolation*: Yes, the alleged event happened—but it should not have; it must be condemned; it cannot be defended. But this is "only an isolated incident." This is not what normally happens, there is no pattern, no system, no routine. The circumstances were special; the victim was atypical; any violations arose from "individual excesses" within the ranks of the police or security forces and are not condoned by the authorities.

2. *Temporal Containment*: Yes, this is what used to take place. In the past—before the government was changed, before we signed this treaty, before we were made aware of human rights criticism—this is the sort of thing that happened, but it could not happen anymore.

3. *Self-Correction*: Yes, we are aware that we have a human rights problem, but we are doing our best to deal with it. This is the strongest form of acknowledgement: The government presents itself as being sensitive, self-correcting, and accountable. It responds to criticisms; has signed and ratified the relevant human rights instruments; passed new domestic laws;

---

22. *Evaluation of the India Campaign* (1993) (Amnesty International internal document) (on file with author).

met with representatives of human rights organizations; set up judicial commissions of inquiry; appointed a human rights commissioner; disciplined, punished, or removed offenders from office.

Such acknowledgement is often genuine enough. In partial transitions to democracy this is often as far as many governments can go—given limited resources, in-built corruption and inefficiency, the fragility of democratic structures, sabotage by the armed forces, or a breakdown of political authority. In these circumstances, human rights organizations concentrate on the partial nature of the acknowledgement and the gap between rhetoric and reality. The recent case of Peru is a classic example. When President Fujimori took office in July 1990, the country had a long legacy of unacknowledged violations, and he pledged a commitment to human rights standards. Subsequent reports about Peru have been structured around a skepticism about these pledges.[23]

An index of the success of the human rights movement is that it increasingly confronts neither a crude denial nor a dismissal of its agenda, but a rhetorical acknowledgement of its legitimacy. A report that has to show that this rhetoric is bogus and self-serving, rather than genuine, is more challenging than the simple exposure of unknown information.

IV. COUNTERING OFFICIAL DENIAL

Government responses contain different permutations of classic denial, counteroffensive, and partial acknowledgement. Each response presents unique problems for organizations planning a counterresponse.

In one sense, despite the increasing influence of the human rights discourse in the international arena, no human rights organization has the power to undermine the standard lines of defense mounted by sovereign states and their patrons. The weapons we advocate—accountability, shame, isolation, economic sanctions, arms, and cultural boycotts—might indeed be effective in bringing about desired improvement in the target country. Their deployment, however, is less often the result of an intellectually convincing report or counterresponse, than a change in the balance of geopolitical and economic interests.

The ways in which powerful governments, most notably the United States, shield their allies and clients (as well as deny their own involvement) presents a particularly discouraging story. No matter how convincing are

---

23. *See* AMNESTY INTERNATIONAL, PERU: HUMAN RIGHTS IN A CLIMATE OF TERROR (1991); AMERICAS WATCH, PERU UNDER FIRE: HUMAN RIGHTS SINCE THE RETURN TO DEMOCRACY (1992).

successive reports about torture in Turkey or massacres by Indonesia in East Timor, there will be no real acknowledgement by the international community. There are numerous examples of countries that are impervious to even the most detailed exposures and deploy the most patently bogus denials.[24]

The independent weight of government denials is heavy enough. The more they are implicitly accepted in the international arena, rather than challenged, the less heart human rights organizations have to write yet another follow-up report or to detail the inadequacies of the government's response to the previous report.

In a sense, the edifice of formal international human rights law is taken itself as the counterresponse to standard defenses, denials, and justifications. These declarations and conventions depend on rejecting the familiar ideological and pragmatic justifications offered for human rights violations. This rejection, however, raises two problems.

First, although human rights prohibitions rule out political justifications (the strong notion of "non-derogability" excludes any justifying circumstances), government appeals to necessity, security, and self-defense are often credible. This makes the principled insistence on a strict human rights line look unconvincing if not naive in many reports. Second, the utilitarian-necessity claim allows for a technical focus on efficient means, routinizing abuses into small practical steps, each one sounding relatively harmless, even desirable. Opposing these policies by an appeal to abstract principles usually looks like an unconvincing luxury.

Most monitoring organizations, though, attempt some form of counterresponse. Sometimes this is *reactive*: the familiar exchanges between international organizations and target governments. This sequence is often intricate and time-consuming. Amnesty International gives detailed guidelines to its members on how to construct a counterresponse to the standard official denials of the original report. For example (referring to a report about torture in Israel): "The accused is an advocate of terrorism"—*but this is irrelevant because we oppose torture in any circumstance*; "the allegations were thoroughly investigated and there had been no deviation from the accepted procedures for interrogation"—*but the accepted procedures themselves are the issue.*

---

24. El Salvador is a well-documented example of such denials. Juan Méndez, former Executive Director of Americas Watch, found the classic denial sequence in the reactions of the Reagan and Bush administrations: "Arguing against all evidence, they have claimed that some of the repellent acts did not happen; that if they happened, they were not perpetrated by government forces but rather by some obscure right-wing force; or that the government forces may have committed atrocities in the past but, thanks to U.S. influence, are now showing greater respect for human rights." Juan Méndez, *Preface to* AMERICAS WATCH, EL SALVADOR'S DECADE OF TERROR ix (1991).

This whole circuit of exchanges will sometimes be published: allegations, government reply, counterresponse.[25] This sequence can go on for years, even indefinitely. Indeed, the growth of human rights bureaucracies *guarantees* that the circuit of paperwork will be prolonged. Israel not only has special civil servants to construct replies to allegations,[26] but recruits volunteers to reply to letters from Amnesty International's volunteers.

The responses also might be *proactive* rather than reactive. The report anticipates the common modes of denial—then builds its replies into the text. This strategy is more refined in the aid and development areas where information routinely anticipates the common denials—for example, that famine is natural, that aid goes to corrupt governments, that helping individuals makes the problem worse. Equivalent proactive counterdenials now often appear in the text of the initial human rights report. These include:

— We have not singled you out for special criticism. We regularly produce equally critical reports about other countries.

— We unequivocally condemn the acts of terror and violence carried out by armed oppositional groups in your country and our organization consistently takes this position elsewhere.

— We are not taking sides in the conflict nor do we favor any particular political solution. Nor have we timed this report provocatively to influence your internal political situation.

— We understand the long history of your conflict and the problems that you are facing today; we know about the atrocities against your citizens and the threats to your security.

— We welcome the improvements that have been made since our last report and we recognize your sincerity and commitment to improving the situation further.

Needless to say, there is no guarantee that these proactive responses will prevent another round of government denial. Indeed, the likeliest result

---

25. For a typical example, see the thirty-page document issued by Amnesty International in October 1991 reproducing (i) extracts from the sections on Israel in the 1990 and 1991 annual reports; (ii) comments by the Human Rights Division of the Israeli Ministry of Justice on these sections; and (iii) Amnesty's responses to these comments. Amnesty International, Israel and the Occupied Territories: Amnesty International's Response to the Comments of the Israeli Ministry of Justice on the Amnesty International Reports, 1990 and 1991 (1991). For further exchanges, see the *Report of the IDF Military Advocate General's Unit to Amnesty International's Report on the Military Justice System in the Administered Territories* (1992) and the IDF responses to the report by the Lawyers Committee for Human Rights, A Continuing Cause for Concern: The Military Justice System in the Occupied Territories (1993).

26. In 1993, the Ministry of Defense published a book-length compendium setting out all its responses to human rights criticisms. *See generally* Israel, the "Intifada" and the Rule of Law (David Yahav et al. eds., 1993).

is to set in motion an even more sophisticated circuit of responses. These texts provide a rich source of material: a mixture of blatant lies, half truths and evasions, legalistic sophistries offered in good faith, ideological appeals, and perfectly credible factual objections.

V. CONCLUSION

As rich as these texts might be for the detached student of the discourse, it is less clear how they advance the human rights cause. There are no simple technical solutions to making this information more effective. Two issues are worth pursuing.

A. Witnessing the Truth

Informative and intellectually convincing as they might be, standard human rights reports and counterresponses—whether anticipating or following official reactions—can do little to undermine the cruder forms of denial and rationalization. The truth, however well documented, will not be accepted as self-evident. Techniques of collecting information might be modern and sophisticated, but human rights organizations are motivated by the old-fashioned Enlightenment faith in the power of knowledge: If only people knew, they would act accordingly. This is just the faith that is undermined by the daily practice of human rights work.

In an electronic age dominated by visual rather than written communication, new technologies for observing, recording and presenting information have obvious potential. They can increase both the public impact and perceived validity of the facts. The faith in information ("if only they knew") becomes "if only they saw." The "Witness Program" of the Lawyer's Committee for Human Rights is a dramatic example of this approach, distributing video cameras to human rights observers to record violations. This should make the facts incontestable: If we have pictures, we have the truth. To stress the benefits of the Witness Program, rock singer Peter Gabriel cited the cover-up of the 1981 El Mozote massacre: "The words were not enough. There were no pictures, no video tape. No proof."[27] He went on:

> A camera in the right hands at the right time at the right place can be more powerful than tanks and guns. In Orwell's *1984*, those in power controlled the people by watching every move. Now the people can watch, witness and report

---

27. Press release on the launching of the Witness Program sponsored by Lawyers for Human Rights, issued at the Reebok Human Rights Awards Ceremony, 10 Dec. 1992.

on those in power. With *Witness* we are serving notice on governments. We are watching that they can no longer keep their deeds hidden, we are watching.[28]

Rhetoric aside, the potential of such techniques are obvious—both in enhancing the credibility of information and, perhaps even more importantly, providing visual material for the mass media. However, there is the "Rodney King effect." Despite the (apparently) obvious video images of police officers beating up an unresisting suspect, the event entered into a legalistic framework when its "obvious" meaning became denied and into an ideological framework where it became justified.

The notion of witnessing and telling the truth that informs the production of human rights information belongs to a simpler era. The task is now more complicated than our traditional methods of reporting allow. On the one hand, the increased international awareness of human rights, the spread of new information technologies, and the globalization of the mass media mean that the sovereign state is being "watched" like never before. On the other hand, the profusion of so many images, the blurring of the lines between fiction and facts (reconstructions, factoids, and documentary dramas), and the relativist excesses of postmodernism and multiculturalism make the representation of old-fashioned human rights information more difficult than ever.

B. Accounting for the Truth

Even if the facts are acknowledged and their framing as human rights violations are not disputed, there is no guarantee that they will evoke the active response that the human rights movement wants.

The problem is that the rationalizations that governments produce are not mere rhetorical flourishes. They are not wholly fictional and they are deeply rooted in national and international political cultures. The typical letters, for example, that ordinary Amnesty International members receive contain the same denials that are found in the official discourse. It sounds reasonable to think "Yes, these allegations sound true—but what else do you expect that government to do with the problem it faces?" Human rights reports about distant places have become institutionalized features of media and public culture. This is what governments usually do; this is what human rights groups usually say.

The consonance between public and official response is obviously even deeper for national organizations working only within their own society. Authoritarian governments rely on enforced compliance; more democratic

---

28. *Id.*

governments rely on passive acceptance of their accounts. No matter, for example, how much human rights conventions insist that no putative threat to public security can justify torture, virtually all citizens will accept the necessity of using any means to extract information if such means might prevent an act of terrorism. No matter how much we criticize accounts such as "obedience to orders," there will be sympathy for soldiers who follow orders.

The limitations of conventional reporting as a way of achieving political changes can be addressed at two levels: first, finding better ways to explain the principles behind human rights norms; second, reexamining the style, format and genre of the human rights report. Are the resources devoted to the circuit of claims and counterclaims a worthwhile investment? Or is this investment only an artifact of the way in which information is presented?

[17]
Crime and Politics: Spot the Difference*

My lecture is about the relationships between crime and politics. It also includes a slightly self-indulgent sub-text: a glance at what happened to some ideas from the 'new criminology' movement which so involved many of us (some present in this audience) thirty years ago – here in the milieu of LSE in the mid-1960s.

I start with two texts – not 'Texts' with a capital T in the literary, post-modernist sense, but texts in the old fashioned way that priests, rabbis and mullahs use for their sermons.

The first is very familiar to criminologists: a much-quoted passage from one of the most influential books of the period, David Matza's *Becoming Deviant* – a text very much resonating the culture of the 1960s (and conceived by Matza while he was a visitor at the LSE in 1967–8). With characteristic irony, he records the uncoupling of modern criminology from politics: 'Among their most notable accomplishments, the criminological positivists succeeded in what would seem the impossible. They separated the study of crime from the workings and theory of the state' (Matza 1969: 143).

My second text is less familiar to criminologists, but more to everyone else. It's from John Le Carré's recent novel *The Night Manager*. This is the scene: the Cold War is over; there is no more pretence at ideology; history has come to an end. The new enemy is the callous international cartels of drug-trafficking, illegal arms-trading and money-laundering. Burr, the agent for the law enforcement division of the revamped British intelligence services, now deals not with the old politics but the new crime. In one scene in Zurich, he is trying to recruit our hero, Jonathan Pine, to help bring to justice a particularly obnoxious dealer in illegal arms and drugs

> Burr was talking about justice. 'When I get to run the world . . . I'm going to hold the Nuremberg trials Part Two. I'm going to get all the arms dealers and shit scientists, and all the smooth salesmen who push the crazies one step further than they thought of going, because it's good for business, and all the lying politicians and lawyers and accountants and bankers, and I'm going to put them in the dock to answer for their lives. And you know what they'll say? "If we hadn't

done it someone else would have." And you know what I'll say? I'll say "Oh, I see. And if you hadn't raped the girl some other fellow would have raped her. And that's your justification for rape. Noted . . ."'. (Le Carré 1994: 84–5)

I will take these two quotes to track two different stories, two apparently opposite but perhaps complementary ways to conceive the relationship between crime and politics.

I will derive from Matza's quote, or rather the uses to which it was put, a brief sociology of knowledge tale: how the first wave of critical criminology from the mid-1960s tried to restore the 'political' to the criminological discourse, to 'bring the state back in'. I will list five ways in which this was done and note the later trajectory of these ideas.

I will derive from John Le Carré a more complicated and speculative point: that somewhere there, in what some of us rather quaintly still refer to as the 'real world', transformations are occurring in the way in which political conflicts are understood and sought to be regulated. These transformations – even when exaggerated – call into question the boundary between crime and politics in more disturbing ways than criminologists imagined.

I. POLITICS IN CRIMINOLOGICAL DISCOURSE

I will distinguish five ways in which the political was originally inserted into the study of crime and deviance:

1. The Hidden Politics of Criminology

The first and most obvious project was to understand the history and status of the criminological discipline itself in political terms.

The evolution of criminological theory from the classical to positivist schools was now located in the broader political economy of the modern state. Oversimplified as some of these early accounts might have been, their general drift remains valid. The impact of Foucault led to a more sophisticated view of the role of criminology in the broader project of 'governmentality'. But today's revisionists (such as David Garland) look for more refined links between knowledge and power, rather than returning to the internalistic intellectual histories.

The question of the current political stance of criminology – as opposed to its hidden political genealogy – has turned out to be more complicated. The original choices, though – between correctionalism, detached scholarship, liberal underdog sympathy and radical social change – remain. Today's left realist criminology might have renounced an outsider status in favour of 'relevance' – but this is hardly a retreat from politics. And the dominant paradigm – now more managerial and

Crime and politics 3

depoliticized than ever (but not simply 'positivist' and not very liberal) — can still be challenged in political terms.

2. *The Politics of Law and Social Control*

The second form of politicization is obvious, non-controversial and hardly needs comment. This is the direction indicated by Matza's reminder about Leviathan: the power of the state to criminalize.

(a) Criminalization The question of criminalization merely drew criminological scholarship into the mainstream of sociological and historical enquiry. Studies about the origins of criminal law, the 'rule of law' or particular laws, became framed either in terms of classic social theory, neo-Marxism or the new social history associated with E.P. Thompson. In all cases, 'crime' became no longer the taken-for-granted construct of positivism, but the object for political deconstruction.

(b) The Origins of Social Control Institutions The same applied to the broader revisionist history of social control structures and ideologies. The juvenile court, the prison, the mental hospital, therapeutic professions, alcohol and drug prohibition . . . and so on: all became subjected to historical scrutiny. Foucault changed the mode of analysis and feminism created a new agenda — but the political drift remains.

(c) Enforcement The importance of the political determinants of law enforcement became taken for granted. You do not have to be a 'critical' criminologist to study patterns of selection and discrimination in police discretion, sentencing or punishment. These are the standard subjects in even the deepest and least sociological backwaters of criminal justice studies or penology. The continued salience of class, race and gender has made the politics of criminal justice even more relevant. This is obvious to any viewer of the O.J. Simpson trial. Even journals like *Newsweek* publish descriptions of the contemporary American justice system as a class struggle, '. . . worthy of some banana republic where the rich often act with impunity and the authorities terrorize the peons at will' (Langbein 1995: 23).

3. *The Political Nature of Crime*

A third and far more complicated notion was the one that soon gave the whole enterprise of politicization a bad name. This was the attempt to rescue the criminal from the positivist assumptions of determinism and pathology. Crime became either the expression, symbol or equivalent of political resistance or the product of the political order of capitalism.

(a) The Criminal as Political Actor The short-lived notion of the criminal as rebel and crypto-political actor was seldom found in its pure form. This

was, however, an identifiable residue from the more anarchist and romantic cultures of the 1960s. A new form of essentialism appeared – an idealist inversion of positivist imagery.

At the extreme, were projections of the criminal as outlaw, hero and Robin Hood; the identification of prisons as incubators of revolution; the Marcusean and Fanonist celebration of liberatory violence. In a less extreme sense, crime and deviance came to be seen as more rational, meaningful and intentional than was allowed by 'agents of social control' or their academic servants. Conventional accounts were seen to mask and mystify the 'essentially' political meaning of the action.

So the new 'fully social' deviant emerged – busy stealing to redistribute private property; attacking the Protestant work ethic by getting stoned; sabotaging factory machines to reassert control over alienated labour; busy in new subcultural theory magically resolving the class contradictions of postwar Britain; busy on the football terraces protesting the transformation of community into commercial spectacle; busy destroying conventional sexual norms; even busy as schizophrenics in undermining the 'lethal gas chamber' of the family. As some of these more extreme versions were called: 'Homage to Catatonia'.

It is easy enough now to caricature these ideas – as I have – and note the absence of much supporting evidence of this political consciousness. It was understandable that later criminologists found these ideas embarrassing: for ignoring the suffering of victims and the particular vulnerability of women, the elderly, the poor and ethnic minorities.

It is unfortunate, however, that the denunciation of these romantic excesses has led to a lack of sensitivity to the political edge that 'ordinary' crime might either take or be attributed with – especially outside its familiar Western settings. The question of when crime can be seen as political remains as opaque as ever. We still have no satisfactory definitions of what is a political rather than an 'ordinary' crime, criminal, trial or prisoner. We therefore miss the theoretical and policy implications of these distinctions. And the matrix of four possibilities as originally constructed, remains:

At the level of the *phenomenon* itself: (i) 'politicization' means an historical change from normatively deviant to self-consciously political narratives (for example the transformation of homosexuality into gay liberation) while the opposite (ii) 'criminalization', means the use of traditional criminal tactics and styles in various forms of political marginality. At the level of *categorization* (social reaction): (iii) 'politicization' means the use of political labels and theories to explain criminal events and actors, while (iv) 'criminalization' ('depoliticization') means the re-allocation of political acts into criminal categories (for example, through terminology such as 'gangs', 'thugs', 'bandits', 'hooligans' or 'crazies').

I will expand later on some rather bizarre twists on this subject. Let me anticipate two:

Crime and politics 5

(i) The original counter-cultural project of endowing the deviant with choice and rationality did not lead very far. But the attack on liberal positivism from the right and the managerial centre succeeded in an astonishing way. Criminologists working for institutions like the Home Office, discovered – to use the title of a book by Ron Clark, one of the model's leading proponents – *The New Reasoning Criminal*. We now have the criminal as consumer and market actor – someone who not only has more rationality than the determined creatures of sociological enquiry, but has *nothing but* choice and rationality. Disembodied from all social context – deprivation, racism, urban dislocation, unemployment are airily listed as 'background factors' – they take their risks, assess their opportunities, have their targets hardened and stay away from others' defensible spaces.

(ii) The second unexpected twist is to find that the use of criminological language in the political realm (depoliticization) has to be taken more seriously. In some accounts of contemporary politics at least, this vocabulary cannot be dismissed as a mere ideological ploy to discredit oppositional forces, but as a credible way to capture certain social changes. I will be returning to these.

(b) Capitalism as criminogenic The causal theory of capitalism as criminogenic had a slightly longer shelf-life than the image of criminal as political hero. True, the original attempts to adapt traditional Marxist concepts to explain working-class property crime and violence have virtually disappeared. But in vocabulary only.

The conceptual base of left-liberal criminology in the USA (Currie 1985) and of left realism in Britain, remains similar. Their causal theory is a political version of the subcultural model and, most especially, the thesis of relative deprivation (Young 1994). The triumph of free-market economies, deepening socio-economic inequalities and – in the middle of this – the discovery of 'the new reasoning criminal', have all drawn attention to the criminogenic features of post-industrial societies (Taylor 1995). In post-communist countries, these corrosive effects have only just started.

Far from politics being removed by this latest round of the 'end-of-ideology', the lethal combination of free market dogma with law and order politics exposes the political dimension of ordinary crime far more clearly than the blurred mirror images of East–West, communism–capitalism, ever did.

4. Crimes of the Powerful: Extending the Definition of Crime

Potentially the most far-reaching of the original attempts to reconnect crime with politics was extending the definition of crime from its narrow legal base to include wider social harms, injuries and injustices. This attempt was encapsulated in the resonant 1960s notion of the 'crimes of the powerful'. Crime in the streets was a mystification; 'real' crime lay elsewhere, in the depredations committed by corporations and by the state.

This claim was only potentially, rather than actually, far-reaching. As I have argued elsewhere (Cohen 1993), early attempts to define the concept of state crime and link it to human rights violations failed because they were too woolly and polemical. In the most-cited version (Schwendinger and Schwendinger 1970), the criteria of social injury and human rights abuse were correctly invoked, but this led to a rhetorical coupling of obvious cases (such as genocide) with the injustices of 'economic exploitation', racism and sexism. Sutherland's famous question 'is white-collar crime, crime?' can be more persuasively translated into 'is state crime, crime?' if we stick to the terrain of formally recognized state violations of human rights.

We might still want to use the term 'crime' as a rhetorical device to describe all forms of institutionalized social injustice. As I will suggest later, though, there are serious problems in glibly applying the criminal law model to political conflict. The terrain of human rights violations offers clearer criteria for regarding genocide, mass political killing, torture and extra-judicial executions as criminal. These are illegalities defined by both domestic and international law. Terms like 'crimes against humanity' and 'war crime' have clear referents. There is an apparatus for enforcement and punishment, however weak in practice.

In any event, for whatever reasons – too vague an extension of 'crimes of the powerful' and also the perverse blindness of Anglo-American criminology about the rest of the world – this particular linkage between crime and politics all but disappeared. Instead of 'crimes of the state' criminologists returned to the familiar territory of 'the state of crime'. Now, external developments (the ascendance of human rights discourse) and internal changes (the pre-occupation with victims) have made the human rights linkage more visible. I will be returning to this subject.

5. *The Politics of Personal Life*

That other resonant 1960s slogan, 'the personal is political', was destined for a less interrupted life than the slogan 'crimes of the powerful'. Originating politically in the civil, gay and women's rights movements and theoretically in the loosely Reichian left-Freudianism of the times, this idea was meant to convey two somewhat different meanings. The first – less significant these days – was a politics of authenticity: personal life should be led in accordance with political convictions. The second – very much the dominant voice of current political and sexual correctness – was to transpose personal and private matters into the political and public realm.

The women's movement became the apotheosis of both these meanings. Gender, sexuality, reproduction, body language, and intimate relationships were politicized in both theoretical and practical terms. In

Crime and politics 7

the world of theory, this led to new ways of conceptualizing power, linking masculinity with violence and deconstructing the boundaries between public and private space. In the world of social control practise, this led to new laws or systems of enforcement dealing with male sexualized violence, discrimination, pornography, sexual harassment, speech codes, etc.

The astonishing growth of the victim movement is a logical extension of this strand. In one sense, this is a victory for C. Wright Mills's original vision of sociology as converting private troubles into public issues. In another sense, as I will suggest, the culture of victimization is a troubling defeat for traditional democratic politics.

II. CRIME IN POLITICAL DISCOURSE

The second part of my lecture reverses the search: looking not for the political dimensions of traditional criminological matters, but for the ways in which the question of crime runs through the substance and discourse of contemporary political life.

Some of these are obvious and beyond dispute. Others suggest transformations as yet unclear in how political conflicts occur and become understood. These blur the boundary between crime and politics in forms more paradoxical than criminologists ever imagined. And they might lead us to prefer – this will be my conclusion – the opposite direction: separating, rather than linking crime and politics.

1. Crime as a Political Issue

The first direction – already obvious thirty years ago and hardly open to dispute – is the embedding of the crime problem into political discourse. The perception of crime as a political threat and the emergence of distinctive political ideologies about crime (crudely, conservative and liberal) can, of course, be traced back to the nineteenth century.

It was not predictable in the 1960s, however, that the crime problem would so come to dominate the contemporary political rhetoric of Western democracies. I doubt that we have fully appreciated the reasons for the potency of law and order issues in election campaigns or the weight of criminal justice policy in the shaping of Thatcher's Britain and Reagan's America (as well as other European countries). Even its critics, or supposedly academic students, have to locate themselves in a new discourse of 'public order'. A British university, Leicester, now has a 'Centre for the Study of Public Order'. Alongside its M.A. in Criminology, this Centre offers an 'M.A. in Public Order' (*sic*) and an 'M.Sc in Security Management and Information Technology'. It lists its interests as 'riots and public disorder, crime and punishment, policing, crime prevention, race and ethnic relations and inner-city issues'. Public order issues are defined as '... the study of how order is sustained in societies as well as considering how and in what circumstances order can be threatened or destroyed'.[1]

Such political location of standard criminological subjects is now taken for granted. This raises many issues that each deserve its own lecture. Let me concentrate on those suggested by the constructionist triangle.

In the first of its corners, there is the actual incidence, severity and risk of criminal victimization. In the second, there is the public perception of the seriousness of the crime problem (crime is increasingly ranked a more important social problem than unemployment, health care, nuclear risk, environmental damage etc). And in the third, there is the rhetorical manipulation of the crime problem and public anxiety in media and political discourse.

What is the congruence between these three corners? Is this public discourse really 'about' crime or rather a metaphor for expressing a wider sense of social dislocation and disorder? The answers to these questions need grounding in particular phases of law and order politics, for example, postwar Britain (Downes and Morgan 1994). Note also the observation that the congruence in America of the Progressive Era between popular understanding, political reform and academic criminology, now no longer exists (Simon and Feeley 1995). For Britain and America, there can be little doubt that the new punitiveness – boot camps, death penalty, longer prison sentences, 'three strikes and you're out', the return of chain gangs – are not simply driven by an increase in crime. But how then to explain the new politics of law and order?

Away from Western democracies, the politics of crime have taken on other forms. The fear of violent and property crime in South Africa – both during and after apartheid – has always been very real as well as a code for political unease. In the former Soviet Union and the post-communist states of Eastern Europe, variants of street and organized crime have quickly been reconstructed as political problems. 'Western-style' crime – Mafia killings, protection rackets, street violence – is now at the centre of popular imagery of Russia. And political discourse is full of Western-style law and order talk. (The most popular pistol sold in a 'gun boutique' in Warsaw is called 'Miami' after the Miami Vice TV series.) There might be some media hype, but all serious accounts (Handelman 1994, Sterling 1994) suggest that the emerging crime problem is real enough.

And its political resonance is explicit. This is a statement from the Russian leadership after the Listyev killing in Moscow in March 1995

> A series of bandit actions and murders committed here ... have provoked the well-founded alarm of society. These crimes can be described as a manifestation of strengthening criminal terror, as a challenge to the course of democractic reform, to the establishment of a civil society. (Quoted from the *Guardian* and *Observer*)

Crime and politics 9

Remember that terms like 'banditry' and 'hooliganism' were precisely those used during the old regime to discredit legitimate political opposition.[2] Politics were criminalized; now crime is politicized.

In other parts of the world, the problems of crime, street violence and drugs, combined with police corruption and inefficiency have led to direct political intervention by the state's armed forces. In Brazil in 1994, for example, the military took over the shanty towns of Rio de Janiero from a totally corrupt local police which had lost control to drug-gangs. The 'urban guerilla warfare', described by Rio's Archbishop, referred not to political conflict, but the power of drug gangs to close shops, schools and election campaigns.

Under similar circumstances elsewhere – as I'll describe later – lawlessness and crime have so destroyed the social fabric that the state itself has withdrawn. Predictions are made that in parts of West Africa, private security businesses and, in the ex-communist world, urban mafias, will become better equipped than municipal police forces to grant physical protection to local inhabitants. A recent journalistic report on Mexico nicely describes the combination of a multitude of legal rules and the government's total inability to enforce them, as 'virtual legality' (DePalma 1995).

Even in more stable democracies, the political resonance of the old 'war on crime' metaphor has become stronger. Many large American cities are routinely described as 'ungovernable' as a result of violence, drugs and a breakdown of policing and social services. There is some exaggeration here – Western capitals are not quite plunged into total disorder[3] – but this rhetoric is now taken for granted. So too is the fusion of crime control policy into routine decisions about urban planning, design and architecture.[4]

Under these circumstances, the 'war against crime' is not just a metaphor, but describes the actual displacement of techniques and personnel from the military apparatus to domestic law enforcement. Part of the military-industrial complex is shifting to what Nils Christie calls the 'corrections-industrial complex' (Elvin 1994). The US National Institute of Justice 1995–1996 Research Plan calls for developing and sharing 'dual-use technologies for law enforcement agencies and military operations other than war' (National Institute of Justice 1995: 20). In June 1994 the Institute convened a conference entitled 'Law Enforcement Technology for the Twenty-First Century'. The conference's subtitle – 'The Less Than Lethal Alternative' – refers to the priority assigned to army chiefs and private corporations to develop non-lethal laser guns and other weapons of pacification.[5] Spin-offs from America's redundant 'Star Wars' satellite navigational system, originally designed as shield against nuclear missiles, are being used by various British police forces in the fight against crime (by tracking car movements to crime scenes).

All this does not mean that crime itself is seen as political in nature. Rather, that more political effort has been displaced onto the terrain of domestic disorder. To cite the *New York Times* (Weiner 1995): the cult of national security represented by the Soviet threat has given way to a cult of personal insecurity which links the hazards of predatory crime with other nameless risks (whether toxic waste, nerve gas in the subway, harmful food and obscurely motivated terrorism).

We need to understand how the mundane politics of crime control fits this wider discourse of order and security. Garland (forthcoming) gives a so-nuanced account about contemporary Britain. His starting point is that during the last 30 years, high crime rates have become a normal social fact. Despite its wholly uneven distribution, crime is accepted not as an aberration, but a routine part of consciousness, an everyday risk to be managed like air pollution and road traffic. There is little confidence in government capacity to 'solve' or 'fight' the problem. What Garland calls the 'crisis of penal modernism', lies in the perceived normality of high crime rates and the long obvious (to any honest criminologist, at least) limits of criminal justice agencies to do anything about this.

The result, he argues (Garland, forthcoming: 4), is an erosion of one of the foundational myths of modern society: that the sovereign state is capable of providing security, law and order and crime control. So new modes of governance develop, especially: (i) the increasing involvement of the private sector, notably in the selling of policing and security as commodities; (ii) the model of crime as a risk to be calculated (by offender and potential victim) or an accident to be avoided rather than a moral aberration needing special explanation; (iii) a 'supply side' policy which seeks to modify the routines of everyday life; (iv) making citizens responsible for crime (through publicity campaigns, self-help groups, volunteers and projects like Neighbourhood Watch and Crime Concern) and (v) the managerial ethos of 'performance indicators' which judge criminal justice agencies by self-referential measures that have nothing to do with reducing crime.

So, expectations are scaled down; the message is that crime control is beyond the state. But why then punitive rhetoric and the fact that the hard core of the traditional system – prisons – keeps expanding? Garland's answer is that at the same time as its administrative institutions have been devising their managerial strategies (with their limited aims of 'risk management'), so the political arm of the state swings into episodes of hysterical and populist denial of these very limitations. In the face of evidence that crime does not really respond to severe sentences or new police powers or greater use of imprisonment, governments still must appeal to the old law and order rhetoric. The short-term political costs of admitting the futility of these methods are unacceptable. So: the sudden and volatile shifts of political mood – responses to popular feelings of rage and frustration after a particularly disturbing crime, cynical manipulations of the symbols of government power, policies that deliberately increase prison populations.

The show of punitive force is used to repress any acknowledgement of

Crime and politics

the state's systemic inability to control crime. State sovereignty over crime is simultaneously denied (transferred to private security corporations or 'responsible citizens') and symbolically reasserted (Garland forthcoming: 19).

2. Corruption and Legitimacy

Political corruption is as old as political power. Yet the post-Watergate era has seen a quite unprecedented and uninterrupted series of public scandals about corrupt government in Western democracies. There might be little in common to diverse events such as Watergate itself and the Iran–Contra affair in the USA, the Scott Inquiry and regular exposure of government 'sleaze' in Britain or the *tangentopoli* scandals in Italy. In some cases, criminal activities (bribery, corruption, embezzlement, theft) were used for personal greed, in others for party political gain, in yet others to subvert basic legal and constitutional rules.

In all cases, though, public perception – aided by a more vigilant media – has raised new questions of legitimacy. This is more than the familiar sequence of muck-raking exposures followed by the cynical view that all politicians are crooked. There are new elements in episodes like the Iran–Contra affair and the official corruption which has totally reshaped Italian politics reverberating in a major corruption scandal even in the quiet democracy of Belgium and reaching the highest level of NATO. There are also allegations that the three-way tie-up between business, political parties and organized crime has stretched to a fourth corner – separatist and terrorist groups. The scale has also become more global. Bodies such as the OECD and the Geneva-based World Economic Forum – concerned by threats to the good name of the free market – are looking for new ways to police international corruption.

The Secretary-General of Interpol noted recently that it is becoming difficult to draw a clear line between what he called 'normal' political business corruption and hard core, organized crime activity. Rhetoric aside, the institutions of criminal justice are involved as never before in regulating public life.[6] Corruption, rather than 'state crime', has become the entry point of criminal justice into government.

3. International Criminal Organization

Here I come to the specific subject raised by the Le Carré quote.

The existence of international criminal organizations is again, not new in itself. And studies of the Mafia and the international drug market have long picked up allegations about government connections, for example, through security services such as the CIA. Standard concepts such as 'narco-terrorism' and new ones such as 'narco-diplomacy' (Griffith 1994) suggest yet other links between crime and politics.

We have not, however, even begun to comprehend the scope of these new transnational networks based on drug cartels, illegal arms dealing, money laundering and political manipulation. There is a worldwide movement of capital and goods uncontrolled and uncontrollable by sovereign states. Its criminal strands are obvious: after oil, the second largest international commodity traded in the world is drugs. In the ex-Soviet Union, illegal arms trading and direct involvement in the black economy have led to a 'criminalized military'. The concept of 'gangster capitalism' is now routine (Handelman 1994). President Yeltsin's comparison of the Dudayev regime in Chechnya to the Colombian Medellin drug cartel is doubly interesting: both for the use of this analogy – and for its proximity to the truth.

There is already a respectable literature on transnational law enforcement. But, not for the first time, journalists and novelists are way ahead of social scientists in depicting this world. Le Carré captures its two features: first, the criminal subversion of legitimate politics by international rackets immune from conventional law enforcement and second, the redeployment of intelligence services from Cold War operations to policing these forms of criminality.

The first feature – the operations themselves – is by definition less visible (coming to public attention only through events such as the BCCI collapse). It is virtually impossible to discover hard facts about all this and no doubt the security services have a vested interest in exaggerating the scale of these operations. But most evidence (Sterling 1994, Naylor 1995) suggests that something new is indeed happening. The second feature – the shift of resources from conventional political threats to crime control, from national security to domestic insecurity – is open knowledge and beyond dispute. Three examples:

(i) The Director General of MI5 in Britain makes regular public statements about the need to expand the agency's role into areas now the responsibility of the police. The agency wants new legislation to allow it to deal with drug-trafficking, money-laundering, computer-hacking, organized crime and even animal rights groups.

(ii) In Germany, new laws have already expanded the internal intelligence operations of the security service and transferred political strategies to domestic crime. In September 1994, the *Bundestag* created a new role for the German foreign secret service (BND) in the fight against serious crime such as terrorism, arms and drug trafficking. Standard legal restrictions on the police would not apply. The Interior Minister, Manfred Kanther, announced that these new laws were needed because the issue was '... no longer the protection of citizens against the "authoritarian state of the nineteenth century" but against "a parallel society of crime"' (quoted in *Fortress Europe* 1994: 2).

(iii) In post-communist countries, former state officials – including, and especially, the most discredited *apparatchniks* from the security services – now openly work for private security companies or sell arms on the commercial market.

Crime and politics 13

The spectre raised by security agencies is that the combination of vast profit, amorality and anachronistic law enforcement could lead to these criminal operations influencing international relations, creating dependencies of national economies and shaping the internal affairs of states or (especially) degenerated states.

Needless to say, all this is insignificant compared with traditional super-power, especially US, sponsorship of government terror in client states.

4. *Crimes of the State – Revisited*

With the collapse of the certainties of Marxism, liberal progressivism and the cold war, 'universal human rights' has become the only surviving meta-narrative. In the 'new world order', traditional conflicts between nations remain, but are increasingly overshadowed by internal state terror and ethnic, nationalist and religious conflicts resulting in atrocities of unimaginable proportions. Eric Hobsbawm (1994) has traced the chronology of today's 'barbarism' from the First World War onwards. He sees both a disruption of the moral rules through which societies regulate their internal social relations and a reversal of the Enlightenment project of finding universal rules.

How do we describe the events of Rwanda, Burundi, the former Yugoslavia, the Caucasus, Haiti, Colombia, Iraq, Somalia, Sudan, large sections of West Africa, Sri Lanka and elsewhere? The theological language of evil and the pictorial language of barbarism, horror and atrocity have been translated into the legalistic terminology of 'human rights violations'. This sounds blander – not 'thou shalt not kill' but 'thou shalt not violate the right to life according to Article 6, Paragraph 1 of the International Covenant' – but at least it offers some institutional safeguards, enforcement and the possibility of prevention.

These mechanisms have been traditionally applied to governments. The term 'human rights violations', though, is broader than 'crimes of the state', including the atrocities committed by armed oppositional groups and those resulting from the breakdown of government monopoly on violence.

Not that these divisions are always clear: the killing of street children and social undesirables in Brazil and Colombia, for example, may be the responsibility of drug barons, gangs, hired mercenaries or shadowy vigilante groups directly connected to the police or army. In Colombia in 1993, death squads of wayward police officers killed some 2,200 'disposables': abandoned street children living as petty thieves, prostitutes, addicts, beggars. Neighbourhood clean-up squads, often hired by local business for 'social cleansing', post notices inviting the community to join the funeral parade for dead delinquents.

Atrocities committed by states against their own citizens are as a matter of habit described as 'criminal'. Take the one example of political killings.

14 — *Stanley Cohen*

Over the last 20 years, millions of people have been murdered or 'disappeared' without trace – in Iraq, Sri lanka, Sudan, Uganda, Burundi, Chad, Indonesia, Guatemala, Peru, the Philippines etc. They were not the victims of war, but their own governments. Human rights reports are now routinely phrased in the language of crime and punishment. Terms such as 'licence to kill', 'murder' and 'serial killings' are used for dramatic effect (Amnesty International 1993).

While some causal theories such as 'crimes of obedience' (Kelman and Hamilton 1989) are helpful, the more interesting questions lie at the definitional level. Three examples:

(i) What is the moral enterprise behind the human rights movement? In simpler times, we used to study the old criminalization to uncover its political interests in middle-class morality and the protection of the interests of capital and the state. But the 'new criminalization' comes from progressive forces – feminism, the environmental movement, consumers, animal welfare, the human rights movement itself. The very social forces which in the 1960s were so critical of Leviathan – which argued for decriminalization – now take as their success the creation of new laws. Why has criminalization become the preferred model to protect liberal values? Routine reports from the United Nations human rights bureaucracy now talk about 'crimes of the powerful'. How have slogans about 'abuses of power' come from the radical margins of the 1960s into the political mainstream?

(ii) What is actually gained by reframing political events in the language of law and crime? In February 1995, at the 50th anniversary of liberation of Auschwitz, an official joint declaration described what happened as 'the greatest crime of the twentieth century'. In 1992, the United Nations Security Council, reacting to reports of the widespread rape of women in Bosnia, 'designated' systematic mass rape as a 'crime against humanity'.[7] What does this renaming imply? What are the implications of making denial of the Holocaust a criminal offence?

(iii) And how appropriate at all is the punitive law model for resolving these political conflicts and making governments responsible for their actions? This question is raised in two dramatic current examples. First, there is the 'justice in transition' debate (Cohen 1995): should societies going through democratization (e.g. South Africa, Eastern Europe, former juntas in Latin America) confront the human rights violations committed by the previous regime by putting individual perpetrators on trial? Second, there is the Tribunal now dealing with atrocities committed in the former Yugoslavia. Although there were precedents in the Nuremberg and Tokyo Tribunals, this is the first truly international criminal jurisdiction to reproduce all features of conventional criminal justice: codification of offences; provision of due process; a victim and witness unit; a 'Detention Unit' in the Hague for inmates. The Tribunal's first report – an extraordinary document – heralds the emergence of new

Crime and politics 15

ideal of individual responsibility in international humanitarian law; it refers to 'system criminality'; it describes its objective as the elimination of the 'root causes of international criminality . . . in the country concerned' (United Nations 1994).

The use of the concept of crime in cases like these is both instinctive and morally appealing. But it is by no means obvious that these mass political conflicts can be translated into the discourse of human rights violations, let alone the particular dialect of the criminal justice system.

5. The New Victimization

In those parts of the world racked by state terror, drug wars and ethnic, nationalist or religious conflict, political violence certainly creates far more victims than regular criminal violence. In more stable democracies, victims are being 'discovered' in somewhat different ways.

First, the same concept of human rights used to describe massive atrocities is applied to the more mundane burdens, deprivations and humiliations of everyday life. A twenty-two stone woman in Chicago sues a cinema for not providing a large enough seat as a 'violation of her human rights'; men who have been circumcised claim that their basic right to bodily integrity was violated at birth without their consent. (They have even formed a liberation movement, RECAP – Restore A Complete Penis.)

Second, the new criminalization has extended the cognitive and legal boundaries of victimization – for example, for women as objects of sexual harassment and children as objects of abuse.

Third, the psycho-therapeutic empire continues to expand its reach, creating new diagnostic categories of illness, personality disorders, eating disorders, learning disorders, dependency and other states. Not just 'repressed memory syndrome' but 'victims of false repressed memory syndrome'; not just 'dependency' but also 'co-dependency'; not just 'serial killer syndrome' but also 'women who love men who kill'.

Some commentators on what has become called the 'nation of victims' (Sykes 1992) or the 'culture of complaint' (Hughes 1993) are too sour and smug. But there are surely profound social consequences in this transfer of private suffering into organized social movements and into public exhibits (such as the confession on Oprah Winfrey and other TV talk shows). For victims, if not for deviants (as we thought in the 1960s), the personal has indeed become political. This culture of victimization emerges from identity politics: groups defining themselves only in terms of their claims to special identity and suffering. And this trend is given a spurious epistemological dignity by the ethic of multiculturalism.

The result of all this is to actually *subvert* the 'politics' that many of us still cling onto – a politics based on such old fashioned Enlightenment meta-narratives as common citizenship and universal rights.

16   *Stanley Cohen*

6. *The Criminalization of Political Conflict*

Our original critique of the depoliticization of the political was easy. Cases such as the psychiatric labelling of dissidents in the Soviet Union were blatant. So too was using the reductivist language of pathology, anomie, alienation or rebellion against paternal authority to discredit and explain away the anti-Vietnam war protest, the counter-culture or the student movement.

But developments over the last decade call for some revision of this critique. Forms of political conflict have emerged in which ideological conviction is no longer seen as central – and where 'criminological' explanations might indeed be relevant.

The most dramatic examples come from the current turmoil of nationalist conflicts and civil wars. For Hobsbawm, these conflicts are neither primarily ideological nor the re-emergence of primordial forces long suppressed by Communism or Western universalism. They are a response to a double collapse

> ... the collapse of political order as represented by functioning states – *any* effective state which stands watch against the descent into Hobbesian anarchy – and the crumbling of the old frameworks of social relations over a large part of the world – *any* framework which stands guard against Durkheimian anomie. (Hobsbawm 1994: 53)

The results are vividly illustrated in widely-discussed journalistic reports such as Kaplan's (1994) on countries (mainly in West Africa) where lawlessness and crime – not political rebellion or experiments with democracy – are the most significant features of a destroyed social fabric. Such reports are full of journalistic hype, but the surface patterns are not in dispute: disease, AIDS, overpopulation, scarcity of resources, refugee movements, erosion of government authority, renegade armies, private security companies, drug cartels. The prospect worse than a coup is 'an anarchic implosion of criminal violence' (Kaplan 1994: 49). Again – remember the 'Miami Vice' pistols sold in Warsaw – the iconography comes from American crime: the most violent slum in Abidjan is called 'Chicago'.

The military historian, Martin van Creveld, finds a transformation of war: for the Chetniks of Serbia, the 'technicals' in Somalia, the Tonton Macoutes in Haiti, war is not primarily fought by nation-states in the name of ideology. In these conditions, urban crime may

> ... develop into low intensity conflict by coalescing along racial, religious, social and political lines. ... Once the legal monopoly of armed force, long claimed by the state, is wrested out of its hands, existing distinctions between war and crime will break down. (van Creveld, quoted in Kaplan 1994: 74)

Crime and politics 17

Low intensity warfare runs into high intensity crime. For many people violence is indeed a form of liberation – close to what Fanon meant, but without the choice that he celebrated.

Who are these people? I deliberately take one description from Hobsbawm – precisely because it was his books on bandits and primitive rebels that were used twenty years ago to find the hidden politics of crime: banditry as 'primitive social protest'. Now observers like Hobsbawm are doing exactly the opposite: describing politics in criminological language. These protagonists make up

> ... a typical contemporary form of the 'dangerous classes,' namely deracinated young males between the ages of puberty and marriage, for whom no accepted or effective rules and limit of behaviour exist any longer: not even the accepted rules of violence in a traditional society of macho fighters. (Hobsbawm 1994: 53).

Recent descriptions by political journalists such as Terzani, Kapuscinski and Ignatieff all confirm this picture. 'Large portions of the former Yugoslavia', writes Ignatieff (1994: 28) '... are now ruled by figures that have not been seen in Europe since late medieval times: the warlord'. He describes the warlords of Serbia and Croatia variously as 'bandits', 'criminals' and 'serial killers' – wandering in a feudal landscape with their postmodern apparatus of carphones and exquisite personal weaponry (supplied, of course, by John Le Carré's villains).

Their followers – influenced by the worst refuse of Western pop culture and ancient hatreds – are described by Ignatieff in terms such as 'adolescent lust' and 'hoodlums'. Of course they are 'nationalists' but their convictions are uninteresting; 'they are technicians of violence rather than ideologues' (Ignatieff 1994: 30). Nationalism is a vocabulary of self-exoneration; atrocities are compelled by fate, paranoia and the tragic necessity of reprisal. There is no brutality which cannot be justified if the words 'nation', 'people', 'rights' and 'freedom' are used.

This explanation does not expunge political history – but places it in context. Nationalist violence offers young, marginalized, unemployable males – the old objects, remember, of criminological theory – an escape from the mediocrity and boredom of backward societies, dislocated by modernization. They assert their masculinity, entering a mythic realm of 'history', intoxicated by destruction and power. As the state monopoly on violence breaks down, the resulting chaos offers young men running the gun culture of checkpoints the chance, Ignatieff speculates, '... of entering an erotic paradise of the all-is-permitted' (Ignatieff 1994: 141).

Even away from the roadblocks, banditry and visible warfare of these parts of the world, similar theoretical contours are being noted. Germany, writes Ignatieff (1994: 10), '... is struggling to contain ethnic nationalism in its modern Western European form: the white racist youth gang.' He interviews a skinhead in Leipzig: 'If he were in Los Angeles or Liverpool, he would be just another teenage gang leader. The nightmare of the new

Germany is that its teenage gangs talk politics' (Ignatieff 1994: 63). But are attacks on foreigners by racist skinheads events that belong 'naturally' to politics and take on a criminal guise – or are they primarily locatable in criminological terms and only secondarily take on a political guise?

Of course this question makes no sense. Studies of racist skinhead groups in Germany (Schmidt 1993) rightly deal both with ideology (racist beliefs, links with organized neo-Nazis) and the subculture of violence, male chauvinism and cruel entertainment of dislocated young men. The same applies to equivalent groups elsewhere. To explain the rioting of English football hooligans in Dublin in February 1995, how much weight should be assigned to traditional models of delinquency – and how much to the youths' racism, their connections with fascist groups (such as the shadowy Combat 17) and their chants of 'no surrender to the IRA'?

Or, to take contemporary terrorism, a subject I have not even touched on, when does ideology shade into pathology? One month's media commentary on four events in early 1995 – the Oklahoma bombing, an ETA bombing in Barcelona, Hamas suicide bombings in Gaza and the Tokyo underground gassing – consisted entirely of variants of the question: how much is criminal, how much is political?

These questions of course make no sense. But others must be posed which do not rely on the touching conception of political ideology that informed the culture of the 1960s: voluntaristic personal conversions, rational choices, wholly disembodied from the social. There is no 'end of ideology'. And observers such as Hobsbawm and Ignatieff may underestimate the power of ideology because of their understandable lack of sympathy for ethnic nationalism and religious fundamentalism. But they are not guilty of stigmatic 'criminalization'. For grasping today's political barbarism, the language of the sociology of crime may be uncomfortably more useful than we would like to think. (And in neither language are there too many rational free market actors.)

CONCLUSION

It would be banal to conclude merely that the boundaries between crime and politics are now more complex than criminologists imagined thirty years ago. The question is what do we make of this complexity?

One answer is suggested by the deconstructionist and post-modernist theories that have so seduced the intellectual avant-garde over this period. For them, 'crime' and 'politics' are always to be placed in inverted commas, to be seen not as terms depicting any identifiable object but as free-floating signifiers, capable of an infinite transferability from one realm to the other. All we can study is the construction of discourses about crime and politics.

This solution is aesthetically appealing – and can be carried quite far, far enough perhaps to make my two lists redundant or interchangeable. It leaves little room, though, to understand the substance of those shifts I have listed, such as the politicization of street crime and criminalization of certain forms of political action.

And it leaves any normative, value, questions even further from reach. In analytical terms, the original enterprise of looking for the links between crime and politics was justified. But do we really want a social order where there is no distinction between the two?

The atrocities that have become daily life in so many parts of the world are an appalling expression of *precisely* the obliteration of any distinction between political dispute and criminal violence. For these countries, the remote prospect of democracy lies in a radical *separation* between crime and politics. This is one way of expressing the ideal of civil society.

And in our own more prosperous and stable democracies, although the stakes are usually lower – 'identity' rather than life or death – more of a separation between public and private lives might also be desirable. Why should 'self-understanding', 'identity' and 'meaning' even *be* public issues? Habermas is right: the state is not a religion and so it has not to give meaning and identity to the citizenry by means of nationalism and patriotism (nor, I would add, by anything else). And the cult of 'the personal is political' – outings, intrusions into privacy, the moral Olympic games between competitors claiming superior status for *their* particular psychic suffering and victimization . . . all this is not really a very promising basis for any public debate about democracy and social justice.

We were right to follow Matza's injunction not to separate the study of crime from 'the workings and theory of the state'. But a world in which politics and crime become indistinguishable is something else.

Stanley Cohen

NOTES

* Centenary Public Lecture in Law and Society, London School of Economics and Political Science, 9 May 1995. I am indebted to the Departments of Law and Sociology for their invitation and to Nils Christie, Ann Peters and Jim Sheptycki for useful references. Another version of this lecture will appear (in German) in Trutz von Trotha (ed.) *Power and The Discourse on Crime: Festschrift for Fritz Sack*.

1. I quote from the Centre's glossy pamphlet which also boasts of its close ties with corporations and the private security industry (Centre for the Study of Public Order 1994).

2. Note, though, that the boundaries between crime and politics during communism were rather complex. As Foucault comments, the Soviet definition as non-political precisely those acts which the rest of world considered political was '. . . at once logical and bizarre' (Foucault 1989: 122). To define criminality in purely political terms – obliterating the distinction between political and non-political offences – would, at first sight, have been more logical.

3. Though one journalist saw the 1994 declaration of a State of Emergency by the Mayor of Washington DC as an appropriate strategy for 'a pocket of the Third World dropped into the United States: ... a one-party state, plagued by daily gun violence, racial tension and financial chaos' (Freedland 1994).

4. Mike Davis's supposedly 'apocalyptic' vision of Los Angeles consists of well-documented evidence of the political power of crime control agencies in major urban planning decisions (Davis 1990).

5. For details on the development of non-lethal laser technology by ARPA (the Pentagon's Advanced Research Projects Agency) for domestic law enforcement, see Kiernan (1994). The aim is for weapons that would 'expand the spectrum between guns and personal persuasion'.

6. For a condensed review of government corruption and judicial intervention during the fifteen years of Conservative rule in Britain, see Gearty (1995).

7. The lack of similar reaction to the mass rape of thousands of women in Burundi in 1994, mainly by Tutsi militia, is a classic episode in the 'politics of ethnic amnesia'.

BIBLIOGRAPHY

Amnesty International, 1993 *Getting Away With Murder: Political Killings and 'Disappearances' in the 1990s.* London: Amnesty International.
Centre for the Study of Public Order 1994 'Current Activities', University of Leicester.
Cohen, Stanley 1993 'Human Rights and Crimes of the State: The Culture of Denial', *Australia and New Zealand Journal of Criminology* 26: 97–115.
Cohen, Stanley 1995 'State Crimes of Previous Regimes: Knowledge, Accountability and the Policing of the Past', *Law and Social Inquiry* 20(1): 7–50.
Currie, Elliot 1985 *Confronting Crime*, New York: Pantheon.
Davis, Mike 1990 *City of Quartz: Excavating the Future in Los Angeles*, London: Vintage.
De Palma, Anthony 1995 'Mexico Lives By Virtual Law', *New York Times*, 26 March: 4.
Downes, David and Morgan, Rod 1994 'Hostages to Fortune: The Politics of Law and Order in Post-War Britain', in M. Maguire et al. (eds) *Oxford Handbook of Criminology*, Oxford: Oxford University Press.
Elvin, Jan 1994 'Corrections-Industrial Complex Expands in the US', *National Prison Project Journal* 10(1): 1–5.
Fortress Europe 1994 'Germany: New Law on "Fight Against Crime"' 28 (October): 1–4.
Foucault, Michel 1989 'The Politics of Soviet Crime', in *Foucault Live: Interviews, 1966–1984*, New York: Semiotext.
Freedland, Jonathan 1994 'DC goes down the fiscal WC', *The Guardian*, 2 February.
Garland, D. (forthcoming) 'The limits of the sovereign state: strategies of crime control in contemporary society', *British Journal of Criminology*. (Page numbers refer to ms.)
Gearty, Conor 1995 'The Party in Government', *London Review of Books* 17 (9 March): 15–18.
Griffith, I. L. 1994 'From Cold War Geopolitics to post-Cold War Geonarcotics', *International Journal, Canadian Institute of International Affairs* XLIX (1): 1–36.
Handelman, Stephen 1994 *Comrade Criminal: The Theft of the Second Russian Revolution*, London: Joseph.
Hobsbawm, Eric 1994 'Barbarism: A User's Guide', *New Left Review* 206: 44–54.
Hughes, Robert 1993 *The Culture of Complaint*, New York: Oxford University Press.
Ignatieff, Michael 1994 *Blood and Belonging: Journeys into the New Nationalism*, London: Vintage.
Kaplan, Robert 1994 'The Coming Anarchy', *Atlantic Monthly* February: 44–76.
Kelman, Herbert C. and Hamilton, V. Lee 1989 *Crimes of Obedience*, New Haven: Yale University Press.
Kiernan, Vincent 1994 'Lasers seen as an aid to law enforcement', *Laser Focus World* September: 49–50.
Langbein, John H. 1995 'Money Talks, Clients Walk', *Newsweek* 17 (April): 21–2.

Crime and politics 21

Le Carré, John 1994 *The Night Manager*, London: Hodder and Stoughton.

Matza, David 1969 *Becoming Deviant*, Englewood Cliff, NJ: Prentice Hall.

National Institute of Justice 1995 *NIJ Research Plan, 1995–6*, Washington DC: US Department of Justice.

Naylor, R. T. 1995 'Loose cannons: Covert Commerce and underground finance in the modern arms black market', *Crime, Law and Social Change* 22(1): 1–57.

Schmidt, Michael 1993 *The New Reich: Violent Extremism in Unified Germany and Beyond*, New York: Pantheon.

Schwendinger, Herman and Schwendinger, Julia 1970 'Defenders of Order or Guardians of Human Rights?' *Issues in Criminology* 7: 72–81.

Simon, Jonathan and Feeley, Malcolm 1995 'True Crime: The New Penology and Public Discourse on Crime', in T. Blomberg and S. Cohen (eds) *Punishment and Social Control*, New York: Aldine de Gruyter.

Sterling, Clare 1994 *Crime Without Frontiers: The Worldwide Expansion of Organized Crime and the Pax Mafiosa*, London: Little Brown.

Sykes, Charles 1992 *A Nation of Victims*, New York: St. Martins Press.

Taylor, Ian 1995 'Critical Criminology and the Free Market: Issues in Social Life and Everyday Crime', in M. Levi et al. (eds) *Contempoary Developments in Criminology*, Cardiff: University of Wales.

Young, Jock 1994 'Incessant Chatter: Recent Paradigms in Criminology', in M. Maguire et al. (eds) *Oxford Handbook of Criminology*, Oxford: Oxford University Press.

United Nations 1994 General Assembly Security Council 'Report of the International Tribunal for the Prosecution of Persons Responsible for Serious Violations of International Humanitarian Law Committed in the Territory of the Former Yugoslavia since 1991', New York, 29 August 1994 (A/49/342/S/1994/1007).

Weiner, Tim 1995 'Fear Itself', *New York Times*, 26 March: 1–3.

[18]
Conference Life: The Rough Guide

There are thousands of journals, there are faxes, satellites, modems, electronic mail, and data retrieval systems. There are Bit-Nets, E-Nets and Inter-Nets. But despite all this new technology, the old fashioned conference—a meeting between live human beings—still endures as the major form of academic communication. All over the world, summer or winter, in hotels or campuses, academics in every discipline gather together for these ritual occasions.

Despite the dominance of this ritual in the rhythm of academic life—the preliminary announcement, pre-registration, getting on the program, sending your abstract, making apologies to your family, arranging your airline ticket, writing your paper, managing the five intense days themselves, the long existential hangover afterwards—the subject has not received any sustained sociological attention.[1] Not even in the agonizing self-referentiality of post modernism has the conference—that quintessential institution of self-reflection—been reflected upon.

This article is a preliminary attempt to identify some features of conference life that merit further study. My data derive mainly from conferences in the social sciences—sociology, criminology, anthropology, psychology—as well as social work and law. Criminology conferences supply my main data-set. As long as governments, foundations and research councils retain their touching faith that the crime problem can be solved by getting people together in hotels to talk about it, these will be rich sources for replication research. I believe, however, that my findings and organizing typology would be applicable to most academic disciplines.

These findings are presented in the form of a guide—using "guide" both in the analytical and normative sense. No one believes anymore that observations

---

First published in Volume 1, 1995, of *The Scottish Journal of Criminal Justice Studies*, the Journal of the Scottish Association for the Study of Delinquency. The editor of *The American Sociologist* wishes to thank Susan Silbey for referring him to this article.

are uncontaminated by the interests of the observer. So, this is like a tourist guide: what is there to be seen ("reality") and how to extract the maximum benefits from the experience.

Following the standard sociological distinction, we might divide "benefit" into its expressive and instrumental dimensions. The conference has two main expressive functions. First, there is the social need for regular gatherings to meet old friends, colleagues, students, research assistants, teachers and lovers—as well as find new ones. Second, there is the purely individual pleasures of travel, good hotels, gourmet food, exotic tourist sights and being away from family and work commitments. Then there are two instrumental functions. The first is to advance your academic career—by listing your conference participation on your *curriculum vitae* or by impressing the powerful by your sheer intellectual brilliance or by actively hustling a job or a publisher's contract. A second instrumental function—advancing intellectual knowledge—needs theoretical reference to complete this typology but in practise plays no part in conference life. I will not refer to this function again.

These functions, needless to say, do not always correlate with each other. There are some extremely enjoyable conferences—an empty program, good food and wine, wonderful beaches, ready access to cheap local drugs—which are of little value on your resume. Alternatively, there are highly select gatherings, filled with powerful and famous patrons, but subject to unspeakable personal discomfort in deserted mountain lodges.

No guide, however comprehensive, can cater to every conference-goer's every need and desire. The following list, arranged in roughly chronological order, presents an introduction to help the newcomer and, hopefully, to stimulate seasoned travellers to further research.

Title

The title of the conference—its name, subject, disciplinary identity, scope, auspices, organizing body, funding agency—is the very first consideration. A simple title, a few words here or there, offers an immediate and often bewildering introduction to the interacting variables of hedonism, interest and career-value. The complexity of this choice can be set out in a six-point typology. Superficially, we might see this as a scale of roughly ascending value—but the title is an open discursive text whose meaning is infinitely negotiable.

(i) Usually of the lowest value, is a title which is closest to your actual field of interest and scholarship. These conferences might be of high intellectual content, but often extremely low in hedonism (no "free time" at all on the program) and of indifferent career value. If the subject is too specific—"Mobility Patterns of Female Turkish Migrant Workers in the Common Market: 1980-1990"— you will be accused of being a mere "specialist" and moreover suspected of inviting yourself to the occasion. In the natural sciences, the specialized workshop—the only twelve people in the world who even understand the subject— is of very high status and desirability. In the social sciences however, this type of "expertise" hardly exists and is anyway regarded with contempt.

(ii) Of better all round value, is the standard annual conference of your national disciplinary association. Something like the American Sociological Association or its equivalent is always a safe bet. These occasions, though, are often dull and repetitive. And as they become larger—especially by the acceptance of every submitted paper to allow participants to receive their travel expenses—they lose whatever pretense they might have had to academic elitism. But for each three of our important conference functions, these occasions can do no harm. And their predictable cyclical appearance in the academic year gives them the highest rating of all for renewal of friendships and other social functions.

(iii) Far more desirable in the era of globalization, is an international conference in your particular discipline, especially if this is held in an exotic place (see below: "Location"). The defects—hours in airport transit corridors, simultaneous translation, official openings addressed by mayors, unpredictable standards of accommodation—are usually compensated by other career and hedonistic advantages. But choices must be made carefully: otherwise an entire week of your life might be wiped out for the sake of one dubious entry on your *curriculum vitae*.

(iv) Career prospects are far more safely enhanced by an international conference which is right outside your disciplinary area. For a sociologist, say, to be invited to an international congress in law, philosophy or medicine is an excellent achievement, almost worth the cost of being cut off from your peer group and being subject to sneering condescension by academics from the higher status discipline. There is also a risk, as with all valuable commodities, of overplaying this choice by being suspected of being unacceptable in your own discipline. This is especially dangerous if the conference subject is of lower ranking than your own. A prominent philosopher, for example, has little to gain at a social work conference.

(v) Even more valuable is a conference—national or international—under what might be called a "transcendental" title—that is, not tied to any subject, discipline or professional association at all. With the current fragmentation of disciplinary identities, these gatherings are becoming more frequent and very easy to be invited to. The more abstract and meaningless the title, the better: terms like "Globalism," "Meta-narrative," "Post-Modernism," "Discourse," "New World Order," "Phallocentrism" and "Hyper-reality" are particularly suitable, either separately or randomly combined. An invitation to a conference of this type which is also set in an exotic location, should not be missed, for example "Deconstructing the North and South," Dakar, July 1996.

(vi) The ultimate invitation, however—the nirvana for all serious conference goers—is to a gathering which has no subject at all. The elite of the world's intelligentsia are important for their ontological existence rather than their interest or competence. These select gatherings are identified just by the name of a place. Thus: "The Salzberg Seminar," "The Jerusalem Dialogue," or "The Prague Forum."

Description

Closely related to the title and subject of the conference is the word chosen to describe the occasion. "Conference," "Congress" and "Meeting" are the most conventional. (The plural "meetings" is—most bizarrely—used by North American academics as a generic to describe any gathering, even a single conference.) Other permutations include "Workshop," "Seminar," "Colloquium" "Forum" and "Symposium." Again, the vaguer the term, the better—with "Dialogue" scoring well above all competitors.[2]

Location

Of equal importance to the question of the conference's title, subject and scope, is the crucial matter of its location. Like choosing the site for the next Olympic games, there is fierce competition between the cities of the globe for staging prestigious international conferences. Preliminary announcements about conferences seem now to be written entirely by tourist agencies.

As suggested above, purely local or national conferences have low status ranking and are less likely to have much hedonistic value. This is especially true when they take place in your own home town. In this event you are likely to find yourself on the Local Organizing Committee—an awful fate which no serious academic should have to face more than once during her or his career (see below: "Role").

Although international conferences are consistently and intrinsically desirable, the exact location offers perplexing dilemmas. The exotic/desirability quotient changes with history, political correctness and fashion. Personal safety has also become a consideration.

Up till the end of the Nineteen Eighties, for example, the Soviet Union and Eastern Europe were always reasonably good choices. The spartan living conditions of Warsaw, Prague, Budapest or Moscow were more than balanced by their esoteric distance and aura of excitement. A specially potent technique was to hint vaguely that your presence at the conference was a cover for supporting the dissident movement. Now, with the collapse of Communism, these cities are becoming more comfortable—but losing some of their dramatic allure. While Moscow and Prague might be shedding special glamour, some of their esoteric quality has now passed to more obscure parts of dismantled Soviet Empire. Kiev, Odessa and Vilnius are excellent choices (though close proximity to Chernobyl is a problem). You should also read the political map very well—or else you might find your hotel room taken over by army snipers.

There are other places which used to be exotic but never politically correct—in particular, various Latin American dictatorships and military juntas. With the transition to democratic regimes, cities like Santiago, Buenos Aires and Rio are now appearing on the conference map. Places like Lima and Bogota are problematic, especially for conferences on narco-terrorism.

The more obscure parts of the Third World remain exotic choices. Dakar,

Manila and Tangier always sound good. Many such locations, however, present some obvious dangers. The best of workshops can be spoilt by armed bandits on the road from the airport, AIDS, drug-war killings, mafia-type kidnappings, malaria and dysentery. Conferences on subjects like poverty, famine and pollution cannot be gracefully attended in countries suffering from poverty, famine and pollution. Since the Salman Rushdie affair, conferences in almost any part of the Islamic world are considered in bad taste.

Some excellent new locations have recently opened up, particularly Johannesburg, Cape Town or anywhere in South Africa. The lifting of the academic boycott offers a unique combination: a long travelling distance, the hint of political commitment (helping to end apartheid), excellent beaches, good wine and an altogether comfortable standard of living.[3]

Traditional cosmopolitan cities—London, Amsterdam, Paris, New York, Barcelona—all remain safe choices. Note, however (see below "Accommodation") that a special warning applies to all locations in Great Britain.

When in doubt, apply one simple criterion, more important even than romantic allure and political correctness: that there will always be something to do, to eat or to see which is more attractive than attending the conference itself.

Accommodation

Smaller conferences give no choice of accommodation. You stay wherever the sessions take place: hotel, villa, ski-lodge, monastery, hostel, theme-park, weekend retreat or university guest house.

Larger conferences, however, present major decisions—often at the reservation stage, months before the event and well before full information is available. Questions of cost, comfort, ostentatiousness and distance from the conference center, present a complex matrix of variables. The safest choice is to stay at whatever hotel the conference is being held, usually a Hilton. This is always convenient for sleeping and social interaction. Other alternatives might leave you stranded next to a noisy sports arena, brothel, airport or railway station or in a distant suburb completely subject to the whims of crooked taxi drivers.

Under no circumstances—except total penury—should you accept "shared accommodation." There is nothing more debilitating than returning to your hotel after a heavy day of discourse and finding your room smelling of tobacco smoke, with cheeseburger remains on the table, beer bottles all over the floor and the other bed occupied by your Bulgarian sociologist room-mate with a 18-year-old local whom he/she has just picked up.

The highest status option, specifically recommended in the Third World or Eastern Europe, is to stay in "Government House" or in your country's Embassy. This accommodation is reserved for the elite of international conference goers. A Canadian visitor, say, intending to travel to a conference in Lagos, should make contact with her Foreign Ministry and arrange to be a guest in the local Embassy.

A special warning about academic conferences held in Great Britain (and some parts of the Commonwealth, such as Australia). Invariably, these conferences take place on university campuses—either in student halls of residence of in "university conference centers" (which is what student halls of residence are called during vacation). The standard of accommodation here ranges from the sordid to the merely ascetic. Rooms are claustrophobically small, beds are too hard or too soft, there is no telephone or television in the room, nor—unbelievably to academics from anywhere else in the world—do you have your own attached bathroom. Toilet facilities and showers have to be shared—often with eight to ten other conference goers. Meals are eaten in canteens or "refectories" which offer no choice at all. (The compulsory breakfast—sweetened tea, two coagulated fried eggs, strips of undercooked greasy bacon, a massive pork sausage, tinned baked beans and three slices of buttered white bread—contain more cholesterol and artificial additives than most health conscious academics consume in an entire semester.)

It is no exaggeration that the average British student accommodation is less comfortable than many prison cells in the U.S.A. or Scandinavia. Unless the conference subject is compelling or the prestige ranking very high (for example, a conference at Oxford or Cambridge) these places should be avoided.

Frequency of Attendance

A certain prestige and reputation for being an eccentric loner is reserved for those academics who refuse all invitations to give papers and never attend conferences at all. The implication is that you are too busy thinking to enter the hustle and bustle of conference life. Unless you already have high transcendental status though, this is a risky game. It might lead to your marginalization and reputation for being arrogant and elitist. And if you are low status and totally unknown, you will remain low status and totally unknown.

There is a clear danger, on the other hand, of going to too many conferences, accepting all invitations. At the extreme (see below: "Psychopathology"), you may become a totally dependent conference junkie. There are some unfortunate souls—well-known figures of contempt on the circuit—who wander the world from conference to conference, with literally no other existence. When not actually at the conference, they spend the rest of their lives scouring bulletins and announcements, writing to offer papers, sending abstracts and even organizing their own conferences.

A reasonable working rule is not to spend more than a thirtieth of your life—an average of one day a month each year—attending conferences.

Being There

The concept of being "on the program" has been refined, reified and fetishized. Only by being on the future program, can you today receive your travel grant and conference expenses. Only by being on the past program can you list this conference participation on your *curriculum vitae* tomorrow.

Your appearance on the program, however, does not—as naive outsiders might assume—actually mean that you are physically present at the conference, still less that you have given your "listed" paper. The program is a text and the concept of "on" has to be severely deconstructed. There are four modes of ontological relationship between being "on" a conference program and being "at" the conference.

The first and most obvious mode, is that you appear on the program—for example, as giving a paper—and you are actually there, in the right city, in the right room, at the right time, and deliver your announced contribution. This mode, though "obvious," is empirically rare and reserved only for the most inexperienced beginners.

The second mode is to be physically there but not to be on the program, nor even to appear in the list of participants. This is an extremely effective technique for high status players. It is obvious that their very presence is what matters and that they are too important to be bothered with the formalities of registration. This is a dangerous game, however, for low status players. For them, it merely reinforces their low status (they were never invited or their papers were rejected) or incompetence (lack of pre-planning or inability to pay the registration fee).

A third ontological mode is to be on the program but not to be there. This is by far the most desirable option of all. It gives you good publicity and name-recognition, it generates expectations ("Will he show up this time?") and creates the aura that you are so incredibly busy and in demand that you have other more important commitments. You also avoid the messy business of airports, the wrong kind of bed and boredom. Above all, your work can never be exposed to any criticism. If used too often, however, this technique can lead to a spoiled identity ("No use inviting her, she never shows up.")

The fourth logical mode—being neither on the program nor being there—offers unknown possibilities that call for further research.

Role

The highest academic status is reserved for the role of opening plenary session address. Other "keynote addresses" are also desirable. A closing address or closing plenary session presents problems if you actually want to say anything: by the last day most participants have drifted home, or are too hung-over and exhausted to pay any attention to the proceedings.

Next in status is the standard lecture, talk, paper or presentation. These can appear in a bewildering variety of permutations, their distinctions known only to a elite cabal of conference organizers. There are special sessions, parallel sessions, thematic sessions, plenary sessions and special plenary sessions; workshops, professional workshops and teaching workshops; seminars, didactic seminars and scholar-to-scholar seminars; roundtables, informal roundtables and breakfast roundtables; panels, open panels and closed panels. Then there are "special poster display presentation sessions." My attention has also been drawn to something called a "Brown Bag Question and Answer Session." Recent years have seen the emergence of new genre, "Author Meets Critics"—a very high status occasion for the author, medium status for critics.

Of somewhat uncertain status, are various other roles such as commentator, discussant, summarizer, rapporteur, chairperson or convener. These roles carry the considerable advantage of being on the program without actually having to prepare anything in advance or do any serious work at all. A disadvantage lies in the impossible demand placed on you to present a coherent discussion of ten completely unconnected papers in five minutes. A role carrying even more extraordinary demands—for some reason, a feature of international criminology conferences or any gathering organized by bodies such as UNESCO or the Council of Europe—is that of "General Rapporteur." You are requested to appear at the Closing Session to summarise the "findings" of the entire five day conference at which some six hundred papers were given in one hundred sessions.[4]

Far worse than being a General Rapporteur is to be on the organizing committee, or the local organizing committee. In advance of the conference, this involves a considerable amount of thankless administrative work, often over a period of years. There are the complex logistics of planning the academic program itself as well as accommodation, catering and transport. You also have to cope with the inflated egos of your "big names" and the special (and often bizarre) demands of just about all your participants. People will request an airport pickup at 3:00 A.M.; the provision of kosher, halal, vegan, low-fat or no-sodium meals; exercise bicycles in their hotel rooms; photocopying in the middle of the night; a high-density mega-sized TV screen for their presentation; or special facilities for their pet dogs.

During the conference itself, you will be subject to endless complaints, demands and whining, especially from those participants who slide into the common conference pattern of childlike dependency and helplessness (see below: "Psychopathology"). You will be asked, over and over, why Panel Session 275 has been moved from the Blue Room at 8:00 A.M. to the Red Room at 8:00 P.M.; you will be told that the hot water does not come out fast enough from the shower; and you will be expected to provide medical treatment for gastric infections, mosquito bites or drug over-doses. You will be bitterly blamed for whatever goes wrong, and you will never be thanked except in the formal closing speeches. Forget it.

Being a Sponsor or on the International Advisory Committee is absolutely safe. The prestige is quite high and the task involves no work at all.

Presentation

In considering how papers are actually presented at conferences, my discussion leaves the realm of the normative and has nothing to do with status, enjoyment, prestige or self-presentation. The issues here are purely technical.

The simple truth is that the standards of presenting papers are so low as to be beyond criticism. It is almost impossible to believe that people who make their living from communication—writing, teaching, supervising, counselling, participating in committee discussions—can have so little idea how to communicate anything. Papers are conventionally presented in what might be called the "conference mumble"—head slightly bowed, body crouched, voice projected inwards, eyes never leaving the paper, the text is rapidly read out, word for word. The same style is followed even if (or especially if) the paper was distributed long in advance and the audience has the written text in front of them. The presentation is visibly autistic; no attention is paid to the audience.

Very few people have the slightest idea how to summarize or pick out the highlights of their own work. Even if they assure you that they spent the entire night before the session getting their presentation "ready," they seem to have no clue about the difference between writing a standard journal-length article and giving a twenty minute talk to a live audience. Invariably, they will use the first ten to fifteen minutes in thanking the chairperson and then reading the "Introduction," which usually consists of a plodding review of the literature. They are then completely astonished—as if they existed in a timeless void (an impression, admittedly, easily induced by conference life)—to discover that they have only five minutes left and have just reached page eight of a forty page text. At this point, the chairperson starts nudging them, looking at the clock or passing notes "ONLY THREE MINUTES MORE PLEASE." Other panelists give dirty looks because their time is being eaten away. By the time this stage is reached, the speaker is hopelessly adrift and can only mumble something about the "full" paper being available at the registration desk.

Some other speakers have a better sense of time, audience and advance planning. They talk clearly and audibly; they stick rigorously to the time limit. But, bewilderingly, they deliberately decide to edit out the most important part of the presentation. A promising sounding paper attracting a large audience—"At Last: A Drug-Abuse Treatment Program that Works"—consists of twenty eloquent minutes devoted to criticizing everyone else's work and then explaining how you got involved in the project, how the research is connected to the subject of the conference and why no one will give you any more funding. This exegesis is concluded with a laconic announcement that you will skip "the actual findings."

There is little more to be said on this sad subject.

Audio-visual Aids

A range of simple technical aids offers the possibility of actually making the presentation interesting—or at least comprehensive. These gadgets have become standard on the conference circuit. Talks are accompanied by tape recordings (ethnomethodological transcripts of patients making telephone appointments with their dentists); overhead projections (tables, graphs, flow charts); slides (artistically blurred shots of vandalized housing estates) or video recordings (hour-long testimonies of distraught victims of AIDS, incest, mugging, child abuse and rape).

If you are working on your home territory, these techniques can be useful enough. At conferences, however—especially international conferences in technologically retarded parts of the world—they should be avoided. The voltage is wrong; tape recorders break down; video sets show VHS rather than BETA; overheads are projected onto dark furled curtains in a sunny room and are either minutely reduced or grotesquely overblown.

Translation

The standard of simultaneous translation at most international academic conferences is appalling. Hours of listening to your headphones will only yield sentences like: "The research we made in the eastern zone confirms... the general organization disposition... taking the findings... um... in devolutionary order of the first population."

If the speaker is using cosmopolitan alternatives to English such as French, Spanish or German, you are advised to dispense with the headphones and pretend you understand. This looks good—and the sound simply flows over you and can be very restful. For talks in Hungarian, Finnish or Turkish, a good recent technique is to plug the conference headphones into a Walkman and listen to Schubert.

Name Tags

Name tags provide a classic example of the rich textual potential of an apparently simple device. The signifier becomes the signified.

Unfortunately, you are usually dependent on the tag prepared by the conference organizers. This gives little room for the manipulation of signs. If the information written on the label is too specific and detailed, and you cannot rewrite it yourself, you should not wear the tag at all. For a high status participant, recognizable by face, body language or profile, this type of detailed information is anyway redundant. For a low status participant, it depresses your status even more, for example: "Ronald Macdonald, Temporary (One Year) Assistant Professor, Department of Criminal Justice Studies, Western Anaheim State University." Compare this to the more concise: "Chomsky, M.I.T."

Reading someone else's name-tag can also be a problem. Assume that you follow the sequences of (a) first, looking at the persons face, second, scanning the name-tag, and third, walking away or (b) scanning the name-tag, looking at the face, and walking away. Neither sequence makes clear whether you are using a polite and legitimate technique to locate someone whom you have arranged to meet (but don't know what he or she looks like)—or whether this is a rather gross style of cruising around until you find someone important enough to engage in conversation.

All these ambiguities can be avoided by simple not wearing or looking at tags.

Demeanor

Goffman's general advice on impression management is particularly well suited to the conference setting. Various forms of role distance are easily employed. The most desirable demeanor to convey is studied situational indifference to the entire proceedings—an indifference, however, which must stop short of real contempt.

At cocktail parties, book exhibitions, and actual sessions, the point is to convey a languid sense of having something much more important on your mind. Writing in a notebook during a session is a useful method—but only for more advanced conference goers. The challenge is to be seen to be writing, but not about anything connected with the subject of the session. Clicking away on your laptop is now becoming more common—but tends to convey a certain over-eagerness and careerism.

Some degree of presence, however, has to be conveyed—especially if you want to be invited again. A good idea is to attend only those sessions where the organizers of the next conference will be present.

Interaction

Related to the subject of demeanor—and, in many senses, the very heart of conference life—is your interaction with other people. However, unlike either demeanor or the academic program itself, social interaction is a realm that can be freed from considerations of status and career-advantage and become a matter of pure enjoyment. The conference is a delightful occasion for making new acquaintances and renewing old friendships. The insulation from normal life allows close interpersonal bonds to develop and mature (see also "Liaisons"). The conference also functions—like a high school reunion—as a way of tracing and remembering your autobiography.

Not that conference interactions are always free of cynical impression management. The initial greeting, for example, becomes an occasion for some people to display their highly cosmopolitan status. Take, for example: the broad smile across a crowded room, the slow approach, the kiss (on both cheeks), the warm bear hug and—loudly—"So good to see you again, Indira. And what's new in the Madras sociology department since my last visit?"

But try not to play or be impressed by these games. Stay close to your friends: talk, walk, tour, eat, drink, inhale, dance, and even go to sessions with them. Always attend their papers (even if you know exactly what they are going to say) and ask friendly questions. Laugh at their tired old jokes. Spend time with your friends talking about your families, your common medical problems, how young you both still look, politics, sexuality in the modern world, the end of history, the meaning of life—anything except your common academic subject. The standard academic conversational line—always useful with a new person or someone of higher or lower status than your own—should be avoided with true friends: "What are you working on now?" If a true friend asks this of you, the best reply is "Oh, you know, the same old stuff."[5]

Conferences bring out the worst in people, and you have to work hard to remain a decent human being.

Spouse Activities

In the era before feminist consciousness, the conference world—like the academic world itself—was resolutely male. Even up to ten years ago, the programs of international conferences would still list special activities and excursions for "wives." While their husbands were solving the problems of pollution, alienation or inflation, these unfortunate women were dragged to visit nursery schools, hospitals, institutions for retarded children, hostels for reformed prostitutes, embroidery collectives or—horror of horrors—folk-dancing festivals.

These excursions have now been de-gendered and listed as being open to "spouses." They should still be avoided at all costs.

Field Trips

A rather special type of excursion—planned for participants rather than their spouses—has become popular at conferences in subjects like social work, criminology and clinical psychology. These are variously termed "field trips," "site visits," or "local observational opportunities."

To supplement their intellectual discussions with some experience of what is still referred to as the "real world," these conference goers may be found wandering around red-light districts, cruising in police patrol cars, sleeping in cardboard boxes with homeless people, observing meetings of Crack Users Anonymous or picking grapes in a farmer's commune.

If this sort of thing appeals to you, go ahead.

Liaisons

The conference liaison—affair, romance, relationship—forms the subject of an underground collection of folklore, oral tradition, rumor and gossip. This knowledge is rarely openly discussed and never analyzed sociologically. At one level, there is nothing very special to explain: conference romances are very similar to the shipboard or holiday romances. The setting is insulated from normal inhibitions, responsibilities, and family ties; there is a sense of adventure, hedonism, and risk-taking; the atmosphere radiates low-level erotic expectations. The conference is a place where you meet the Other—you meet him or her intensely, you are cut off from the real world, you say goodbye and you get into the taxi to return home. The conference sequence, therefore, is not only conducive to the affair but actually reproduces its distinctive social features.[6]

There are no special techniques for making initial contacts or opening moves. The familiar scripts of eye contact, body language and verbal ambiguity are, however, perilous in an academic institution so especially sensitive to issues of political correctness and sexual harassment.

The main settings for the initial encounters are restaurants, bars and the opening reception. Academic sessions themselves offer a more interesting range of possibilities. A pass from lecturer-to-audience or audience-to-lecturer—usually through the "Fixed Gaze" technique—is hazardous because of questions of power, inequality and hierarchy. It is much safer and more rewarding to remain within audience-to-audience transactions. The initial approach will often take place through a furtive passing of notes. A conventional, but trusted, technique is the expression of putative mutual role distance. Thus: "From the way you look, I can't be the only one thinking that this whole session is a load of mundane rubbish." This almost always evokes a "like-minded" response: "God, yes. Why do we keep coming to these things, year after year?" This expected response does not always come ("That's my wife/husband giving the paper," "I convened the session," or simply a frozen stare)—but if it does, the rest is history.

After the initial consummation, however, maintaining the liaison during the rest of the conference is not easy. Here, the occasion begins to take on the worst features not just of holiday or shipboard romances, but also office or campus romances. The main problem is maintaining discretion and avoiding embarrassment in a confined social space. Close familiarity looks suspicious as does conspicuous distancing. The conference message board is a useful way of keeping contact, but care must be taken to address the recipient very precisely and to seal the message. Mistaken identity or deliberate nosiness might otherwise reveal certain indiscreet communications: "Michael—last night was wonderful. Will you be at Susan's (boring!) session on the welfare state this afternoon? Love, J."

Avoidance and retreat present acute problems in the total institutional setting of the conference. If either party wishes to retreat gracefully after the first night, there is nowhere to hide. This problem can be solved by starting the liaison only on the last night of the conference. The opposite problem is situational transfer. There might be a mutual desire to continue the relationship, but the heady emotions and sense of deep affinity evoked in a beach hut in the Caribbean cannot be easily reproduced in another location. E-Mail terminations are frequent.

Note also the special—and rather embarrassing—version of the Marienbad syndrome (see below: "Psychopathology"). The repetitious nature of conferences sometimes induces a trance-like amnesia about whether the person you are approaching is or is not someone whom you have already "encountered." This leads, respectively, to the false positive and false negative errors. The false positive is: "God, I just can't tell you how often I've thought about you since last year's M.E.S.A." The false negative is: "Hi. You look as if this is your first A.S.A. meeting." The only response to both types of error is a cold stare.

Because of such hazards and recent trends (such as AIDS and the new asceticism) the conference liaison is less popular than it used to be. But at its best, it offers a unique form of social interaction. A legendary tale on the British social science circuit, for example, concerns a couple who sustained an intense and loving relationship over fifteen years—having no contacts whatsoever over this period outside the annual four day conference of their academic association.

Arrival and Departure

The apparently mundane logistics of how to arrive and then depart from the conference require subtle planning. The general rule is "arrive late, depart early." This is an easy way of giving the impression of having a demanding, busy schedule in which this conference is a mere passing event. The technique is particularly effective when accompanied by hints of other (more important) conferences before or afterwards. It is especially desirable to be invited to a post-conference workshop. This gives the impression that here is where the really important issues—beyond the grasp of the masses at the conference itself—will actually be resolved.

Avoid, however, coming *too* late to the conference. This runs the risk of your hotel room being allocated to someone else, not having any meal tickets, or missing important participants who are leaving early.

In addition to other conferences or academic engagements, it is now becoming politically correct to demonstrate a deep commitment to family life. Your children can appear on the second to last day of the conference, and you can conspicuously depart with them for skiing, scuba diving or camping.

Expenses

Never pay for a conference out of your own money. Getting a travel grant from your institution or research council is fine; the best is to be invited with all expenses paid including a *per diem*. It is cheap and tasteless to request receipts for small expenses like $3.50 taxi fares. Try to be reimbursed for your claims on the spot; otherwise you are destined to months of embarrassing correspondence.

Psychopathology

The psychopathology of conference life is worth separate attention.

The most general pathological syndrome is known colloquially as being "conferenced out." At the subjective level, this state is marked by intense and chronic tiredness, listlessness, hunger in the middle of the night (uncorrelated to jet lag), spatial and temporal disorientation, extreme mood swings and a sense of deep unreality. Its external diagnostic signs include a glazed look, slow walking, the deepening of facial lines, creased clothes and—at the extreme—hand tremors. Verbal expressions include "What am I doing here?" "Dear God, never again," and—at the extreme—"If only I could get home to my family."

Another constellation of symptoms—sometimes accompanying the general state of being conferenced-out, sometimes appearing separately—is an extreme regression to childlike and even infantile states of helplessness and dependency. This takes the form of an inability to understand the simplest instructions and a total loss of all social skills. Grown up and otherwise socially competent adults wander down corridors looking for rooms; they continually accost conference organizers to ask the way to the toilet, the dining room or the registration desk; they are always losing their name tags, meal tickets, hotel keys, travellers cheques and passports. They plague the conference travel office with requests to reconfirm their return flights. They forget when the conference is due to end.

There is an extreme form of disorientation known as "conference deja-vu" or the Marienbad syndrome (see above: "Liaisons"). This consists of an inability to remember whether you've been at the same conference with different people in the previous year or a different conference with the same people two years ago. Conversational openings such as "Oh yes, we met last year at the Legal Studies meetings in Bratslava" might be followed by (a) "I've never been to Bratslava." (b) "I was in Bratslava six years ago," or (c) "I was in Bratslava last year, but I've never met you in my life." Any variant of these three replies can induce an immediate identity-panic state or else deepening anxiety about Alzheimer's disease.

Variations of the Marienbad syndrome are particularly marked among academics who are literally addicted to conference life (see above: "Frequency"). There are some people who are unable to survive outside the conference world. Given the limited time span of most conferences—a maximum of six days—these sad creatures are doomed to wander the earth in search of their next fix. There is a story—no doubt apocryphal—of Canadian social scientist seen in the transit lounge of Zurich airport unable to remember whether he was getting a connection to or from a semiotic congress in Strasbourg.

The only known treatment is complete withdrawal. A period of at least two years spent in your own university and with your own family will allow most symptoms to fade away.

All the subjects raised in this article require further research. I am offering only a preliminary typology, primarily of nosological and didactic value. A full explanatory schema demands serious comparative and historical work. The beginning of such work are being carried out by the Geneva Institute of Meta Communication, and I am grateful for access to their preliminary data archive of ego-documents about conference life.

Notes

An earlier version of this article was given as a paper at the "Odessa Conference on Global Meta-Communication" organized by the Institute in July 1994. The Institute has just issued a "call for papers" for the Follow Up Conference to be held in Jakarta in 1998. Selected papers from this conference will be published in a special issue of the journal *Ulysses*.

1. Novelists, on the other hand, especially the British "campus novelists," have given much attention to conference life. See, especially the David Lodge trilogy, *Changing Places*, *It's a Small World* and *Nice Work*. More recently, there is Malcolm Bradbury, *Doctor Criminale* (London, Penguin, 1993). A major part of this novel takes place in academic conferences, most notably at "Barolo," a thinly disguised version of the Bellagio conference center.
2. Next on the conference horizon, is the "quadrilogue." The North-South Centre in Lisbon is " . . . a quadrilogue

partnership of Government, Parliamentarians, NGO's and Local Authorities." The Centre has its own Centre, the "European Centre for Global Interdependence and Solidarity" which, in January 1994, organized in Rome an "International Symposium on Transmeditteranean Interdependence and Partnership." Really.
3. As my friend and colleague from UCLA, Richard Abel, replied to a question about why he was doing research in South Africa: "It's the only place where there's a revolution and they speak English."
4. At one conference I recently attended, the General Rapporteur solved this problem by spending his entire allocated half hour giving a classified count of all the papers on the program: "There were 40 papers on women, 27 papers on prison, 9 papers on women in prison..." (Incredibly, no one in the audience walked out).
5. Brecht gives the definitive answer: "'What are you working on?' Herr Keuner was asked. 'I'm having a lot of trouble,' answered Herr Keuner, 'I'm getting ready for my next mistake.'" Bertold Brecht, *Anecdotes of Herr Keuner*.
6. "In a sense every congress, like every love affair (and the two are often closely connected), is different." Bradbury, *Doctor Criminale*, p. 226.

[19]
Moral Panics as Cultural Politics

Folk Devils and Moral Panics was published in 1972. It was based on my PhD thesis, written in 1967–69 and the term 'moral panics' very much belongs to the distinctive voice of the late Sixties.[1] Its tone was especially resonant in the subjects then shared by the new sociology of deviance and the embryonic cultural studies: delinquency, youth cultures, subcultures and style, vandalism, drugs and football hooliganism.

When the **Second Edition** appeared in 1980, I wrote an Introduction ['Symbols of Trouble', reprinted here unchanged] that dealt almost entirely with the 'Folk Devils' part of the book's title (the Mods and Rockers), especially the developments in subcultural theories of delinquency associated with the Birmingham Centre for Contemporary Cultural Studies. In this Introduction to the **Third Edition**, I deal only with the 'Moral Panics' part of the title: reviewing uses and criticisms of the concept over the last thirty years. This is followed by a *Selected Reading List*.

There are three overlapping sources for this review:

First, is the stuff itself, thirty years of moral panics. Whether or not the label was applied and/or contested at the time or afterwards, there are clusters of reactions that look very much like 'classic' moral panics.

Second, the same public and media discourse that provides the raw evidence of moral panic, uses the concept as first-order description, reflexive comment or criticism.[2] These are short-term reactions to the immediate ('the current moral panic about paedophiles') and long-term general reflections on the 'state-of-our-times'.

Third, is the meta-view from academic subjects, notably media and cultural studies, discourse analysis and the sociology of deviance, crime and control. Here the concept has been adapted and adopted, expanded and criticized, and included as a 'Key Idea' in sociology and a standard entry in textbooks and dictionaries.[3]

viii   *Introduction to the Third Edition*

Calling something a 'moral panic' does not imply that this something does not exist or happened at all and that reaction is based on fantasy, hysteria, delusion and illusion or being duped by the powerful. Two related assumptions, though, require attention – that the attribution of the moral panic label means that the 'thing's' extent and significance has been exaggerated (a) in itself (compared with other more reliable, valid and objective sources) and/or (b) compared with other, more serious problems. This labelling derives from a wilful refusal by liberals, radicals and leftists to take public anxieties seriously. Instead, they are furthering a politically correct agenda: to downgrade traditional values and moral concerns.

Carry on Panicking

The objects of normal moral panics are rather predictable; so too are the discursive formulae used to represent them. For example:

They are *new* (lying dormant perhaps, but hard to recognize; deceptively ordinary and routine, but invisibly creeping up the moral horizon) – but also *old* (camouflaged versions of traditional and well-known evils). They are damaging *in themselves* – but also merely *warning signs* of the real, much deeper and more prevalent condition. They are *transparent* (anyone can see what's happening) – but also *opaque*: accredited experts must explain the perils hidden behind the superficially harmless (decode a rock song's lyrics to see how they led to a school massacre).

The objects of moral panic belong to seven familiar clusters of social identity:

1. Young, Working-class, Violent Males

Working-class yobs are the most enduring of suitable enemies. But the roles they played over these decades – football hooligans, muggers, vandals, loiterers, joy riders and mobile phone snatchers – were not represented by distinctive subcultural styles. There is too much fragmentation to identify dominant subcultures. Loyalties – whether to fashion, musical style, or football – are too diffuse to match each other. Under the exclusionary regimes set up in the Thatcher years and adapted by New Labour, the losers drop quietly off the board, too quietly for any public displays like the Mods and Rockers. Each of the 1992 riots on out-of-town council estates (in Bristol, Salford and Burnley) was short-lived and self-contained. Only the identities and barriers of race have been further strengthened. With the constant exception of football hooliganism, most crowd scenes of these years (mobs, riots, public disturbance) have been organized on ethnic lines (Brixton, Leicester and Bradford).

Away from the crowds two very different cases stand out, both known by the names of the victims. One, the Jamie Bulger story, was utterly unique, yet triggered off an immediate and ferocious moral panic; the other, the Stephen Lawrence case, despite being indeed a harbinger of things to come, produced a late, slow running and ambiguous reaction, never reaching full panic status.

On 12 February 1993, two 10-year-old boys, Robert Thompson and Jon Venables, led away 2-year-old James Bulger from a shopping centre in Bootle (Liverpool). They walked with him for some two and a half miles to a railway line and then battered him to death. The number of 'Children Who Kill Children' is minute and not increasing. It was precisely the rarity of the event and its context that made it so horrible. Long before the trial began in November the Bulger story had become a potent symbol for everything that had gone wrong in Britain: a 'breed' of violent children, whether feral or immoral; absent fathers, feckless mothers and dysfunctional underclass families; the exploitation of children by TV violence and video nasties; anomic bystanders – on the grainy screen of the defective CCTV they watch as the toddler (arm stretched up, between the two older boys, one in step, the other moving grimly ahead) is led to his death.

The Sun instantly called for 'a crusade to rescue a sick society'. A few days later, the shadow Home Secretary, Tony Blair, referred to the week's news as 'hammer blows struck against the sleeping conscience of the country, urging us to wake up and look unflinchingly at what we see'. *The Independent* (21 February 1993) used Blair's phrase to headline its leading article '*The Hammer Blow To Our Conscience*'. 'Britain is a worried country,' it stated, 'and it has a good deal to be worried about.' By the end of the week, Britain was 'examining the dark corners of its soul' (*The Economist*, 27 February 1993). The only bit of late modernist reflexivity came from someone who makes a living from moralizing: Archbishop George Carey warned about the dangers of 'lapsing into moral panic'.

One such danger is a ready susceptibility to simple explanations. A throwaway remark by the trial judge – 'I suspect that exposure to violent video films may in part be an explanation' – quickly became a factoid that the last video rented by one of the boys' father was *Child's Play 3* (a nasty video indeed in which a child 'kills' a manic doll). This had 'chilling parallels' to the murder of Jamie Bulger; the two boys 'may' have watched it (*Daily Mail*, 26 November 1993). The panic turned on media violence. *The Sun* staged a public burning of horror videos; reports claimed that *Child's Play* had been removed from video shops; Scotland's largest video chain burnt its copies. Four months later, a senior Merseyside police inspector revealed that checks on the family homes and rental lists showed that neither *Child's Play* nor anything like it had been viewed.

The search for meaning and causes is of course not always spurious, simple-minded or mythical. Public opinion, social scientific theories and poetic imagination[4] had to strain themselves to make sense of such an event. But during moral panics and media frenzies the atypical case is compressed into general categories of crime control (such as 'juvenile violence'). The explanatory theory is based on too few cases; injustice results by targeting too many cases.

Stephen Lawrence was an 18-year-old black youth from South London. On the evening of 22 April 1993, while standing at a bus stop with a friend he was taunted with racial abuse by a group of five or six white youths. They then stabbed him in the chest and he died some hours later.

This was to become another boundary marking case. It was not as unusual as the Bulger story, but just as rich and received more intense public and media exposure over a much longer period. The visible failure to bring the known group of suspects to trial led to continuous revelations of police incompetence and racism. After six years of persistent campaigning and claims-making (by various civil liberties organizations, anti-racist groups and the local black community including Stephen Lawrence's parents), an inquest, a botched private prosecution, a flawed internal police review, and a Police Complaints Authority investigation, eventually a £3 million Judicial Inquiry was set up (chaired by a retired judge, Sir William Macpherson). It published its 335-page Report in February 1999.[5] The Report generated enormous public attention and an iconic policy agenda still refers to policing 'after Macpherson' or 'after the Stephen Lawrence Report'.[6]

At first glance, all the ingredients for a moral panic were in place. The Report itself took a moral stand against the persistent racism it had identified. For example: 'Stephen Lawrence's murder was simply and solely and unequivocally motivated by racism. It was the deepest tragedy for his family. It was an affront to society, and especially to the local black community in Greenwich' (Para. 1.11); 'Nobody has been convicted of this awful crime. This is also an affront both to the Lawrence family and the community at large' (Para. 1.12). Professional incompetence and poor leadership were important reasons for the police failure, but the overarching problem was 'pernicious and persistent institutional racism', police failure to respond to the concerns of ethnic minorities and 'discrimination through unwitting prejudice, ignorance, thoughtlessness and racist stereotyping' (Para. 6.34).

Introduction to the Third Edition xi

Why did all this not quite add up to a moral panic? Despite the continued use of Stephen's name, public attention shifted from the victim to the police. With the quick departure from the scene of the suspected offenders (their culture of violence and racism soon forgotten) the police became the *only* object of attention. The Macpherson Report found a divided organization sending out contradictory and confusing messages marked by an 'alarming inability to see how and why race mattered'.[7] Precisely because of this 'inability' the police could hardly be expected to carry the full burden of the Lawrence fiasco, and even less, the damaging indictment of 'institutionalized racism'. There was no one else to blame – but the police were just unsuitable as folk devils. Moreover they had the power to deny, downplay or bypass any awkward claims about their culpability.[8]

The right wing press, especially the *Daily Mail* and the *Daily Telegraph*, claiming to speak on behalf of all British society, directly aided the police. These papers applied, with astonishing accuracy, methods that could appear in a manual on '*How To Prevent a Moral Panic*'. The notion of 'institutionalized racism' was denounced as meaningless, exaggerated and too sweeping; the term could stir up resentments among ordinary people (stigma and deviancy amplification theory); it besmirches the whole police force because of a few blameworthy individuals; the British are a tolerant people who have marginalized the far right and allowed racial minorities to be integrated and accepted. The Report, proclaimed the *Telegraph*, could have come from a 'loony left borough'. Some of its conclusions 'bordered on the insane'. Macpherson (a witch finder looking for thought-crimes) was a useful idiot duped by the 'race relations lobby' (*Sunday Telegraph* 21 and 28 February 1999 and *Daily Telegraph*, 26 February 1999).

In the end, the Lawrence case lacked three of the elements needed for the construction of a successful moral panic. First, a *suitable enemy*: a soft target, easily denounced, with little power and preferably without even access to the battlefields of cultural politics. Clearly not the British police. Second, a *suitable victim*: someone with whom you can identify, someone who could have been and one day could be anybody. Clearly not inner-city young black males. Third, a consensus that the beliefs or action being denounced were not insulated entities ('it's not only this') but integral parts of the society or else could (and would) be unless 'something was done'. Clearly if there was no institutionalized racism in the police, there could not be in the wider society.

xii *Introduction to the Third Edition*

2. School Violence: Bullying and Shootouts

The 'Blackboard Jungle' (the name of the 1956 movie) has long served, in Britain and the USA, as a vivid image about the menacing violence of inner-city schools. Violence is seen as a constant daily backdrop: pupils against each other (bullying, playing dangerous macho games, displaying weapons); teachers against pupils (whether formal corporal punishment or immediate rage and self-protection).

There have been sporadic outcries about this backdrop of school violence and related problems such as truancy, large-scale social exclusion into special classes or units and more recently the neighbourhood pusher selling drugs at the school gate. Fully-fledged moral panics need an extreme or especially dramatic case to get going. The age-old rituals of bullying in classroom and playground (girls, for once, getting a fair share of attention) are usually normalized until serious injury or the victim's suicide.

A recent example is the run of high school massacres and shooting sprees. The first images – from the USA in the mid-nineties – were quite unfamiliar: school grounds taped off by police; paramedics rushing to wheel off adolescent bodies; parents gasping in horror; kids with arms around each other; then the flowers and messages at the school gates. In the late nineties, when these events were still rare, each new case was already described as 'an all-too-familiar story'. The slide towards moral panic rhetoric depends less on the sheer volume of cases, than a cognitive shift from 'how could it happen in a place like this?' to 'it could happen anyplace'. In the USA at least, the Columbine Massacre signalled this shift.

On 20 April 1999 two male students dressed in black (one 17 years old, the other just 18) walked into the 1,800 student Columbine High School in the quiet town of Littleton, Colorado. They were armed with shotguns, a handgun and a rifle. They started shooting, initially targeting known athletes, killing a teacher and twelve fellow students and then shot themselves. How could this have happened? As *Time* magazine posed the question: 'The Monsters Next Door: What Made them Do It?' (3 May 1999). British newspaper headings (the archetypal carriers of moral panics) had already covered a range of explanations. On the print day after the event (22 April) the *Daily Mail* went for ideological motivation ('Disciples of Hitler'). *The Independent* preferred psychopathology ('The Misfits Who Killed For Kicks') as did the *Sunday Times* (25 April): 'Murderous Revenge of the Trench-coat Misfits'. *The Guardian* side-stepped the problem of motivation and went for the liberal middle path issue: 'The Massacre that Challenges America's Love Affair with the Gun' (22 April).

Introduction to the Third Edition xiii

This scurrying around for a causal theory – or, at least, a language for making sense – is found in all moral panic texts. If indeed, in President Clinton's words, Columbine had 'pierced the soul of America' we must find out why *this* event happened and how to stop it happening *elsewhere*. Moreover, if this happened in a place like Columbine (and most school massacres do happen in such ordinary places) then it could well happen elsewhere.

As these stories unfold, experts such as sociologists, psychologists and criminologists are wheeled in to comment, react and supply a causal narrative. Their ritual opening move – 'putting things in perspective' – is not usually very helpful: 'Schools Still Safest Place For Children; Many More Dead at Home Than in Classroom.'

3. Wrong Drugs: Used by Wrong People at Wrong Places

Moral panics about psychoactive drugs have been remarkably consistent for something like a hundred years: the evil pusher and the vulnerable user; the slippery slope from 'soft' to 'hard' drugs; the transition from safe to dangerous; the logic of prohibition. New substances are just added to the list: heroin, cocaine, marijuana and then the Sixties drugs of amphetamines (very much the Mod pill) and LSD. Then a string of substances: designer drugs, PCP, synthetic drugs, ecstasy, solvents, crack cocaine and new associations: acid-house, raves, club culture, 'heroin chic' supermodels.

In Britain, Leah Betts joined James Bulger as a melodramatic example of a moral panic generated by the tragic death of one person. On 13 November 1995, 18-year-old Leah Betts collapsed soon after taking an ecstasy tablet in a London nightclub, was taken to hospital and went into a coma. By the next day – for reasons not altogether clear – the story made instant panic headlines: the anguish of Leah's parents; the evil pushers of poison; the insistent message 'it could be your child'. Leah died two days later. Her parents began to appear regularly in the media to warn of the dangers of ecstasy. They became instant experts and moral guardians – disagreeing with them would be insensitive to their grief. The warning was symbolically sharpened by Leah's respectable home background: father an ex-police officer, mother had worked as a drug counsellor. This meant, explained the *Daily Express*, that drugs were a 'rotten core in the heart of middle England'. Leah was the girl next door.

This episode has been much analysed: the story itself, the media reaction, the left liberal counter-reaction (attacking the media-spread panic) and even a left liberal reaction against the counter-reaction for being just a mirror-image, merely inverting one simple message into another equally simple.[9]

xiv *Introduction to the Third Edition*

Instead of: a monolithic popular youth culture promotes drug use and normalizes other anti-social actions and attitudes, we have: panic coverage by a monolithic media promotes a false consensus that alienates occasional drug users into further marginalization.

This was to be a long-running story. Nearly six months later, anxieties were still being raised: 'Even the best parents, raising the most level-headed children, fear that one of them somehow might be next weekend's Leah Betts, who died after taking Ecstasy' (*Daily Telegraph*, 12 April 1996). Fourteen months after Leah's death, the pop star Noel Gallagher had to apologize to her parents for saying that ecstasy use was commonplace and harmless among some young people. In March 2000, about five years after the event, Leah's mother was widely quoted as 'hitting out' at a Police Federation inquiry that suggested relaxing some drug laws. Leah's father was still a recognizable authority: 'Ecstasy Victim's Dad in Drug Danger Alert' (*Birmingham Evening Mail*, 12 October 2000); 'Leah Drug Death Dad Not here to Preach' (*Bolton, UK Newsquest Regional Press*, 18 May 2001).

4. Child Abuse, Satanic Rituals and Paedophile Registers

The term 'child abuse' contains many different forms of cruelty against children – neglect, physical violence, sexual abuse – whether by their own parents, staff in residential institutions, 'paedophile priests' or total strangers. Over the last decade, public perceptions of the problem have become increasingly focused on sexual abuse and sensationally atypical cases outside the family.

Reactions to the sexual abuse of children rest on shifting moral grounds: the image of the offender changes; some victims appear more suitable than others.[10] A series of stories over the last twenty years about serious abuse in children's homes and other residential institutions revealed not panic or even anxiety, but a chilling denial. The victims had endured years of rejection and ill-treatment by their own parents and the staff supposed to care for them. Their complaints to senior staff and local authority officials and politicians were met with disbelief, collusion and a tight organizational cover-up. There have been repeated waves of denial, exposure then denunciation. The same pattern applies to those traditional folk devils, paedophile priests.[11]

In the mid-1980s, however, a succession of highly publicized child deaths under more 'ordinary' circumstances, led to a very different type of panic. Into the familiar criminal triangle – child (innocent victim); adult (evil perpetrator) and bystanders (shocked but passive) – appears the social worker, trying to be

Introduction to the Third Edition xv

rescuer but somehow ending up being blamed for the whole mess. Social workers and social service professionals were middle-class folk devils: either gullible wimps or else storm troopers of the nanny state; either uncaring cold hearted bureaucrats for not intervening in time to protect the victim or else over-zealous, do-gooding meddlers for intervening groundlessly and invading privacy.

The Cleveland child sexual abuse scandal of 1987 marked the peak of this period and condensed its themes: the tensions between social work, medicine and the law; social workers as anxious, demoralized and particularly vulnerable as a predominantly female profession.[12] For three months from April that year, a cluster of some 120 children (average age between 6 and 9) had been diagnosed as having been sexually abused in their families. In June, a local newspaper published a story about confused and angry parents who claimed that their children had been taken from them by local authority social workers on the basis of a disputed diagnosis of sexual abuse made by two paediatricians in the local hospital. The *Daily Mail* ran the story on 23 June ('Hand Over Your Children, Council Orders Parents of 200 Youngsters').

The resulting moral panic became a pitched battle of claims and counter-claims. So busy were the key players in fingering each other — social workers, police, paediatricians, doctors, lawyers, parents, local and national politicians, then a judicial inquiry — that there was not even minimal consensus about what the whole episode was about.

Another episode was more fictitious and one of the purest cases of moral panic. Superimposed on the very real phenomenon of childhood sexual abuse and incest, came the 'recovered memory' of childhood incest: bitter debates about the existence of repressed (and recovered) memories of childhood sexual abuse. In these therapeutic interstices, came the story of 'ritual child abuse', 'cult child abuse' or 'Satanic abuse'. In around 1983, disturbing reports began circulating about children (as well as adults in therapy who were 'recovering' childhood memories) alleging that they had been sexually abused as part of the ritual of secret, Satanic cults, which included torture, cannibalism and human sacrifice. Hundreds of women were 'breeders'; children had their genitals mutilated, were forced to eat faeces, were sacrificed to Satan, their bodies dismembered and fed to participants — who turned out to be family members, friends and neighbours, day-care providers and prominent members of the community. Claims-making for various parts of this story joined conservative Christian fundamentalists with feminist psychotherapists.

One form of sexualized violence against children does not generate counter-claims about its existence nor any moral disagreement: the abduction and

xvi *Introduction to the Third Edition*

sexual killing of children, especially girls. This strikes a depth of horror in us all. There is a panicky sense of vulnerability – both in the sense of statistical risk (these events seem to be happening more often) and emotional empathy (How would I feel if this happened to my child?). The script becomes more familiar: child disappears on way home from school; the police set up investigation team; school friends, neighbours, teachers interviewed; frantic, distraught parents make appeals on TV; members of public join police in searching fields and rivers . . .

These offenders are pure candidates for monster status. The July 2000 abduction and murder of 8-year-old Sarah Payne led to the *News of the World* 'crusade' (its own word), a series of classic texts of monster-making. The 23 July front page reads: 'NAMED AND SHAMED. There are 110,000 child sex offenders in Britain . . . one for every square mile. The murder of Sarah Payne has proved police monitoring of these perverts is not enough. So we are revealing WHO they are and WHERE they are . . . starting today.' The lists of names and the rows of photos reflect what the paper assumes and constructs as the primeval public anxiety: 'DOES A MONSTER LIVE NEAR YOU?' Check the list, then read on: 'WHAT TO DO IF THERE IS A PERVERT ON YOUR DOORSTEP.' The paper called for information about convicted sex offenders to be made publicly available and itself published over the next two weeks photos, names and addresses of 79 convicted sex offenders.

Many obvious and worrying issues were raised: how the list was constructed (partly from Scout Association records: *Scouting Out the Beasts*, the paper explained); how downloading child porn or the seduction of a 14-year-old schoolboy by his mid-thirties female teacher belong to the same category as the sexual murder of a child; the counter-productive effect of driving already monitored offenders underground; the media's own freedom to publish. The special dangers of vigilantism and lynch mobs soon appeared with crowd protests calling for named and shamed offenders to be moved out of neighbourhoods or council housing estates. Attention focused on the Paulsgrove estate near Portsmouth – where each night for a week crowds of up to 300 marched upon houses of alleged paedophiles.

Public figures had to express sympathy with the parents and share their moral revulsion but also distance themselves from the mob. This was easily done by repeating the inherently negative connotations of lynch mob and mob rule, the primitive, atavistic forces whipped up by the *News of the World*.[13] The rational polity is contrasted to the crowd: volatile, uncontrollable and ready to explode.

Introduction to the Third Edition xvii

5. Sex, Violence and Blaming the Media

There is a long history of moral panics about the alleged harmful effects of exposure to popular media and cultural forms – comics and cartoons, popular theatre, cinema, rock music, video nasties, computer games, internet porn.[14] For conservatives, the media glamorize crime, trivialize public insecurities and undermine moral authority; for liberals the media exaggerate the risks of crime and whip up moral panics to vindicate an unjust and authoritarian crime control policy. In these 'media panics', the spirals of reaction to any new medium are utterly repetitive and predictable. With historical incorporation: 'the intense pre-occupation with the latest media fad immediately relegates older media to the shadows of acceptance.'[15]

The crude model of 'media effects' has hardly been modified: exposure to violence on this or that medium causes, stimulates or triggers off violent behaviour.[16] The continued fuzziness of the evidence for such links is overcompensated by confident appeals to common sense and intuition. When such appeals come from voices of authority (such as judges) or authoritative voices (experts, professionals, government inquiries) the moral panic is easier to sustain, if only by sheer repetition. The prohibitionist model of the 'slippery slope' is common: if 'horror videos' are allowed, then why not 'video nasties?' Child pornography will be next and finally the legendary 'snuff movies.' Crusades in favour of censorship are more likely to be driven by organized groups with ongoing agendas.

Some recent media panics are more self-reflective – anticipating having to defend themselves against the accusation of spreading a moral panic. The media play a disingenuous game. They know that their audiences are exposed to multiple meanings and respond differently to the 'same' message. They use this knowledge to support their indignation that they could have any malignant effect; they forget this when they start another round of simple-minded blaming of others. The powerful, increasingly homogenized and corporate news media blame *other* media forms. But their own effect is the most tangible and powerful, shaping the populist discourse and political agenda-setting. This has happened most obviously in my next two examples: welfare cheats and bogus asylum seekers.

6. Welfare Cheats and Single Mothers

The cutbacks in welfare state provisions during the Thatcher years were accompanied by the deliberate construction of an atmosphere of distrust.

xviii *Introduction to the Third Edition*

Widespread folk beliefs – the assumption that significant numbers of welfare claims were bogus or fraudulent, made by people taking advantage of ('ripping off') the welfare state – were given official credibility. Governments confirmed the need for institutional practices (laws, administrative procedures) that would firmly and reliably weed out the fake from the real. Legal changes assume, along with the public culture, 'not just that each claimant is *potentially* a fraudster but that he/she is probably so'.[17]

'Welfare cheats', 'social security frauds' and 'dole scroungers' are fairly traditional folk devils. So too are unmarried mothers. Over the 1980s, though, there was a 'kind of subdued moral panic' about young, unemployed girls becoming pregnant, staying single and taking themselves out of the labour market by opting for full-time motherhood, becoming dependent on welfare benefits rather than a male breadwinner.[18] The campaign ran most stridently from 1991 to 1993. Conservative politicians explicitly linked the goal of reducing government expenditure with moral exhortation for people to take responsibility for their own lives. 'Girls' were depicted as getting pregnant in order to be eligible for state benefits, even 'extra handouts' or to jump the queue for public housing. The 1993 'Back to Basics' campaign in Britain cynically constructed the single mother as a potent moral threat.[19] The abuse directed at lone parents led an *Independent* editorial (11 October 1993) to note that 'Conservative politicians are subjecting them to a vilification that would be illegal if addressed to racial minorities.'

The image of single mothers as irresponsible adults and ineffective parents helps to legitimize and entrench shrinking public provisions.[20] There are further causal leaps: 'feckless mothers' get pregnant to obtain state welfare; they raise children who will be the criminals of the future; absent fathers are present somewhere, unemployed and also living off the state. All this points to the same underclass culture that created the problem in the first place. But the real problem is none other than: the future of the nuclear family.

7. *Refugees and Asylum Seekers: Flooding our Country, Swamping our Services*

In media, public and political discourse in Britain the distinctions between immigrants, refugees and asylum seekers have become hopelessly blurred. Refugee and asylum issues are subsumed under the immigration debate which in turn is framed by the general categories of race, race relations and ethnicity. The framing itself does not necessarily imply racism. There are domains of British society where racism is subdued or at least contested. Conservatives

Introduction to the Third Edition xix

may well flirt with the idea that 'political correctness' is a leftist moral panic, but political instinct tells them to condemn their members for telling racist jokes.

No such sensitivity is extended to refugees and asylum seekers. Over the 1990s and throughout Europe a 'hostile new agenda' emerged.[21] At one level, there is the repeated and ritualistic distinction between genuine refugees (still entitled to compassion) and bogus asylum seekers (no rights, no call on compassion). But this distinction hides the more profound sense in which the once 'morally untouchable category of the political refugee'[22] has become deconstructed.

Governments and media start with a broad public consensus that *first*, we must keep out as many refugee-type of foreigners as possible; *second*, these people always lie to get themselves accepted; *third*, that strict criteria of eligibility and therefore tests of credibility must be used. For two decades, the media and the political elites of all parties have focused attention on the notion of 'genuineness'. This *culture of disbelief* penetrates the whole system. So 'bogus' refugees and asylum seekers have not really been driven from their home countries because of persecution, but are merely 'economic' migrants, attracted to the 'Honey Pot' of 'Soft Touch Britain'.

In tabloid rhetoric, especially the *Daily Mail* (whose campaign of vilification is too deliberate and ugly to be seen as a mere moral panic), the few nuances in these assumptions disappear: the untypical is made typical; the insulting labels are applied to all. (The bogus/genuine dichotomy appeared also in 58 per cent of all relevant articles over 1990–1995 in *The Guardian*, *The Independent* and *The Times*; one-third of *Guardian* and *Independent* references either criticized this idea or were citing others.[23])

This area is crucially different from my other six examples. First, although there have been intermittent panics about specific newsworthy episodes, the overall narrative is a single, virtually uninterrupted message of hostility and rejection. There is a constant background screen, interspersed with vivid little tableaux: Tamils at the airport, stripping in protest; Kurds clinging to the bottom of Eurostar trains; Chinese suffocating to death in a container lorry. Second, these reactions are more overtly political than any others – not just because the problem is caused by global political changes, but because the reactions have a long history in British political culture. Moreover, successive British governments have not only led and legitimated public hostility, but spoken with a voice indistinguishable from the tabloid press.

The media's lexicon of verbal abuse has kept up a constant level of bigotry. A recent analysis shows Scottish newspapers highlighting the same negative

xx   *Introduction to the Third Edition*

words and racial stereotypes; presenting asylum myths as fact; openly hostile about the presence of asylum seekers in Britain and openly suggesting they go back to their country of origin.[24] (Note though that only 44 per cent of references were judged as wholly negative, 21 per cent as balanced and 35 per cent as positive.)

A socio-linguistic study in a quite different cultural context – Austrian newspaper reports on the Kurdish asylum seekers in Italy in 1998 – nicely identifies the 'metaphors we discriminate by'.[25] Three dominant metaphors portray asylum seekers as *water* ('tidal waves'), as *criminals* or as an *invading army*. The repetition of these themes in relatively fixed lexical and syntactic forms shows them as the 'natural' way of describing the situation. The 'naturalization' of particular metaphors can blur the boundaries between the literal and the non-literal.

Similar metaphors – plus a few others – appear in British newspapers:

- Water is represented as *Flood, Wave, Deluge, Influx, Pour(into), Tide* and *Swamp*. As in 'Human Tide Labour Would Let In' (*The Sun*, 4 April 1992).
- Refugees are more criminal and more violent: 'Thousands have already [come to Britain] bringing terror and violence to the streets of many English towns' (*Sunday People*, 4 March 2001). 'An asylum free-for-all is a time bomb ticking away . . . that could one day explode with terrifying public violence' (*Scottish Daily Mail*, 13 April 2000). Their primal dishonesty is that they are *Cheats, Fakes, Bogus* and *Liars*. 'Fury as 20,000 Asylum cheats beat the System to Stay in Britain; Get them Out' (*Daily Express*, 30 July 2001).
- Refugees are *Scroungers* and *Beggars*, always looking for *Handouts* and trying to *Milk* the system.
- This is easy because Britain is a *Haven* with generous provisions (*Milk and Honey*) and is such a *Soft Touch*: 'Don't Let Britain Be A Soft Touch' (*Sunday Mirror*, 4 August 2001); 'Labour has made UK a haven for Refugees' (*Daily Mail*, 7 August 1999); Britain as 'the number one destination for asylum-seekers' (*Daily Telegraph*, 19 February 2001); 'the Costa del Dole for bogus refugees' (*Scottish Sun*, 11 April 2000).
- These metaphors and images are usually combined: 'Soft Touch That Lets in the Refugee Tricksters' (Press Association, 4 November 1999); 'Bogus Asylum Seekers That Keep on Flooding Into Britain: Britain a Soft Touch on Asylum' (*Daily Express*, 26 April 2001); 'We resent the scroungers, beggars and crooks who are prepared to cross every country in Europe to reach our generous benefits system' (*The Sun*, 7 March 2001).

Introduction to the Third Edition xxi

- The headlines of 'Straight Talking', David Mellor's regular column in the *People* make up a collage of these themes: 'Why we must turn back the Tide of Dodgy Euro Refugees' (29 August 1999); 'Send Spongers Packing Before We Are Over-run' (13 February 2000); 'Kick Out All This Trash' (5 March 2000). Then, after all this, 'When Telling the Truth is Called Racism' (16 April 2000).

The immediate effects of such sustained venom are easy to imagine, but harder to prove. In three days in August 2001 a Kurdish asylum seeker was stabbed to death on a Glasgow housing estate and two other Kurds attacked. The UNHCR issued a statement saying that this was predictable given the 'climate of vilification of asylum seekers that has taken hold in the UK in recent years'. This branding has become so successful that the words 'asylum seeker' and 'refugee' have become terms of abuse in school playgrounds.

Because this area is so obviously political, a strong opposition has been generated. Many NGOs – from human rights, civil liberties and anti-racist directions – give explicit attention to combating the pernicious effects of panic discourse. More specialist groups such as the Press Trust and RAM (Refugees, Asylum-seekers and the Mass Media) work only on countering media images and myths.

In May 2002, the Labour government announced a new round of plans under the slogan of 'zero acceptance': shut the Sangatte refugee camp on the French side of the Channel Tunnel; intercept boats carrying illegals; speed up deportation procedures. Under the heading 'Asylum: 9 out of 10 are Conmen' the *Daily Star* (22 May 2002) launched a typical side panic against 'turncoat immigration officers'. Immigration officers, trained at the taxpayers' expense, are quitting their jobs and using their expertise to set up lucrative consultancies to advise waves of bogus asylum seekers on how to beat the system.

Extensions

The concept of moral panic evokes some unease, especially about its own morality. Why is the reaction to Phenomenon A dismissed or downgraded by being described as 'another moral panic,' while the putatively more significant Phenomenon B is ignored, and not even made a candidate for moral signification?

These are not just legitimate questions but *the* questions. Like the folk objections against labelling, social constructionist or discourse theory in general, they strengthen the very position they are trying to attack. Such

xxii *Introduction to the Third Edition*

questions can only be posed if the lack of congruence between *action* (event, condition, behaviour) and *reaction* is correctly understood to be normal and obvious. To point to the complexities of the relationship between social objects and their interpretation is not a 'criticism' but the whole point of studying deviance and social control. Some trivial and harmless forms of rule-breaking can indeed be 'blown out of all proportion'. And yes, some very serious, significant and horrible events – even genocide, political massacres, atrocities and massive suffering – can be denied, ignored or played down.[26] Most putative problems lie between these two extremes – exactly where and why calls for a comparative sociology of moral panic that makes comparisons within one society and also between societies. Why, thus, does rate X of condition Y generate a moral panic in one country but not in another with the same condition?

All this certainly demands a rather clearer definition of the concept. Commentators have distinguished the separate elements in the original definition:[27] (i) *Concern* (rather than fear) about the potential or imagined threat; (ii) *Hostility* – moral outrage towards the actors (folk devils) who embody the problem and agencies (naïve social workers, spin-doctored politicians) who are 'ultimately' responsible (and may become folk devils themselves); (iii) *Consensus* – a widespread agreement (not necessarily total) that the threat exists, is serious and that 'something should be done'. The majority of elite and influential groups, especially the mass media, should share this consensus. (iv) *Disproportionality*: an exaggeration of the number or strength of the cases, in terms of the damage caused, moral offensiveness, potential risk if ignored. Public concern is not directly proportionate to objective harm. (v) *Volatility* – the panic erupts and dissipates suddenly and without warning.

I will return to these elements, especially the last two. Before that, a list of more sophisticated theories not available thirty years ago.

1. Social Constructionism

Folk Devils and Moral Panics was informed by the sixties fusion of labelling theory, cultural politics and critical sociology. Today's students of moral panics do not have to engage with this theoretical mix-up. They can go straight into the literature on social constructionism and claims-making.[28] This is a well-developed model for studying the contested claims that are made – by victims, interest groups, social movements, professionals and politicians – in the construction of new social problem categories.

Introduction to the Third Edition xxiii

Typical cases include: drunken driving, hate crime, stalking, environmental problems, psychiatric categories such as PTSD (Post Traumatic Stress Disorder) and various dependencies, eating disorders and learning disorders. Moral enterprise comes from many different directions: traditional 'disinterested' forces (such as the helping professions), interest groups (such as pharmaceutical companies) and the rainbow coalition of multi-cultural and identity groups, each claiming its own special needs and rights. The rhetoric of victim-hood, victim and victimization is the common thread in these newer forms of claim-making: secondary victims, such as Mothers Against Drunk Driving (MADD) look for tougher punishment; animal rights campaigners look for the criminalization of cruelty towards victims who cannot speak; putative victims, such as sick Gulf War veterans, want official recognition of their syndrome and consequent compensation.

Social problem construction always needs some form of enterprise. It does not, however, need a moral panic. When this rather special mode of reaction takes place, it may strengthen (and then be absorbed by) the construction process. Or it never reaches this point – remaining a shriek of indignation that leads nowhere.

'But is there anything out there?' Constructionists have a range of well-rehearsed responses to this question. In the 'strong' or 'strict' version there are constructs and nothing but constructs all the way down; the sociologist is merely another claims-maker; in 'weak' or 'contextual' constructionism, the sociologist can (and should) make reality-checks (to detect exaggeration) while simultaneously showing how problems are socially constructed. I would also distinguish between *noisy* constructions – where moral panics appear (usually at an early stage) and may be associated with a single sensational case – and *quiet* constructions, where claims-makers are professionals, experts or bureaucrats, working in organizations and with no public or mass media exposure.

2. Media and Cultural Studies

At their point of origin in the sixties, concepts like 'moral panic' and 'deviancy amplification' were symbiotically linked to certain assumptions about the mass media. Vital causal links were taken for granted – notably that the mass media are the primary source of the public's knowledge about deviance and social problems. The media appear in any or all of three roles in moral panic dramas: (i) *Setting the agenda* – selecting those deviant or socially problematic events deemed as newsworthy, then using finer filters to select which of these events are candidates for moral panic; (ii) *Transmitting the images* – transmitting the

xxiv *Introduction to the Third Edition*

claims of claims-makers, by sharpening up or dumbing down the rhetoric of moral panics; or (iii) *Breaking the silence, making the claim*. More frequently now than three decades ago, the media are in the claims-making business themselves. Media exposures – whether *The Guardian's* tale of government sleaze or *The Sun's* headline 'Would You Like a Paedophile as Your Neighbour?' – aim for the same moral denouement: 'We Name the Guilty Men.'

These years have seen major developments in discourse theory and analysis. I would now be expected to *interrogate* the speeches by Brighton magistrates or editorials from the *Hastings Observer* as *texts* or *narratives* in order to *problematize* their *mediated representation* of the *distant other's* stance to a *posited external world*. All this is far away from what I now see as the book's weakest link: between moral panics and folk devils. The many robust critiques of simple 'stimulus/response' and 'effects' models have hardly touched the thin idea of media-induced deviancy amplification. This is not causation in the constructionist sense – moral panics 'cause' folk devils by labelling more actions and people – but causation in the positivist sense and without the inverted commas. This psychology still uses concepts such as triggering off, contagion and suggestibility. Later cognitive models are far more plausible. For those who define and those who are defined, sensitization becomes a matter of cognitive framing and moral thresholds. Rather than a stimulus (media message) and response (audience behaviour) we look for the points at which moral awareness is raised ('defining deviance up') or lowered ('defining deviance down').

These years have also seen some substantive changes in the media coverage of crime, deviance and social problems. One study of crime reporting in Britain over the last five decades finds that crime is increasingly portrayed as a pervasive threat not just to its vulnerable victims, but to ordinary people in everyday life.[29] Attention shifts away from offence, offender and the criminal justice process and towards a victim-centred cosmology. If the offenders' background, motivation and context become less salient so they are easier to demonize. This contrast between dangerous predators and vulnerable innocents allows the media to construct what Reiner terms 'virtual vigilantism'. This can be seen throughout the new realities of 'tabloid justice'[30] and in the victim culture encouraged by talk shows such Jerry Springer's.

These Durkheimian boundary setting ceremonies continue to be staged by the mass media. But they have become desperate, incoherent and self-referential. This is because they run against shifts in media representation of crime and justice since the late sixties: the moral integrity of the police and other authorities is tarnished; criminality is less an assault on sacred and

Introduction to the Third Edition xxv

consensual values than a pragmatic matter of harm to individual victims. Above all, crime may be presented as part of the wider discourse of risk. This means that moral panic narratives have to defend a 'more complex and brittle' social order, a less deferential culture.

3. Risk

Some of the social space once occupied by moral panics has been filled by more inchoate social anxieties, insecurities and fears. These are fed by specific risks: the growth of new 'techno-anxieties' (nuclear, chemical, biological, toxic and ecological risk), disease hazards, food panics, safety scares about travelling on trains or planes, and fears about international terrorism. The 'risk society' — in Beck's well-known formulation — combines the generation of risk with elaborated levels of risk management plus disputes about how this management is managed. The construction of risk refers not just to the raw information about dangerous or unpleasant things but also to the ways of assessing, classifying and reacting to them. Newly refined methods of predicting risk (like actuarial tables, psychological profiling, security assessments) become themselves objects of cultural scrutiny. If these methods reach quite different conclusions — Prozac is a safe drug; Prozac is a dangerous drug — the discourse shifts to the evaluative criteria or to the authority, reliability and accuracy of the claims-maker. Even further from the original 'thing' the shift takes a moral turn: an examination of the character and moral integrity of the claims-makers: Do they have a right to say this? Is their expertise merely another form of moral enterprise?

Reflections on risk are now absorbed into a wider culture of insecurity, victimization and fear. Both the technical question of risk analysis and the wider culture of risk-talk, have influenced the domain of deviance, crime and social control. This is self-evident in crime control policies such as *Situational Crime Prevention* that are grounded in the model of risk and rationality. Contemporary crime control ideology has not been wholly taken over by the 'new penology', based on prevention, rational choice, opportunity, actuarial modelling, etc. In one view, these new methods of governance and management are still being 'interrupted' by episodic spasms of old morality. Another view sees the theorists and managers of the criminal justice system employing the rhetoric of risk while the public and mass media continue with their traditional moral tales.[31] Neither view does justice to the now stylized (almost self-parodying) screams of tabloid panics nor the real anger, resentment, outrage and fear of the crowd banging the sides of the security van outside the trial of a sex offender.

xxvi *Introduction to the Third Edition*

The global scope of the risk society, its self-reflective quality and its pervasiveness create a new backdrop for standard moral panics. Perceptions of heightened risk evoke images of panic. And in populist and electoral rhetoric about such issues as fear of crime, urban insecurity and victimization, the concepts of risk and panic are naturally connected. The realm of political morality, however, is just about distinctive enough for the BSE ('mad cow disease') or foot and mouth disease panics not to be *moral* panics. Only if risk analysis becomes perceived as *primarily* moral rather than technical (the moral irresponsibility for taking this risk) will this distinction wither away. Some argue that this has already happened. The story of HIV-AIDS shows how the clearly organic nature of the condition can be morally constructed and result in changed value positions about sexuality, gender and social control. The demography of risk was informed from the outset by the ascription of moral failures to homosexuals and other groups.

This is not quite the same as claiming that the language of the risk society has taken over or should take over the moral framework.[32] Public talk about child neglect, sexual abuse or predatory street crime strongly resists the language of probabilities. Clever statistics about your low risk of becoming a victim are no more consoling than a message from medical epidemiology that you are in a low risk category for the disease that you are actually suffering.

More interesting than 'applying' risk theory to the study of moral panics is to remember that most claims about relative risk, safety or danger depend on political morality. As Douglas originally argued, substantial disagreements over 'what is risky, how risky it is and what to do about it' are irreconcilable in purely objective terms. Moreover the perception and acceptance of risk is intimately tied to the question of who is perceived to be responsible for causing the hazard or damage to whom.[33] This allocation of blame is intrinsic to moral panics.

Criticisms

Armed or not with these newer theoretical extensions, we can approach some recurring criticisms of moral panic theory.

1. Why 'Panics?'

In disputes about definition, the term 'panic' has caused unnecessary trouble. I believe that it still makes some sense as an extended metaphor and furthermore, that there are indeed similarities between *most* moral panics and *some* other panics.

Introduction to the Third Edition xxvii

The term is unfortunate, though, because of its connotation with irrationality and being out of control. It also evokes the image of a frenzied crowd or mob: atavistic, driven by contagion and delirium, susceptible to control by demagogues and, in turn, controlling others by 'mob rule'. Newspaper reports over the last decade have referred to: *in the grips (or climate) of a moral panic . . . hit the moral panic button . . . a moral panic has broken out (or struck, been unleashed) . . . moral panic merchants (or mongers) . . . seized by a moral panic.* I invited further criticism by using two rather special examples of mass panics: first, collective delusions and urban myths — implying that these perceptions and beliefs were based on hallucinations, entirely imagined realities and second, natural disasters — evoking images of a hysterical crowd, utterly out of control, running for their lives from an imminent danger.

After being at first apologetic and accepting the downgrade of 'panic' to a mere metaphor, I remain convinced that the analogy works. Recent sociological literature on disasters and environmental problems has broadened the definition of the social. This is a denaturalization of nature. The contingencies of ordinary social life — the divisions of power, class and gender — influence the risks and consequences of exposure to such events. Models of 'environmental justice' show how dangers such as proximity to nuclear waste are socially determined. And just as Erikson used seventeenth century witch-hunts and religious persecution to understand how deviance and social control test and reinforce moral boundaries (see Chapter 1) he later showed how catastrophes may be treated as social events.[34] These 'technical' disasters are 'the new species of trouble', in contrast to traditional 'natural' disasters. They have become 'normal accidents', catastrophes embedded within the familiar: the collapse of a football stand, a rail crash, a bridge falling, the sinking of a channel ferry, a botched cancer screening programme. The resultant reactions are not as homogenous, automatic or simple as they are supposed to be in contrast with the complexities of moral discourse. Indeed the reactions are similar to the highly contested terrain of all moral panics.[35]

The criteria by which certain media driven narratives are easily recognized as moral panics need more careful explanation: drama, emergency and crisis; exaggeration; cherished values threatened; an object of concern, anxiety and hostility; evil forces or people to be identified and stopped; the eventual sense of the episodic and transitory, etc. Many such criteria are self-evident. Thompson correctly notes, though, that two of them are genuinely problematic: first, *disproportionality* and second, *volatility*.[36] While conservatives complain that moral panic theorists use disproportionality in a highly selective way that barely hides their left liberal political agenda, the critique of volatility xxviii *Introduction to the Third Edition*

comes from radicals to whom the assumption of volatility is not solid or political enough.

2. *Disproportionality*

The very usage of the term moral panic, so this argument starts, implies that societal reaction is disproportionate to the actual seriousness (risk, damage, threat) of the event. The reaction is always *more* severe (hence exaggerated, irrational, unjustified) than the condition (event, threat, behaviour, risk) warrants. Why is this just assumed? And on what grounds is the sociologist's view always correct, rational and justified?

Even in these limited terms, the assumption of disproportionality is problematic. How can the exact gravity of the reaction and the condition be assessed and compared with each other? Are we talking about intensity, duration, extensiveness? Moreover, the argument goes, we have neither the quantitative, objective criteria to claim that R (the reaction) is 'disproportionate' to A (the action) nor the universal moral criteria to judge that R is an 'inappropriate' response to the moral gravity of A.

This objection makes sense if there is nothing beyond a compendium of individual moral judgements. Only with a prior commitment to 'external' goals such as social justice, human rights or equality can we evaluate any one moral panic or judge it as more specious than another. Empirically, though, there are surely many panics where the judgement of proportionality can and should be made – even when the object of evaluation is vocabulary and rhetorical style alone. Assume we know that, over the last three years, (i) X% of asylum seekers made false claims about their risk of being persecuted; (ii) only a small proportion (say 20 per cent) of this subgroup had their claims recognized; and (iii) the resultant number of fake asylum seekers is about 200 each year. Surely then the claim about 'the country being flooded with bogus asylum seekers' is out of proportion.

This, needless to say, is not the end of the matter: the counter-claim may lead only to another round of claims-swapping. But this does not make questions of proportion, congruence and appropriateness unimportant, irrelevant or out of date (because all there is, after all, is representation). The core empirical claims within each narrative can usually be reached by the most rudimentary social science methodology. It would be perverse to dismiss such findings merely as one 'truth claim' with no 'privileged status'. Claims about past statistical trends, current estimates and extrapolations to the future are also open to scrutiny.

Introduction to the Third Edition xxix

The problem is that the nature of the condition – 'what actually happened' – is not a matter of just how many Mods wrecked how many deck-chairs with what cost, nor how many 14-year-old girls became ill after taking which number of ecstasy tablets in what night club. Questions of symbolism, emotion and representation cannot be translated into comparable sets of statistics. Qualitative terms like 'appropriateness' convey the nuances of moral judgement more accurately than the (implied) quantitative measure of 'disproportionate' – but the more they do so, the more obviously they are socially constructed.

The critics are right that there is a tension between insisting on a universal measuring rod for determining the action/reaction gap – yet also conceding that the measurement is socially constructed and all the time passing off as non-politically biased the decision of what panics to 'expose'.

3. Volatility

Every critique from the 'left' starts by citing *Policing the Crisis*, the 1978 study by Hall and his colleagues about media and political reactions to street violence, especially mugging, carried out by black youth. This critique contrasts labelling theory's supposed separate and free-floating moral panics, each dependent on the whims of moral enterprise (Satanic cults this week, single mothers the week after) with a theory of state, political ideology and elite interests, acting together to ensure hegemonic control of the public news agenda. Far from being isolated, sporadic or sudden, these are predictable moves from one 'site' of tension to another; each move is patrolled by identical and integrated interests.

In some theories, this is less a contrast than a sequence. Discrete and volatile moral panics might indeed once have existed but they have now been replaced by a generalized moral stance, a permanent moral panic resting on a seamless web of social anxieties. The political crisis of the state is displaced into softer targets, creating a climate of hostility to marginal groups and cultural deviance. Even the most fleeting moral panic refracts the interests of political and media elites: legitimizing and vindicating enduring patterns of law and order politics, racism and policies such as mass imprisonment.[37] The importance of the media lies not in their role as transmitters of moral panics nor as campaigners but in the way they reproduce and sustain the dominant ideology.

This sequential narrative – from discrete to generalized, volatile to permanent – sounds appealing. But when did it happen? And what exactly was the shift? Thompson's claim, for example, that moral panics are succeeding each other more rapidly does not deny their volatility. His claim that they xxx *Introduction to the Third Edition*

are becoming more all pervasive (panics about child abuse extend to the very existence of the family) is not, however, a shift because the appeal to pervasiveness ('it's not only this') was a defining feature of the concept.

The notion of a 'permanent moral panic' is less an exaggeration than a oxymoron. A panic, by definition, is self-limiting, temporary and spasmodic, a splutter of rage which burns itself out. Every now and then speeches, TV documentaries, trials, parliamentary debates, headlines and editorials cluster into the peculiar mode of managing information and expressing indignation that we call a moral panic. Each one may draw on the same stratum of political morality and cultural unease and – much like Foucault's micro-systems of power – have a similar logic and internal rhythm. Successful moral panics owe their appeal to their ability to find points of resonance with wider anxieties. But each appeal is a sleight of hand, magic without a magician. It points to continuities: in space (*this sort of thing . . . it's not only this*) backward in time (*part of a trend . . . building up over the years*) a conditional common future (*a growing problem . . . will get worse if nothing done*). And for a self-reflexive society, an essential meta-message: *This is not just a moral panic*.

The element of volatility should be studied in two ways. First, why do full-blown panics ever end? My original answers were only guess-work: (i) a 'natural history' which ends with burn out, boredom, running out of steam, a fading away (ii) the slightly more sophisticated notion of cycles in fashion – like clothing styles, musical taste; (iii) the putative danger fizzles out, the media or entrepreneurs have cried wolf once too often, their information is discredited; (iv) the information was accepted but easily reabsorbed whether into private life or public spectacle – the end result described by the Situationists as *recuperation*. A second question concerns failed moral panics. Why despite having some ingredients, did they never quite take off: alcopops; computer hackers; cults, new age travellers; lesbian mums; commercial surrogate births; the Dunblane school shooting; baby-snatching from hospitals; cloning . . .

The volatility issue needs careful steering. If the idea of panic is domesticated under the dull sociological rubric of 'collective behaviour', the political edge of the concept is blunted. In this tradition, a moral panic merely reflects fears and concerns that are 'part of the human condition', or the 'maverick side of human nature' and 'operates outside the stable, patterned structures of society'.[38] The opposite is true: without the 'stable, patterned structures' of politics, mass media, crime control, professions and organized religion, no moral panics could be generated or sustained.

McRobbie and Thornton are correct that today's more sophisticated, self-aware and fragmented media make the original notion of the spasmodic ('every

Introduction to the Third Edition xxxi

now and then') panic out of date.[39] 'Panic' is rather a mode of representation in which daily events are regularly brought to the public's attention:

> They are a standard response, a familiar, sometimes weary, even ridiculous rhetoric rather than an exceptional emergency intervention. Used by politicians to orchestrate consent, by business to promote sales . . . and by the media to make home and social affairs newsworthy, moral panics are constructed on a daily basis.[40]

But surely not quite a 'daily basis'. Moral panic theory indeed must be updated to fit the refractions of multi-mediated social worlds. But the unexpected, the bizarre and the anomalous happen: the James Bulger murder is neither a daily event nor a familiar story. The repertoire of media and political discourses has to design special conventions to translate anomalies into everyday, long-term anxieties. But they still have to remain within the format of the transitory and spasmodic – the essence of news.

The fragmentary and the integrated belong together: moral panics have their own internal trajectory – a microphysics of outrage – which, however, is initiated and sustained by wider social and political forces.

4. Good and Bad Moral Panics?

The criticism that 'moral panic' is a value-laden concept, a mere political epithet, deserves more complicated attention than it receives. It is obviously true that the uses of the concept to expose disproportionality and exaggeration have come from within a left liberal consensus. This empirical project is concentrated on (if not reserved for) cases where the moral outrage appears driven by conservative or reactionary forces. For cultural liberals (today's 'cosmopolitans'), this was an opportunity to condemn moral entrepreneurs, to sneer at their small-mindedness, puritanism or intolerance; for political radicals, these were easy targets, the soft side of hegemony or elite interests. In both cases, the point was to expose social reaction not just as over-reaction in some quantitative sense, but first, as *tendentious* (that is, slanted in a particular ideological direction) and second, as *misplaced* or *displaced* (that is, aimed – whether deliberately or thoughtlessly – at a target which was not the 'real' problem).

As the term itself became diffused and explicitly used in the media, the liberal/anti-authority origin of its birth made it more openly contested. A popular strand in Thatcherite Conservatism was indeed to uphold *exactly* the meta-politics and causal theories that fuelled moral panics and to attack the derogatory use of the concept as a symptom of being 'out of touch' with public opinion and the fears of 'ordinary people'. This populist rhetoric remains in New Labour — with the attractive twist that many with roots in *Guardian* liberalism (and who had used the concept earlier) now turn on the 'jargon-laden left' for using the term so selectively.

In the British public arena the debate is frozen at this level of journalistic polemics. An imaginary sequence:

- *The Sun* reports that a 14-year-old school-girl in Oldham attacked a male teacher with a pair of scissors after he reprimanded her for using dirty language. The teacher's wound needed hospital treatment. The girl is 'of Asian origin'; the teacher is white. The police are investigating the incident; the local MP claims that such violent attacks by girls have doubled in this year. The story, with standard elaborations (the girl's father was an asylum seeker; teachers in other schools were too scared to speak out), runs in the tabloids for two more days.
- On the fourth day, *The Guardian* publishes an op-ed article by one of its think-piece journalists. She urges caution before a fully-fledged moral panic breaks out. The police, the school, the education authority and the police deny that such incidents are increasing; no one knows where the MP got his statistics. The teacher's wound was superficial. Such irresponsible reporting plays into the hands of extremist parties running for the local election. The *real* problems in places like Oldham are institutionalized racism in the schools and the special pressures that immigrant parents place on their daughters.
- On the day after, a *Daily Telegraph* editorial denounces the *Guardian* piece for deliberately trying to evade and distort the issue in the name of political correctness. Once again, the label of 'moral panic' is being used to play down the fears and anxieties of ordinary people — teachers, pupils, parents — who have to live every day in an atmosphere of violence. It now appears that the local schoolteachers' union had warned two months ago that school violence was driving teachers into leaving the profession.

This sequence allows for somewhat different readings of the relationships between moral panics and political ideology. (i) The weakest version sees the concept as a neutral descriptive or analytical tool, no different from other terms in this area (such as 'campaign' or 'public opinion'). It just so happens that the term has been used by left liberals (and their sociological cronies) to

Introduction to the Third Edition xxxiii

undermine conservative ideologies and popular anxieties by labelling their concerns as irrational. But the term remains neutral and its usage could easily be reversed. (ii) In a slightly stronger version, the liberal appropriation of the term has gone too far for any reversal. We cannot expect to find conservatives trying to expose liberal or radical concerns as being 'moral panics'. (iii) A third version goes further. The genealogy of the term, its current usage and its folk meaning allow for one reading only: the term is not just 'value laden' but intended to be a critical tool to expose dominant interests and ideologies. The school violence sequence depicts one round in the battle between cultural representations.

These positions rest on shifting sands. In some cases, the logic of labelling social reaction as a moral panic may indeed lead to varieties on non-intervention (leave things alone): either because reaction is based on literal delusion or because the problem does not deserve such extravagant attention. The difficult cases are more interesting – the existence of the problem is recognized, but its cognitive interpretation and moral implications are denied, evaded or disputed.

Such reactions form exactly the discourse of denial: *literal denial* (nothing happened); *interpretative denial* (something happened, but it's not what you think) and *implicatory denial* (what happened was not really bad and can be justified). Instead of exposing moral panics, my own cultural politics entails, in a sense, *encouraging* something like moral panics about mass atrocities and political suffering – and trying to expose the strategies of denial deployed to prevent the acknowledgement of these realities. All of us cultural workers – busily constructing social problems, making claims and setting public agendas – think that we are stirring up 'good' moral panics. Perhaps we could purposely *recreate* the conditions that made the Mods and Rockers panic so successful (exaggeration, sensitization, symbolization, prediction, etc.) and thereby overcome the barriers of denial, passivity and indifference that prevent a full acknowledgement of human cruelty and suffering.

The pathetic ease and gullibility with which the mass media are lured into conventional moral panics may be contrasted to the deep denial behind their refusal to sustain a moral panic about torture, political massacres or social suffering in distant places. Public and media indifference are even attributed to deep states such as 'compassion fatigue'.[41] Moeller describes a cognitive and moral stupor in which attention thresholds have risen so rapidly that the media try even more desperately to 'ratchet up' the criteria for stories to be covered. In the hierarchy of which events and issues will be covered, a footballer's ankle injury will get more media attention than a political massacre.

xxxiv *Introduction to the Third Edition*

Sometimes (as Moeller shows in her analysis of the coverage of the Bosnian and Rwandan stories) the media try to create moral concern, but struggle against a palpable audience denial. This was less compassion fatigue than compassion avoidance: 'confronted with the images of putrefying corpses or swollen bodies bobbling along river banks they looked away – even when they believed that the story was important.'[42] The shifting thresholds of attention she describes – the bewildering ways in which compassion rises and falls, the blurred boundaries of what is accepted as normal – look just like the volatility of moral panics.

I concluded my book with a vague prediction that more 'nameless' folk devils would be generated. The current causes of delinquency are clearer now: the climate of distrust and Darwinian individualism generated by Thatcherism and sustained in New Labour; under-regulated market economies; privatization of public services, welfare state cutbacks, growing inequality and social exclusion. Delinquents are nameless not in the banal sense that I meant (not being able to predict the names of the subcultural styles that would replace 'Mod' and 'Rocker') but because they remain as anonymous as the schools, housing estates, urban sprawls from which they came. Pictorial and verbal imaginations are applied more readily to the naming of social controls: Crime Watch, Situational Crime Prevention, Closed Circuit Television, Zero Tolerance, Three Strikes and You're Out, Anti Social Behaviour Orders. Social policies once regarded as abnormal – incarcerating hundreds of asylum seekers in detention centres, run as punitive transit camps by private companies for profit – are seen as being normal, rational and conventional.

The idea that social problems are socially constructed does not question their existence nor dismiss issues of causation, prevention and control. It draws attention to a meta debate about what sort of acknowledgement the problem receives and merits. The issue indeed is *proportionality*. It is surely not possible to calibrate exactly the human costs of crimes, deviance or human rights violations. The shades of intentionally inflicted suffering, harm, cruelty, damage, loss and insecurity are too complex to be listed in an exact, rational or universally accepted rank order of seriousness. But some disparities are so gross, some claims so exaggerated, some political agendas so tendentious that they can only be called something like, well, 'social injustice'.

Sociologists have no privileged status in pointing this out and suggesting remedial policies. But even if their role is relegated to being merely another claims-maker, this must include not only exposing *under-reaction* (apathy, denial and indifference) but making the comparisons that could expose *over-reaction* (exaggeration, hysteria, prejudice and panic). These 'reactions' may be

Introduction to the Third Edition xxxv

compared to the perceptual realm occupied by the sociology of risk: assessing not the risk itself nor its management, but the ways it is perceived. Even if there is no question of physical danger (death, infliction of pain, financial loss), the drawing and reinforcement of moral boundaries is as similar as Mary Douglas's comparison between physical and moral pollution. People's perceptions of the relative seriousness of so many different social problems cannot be easily shifted. The reason is that cognition itself is socially controlled. And the cognitions that matter here are carried by the mass media.

This is why moral panics are condensed political struggles to control the means of cultural reproduction. Studying them is easy and a lot of fun. It also allows us to identify and conceptualize the lines of power in any society, the ways we are manipulated into taking some things too seriously and other things not seriously enough.

Notes and References

1. The term 'moral panic' was first used by Jock Young in 'The Role of the Police as Amplifiers of Deviancy, Negotiators of Reality and Translators of Fantasy', in S. Cohen (Ed.), *Images of Deviance* (Harmondsworth: Penguin, 1971), p. 37. We both probably picked it up from Marshall McLuhan's *Understanding Media*, published in 1964.
2. Between 1984 and 1991 (inclusive) there were about 8 citations of 'moral panic' in UK newspapers; then 25 in 1992, then a sudden leap to 145 in 1993. From 1994 to 2001, the average was at 109 per year.
3. Kenneth Thompson's *Moral Panics* (London: Routledge, 1998), appeared in the Routledge 'Key Ideas' series. For definitions, see Allan G. Johnson, *Blackwell Dictionary of Sociology* (Oxford: Blackwell, 2000) and Karim Murji, 'Moral Panic' in *Dictionary of Criminology*, London, Sage, 2001.
4. Blake Morrison, *As If* (Cambridge: Granta, 1997).
5. Sir William Macpherson, *The Stephen Lawrence Inquiry* (London: HMSO, 1999).
6. Two useful examples: Eugene McLaughlin and Karim Murji, 'After the Stephen Lawrence Report', *Critical Social Policy* 19 (August 1999), pp.371–85; Alan Marlow and Barry Loveday (Eds), *After Macpherson: Policing After the Stephen Lawrence Inquiry* (Lyme Regis: Russell House Publishing, 2000).
7. McLaughlin and Murji, op. cit. p.372.
8. As *The Sun*'s front page proclaimed: 'Britain Backs Our Bobbies: Sun Poll Boosts Under-Fire Cops' (1 March 1999).
9. Karim Murji, 'The Agony and the Ecstasy: Drugs, Media and Morality', in Ross Coomber (Ed.), *The Control of Drugs and Drug Users: Reason or Reaction?* (London: Harwood Publishers, 1998).

xxxvi *Introduction to the Third Edition*

10 Phillip Jenkins, *Moral Panic: Changing Concepts of the Child Molester in Modern America* (New Haven, Yale University Press, 1998).

11 See Phillip Jenkins, *Pedophiles and Priests: Anatomy of a Contemporary Crisis* (Oxford: Oxford University Press, 1996).

12 For two different, but complimentary, views see Beatrix Campbell, *Unofficial Secrets: Child Sexual Abuse – The Cleveland Case* (London: Virago, 1989) and Nigel Parton, *Governing the Family: Child Care, Child Protection and the State* (London: Macmillan, 1991), especially Chapter 4 'Sexual Abuse, the Cleveland Affair and the Private Family'.

13 For an analysis of newspaper coverage of the series of 'anti-paedophile crowd actions' in Britain over summer 2000, see John Drury, '"When the mobs are looking for witches to burn, nobody's safe" talking about the reactionary crowd', *Discourse and Society* 13, 1 pp. 41–73.

14 On the history of media panics about the appearance of new forms of media, see Kirsten Drotner, 'Modernity and Media Panics', in M. Skovmand and K.C. Schroder (Eds), *Media Cultures: Reappraising Traditional Media* (London: Routledge, 1992) and 'Dangerous Media? Panic Discourses and Dilemmas of Modernity', *Pedagogica Historica* 35, 3 (1999), pp. 593–619.

15 Drotner, op. cit. p.52.

16 For a recent review (concentrating on highly publicized violent crimes) see Martin Barker and Julian Petley (Eds), *Ill Effects: The Media-Violence Debate* (London: Routledge, 2001).

17 Grainne McKeever, 'Detecting, Prosecuting and Punishing Benefit Fraud: The Social Security Administration (Fraud) Act 1997', *Modern Law Review* 62 (March 1999), p.269.

18 Angela McRobbie, 'Motherhood, A Teenage Job', *Guardian* (5 September 1989).

19 A. Ward, *Talking Dirty: Moral Panic and Political Rhetoric* (London: Institute for Public Policy Research, 1996).

20 P.M. Evans and K.J. Swift, 'Single Mothers and the Press: Rising Tides, Moral Panic and Restructuring Discourses', in S.M. Neysmith (Ed.), *Restructuring Caring Labour: Discourse, State Practice and Everyday Life* (Oxford, OUP, 2000).

21 J. Doly *et al.*, *Refugees in Europe: The Hostile New Agenda* (London: Minorities Rights Group, 1997).

22 Robin Cohen, *Frontiers of Identity: The British and the Others* (London: Longman, 1994).

23 Ron Kaye, 'Redefining the Refugee: The UK Media Portrayal of Asylum Seekers', in Khalid Koser and Helma Lutz (Eds), *The New Migration in Europe: Social Constructions and Social Realities* (London: Macmillan Press, 1998), pp. 163–82.

24 See the report by Oxfam's UK poverty programme in Scotland, *Asylum: the Truth Behind the Headlines* (Oxfam, February 2001). This project monitored six

Introduction to the Third Edition xxxvii

Scottish papers over a two-month period (March–April 2000): a total of 263 articles on asylum and refugee issues.

25 E. El Refaie, 'Metaphors we Discriminate by: Naturalized Themes in Austrian Newspaper Articles about Asylum Seekers', *Journal of Sociolinguistics* 5, 3 (August 2001), pp. 352–71.
26 Stanley Cohen, *States of Denial: Knowing About Atrocities and Suffering* (Cambridge: Polity, 2001).
27 For example, Erich Goode and Nachman Ben-Yehuda, *Moral Panics: The Social Construction of Deviance* (Oxford: Blackwell, 1994).
28 See **Selected Reading List** below for references on constructionism.
29 Robert Reiner, 'The Rise of Virtual Vigilantism: Crime Reporting Since World War II', *Criminal Justice Matters* 43 (Spring 2001).
30 Richard.L. Fox and Robert Van Sichel, *Tabloid Justice: Criminal Justice in an Age of Media Frenzy* (Boulder: L. Rienner Publishers, 2001).
31 David Garland, *The Culture of Control* (Oxford: Oxford University Press, 2001).
32 Sheldon Unger, 'Moral Panic versus the Risk Society: Implications of the Changing Sites of Social Anxiety', *British Journal of Sociology* 52, pp. 271–292.
33 Mary Douglas's main publications on the subject (*Risk and Culture* and *Risk and Blame*) are presented in Richard Farndon, *Mary Douglas: An Intellectual Biography* (London: Routledge, 1999), pp 144–67.
34 Kai T. Erikson, *Everything in Its Path: Destruction of Community in the Buffalo Creek Flood* (New York: Simon and Schuster, 1976).
35 See Phil Scraton, *Hillsborough: The Truth* (Edinburgh: Mainstream, 2001).
36 Thompson, op. cit. pp. 8–11.
37 See William J. Chambliss, 'Crime Control and Ethnic Minorities: Legitimizing Racial Oppression by Creating Moral Panics', in Darnell Hawkins (Ed.), *Ethnicity, Race and Crime* (Albany: State University of New York Press, 1995).
38 Goode and Ben-Yehuda, op. cit. p.104.
39 Angela McRobbie and Sarah L. Thornton, 'Rethinking "moral panic" for multi-mediated social worlds', *British Journal of Sociology* 46 (December 1995), pp. 559–74.
40 ibid. p. 560.
41 Susan D. Moeller, *Compassion Fatigue: How the Media Sell Disease, Famine, War and Death* (New York: Routledge, 1999).
42 ibid. p. 306.

Thanks to Kate Steward and Andy Wilson for their help with this 'Third Edition'.

[20]
Post-Moral Torture:
From Guantanamo to Abu Ghraib

The history of torture – like all social institutions ever regarded as deviant, taboo or immoral – can be visualised in three ways. The first is a history of the deed – those diverse, many but rather special forms of human violence that are designated (seldom with total agreement) as being 'torture'. The second history deals with the oscillation between the extremes of tolerance and prohibition. Since the presumed disappearance after the Enlightenment of judicially approved torture, this has been told as a narrative of successful control. (Which meant ignoring the not-so-secret histories of tolerated torture under colonialism.) This is a story of moral restraint and stigmatisation; punishment, abolition and ban; regulation and prevention. By the mid twentieth century, the era of human rights declarations and prohibitions had signalled victory for the abolitionist case: the ban was supposed to be universal and absolute. There were no circumstances whatsoever in which torture could be justified. Or at least not if the torturers and their masters were – as they obviously were – Bad People.

This was just the time (1949) of Orwell's famous warning about Good People doing Bad Things. He did not mean the micro-sociology of torture: the situational pressures (later explored in the *Milgram and Zimbardo* tradition) that induce ordinary people to conform because of obedience to authority. He obviously meant the grand narratives of patriotism, liberty, freedom and democracy. Long-abandoned practices like torture, Orwell wrote, would not only became common again, but would be '…tolerated and even defended by people who considered themselves enlightened and progressive'.

This is why there has to be a third history of torture: the words that justify the deeds. Good ('enlightened', 'progressive') societies were liberal and democratic; their Bad Deeds required – at the very least – justifications that other liberal democratic societies could accept. These justifications had to be crafted within the special dialects and rituals of liberal legality. This calls for something far more remarkable than learning how to talk legal language ('Does this correspond with Article 23, Clause (b) of the VP Convention?'). Democratic leaders who authorised the violation had to learn voodoo talk: yes, we understand and affirm that a total prohibition on torture means just that: there can be no exceptions, not under any circumstances. But what we are doing isn't really torture and anyway is morally justifiable under the special circumstances we find ourselves in (in these terrible times).

By the third quarter of the century, three emblematic cases of this type appeared – each generating a rich list of items for future lexicons of *Democratic Justifications For Torture* 'First, there were the 'special procedures'

TORTURE: FROM GUANTANAMO TO ABU GHRAIB

(probably the most brutal violence ever used on this scale) used by France to defend its 'civilising mission' in Algeria; second, Israel's not so moderate 'moderate physical pressure' used against Palestinians in the occupied territories. And finally the slow, but long-running, story of the British in Northern Ireland, with its repertoire of 'depth interrogations'

Torture was a prominent feature of the Latin American military dictatorships, notably Argentina, Uruguay and Brazil. But the justificatory language of divine violence, purge, salvation, cleansing and 'national security' (in its fascist, rather than democratic version) needed no fancy legal manoeuvres, either at the time or afterwards. The collapse of these regimes and the subsequent 'transitions' to democracy in Latin America, South Africa and the Soviet Empire did not direct much attention to torture as a separate issue. Only in the aftermath of September 11, 2001, the global war against terrorism and the revelations about the abuse of detainees in Guantanamo, did massive public attention turn towards the subject. Were these detainees being tortured, or was this merely humiliation, degradation, abuse, ill-treatment (or their more or less legal equivalent, '…cruel and unusual punishment'?) What exactly was 'All the appropriate pressure' being placed on Khalid Shaikh Mohammed in March 2003. When was such 'stress and duress' allowed and justified? And how severe did it have to be to enter the category of torture?

The two features that characterise the first period from Guantanamo are *media saturation* and *ethical populism*.

Media saturation refers to the sheer amount of space devoted over this three-year period to news items, talk shows, documentaries, etc. As the *New York Times*: detected 'Torture Seeps Into Discussion by News Media' (5th November 2001) The horrors of 9/11 gave this discussion a sense of urgency, of being long overdue. Integral parts of the war against terror were information-gathering, risk analysis, early warnings, reliable intelligence. It was unfortunate that these methods might need some degree of torture; but it was better to debate all this in the open. 'Time to Think About Torture,' said *Newsweek* (5 November 2001). A subject seen as too squeamish, arcane and remote remote should enter the agenda of everyday thinking. In response to criticism about the lack of news coverage of torture, Jim Murphy (the executive producer of CBS *Evening News* with Dan Rather) had already anticipated the restructuring of family dinners. Speculation about torture and discussion of its merits, he said, were for now best left to talk shows and columnists, not the news: 'It's like the conversation you or I would have at dinner: 'I wonder if we should torture?'

Media saturation also demands more pictorial images. Orwell showed that the euphemism and vagueness of Newspeak was needed '…if one wants to name things without calling up mental pictures of them'. Phrases like 'stress and duress' were as blandly non-pictorial as 'moderate physical pressure'. 'In this autumn of anger,' wrote Jonathan Alter (*Newsweek*, 5 November 2001) 'even a liberal can

STANLEY COHEN

find his thoughts turning to … torture. OK, not cattle prods or rubber hoses, at least not here in the USA but something…'

But what? 'All appropriate pressure' was hardly pictorial, although 'appropriate' was the appropriate Clintonesque term for designating something vaguely wrong. Soon, a number of separate techniques were mentioned: hooding… withdrawal of painkillers ….beating and shaking… sleep deprivation…harsh lights…loud noise…sensory deprivation…'position abuse'. An excellent ad-agency phrase was invented by Wayne Madsen (a former US navy intelligence officer)'torture lite'. If this term does cover these techniques, then there is clearly something wrong with international definitions of torture. 'Torture lite' may be used in all innocence but it usually requires the same bad faith as 'diet Coke' or 'fat-free cheesecake.' It is difficult to imagine, even harder to incorporate into legal and public discourse, a clear definition of 'justified' torture: this amount of pain; using this technique; to these parts of the body; over a certain time. This is not an aesthetic or descriptive problem but overcoming the taboo about being too explicit about *what odd behaviour your culture will permit*. It required the moral authority of a Harvard University law professor to set out a pictorial description of inserting sterilized needles under fingernails.

By *ethical populism* I mean the spread and popularisation of liberal-legal justifications. None of these is new but they were once more confined to legal settings, United Nations diplomatic deals, first-year university ethics courses or ritual exchanges between human right organisations and offending governments. Audiences are primed to neutralise any scruples by two disarming arguments: (1) The September 11 disaster and the birth of Islamic fundamentalist terrorism caught us by surprise, it might have been prevented and must be prevented from happening again. Only the inflexibility and absolutism of liberals, human rights organisations and the United Nations gets in the way. (2) At the same time, the audience is assured that nothing radical or even new is coming up for their approval. Don't they understand that all this stuff has been used already? So smart up, get wise, be as cynical as Alan Dershowitz: 'If anybody has any doubt that our CIA over time has taught people to torture, has encouraged torture, has probably tortured in extreme cases, I have a bridge to sell you in Brooklyn.' These are three standard examples:

The ticking bomb story is the best known: you have captured a terrorist who knows where/when a bomb is about to explode; can you torture him to save 50 lives? This story becomes exaggerated and simplified; above all, the number of times this opportunity presents itself is greatly exaggerated.

Self-preservation – the doctrine of security, necessity and self defence, the slogan 'the constitution is not a suicide pact' – all these principles are embedded in the notion of the 'third way' and the logic of regulation. In 1987, an Israeli judicial commission on torture – the Landau Commission – worked out a model used explicitly (by Alan Dershowitz and others) from the early days of Guantanamo Bay.

The first position is tolerance and laissez-faire. We give the security services a free hand to operate in a twilight zone outside the realm of law. This means coming right out to acknowledge that torture had indeed been used in this situation (however reluctantly) , and that all decisions about when it was appropriate would be left to the security services. But that was not viable. No Israeli government now nor any other present democratic government could abandon all political or legal control over such a practice. This would be the road to fascism '... sliding towards methods practised in regimes which we abhor' [*Landau Commission*, para.4.2]

The second idea was to deny that it happened at all, to keep on saying, whatever the evidence, that it was prohibited and therefore couldn't exist. We repeat the absolute ban ... but turn a blind eye. This was surely in Landau's words 'the way of the hypocrites'.

Now we arrive at the third way: interrogation is regulated and supervised by judicial bureaucrats. This means regulation, control, restrictions, guidelines. Neither total prohibition nor total discretion to the agents. In Alan Dershowitz's version, authorities apply to the judge for a 'torture warrant' on a case-to-case basis: 'I'm not in favour of torture, but if your'e going to have it, it should damn well have court approval ... If we have torture, it should be authorised by law (*Los Angeles Times*). The question becomes whether it is worse for that torture to be conducted in secret and then publicly denied, as the French did in Algeria, or for the government to acknowledge that it is making an exception to the general prohibition against torture in this case. There is no 'good' realistic third alternative. This is a classic 'choice of evils'....

When the first words and images about Abu Ghraib appeared in May 2004, much of the initial shock came from sheer surprise. None of us had ever seen anything like this. Now, after seeing so much analysis and exegesis, the novelty fades but the revulsion is deeper: the hooded, naked, manacled men huddle by cell gates; the grinning US soldiers point at the prisoners' genitals; the off-stage photographer obsessively records each move; dogs are about to attack naked men in their cells. I must admit to my own private reaction: these are the only atrocity images that I have seen that I literally cannot bear to see again.

What was going on? The humiliation and sadism did not seem to cause serious physical pain yet it didn't fit the vague notion of 'torture lite'. And the techniques of degradation did not seem to come from training courses of the kind that Ron Crelinsten has studied: 'They taught us psychological methods – to study the fears and weaknesses of a prisoner. make him stand up, don't let him sleep, keep him naked and isolated, put rats and cockroaches in his cell, give him bad food, serve him dead animals, throw cold water on him, change the temperature. The Americans didn't accept any physical torture.'

But these manuals and courses include familiar items in the repertoire of torture – heavy or lite. Their rationale is as instrumental as Guantanamo (or Belfast or Buenos Aires). The cruelty may seem gratuitous,redundant or even

STANLEY COHEN

counter-productive, but even if not planned, it is planned for. We cannot make sense of Abu Ghraib by looking for totalistic theories that assume that every move was known, choreographed and co-ordinated by Secretary of State Rumsfeld. In Seymour Hersch's *New Yorker* articles we learn that Rumsfeld, the CIA, the Deprtment of Defence indeed intended a programme of humiliation, including sexual humiliation like this in order to intimidate detainees into informing on each other. And, like old fashioned conspirators, they took pains to cover their tracks. What went wrong was the *camrecorders*. Using them was stupid enough; letting them leak out was stupid beyond belief.

We must visualise the highly fragmented scene so characteristic of modern warfare, atrocities and political violence. The agents on the ground are informed by a package deal of motives in which the calculating instrumental reality of the neo-cons (symbolised by Rumsfeld impersonating Peter Sellers playing Dr Stranglelove) has only a small walk-on part. Their main inspiration is as Joanna Bourke describes: the carnival; the spectacle of unrestrained ludic sexuality; trick shop horrors; the fake jungles of reality television; the rewarded narcissism and cruelty of 'Big Brother' and 'I'm a Celebrity … Get Me Out Of Here'. A maniacal Jerry Springer presides as blacks, chicanos and 'trailer trash' whites find their surrogate targets in hapless Iraqi detainees.

I hope that it does not sound too pretentious to see Guantanamo and Abu Ghraib as standing along the fault lines in the American Empire: neo-liberal rationality in the centre; madness at the multicultural edges. Neither project is too interested in moral justifications. As Bourke first described the Abu Ghraib scene: 'There is no moral confusion here: the photographers don't even seem aware that they are recording a war crime.' There is no suggestion that the scene is morally skewed; aesthetics of porno protects them from blame.' (*Guardian* 7 May, 2004). The leadership has made a rational calculation: we can do what we like. Why waste resources on lawyers who'll conclude anyway (as Rodley shows) that Constitutional considerations are less important than international norms?

The chilling statement 'bad things happen' was generally taken as Rumsfeld's refusal to engage with the moral issues about prison conditions, detention practice and torture. In fact he did not say this nor (though it was heard in the same fortnight) did it refer to Abu Ghraim. On May 20 2003, in a remote stretch of desert near Faluja west of Bagdad, an American Marine Division attacked a group of Iraqis who said that they were guests at a wedding. Some 20 'military aged males' were killed. Major General James Mattis, commander of the 1st Marine Division, was scathing about suggestions that these were bona fida wedding guest. How many people would go into the desert for a wedding? Reporters then asked him about footage on Arab TV showing a child's body lowered into grave: This was his reply: 'I have not seen the pictures but bad things happen in wars. I don't have apologise for the conduct of my men.'

'Bad things happen' – the polite form of 'shit happens' – is not just a radical denial of accountability. It refuses to see the salience of human rights principles at all. The so-called 'hypocrites' way on torture (proclaiming the righteousness of a prohibition while knowingly evading it) at least recognizes the existence of the problem. Salim, the East African trader in VS Naipaul's novel *A Bend in the River,* has no illusions about the pre-colonial cruelty of the Africans; they never lied because they never assessed themselves. But the Europeans could do one thing and say something quite different. 'The Europeans wanted gold and slaves, like everybody else, but at the same time they wanted statues put up to themselves as people who had done good things for the slaves. Beng an intelligent and energetic people…. They could express both sides of their civilisation and they got both the slaves and the statues'

A final terrible thought on the democracy of representation. The videocam recorder follows the low life s/m scenes of Abu Ghraib; the offenders and a universal audience of voyeurs seem to share these cultural meanings; all over the world the sickening sights of violent pornography (described by Gunhammer) are easily available (you can watch the rape of a girl on a website and for $4.50 change her identity from Thai, to Korean to Vietnamese). And there on the screen are the Others – the terrorists, cultists, freedom fighters, separatists, urban guerillas. And what are they doing? Beheading captives on television; phographing hostages begging for their lives; sending 3-D photos of their victims's ears. Did they learn this from us or did we pick it up from them? Or are we both under the same zombie's spell? I doubt that it would do much harm for a journal concerned with the value of human rights and free expression to at least look at these questions. ❑

[21]
Carry on Panicking

Address on receiving the Award for "Outstanding Achievement" from the British Society of Criminology at its Annual Conference, Cardiff, 29 June 2009

Introduction

I am very grateful to British Society of Criminology for giving me this award. I truly value this as an honour from my colleagues. I owe special thanks to David Downes for his support and generosity of spirit over the forty five years since my early graduate student days at LSE. Thanks also to those of you "out there" - my friends, ex-colleagues and ex-graduate students - for your support, loyalty and enthusiasm.

What do you say in a 20 minute "acceptance" talk for a prize that no one has received before? A competition that you hadn't heard of? What is the right note to strike? There are many publicized prizes and awards these days - whether in the arts, literature, academic disciplines, sports, public service etc. Surely I could draw on an existing template?

1. Obedient Servant Rewarded
This is the most often used, conformist and conventional of all narratives. Just an ordinary bloke or girl gradually climbs the right ladders, patiently playing according to the rules. This culminates in the appropriate reward. Everyone in her path has been marvellously helpful; every item on her CV (articles, research grants) is tested to be RAE positive and inexorably counts towards the end result[1].

2. Coming in from the Cold
This is about the youthful rebel: in some romantic versions he is the outsider, unrecognized, on the margins, dismissed either as a harmless nutter or a dangerous heretic, ostracized or ignored by his colleagues. In the less dramatic version, his work is seen as dull and boring, not "serious" enough to be taken seriously. But things change. In one narrative, he himself changes: - he adapts, tones down and compromises until he eventually melts into his environment. In this remaking of himself, he might denounce his own past (I will return later to the example from my generation: the renunciation of values supposedly connected to the loosely termed "Sixties"). In another narrative, the award-winner will tell you that he was right all the time and has remained utterly consistent. The change has come from outside – the hegemony of the old guard has gone (or in some stories, there has even been a "paradigm shift"), thus exonerating your original position.

3. Ironic Gesture
There is, of course, the possibility of refusing the award on ideological grounds. The refusal though must be public; there is no political gain in a private letter (you might just as well have pleaded swine-flu). There are many ideological grounds for refusal: the award (honour or money) is tainted (for example, the sponsor is involved with the arms trade); your fellow academics or artists are banned; a

---

[1] In the early Seventies, the head of a well known Sociology Department, would refer to articles written by staff since the last departmental meeting as "goals scored."

gesture of solidarity with whatever group is being currently oppressed and victimized. In addition to refusal, there is the option of ironic refusal. My acceptance of a prize - so I tell a credulous post-modernist audience - only *looks* like I'm being used to give moral credibility to the sponsoring organization or government.

But none of these models seemed to fit me. This, of course, is for others to judge but I don't think that my work has been conformist, nor have my values changed much. As for the option of refusal, well - as much as I researched the CV's and backgrounds of the BSC Executive Committee - I couldn't find anything incriminating. The BSC has not done bad things, not offended anybody, nor been undemocratic. It seems an exemplary professional association.

My assertion that my values have not changed expresses my particular aversion to the current "coming of age" trope[2] which denounces the values of the Sixties as naïve, adolescent, romantic, anarchistic and utopian. So they were, as Abby Hoffman famously remarked, but we were still right.

Last year, I gave a graduation day address to sociology students at Middlesex University. I talked about the clichéd advice that dominated these occasions: "Put your three years at university behind you; it's time to enter the real world." I told the students to please pay no attention to this advice. It's just another form of social control to stop you from continuing to appreciate the values that you should have picked up in any decent university - care for learning in itself; scepticism about accepted knowledge; the personal qualities of tolerance and friendship; the political values of fairness and social justice. Above all, they should question the notion that their three years of university were not "real", that university life was somehow "artificial". But what is taken as "real" life - A mental hospital? Perhaps the Houses of Parliament during the expenses story? A training school for suicide bombers? Or maybe reality television, watching a group of your fellow human beings degrade themselves and each other in front of audiences of 12 million?

I warned them - as I warn you - to beware of the people whom Saul Bellow calls *reality instructors*: You know those people who are always grabbing you to tell you "What Things Are Really Like": the cops, doctors, judges and journalists who instruct you on how things work "out there". The criminological version of "out there" is sitting in the back of a police van.

I said that those models of award-acceptance speeches didn't fit me. Allow me to end with the narrative of change and continuity which led up to the work I'm doing now. I promise not to instruct you about what is really real; my subject is rather what is really *important*.

Moral Panics

Folk Devils and Moral Panics was surely a child of its time and place. At the end of the Seventies I went to live in Israel for what turned out seventeen years. As this period moved along, so the book and its cultural milieu seemed more and more remote. Even the dumbest and most otiose sociology does not require a theory to "explain" the differences between Britain in the Sixties and Israel in the Eighties. I am merely trying to think aloud (and in print) about the complex links between biography and external social reality.

In the mid-Nineties, I returned to London and to teaching criminology, deviance and social control courses at the LSE. I tried to reconstruct for my students the texts and contexts of labelling theory, the

---

[2] A particular application - with the same social control functions - of the great wisdom that "If you are not a socialist when you are twenty, then you haven't got a heart; if you are still a socialist when you are forty, then you haven't got a head".

NDC, new deviancy theory and the new criminology. From my vantage point now, the criticism of our supposed liberal tolerance looks more interesting. The first wave of radical theorists had indeed argued that *too much* stuff was being (to use some ugly but useful terms) criminalized, deviantised or problematised): defining deviance up, as this was later called. The point is not whether we approve; nor whether we can sympathize, nor whose side we are on. Nor is everything simply a matter of political stance: non-interventionism can be justified by conservatives (not the responsibility of governments, leave it to the market); liberals (civil rights are threatened, private life is not the business of the state; and radicals (distrust of the repressive state apparatus, the crime problem requires not legal tinkering but radical change of whole society).

The eclectic elements in the original discourse - symbolic interactionism, socialism, restorative justice - hardly added up to a coherent social policy. Social policy is by definition interventionist - which means *doing something* about the problem, for example: moral enterprise to stop the problem from being normalised, further enterprise to draw attention to its seriousness, new laws, prohibitions or sanctions; improving the criminal justice and other social control systems. But these responses only make sense if you have taken the problem seriously. This recognition soon prompted the radical model to develop its own internal self correction. Therefore the phase of "left realism" and "taking crime seriously".

The pristine rhetoric was "against" the moral panic: there's no need to panic, calm down, it's not that serious, it's not the end of the world, there are more serious problems. The liberal and radical exposures of moral panic was informed by discovery or recovery of victims - especially under the driving force of feminism. The (still expanding) literature on victims, harm, danger and risk began to examine the empirical base for what has been on the agenda of ethics and moral philosophy for centuries.

Denial

The phenomena that concerned me in *States of Denial* were undisputedly serious - torture, genocide, ethnic violence, terror, political massacres, atrocities of all types, "social suffering" resulting from poverty, racism as well as natural disasters. And just as I had written more about moral panics than folk devils, I was now dealing with reactions to these phenomena (my subtitle is *Knowledge About Atrocities And Suffering*) rather than the phenomena themselves. I don't want to repeat what the book says about how my life in Israel influenced my whole subject, nor about the concept of denial. My viewpoint here is much narrower: the hidden continuities and overlaps between these two books.

The most obvious link, is that the entire human rights enterprise is a product of social construction. The legalistic ownership of the problem is conveyed in the relatively recent term "human rights violations". This translates the traditional moralistic language of sin and evil into the legal dialect. In the public realm, however, this translation hardly ever works: participation in genocide, for example, is not convincingly described as a "human rights violation". The more pictorial languages of atrocity and social suffering are obviously more appropriate.

In any event, the work of humanitarian organizations and the media is clearly a form of moral enterprise; there are moral crusades and campaigns. But are there moral panics? And is there anything helpful in conceptualizing them as the "opposite" of denial? I was prompted to ask these questions by current versions of the standard critique that the concept of moral panic is inherently normative, political and value-loaded. The Melanie Phillips version is best known: the left-liberal elitists (who, of course, dominate the media) have simply applied the label of moral panic in a selective and biased way to the wholly justified reactions of ordinary people to real problems.

Hysterical as the "right realist" position may be, there a peculiar sense in which Phillips is correct. When these left liberals study or support social movements - say, in favour of animal rights or the heavier criminalization of domestic violence - they will hardly describe them moral panics.[3] The category of moral panic is, however, "objective" in the sense that the criteria for defining some social reactions as moral panics and others not, can be set out and applied by any observer. Thus there can theoretically be "negative moral panics" (the traditional ones that criminologists so readily detect, expose and criticize) but also "positive moral panics": the ones that we approve.

The problem, so one argument goes, lies in the particularly negative connotations of the word "panic": hysteria, exaggeration, crowd behaviour, delusion and - above all - irrationality. Lets see what happens if we use alternative words: yes, it does makes considerably more sense to talk of an "approved crusade" than an "approved panic". But this loses the particular connotations of "panic" that you want to retain!

All these tricky matters become trickier if we compare moral panic with denial. I have argued that denial in the personal realm is morally nuanced and ambiguous; there are defensible and positive functions. In the public realm, however, denial always has to be denounced as the enemy. This, of course, begs the question about the difference between private and public. And in the realms of social life that interest me most - at the interface between the personal and the political - it is near-impossible to use some words in a neutral way: passivity, inertia, silence, normalization, collusion, cover-up, turning a blind eye, the bystander effect, compassion fatigue. The opposite of all this is acknowledgement of the truth and acting accordingly. But to dwell nowadays on matters like "the truth" is to invite theoretical questions way beyond my reach. Let me rather examine the concept at work.

Climate Change

The emergence of climate change as a major public problem, no doubt needs setting in the wider discourse about ecology, environmentalist social movements and green politics. I use this only as a more specific case study of denial and moral panic. I don't know the literature well enough to do more than list some points of entry:

1. Climate change seems to fit the social constructionist model. There were all the familiar stages in the natural history of social problem construction; there are identifiable moral entrepreneurs - whether individuals (politicians, activists, scientists) and organizations; there are claims-makers, contesting not only rival models of knowledge, policy and risk-management, but also the most basic claims about the problem's existence.

2. The rhetoric about climate change draws on the classic moral panic repertoire: disaster, apocalyptic predictions, warning of what might happen if nothing is done, placing the problem in wider terms (the future of the planet!). According to Tom Burke, climate is: "the most serious threat to humanity since the invention of nuclear weapons."

3. Truth claims are made as facts beyond questioning. The facts are so obvious, that "the task of climate change agencies is not to persuade by rational argument, but in effect to develop and

---

[3] The political ambiguities in moral panic theory have been well discussed in the literature. See, for example, the recent Special Issue of the British Journal of Criminology, 49(1), January 2009.

nurture a new 'common sense'....*The* "facts" need to be treated as so taken-for-granted that they need not be spoken.[4]

4. Within the environmentalist movement itself, there is an explicit discourse about climate change denial. There is a "Climate Change Denial Website" and a Google search yields 390,000 entries. My book on denial is much cited - an ironic flattery because I clearly express my own lack of enthusiasm about the environmental cause.

5. The discourse about climate change is quite unusual in concentrating so much on what I called *literal denial*. The core of the climate change movement is the construction of any sort of doubt, qualification or disagreement as denial. And they mean not just the passive denial of indifference, but the active work of "denialists". Sceptics are demonized: treated like retarded or crazy persons, people who just don't get it. Taking his cue From Al Gore, here is David Miliband: those who deny climate dangers are "the flat earthers of the twenty-first century", A group of Australian activists and journalists have suggested that climate change denial should become a crime like Holocaust Denial; deniers should be brought before a Nuremberg-style court. We must make them responsible for the thousands of deaths which will happen if global warming alarm not heeded.

6. Most important of all: the environmental cause is winning hearts and minds. A new part in the moral edifice of society is close to being created. The process of social problem construction is just about complete. Moral entrepreneurs though, will have to remain active - for example, combating climate change denial. But the discourse of the major institutions of society has been changed; for example: the curricula of schools, the public face of big business, the greening of party politics, the very existence of separate government departments of ministries; and of course, the morality plays of the mass media. (A recent *Observer* Sunday Supplement was described as a guide for ethical living. The entire magazine was devoted to environmental causes, instructions on how to live good life. In an ethical life, you learn to put your computer on standby, to give up your electric toothbrush and keep a record of your carbon footprints.)

All this invites two types of question. The *empirical* question is whether the environmental appeal is competing with humanitarian causes for public support or has its own constituency. The *normative* question - forgive this Walt Disney simplification - is which of these you would choose to worry about and which you would rather deny.

Moving On

Here, after a journey into the past, is where we have reached:

The critique behind the concept of moral panics, is that too much attention (human resources, moral indignation, social construction) is given to the particular problem at issue. The critique behind the concept of denial is too little attention of the same type is given to a particular problem.

Taking off from denial theory, I'm continuing to work on the "particular problem" of public response to representations (by humanitarian organizations and the mass media) of the suffering of distant others. I'm reading more about selective attention, moral judgement and the ethics of responsibility to others. The point is to locate these individual matters in specific social and political contexts.

---

[4] Ereaut, G. and Segnit, N. (2006) *Warm Words: How are we telling the climate story and can we tell it better?* London: Institute for Public Policy Research.

This might be a long way from criminology. But so be it. It might seem strange, but for many of us, criminology has been the best starting point to arrive at these wider questions. This is why I'm pleased to accept an award in *criminology*.

Stanley Cohen, London, August 2009

Name Index

Abel, Richard 129, 133, 159, 163–4, 165, 167–8
Adlam, D. 152
Adorno, Theodor xii
Alfonsín, Raoul 215
Ali, Khaled al-Sheikh 174
Ali, Muhammad lxii
Alter, Jonathan 348–9
Althusser, Louis xlviii
Anderson, P. 34
Anitua, G. I. xxi
Arendt, Hannah 65
Arevalo, Cerezo 205
Aylwin, Patricio 215, 237

Baldwin, James 2
Barak, Aharon 177
Barbie, Klaus 219, 231
Bartky, S. L. 154
Bauman, Zygmunt xxvin16, 156
Bayer, R. 129
Beck, R. 126–7, 128
Beck, Ulrich 333
Becker, Howard S. xlviii, 1, 7, 11, 27–8, 41, 46, 141
Beer, Dame Gillian xlii
Beit Hallahmi, B. 139
Bellow, Saul 356
Ben-David, Joseph lv
Ben-Yehuda, Nachman xxi, lviii
Berlin, Isaiah 65, 122–3
Bernal Sarmiento, C. E. xxi
Betts, Leah 321–2
Biko, Steve 237
Blair, Tony 317
Bonger, Willem 49, 181, 201
Bordaglio, 154
Bordo, S. 154
Boris, 154
Bottomore, T. 59–60
Bottoms, A. E. 137
Bourke, Joanna 351–2
Braithwaite, John 234, 238

Brophy, J. 152
Brosnan, D. 194
Bukowski, Charles xxvin6
Bulger, Jamie 317–18, 339

Calley, William 68–9
Carey, George 317
Carlen, Pat xxvin16
Carson, W. G. 32, 38
Carte, G. E. 29
Ceausescu, Nicolae 244
Chinkin, Christine lvi
Chomsky, Noam 251
Christie, Nils xv, 285
Chunn, D. E. 152
Clark, Ron 281
Clarke, R. V. G. 136
Clinton, Bill 321
Cohen, Clive xliv, xlvi–xlvii, li
Cohen, Jessica xli, li, liv–lv, lix
Cohen, Judith xli, xlvii, li, liii, liv, lvi, lix, lx
Cohen, Ray xl
Cohen, Robin xxi, xliii, xliv, xlvi–xlvii, li, liii, lv, lvi, lvii–lviii, lix, lx
Cohen, Ruth (née Kretzmer) xli, xlvii, liii, liv–lv, lvi, lviii–lix
Cohen, Sie xl
Cohen, Stanley xi–xxii; *Against Criminology* xii, xlv; 'Alternatives to punishment – The abolitionist case' xviii, 159–69; *Anarchy* xlv; bibliography xxviii–xxxvi; B'Tselem report xviii–xix, xx; *Canadian Criminology Forum* xx; Centenary Lecture xix–xx; 'Conference Life' xx, 299–314; 'Crime and Politics' xx, 277–97; 'Crime and Punishment: 1. How can we balance justice, guilt and tolerance?' xvii, 65–70; 'Crime and Punishment: 2. Community control – a new utopia' xvii–xviii, 71–7; 'Crime and Punishment: 3. Some modest and unrealistic proposals' xvii, 79–87; 'Criminology and the Sociology of Deviance in Britain' xvii, 25–64; 'The

critical discourse on social control' xviii, 147–57; *Denial and Acknowledgement* xix, xx; dissertation xi, xvi, xx, xxviin17, xl, xlviii; *Escape Attempts* xiii, xiv, xxvn3; *Festschrift* xxi, xxxix; 'fishing net'-metaphor xviii; *Folk Devils and Moral Panics* xx, xxi–xxii, xl, 315, 330, 356; 'Government Responses to Human Rights Reports' xix, 249–75; 'Intellectual Skepticism and Political Commitment' xix, 181–203; Israel liii–lviii; 'Mods, Rockers and the Rest' xvi, 1–10; 'Moral panics as cultural politics' xx, 315–45; *Neue Kriminalpolitik* xxi; obituaries xxi; Outstanding Achievement Award xii, xiv, xx, xlii, 355–60; photography xxxviii; 'Pioneers of Qualitative Research' xxi; 'Postmoral torture: From Guantanamo to Abu Ghraib' xx, 347–53; *The Power to Punish* xviii; *Prison Secrets* xiii; *Psychological Survival* xiii, xliv; 'The punitive city' xvii–xviii, lviii, 89–113; Sellin-Glueck Award xlii; 'Social-Control Talk: Telling Stories about Correctional Change' 115–46; South Africa xlvi–xlvii; 'Stan Cohen Collection' xxii; 'State crimes of previous regimes' xix, 205–48; *States of Denial* xix, xx, xxi, xlii, lii, lvii, 357, 359; 'Talking about torture in Israel' xix, 171–80; 'Vandalism – 1. The Politics of Vandalism' xvi–xvii, 11–15; 'Vandalism – 2. The Nature of Vandalism' xvi–xvii, 17–20; 'Vandalism – 3. Can it be controlled?' xvi–xvii, 21–4; *Visions of Social Control* xviii, xx, xxvn3, xxvin8, lviii; Willem Bonger Memorial Lecture xvi, xix, xxi, xxvin15
Comfort, Megan lii, lx–lxi
Cooper, David 22
Cooper, Tommy lxii
Crelinsten, Ron 350
Cressey, D. R. 39, 42, 99
Croft, J. 34
Cronje, Geoff 202n2
Currie, Elliot 281

Daems, T. xxi
Danner, Mark 255
Davis, D. B. 122
Davis, F. 125
de Beauvoir, Simone 244

de Haan, W. 168
de Klerk, F. W. 237, 239
DePalma, Anthony 285
Derrida, Jacques 194
Dershowitz, Alan 349–50
Diamond, I. 153
Donzelot, J. 128, 132
Dorfman, Ariel 217
Douglas, J. D. 56
Douglas, Mary 334, 343
Downes, David xxi, xxviin11, xl, xlv, xlvii, l, liii–liv, 22, 35, 39, 45, 48, 284, 355
Durkheim, Emile li, 46

Edelman, M. 141
Eichmann, Adolf 244, 245
Eisenstadt, Shmuel Noah lv
Ellsberg, Daniel 180
Elvin, Jan 285
Empey, L. T. 106
Engels, Friedrich 49, 122
Erikson, Kai xlviii, 46, 335
Etzioni, A. 138, 141
Eysenck, Hans 42, 44

Feeley, Malcolm li–lii, liv, lv, 284
Feldman, Avigdor 176
Feyling, R. xxi
Finkielkraut, Alain 219, 231
Foucault, Michel xx, xxvn3, xxvin12, li, lviii, 71, 85, 89, 90, 109, 110, 117, 121, 123, 128, 132, 141, 150, 151, 152–4, 160, 164, 180, 183, 197, 200, 214–15, 242, 278–9, 338
Franke, Herman xi, xxi
Freud, Sigmund li, 46
Friedenberg, Edgar 14
Frith, S. xvii
Fujimori, Alberto 268, 270

Gabriel, Peter 273–4
Galanter, Marc 159, 164, 166–7
Gallagher, Noel 322
Garland, David xxi, xxviin14, 149, 153, 278, 286–7
Gavigan, S. A. M. 152
Gaylin, W. 111n1, 133
Gearty, Conor lii–liii, lxi
Gibbens, T. C. N. 36
Gitlin, T. 197

Glover, Edward 37
Glueck, Eleanor 43–4
Glueck, Sheldon 43–4
Godwin, William xliv
Goffman, Erving xxvn3, xlviii, xlix, 25, 238, 309
Golan, Daphna xiii, xviii–xix, xx, xxi, 174–5
Goldstein, Dov 176
Gordon, R. W. 150, 191
Goren, Shlomo 177
Goring, Charles 30–1, 40, 42, 43
Goudsblom, Jaap xxvin16
Gouldner, A. 51, 59
Greenberg, D. F. 100, 124
Griffith, I. L. 287
Gross, Martin 90
Grünhut, Max 34, 35

Habermas, Jurgen 295
Hall, Stuart xxi, 45, 337
Halloran, J. D. 45
Hamilton, V. Lee 290
Hammarberg, Thomas xxi, xliii
Hammerman, Ilana 179–80
Handelman, Stephen 284, 288
Hargreaves, David 22
Hassan II, King 248
Havel, Vaclav 216, 223–4, 226, 246n69
Heidensohn, Frances lxi–lxii
Hersch, Seymour 351
Higgins, J. 116
Hitler, Adolf 218
Hobsbawm, Eric 12, 289, 292, 293, 294
Hoffman, Abby 356
Honecker, Erich 230
Hood, R. 57–8
Horowitz, I. L. 26, 49
Hudson, B. xxi
Hughes, Robert 291
Hulsman, Louk 159, 162, 164, 165, 168

Ignatieff, Michael 117, 120–1, 293–4

James, William 1
Jeffrey, C. R. 136
Jit, Mohammed 175
Jones, H. 32, 42–3
Jubany, Olga xlv, li

Kahane, Meir 177
Kaplan, Robert 292
Kapuscinski, Ryszard 293
Kellough, G. xvi, xx, xxv–xxvin5
Kelman, Herbert C. 290
Kermode, Frank 197
Kirchheimer, O. 121
Kittrie, N. N. 90
Krausz, E. 48
Kremnitzer, Mordechai 173
Kretzmer, David liv
Krinsky, C. xxi
Kundera, Milan 246
Kuper, Adam xliii, xlvi, xlix, l, lv–lvi, lviii

Laber, Jerri 225
Laing, Ronald xlviii, li, 11, 51
Landau, Moshe 172–3, 176–7, 178
Langbein, John H. 279
Lasch, C. 122, 128, 132
Lawrence, Stephen 317, 318–19
Le Carré, John 277–8, 288, 293
Leach, E. R. 142–3
Lemert, Edwin xlviii, 1, 5, 11, 13, 15, 27, 28, 51
Lissenberg, Elisabeth xxvin15
Livnat, Limor 177, 178
Lombroso, Cesare 30, 31

McCarthy, Mary 68–9
McDermott, V. xxi, 99
Mack, Raymond 86
McKelvey, B. 119
MacKinnon, C. 193
McLaughlin, E. xxi
McMahon, M. xvi, xx, xxv–xxvin5
Macpherson, William 318–19
McRobbie, Angela 338–9
Madsen, Wayne 349
Mandela, Nelson 233
Mandelstam, Nadezhda 234–5
Mannheim, Hermann 31, 32, 34, 35, 37, 39, 46
Maran, Rita 173–4
Marcuse, Herbert xii, 153
Margalit, Dan 177
Martin, B. 196
Martin, John 18, 20
Marx, Karl xlviii, 49, 122
Masseru, Emilio 244

Mathews, R. 152
Mathiesen, Thomas xvi, 117, 191
Mattis, James 352
Matza, David xiii, xx, xlviii, xlix, 14, 27, 28–9, 30, 39, 42, 51, 56, 68, 277–9, 295
Mayhew, P. 136
Mays, 35, 48
Mead, George Herbert xlviii
Medina, Ernest 68–9
Mellor, David 329
Melossi, D. 121, 148
Menem, Carlos 228
Merton, R. 47
Messinger, S. L. 155
Michnik, Adam 241
Miliband, David 359
Mill, J. S. 67
Miller, Emmanuel 37
Miller, P. 152
Miller, Walter 13
Mills, C. Wright 126, 283
Minson, J. 151
Moeller, Susan D. 341–2
Mohammed, Khalid Shaikh 348
Molotch, Harvey xxi, xlv, 1
Moon, Claire xxi, lii, lvii, lxi
Morgan, Rod 284
Morris, E. K. 136
Morris, Terence xxvin11, xl, 1, 34–5, 38–9, 45–6, 48
Munro, B. xxi
Murphy, Jim 348

Nafsu, Izzat 172
Nagel, Thomas 216
Naylor, R. T. 288
Neier, Aryeh 233
Newburn, Tim liii, lxii
Newman, O. 139
Nisbet, R. A. 125, 143n1
Nixon, Richard 68
Norris, C. 194–5
Novelozo, A. xxi
Nozick, Robert 130
Nuttall, Jeff 51

Olson, F. 193
Ophir, Adi 178–9
Ophul, Marcel 244

Orwell, George 134–5, 139, 173, 175, 180, 242, 259, 260, 347

Park, Robert 1
Parker, Tony 45
Pashukanis, Evgenii xlviii
Pavarini, M. 121
Payne, Sarah 324
Peters, Edward 171
Phillips, Melanie 357
Pinochet, Augusto 227
Plant, R. 125
Platt, A. 130
Polsky, Ned 1, lxii, 47
Potter, G. xxi
Poulantzas, Nico xlviii
Probyn, Walter xxvn1

Quinby, L. 153

Radzinowicz, Leon xvii, 32, 33, 34, 35, 37, 40, 43, 45, 56
Rather, Dan 348
Rawls, John 130
Rock, Paul xiii, xvi, xxvin9, xxxix–lxii
Rodley, Nigel 352
Rorty, Richard 196, 198
Rose, N. 152, 154
Rosen, Roly 179–80
Rosenberg, Harold 244, 245
Rothman, David xxvin12, 90, 97, 117, 119–21, 122, 137
Rumsfeld, Donald 351, 352
Rusche, G. 121
Ryle, Gilbert 83

Sachs, Albie 238
Sacks, Oliver 243
Sainsbury, Peter 39
Samenow, S. E. 136
Sartre, Jean-Paul 244
Savage, M. xvii
Scarry, Elaine 171
Schmidt, Michael 294
Schur, E. M. 2
Schutz, Alfred lx
Schwendinger, Herman 282
Schwendinger, Julia 282
Scott, D. xxi

NAME INDEX

Scott, P. 39
Scull, Andrew xiii, xvii, xxvin12, 90, 103, 111n4, 117, 121, 122, 124, 128
Seiter, R. P. 136
Sennet, R. 132
Seu, Irene Bruna xiii, lii
Shalev, Sharon lii, lix, lx
Sharon, Arik 177
Shavit, Ari 176
Shover, N. 116
Simmel, Georg xxvn3
Simon, Jonathan 284
Simpson, O. J. 279
Skolnick, Jerome H. 27, 29
Smart, B. 121
Smart, C. 152
Snare, A. 133
Sparks, Richard xlix, 57–8
Spierenburg, Pieter 153
Spitzer, S. 121, 153, 243, 245–6
Springer, Jerry 332, 352
Stang, D. T. 133
Stedman-Jones, G. 116
Steiner, George 193
Steinert, Heinz 159, 162–3, 164, 165, 167, 168
Steinfels, P. 131
Sterling, Clare 284, 288
Stroessner, Alfredo 214
Super, G. xxi
Sutherland, Edwin 282
Sykes, Charles 291
Szasz, Thomas 90

Takagi, P. 130
Tannenbaum, Blanche 177
Tannenbaum, Frank 7
Taylor, I. 200, 281
Taylor, Laurie xiii–xiv, xvii, xx–xxi, xxi, xxvn3, xliv, xlix, l, lxi
Taylor, Steve xxi–xxii
Terzani, Tiziano 293
Thompson, E. P. 279
Thompson, Kenneth xxi, 337–8
Thompson, Paul xv, xvi, xviii, xxi, xxvin9
Thompson, Robert 317–18
Thornton, Sarah L. 338–9
Toby, Jackson 44
Touvier, Paul 211n4

Trasler, G. 45
Trilling, Lionel 84
Tucker, Benjamin 237–8

Urban, Jan 236

van Creveld, Martin 292
van Dijk, Jan 187–8, 193
van Weringh, Jac xxvin16
Venables, Jon 317–18
Verdi, Giuseppe lxii
von Hirsh, Andrew 69

Wade, Andrew 20
Walker, N. 32, 35, 40–1, 45
Waller, Irvin xlix
Waltzer, M. 131–2, 200
Ward, Colin xliv
Weber, Max 241
Weiner, Tim 286
Weschler, Lawrence 216
West, D. J. 32, 39
Weston, N. A. 155
Wiles, Paul xliv, 32, 38
Wilkins, L. 2, 10
Williams, B. 198
Williams, John xlix
Willmott, 48
Wilson, J. Q. 137, 138
Winfrey, Oprah 291
Wolf, Christa 226
Wolfenden, John 67
Wolfgang, M. E. 39
Wolpe, Harold xvi
Wright, M. 37

Yablonsky, L. 8
Yeltsin, Boris 288
Yochelson, S. 136
Young, Jock xiii, xxi, xlvii, 52, 181, 188, 202n5, 281
Young, P. xxvin

Zahn, Ernest xxvin16
Zalaquett, Jose 220, 241
Zamir, Yitzhak 177